The American Revolution

Explorations in the History of American Radicalism

Explorations in the History of American Radicalism

Dissent (1968)
Edited by Alfred F. Young

The American Revolution (1976)
Edited by Alfred F. Young

THE
AMERICAN
REVOLUTION

Explorations in the History of
AMERICAN RADICALISM

Edited by

Alfred F. Young

Northern Illinois University Press

DeKalb 1976

Several passages in Ira Berlin's "Revolution in Black Life" are reprinted from *Slaves Without Masters,* copyright © 1974 by Ira Berlin. Reprinted by permission of Pantheon Books, a Division of Random House, Inc.

Maps within the essay by Marvin L. Michael Kay are from Harry Roy Merrens, *Colonial North Carolina in the Eighteenth Century,* copyright © 1964 by University of North Carolina Press. Reprinted with permission.

Library of Congress Cataloging in Publication Data
Main entry under title:

The American Revolution: explorations in the history of
    American radicalism.

    Half title: Explorations in the history of American
radicalism.
    Includes bibliographies and index.
    1. United States—History—Revolution, 1775–1783—
Addresses, essays, lectures.   2. Radicalism—United
States—Addresses, essays, lectures.   I. Young,
Alfred Fabian, 1925–
E208.A43   973.3   75-45359
ISBN 0-87580-057-2
ISBN 0-87580-519-1 pbk.

First Printing April 1976
Second Printing May 1976

Copyright © 1976 by Northern Illinois University Press
Published by the Northern Illinois University Press,
DeKalb, Illinois 60115
Manufactured in the United States of America

CONTENTS

Outsiders

The American Revolution
Explorations in the History of American Radicalism

Foreword

This is a volume of original essays exploring radical themes in the era of the American Revolution. These essays deal with three sorts of subjects: radical movements, groups and social classes at "the bottom" or on the outside of colonial society, and the policies of those in power towards radicalism and towards these groups. Each essay in this volume stands on its own merit. Each has a brief introduction by the author explaining what he or she is trying to do and how it fits into the larger exploration he or she is engaged in. There is a need, therefore, only for a short foreword explaining the basis on which scholars were asked to contribute to this volume. In the Afterword, I offer some comment on what the essays suggest to me as to an overall way of exploring the complexities of the American Revolution.

While I have not attempted to create a book with a single point of view, I have certain assumptions as to what sort of scholarship needs to be done, and the reader is entitled to know the principles that guided me in soliciting contributions and sifting manuscripts.

First, how is "radicalism" being defined? There are two ways in which the term is commonly used by historians who study the Revolution. In the first meaning, radicalism is applied to those individuals—like the Sons of Liberty and Samuel Adams—who were the most anti-British in the decade before 1776: the strongest in their protest against British measures, the most extreme in their methods of resistance (including the mobilization of popular movements), and the earliest to entertain notions of "independency." Opposed to them were moderates or conservatives—contemporaries sometimes called them "the cool, considerate men"—who wanted to confine the protest against Britain to proper channels, who were alarmed at extremist methods, and who were reluctant to give up the prospect of reconciliation. When the lines were drawn in 1775–76, many such conservatives chose independence; others became Tories.

In the second meaning, "radical" is applied by historians to all those without power who were interested in "who shall rule at home" as well as in "home rule" (to take Carl Becker's old but still useful phrase), or to those who were unfree and who sought personal freedom rather than freedom for the colonies. In this latter sense, the term is applied to those groups and individuals who—in the decade before 1776, during the war, and in the decade after—came in conflict with those at the top of colonial society (the elites, the aristocracy, the ruling classes). Contemporaries did not call such people "radical"; rather they used a number of derogatory terms such as "democratical," "popular," or "leveller."

Those who took a radical stand against Great Britain were not necessarily radical on internal matters; quite the contrary. And conversely, those who were radical on internal matters were not necessarily radical towards Britain or even part of the patriot movement. Neither of these contrary trends is very well known in the prevailing popular version of the Revolution. The essays in this book are concerned primarily with the second sort of radicals—those seeking internal change. But inevitably, and by design, they also deal with the first sort; in fact, the complex relationship between internal and external radicalism forms one of the major themes of the volume.

Second, my assumption is that the principal task confronting scholars of American radicalism is to analyze it, which means to identify and define it and to explain not only its successes but also its limitations and failures. The history of American radicalism has long been buried or blurred by a liberal-conservative consensus. The platitude that "the only radicals America glorifies are dead radicals" is not true even for the Revolution. Thomas Paine, if he is no longer called "a filthy little atheist" (as he was by Theodore Roosevelt), is consigned by most historians to the fringes of the Revolution as a person of marginal influence. Samuel Adams is still prisoner of the cliché "mob organizer." And what of Hermon Husband, North Carolina Regulator; Ebenezer MacIntosh, Boston shoemaker and organizer of the Stamp Act demonstrations; William Prendergast, Hudson Valley tenant leader; John Leland, Virginia's democratic evangelical Baptist minister; or Dr. Thomas Young, deist and democrat, whose career spanned the Hudson Valley, Boston, and Philadelphia—how many historians can assign them their proper place in the mosaic of the Revolution?

Most Americans have been taught to approach the Revolution in a mood of reverence and self-congratulation. At the same time, it can be said that twentieth-century dissenters have had their own difficulties in coming to grips with the American radical tradition and, in particular, with the Revolution, swinging as they have from the glorification of the radical tradition in the 1930s, to a denigration of "Amerika" (spelled symbolically with a "k") in the 1960s, and back to an attempted reidentification with the tradition of the Revolution in the 1970s. Those who think of themselves as belonging in the radical tradition have had a hard time deciding who were the radicals. It is understandable. So have the historians. The mood of this volume is neither one of celebration nor one of denigration. Rather it is one of discovery, definition, and analysis; and it is this mood that will, in the long run, restore some badly neglected and distorted American history to the place it deserves.

Third, radical movements are only going to be understood when one examines the social classes and groups—ethnic, religious, and by gender—that sometimes were the carriers of radicalism and as often were not. This volume, therefore, is weighted with essays focusing on what has been called "history from the bottom up"—on those groups at the bottom of white society: in the cities, the lower and "middling" classes; in the countryside, poor farmers, both those who owned land and those who either rented or had uncertain title to it; and on the "outsiders" to white male society: blacks, Indians, and women. Some scholars in this volume assume the task of exploring the nature of radicalism in a particular group; others have the equally important task of explaining a negative—the absence of any overt radicalism: why there was no woman's rights movement and why the Revolution was largely irrelevant to women; or of explaining the conflict among radicals, for example, in the complex world of Thomas Paine's Philadelphia, where artisans were divided against each other.

To come to grips with problems such as these, I have sought out scholars who are attempting to see their subjects in the larger context of colonial and revolutionary society. The new radical culture of evangelical religion among the common folk of Virginia is contrasted to the culture of the "gentle folk" at the top; Boston's crowds are examined in interaction with Boston's leaders; the political economy of the merchants is dealt with in conjunction with the thinking of the artisans and farmers; the "disaffected" in the wartime South are seen together with the patriot gentry trying to establish social control.

Fourth, among the assumptions that have shaped this collection is that if one is to get at the consciousness of those down below, it is as important to study their ideas and culture as it is to study their material circumstances. It should not, of course, be an either/or choice. We need a great deal more hard data, quantitatively measured, about the conditions of all classes and ethnic groups and of the women of the revolutionary era. Some of our essayists contribute to this task. But one can quantify just so much. And if the emphasis in this volume is elsewhere, it is because quantitative scholars have done little with the movements of the Revolution and because some quantifiers (who claim to be getting at the "minds" of the poor and the unfree) work on the unstated "belly" assumption: that those at the bottom of society respond primarily to material deprivation and have neither systems of ideas nor traditions nor culture.

The creative and quite diverse scholarly works of E. P. Thompson, Eric Hobsbawn, George Rudé, and Christopher Hill have shown otherwise for the English plebeian classes, and in doing so, they have re-opened the entire question of radicalism in a period germane to students of the American Revolution. Four of our contributors are applying such insights, also in diverse ways, in their explorations of the cultural history of those down below in America. Toward this end, they make use of sources that scholars have only begun to tap—such as the memoirs of ordinary people; or they focus on things that have to be read in a new way—the dynamics of crowds, the rhetoric of a Thomas Paine, the "body language" at evangelical meetings. It is a line of scholarship much worth encouraging.

Fifth, our understanding of the Revolution can profit from the perspectives brought to it from "outsiders." I use the term in two senses: scholars who are not Americans, or American scholars who have had the advantage of living and working outside their country; and I have invited outsiders in a second sense: scholars who have hitherto done their major work outside the historic period of the Revolution but who have been drawn to it in order to cope with a long-range problem in American history that is their principal interest: the declining status of women; the sources of nineteenth-century radicalism; the "cant of conquest" in the white invasion of America; the origins of free black institutions. It is not so much that all these outsiders bring a sense of detachment to the Revolution but rather that they show how very different the Revolution can look when one views it from another perspective.

This volume is a sequel to *Dissent: Explorations in the History of American Radicalism* (Northern Illinois University Press, 1968), which brought together essays that ranged over two centuries of American history. The principal and overriding criterion in soliciting contributions remains the same in this volume: scholars must be currently involved in an ongoing exploration of their subject.[1] Some of the authors present what might be called an interim report on research in progress, and in such cases their occasional tentativeness or uncertainty should be accepted as an invitation to further inquiry. Their aim is to raise questions, not to foreclose them.

The four other criteria for contributions differ somewhat from those used for the earlier collection. These essays were written especially for this volume; all appear in print here for the first time. Second, they are all confined to one era, albeit broadly defined; in fact, one possible conclusion is that taken together the essays point to the need to redefine the revolutionary era in such a way as to encompass important radical themes. Third, they are based on a broader conception (explained above) of what should be investigated in order to understand radicalism. And, finally, contributors have been urged to write not for their fellow specialists but for the large, general audience that the reception of *Dissent* showed to be interested in serious analysis of American radicalism.

I have made no effort to select authors who share a single overall approach to the American Revolution, to American radicalism, or to American history in general. That would hardly be possible even if it were desirable. Indeed, when I extended invitations, I did not know the overall point of view of most of the authors (and, for a few, still do not). In dealing with prospective contributors, I invited them to tell me what should go into an essay for a volume of this sort. At no time did I ask a scholar to prove a particular thesis or otherwise tailor his or her work to my preconceptions of the Revolution. I have argued with the authors when I disagreed with them, and pointed out aspects of their subject I thought deserved further attention, but I confined myself to what I think an editor's principal function should be: challenging scholars to make their case convincing and in the clearest possible language. I am not sure I agree with all the arguments advanced; obviously, I think they all deserve a hearing. The essayists are responsible neither for the company I have thrown them in with nor for the comments on the Revolution their scholarship has inspired in my "Afterword."

This volume is not intended as a presentation of a so-called radical point of view on the Revolution; nor is it intended to be an interpretation of the Revolution as fundamentally radical or conservative. Taken all together, the essays may not add up to any interpretation of the Revolution at all; they certainly do not add up to any interpretation that can be easily labeled.

All of this has to be said, unfortunately, because, as it has been pointed out by Bernard Bailyn (with whose overall interpretation of the Revolution a number of the writers in this volume—including the editor—take issue), "A special species of writing has grown up devoted to analyzing the historiography of the Revolution" which has "an uncontrollable inner dynamic: trends or schools are detected and criticized before they are fully developed, sometimes before their original authors are themselves aware they are contributing to a trend." One consequence is that "new contributions are at times dismissed out of hand or swallowed whole instead of being absorbed carefully."[2]

Another consequence is that new contributions are immediately labeled. There exists a species of commentators—glib book reviewers, media reporters on trends in history, and some students of "historiography"—who think they have contributed to the world's understanding when they have determined what particular pigeonhole a book belongs in. Mailboy pigeonholing of this sort is an intellectual dead end rather than an invitation to thought and further inquiry. The fact that none of the individual essays can be easily labeled and that the collection as a whole does not fall easily into any existing school of interpretation may well be one of the virtues of this entire exploration. Each scholar is offering findings on a search that has only begun. And while it may be discouraging, at first, for the general reader to learn that after 200 years historians still feel there is a great deal we don't know about the American Revolution, after a second thought, it should be encouraging—and even exciting—to discover how much more there is to the Revolution than the stereotypes the textbooks and mass media continue to present.

It is far too early to say what synthesis of the Revolution may ultimately result from the separate lines of inquiry underway by these and other scholars. Yet it is possible to say that the essays point in the direction of a Revolution that was more complex, more meaningful, and far more challenging to traditional notions than anything we have imagined.

1. I wish to express my appreciation to the following who have been helpful in identifying scholars who have been working on subjects germane to the themes of this volume: John Bracey, Joseph Ernst, Eugene Genovese, Herbert Gutman, Merrill Jensen, Jesse Lemisch, Gerda Lerner, Jackson Turner Main, Kenneth Owens, Willie Lee Rose, Thad Tate, and William A. Williams; to all the scholars in the volume who shared in discussing each other's essays, as well to my graduate students Mark Jones, Stephen Rosswurm, and Walter Wallace; to my wife, Marilyn Mills Young, and to J. Carroll Moody, who helped me clarify the "Foreword" and the "Afterword"; and to Jesse Lemisch, who has helped me clarify many of my ideas about doing "history from below."

2. Bernard Bailyn, "Lines of Force in Recent Writing on the American Revolution," report to the Fourteenth International Congress of Historical Sciences, San Francisco, August 1975, pp. 4, 25.

Common Folk
and Gentle Folk

Social Change and the Growth of Prerevolutionary Urban Radicalism

Gary B. Nash

The symbol of mechanic pride in the "productive arts," which appeared as the central motif on the membership certificate of the General Society of Mechanics and Tradesmen of New York City, organized in 1786. Taken from a reissue of the certificate by the Society.

My own work in colonial history began with an emphasis on elite groups. My first book, *Quakers and Politics: Pennsylvania, 1681–1726,* tried to show how English Quakers transplanted their culture to the Delaware River Valley and how political factionalism, rather than consensual politics, transformed it. The emphasis was on those in the upper stratum of Pennsylvania society.

When, in 1966, I moved from Princeton to Los Angeles to teach at the University of California, I became deeply involved in the Civil Rights movement, and particularly in interracial attempts to bring from the ashes of the Watts Revolt of 1965 a community-based movement that might initiate changes in a society where racism was deeply institutionalized. At the same time, I found that my students were far more diverse than in the East—diverse in terms of race, class, sex, age, and cultural background. My courses in the history of colonial and revolutionary America began to change under this dual influence. I realized that in my own study I had passed over important aspects of the American past and that these areas of historical concern were often the ones most relevant to the lives of my students.

In my scholarship since 1966, I have tried to fashion a broad interpretation of early American history that integrates the history of Indian, African, and European peoples, who interacted dynamically over a period of several centuries. This is the theme of my recent book, *Red, White, and Black: The Peoples of Early America* (Prentice Hall, 1974). Another vein of my work, which will eventually appear in a book entitled "Urban Lives: Social Change, Politics, and Popular Culture Before the Revolution," deals with the interplay of various social groups in three colonial seaports from 1680 to 1770. I have tried to be sensitive to the complexity of the urban experience, showing how people of different levels of society responded to changes that transformed the seaboard towns in the century before the American Revolution. Laborers are as important as merchant princes in this approach, for each was involved in fabricating a culture that met their needs. Interested students can preview this work-in-progress in the articles mentioned in the footnotes of the essay that follows.

Gary B. Nash (Ph.D., Princeton University, 1964), teaches at the University of California, Los Angeles. He has held fellowships from the Guggenheim Foundation and American Council of Learned Societies.

Recent studies of the American Revolution have relied heavily on the role of ideas to explain the advent of the American rebellion against England.[1] The gist of the ideological interpretation of the Revolution is that colonists, inheriting a tradition of protest against arbitrary rule, became convinced in the years after 1763 that the English government meant to impose in America "not merely misgovernment and not merely insensitivity to the reality of life in the British overseas provinces but a deliberate design to destroy the constitutional safeguards of liberty, which only concerted resistance—violent resistance if necessary—could effectively oppose."[2] It was this conspiracy against liberty that "above all else...propelled [the colonists] into Revolution."[3]

An important corollary to this argument, which stresses the colonial defense of constitutional rights and liberties, is the notion that the material conditions of life in America were so generally favorable that social and economic factors deserve little consideration as a part of the impetus to revolution. "The outbreak of the Revolution," writes Bernard Bailyn, a leading proponent of the ideological school, "was not the result of social discontent, or of economic disturbances, or of rising misery, or of those mysterious social strains that seem to beguile the imaginations of historians straining to find peculiar predispositions to upheaval." Nor, asserts Bailyn, was there a "transformation of mob behavior or of the lives of the 'inarticulate' in the pre-Revolutionary years that accounts for the disruption of Anglo-American politics."[4] Another historian, whose focus is economic change and not ideas, writes that "whatever it might have been, the American Revolution was not a rising of impoverished masses—or merchants—in search of their share of the wealth. The 'predicament of poverty,' in Hannah Arendt's phrase, was absent from the American scene"—so much so that even though the "secular trend in the concentration of wealth created an increasing gulf between the rich and the poor over the years separating 1607 and 1775, the fact remains that not only were the rich getting richer but the poor were also, albeit at a slower rate."[5]

One of the purposes of this essay is to challenge these widely accepted notions that the "predicament of poverty" was unknown in colonial America, that the conditions of everyday life among "the inarticulate" had not changed in ways that led toward a revolutionary predisposition, and that "social discontent," "economic disturbances," and "social strains" can generally be ignored in searching for the roots of the Revolution. I do not suggest that we replace an ideological construction with a mechanistic economic interpretation, but argue that a popular ideology, affected by rapidly changing economic conditions in American cities, dynamically interacted with the more abstract Whig ideology borrowed from England. These two ideologies had their primary appeal within different parts of the social structure, were derived from different sensibilities concerning social equity, and thus had somewhat different goals. The Whig ideology, about which we know a great deal through recent studies, was drawn from English sources, had its main appeal within upper levels of colonial society, was limited to a defense of constitutional rights and political liberties, and had little to say about changing social and economic conditions in America or the need for change in the future. The popular ideology, about which we know very little, also had deep roots in English culture, but it resonated most strongly within the middle and lower strata of society and went far beyond constitutional rights to a discussion of the proper distribution of wealth and power in the social system. It was this popular ideology that undergirded the politicization of the artisan and laboring classes in the cities and justified the dynamic role they assumed in the urban political process in the closing decades of the colonial period.

It is toward understanding this popular ideology and its role in the upsurge of revolutionary sentiment and action in the 1760s that this essay is devoted. Our focus will be on the three largest colonial cities —Boston, New York, and Philadelphia. Other areas, including the older, settled farming regions and backcountry, were also vitally important to the upwelling of revolutionary feeling in the fifteen years before 1776 and in the struggle that followed. But the northern cities were the first areas of revolutionary ferment, the communication centers where newspapers and pamphlets spread the revolutionary message, and the arenas of change in British North America where most of the trends overtaking colonial society in the eighteenth century were first and most intensely felt.

To understand how this popular ideology swelled into revolutionary commitment within the middle and lower ranks of colonial society, we must first comprehend how the material conditions of life were changing for city dwellers during the colonial period and how people at different levels of society were affected by these alterations. We cannot fathom this process by consulting the writings of merchants, lawyers, and upper-class politicians, because their business and political correspondence and the tracts they wrote tell us almost nothing about those below them in the social hierarchy. But buried in more obscure documents are glimpses of the lives of both ordinary and important people—shoemakers and tailors as well as lawyers and merchants. The story of changing conditions and how life in New York, Philadelphia, and Boston was experienced can be discerned, not with perfect clarity but in general form, from tax, poor relief, and probate records.

I

The most generally recognized alteration in eighteenth-century urban social structures is the long-range trend toward a less even distribution of wealth. Tax lists for Boston, Philadelphia, and New York, ranging over nearly a century prior to the Revolution, make this clear. By the early 1770s the top 5 percent of Boston's taxpayers controlled 49 percent of the taxable assets of the community, whereas they had held only 30 percent in 1687. In Philadelphia the top twentieth increased its share of wealth from 33 to 55 percent between 1693 and 1774. Those in the lower half of society, who in Boston in 1687 had commanded 9 percent of the taxable wealth, were left collectively with a mere 5 percent in 1771. In Philadelphia, those in the lower half of the wealth spectrum saw their share of wealth drop from 10.1 to 3.3 percent in the same period. It is now evident that the concentration of wealth had proceeded very far in the eighteenth-century cities.[6]

Though city dwellers from the middle and lower ranks could not measure this redistribution of economic resources with statiscal precision, they could readily discern the general trend. No one could doubt that upper-class merchants were amassing fortunes when four-wheeled coaches, manned by liveried Negro slaves, appeared in Boston's crooked streets, or when urban mansions, lavishly furnished in imitation of the English aristocracy, rose in Philadelphia and New York.[7] Colonial probate records reveal that personal estates of £5000 sterling were rare in the northern cities before 1730, but by 1750 the wealthiest town dwellers were frequently leaving assets of £20,000 sterling, exclusive of real estate, and sometimes fortunes of more than £50,000 sterling—equivalent in purchasing power to about 2.5 million dollars today.[8] Wealth of this magnitude was not disguised in cities with populations ranging from about 16,000 in Boston to about 25,000 in New York and Philadelphia and with geographical expanses half as large as public university campuses today.

While urban growth produced a genuinely wealthy upper class, it simultaneously created a large class of impoverished city dwellers. All of the cities built almshouses in the 1730s in order to house under one roof as many of the growing number of poor as possible. This was the beginning of a long trend toward substituting confinement in workhouses and almshouses for the older familial system of direct payments to the poor at home. The new system was designed to reduce the cost of caring for a growing number of marginal persons—people who, after the 1730s, were no longer simply the aged, widowed, crippled, incurably ill, or orphaned members of society, but also the seasonally unemployed, war veterans, new immigrants, and migrants from inland areas seeking employment in the cities. These persons, whose numbers grew impressively in the 1750s and 1760s, were now expected to contribute to their own support through cloth weaving, shoemaking, and oakum picking in city workhouses.[9]

Beginning in Boston in the 1740s and in New York and Philadelphia somewhat later, poverty scarred the lives of a growing part of the urban populations. Among its causes were periodic unemployment, rising prices that outstripped wage increases, and war taxes which fell with unusual severity on the lower classes. In Boston, where the Overseers of the Poor had expended only £25–35 sterling per thousand inhabitants in the 1720s and 1730s, per capita expenditures for the poor more than doubled in the 1740s and 1750s, and then doubled again in the last fifteen years of the colonial period. Poor relief rose similarly in Philadelphia and New York after 1750.

In the third quarter of the eighteenth century poverty struck even harder at Boston's population and then blighted the lives of the New

York and Philadelphia laboring classes to a degree unparalleled in the first half of the century. In New York, the wartime boom of 1755–1760 was followed by postwar depression. High rents and unemployment brought hundreds of families to the edge of indigency. The incidence of poverty jumped more than fourfold between 1750 and 1775. By 1772 a total of 425 persons jostled for space in the city's almshouse, which had been built to accommodate about 100 indigents. In Philadelphia, in the decade before the Revolution, more than 900 persons each year were admitted to the city's institutions for the impoverished —the almshouse, workhouse, and Hospital for the Sick Poor.[10] The data on poor relief leaves little room for doubt that the third quarter of the eighteenth century was an era of severe economic and social dislocation in the cities, and that by the end of the colonial period a large number of urban dwellers were without property, without opportunity, and, except for public aid, without the means of obtaining the necessities of life.

The economic changes that redistributed wealth, filled the almshouses to overflowing, and drove up poor rates, also hit hard at the lower part of the middle class in the generation before the Revolution. These people—master artisans rather than laborers, skilled shipwrights rather than merchant seamen, shopkeepers rather than peddlers—were financially humbled in substantial numbers in Boston beginning in the 1740s and in Philadelphia and New York a dozen years later.

In Boston, this crumbling of middle-class economic security can be traced in individual cases through the probate records and in aggregate form in the declining number of "taxables." In that city, where the population remained nearly static, at about 15,500 from 1735 to the Revolution, the number of "rateable polls" declined from a high of more than 3,600 in 1735, when the city's economy was at its peak, to a low of about 2,500 around mid-century. By 1771, Boston's taxables still numbered less than 2,600.[11] This decline of more than a thousand taxable adults was not caused by loss of population but by the sagging fortunes of more than 1,000 householders—almost one-third of the city's taxpaying population. Boston's selectmen made this clear in 1757 when they pointed out that "besides a great Number of Poor...who are either wholly or in part maintained by the Town, & so are exempt from being Taxed, there are many who are Rateable according to Law...who are yet in such poor Circumstances that

Considering how little business there is to be done in Boston they can scarcely procure from day to day daily Bread for themselves & Families."[12]

In Philadelphia, the decay of a substantial part of the "middling sort" similarly altered the urban scene, though the trend began later and did not proceed as far as in Boston. City tax collectors reported the names of each taxable inhabitant from whom they were unable to extract a tax, and the survival of their records allows for some precision in tracing this phenomenon. Taxpayers dropped from the rolls because of poverty represented less than 3 percent of the taxables in the period before 1740, but they increased to about 6 to 7 percent in the two decades beginning in 1740, and then to one in every ten taxpayers in the fifteen years before the Revolution.[13]

The probate records of Boston and Philadelphia tell a similar tale of economic insecurity hovering over the middle ranges of urban society.[14] Among these people in Boston, median wealth at death dropped sharply between 1685 and 1735 and then made a partial but uneven recovery as the Revolution approached. The average carpenter, baker, shopkeeper, shipwright, or tavernkeeper dying in Boston between 1735 and 1765 had less to show for a lifetime's work than his counterpart of a half century before. In Philadelphia, those in the lower ranges of the middle class also saw the value of their assets, accumulated over a lifetime's labor, slowly decline during the first half of the eighteenth century, though not so severely as in Boston. The startling conclusion that must be drawn from a study of nearly 4,500 Boston and Philadelphia inventories of estates at probate is that population growth and economic development in the colonial cities did not raise the standard of living and broaden opportunities for the vast majority of people, but instead conferred benefits primarily upon those at the top of the social pyramid. The long-range effect of growth was to erode the personal assets held at death by those in the lower 75 percent of Boston society and the lower 60 percent of Philadelphia society. Though many city dwellers had made spectacular individual ascents from the bottom, in the manner of Benjamin Franklin of Philadelphia or Isaac Sears of New York, the statistical chances of success for those beginning beneath the upper class were considerably less after the first quarter of the eighteenth century than before. The dominating fact of late colonial life for many middle-class as well as most lower-class city folk was not economic achievement but economic frustration.

II

Understanding that the cities were becoming centers of frustrated ambition, propertylessness, genuine distress for those in the lower strata, and stagnating fortunes for many in the middle class makes comprehensible much of the violence, protest, and impassioned rhetoric that occurred in the half-generation before the colonial challenge to British regulations began in 1764. Upper-class colonists typically condemned these verbal attacks and civil disorders as the work of the "rabble," the "mob," the "canaille," or individuals "of turbulent disposition." These labels were used to discredit crowd activity, and historians have only recently recognized that the "rabble" often included a broad range of city dwellers, from slaves and servants through laborers and seamen to artisans and shopkeepers—all of whom were directly or indirectly expressing grievances.[15] Cutting across class lines, and often unified by economic conditions that struck at the welfare of both the lower and middle classes, these crowds began to play a larger role in a political process that grew more heated as the colonial period came to an end.[16] This developing consciousness and political sophistication of ordinary city dwellers came rapidly to fruition in the early 1760s and thereafter played a major role in the advent of the Revolution.

Alienation and protest had been present in the northern cities, especially during periods of economic difficulty, since the early eighteenth century. In Boston, between 1709 and 1713, townspeople protested vigorously and then took extralegal action when Andrew Belcher, a wealthy merchant, refused to stop exporting grain during a bread shortage in the city. Belcher had grown fat on war contracts during Queen Anne's War, and when he chose to export grain to the Caribbean, at a handsome profit, rather than sell it for a smaller profit to hungry townspeople, his ships were attacked and his warehouses emptied by an angry crowd. Rank had no privileges, as even the lieutenant-governor was shot when he tried to intervene. Bostonians of meagre means learned that through concerted action, the powerless could become powerful, if only for the moment. Wealthy merchants who would not listen to pleas from the community could be forced through collective action to subordinate profits to the public need.[17]

After the end of Queen Anne's War, in 1713, Boston was troubled by postwar recession and inflation, which cut into the wages of working people. Attempts to organize a land bank in order to increase the scarce circulating medium in Boston were opposed by wealthy men, many of them former war contractors. Gathering around the unpopular governor, Paul Dudley, these fiscal conservatives blamed the hard times on the extravagant habits of "the Ordinary sort" of people, who squandered their money on a "foolish fondness of Forreign Commodities & Fashions" and on too frequent tippling in the town's taverns.[18] But such explanations did not deceive returning war veterans, the unemployed, or those caught in an inflationary squeeze. They protested openly against men who made their fortunes "by grinding the poor," as one writer expressed it, and who studied "how to oppress, cheat, and overreach their neighbours." "The Rich, Great, and Potent," stormed this angry spokesman, "with rapacious violence bear down all before them, who have not wealth, or strength to encounter or avoid their fury."[19] Although the land bank movement failed in 1720, it was out of this defeat that the Boston Caucus, the political organization designed to mobilize the middle- and lower-class electorate in the decades to come, arose.[20]

In Philadelphia, economic issues also set the mechanic and laborer against the rich as early as the 1720s. When a business recession brought unemployment and a severe shortage of specie (the only legal circulating medium), leading merchant-politicans argued that the problem was moral in nature. If the poor were unemployed or hungry, they had their own lack of industry and prudence to thank, wrote James Logan, a thriving merchant and land speculator. "The Sot, the Rambler, the Spendthrift, and the Slip Season," he charged, were at the heart of the slump. Schemes for reviving the economy with emissions of paper money were reckless attempts to cheat those who worked for their money instead of drinking their time away.[21]

But, as in Boston, the majority of people were not fooled by such high-toned arguments. Angry tracts appeared on both sides of the debate concerning the causes and cure for recession. Those who favored paper money and called for restrictions on land speculators and monopolizers of the money market made an attack on wealth itself an important theme. Logan found bricks flying through his windows and a crowd threatening to level his house. Meanwhile, he looked on in disgust as Governor William Keith organized a political caucus, encouraged laboring men to participate in politics, and conducted a campaign aimed at discrediting Logan and other wealthy merchants.[22]

"It is neither the Great, the Rich, nor the Learned, that compose the Body of any People, and . . . civil Government ought carefully to protect the poor, laborious and industrious Part of Mankind," Keith cautioned the Assembly in 1723.[23] Logan, formerly respected as William Penn's chief proprietary officeholder, a member of council, a judge of the colony's highest court, and Pennsylvania's most educated man, now found himself reviled in widely distributed tracts as "Pedagogus Mathematicus"—an ambitious, ruthless elitist. He and his henchmen, cried the pamphleteers, deserved to be called "petty Tyrants of this Province," "Serpents in the Grass," "Rich Misers," "Phenomena of Aristocracy," "Infringers of our Priviledges," and "Understrappers of Government."[24]

In a striking inversion of the conventional eighteenth-century thinking that only the rich and educated were equipped to hold high political offices, the Keithian faction urged the voters to recognize that "a mean Man, of small Interest, devoted to the faithful Discharge of his Trust and Duty to the Government" was far more to be valued than rich and learned men.[25] For the rest of the decade the anti-Logan forces, organized into political clubs in Philadelphia, held sway at the annual elections and passed legislation to relieve the distress of the lower-class unemployed and middle-class debtors. Members of the Philadelphia elite, such as Logan and merchant Isaac Norris, hated the "new vile people [who] may be truly called a mob," and deplored Keith's "doctrine of reducing all to a level."[26] But they could no longer manage politics from the top. The "moral economy of the crowd," as E. P. Thompson has called it—the people's sense that basic rules of equity in social relations had been breached—had intervened when the rich would do nothing to relieve suffering in a period of economic decline.[27]

When an economic slump beset New York in the 1730s, causing unemployment and an increase in suits for debt, the reaction was much the same as in the other cities. The John Peter Zenger trial of this era is best remembered as a chapter in the history of the freedom of the press. But central to the campaign organized by Zenger's supporters were the indictment of the rich and the mobilization of the artisanry against them. A 1734 election tract reminded the New York electorate that the city's strength—and its future—lay with the fortunes of "Shuttle" the weaver, "Plane" the joiner, "Drive" the carter, "Mortar" the mason, "Tar" the mariner, "Snip" the tailor, "Smallrent" the fair-minded landlord, and "John Poor" the tenant. Pitted against them were "Gripe the Merchant, Squeeze the Shopkeeper, Spintext and Quible the Lawyer."[28] In arguments reminiscent of those in Philadelphia a decade before, the Lewis Morris faction counseled the people that "A poor honest Man [is] preferable to a rich Knave." Only by electing men responsive to the needs of the whole community, the Morrisites advised, could New Yorkers arrest the forces that were impoverishing the artisan class while fattening the purses of merchants and moneylenders. The conservative clergy of the city advised working people to pray harder in difficult times, but the Morrisite pamphleteers urged the electorate to throw out of office those "people in Exalted Stations" who looked with disdain upon "those they call the Vulgar, the Mob, the herd of Mechanicks."[29]

Attacks on wealth and concentrated power continued in New York through 1737. The opulent and educated of the city were exposed as self-interested and oppresive men, not the public-minded community servants that conventional political philosophy prescribed. Though the leaders of the Morris faction were themselves men of substantial wealth, and though they never advocated a truly popular form of politics, their attacks on the rich and their organization of artisan voters became imbedded in the structure and ideology of politics.[30]

A decade later, political contention broke out again in New York City and attacks on the wealthy and well-born were revived. To some extent the political factionalism in the period from 1747 to 1755 represented a competition for power and profit between different elements of the elite. DeLanceys were pitted against Coldens, and Alexanders against Bayards, in a game where the stakes were control of land in neighboring New Jersey, the profits of the Iroquois fur trade, and the power of the assembly in opposition to the governor and his clique of officeholders. But as in earlier decades, the success of these intra-elite struggles depended upon gaining support from below. In appealing to the artisans and tradesmen, especially during periods of economic decline, bitter charges surfaced about the selfishness of wealthy men and the social inequities in society which they promoted.[31] Cadwallader Colden's *Address to the Freeholders* in 1747 inveighed against the rich, who did not build their fortunes "by the honestest means" and who had no genuine concern for the "publick spirit." Colden attacked the wealthy, among whose ranks he figured importantly, as tax dodgers who indulged in wanton displays of wealth and gave little thought to the welfare of those below them. "The midling rank of mankind," argued Colden, was far more honest, dependable, sober, and public spirited "in all Countries," and it was therefore best to trust "our Liberty & Property" to them rather than to New York's "rich jolly or swaggering companions."[32]

In Boston, resentment against the rich, focusing on specific economic grievances, continued to find voice in the middle third of the century. Moreover, since the forming of the caucus a generation before, well-coordinated street action channeled the wrath of townspeople against those who were thought to act against the interest of the commonality. In the 1730s an extended debate erupted on establishing a public market where prices and marketing conditions would be controlled. Many Bostonians in the lower and middle strata regarded a regulated public market as a device of merchants and fiscal conservatives to drive small retailers from the field and reap the profits of victualing Boston themselves. Though they lost their cause after a number of bitter debates and close votes at the town meeting in the mid-1730s, these humbler people, who probably included many without a vote, ultimately prevailed by demolishing the public market on Dock Square in 1737.[33] The attack was accompanied by much "murmuring agt the Government & the rich people," lamented Benjamin Colman, an advocate of the regulated market and a member of the conservative faction. Worse yet, "none of the Rioters or Mutineers" could be discovered. Their support was so broad that they promised that any attempt to arrest or arraign the saboteurs would be met by "Five Hundred Men in Solemn League and Covenant," who would resist the sheriff and destroy any other markets erected by wealthy merchants. The timbers of the public market which fell before the night raiders in 1737 showed how widely held was the conviction that only this kind of civil disobedience would "deliver the poor oppressed and distressed People out of the Hands of the Rich and Mighty."[34]

The Land Bank controversy from 1740 to 1742 further inflamed a wide segment of Boston society. Most of the colony, including Boston, favored a land bank which would relieve the economic distress of the period by issuing more paper money and thus continuing the inflationist policies of the last twenty years. In opposition stood a group of Boston merchants, who "had railed against the evils of paper money" for years and now "damned the Bank as merely a more invidious form of the soft money panacea typically favored by the province's poor and unsuccessful."[35] One of their spokesman, William Douglass, reflected the elitist view by characterizing the dispute as a struggle between the "Idle & Extravagant who want to borrow money at any bad lay" and "our considerable Foreign Traders and rich Men."[36]

Even though the inflationists swept the Massachusetts assembly elections of 1740 and 1741, they could not overcome the combined opposition of Governor Jonathan Belcher, a group of wealthy merchants, and officials in England. In the end, the Land Bank movement was thwarted. The defeat was not lightly accepted or quickly forgotten by debtors and Bostonians of modest means. Three years later, a committee of the Boston town meeting, which had consistently promoted inflated paper currency as a means of relief for Boston's numerous debtors, exploded with angry words at another deflationist proposal of the mercantile elite: "We cannot suppose, because in some extraordinary Times when a Party Spirit has run high there have been some Abuses of Our Liberties and Priviledges, that therefore We should in a Servile Manner give them all up. And have our Bread & Water measured out to Us by those Who Riot in Luxury & Wantonness on Our Sweat & Toil and be told by them that we are too happy, because we are not reduced to Eat Grass with the Cattle."[37]

The crowning blow to ordinary Bostonians came in 1748 when Thomas Hutchinson, the principal architect of the monetary policy favored by the wealthiest merchants, engineered a merciless devaluation of Massachusetts currency as a cure to the continuing inflation, which by now had reduced the value of paper money to a fraction of its face value. With many persons unemployed, with poverty afflicting hundreds of families, and with Hutchinson personifying the military contractors who had reaped fortunes from King George's War (1739–1747) while common people suffered, popular sentiment exploded. The newspapers carried a rancorous debate on the proposed devaluation, street fights broke out when the new policy was instituted, and Hutchinson was personally threatened on several occasions.[38] An anonymous pamphleteer put into words the sentiment of many in the city who had watched the gap widen between rich and poor during hard times. "Poverty and Discontent appear in every Face, (except the Countenances of the Rich), and dwell upon every Tongue." A few men, fed by "Lust of Power, Lust of Fame, Lust of Money," had grown rich by supplying military expeditions during the last war and had now cornered the paper money market and manipulated the rates of exchange for English sterling to their own profit. "No Wonder such Men can build Ships, Houses, buy Farms, set up their Coaches, Chariots, live very splendidly, purchase Fame, Posts of Honour," railed the pamphleteer. But such "Birds of prey . . . are Enemies to all Communities—wherever they live."[39]

The growing sentiment in the cities against the wealthy was nourished by the Great Awakening—the outbreak of religious enthusiasm throughout the colonies beginning in the late 1730s. Although this eruption of evangelical fervor is primarily identified as a rural phenomenon, it also had powerful effects in the cities, where fiery preachers such as George Whitefield and Gilbert Tennant had their greatest successes. We have no study as yet of the Great Awakening in the cities, but clues abound that one important reason for its urban appeal was the fact that the evangelists took as one of their primary targets the growth of wealth and extravagance, accompanied by a dwindling of social concern in colonial America. Nowhere was this manifested more noticeably than in the cities.[40]

The urban dwellers who thronged to hear George Whitefield in Philadelphia in 1739 and 1741 and those who crowded the Common in Boston to hear Whitefield and the vituperative James Davenport in the early 1740s were overwhelmingly from the "lower orders," so far as we can tell. What accounts for their "awakening" is the evangelists' presentation of a personal religion where humble folk might find succor from debt, daily toil, sickness, and want, and might express deeply felt emotions in an equality of fellowship. At the same time, the revivalist preachers spread a radical message concerning established authority. City dwellers were urged to partake in mass revivals, where the social distance between clergyman and parishoner and among worshippers themselves was obliterated. They were exhorted to be skeptical toward dogma and to participate in ecclesiastical affairs rather than bow passively to established hierarchy.[41]

Through the Great Awakening, doctrinal controversy and attacks on religious leaders became widely accepted in the 1740s. In Boston the itinerant preacher James Davenport hotly indicted the rich and powerful and advised ordinary people to break through the crust of tradition in order to right the wrongs of a decaying society. It was the spectre of unlearned artisans and laborers assuming authority in this manner that frightened many upper-class city dwellers and led them to charge the revivalists with preaching levelism and anarchy. "It is . . . an exceedingly difficult, gloomy time with us . . .," wrote one conservative clergyman from Boston. "Such an enthusiastic, factious, censorious Spirit was never known here. . . . Every low-bred, illiterate

Person can resolve Cases of Conscience and settle the most difficult Points of Divinity better than the most learned Divines."[42]

Such charges were heard repeatedly during the Great Awakening, revealing the fears of those who trembled to see the "unthinking multitude" invested with a new dignity and importance. Nor could the passing of the Awakening reverse the tide, for this new sense of power remained a part of the social outlook of ordinary people. In fact, the radical transformation of religious feeling overflowed into civil affairs. The new feeling of autonomy and importance was bred in the churches, but now it was carried into the streets. Laboring people in the city learned "to identify the millenium with the establishment of governments which derived their power from the people, and which were free from the great disparities of wealth which characterized the old world."[43]

III

The crescendo of urban protest and extralegal activity in the prerevolutionary decades cannot be separated from the condition of people's lives. Of course those who authored attacks on the growing concentration of wealth and power were rarely artisans or laborers; usually they were men who occupied the middle or upper echelons of society, and sometimes they were men who sought their own gain— installment in office, or the defeat of a competitor for government favors. But whatever their motives, their sharp criticisms of the changes in urban society were widely shared among humbler towns-people. It is impossible to say how much they shaped rather than reflected the views of those in the lower half of the social structure— urban dwellers whose opportunities and daily existence had been most adversely affected by the structural changes overtaking the colonial cities. But the willingness of broad segments of urban society to partic-ipate in attacks on narrowly concentrated wealth and power—both at the polls where the poor and propertyless were excluded, and in the streets where everyone, including women, apprentices, indentured servants, and slaves, could engage in action—should remind us that a rising tide of class antagonism and political consciousness, paralleling important economic changes, was a distinguishing feature of the cities at the end of the colonial period.

It is this organic link between the circumstances of people's lives and their political thought and action that has been overlooked by historians who concentrate on Whig ideology, which had its strongest appeal among the educated and well-to-do. The link had always been there, as detailed research into particular communities is beginning to show. But it became transparently clear in the late colonial period, even before England began demanding greater obedience and greater sacrifices in the colonies for the cause of the British Empire. The connection can be seen in New York in the 1760s, where the pleas of the impoverished against mercenary landlords were directly expressed in 1762, and where five years later the papers were pointing out that while the poor had vastly increased in recent years and while many families were selling their furniture at vendue to pay their rent, carriage owners in the city had grown from five to seventy.[44] The link can also be seen in Philadelphia, where growing restlessness at unemployment, bulging almshouses, rising poor taxes, and soaring prices for food and firewood helped to politicize the electorate and drew unprecedented numbers of people to the polls in the last decade of the colonial period.[45]

However, it was in Boston, where poverty had struck first, cut deepest, and lasted longest, that the connection between changing urban conditions and rising political radicalism is most obvious. That it preceded the post-1763 imperial debate, rather than flowing from it, becomes apparent in a close examination of politics in that city between 1760 and 1765.

The political factionalism of these years has usually been seen as a product of the accession of Francis Bernard to the governorship in 1760 and the subsequent appointment of Thomas Hutchinson to the chief justiceship of the colony over the claims of James Otis, Sr., who thought he had been promised the position. Hutchinson, already installed as lieutenant-governor, judge of probate, president of the provincial council, and captain of Castle William, now held high office in all three branches of government—executive, judicial, and legislative. The issues, as historians have portrayed them, were plural officeholding, prosecution of the colony's illegal traders under writs of assistance, and, ultimately, the right of England to fasten new imperial regulations on the colony.[46] But running beneath the surface of these arguments, and almost entirely overlooked by historians, were issues that had far greater relevance to Boston's commonality.

For ordinary Bostonians, Thomas Hutchinson had long been regarded as a man who claimed to serve the community at large but
devised policies which invariably benefitted the rich and hurt the poor.
As far back as 1738, Hutchinson had disregarded instructions from the
town meeting and pressed the General Court to pass deflationary
measures which hurt the pocketbooks of common people, particularly
those in debt. Hutchinson continued his hard money campaign in the
1740s. During the 1747 impressment riot, when an angry crowd took
control of Boston and demanded the release of some fifty of the town's
citizens seized for service in His Majesty's ships, Hutchinson lined up
behind the governor in defense of law and order. Alongside other
merchants who were chalking up handsome profits on war contracts
issued by Governor William Shirley, Hutchinson now stood at the
governor's side as his house was surrounded by a jeering, hostile
crowd that battered the sheriff and then "swabb'd in the gutter" and
locked in the town stocks a deputy sheriff who attempted to disperse
them. Hutchinson and his future brother-in-law, Andrew Oliver,
joined two other merchants in drafting a report condemning the impressment proceedings as a "Riotous Tumultuous Assembly" of "Foreign Seamen, Servants, Negroes, and Other Persons of Mean and Vile
Condition."[47]

One year later, Hutchinson became the designer and chief promoter of a plan for drastically devaluing Massachusetts currency. Enacted into law after bitter debate, the hard money plan was widely seen
as a cause of the trade paralysis and economic recession that struck
Boston in the early 1750s. Hutchinson's conservative fiscal measure
was roundly attacked in the Boston press and specifically criticized for
discriminating against the poor. Four months after the Hutchinson
plan became law, Boston's voters turned him out of the House. Shortly
thereafter, when his home mysteriously caught fire, a crowd gathered
in the street, cursing Hutchinson and crying, "Let it burn!" A rump
town meeting sardonically elected Hutchinson tax collector, a job
which would take him out of his mansion and into the streets where
he might personally see how laboring-class Bostonians were faring
during hard times.[48]

The animosity against Hutchinson continued during the next
decade, because he aligned himself with a series of unpopular issues
—the excise tax of 1754, the Albany Plan of the same year, and another
devaluation scheme in 1761.[49] More than anyone in Boston in the
second third of the eighteenth century, Thomas Hutchinson stood in
the common people's view as the archetype of the cold, grasping,

ambitious, aristocratic merchant-politician who had lost touch with his humbler neighbors and cared little whether they prospered or failed.

Fanning the flames of rancor toward Hutchinson in the early 1760s was his leadership of a small group of conservative merchants and lawyers, known in the popular press as the "Junto." These men were known not only for fiscal conservatism but for their efforts to dismantle the town meeting system of government in Boston in order to enlarge their power while curbing that of the middle and lower classes. Most of them were friends of the new governor, Francis Bernard, enjoyed appointments in the provincial government, belonged to the Anglican church, and were related by blood or marriage. Among them were Hutchinson, Andrew and Peter Oliver, Eliakim Hutchinson, Charles Apthorp, Robert Auchmuty, Samuel Waterhouse, Charles Paxton, Thomas Flucker, John Erving, Jr., Edmund Trowbridge, and Chambers Russell.

The move to overthrow the town meeting in 1760 had deep roots. In 1715 and again in the early 1730s conservative merchants had argued that Boston should substitute a borough government for the town meeting. Under municipal incorporation, a system of town government widely used in England as well as in Philadelphia, appointed alderman would serve life terms and would elect the mayor. Under such a plan most municipal officers would be appointed rather than elected. The proposal was designed to limit popular participation in government and transfer control of the city to the elite, whose members argued that they would institute greater order and efficiency.[50]

Both earlier attempts to scrap the town meeting had been staunchly attacked by pamphleteers, who warned that such "reforms" would give exorbitant power to men whose wealth and elevated social status were frail guarantees that they would act in the public interest. The gulf between the rulers and the ruled, between the rich and poor, would only increase, they prophesied, and the people would pay a fearful price for abdicating their political rights. Those who favored incorporation, argued a pamphleteer in 1715, despised "Mobb Town Meetings," where the rich, if they wished to participate, had to mingle with less elevated townspeople. They wished to substitute the rule of the few so that "the Great Men will no more have the Dissatisfaction of seeing their Poorer Neighbours stand up for equal Privilege with them." But neither in 1715 nor in the early 1730s could the elite push through their reorganization of town government.[51]

The town meeting continued to rankle those who regarded laboring people as congenitally turbulent, incapable of understanding economic issues, and moved too much by passion and too little by reason to make wise political choices. Governor Shirley expressed this view most cogently after the demonstration against British impressment of Boston citizens in 1747: "What I think may be esteemed the principal cause of the Mobbish turn in this Town is its Constitution; by which the Management of it is devolv'd upon the populace assembled in their Town Meetings . . . where the meanest Inhabitants . . . by their constant Attendence there generally are the majority and outvote the Gentlemen, Merchants, Substantial Traders and all the better part of the Inhabitants; to whom it is irksome to attend." When so many workingmen, merchant seamen, and "low sort of people" could participate in town meetings, the governor lamented, what could be expected but "a factious and Mobbish Spirit" that kept educated and respectable people away?[52]

In 1760, five months before Hutchinson's appointment as chief justice, the conservative "Junto" made another attempt to gain control of the town government. Realizing that common Bostonians could not be gulled into surrendering their political rights, the "Junto" plotted a strategy for swinging the May elections in Boston and sending to the General Court four representatives who would convince the House to pass a law for incorporating Boston. A "Combination of Twelve Strangers," who called themselves "The New and Grand Corcas," warned the populist *Boston Gazette*, were designing to "overthrow the ancient Constitution of our Town-Meeting, as being popular and mobbish; and to form a Committee to transact the whole Affairs of the Town for the future." In order to control the elections, the article continued, the "Junto" would attempt to keep "tradesmen, and those whom in Contempt they usually term the Low lived People," from voting. They would challenge their eligibility at the polls, attempt to buy their votes, and threaten them with arrest and loss of their jobs.[53] As Samuel Adams later remarked, it was obvious that Hutchinson was bent on destroying the "Democratic part" of government.[54] On the eve of the election, the "Committee of Tradesmen," working with the "old and true Corcas," used the press to urge Boston's working people to stand up to these threats. The artisans should "put on their Sabbath Cloathes . . . wash their Hands and faces that they may appear neat and cleanly," spurn the vote-buying tactics of the "Junto," and elect men who represented their interests.[55]

A record number of voters turned out on 13 May 1760, as both factions courted the electorate. The result was indecisive. Royall Tyler, vociferously opposed by the Anglican "Junto," was reelected. But

Benjamin Prat and John Tyng, who during the preceding year had taken an unpopular stand on sending the province ship to England, lost their seats to two moderates, Samuel Welles and John Phillips, who were supported by the Hutchinsonians. The conservatives had succeeded to this extent in creating a "popular" issue and using it to rally the electorate against two of the Caucus's candidates. It was enough to hearten the Hutchinsonians, who now had reason to anticipate other electoral successes, and to galvanize the anti-Hutchinsonians into redoubling their efforts among Boston's electorate.

In the period immediately after the 1760 election, James Otis made his meteoric rise in the "popular" party in Boston, leading the fight to curb the growing power of the Hutchinsonian circle. The Otis-Hutchinson struggle has usually been interpreted as a fight over the regulation of trade and oligarchic officeholding, or, more recently, as the culmination of a long-standing interfamily competition. In both interpretations Otis appears as a sulphurous orator and writer (either brilliant or mad according to one's views), who molded laboring-class opinion, called the "mob" into action, and shaped its behavior. To a large extent, however, Otis was only reflecting the perceptions and interests of common Bostonians in his abusive attacks on the lieutenant governor and his allies. For two years after the 1760 elections, which were dangerously indecisive from the viewpoint of the "popular" party, Otis filled the *Gazette* with vitriolic assaults on the Hutchinson clique, each fully answered in the conservative *Evening-Post.* Woven into Otis's offensive was the theme of resentment against wealth, narrowly concentrated political power, and arbitrary political actions which adversely affected Boston's ordinary people. But rather than seeing this campaign solely as an attempt to mobilize the artisans and laborers, we should also understand it as a reflection of opinion already formed within these groups. For years Boston's common people had shown their readiness to act against such oppression—in preventing the exportation of grain, in destroying the public market, and in harassing arbitrary officeholders. Otis, keenly aware of the declining fortunes and the resentment of ordinary townspeople, was mirroring as well as molding popular opinion.

In 1763 the Hutchinson circle made another attempt to strike at the town meeting system of politics, which was closely interwoven with the Boston Caucus. Election messages in the *Evening-Post* urged the electorate to "keep the Public Good only in View" while burying "in everlasting Oblivion" old prejudices and animosities. But this much said, the paper ran a scathing "expose" of the Caucus, which read like

the confessions of an ex-Communist. Allegedly written by a former
member of the Caucus, it explained how Caucus leaders conducted all
political affairs behind closed doors and in smoke-filled rooms. Then,
"for form sake," the leaders "prepared a number of warm disputes . . .
to entertain the lower sort; who are in an ecstasy to find the old Roman
Patriots still surviving." All townspeople were invited to speak at these
open meetings, it was claimed, but to oppose Caucus leaders was to
earn their "eternal animosity" and end forever any chance of obtaining
town office. Democracy, as practiced by the Caucus, was nothing but
sham, mocked the *Evening-Post* writer.[56]

The attempt to "expose" the Caucus as a dictatorial clique, with
little genuine interest in the laboring classes, failed miserably. The
Caucus responded by organizing its most successful roundup of voters
in Boston's colonial history. On election day, 1,089 voters went to the
poll, a number never to be exceeded even in the tumultuous years of
the following decade. They drubbed the candidates favored by the
Hutchinsonians. James Otis, the leading anti-Hutchinsonian, got the
largest number of votes and was installed as moderator of the town
meeting—a token of the confidence in which he was held for his open-
handed attacks on Hutchinson.[57]

The bitter Otis-Hutchinson fight of the early 1760s, carried on
before English imperial policy became an issue in Massachusetts, revolved around a number of specific issues, including the replacement
of William Bollan as provincial agent, the establishment of an Anglican
mission in the shadow of Harvard College, the multiple offices held by
Hutchinson and his relatives, the writs of assistance, and other problems. But more fundamentally, the struggle matched two incompatible
conceptions of government and society. Developed during the controversies of preceding decades, these conceptions were spelled out in an
outpouring of political rhetoric in the early 1760s and in the crystalli-
zation of two distinct factions.

James Otis, Samuel Adams, Royall Tyler, Oxenbridge Thacher,
and a host of other Bostonians, linked to the artisans and laborers
through a network of neighborhood taverns, fire companies, and the
Caucus, espoused a vision of politics that gave credence to laboring-
class views and regarded as entirely legitimate the participation of
artisans and even laborers in the political process.[58] This was not a new
conception of the rightful political economy, but a very old one. The
leaders of this movement were merely following in the footsteps of
earlier popular leaders—from John Noyes to Elisha Cooke to James

Allen. The town meeting, open to almost all property owners in the city and responsive to the propertyless as well, was the foundation of this system. By no means narrowly based, the "popular" party included many of the city's merchants, shopkeepers, lawyers, doctors, clergymen, and other well-to-do men. They provided leadership and filled the most important elective offices—overseers of the poor, tax assessors, town selectmen, and delegates to the House of Representatives. Lesser people filled minor offices and voiced their opinions at the town meetings where they were numerically dominant.

For the conservative merchants and lawyers, led and personified by Thomas Hutchinson, the old system spelled only chaos. "Reform" for these men meant paring back the responsibilities of the town meeting, substituting appointive for elective officeholders, restricting the freedom of the press, and breaking down the virulent anti-Anglican prejudice that still characterized the popular party. Like their opponents, members of the "prerogative" party had suffered as Boston's economy stagnated after 1740. But they saw the best hope for reviving the economy in handing over the management of town government to the wealthy and well-born exclusively. To see Otis address the crowd and to witness "the Rage of Patriotism...spread so violently...thro' town and country, that there is scarce a cobler or porter but has turn'd mountebank in politicks and erected his stage near the printing-press" was their vision of hell.[59]

Between 1761 and 1764 proponents of the "popular" and "prerogative" conceptions of politics engaged in a furious battle of billingsgate that filled the columns of the *Gazette* and *Evening-Post.* It is easy to be diverted by the extreme forms which the scurrility took. Charges of "Racoon," "stinking Skunk," "Pimp," "wild beast," "drunkard," and dozens of other choice titles were traded back and forth in verbal civil war. But more important than this stream of epithets was the deep-seated, class-tinged animosity which the polemical pieces exposed: hatred and suspicion of laboring people on the part of the Hutchinsonians; suspicion and hatred of the wealthy, Anglican, prerogative elite held by the common people.

Thus, Thomas Pownall, the popular governor from 1757 to 1760, was satirized by a conservative for confusing class lines by going aboard ships in Boston harbor to talk with "common people about ship-affairs" and mingling in the streets with the "dirtiest, most lubberly, mutinous, and despised part of the people."[60] The anti-Hutchinsonians, on the other hand, urged Bostonians to oppose "The

Leviathan in power [Hutchinson], or those other overgrown Animals, whose influence and importance is only in exact mathematical proportion to the weight of their purses."[61] The Caucus, decried a Hutchinsonian, talked incessantly about the right "for every dabbler in politicks to say and print whatever his shallow understanding, or vicious passions may suggest, against the wisest and best men—a liberty for fools and madmen to spit and throw firebrands at those of the most respectable and most amiable character."[62] In retort, Otis, speaking as a mechanic, poured out his resentment: "I am forced to get my living by the labour of my hand; and the sweat of my brow, as most of you are and obliged to go thro' good report and evil report, for bitter bread, earned under the frowns of some who have no natural or divine right to be above me, and entirely owe their grandeur and honor to grinding the faces of the poor, and other acts of ill gotten gain and power."[63] In reply, the conservatives charged anarchy: "The day is hastening, when some who are now, or, have lately been the darling idols of a dirty very dirty witless rabble commonly called the little vulgar, are to sink and go down with deserved infamy, to all posterity."[64] This was doubtful, retorted a writer in the *Gazette:* the problem was that the rich were obsessed with money and "couldn't have the idea of riches without that of poverty. They must see others poor in order to form a notion of their own happiness." Thus, in what was once a flourishing town, "a few persons in power" attempted to monopolize politics, and promoted projects "for keeping the people poor in order to make them humble. . . ."[65]

This reciprocal animosity and mistrust, suffusing the newspapers and pamphlets of the late colonial period, reveals the deeply rooted social tensions that Bostonians would carry into the revolutionary era. These tensions shaped the ways in which different social groups began to think about *internal* political goals once the conflict against *external* authority began. In the end, the Hutchinson faction, looking not to the future but staring into the distant past, faced an impossible task—to convince a broad electorate that the very men who had accumulated fortunes in an era when most had suffered were alone qualified to govern in the interest of the whole community. Lower- and middle-class Bostonians had heard fiscal conservatives and political elitists pronounce the same platitudes for half a century. Even now, a generation before James Madison formally enunciated an interest-group theory of politics, they understood that each group had its particular interest to promote and that aristocratic politicians who claimed to work for the commonweal were not to be trusted. Such men employed the catchwords of the traditional system of politics—"public good," "community," "harmony," and "public virtue"—to cloak their own ambitions for aggrandizing wealth and power.[66] The growing inequalities of wealth in Boston, which could be readily seen in the overcrowded almshouse and flocks of outreliefers in contrast to the urban splendor of men like Hutchinson and Oliver, were proof enough of that.

IV

Only by understanding the long animosity that the common people of Boston held for Thomas Hutchinson and his clique can sense be made of the extraordinary response to the Stamp Act in Boston in August 1765—the systematic destruction of the houses of Hutchinson and other wealthy and conservative Boston officials—and of the course of revolutionary politics in the city in the years that followed. It is possible, of course, to revert to the explanation of Peter Oliver, who, at the time, argued that "the People in general . . . were like the Mobility of all Countries, perfect Machines, wound up by any Hand who might first take the winch."[67] In this view, the crowd was led by the nose by middle- and upper-class manipulators such as Otis and Samuel Adams, and used to further their own political ambitions. In this Newtonian formulation, the crowd could never be self-activating, for thought and planned action could have their source only in the minds of educated persons.[68]

Such explanations, however, bear no relationship to the social realities in Boston at the time or to the long history of popular protest in the city. Again and again in the eighteenth century the Boston crowd had considered its interest, determined its enemies, and moved in a coordinated and discriminating way to gain its ends through street action. It was frequently supported in this by men higher up on the social scale—men who shielded the crowd leaders from subsequent attempts of the authorities to punish them.[69] Thus, several socioeconomic groups, with interests that often coincided but sometimes diverged, found it profitable to coordinate their actions.

The attacks on Andrew Oliver's house on the evening of 14 August 1765, and on Hutchinson's house twelve days later, were entirely consistent with this pattern of politics. On the evening of 14 August,

the crowd, led by the shoemaker Ebenezer MacIntosh, culminated a
day of protest against the Stamp Act by reducing Oliver's mansion to
a shambles. Accompanied by the sheriff, Hutchinson attempted to stop
the property destruction. For his trouble, he was driven off with a
hailstorm of stones. Less than two weeks later it was Hutchinson's
turn. Forcing him and his family to flee, the crowd smashed in the
doors with axes, reduced the furniture to splinters, stripped the walls
bare, chopped through inner partitions until the house was a hollow
shell, destroyed the formal gardens behind the house, drank the contents of the wine cellar, and carried off every moveable object of value
except some of Hutchinson's books and papers, which were left to
scatter in the wind. Not a person in Boston, neither private citizen nor
officer of the law, attempted to stop the crowd. Its members worked
through the night with almost military precision to raze the building,
spending three hours alone "at the cupola before they could get it
down," according to Governor Bernard.[70]

Historians agree that in destroying the Boston mansions of Oliver
and Hutchinson, the crowd was demonstrating against the Stamp Act.
Oliver had been appointed Stamp Collector, and Hutchinson, though
he publicly expressed his view that the act was unwise, had vowed to
use his authority as lieutenant-governor to see it executed. But in
conducting probably the most ferocious attack on private property in
the history of the English colonies, the crowd was demonstrating
against far more than Parliamentary policy. Stamp collectors were
intimidated and handled roughly in many other cities. But nowhere
else did the crowd choose to destroy property on such a grand scale
and with such exacting thoroughness. The full meaning of these attacks can be extracted only by understanding the long-standing
animus against the Oliver-Hutchinson circle. Beyond intimidating
British officialdom, the crowd was giving vent to years of hostility at
the accumulation of wealth and power by the aristocratic, Hutchinson-
led prerogative faction. Behind every swing of the ax and every hurled
stone, behind every shattered plate and splintered mahogany chair lay
the fury of a Bostonian who had read or heard the repeated references
to the people as "rabble," and who had suffered economic hardship
while others grew rich. The handsome furnishings in the houses of
Hutchinson, Oliver, and others that fell before the "Rage-intoxicated
rabble," as one young upper-class lawyer put it, provided psychological recompense for those Bostonians who had lost faith that opportunity or equitable relationships any longer prevailed in their city.[71]

The political consciousness of the crowd and its use of the Stamp Act protests as an opportunity for an attack on wealth itself were remarked upon again and again in the aftermath of the August crowd actions. Fifteen houses were targeted for destruction on the night of 27 August, according to Governor Bernard, in what he thought had become "a War of Plunder, of general levelling and taking away the Distinction of rich and poor." "Everything that for years past, had been the cause of any unpopular discontent was revived," he explained; "and private resentments against persons in office worked themselves in, and endeavoured to exert themselves under the mask of the public cause."[72] On the same day, the governor warned that unless "persons of property and consideration did not unite in support of government"—by which he meant that a way must be found to employ the militia or some kind of *posse comitatus* to control crowd actions—"anarchy and confusion" would continue in "an insurrection of the poor against the rich, those that want the necessities of life against those that have them."[73] On 10 September, two weeks after the destruction of Hutchinson's house, another Boston merchant wrote that "the rich men in the town" were seized with apprehension and "were moveing their cash & valuable furniture,&c" to the homes of poorer friends who were above suspicion.[74]

Seen in the context of three generations of social and economic change in Boston, and set against the drive for power of the Hutchinson-Oliver faction in Massachusetts, the Stamp Act riots provide a revealing example of the "moral economy of the crowd" in the early stages of the revolutionary movement. Members of the Boston "mob" needed no upper-class leaders to tell them about the economic stagnation of the late colonial period that had been affecting their lives and the structure of opportunity in the town. Nor did they need to destroy the homes of Oliver and Hutchinson in order to obtain the promise of these officeholders to hold the Stamp Act in abeyance. Instead, the crowd paid off some old debts and served notice on those whom it regarded as enemies of its interests.[75] It was the culminating event of an era of protest against wealth and oligarchic power that had been growing in all the cities. In addition, it demonstrated the fragility of the union between protesting city dwellers of the laboring classes and their more bourgeois partners, for in the uninhibited August attacks on property, the Boston crowd went much farther than Caucus leaders such as James Otis and Samuel Adams had reckoned or wished to countenance.[76]

V

In the other cities the growing resentment of wealth, the rejection of an elitist conception of politics, and the articulation of artisan- and laboring-class interests also gained momentum after 1765. These were vital developments in the revolutionary period. Indeed, it was the extraordinary new vigor of urban laboring people in defining and pursuing their goals that raised the frightening spectre of a radicalized form of politics and a radically changed society in the minds of many upper-class city dwellers, who later abandoned the resistance movement against England that they had initially supported and led.

That no full-fledged proletarian radical ideology emerged in the decade before the Revolution should not surprise us, for this was a preindustrial society in which no proletariat yet existed. Instead, we can best understand the long movement of protest against concentrated wealth and power, building powerfully as social and economic conditions changed in the cities, as a reflection of the disillusionment of laborers, artisans, and many middle-class city dwellers against a system that no longer delivered equitable rewards to the industrious. "Is it equitable that 99, rather 999, should suffer for the Extravagance or Grandeur of one," asked a New Yorker in 1765, "especially when it is considered that Men frequently owe their Wealth to the impoverishment of their Neighbors?"[77] Such thoughts, cutting across class lines, were gaining force among large parts of the urban population in the late colonial period. They were directed squarely at outmoded notions that only the idle and profligate could fail in America and that only the educated and wealthy were entitled to manage political affairs.

But the absence of clearly identifiable class consciousness and of organized proletarian radicalism does not mean that a radical ideology, nurtured within the matrix of preindustrial values and modes of thought, failed to emerge during the Revolution. Though this chapter in the history of the Revolution is largely unwritten, current scholarship is making it clear that the radicalization of thought in the cities, set in motion by economic and social change, advanced very rapidly once the barriers of traditional thought were broken down. A storm of demands, often accompanied by crowd action to insure their implementation, rose from the urban "tradesmen" and "mechanicks": for the end of closed assembly debates and the erection of public galleries in the legislative houses; for published roll-call votes which would indicate how faithfully elected legislators followed the wishes of their constituents; for open-air meetings where laboring men could help devise and implement public policy; for more equitable laying of taxes; for price controls instituted by and for the laboring classes to shield them from avaricious men of wealth; and for the election of mechanics and other ordinary people at all levels of government.[78]

How rapidly politics and political ideology could be transformed, as colonists debated the issue of rebellion, is well illustrated by the case of Philadelphia. In one brief decade preceding the Revolution the artisanry and laboring poor of the city moved from a position of clear political inferiority to a position of political control. They took over the political machinery of the city, pushed through the most radical state constitution of the period, and articulated concepts of society and political economy that would have stunned their predecessors. By mid-1776, laborers, artisans, and small tradesmen, employing extralegal measures when electoral politics failed, were in clear command in Philadelphia. Working with middle-class leaders such as James Cannon, Timothy Matlack, Thomas Young, and Thomas Paine, they launched a full-scale attack on wealth and even on the right to acquire unlimited private property. By the summer of 1776 the militant Privates Committee, which probably represented the poorest workers, became the foremost carrier of radical ideology in Pennsylvania. It urged the voters, in electing delegates.for the constitutional convention, to shun "great and overgrown rich men [who] will be improper to be trusted, [for] they will be too apt to be framing distinctions in society, because they will reap the benefits of all such distinctions."[79] Going even further, they drew up a bill of rights for consideration by the convention, which included the proposition that "an enormous proportion of property vested in a few individuals is dangerous to the rights, and destructive of the common happiness, of mankind; and therefore every free state hath a right by its laws to discourage the possession of such property."[80] For four years, in an extremely fluid political scene, a radicalized artisanry shaped—and sometimes dominated—city and state politics, while setting forth the most fully articulated ideology of reform yet heard in America.[81]

These calls for reform varied from city to city, depending on differing conditions, past politics, and the qualities of particular leaders. Not all the reforms were implemented, especially those that went to the heart of the structural problems in the economy. Pennsylvania, for example, did not adopt the radical limitation on property holding.

But that we know from hindsight that the most radical challenges to the existing system were thwarted, or enjoyed only a short period of success, does not mean that they are not a vital part of the revolutionary story. At the time, the disaffected in the cities were questioning some of the most fundamental tenets of colonial thought. Ordinary people, in bold opposition to their superiors, to whom custom required that they defer, were creating power and suggesting solutions to problems affecting their daily lives. As other essays in this book explain, how far these calls for radical reform extended and the success they achieved are matters that historians have begun to investigate only lately. But this much is clear: even though many reforms were defeated or instituted briefly and then abandoned, political thought and behavior would never again be the same in America.

In preparing this essay I profited greatly from the criticism of James A. Henretta, Jesse Lemisch, Stephen Patterson, and Alfred Young.

   1. See, for example, Bernard Bailyn, *The Ideological Origins of the American Revolution* (Cambridge: Harvard University Press, 1967); Bailyn, *The Ordeal of Thomas Hutchinson* (Cambridge: Harvard University Press, 1974); Pauline Maier, *From Resistance to Revolution: Colonial Radicals and the Development of American Opposition to Britain, 1765–1776* (New York: Alfred A. Knopf, 1972); Richard D. Brown, *Revolutionary Politics in Massachusetts: The Boston Committee of Correspondence and the Towns, 1772–1774* (Cambridge: Harvard University Press, 1970).
   2. Bailyn, "The Central Themes of the American Revolution: An Interpretation," in Stephen G. Kurtz and James H. Hutson, eds., *Essays on the American Revolution* (Chapel Hill: University of North Carolina Press, 1973), p. 12.
   3. Bailyn, *Ideological Origins of the Revolution,* p. 95.
   4. Bailyn, "Central Themes of the American Revolution," p. 12.
   5. John J. McCusker, "Sources of Investment Capital in the Colonial Philadelphia Shipping Industry," *Journal of Economic History* 32 (1972): 156–57.
   6. For Boston, see James A. Henretta,"Economic Development and Social Structure in Colonial Boston," *William and Mary Quarterly,* 3d ser. 22 (1965): 75–92. The Boston data has been reexamined and compared with similar data from New York and Philadelphia in Gary B. Nash, "Wealth and Poverty in Three Colonial Cities: The Social Background to Revolution," *Journal of Interdisciplinary History* 8 (1976).
   7. For the rise of urban affluence, see Carl Bridenbaugh, *Cities in Revolt: Urban Life in America, 1743–1776* (New York: Alfred A. Knopf, 1955), chap. 6. A revealing individual case is studied in Nicholas B. Wainwright, *Colonial Grandeur in Philadelphia: the House and Furniture of General John Cadwalader* (Philadelphia: Historical Society of Pennsylvania, 1964).
   8. Wills and inventories for almost 1,400 eighteenth-century Philadelphians are in the Office of the Recorder of Wills, City Hall Annex, Philadelphia. More than twice that number are available for Boston at the Office of the Recorder of Wills, Suffolk County Court House, Boston.
   9. Raymond A. Mohl, "Poverty in Early America, A Reappraisal: The Case of Eighteenth-Century New York City," *New York History* 50 (1969): 5–27. The data and conclusions on poverty and poor relief in the following paragraphs are discussed more fully in Nash, "Wealth and Poverty," and Gary B. Nash, "Poverty and Poor Relief in Pre-Revolutionary Philadelphia," *William and Mary Quarterly,* 3d ser. 33 (1976).

10. Data derived from Records of the Pennsylvania Hospital for the Sick Poor, 1751–1828, American Philosophical Society (microfilms); and Records of the Contributors for the Better Relief and Employment of the Poor, 1767–1778, City Archives, Philadelphia.

11. William H. Whitmore et al., eds., *Reports of the Record Commissioners of Boston,* 39 vols. (Boston, 1878–1902), 14:13, 100, 280; Lemuel Shattuck, *Report to the Committee of the City Council Appointed to Obtain a Census of Boston for the Year 1845* (Boston, 1846), p. 5; G. B. Warden, *Boston, 1689–1776* (Boston: Little, Brown, and Co., 1970), pp. 128, 325n.

12. *Record Commissioners of Boston,* 12:178; 14:302.

13. County Commissioners of Philadelphia, Minutes, 1718–1766, City Archives, Philadelphia; Minutes, 1771–1774, Historical Society of Pennsylvania; Minutes, 1774–1776, Pennsylvania State Archives, Harrisburg.

14. The following discussion of probated wealth is drawn from a much fuller treatment in Nash, "Wealth and Poverty."

15. Gordon S. Wood, "A Note on Mobs in the American Revolution," *William and Mary Quarterly* 23 (1966): 635–42; Pauline Maier, "Popular Uprisings and Civil Authority in Eighteenth-Century America," ibid., 27 (1970): 3–35.

16. Jesse Lemisch, "Jack Tar in the Street: Merchant Seamen in the Politics of Revolutionary America," *William and Mary Quarterly* 25 (1968): 371–407; Warden, *Boston,* chaps. 6–8; Gary B. Nash, "The Transformation of Urban Politics, 1700–1765," *Journal of American History* 60 (1973): 605–32.

17. *Record Commissioners of Boston,* 8:99–104; 11:194–97; Warden, *Boston,* p. 66.

18. *The Present Melancholy Circumstances of the Province...* (Boston, 1719); Everett Kimball, *The Public Life of Joseph Dudley: A Study of the Colonial Policy of the Stuarts in New England, 1660–1715* (New York: Longmans, Green and Co., 1911), pp. 161–78.

19. *A Letter to an Eminent Clergy-Man...* [Boston, 1721]; see also the series of pamphlets published from 1719 to 1721 reprinted in Andrew McFarland Davis, *Colonial Currency Reprints, 1682–1751,* 4 vols. (Boston: The Prince Society, 1910–1911), 1:367–452; 2:3–334.

20. Warden, *Boston,* pp. 91–96; Warden, "The Caucus and Democracy in Colonial Boston," *New England Quarterly* 43 (1970): 19–33.

21. Logan, *A Dialogue Showing What's Therein to be Found* (Philadelphia, 1725); in *A Charge From the Bench to the Grand Jury* (Philadelphia, 1723), Logan argued that the high wages demanded by artisans and laboring men were also a cause of the depression.

22. Thomas Wendel, "The Keith-Lloyd Alliance: Factional and Coalition Politics in Colonial Pennsylvania," *Pennsylvania Magazine of History and Biography* 92 (1968): 289–305; Nash, "Transformation of Urban Politics," pp. 606–8.

23. Gertrude MacKinney, ed., *Votes and Proceedings of the House of Representatives of the Province of Pennsylvania, Pennsylvania Archives,* 8th ser. (Harrisburg, 1931–1935), 2:1459. For the attack on Logan's house, see Logan to James Alexander, 23 October 1749, Logan Letter Book, 1748–1750, Historical Society of Pennsylvania.

24. *The Triumverate of Pennsylvania: In a Letter to a Friend in the Country* (Philadelphia, 1728); also *A Dialogue Between Mr. Robert Rich and Roger Plowman* (Philadelphia, 1725).

25. David Lloyd, *A Vindication of the Legislative Power* (Philadelphia, 1725); the attacks on accumulated wealth and power were continued in [William Keith], *The Observators Trip to America* (Philadelphia, 1725); Keith, *A Modest Reply to the Speech of Isaac Norris ...* (Philadelphia, 1727); [Keith], *Remarks upon the Advice to the Freeholders* of the Triumvirate... (Philadelphia, 1729).

26. Logan to John Penn, 17 November 1729, *Pennsylvania Magazine of History and Biography* 34 (1910): 122–23; Norris to Joseph Pike, 28 August 1728, Norris Letter Book, 1716–1730; David Barclay to Thomas Penn, [1727], Penn Papers; Official Correspondence, 2:43, Historical Society of Pennsylvania.

27. Thompson, "The Moral Economy of the English Crowd in the Eighteenth Century," *Past and Present,* no. 50 (1971) pp. 76–136.

28. Timothy Wheelwright [pseud.], *Two Letters on Election of Alderman* [New York 1734].

29. *New-York Journal,* 18 March, 20 May, 8 July 1734; for a general consideration of New York City politics in this era, see Patricia U. Bonomi, *A Factious People: Politics and*

Society in Colonial New York (New York: Columbia University Press, 1971), pp. 112–34.

30. *New-York Journal,* 8, 15 July 1734; 3 March 1735; 30 May 1737. The fullest discussion of this era is Beverly McAnear, "Politics in Provincial New York, 1689–1761," (Ph.D. diss., Stanford University, 1935), pp. 420–88.

31. Bonomi, *A Factious People,* chap. 5; *New-York Gazette, or the Weekly Post-Boy,* 25 January 1747/48.

32. Colden, *An Address to the Freeholders* (New York, 1747); *New-York Evening Post,* 21 December 1747; *New-York Mercury,* 7, 21 January 1754; *New-York Gazette,* 14 January 1754; *New-York Post-Boy,* 22 April 1754; McAnear, "Politics in Provincial New York," pp. 535–36.

33. Warden, *Boston,* pp. 116–22; Dirk Hoerder, "People and Mobs: Crowd Action in Massachusetts during the American Revolution, 1765–1780," (Inaugural-diss., University of Berlin, 1971), pp. 94–102.

34. Warden, *Boston,* p. 122; *The Melancholy State of this Province...* ([Boston], 1736), p. 9.

35. Robert Zemsky, *Merchants, Farmers, and River Gods: An Essay on Eighteenth-Century American Politics* (Boston: Gambit, 1971), pp. 118–19; for the Land Bank, see also George A. Billias, *The Massachusetts Land Bankers of 1740* (Orono, Me.: University of Maine, 1959).

36. [Douglass], *Postscript To a Discourse concerning the Currencies of the British Plantations in America* ([Boston, 1740]), pp. 59–60.

37. Minutes of the Boston Town Meeting, in Justin Winsor et al., *The Memorial History of Boston,* 3 vols. (Boston, 1880–1883), 2:489–90.

38. *Boston Gazette,* 4, 11 December 1749; 9 January, 13, 20 March 1750; *Boston Evening-Post,* 18 December 1749; 12, 19 March 1750; *Boston Independent Advertiser,* 18, 25 September 1749; *Boston Weekly News-Letter,* 1 February 1750; Warden, *Boston,* pp. 139–41; Peter Orlando Hutchinson, ed., *The Diary and Letters of His Excellency Thomas Hutchinson,* 2 vols. (London, 1883–1886), 1:54. Hutchinson's account of his role in the devaluation is in his *History of the Colony and Province of Massachusetts-Bay,* ed. Lawrence Shaw Mayo, 3 vols. (Cambridge: Harvard University Press, 1936), 2:334–37; 3:6–7. Hutchinson later recounted that his friend, William Bollan, warned him to retire to his summer mansion at Milton in order to avoid being mobbed by his townsmen. Hutchinson to Bollan, 27 December 1765, Massachusetts Archives, 26:187.

39. Vincent Centinel [pseud.], *Massachusetts in Agony: Or, Important Hints To the Inhabitants of the Province: Calling aloud For Justice to be done to the Oppressed...* (Boston, 1750), pp. 3–5, 8, 12–13. The best account of Hutchinson's hard money policy and its repercussions in Boston is Malcolm Freiberg, "Thomas Hutchinson and the Province Currency," *New England Quarterly* 30 (1957): 196–206.

40. The best places to begin a study of the urban dimension of the Great Awakening are Alan Heimert, *Religion and the American Mind from the Great Awakening to the Revolution* (Cambridge: Harvard University Press, 1966); and Dietmar Rothermund, *The Layman's Progress: Religious and Political Experience in Colonial Pennsylvania, 1740–1770* (Philadelphia: University of Pennsylvania Press, 1961).

41. Rothermund, *Layman's Progress,* pp. 55–60, 81–82; Heimert, *Religion and the American Mind,* pp. 27–58, 239–93. The process of mental transformation was not confined to the cities of course. See Richard L. Bushman, *From Puritan to Yankee: Character and the Social Order in Connecticut, 1690–1765* (Cambridge: Harvard University Press, 1967); and Rhys Isaac, "Preachers and Patriots: Explorations in Popular Culture and Revolution in Virginia, 1774–1776," in this volume.

42. For Davenport, see *Boston Evening-Post,* 2 August 1742. The response of the frightened Charles Chauncy is quoted in John C. Miller, "Religion, Finance, and Democracy in Massachusetts," *New England Quarterly* 6 (1933): 52–53.

43. Eric Foner, "Tom Paine's Republic: Radical Ideology and Social Change," in this volume.

44. *New-York Gazette or Weekly Post-Boy,* 26 August 1762; 13, 20 August 1767; *New-York Journal,* 18 November, 17, 24, 31 December 1767; 7, 21 January 1768; Pierre Du Simitiere Papers, Historical Society of Pennsylvania, for carriage owners.

45. Nash, "Transformation of Urban Politics," pp. 626–29.

46. The most important contributions are Malcolm Freiberg, "Thomas Hutchin-

son: The First Fifty Years (1711–1761)," *William and Mary Quarterly* 15 (1958): 35–55; John A. Schutz, *Thomas Pownall, British Defender of American Liberty: A Study of Anglo-American Relations in the Eighteenth Century* (Glendale, Calif.: A. H. Clark Co., 1951); Ellen E. Brennan, *Plural Office-Holding in Massachusetts, 1760–1780: Its Relation to the "Separation" of Departments of Government* (Chapel Hill: University of North Carolina Press, 1945); John J. Waters, Jr., *The Otis Family in Provincial and Revolutionary Massachusetts* (Chapel Hill: University of North Carolina Press, 1968); and Waters and Schutz, "Patterns of Massachusetts Colonial Politics: The Writs of Assistance and the Rivalry between the Otis and Hutchinson Families," *William and Mary Quarterly* 24 (1967): 543–67.

47. Warden, *Boston*, p. 136; *Boston Record Commissioners* 14:127.

48. *Boston Gazette*, 9 January 1750; *Boston Weekly News-Letter*, 7 July 1748; *Boston Evening-Post*, 11, 18 December 1749. See also Herman J. Belz, "Currency Reform in Massachusetts, 1749–50," *Essex Institute Historical Collections*, 103 (1967): 66–84; and Freiberg, "Thomas Hutchinson and the Province Currency," pp. 199–206. The election of Hutchinson as tax collector, an office from which he was exempt by law as a member of the governor's council, was reported in *Boston Weekly Post-Boy*, 25 December 1749.

49. In 1759 Hutchinson himself noted the bitter opposition to him in Boston. Hutchinson to Israel Williams, 14 June 1759, Israel Williams Letters, Massachusetts Historial Society, 2:150. The attacks on Hutchinson's 1761 devaluation scheme are in *Boston Gazette*, 21, 28 December 1761; 11 January 1762; and [Oxenbridge Thacher], *Considerations on Lowering the Value of Gold Coins. . .* [Boston, 1762]. See also Hugh F. Bell, "A Personal Challenge: the Otis-Hutchinson Currency Controversy of 1761–1762," *Essex Institute Historical Collections* 106 (1970): 297–323.

50. Warden, *Boston*, pp. 73–77, 104–11.

51. *A Dialogue Between a Boston Man and A Country Man* ([Boston], 1715); *Trade and Commerce Inculcated. . .* (Boston, 1731).

52. Charles H. Lincoln ed., *Correspondence of William Shirley*, 2 vols (New York, 1912), 1:418–22.

53. *Boston Gazette*, 5, 12 May 1760.

54. Quoted in John C. Miller, *Sam Adams; Pioneer in Propaganda* (Stanford, Calif.: Stanford University Press, 1936), p. 27.

55. *To the Freeholders of the Town of Boston* (Boston, 1760); *Boston Gazette*, 12 May 1760.

56. *Boston Evening-Post*, 21 March 1763.

57. *Boston Gazette*, 16 May 1763.

58. On the Caucus, see Warden, "The Caucus and Democracy in Colonial Boston"; and Alan and Katherine Day, "Another Look at the Boston 'Caucus,' " *Journal of American Studies* 5 (1971): 19–42.

59. *Boston Evening-Post*, 7 March 1763.

60. Tom Thumb [Samuel Waterhouse], *Proposals for Printing. . . by Subscription the History of Vice-Admiral Thomas Brazen. . .* ([Boston], 1760).

61. *Boston Gazette*, 28 December 1761. See also [Oxenbridge Thacher], *Considerations on the Election of Counsellors, Humbly Offered to the Electors* ([Boston], 1761).

62. *Boston Evening-Post*, 14 March 1763.

63. *Boston Gazette*, 11 January 1762, Supplement.

64. *Boston Evening-Post*, 14 March 1763.

65. *Boston Gazette*, 28 February 1763.

66. The best explication of coexisting "antipartisan theory and partisan reality" during this period is in Stephen E. Patterson, *Political Parties in Revolutionary Massachusetts* (Madison, Wis.: University of Wisconsin Press, 1973), chap. 1.

67. Peter Oliver, *Origins & Progress of the American Rebellion: A Tory View*, eds. Douglass Adair and John A. Schutz (Stanford, Calif.: Stanford University Press, 1967), p. 65. This is a view found in most modern histories of the period.

68. In most of the recent literature of the early revolutionary period in Boston, and especially in John C. Miller, *Sam Adams;* and Hiller Zobel, *The Boston Massacre* (Boston: W. W. Norton and Co., 1970), the crowd is characterized as mindless, manipulable, and antirational. For a discussion of how the crowd is treated in Zobel's book and several other recent works, see Jesse Lemisch, "Radical Plot in Boston (1770): A Study in the Use of Evidence," *Harvard Law Review* 84 (1970): 485–504; and Edward Countryman,

"The Problem of the Early American Crowd," *Journal of American Studies* 7 (1973): 77–90.

69. Pauline Maier, "Popular Uprisings and Civil Authority in Eighteenth-Century America," *William and Mary Quarterly* 27 (1970): 3–35; in many ways the Boston crowd resembles the preindustrial "city mob" described by E. J. Hobsbawm in *Primitive Rebels: Studies in Archaic Forms of Social Movement in the 19th and 20th Centuries* (New York: W. W. Norton and Co., 1965), chap. 7. Nothing illustrates better the support which the lower-class participants in crowd action received from those above them than the consistent refusal of the grand jury in Boston to indict rioters.

70. The Stamp Act riots are best described, though analyzed differently, in Edmund S. and Helen M. Morgan, *The Stamp Act Crisis; Prologue to Revolution* (Chapel Hill: University of North Carolina Press, 1953), pp. 160–69; Warden, *Boston*, pp. 165–69; Zobel, *Boston Massacre*, pp. 24–47; and George P. Anderson, "Ebenezer Mackintosh: Stamp Act Rioter and Patriot," *Publications* of the Colonial Society of Massachusetts, 26 (1924–1926): 15–64.

71. Josiah Quincy, Jr., *Reports of Cases Argued in the Superior Court... Between 1761 and 1772...,* Samuel M. Quincy, ed. (Boston, 1865), p. 169.

72. Bernard to the Board of Trade, 31 August 1765, in William Cobbett, ed., *The Parliamentary History of England,* 16 (London, 1813), pp. 129–31.

73. Bernard to Halifax, 31 August 1765, Francis Bernard Papers, 4:158ff, Houghton Library, Harvard University, quoted in Bailyn, *Hutchinson,* p. 37n.

74. James Gordon to William Martin, 10 September 1765, Massachusetts Historical Society *Proceedings,* 2d ser. 13 (1899–1900): 393.

75. A month after the destruction of his house Hutchinson admitted that some of those who in 1749 and 1750 had "threatened me with destruction" had "retained their rancor ever since and are supposed to have been aiders and abettors if not actors in the late riot." Hutchinson to Henry Seymour Conway, 1 October 1765, Massachusetts Archives 26:155. Four years earlier Hutchinson had noted that his unpopularity was largely attributable to his hard money policy in the late 1740s. Hutchinson to William Bollan, 14 December 1761, ibid., 26:24.

76. Patterson, *Political Parties in Revolutionary Massachusetts,* chap. 3.

77. *New-York Gazette,* 11 July 1765, quoted in Bernard Friedman, "The Shaping of the Radical Consciousness in Provincial New York," *Journal of American History* 56 (1970): 794.

78. The calls for political reform are best treated in J. R. Pole, *Political Representation in England and the Origins of the American Republic* (New York: MacMillan and Co., 1966); for price controls, Hoerder, "People and Mobs: Crowd Action in Massachusetts"; John K. Alexander, "The Fort Wilson Incident of 1779: A Case Study of the Revolutionary Crowd," *William and Mary Quarterly* 31 (1974): 589–612; and Anne Bezanson, "Inflation and Controls During the American Revolution in Pennsylvania, 1774-1779," *Journal of Economic History* 8, Supplement (1948): 1–20.

79. *To the Several Battalions of Military Associators in the Province of Pennsylvania* (Philadelphia, 1776), quoted in Merrill Jensen, "The American People and the American Revolution," *Journal of American History* 57 (1970): 29. Four months later, the radical party in Philadelphia urged the voters "to chuse no rich men and [as] few learned men possible to represent them in the [state constitutional] Convention." *Pennsylvania Packet,* 26 November 1776. The best accounts of the Privates Committee are in David Hawke, *In the Midst of a Revolution* (Philadelphia: University of Pennsylvania Press, 1961); R. A. Ryerson, "Political Mobilization and the American Revolution: The Resistance Movement in Philadelphia, 1765 to 1776," *William and Mary Quarterly* 31 (1974): 565–88.

80. *An Essay of a Declaration of Rights...* (Philadelphia, 1776), quoted in Jensen, "The American People and the American Revolution," pp. 32–33.

81. The standard account of this process is J. Paul Selsam, *The Pennsylvania Constitution of 1776: A Study in Revolutionary Democracy* (Philadelphia: University of Pennsylvania Press, 1936). Recent work is extending and revising Selsam's analysis; see especially, Ryerson, "Political Mobilization"; Alexander, "The Fort Wilson Incident of 1779"; and the essay on Thomas Paine by Eric Foner in this volume.

"Out of the Bounds of the Law": Northern Land Rioters in the Eighteenth Century

Edward Countryman

The colonial farmer at the plough, as depicted on the title page of *John Tobler's Almanack*, published in many editions by Christopher Sower at Germantown, Pennsylvania, between 1742 and 1759. Library of Congress.

Although I am a native American, I have spent my professional life since graduate school "on the outside," first in New Zealand and now in Great Britain. I suppose that that gives me an outsider's view of the sort of thing I study in this essay, and there is no question that I have been heavily influenced by such European Marxist historians as Edward Thompson, Albert Soboul, George Rudé, and E. J. Hobsbawm. The point may be reinforced by the fact that, as I write this preface, my university is in the midst of a student crisis of the sort not known in the States since 1970. But at the same time, my thinking about upheaval also reflects the work of systemic and behavioral analysts like Samuel P. Huntington, Ted Robert Gurr, and David Easton.

My interest in crowd studies is a basic element in my development as a historian. My doctoral thesis was a purely institutional study, looking at the New York State Legislature in the years following independence and paying little attention to problems outside the formal structure of political institutions. Its major feature was an attempt, through quantitative behavioral analysis, to resolve the rather hackneyed question of whether there were political parties in New York during the confederation period; but the most fruitful result of my venture into cliometrics was the realization that before I could understand either institutions or parties within them, I had to go back to the people at large and to their relationship to the collapse of old institutions and to the creation of new ones. I had assumed that the New York government was stable and "legitimate" from its inception, but I found that it was not. This essay is an attempt to understand a major facet of why it was not, and it ties into another essay in which I attempt to explain how and when the new institutions did take hold.

I am presently at the writing stage of a full-length project which will bring together these themes of destruction and creation and transformation. I think it will offer a fresh perspective on how much a revolution the American Revolution was.

Edward Countryman (Ph.D., Cornell University, 1971), teaches in the Joint School of Comparative American Studies at the University of Warwick, England.

Sometime in November 1749 a crowd of men gathered at the home of Abraham Phillips, a small farmer who lived at Horseneck, New Jersey. They pulled down his fences, loosed his hogs, spat in his face, knocked over a foundation that he had laid for an oven, and finally tore off part of the roof of his house and disheveled the house's contents. The rioters had declared previously that they "were going to tear Brom [Phillips] all to pieces."[1] On 26 August 1765, another crowd, this time in Boston, thoroughly sacked the mansion of Thomas Hutchinson, one of the most notable of the sons of Massachusetts.[2] And early in November 1771 Ethan Allen and Remember Baker, leaders-to-be of the Green Mountain Boys, led a small crowd (only nine men strong) to the house of Charles Hutchesson, a sometime corporal in a Highland regiment, who was trying to set himself up as a farmer near New Perth, on New York's northern frontier. Setting the house on fire, they told Hutchesson that "they had resolved to offer a burnt sacrifice to the Gods of the World."[3] Three different crowds, three different victims, and clearly Phillips, Hutchinson, and Hutchesson had little in common —besides having their houses destroyed. As George Rudé has recently pointed out, the very fact that early American crowds chose, like their English counterparts, to pull down houses shows how very Anglo-Saxon their behavior was.[4] But with crowds choosing victims as disparate as Phillips, Hutchinson, and Hutchesson, it seems that it is at that point that the problem of understanding them begins.

Not surprisingly, we know far more about the destruction of Thomas Hutchinson's house than about the others. The lieutenant-governor was a prominent and powerful man, the sort about whom lengthy biographies can be written,[5] and Boston's Stamp Act riots, during which his house was destroyed, were among the most dramatic

events in the coming of the American Revolution. One can make a
good case, however, that we need to know as much about rural crowds
of the sort that attacked Phillips and Hutchesson as about urban ones,
both for their own sake and for the sake of a fuller understanding of
the Revolution. Not the least reason for saying this is the fact that
despite their enormous political significance during the revolutionary
period, the people of Boston, New York, Philadelphia, Newport, and
Charleston formed only a tiny proportion of the whole population of
British America. It was the city crowd that gave punch to the movement
against Great Britain during the 1760s and early 1770s, but not until
the countryside joined in (in 1774 and 1775) did the movement find
the strength to topple the existing order and become fully revolutionary.[6] At the same time, it was this rural mobilization that led to the
most bitter internal disputes of the period, both between patriot and
loyalist Americans, and within the patriot camp itself.[7] The task here
is to consider the background to both the mobilization and the bitterness, at least in part.

A good part of that background, in the northern provinces, was
to be found in land rioting, most especially in the cases of the mid-
century New Jersey land riots, the Hudson Valley tenant disturbances
of the 1750s and 1760s, and the insurgency in northeastern New York
that began in 1764 and (by 1777) had led to the dismemberment of
the state and the creation of Vermont. Excellent studies have been
done of all these actions,[8] but there has been little effort to synthesize
what we know about them and to compare them with their eighteenth-
century counterparts in American cities and on the other side of the
Atlantic.[9] This essay will attempt such a synthesis, concentrating on
what the rioters did and how they did it, and trying to relate these
things to the sorts of men they were. It will look at the background of
the insurgencies, at the internal structure of the crowds, at their targets, at their attitudes to authority, and at authority's attitudes towards
them. That done, it will be possible to offer some speculations on their
deeper significance and on the rural crowd's place in the Revolution.

I

We are dealing with land riots, not with bread riots, and that fact
immediately sets the American rural crowd off from its counterparts
in both western Europe and urban America. In eighteenth-century

France and England, country people turned out characteristically in response to food shortage, and when good cheap bread was available there was little rioting. Although such crowds had well-developed ideas about what was right and what was wrong—a "moral economy" — they rarely became politicized, and, as E. P. Thompson suggests, astute local notables could respond to them in a positve, if paternalistic, way. Crowds themselves quite often expected such responses.[10] Crowds in colonial American cities could likewise riot over bread, though they also took to the streets for other reasons. It has been suggested that their social role was quasi-functional, the crowd in effect acting as an extension of government and on behalf of the community.[11] But in the northern American countryside the problem behind crowd action was not provisions, or whorehouses, or press-gangs; it was how and under what conditions and by whom a limited amount of land would be owned and occupied.

In New Jersey the question was whether the land around Newark and Elizabethtown would be held under title derived from the elite East New Jersey Proprietors, the beneficiaries of a seventeenth-century grant made by the Duke of York. The roots of the insurgency lay in conflicting grants made at the same time by the duke's governor, but by the 1740s the rioters were claiming that the land was theirs by direct Indian purchase. By the proprietors' own testimony, the implementation of their rights would have meant a crushing burden on small holders. They spoke of their land as being worth nearly a pound per acre and estimated the arrears of quitrents due in New Jersey at £15,000. Small wonder that the insurgents preferred Indian titles, which permitted sales of land at a tiny fraction of the proprietors' price![12] In the Hudson Valley the issue was the very existence of the manors and patents that made New York's land system unique in America. Their owners designed to have them occupied by tenants, and although they could offer attractive terms to newcomers, these terms were not intended to lead to freehold ownership. They often included humiliating vestiges of medieval tenant subservience, without the owners offering the physical protection that once had presumably justified such subservience. It was common knowledge in New York that at least some of these tracts had been obtained by blatant fraud. The validity of others was brought into question in mid-century by conflicting Indian titles (claimed by the Indians themselves), by the known hostility to the tracts of English officialdom, and by the problem of where New York ended and where New England began.[13]

The region that became Vermont was claimed, until 1764, by both New Hampshire and New York, and by the time that the Crown resolved the dispute in New York's favor, the two provinces had made many overlapping grants in it. The insurgency that wracked the district after 1764 sprang from the resistance of New Hampshire grantees who knew that submitting to New York would mean the loss of much of their land to New York City speculators. They knew, too, that any land they might hold under New York title would be subject to a far heavier quitrent that that due under a New Hampshire one. By 1776, New York's Royal governors had granted 2,115,610 acres in the region, all but 180,620 of them in direct defiance of a Royal order of 1767 that prohibited any further grants there. The order had been given in the vain hope of opening the way to a settlement.[14]

In none of these cases could the basic issue be compromised, for either the land would be held by or from the East Jersey proprietors, the Hudson Valley landlords, and the New York grantees, or it would not. And in all three cases the better legal position and the institutions of the province were on the side of the big owners. A recent exciting essay has suggested that by mid-century such great owners were revivifying the medieval technicalities of their tenure and bringing about a "feudal revival" in America.[15] It can be seen that the insurgents were responding not to sudden crises or short-term irritations but rather to structural conditions basic to their existing societies and to major trends in their development.

This helps to explain the fact that all three cases involved not sporadic rioting but rather movements that lasted for years. Organization is implicit in such staying power, and these rural crowds were organized to a remarkably high degree. The Hudson Valley rioters were perhaps the least structured of the three; the movement there was certainly the least permanent, flaring up in the 1750s, and then subsiding for several years before erupting into the great revolt of 1766. Yet clearly recognized leaders such as Michael Hallenbeck, Josiah Loomis, and Robert Noble emerged on Livingston Manor and neighboring Rensselaerwyck during the first wave, and as it was subsiding in 1762, "the club" was self-conscious enough to appoint "an agent to go for them to New York City in order to procure title from the Governor for the land at Taghkanick." The great rising of 1766 was preceded by the choice of William Prendergast, a Dutchess County farmer, as its leader, by the setting up of a committee of twelve to aid him, by the formation of militia companies, and by the election of captains for them. When they took to the field, the rioters tried captured enemies before popular courts. And they knew the importance of solidarity, for "It was the resolution of the mob that if any tenants setld without the Rest they should be destroyed."[16]

The insurgents in New Jersey and in the New Hampshire Grants went well beyond this, developing highly complex and lasting structures. The Jerseymen had a coordinating committee long before they turned to violence, and they showed in 1746 that their military organization was stronger than the official milita. This was a matter of competing loyalties, for the same men made up both bodies. When militia officers tried to quell a disturbance by ordering their men—the rioters—to fall into ranks, the crowd's leader, Amos Roberts, countered by calling "everyone who was on his list" to follow him. When some 300 did so, the officers were left to themselves. The next year, 1747, saw reports that the rioters "had built a Goal back in the Woods," and that they planned to imprison their enemies "& then see who durst fetch them out." By 1748 the insurgents had divided themselves "into three Wards & a trustee in each Ward for raising of money," and again in 1749 it was reported that they were operating a tax system. Their enemies appreciated their sophistication, and one of them summed it up in 1748 with the comment that "it appears that they had erected Courts of Judicature, & determined causes by hearing of one side, but intended for the future, to hear both sides; that they had taken upon them to choose their militia officers . . . that they pay taxes to their Committees."[17]

When inhabitants of Bennington resisted the running of a New York survey line in October 1769, they were led by their town committee. It was estimated that by this time the number of New Hampshire title holders had increased between five and tenfold over that of 1764, and these grantees were developing the full spirit of New England local life. During 1772 and 1773 the insurgents took formal military shape as the Green Mountain Boys, and by 1773 the insurgents had established courts "appointed by their own authority," courts which tried enemies of the movement and punished them, sometimes savagely. One wretched Yorker suffered 200 lashes on his bare back simply because he acted as a New York justice of the peace.[18]

These movements, in short, created counter-governments that exercised or tried to exercise almost all of the functions that government was expected to carry out in the eighteenth century. But to return to the pulling-down of houses, the proper question to ask is, "What sort of houses did the crowds pull?" The problem is whether in victimizing the likes of Abraham Phillips and Charles Hutchesson, they were merely bullying defenseless individuals (which is what Phillips and Hutchesson would have said) or whether one can find a rational pattern in their choice of targets.

In all three of these affairs there were prominent men whom the crowd identified as its chief enemies. In New Jersey they included Robert Hunter Morris, James Alexander, and Samuel Nevill. Morris was chief justice of the province, and he and Alexander, who had been John Peter Zenger's original lawyer in his famous trial defending freedom of the press, dominated both the provincial council and the board of proprietors. Nevill was a county judge and a leading figure in the provincial assembly. It was Alexander and Morris who were responsible for bringing the barrage of eviction suits that sparked off the troubles, suits of which one observer said that "this carried Terror on the face of it." It was Alexander and Morris who encouraged others to settle in the places of evictees, who wrote tract after tract condemning the rioters, and who gathered the copious documentation that tells us most of what we know about them.[19] All the great landlords of the east bank of the Hudson drew the ire of their tenants at one point or another, from the easy-going paternalist Henry Beekman to Roger Morris and Beverly Robinson, upstart sons-in-law of the Philipse family whose rash eviction orders—again the theme of sudden evictions—set off the 1766 rising.[20] But most of all, the valley's social order was symbolized in the Livingston and Van Rensselaer families, whose manors of Livingston and Rensselaerwyck, each represented in the provincial assembly by a member of the family, bestrode the upper reaches of the valley from Rhinebeck to well above Albany. The anger felt by the tenants of these manors toward their landlords was especially long-lasting and deep.[21] And in the case of the New Hampshire Grants, hatred focused on John Tabor Kempe, attorney-general of New York, and on James Duane, lawyer, politician, and land operator. Kempe bore chief responsibility for imposing New York authority on the region, and during the 1760s and 1770s Duane was speculating there in a grand way, both under his own name and through dummies.[22]

Only rarely were these figures accessible to the rioters. There was a report in 1748 of a plot "to pull down the house of Saml Nevill Esqr." A year before, one of the rioters said that if the proprietor John Coxe should cause any more people to be jailed "they wod go . . . & pull Coxe's House down abot his Ears."[23] The great men could most easily be attacked in the Hudson Valley, where they and their property and servants were far from safe. In 1755 crowds kidnapped iron workers employed by the manor lord Robert Livingston, Jr., and warned men repairing his dam to go, lest they too be taken. Two years later, Livingston was so frightened that he requested a company of fifty men from the governor as a guard. During the 1766 rising 200 men on Livingston Manor "marched to murther the Lord . . . and level his house" but were dispersed; a few months previously there was even talk of pulling down the city homes of some of the landlords.[24] In both New Jersey and the Hudson Valley, rioters destroyed trees belonging to the landlords; Joseph Paine, who "Girdled, & cutt down several thousands" belonging to Robert Livingston, told the lord's servants "that the trees were his & he would go & distroy the timber as he pleased & Robert Livingston kiss his a—s."[25]

But such direct attacks rarely succeeded, and for the most part the rioters had to vent their anger in the manner of the Jerseyman who said of Samuel Nevill, "Damn him for a Son of a Bitch, I wish I cod see him, I'd be the death of him."[26] More commonly, the rioters acted to prevent occupation and cultivation of the land by men who had leased or purchased it from the great ones. Sometimes this meant destruction, sometimes it meant turning the occupants out and installing others in their places, and sometimes it meant harassing them by spoiling their crops and pulling down their fences. In New Jersey it was common to give the intended victim the chance to repudiate his proprietary title and join the movement. Such was the case with Abraham Phillips, with Edward Jefferies, visited by the crowd on 5 August 1746, and, it would appear, with many others.[27] Both there and in the Hudson Valley the rioters were more likely to leave the property standing, with new occupants, than to destroy it. The main exception was property that belonged directly to the lord. When Robert Livingston, Jr., evicted his tenant Jan Hallenbeck in 1755, he sent his hands to plow Hallenbeck's lands for wheat and repair fences. Hallenbeck, however, returned, destroying wheat and tearing down the fences. But more characteristic were the cases of Johannes Van Deusen, dispossessed by the rioters in favor of one of their own in 1755, or of the loyal tenants whom Josiah Loomis warned to leave in 1762.[28] Similarly, when Robinson and Morris began evicting in 1766, "armed mobs visited the homes where men had been ejected, dispossessed the new tenants . . . and restored the orginal occupants." Forcible dispossession, tearing down houses, and destroying crops were all landlord tactics as well, and during the 1750s

Hudson Valley rioters could maintain that the word was a better description of landlords' men than of themselves.[29]

In "the Grants" the insurgents likewise operated at levels ranging from petty harassment to the vicious whipping already noted. They could draw fine distinctions, deciding in one instance not to burn a house down but merely to remove its roof, and they could wreak thoroughgoing havoc, as in the case of Otter Creek, a Yorker village sacked so thoroughly in 1772 that even the millstones were broken and thrown into a stream.[30] But unlike rioters in New Jersey and the Hudson Valley, the Green Mountain Boys never gave their victims the chance to join them.

The law was likewise a target. Breaking of jails was so much standard procedure in New Jersey that one jail keeper noted that the crowd "went off Huzzawing but not for King George as they had done at former breakings of the Gaol." Jail breaking did not always mean indiscriminate release; the crowds sought to free specific men, such as Samuel Baldwin, one of their committeemen arrested in early 1746 and rescued by a crowd of 150, "with clubbs, Axes and Crow barrs," or Abraham Anderson, rescued by 100 men, or John Bainbridge, freed from a Perth Amboy jail in June 1747 by a crowd estimated at 200.[31] The 1750s rioters on Rensselaerwyck and Livingston Manor several times rescued their fellows from the custody of the Albany County sheriff, and on one occasion they carted the sheriff himself off as a prisoner to a Massachusetts jail. The 1766 rising saw "all the jails broke open" on the east bank of the Hudson between New York City and Albany.[32]

After 1770 it was impossible for New York to make her writ run on the western side of the Green Mountains, and Colonel Nathan Stone, a prominent figure in the town of Windsor, warned that "he was determined that no writs or Precepts" from New York courts would operate in Windsor, on the west bank of the Connecticut River. When Yorker officials did try to make an arrest, a bloody affray, such as the one that mutilated Remember Baker in 1772, was likely to result.[33] Nathan Stone and an armed crowd attended a sitting of the court of Cumberland County, which New York had created as a local government for part of the region, in order to deny the court's authority and to kidnap the Yorker attorney whom they believed to be its eminence grise. Half a decade later, in March 1775, another sitting of the same court was broken up when ninety insurgents occupied the courthouse at Westminster. When the county sheriff and an armed posse recaptured the building, two rioters were killed and several others wounded. Some 500 insurgents quickly gathered, once again seizing the courthouse, and this time sending the magistrates and sheriff to a Massachusetts jail.[34]

Thus there were certain types of property that northern land rioters regularly attacked—property rather than people. They were capable of violence to other human beings, but despite talk of "murthering" Robert Livingston, of being "the death" of Samuel Nevill, and of leaving everyone in a Yorker settlement a corpse,[35] the evidence suggests that when land rioting brought death, the victim was likely to be a rioter. Both sides went armed, but the authorities were quicker to use their guns, and these authorities made up the second class of typical targets. The rioters knew the seriousness of their attitude toward authority. One Jerseyman was quoted in 1749 as saying that he "Wis'd they (meaning the Authority) had fired upon them the said Rioters, for if they had they never should have seen such work, *for* if *they would have destroy'd them all* and drove them into the sea."[2] When William Prendergast was cautioned that requiring a victim to swear on oath "might be agt. the King," he replied that "if the King was there he would serve him . . . that Mobs had overcome Kings before and why should they not overcome."[36] The Westminster court closers, like Colonel Stone five years before, "would not, under the present circumstances, suffer any Magistrate at all," and Remember Baker said that the Grants people "lived out of the Bounds of the Law." And as Ethan Allen put it most succinctly to Charles Hutchesson, "God Damn your Governour, Laws, King, Council & Assembly."[37]

Men in authority took the rioters equally seriously. Their rhetoric, most especially that of the Jersey proprietors, was full of declarations about the riots threatening the destruction of all government and all society. In 1746 Samuel Nevill told the New Jersey Assembly that a petition against the proprietors was "a scandalous, false, abusive and inveterate libel, upon a Set of Gentlemen" and a "Notorious libel upon the Crown of England." The libel was inspired by "some crafty, subtle incendiaries," men "tinctured with the Spirit and Seeds of Sedition." The next year, as judge of the Middlesex County Court, Nevill was charging a grand jury that was to consider the riots with phrases like "the Natural ill will to superior Power and the inbred Malice to Authority." The first publication of the proprietors declared that the insurgents' invocation of Indian land titles was high treason and toward the end of 1747 the Provincial Council, very much a stronghold of the proprietors, described the riots as "bold & daring Attempts to throw off his Majesties Authority and their dependence on the Crown of Brittain."[38] This was the sort of language that reached official eyes in London, and it is no surprise to find the Board of Trade describing the Jersey rioters as "chiefly the dregs of the People, and many of them Irish."[39]

Such rhetoric was accurate, not hysterical. The rioters had no doubt that they could not live with landlord domination and with the political institutions that supported it, and, legally speaking, they were indeed committing treason when they took over government's tasks.[40] The Jerseymen admitted as much when, in a long self-justification, they invoked philosopher John Locke on the relationship between property and government, denied the right of the Crown to grant Indian lands with the charge that it was a "Royal Fraud," and stated that "When Property is made uncertain and precarious this band [of government] is broken."[41]

The authorities matched their words with action. When the sheriff of Albany County led a posse to Bennington to make an arrest in 1771, its roster read like a who's who of the local power structure. It included Robert Yates, attorney and future member of the Philadelphia Convention; John Roorback, alderman and justice of the peace; Mayor Abraham C. Cuyler of the city of Albany; Christopher P. Yates, attorney and future assemblyman, and Gysbert G. Marselis, alderman and justice of the peace, to mention a few.[42] British troops were used to crush the tenant rising in 1766,[43] and remembering that success, New York officials begged Generals Thomas Gage and Frederick Haldimand for troops to use against the Green Mountain Boys in 1773 and 1774. The British had other problems to worry about by then, and one of them, with an irony he could hardly have intended, pointed out to Lieutenant-Governor Cadwallader Colden that if the civil authority was that weak there was little point in bringing the troops in.[44]

Another New York response was the passage in 1774 of a fearsome riot and treason law for the New Hampshire Grants area, a law that declared forfeit the lives of eight leaders (whom it named) if they did not surrender themselves, and which also imposed the death penalty for a host of offences if they were committed in the region.[45] This was modeled on the response of Parliament to the Stuart rebellions of 1715 and 1745, and it was not the first time that the homeland's example was invoked. In 1748 James Alexander proposed to fellow proprietor John Coxe that "the best presidents [precedents]" for dealing with the Jersey rioters were "those given by the Brittish [sic] Parliament—they, after the late rebellion [1745], made Acts of Attainder of Persons by name, if by a certain date they did not deliver themselves...Querie, if the like step may not be proper to the next Assembly." Crowd leader Amos Roberts, Alexander thought, "ought to suffer without Mercy."[46] If the rebels learned what was planned for them, one can only hope that they appreciated its grim irony, for Alexander himself had come to America after the 1715 rebellion—as a Jacobite refugee.[47]

These land riots were serious affairs, and both sides knew it. The problem was the division and tenure of land, and in early America that was basic. Since in each case one side was composed of wealthy, prominent, and powerful men, and since these men had the authority of government with them, the rioting took on profound political importance as well, importance complicated in the two New York affairs by the uncertainty of the province's eastern boundary. And in all three cases the enemies of the rioters were willing to use nearly any tactic to quell them, for real issues of property and of power were at stake.

II

Rioters in all three affairs made it plain enough that they thought of what they were doing in class terms. A man named Moss Kent, giving testimony at the trial of the insurgent leader William Prendergast in 1766, declared that farmers evicted by the landlords "had an equitable Title but could not be defended in a Course of Law because they were poor and...poor men were always oppressed by the rich" and that "when they went to New York they expected to be assisted by the poor people there." Prendergast himself was quoted as saying that "it was hard they were not allowed to have *any property*" and that he pitied poor people who were turned out of possession, for "there was no law for poor men."[48] Defenders of the Jersey rioters likewise thought in terms of poor and rich,[49] and in both places English precedent was invoked: "The King himself was unable to quell mobs in England, by any other ways than granting their desires."[50] And the Green Mountain people described themselves as "a poor people... fatigued in settling a wilderness country," and their enemies as "a number of Attorneys and other gentlemen, with all their tackle of ornaments, and compliments, and French finesse."[51]

Yet historically American strife has been characterized at least as much by ethnocultural and racial content as by class concerns. From the time of John Smith and John Winthrop to the present day, one finds Americans spilling blood and smashing property because of skin color, religion, and ancestry, and the question of whether eighteenth-century rural rioting involved these things deserves serious consideration. Several scholars have seen as the starting point for understanding the New York riots the presence not of two classes but rather of two cultures, Yorker and Yankee. Friction and violence developed, they suggest, because land-hungry New Englanders pushed their way into eastern New York and tried, once there, to impose their own way of doing things on Yorkers, both tenant and landlord.[52]

In some rural rioting, such as the Paxton Boys affair in Pennsylvania in 1764, the predominance of the ethnocultural and racial element is plain,[53] but the suggestion here is that in land rioting the matter was more complex. The Livingston family, James Alexander, and Charles Hutchesson were all either Scots or of Scottish descent, and hatred of Scots was a basic thing in English popular feeling at the time[54]; had it, like the technique of house-pulling, crossed the Atlantic? The anti-Scot theme emerged elsewhere in eighteenth-century America, including in the well-known hatred of Lord Bute in the Stamp Act riots, in North Carolina during the Regulation, in the Paxton Affair, and in Virginia and western New York during the Revolution. In the last, it helped bring on seven years of vicious civil war. Yet the Scots that the Virginians hated were Norfolk merchants, as well as Caledonians, and the patriot settlers west of Albany fought Sir William Johnson's Catholic Highlanders because they supported Sir William's sons in their arrogant claim to dominate the region. The spirit of the baronet's heirs is reflected in the "hearty horsewhipping" that Sir John Johnson gave in 1775 to "one Mr. Visher," a candidate for a commission in the revolutionary militia, for "impertinence," and in Sir John then "very cooly" getting into his carriage and driving off.[55] Clearly the clash of Catholic Highlander and Protestant German, Dutchman or Yorker, and the penchant of the Scots for flaunting their distinctiveness by wearing the kilt, were not the only causes of bitterness in the Mohawk Valley. So, too, with those other Caledonians, James Alexander, the Livingston family, and Charles Hutchesson. They were all Celts, but it was more important that they were landlords and landlords' men.

But the real problem was Yankees, not Scots. The New Hampshire Grants, the eastern reaches of the Hudson Valley, and the Newark region of New Jersey were indeed all full of New Englanders, and this certainly explains the absolute refusal of the rioters in the first to allow prospective victims the choice of joining them. The Green Mountain Boys knew they were New Englanders and that settlers under New York auspices were forever outside the fold. But though this tribalism explains the area's special ferocity, it does not explain the whole of the movement, and, apart from that ferocity, the evidence suggests that ethnic grounds played little role in determining the choice of victims and the treatment meted out to them.[56]

Outside of the grants, the crowds themselves were mixed. William Prendergast had migrated from Ireland and had married a Dutchess County Quaker woman,[57] and Michael Hallenbeck, one of the biggest thorns in Robert Livingston's side, was of Dutch descent and had been a Livingston tenant for more than three decades.[58] Even the bearing of an obviously English name is no sure sign that its owner was a newly arrived Yankee troublemaker. Robert Noble, bane of the Van Rensselaers, was described by John Van Rensselaer as having been his tenant for six or seven years; Joseph Paine, who destroyed Livingston's trees, had been a long-term tenant; Jacob Knight, involved in the abduction of the ironworkers, was apparently Robert Livingston's personal servant.[59] Some half of the persons named in the records in O'Callaghan's *Documentary History* as being rioters during the 1750s bore Dutch names, and when 500 Loyalist tenants rose in support of the king and in hope of freeholds in 1777, ethnicity had been completely defused as an issue. The Albany area Dutch were both Loyalists and patriots.[60] One likewise finds non-Englishmen among the Jersey rioters. One of their public addresses was signed by Simeon Wyckoff, Cornelius DeHart, and Robert Schermerhorne, and on one occasion their enemies made fun of them by using a heavy Dutch dialect in a newspaper essay.[61]

Thus the land riots were ethnic only in a very qualified way. But if one stresses the culture of those rioters who were Yankees rather than their simple ethnicity, then the trail blazed by the historian Dixon Ryan Fox can lead to some fresh insights. The crowds did include many New Englanders who behaved in remarkably similar ways—popular behavior is usually rooted in popular culture. The sparkling collection of recent studies on the social and cultural history of early New England gives a basis for relating Yankee popular culture to the riots.

The most important point is the self-conscious traditionalism of

New England's local social and political life. When they were founded in the seventeenth century as "closed, corporate, Christian, utopian communities"—in Kenneth Lockridge's phrase— New England towns were intended to be refuges from the disruption that modernization was bringing to Stuart England. Their way stressed consensus, harmony, internal agreement, and focus on the whole rather than on the individual, and during the seventeenth century their static and noncommercial life-style was more or less in harmony with these values.[62] By 1700, however, their experiment was failing, as open-field farming was replaced by the enclosed farm and by nonagricultural business, as new wealth and new poverty took shape, as overcrowding brought heavy pressure on the land, and as, in demographic terms, the quality of life decayed. Meanwhile, the monopoly of faith once held by the Congregational Church was in full flight, as Anglicans, Baptists, Quakers, Presbyterians, and sectarians set themselves up.[63]

These changes, and parallel ones in politics,[64] meant the destruction of the communal way of life that had supported New England's early values of harmony and stability, but the old ways of thinking and feeling died hard. As a number of scholars have shown, family and emotional ties kept many men and women in the old communities despite the bleak future they offered, despite the fact that "New England had to expand or die."[65] Those who did move north or west continued to organize themselves in towns. Much emphasis has properly been laid on the fact that these towns were owned, at the outset, by speculators and not by community builders; but once a town was incorporated absentees were excluded from its public life and community decision-making was once again possible.[66] Kent, Connecticut, at its founding in 1738, hardly had the fullness of utopianism that had been present in Dedham, Massachusetts, a century earlier, but the political stability and insularity that were to be found in both Kent and nearby Windham in succeeding years lead one to think that, in an attenuated form at least, the old values were there.[67] Even the tumultuous religious revival of the 1740s, which we call the Great Awakening, though it sundered churches and whole villages, included a strong thrust toward recapturing the sense of fraternity that was draining out of New England.[68] The suggestion here is that although by mid-century the old order was moribund in New England, popular culture included a real disposition toward resistance to change away from it.

But seventeenth-century Puritanism had been radical as well as nostalgic, producing wild men and women who turned the English world upside down, as well as the contented inhabitants of utopias in Massachusetts, producing Anne Hutchinson as well as John Winthrop, and this theme, too, seems to have survived. Anne Grant, a young member of the Hudson Valley aristocracy, noted this when she commented on the Yankees entering New York that "Obadiah or Zephaniah from Hampshire or Connecticut . . . came in without knocking, sat down without invitation, and lighted their pipe without ceremony; then talked of buying land; and finally began a discourse on politics which would have done honour to Praise God Barebones, or any of the members of his Parliament."[69] And both radicalism and nostalgia showed themselves in the land riots.[70] In all three of the affairs discussed in this essay one can see a conjuncture, perhaps (in Michael Kammen's phrase) a biformity, of the themes of private property and individualistic acquisition (which were the essence of the coming American social order) with those of community and fraternity. Historians who favor New York on the Grants issue never tire of pointing out that Ethan Allen and friends had much to gain if their Onion River Land Company succeeded, and that for the Grants settlers buying and selling land was a favorite pastime. But for the most part these men were "settler-proprietors,"[71] petty speculators at most, and where Vermont towns were settled by whole groups, as happened,[72] the group's primacy may be assumed.

But once in the Grants, the settlers found themselves confronting New York institutions and practices that negated both private ambition and the New England way. For one thing, New York proposed to people to develop the region by what amounted to a dilute form of her great tract system, with the addition of absentee ownership,[73] and the hatred of the Yankees for James Duane shows how well they knew it. For another thing, New York intended to govern it by county courts, and erected the counties of Charlotte, Cumberland, and Gloucester for the purpose. New York law did provide for townships and town meetings,[74] but power was to be centered in the courts, and men like Philip Schuyler, Philip Skene, and William Duer, who made up the first bench in Charlotte, had little in common with Yankees. One can feel the bitterness with which Nathan Stone said that no one had ever asked for Cumberland County to be set up and that "the making of a county was a sham."[75]

Again the Hudson Valley was more complex. Frontier crudity was long gone there and, with the Hudson River to serve as its artery, commerce flourished. By mid-century, New York was growing large amounts of wheat for export and to feed New York City and Albany, and this commercial agriculture was the essence of manor life. Yet this was itself coupled with neotraditionalist attitudes, not Yankee communalism but rather the hierarchical ones espoused by the Livingston family and their ilk. These attitudes showed themselves in the quaint notion of the lord of Livingston Manor, in that even after independence his family deserved its own seat in the New York Assembly, and in his sniffling about "insolent" tenants who refused to perform road service.[76] They showed themselves in the conspicuous consumption of an heiress marrying under a gold canopy while "as on rent day the tenants gathered before the manor hall."[77] They showed themselves most of all in the reluctance of the great families to sell their land and in the humiliating terms of the leases that they granted, leases that ultimately meant wealth for the lessors.[78]

But commercialization could only mean that the "expectant capitalists" among the tenants would want development along the path that Pennsylvania, and even the west bank of the Hudson, had already taken, toward a society of freehold family farms, with no nonsense about corvée service and insolence.[79] And the New England influx meant efforts toward the creation of a town life that could not live easily with the ethos of the landlords. The first was very much the goal of the 1766 rioters and the tenant Loyalists of 1777. On the second count, one finds Livingston tenants petitioning Boston for grants on a town basis in 1753, Michael Hallenbeck going there to get leave to lay out a township in 1754, and Van Rensselaer tenants planning to adopt New England ways in 1755.[80] The two themes were not, of course, irreconcilable. And as far as New Jersey, it has been suggested that it is in the Newark area rather than in New England itself that one finds "Yankee villages turned inward upon themselves and divorced from broader political life." It was these well-settled villages that faced the threat of being shattered by the proprietors' ejectment suits in the 1740s.[81]

Scraps, hints, suggestive vignettes: these bits of information from widely scattered sources do no more than permit one to make sense of them in a very tentative way. There is, however, good evidence that some insurgents were thinking along some of these lines. We have already seen the Jerseymen quoting Locke's *Second Treatise* and drawing out its revolutionary implications. On the other theme, that of communalism, "The Vision of Junus, The Benningtonite," a mock-Biblical essay that was published in late 1772, spoke of the "Holy Hill of Bennington," of "the People of the L——d" who dwelt there, and of the hatred that the heathen Albanians, Schanachidyans, and Kinder-hookites felt for them. Parody, surely, but coming from a people who would soon produce Joseph Smith and William Miller, the founders of Mormonism and Seventh-day Adventism, it is not to be dismissed lightly.[82]

Two longer pieces likewise defended the insurgences in communitarian terms. One of these was a sermon preached to the leaders of Vermont as they were about to constitute their state in 1777, and the other was a tract written in defense of the New Jersey rioters in 1746. Griffin Jenkins, who wrote the Jersey tract, was apparently a home-grown William Blake; in places his prose nearly dissolves into mysticism, and two of the piece's four sections are poetic religious meditations. The essay's readers are addressed in Quaker-style plain speech. In contrast, the sermon that the Reverend Aaron Hutchinson preached to the Vermonters is a model of Puritan formal style, as modified by the Commonwealth political tradition. Yet both Hutchinson and Jenkins justified the resistance of their rioters in terms of the internal love and mutual agreement that bound their communities together, and of the need to protect these precious qualities against both outside enemies and internal divisiveness. Hutchinson appealed frankly to the New England tribalism of his listeners. Jenkins wrote that "going to law is one of those lawful things, which is very difficultly manag'd without Sin," rebuked the proprietors for the covetousness and dissent that they had brought in, and praised the people for "joining together to defend their Plantations with the utmost Vigour."[83] Any of these themes of Jenkins and Hutchinson would have fitted perfectly into the New England towns that have been called "peaceable Kingdoms."[84]

We may even reopen the question of whether we are dealing with peasants, or at least with peasant attitudes. Specialists in peasant studies—like specialists in most things— agree only that they disagree on what a peasant is, but the term appears to be as useful to describe human beings in the modern Caribbean or Vietnam as it is for thirteenth-century France or England.[85] What needs to be stressed is that peasant and feudal serf are not synonymous terms, that peasant grievances can extend to far more than rack rent, and that peasant protest does not necessarily take the form of a jacquerie. As Samuel Huntington puts it, in words that bear extended quotation, a peasantry caught up in modernization is a force of enormous revolutionary potential:

In agrarian society, a more equitable distribution of ownership is the prerequisite to economic growth. It is precisely for this reason that the tensions of the countryside are potentially so much more revolutionary than those of the city. The industrial worker cannot secure personal ownership or control of the means of production; this, however, is precisely the goal of the peasant. The basic factor of production is land; the supply of land is limited if not fixed; the landlord loses what the peasant acquires. Thus the peasant. . . has no alternative but to attack the existing system of ownership and control.[86]

A good case has already been offered for applying the term to early New Englanders,[87] and the Hudson Valley landlords certainly envisaged their tenants as playing the role of a peasantry. The New Hampshire grantees even described themselves as "hard labouring, industrious, honest peasants."[88] Moreover, some of the rioters showed the typical peasant belief that the king, if only he could know, would be on their side. "Junus the Benningtonite" spoke of "Duane and Kemp," who strove "to set the Lord's anointed against his people, falsely accusing them before the Court of Great Britain," and rioters in New Jersey believed that what they were doing would make the king see that his subjects were "wronged or oppressed, or else they would never rebell against my laws."[89] Despite the realities of Anglo-American politics, their hope may not have been wholly misplaced; it was, after all, a royal pardon that saved William Prendergast from the brutal death to which a New York court sentenced him in 1766.[90]

And most important, the problem in all three cases was the classic one in peasant revolution of who would have the land and the political and social power that went with it. On that count it perhaps makes little difference whether the rioters themselves saw their model of an alternative to landlord domination in the communal life of early Dedham, in the burgeoning individualism of early Pennsylvania, or, as seems most likely, in an uneasy mixture of two. But what had the land rioters to do with the American Revolution?

III

It depends on how we define the Revolution. If we see it solely as the winning of independence, then land rioters were either irrelevant or actually hostile. As Staughton Lynd has forcefully shown, Hudson

Valley tenants frequently combined social radicalism with political Toryism in the late 1770s, supporting the king in the hope that a British victory would crush the power of the Whig landlords and bring a redistribution of their estates.[91] Any specialist knows that Ethan Allen, despairing in the early 1780s that Congress would ever recognize Vermont, and fearful that New York would succeed in reimposing her authority, embarked on serious negotiations with the British. In each case the local issue was seen as more important than the imperial one. The New Jersey affair, taking place a full generation before the Revolution, had no direct relationship to it, save that the riots may have helped to convince the young British politician Charles Townshend that the Americans needed control from outside. In 1767, Townshend would get a chance to put his ideas into practice, with disastrous results, but the main historian of the New Jersey riots agrees with other specialists in the state's history that a legal settlement in 1771 in favor of the proprietors was "the last heard of the entire controversy."[92]

But, to borrow again from Huntington, "It takes more than one revolutionary group to make a revolution . . . one social group can be responsible for a coup, a riot or a revolt, but only a combination of groups can produce a revolution."[93] It may be more in line with what happened in many parts of America to conceive of the Revolution not just as the sundering of the imperial tie and the creation of republican constitutions but also in terms of the rapid and often violent mobilization into public life of many different groups, of the collapse in the face of this mobilization of one set of institutions, and of the painful legitimization as well as the creation of another set. Some very recent scholarship is working along these lines.[94] In these processes, rural crowds, including our land rioters, played a major, albeit frightfully complex, role.

Prior to the final crisis in 1774 and 1775, country people had very little to do with the main movement, but nonetheless there was significant rural action during the 1760s and 1770s in both Carolinas, western Pennsylvania, the Hudson Valley, and the Green Mountains. The effect of this action was to challenge and undermine the authority of provincial institutions and leaders at the same time that urban crowds were challenging the British government. In New York, for instance, only the counties west of the Hudson and those on Long Island went undisturbed in 1765 and 1766. Great Britain's Coercive Acts in 1774 and the resort to arms the following year served to bind the urban and rural movements into one large question and to mobilize country people who had hitherto remained quiet. For the Green Mountain rebels it meant a chance to identify their own cause with the larger one through Ethan Allen's dramatic capture of Fort Ticonderoga, and through repeated insistence that the Yorker officials whose lives they made miserable were tools of the British. They charged, for instance, that the judges and sheriff whom they imprisoned after the Westminster Court closing had been blocking communications between themselves and the revolutionary committees that were taking shape elsewhere, and in 1777 Aaron Hutchinson cast before their leaders an imagined vignette in which Yorkers plotted to do their part in the great British conspiracy against liberty.[95]

In Dutchess and Albany counties the showdown meant politicization of tenants on the Tory side. It meant the creation of a patriot militia, which was so unreliable that its commanders did not dare to call it out. It meant safe passage from cottage to cottage for astute British agents offering the tenants their landlord's land if they would support the king.[96] In Tryon County, in western New York, it meant the complete polarization of a society that had been, until that time, utterly quiet. The mobilization began in late 1774 with the formation of a tiny secret committee of middle-class farmers and professionals; by the next summer it had reached the point of patriots sending to Albany for cannon to attack the fortified Johnson house. Here the insurgents were not tenants but rather small independent farmers. Nonetheless, the Mohawk Valley had been as much the preserve of the Johnson family as Albany County was of the Van Rensselaers and Livingstons.[97] Thus 1775 and 1776 saw not merely the end of the power of Governor William Tryon and the replacement of the Provincial Assembly by a revolutionary congress but also the complete collapse of local government and society in Westchester, Dutchess, Albany, Charlotte, Cumberland, Gloucester, and Tryon counties, not to mention the cities of New York and Albany.

This radical disintegration was completed in late 1776 and 1777 by the decision of the Vermonters to go it alone, and also by the British occupation of Long Island, New York City, Staten Island, and southern Westchester County, an action that had the full support of the people of Kings, Queens, and Richmond counties. The net result of Vermont secession, Mohawk Valley civil war, renewed Hudson Valley tenant strife, and British occupation was a thorough redefinition of what New York was, and in this redefinition rural crowds had played a major role.

Nor did their impact stop there. Rural radicals had little to do with the shaping of New York's new constitution: that document was drafted in the dreadful winter of 1776–1777 by men on the run, men with neither the chance nor the inclination to pay attention to the ideas of land rioters.[98] By that time the Vermonters and the tenant Loyalists had in any case read themselves out of the state. But in Vermont itself rural radicals had a perfect, unfettered chance to institutionalize their ideas on public life, and the result was a constitution that marked the outer limits of American radical republicanism. The Vermont constitution is usually dismissed as a mere copy of the Pennsylvania Constitution of 1776; yet in itself this is significant. One of the main authors of the Pennsylvania charter, and the man who recommended it to the Vermonters, was Dr. Thomas Young, physician and professional revolutionary. A native of Ulster County, New York, his career had led him first to eastern Dutchess County, across the Hudson, and then to Albany, Boston, and Philadelphia. In all three cities he served on revolutionary committees, and he was in on the action from 1765 to 1776. One needs little further illustration of how radical ideas got from place to place.[99]

Young apparently received his political education from New England rural culture and from landlord-tenant strife. While he was living in Amenia, New York, he made friends with Ethan Allen, who was just across the Connecticut line at the time. One result was collaboration on the rationalist tract known as *Ethan Allen's Bible.*[100] Another was Young's involvement in a Green Mountain land scheme that was being floated under Massachusetts auspices by Col. John Henry Lydius of Albany. By 1764, this scheme had run into opposition from the New York government, and in that year Young published a tract in its defense. What is most noteworthy in the tract is the way in which Young fell back to first principles, his basic premise being that in America the only really sound land title was one derived from Indian purchase or grant. The land was not the king's either to grant or to tax by means of quitrents, and since Lydius had a good Indian title, neither was it the property of the "gentlemen in the province of *New-York*" who were behind their province's opposition to Lydius, and who, Young maintained, opposed settlement by poor industrious people in the hope of speculative gain for themselves. In this first sign of his developing attitudes, Young thus blended an attitude of no-great-reverence for the Crown with an intense hostility to New York's land grandees. A dozen years after that first tract, in 1776, Young was publicly condemning "men of some rank" who sought to recreate "the system of Lord and Vassal or *principal* and *dependent*."[101] Throughout the intervening decade he supported the Green Mountain insurgents.

This was the man who played a major role in the writing of the Pennsylvania constitution. In April 1777 he addressed a short pamphlet to the Vermonters, who had just declared themselves independent, recommending Pennsylvania to them as "a model which, with a very little alteration will . . . come as near perfection as anything yet concerted by mankind." Most especially he saw it as preferable to the charters of Connecticut and Rhode Island—those two documents beloved of historians who see nothing but continuity in the Revolution —because "in the one case the Executive power can advise and in the other compel. For my own part I esteem the people at large the true proprietors of governmental power."[102] Young thus cast away the whole intellectual baggage of interests and orders, of depraved human nature, and of a "senatorial part of society" that many other American leaders carried into independence with them.[103] But at the same time that the Vermonters were enthusiastically accepting his ideas, the Continental Congress, under pressure from New York, was condemning both Young's pamphlet and the Vermont movement itself.[104] Young was apparently responsible for the Vermont constitution's provision forever disqualifying from representing the state any man who accepted an office in Congress's gift while sitting in it. But it was the Vermonters themselves who tied together the themes of radical individualism and of New England communalism, by providing for both manhood suffrage and for representation in the state assembly on the corporatist principle of one town, one representative.[105]

In New York, land rioters were much further from the locus of power, both during the shaping of the new order and after it went into effect. Tory tenants in the Hudson and Mohawk valleys responded with spy networks, with an underground railroad to the British lines, with organized escapes to New York City, with support for Generals John Burgoyne and Sir Henry Clinton, with kidnappings and burnings, and with actual guerrilla warfare.[106] This was met with as much repression as the new state could muster, both political and military. But not all discontented tenants were Loyalists, and the support of country people was absolutely vital if the new order was to stand. As the war years passed, the state legislature and Governor George Clinton undertook more and more policies calculated to please their rural constituents. Two of the most popular involved the confiscation of the estates of many Tory landlords (including the DeLancey, Philipse, Skene, and Johnson families) and their eventual sale,[107] and a radical change in the state's taxation system. This brought taxation not according to the worth of a man's estate but rather according to "circumstances and other abilities to pay taxes, collectively considered."[108] It amounted to an invitation to assessors, who were popularly chosen, to discriminate at will in levying taxes against great owners, and during the 1780s it was a major bone of contention in the state's politics. It was first adopted in 1780 against the wishes of nearly all of the state's leaders, but with the support in the assembly of the delegates from all of the counties of strife: Albany, Tryon, Dutchess, and Charlotte.[109] When Governor Clinton finally endorsed the principle in 1783 it amounted to his declaration of political war on the landlord families whose cooperation and in some cases friendship he had enjoyed. What is certain is that both confiscation, which hit at Tory landlords, and radical taxation, which hit at Whig ones, were immensely popular, and that they had the effect of showing discontented country people that the law could work for as well as against them. New York's land problems would not be finally solved until the 1840s, but in bringing about radical taxation and confiscation, rural discontent had played a major role in determining the kind of place New York was to be.

In conclusion, we can say that northern rural crowds played a major role in the political and social life of revolutionary America. Their direct social concerns were not those of crowds in either rural England and France or urban America, and only in the final crisis did their interests become bound up with the imperial question; indeed, during the decade of imperial tension the revolutionary leaders in Boston and New York City feared rural crowds and all that they stood for. But by their very existence they helped to add to the atmosphere of general crisis, the sense of many colonists that something was wrong with the standing order,[110] and when the mid-1770s saw the merger of social and political issues, the independence crisis came to mean much more than just the installation of new men in old places, or the giving of new titles to old men. The appearance of such a profound internal dimension puzzled and worried the city intellectuals and merchants who had earned the title of radicals during the imperial confrontation, but by then the Revolution was no longer their exclusive property, if ever it had been.[111] And because it was not, it was all the more a revolution.

I want to thank J. R. Pole and his seminar in Cambridge; Peter Marshall and the American Studies group, Manchester, and George Rudé for comments on earlier drafts of this essay. I owe special gratitude to Joel Silbey for extended discussions in London during the winter of 1973–1974 and for many stimulating suggestions.

1. Affidavit of Abram Phillips, 9 December 1749; affidavit of Thomas Gould, 9 December 1749, *Documents Relating to the Colonial History of the State of New Jersey, 1746–1751*, ed. William A. Whitehead [New Jersey Archives, 1st ser., 7] (Newark: Daily Advertiser Printing House, 1883), pp. 370–76 [Hereafter cited as *NJA*, 7].

2. For the most recent of many accounts, see Bernard Bailyn, *The Ordeal of Thomas Hutchinson* (Cambridge: Harvard University Press, 1974).

3. Warrant by Alexander McNaughton, J. P., 12 December 1771, *Documentary History of the State of New York*, ed. E. B. O'Callaghan, 4 vols. (Albany: Weed, Parsons & Co., 1851), 4:745–47. pk@Hereafter cited as *OCDH*.]

4. Review of Pauline Maier, *From Resistance to Revolution*, *William and Mary Quarterly*, 3rd ser. 30 (1973): 153.

5. See Bailyn, *The Ordeal of Thomas Hutchinson*.

6. "Revolutionary" and "revolution" are used here primarily in the political sense suggested by Peter Amann and Samuel P. Huntington and by Lenin. Amann uses the word to refer to a situation in which no single set of institutions possesses a generally accepted claim to a monopoly of power, and Huntington and Lenin both stress the importance of massive popular convulsion in shattering existing institutions and bringing such a situation about. See Amann, "Revolution: A Redefinition," *Political Science Quarterly* 77(1962): 36–53; Huntington, *Political Order in Changing Societies* (New Haven: Yale University Press, 1968), pp. 264–343; and Lenin, *The State and Revolution: The Marxist Theory of the State and the Tasks of the Proletariat in the Revolution* (Moscow: Progress Publishers, 1972). For further discussion see below, section III.

7. Cf. Piers Mackesy, *The War for America, 1775–1783* (Cambridge: Harvard University Press, 1964), and Robert J. Taylor, *Western Massachusetts in the Revolution* (Providence: Brown University Press, 1954).

8. See Gary S. Horowitz, "New Jersey Land Riots, 1745–1755," (Ph.D. diss., Ohio State University, 1966); Irving Mark, *Agrarian Conflict in Colonial New York* (New York: Columbia University Press, 1940); Staughton Lynd, *Anti-Federalism in Dutchess County New York, A Study of Democracy and Class Conflict in the Revolutionary Era* (Chicago: Loyola University Press, 1962); and *Class Conflict, Slavery and the United States Constitution, Ten Essays* (Indianapolis and New York: Bobbs-Merrill, 1967); Dixon Ryan Fox, *Yankees and Yorkers* (New York: New York University Press, 1940); Patricia U. Bonomi, *A Factious People, Politics and Society in Colonial New York* (New York: Columbia University Press, 1971); and Matt Bushnell Jones, *Vermont in the Making, 1750–1777* (Cambridge: Harvard University Press, 1939).

9. Mention must be made of the perceptive comparisons made by Irving Mark in his *American Conflict in Colonial New York*. See especially pp. 115 and 140.

10. E. P. Thompson, "The Moral Economy of the English Crowd in the Eighteenth Century," *Past & Present*, no. 50 (February 1971), pp. 76–136. I have also drawn heavily on George Rudé, *The Crowd in History* (New York: John Wiley & Sons, 1964).

11. *Pauline Maier, From Resistance to Revolution: Colonial Radicals and the Development of American Opposition to Britain, 1765–1776* (New York, Alfred A. Knopf, 1972); for an astute criticism, see Eric Foner, "Battle Over the Revolution," *New York Review of Books* 20, no. 2 (22 February 1973), pp. 35–37.

12. Horowitz, "New Jersey Land Riots," chapter 1; Publication of the Council of Proprietors of East New Jersey, 25 March 1746, *Documents Relating to the Colonial History of the State of New Jersey 1738–1747*, ed. William A. Whitehead [*New Jersey Archives*, 1st ser. 6] (Newark: Daily Advertiser Printing House, 1882), pp. 297–323. [Hereafter cited as *NJA* 6].

13. For factors weakening the claim of the great landlords, see Bonomi, *A Factious People*, pp. 200–211; for the Indian claim, see petition of Benjamin Kokkkowenaunaut et al. to Sir Henry Moore, 1 April 1765; Benjamin Kokkkowenaunaut to Volkert Douw, Mayor of Albany, 30 June 1766; Benjamin Kokkkowenaunaut et al. to Governor Bernard, 1 July 1766; and Sir William Johnson to Governor Moore, 20 July 1768, all British

Museum, Add. MS. 22679 and "Narrative of the Controversy between Daniel Ninham . . . and Messrs. Roger Morris, Beverly Robinson, and Philip Philipse," British Museum, Lansdowne MS. 707.

14. Hiland Hall, "New York Land Grants in Vermont, 1765–1776," *Collections of the Vermont Historical Society*, 2 vols. (Montpelier: printed for the society, 1870–71), 1:145–59; Lord Shelburne to Sir Henry Moore, 11 April 1767, *OCDH* 4:589–90; Order in Council, 24 June 1767, ibid, 609–11. The New York quitrent was 2/6 sterling per hundred acres; that of New Hampshire was one ear of Indian corn from the town for ten years and thereafter 1/- proclamation money per hundred acres.

15. Rowland Berthoff and John M. Murrin, "Feudalism, Communalism and the Yeoman Freeholder: The American Revolution Considered as a Social Accident," in Stephen G. Kurtz and James H. Hutson, eds., *Essays on the American Revolution* (Chapel Hill: University of North Carolina Press, 1973), pp. 256–88.

16. James Elliott to Robert Livingston, Esq., 20 March 1762, *OCDH*, 3:826–27; Lynd, *Anti-Federalism*, p. 49; Bonomi, *A Factious People*, 221–22; Irving Mark and Oscar Handlin, eds., "Land Cases in Colonial New York, 1765–1767, The King v. William Prendergast," *New York University Law Quarterly Review* 9 (1942): 178.

17. "Communication of the Rioters About the Riot in Newark," 17 February 1745/6, *NJA* 6:292–96; James Alexander and Robert Hunter Morris, "State of the Facts, Concerning the Late Riots at Newark in the County of Essex, & in other parts of New Jersey; 24 December 1746," ibid., p 403; affidavit of Sarah Martin, 20 July 1747, ibid., pp. 469–70; affidavit of Abraham Shotwell, 2 December 1748, *NJA* 7:179–80; "A Second Addition to, or Continuac'on of, The Brief State of Facts . . . ," ibid., p. 281; "A State of Facts Concerning the Riots and Insurrections in New Jersey . . . ", ibid., pp. 217, 225.

18. Affidavit of James Breakenridge and Samll Robinson, 14 February 1770, *OCDH* 4: 617–19; Depositions of Ebenezer Cole, 27 February and Samll Wells, 2 March 1771, ibid., pp. 679–85, 696–99; Charles A. Jellison, *Ethan Allen, Frontier Rebel* (Syracuse: Syracuse University Press, 1969), p. 43; deposition of Benjamin Hough, 7 March 1775, *American Archives*, comp. Peter Force, 9 vols. (Washington, D.C.: M. St. Claire Clarke and Peter Force, 1837–1853), 2:215–18.

19. "Henricus Aenfiender," *The N.Y. Gazette Revived in the Weekly Post Boy*, 26 February 1750, reprinted in *Documents Relating to the Colonial History of the State of New Jersey, Extracts From American Newspapers Relating to New Jersey*, ed. William Nelson, (Paterson: The Press Printing and Publishing Company, 1895) [*New Jersey Archives* lst ser. 12], p. 607. [Hereafter cited as *NJA* 12]; *NJA* 6 and *NJA* 7, both passim.

20. Bonomi, *A Factious People*, pp. 166–71, 192–95, 211–13, 220; Mark, *Agrarian Conflict*, pp. 131–32.

21. Staughton Lynd, "Who Should Rule at Home? Dutchess County, New York, in the American Revolution," and "The Tenant Rising at Livingston Manor, May 1777," in his *Class Conflict*, pp. 25–61 and 63–77.

22. It must be noted that save for Philip Schuyler and Sir William Johnson everyone who was "anyone" in New York, from Isaac Sears to Thomas Jones, was involved in the area. See the names indexed in *New York Land Patents 1688–1786 Covering Land Now Included in the State of Vermont*, ed. Mary Greene Nye [*State Papers of Vermont*, VII] (n.p. Ryson C. Myrick, 1947).

23. "A State of the Facts," *NJA* 7:215; affidavit of Wm Deare and Jarritt Wall, 20 July 1747, *NJA*, 6:467–68.

24. Dirck Swart to Mr. Livingston, 6 May 1755, *OCDH* 3:791–92; affidavit of Robert Livingston, 8 May 1755, ibid., pp. 792–93; Robert Livingston to Governor Hardy, 9 November 1755, ibid., pp. 813–14; extract from Provincial Council Minutes, 14 May 1757, ibid., pp. 819–20; journals of Captain John Montresor, 28 June, 29 April 1766, *The Montresor Journals*, ed. G. D. Scull [*Collections* of the New-York Historical Society for the year 1881] (New York: printed for the society, 1882), pp. 375, 363.

25. Robert Livingston to Sir Charles Hardy, 23 November 1755, *OCDH* 3:815.

26. Affidavit of Andrew Kelly, 20 July 1747, *NJA* 6:468.

27. "State of the Facts About the Riots . . . 24 December 1746," *NJA* 6:415; "State of the Facts Concerning the Riots . . ." (1748) *NJA* 7:213–14, 216.

28. Robert Livingston to Lt. Gov. DeLancey, 23 June 1755, *OCDH* 3:808–12; Robert VanDusen to Robert Livingston, 29 October 1755, ibid., p. 812; affidavit of Peter

Livingston, 21 November 1755, ibid. pp. 817–18; Robert Livingston to Peter Livingston and James Duane, 22 March 1762, ibid., pp. 825–26.

29. Lynd, *Anti-Federalism in Dutchess County,* p. 50; Lt. Gov. Phips to Lt. Gov. DeLancey, 28 April 1755, *OCDH* 3:789; John Halenbake to Mr. Ingersol, 19 May 1755, ibid., pp. 799–800; report of Massachusetts Legislature, 11 September 1753, ibid., pp. 754–56.

30. Affidavit of Jacob Marsh, 6 December 1773, *OCDH* 4:862–64; James Henderson to Mr. Mackintosh, 12 August 1773 and accompanying documents, ibid., pp. 842–54.

31. Affidavit of John Styles, 1 December 1748, *NJA* 7:178–79; communication of the Rioters about the Riot in Newark, 17 February 1745–1746, *NJA* 6:294–95; State of the Facts, 24 December 1746, ibid., pp. 416–17; Judge Nevill's Charge to Grand Jury of Middlesex County, June 1747, ibid., pp. 459–60.

32. Affidavit of Sheriff Yates, 13 February 1755, *OCDH* 3:777–78; affidavit of John Van Rensselaer, 22 February 1755, ibid., pp. 780–82; journals of John Montresor, 29 June 1766, *The Montresor Journals,* p. 376.

33. Affidavit of Samuel Wells, 9 August 1770, *OCDH* 4:641–45; affidavit of Samuel Willoughby, 17 May 1771, ibid., pp. 710–11; affidavit of Robert Yates, 7 October 1771, ibid., pp. 732–34; Joseph Lord to Governor Tryon, 29 January 1771, ibid., pp. 757–59.

34. Affidavit of Samuel Wells, 1770, ibid., 4:641–45; affidavit of John Grout, 9 August 1770, ibid., pp. 637–40; affidavit of Oliver Church and John Hancock, 22 March 1775, deposition of John Griffin, 27 March 1775, Cadwallader Colden to Lord Dartmouth, 5 April 1775, ibid., pp. 904–16. Cadwallader Colden believed that the Westminster Court closing of 1775 was more related to the court closings with which western Massachusetts had just responded to the Massachusetts Government Act than to the insurgency against New York. Following Richard D. Brown's interpretation of these events this would mean that the insurgents were primarily concerned about unconstitutional authority. See his *Revolutionary Politics in Massachusetts, The Boston Committee of Correspondance and the Towns, 1772–1774* (Cambridge: Harvard University Press, 1970). I criticized this view in my "The Problem of the Early American Crowd," *Journal of American Studies* 7 (1973): 77–90, and a better discussion has been offered in Stephen E. Patterson, *Political Parties in Revolutionary Massachusetts* (Madison: University of Wisconsin Press, 1973), pp. 91–124. In any case, it was New York authority that was being denied at Westminster.

35. Mark, *Agrarian Conflict,* p. 185.

36. Deposition of Ebenezar Salter, 20 July 1749, *NJA* 7:450–52 [Emphasis in the original]; Mark and Handlin, "Land Cases in New York," p. 187.

37. Deposition of Benjamin Hough, 7 March 1775, *American Archives* 2:216; Mark, *Agrarian Conflict,* p. 184; warrant by Alexander McNaughton, J.P., 12 November 1771, *OCDH* 4:745–47.

38. Speeches of Samuel Nevill to the New Jersey Assembly, 26 April 1746, *NJA* 6:324, 325, 333, 343; publication of the Council Proprietors, 25 March 1746, ibid., pp. 320–21; Judge Nevill's charge to the Grand Jury, June 1747, ibid., p. 458; Provincial Council to Governor Belcher, *NJA,* pp. 81–82.

39. Representation of the Lords of Trade to the Privy Council 1 June 1750, *NJA* 7:469.

40. Pauline Maier, "Popular Uprisings and Civil Authority in Eighteenth-Century America," *William and Mary Quarterly,* 3rd ser. 27 (1970): 21.

41. Answer of the Rioters to the Publication of the Proprietors and Speech of Samuel Nevill (August 1747), *NJA* 7:42, 39, 41.

42. Affidavits of Robert Yates et al., October 1771, *OCDH* 4:731–43.

43. Lynd, *Anti-Federalism,* p. 50; Mark, *Agrarian Conflict,$ pp. 143–50.*

44. Resolution of Provincial Council, 31 August 1773,General Haldimand to Governor Tryon, 1 September 1773, *OCDH* 4:843–45.

45. New York Colonial Laws, Ch. 1660, *The Colonial Laws of New York From the Year 1664 to the Revolution.* 5 vols. (Albany: James B. Lyon, 1894), 5:647–55; excerpt from minutes of General Meetings in Manchester, 1 March 1774 and Arlington, 3rd Wednesday in March 1774 and Remonstrance of Ethan Allen and others, 26 April 1774, *Vermont State Papers* (1823), pp. 37–42, 49–54; a local versifyer named Thomas Rowley wrote the

following poem on the act:

> When *Caesar* reigned King at *Rome*/ *St Paul* was sent to hear his doom;/ But *Roman* laws in a criminal case,/ Must have the accuser face to face,/ Or *Caesar* gives a flat denial—/But here's a law made new of late,/ Which destines men to awful fate,/ And hangs and damns without a trial,/ Which made me view all nature through,/ To find a law where men were ti'd,/ By legal act which doth exact,/ Men's lives before they're try'd,/ Then down I took the sacred book,/ and turn'd the pages O'er,/ But could not find one of this kind,/ By God or man before.

Vermont State Papers (1823), p. 54.

46. James Alexander to John Coxe, 5 July 1748, *NJA* 7:154–56.

47. Ian Charles Cargill Graham, *Colonists From Scotland: Emigration to North America, 1707–1783* (Ithaca: Cornell University Press, 1956), p. 145. But it must be noted that in 1754 Alexander himself was accused of instigating crowd action over lands that were in dispute between New York and New Jersey. New York Assembly Journal, session of October, 1754, Public Record Office, C.O. 5, 1216.

48. Mark and Handlin "Land Cases in Colonial New York," pp. 175, 191.

49. Griffin Jenkins, "A Brief Vindication of the Purchasers Against the Proprietors in a Christian Manner," *NJA* 6:266–92; "Henricus Aenfiender," *The New York Gazette Revived in the Weekly Post Boy*, 26 February 1750, reprinted *NJA* 12:607.

50. Information of Solomon Boyle, 18 October 1749, *NJA* 7:426–28; "A State of Facts Concerning the Riots and Insurrections in New Jersey," (1748), ibid., p. 217.

51. Ethan Allen, Seth Warner, Remember Baker, and Robert Cochran to Governor Tryon, 5 June 1774, *Vermont State Papers* (1823), pp. 24–29.

52. Fox, *Yankees and Yorkers*, passim; Bonomi, *A Factious People*, pp. 196–228.

53. See the fiercely anti-Scotch-Irish invective in some of the documents collected as the *Paxton Papers*, ed. John R. Dunbar (The Hague: Nijhoff, 1957).

54. See Rudé, *The Crowd in History*, p. 63.

55. Joseph Chux (?) to unspecified addressee in London, 25 January 1776, British Museum, Add. MS. 29327.

56. Arguing from a lack of evidence is a difficult thing, but only in the case of the Paxton boys is there ethnic invective in the evidence left behind by northern rural crowds. Patriots in the Mohawk Valley pointed out that Sir William Johnson's tenants were Catholics, but, as already suggested, Catholicism was not the only problem in that region. Contrast this with the argument offered in David Grimstead, "Rioting in its Jacksonian Setting," *American Historical Review* 77 (1972): 361–97.

57. Bonomi, *A Factious People*, 221 n.

58. Robert Livingston to Lt. Gov. DeLancey, 12 February 1754, *OCDH* 3:767.

59. Affidavit of John Van Rensselaer, 22 February 1755, *OCDH* 3:780–82; Robert Livingston to Governor Hardy, 23 November 1755, ibid., pp. 814–17; Dirck Swart to Mr. Livingston, 6 May 1755, ibid., pp. 791–92. One could also mention William Rees (or Reece or Race), a tenant of three generations of Livingstons, who lost his life at the hands of a party led by John Van Rensselaer in 1755. See John Van Rensselaer to Lt. Gov. DeLancey, 18 April 1755, ibid, pp. 788–89, and Lt. Gov. DeLancey to Lt. Gov. Phips, 12 May 1755, ibid, pp. 793–95.

60. Alice P. Kenney, "The Albany Dutch, Loyalists and Patriots," *New York History* 42 (1961): 331–50; Staughton Lynd, "The Tenant Rising at Livingston Manor," in *Class Conflict*, pp. 63–77. It is also noteworthy that the ethnic issue lost its saliency in New York City politics between 1700 and 1760. See Gary B. Nash, "The Transformation of Urban Politics 1700–1765," *Journal of American History* 60 (1973–1974): 611.

61. Address to Governor Belcher (1747) from the Committee of the Disaffected, *NJA* 7:63–64; *The New York Gazette Revived in the Weekly Post Boy*, 12 October 1747, reprinted *NJA* 12:406–10.

62. See most especially Kenneth Lockridge, *A New England Town: the First One*

Hundred Years. Dedham, Massachusetts, 1636–1736 (New York: W. W. Norton & Co., 1970), part 1; see also Stephen J. Foster and Timothy H. Breen, "The Puritans' Greatest Achievement: A Study of Social Cohesion in Seventeenth-Century Massachusetts," *Journal of American History* 60 (1973–1974): 3–22.

63. These comments, like those immediately above, are drawn from a wide range of secondary sources, including the work of Kenneth Lockridge, Philip J. Greven, Jr., Sumner Chilton Powell, James A. Henretta, Richard J. Bushman, John M. Murrin, Dirk Hoerder, Rowland Berthoff, Alan Heimart, J. M. Bumstead, and William J. McLoughlin. None of them bears the slightest responsibility for my attempt at synthesis.

64. Kenneth Lockridge and Alan. H. Kreider, "The Evolution of Massachusetts Town Government, 1640 to 1740," *William and Mary Quarterly*, 3rd ser. 23 (1966): 549–74; John M. Murrin, "Review Essay," *History and Theory* 11:267–70.

65. Edward M. Cook, Jr., "Social Behavior and Changing Values in Dedham, Massachusetts, 1700 to 1775," *William and Mary Quarterly*, 3rd Ser. 27 (1970): 546–80; Philip J. Greven, Jr., *Four Generations: Population, Land and Family in Colonial Andover, Massachusetts* (Ithaca: Cornell University Press, 1970); Lockridge, *A New England Town*, part 2; James A. Henretta, "The Morphology of New England Society in the Colonial Period," *Journal of Interdisciplinary History* 2 (1971–1972): 391.

66. Charles S. Grant, *Democracy in the Connecticut Frontier Town of Kent* (New York: Columbia University Press, 1961), pp. 22–27.

67. Grant, *Kent*, pp. 128–40; Lockridge, *A New England Town*, part 1; William F. Willingham, "Deference Democracy and Town Government in Windham, Connecticut, 1755–1786," *William and Mary Quarterly*, 3d ser. 30 (1973): 401–22.

68. Alan Heimert, *Religion and the American Mind, From the Great Awakening to the Revolution* (Cambridge: Harvard University Press, 1966).

69. Quoted by Alfred F. Young in *The Democratic Republicans of New York: The Origins, 1763–1797* (Chapel Hill: University of North Carolina Press, 1968), pp. 260–61.

70. Many of the themes that were developed more fully in New Jersey, the Hudson Valley, and the Grants first emerged in a brief flurry of popular action in Connecticut in 1722. A minor land dispute between Major John Clark and Captain Jeremiah Fitch led to the jailing of Fitch and the threatening of the land tenure of men whose titles were similar to his. On 22 October about fifty men marched to Hartford, demanded Fitch's release, and then made a general jail delivery. When the sheriff of Hartford County attempted to arrest the jail breakers, he was beaten. One result was the swift passage of a riot act, which all town clerks were required to read at their town's annual election meeting. *The Public Records of the Colony of Connecticut From May 1717 to October 1725*, ed. Charles J. Headly (Hartford: Hartford Press of Case, Lockwood & Brainard, 1872), pp. 346–48 n.

71. Grant, *Kent*, pp. 12–28.

72. Douglas E. Leach, *The Northern Colonial Frontier, 1607–1763* (New York: Holt, Rinehart and Winston, 1966), p. 206.

73. As noted above, the amount of land given out by New York's Royal Governors in defiance of the Order-in-Council of 1767 was enormous. William Smith, Jr., the historian and lawyer, was well aware of the moral and ethical problems involved in this, but he eventually shrugged his shoulders and joined in this eighteenth century great barbecue. See his *Historical Memoirs from 16 March 1763 to 9 July 1776*, ed. William H. W. Sabine (New York: Colborn & Tegg, 1956), entries for 2 December 1771, pp. 110–11; 16 April 1771, pp. 183–84; 16 May 1774, pp. 185–86; and 14 June 1774, pp. 187–88, and William Smith to Philip Schuyler, 9 July 1774, ibid., pp. 188–89. A typical case is to be found in the New York grant town of Socialborough, a tract of forty-eight thousand acres given to forty-nine men by Sir Henry Moore. The grantees included Thomas Jones, Isaac Low, John DeLancey, Frederick Van Cortlandt, John Jay, James Duane, Robert Cambridge Livingston, and Egbert Benson. Nye, *New York Land Patents*, pp. 208–13. A mere listing of the grantees only scratches the surface because of the widespread use of dummies. Thus a pre-Vermont source charged that the grant of the town of Norbury, in which Duane was interested, was really a cover for a grant by Governor Tryon to himself. Nye, *New York Land Patents*, pp. 336–39; Hall, "New York Land Grants," *Collections of the Vermont Historical Society*, 1:156; another sign of what was intended for the region is to be found in the dispute among New York grantees over

the location of the County Town of Charlotte County. Colonel John Reid, writing on behalf of the former Governor Lord Dunmore, asked Governor Tryon that it be located on Dunmore's land, and promised that if it were, Dunmore would erect the necessary public buildings. Reid to Governor Tryon, 7 April 1772, *OCDH* 4:771–73. Philip Skene, one of the few major New York grantees who actually lived in the region, wanted it at his town of Skenesborough, and submitted a set of petitions which mentioned that Skene himself maintained a baronial household of forty-four persons and that he had seventy-one tenants. Petitions for the erection of Skenesborough as County Town of Charlotte County, ibid., pp. 818–21.

74. Patricia Bonomi deserves credit for pointing out that town-style government could be found in New York as well as in New England. *A Factious People*, pp. 28–39. See New York colonial Laws, chaps. 2 and 3, *Colonial Laws*, 1:224–26. There seem, however, to be several points of contrast with New England practice. Although the law provided for town meetings for elections and the making of local ordinances, these meetings do not seem to have taken on the self-consciousness of their New England counterparts. Towns were not units of representation in New York, and they were subject to considerable outside control. In the Grants the extent of such control is demonstrated in the case of Kingsland, a grant to King's College. The governors of the college decreed in 1772 that the town would be laid in a nucleated village pattern, and specified the size of town and farm lots; by contrast, in seventeenth-century New England the pattern of land distribution had been a matter for local decision. Order of the Board of Governors, 17 February 1772, *OCDH* 4:767–68. Another point of contrast is to be found in the relative simplicity of New Hampshire and, after independence, Vermont grants vis-a-vis New York ones. Compare the Princetown patent [New York, 1765], Nye, *New York Land Grants*, pp. 31–36, with the Poultney charter [New Hampshire, 1761], *The New Hampshire Grants, Being Transcripts of the Charters of Townships . . .*, ed. Albert Stillman Batchellor (Concord, 1895) [*New Hampshire State Papers*, 26], pp. 355–58 and the Fairhaven Charter [Vermont, 1779], *Charters Granted by the State of Vermont*, (Bellows Falls, Vt., 1922) [*State Papers of Vermont*, 2].

75. Affidavit of Samuel Wells, 9 August 1770, *OCDH* 4:641. Stone's point must be taken rhetorically, for in 1766 he had in fact participated in a petition to the New York Government for the erection of county government in the Grants. "New York Assembly Journal," 11 June 1766, Public Record Office, C.O. 5 1217.

76. William Smith, *Historical Memoirs from 12 July 1776 to 25 July 1778*, ed. William H. W. Sabine (New York: Colborn & Tegg, 1958), entry for 13 May 1777, p 136; Bonomi, *A Factious People*, 191 n.

77. Alice C. Desmond, "Mary Philpse: Heiress," *New York History* 28 (1947): 26, quoted in Lynd, "Who Should Rule at Home?" pp. 27–28.

78. Lynd, "Who Should Rule at Home?" pp. 29–31, and "The Tenant Rising at Livingston Manor," pp. 66–67; Mark, *Agrarian Conflict*, chaps. 2 and 3. As I was shaping this part of my argument, I read the essay by Barthoff and Murrin noted above (n. 15) and found that I was walking a trail that they had already blazed. The great merit of their work over anything that I had thought of lies in the way in which they show the effects of the Revolution not only on the neo-feudal revival, which had been of interest to me, but also on the nostalgic communalism which I see as a major standpoint for popular criticism of neo-feudalism. Both of these gave way, Berthoff and Murrin suggest, before a new social model based on the concept of the "virtuous individual." At that point the path to the nineteenth century was clear.

79. See James T. Lemon, *The Best Poor Man's Country, A Geographical Study of Early Southeastern Pennsylvania* (Baltimore: Johns Hopkins Press, 1972).

80. Memorial of Robert Livingston, 31 May 1753, *OCDH* 3:740; Robert Livingston to Lt. Gov. DeLancey, 12 February 1754, ibid, p. 767; affidavit of John Van Rensselaer, 22 February 1755, ibid., p. 780.

81. Murrin, "Review Essay," p. 274.

82. "The Vision of Junus, the Benningtonite," *Connecticut Courant*, 22 September 1772, reprinted in *Collections of the Vermont Historical Society* 1:105–8.

83. Griffin Jenkins, "A Brief Vindication of the Purchasers Against the Proprietors in a Christian Manner," *NJA* 6:266–92; Aaron Hutchinson, "A Well Tempered Self-Love, a Rule of Conduct Towards Others," a sermon preached on 2 July 1777 before the Vermont State Convention at Windsor, *Collections of the Vermont Historical Society*

1:67–101. On several occasions New Jersey proprietors suspected that the local minister was backing the crowd, and some thought that "Griffin Jenkins" was his pseudonym. See James Alexander to David Ogden, 1 September 1747, *NJA* 7:53–54, and affidavit of Thomas Miller and Thomas McConnell, 4 April 1747, *NJA* 6:430–32.

84. Michael Zuckerman, *Peaceable Kingdoms: New England Towns in the Eighteenth Century* (New York: Alfred A. Knopf, 1970).

85. See the articles contained in the first number of newly-founded *Journal of Peasant Studies.*

86. Huntington, *Political Order in Changing Societies,* pp. 298–99.

87. Lockridge, *A New England Town,* chap. 1.

88. Resolutions of a meeting at Bennington, 14 April 1774, *Vermont State Papers* (1823), p. 40.

89. "The Vision of Junus," *Vermont Historical Society Collections* 1:106; Jenkins, "Brief Vindication," *NJA* 6:284; depostion of Solomon Boyle, 10 March 1747, *NJA* 7:422–23.

90. Lynd, *Anti-Federalism,* pp. 37–38, 50–51.

91. Lynd, "The Tenant Rising at Livingston Manor."

92. Robert J. Chaffin, "The Townshend Acts of 1767," *William and Mary Quarterly,* 3rd ser. 27 (1970): 93; Horowitz, "New Jersey Land Riots," p. 214; Richard P. McCormick, *New Jersey From Colony to State, 1609–1789* (Princeton: Van Nostrand, 1964), passim.

93. Huntington, *Political Order in Changing Societies,* p. 277.

94. On popular mobilization, see Kenneth Lockridge, "Social Change and the Meaning of the American Revolution," *Journal of Social History* 6 (1973): 403–39, and R. A. Ryerson, "Political Mobilization and the American Revolution: The Resistance Movement in Philadelphia, 1765–1776," *William and Mary Quarterly,* 3d ser. 31 (1974): 565–88. On the collapse of old institutions and the legitimation of new ones, see my essay "Consolidating Power in Revolutionary America: The Case of New York, 1775–1783," *Journal of Interdisciplinary History,* forthcoming (1976).

95. "A Relation of the Proceedings of the People of the County of Cumberland and Province of New York," Force *American Archives,* 4th ser., 2:218–22; Hutchinson, "A Well Tempered Self-Love," *Collections of the Vermont Historical Society* 1:67–101.

96. Samuel Dodge to the president of the New York Provincial Congress, 5 December 1775, *Journals of the Provincial Congress, Provincial Convention, Committee of Safety and Council of Safety of the State of New York,* 2 vols. (Albany: Thurlow Weed, 1842), 2:106.

97. See *The Minute Book of the Committee of Safety of Tryon County,* ed. J. Howard Hanson and Samuel Ludlow Frey (New York: Dodd, Mead, 1905), passim., especially entry for 25 August 1775, pp. 49–51, and Robert William Venables, "Tryon County, 1775–1783: A Frontier in Revolution," (Ph.D. diss., Vanderbilt University, 1967).

98. See Bernard Mason, *The Road to Independence, the Revolutionary Movement in New York, 1773–1777* (Lexington: University of Kentucky Press, 1966), chapter 7, and Edward Francis Countryman, "Legislative Goverment in Revolutionary New York, 1777–1788," (Ph.D. diss., Cornell University, 1971), chap. 3.

99. On Young's background, see Henry Herbert Edes, "Memoir of Dr. Thomas Young, 1731–1777," *Publications of the Colonial Society of Massachusetts,* 11, *Transactions, 1906–1907* (Boston, Published by the Society, 1910), pp. 2–54, and David Freeman Hawke, "Dr. Thomas Young—Eternal Fisher in Troubled Waters, Notes for a Biography," *New-York Historical Society Quarterly* 54 (1970): 7–29.

100. *Reason the Only Oracle of Man, Or a Compendious System of Natural Reglion (1785).*

101. [Thomas Young], "Some Reflections on the Disputes Between New York, New Hampshire and Col. John Henry Lydius of Albany," (New Haven: Benjamin Mecom, 1764, Evans No. 9889). Young was one of many who charged the great landlords with retarding settlement in the hope of speculative gain. For modern arguments to the contrary, see Sun Bok Kim, "A New Look at the Great Landlords of Eighteenth-Century New York," *William and Mary Quarterly,* 3d ser. 27 (1970): 581–614, and Bonomi, *A Factious People,* pp. 180–200. Young quote of 1776 cited by Eric Foner, "Tom Paine's Republic," in this volume.

102. Thomas Young, "To the Inhabitants of Vermont, A Free and Independent State, bounding on the River Connecticut and Lake Champlain," (Broadside, Philadelphia, 11 April 1777, Evans number 15649).

103. Gordon S. Wood, *The Creation of the American Republic, 1776–1787* (Chapel Hill: University of North Carolina Press, 1969) parts 1 and 2, especially pp. 206–14.

104. Edes, "Memoir of Young," pp. 46–48.

105. Jones, *Vermont in the Making,* pp. 389–90; Chilton S. Williamson, *American Suffrage From Property to Democracy* (Princeton: Princeton University Press, 1960), pp. 98–99.

106. I develop this point at greater length in "Consolidating Power in Revolutionary America"; see also Lynd, "The Tenant Rising at Livingston Manor."

107. On this, see Lynd, *Anti-Federalism,* chap. 4, and Beatrice Reubens, "Pre-Emptive Rights in the Disposition of a Confiscated Estate: Philipsburgh Manor, New York," *William and Mary Quarterly,* 3d ser. 22 (1965): 435–56.

108. *Laws of the State of New York,* Sessions 1–11, *Records of the States of the United States,* ed. William Sumner Jenkins (Washington: The Library of Congress Photoduplication Service, 1949), New York B.2, reel 6. 3d sess., chap. 47.

109. See the roll call analysis in my "Legislative Government in Revolutionary New York," pp. 274–75.

110. See Gordon S. Wood, "Rhetoric and Reality in the American Revolution," *William and Mary Quarterly,* 3d ser 23 (1966): 26, 31.

111. Patterson, *Political Parties in Revolutionary Massachusetts,* pp. 153–247; see also Dirk Hoerder, "People and Mobs: Crowd Action in Massachusetts During the American Revolution, 1765–1780," (Ph.D. diss., Free University Berlin, 1971), passim.

The North Carolina Regulation, 1766-1776: A Class Conflict

Marvin L. Michael Kay

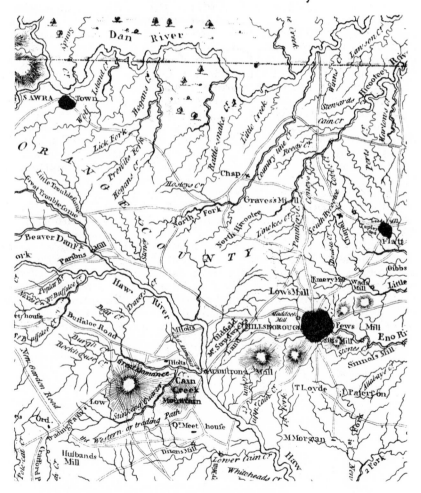

The site of the Battle of the Alamance, in 1771, at which troops of the royal Governor of North Carolina crushed the Regulator movement. From Abraham Collet's *A Compleat Map of North Carolina 1770.* North Carolina Department of Archives and History.

I have been studying colonial North Carolina since 1960, dealing in various ways with its institutions, its demography, and with those who held power and the movements that challenged them. Some of the findings of the first phase of this research may be found in my dissertation, "The Institutional Background to the Regulation in North Carolina" (1962), and a number of articles listed in the footnotes to this essay. These articles were done during my four-year stay at the University of Queensland, Australia.

In recent years I, as well as others, have turned to quantitative analysis wherever appropriate and, like others, have had to develop the necessary tools. In this slow process I came to recognize that a single individual cannot work adequately with the enormous amounts of data that require quantification. I have therefore undertaken dual and multiple studies with several other scholars: Lorin Lee Cary (Department of History) and Calman Winegarden (Department of Economics), both of the University of Toledo, and William S. Price of the North Carolina Department of Archives and History. The manuscripts which are the first fruits of these collaborative efforts and form the basis of some of the conclusions of this essay are also listed in the footnotes. I am happy to acknowledge my debt to these colleagues, and to my daughter, Melisande, and my graduate assistants who helped collect and assemble much of the data, and to my wife, Elizabeth Ruth, who has helped in editing these studies. The first book that will emerge from this collaborative work will be *Slavery in North Carolina, 1748–1772*, with Lorin Lee Cary. The second, of which I will be the sole author, is *The North Carolina Regulators, 1766–1776.*

I have made use of quantitative analysis, but, as this essay makes clear, I believe there is no substitute, in dealing with sociopolitical movements, for studying what people did and what they said. I feel it is necessary to wed this so-called traditional approach to the newer tools, especially if one is to deal successfully with the question of class consciousness, which is at the heart of this essay and which, in my opinion, has been obscured by several schools of historians, old and new.

Marvin L. Michael Kay (Ph.D., University of Minnesota, 1962) teaches history at the University of Toledo. His most recent grants are from the University of Toledo and the American Philosophical Society.

The North Carolina Regulation was an organized movement of white farmers which swept the three western counties of Orange, Anson, and Rowan from 1766 until 1771, when it had the support of 6,000 to 7,000 men out of a total white taxable population of about 8,000.[1] As might be expected in a popular movement that lasted five years, the Regulation also attracted sympathetic but less organized backing in seven surrounding counties.[2] During this time participants gained awareness and broadened their program while adopting a variety of methods of protest: moving through legal political pressure applied directly upon local officials; law suits; civil disobedience; limited acts of violence; petitions to the governor, council, and assembly; election campaigns; and finally a military confrontation at the since famous Battle of the Alamance, on 16 May 1771, in which an armed force of Regulators was defeated by an army of loyal militia, led by the royal governor, in a two-hour battle.[3]

The Regulator movement was not, as it is usually described, a sectional struggle between western farmers and the aristocratic easterners who controlled provincial government.[4] Rather, the Regulators were class-conscious white farmers in the west who attempted to democratize local government in their respective counties and to replace their wealthy and corrupt elected officials with farmer representatives who would serve the interests of the farmers and, hence, all the people. They did, in time, also assail the governor, and obliquely the eastern elite, but this was simply an acknowledgment that many problems were provincial in origin and, therefore, demanded provincial rather than local solutions. Thus, the dissenting farmers eventually fought against their wealthy and powerful exploiters wherever they lived, east and west, but they never regarded the conflict as sectional.

The class consciousness of the Regulators reflected both the existing maldistribution of wealth and power and the prevailing ideology of an age that openly asserted the necessity and benevolence of upper-class rule and demanded that "the people" defer to rule by their "betters."[5] The apostasy of the Regulators was to proscribe upper-class rule as malevolent and then to replace class deference with class conflict.

The Regulators were able to reject deferential attitudes, in part because in the more recently settled western counties, where wealth was growing rapidly, the ruling class was neither as long established nor as wealthy as its counterpart in the east.[6] Wealth was inequitably distributed in all sections of the province, but the range was narrowest in the west, and the area had the province's largest concentration of small-to-middling non-slaveholding farmers. When they felt themselves exploited, therefore, they had both the numbers and relative lack of inhibitions to protest vigorously.

The ethos of the age together with the bitter class antagonisms and refusal of Regulators to defer to the ruling class led them to use the class terms they did use to describe themselves and their adversaries. They saw themselves as "farmers," as "planters" (a term with none of the later connotations associated with large plantation owners), as "poor Industrious peasants," as productive hardworking "labourers," as "the wretched poor," as "poor ["oppressed"] people," and as "poor ["helpless"] families."[7]

While they did not reject the accumulation of land, slaves, and liquid wealth, and normally either owned, rented, or squatted on the land they worked, the Regulators saw no inconsistency in insisting that they were "labourers" and "poor peasants." As laborers, they characterized themselves and their class as the producers in society, and all others were either economic dependents or parasites. Use of the term "peasants" and the stress upon "family" suggest both their sense of community and the permanence of their economic condition. Community and family, joined with deference, were important elements of the conservative ideology of the period. However, the Regulators, in rejecting deference, were free to use their belief that they comprised a community of laboring peasants to develop a radical attack upon the ruling class. And, during this transitional period in Anglo-American history, when liberal capitalistic values were gaining acceptance, the Regulators' petty capitalistic/acquisitive thrust, though in tension with the peasant values, acted as a catalyst to deepen class tensions and further encourage Regulator demands for democracy.

As a corollary of their view of themselves, Regulators saw their western opponents (and by extension, antagonists throughout the province) as expropriators of the fruits of "the people's" labor—"rich and powerful, . . . designing Monsters in iniquity" who (practicing "every Fraud, and . . . threats and menaces") parasitically were "dependent in their Fortunes, with great Expectations from others . . . "[8] Such men could be wealthy farmers or persons in other occupations. More often, Regulators saw that most of the wealth accumulated by the affluent in the western counties was gained by multiple economic pursuits: store-owning, the practice of law, land speculation, milling, tavern keeping, and money lending, all in addition to or instead of farming. Consequently, although the Regulators attacked the rich in general, they assailed in particular those they considered nonproductive, especially merchants and lawyers. The Regulators, however, never understood their enemies solely in economic terms. They believed that the wealthy also controlled the political and legal systems and used this control to aggrandize themselves further at the expense of the poor farmers. Thus, much of the Regulators' attack was concentrated upon the affluent county officers.

Rhetoric does not always describe what is. But Regulator insistence on the interrelation of wealth and political power, this essay will argue, coincided with reality. In North Carolina the royal governor and council appointed the affluent to local militia and civil posts. These men, in turn, ensured their continued appointment in part by their control over the executive, administrative, legislative, judicial, police, and military functions of each county. Invariably these same officials were elected to the vestry and assembly as a consequence of the dexterous use of their wealth and appointive power, including effective control over the nominating and electoral processes, joined with the habitual attitudes of deference on the part of the people. Elected officials, as the Regulators argued, were those "whose highest Study is the Promotion of their wealth" and who would consequently allow "the Interest of the Public, when it comes in Competition with their private Advantages . . . to sink."[9]

Officials pursued public policies which added to private fortunes in many ways: by the awarding of public contracts to favorites; by locating and building roads, bridges, harbors, ferries, and towns to convenience the rich and powerful; by issuing licenses for mills to favorites; by insuring that the public offices the wealthy controlled were remunerative; by granting compensations to masters for executed slaves; and by awarding exorbitant commissions to a favored few to handle the mechanics of currency emissions.[10]

Affluent officeholders also exploited more directly their poorer and weaker constituents. They collected unlawful taxes and fees and corruptly handled public monies. Such actions not only stole money from the people, but also further increased the tax levels that had remained high after the French and Indian War to pay off war debts and to finance growing, peacetime public expenditures. The ruling provincial elite also early instituted a regressive tax system that depended primarily upon poll taxes, duties, fees, and work levies—all of which disproportionately and harshly burdened the poor. The scarcity of currency, though not a deliberate policy of the elite, made even greater the burden of taxation on the poor, especially those in the west who were farthest from the centers of commerce.[11] Moreover, creditors, merchants, lawyers, and public officers brought an increasing number of court suits against indebted farmers, while lawyers and officers charged exorbitant or extortionate court fees.[12] All these groups cooperated in distraining exorbitant amounts of property from moneyless farmers and corruptly selling the property at public auctions below its value to members of the in-group—with nothing returned to the victims. The wealthy and powerful were able to maintain these conditions both by passing biased laws and by manipulating the application of these statutes.[13] For example, small claims procedures would have been expensive even if court officers had acted honestly and with moderation, but statutes concerning fees were sufficiently vague to invite misconstruction and misconduct by officers and lawyers.[14]

These matters formed the substance of Regulator protest. Their grievances were thus rooted in class, not sectional differences and exploitation. This is why they did not challenge the disproportionately small number of western representatives in the assembly. In 1769, when the Regulators urged dividing western counties to create additional counties, their goal was not to gain parity in representation, but to decrease the size of counties in order to provide western farmers with readier access to public facilities.[15]

In support of this argument, this essay will explore first, the pattern of the distribution of wealth and political power in the Regulator counties, and second, the policies put forth by the Regulators and their adversaries as the conflict unfolded between 1766 and 1771. Thirdly, the essay will explore the complex and far less certain relationship between the conflict of Regulator and anti-Regulator and the coming of the American Revolution. I will suggest that the Regulators in 1776 may not fit any more neatly into the categories historians have placed them than they fit the categories they are assigned for 1766–1771.

I

Historians who have offered a sectional interpretation of the Regulator movement have traditionally stressed the contrast between the western and eastern counties. Selecting data to justify their interpretation and using inadequate quantitative techniques, they have exaggerated the demographic and class differences between east and west, overstated the homogeneity of property holdings within the western counties, and virtually ignored variations within regions throughout the province. As a result, these historians have been incapable of describing systematically the objective class characteristics of the western counties in general, or of the Regulators and their adversaries in particular.[16]

What follows is an analysis primarily based on quantifiable data that will cover the following: (1) economy and demography, (2) wealth distribution in the western counties where the Regulators were organized, (3) the pattern of political power in these counties, (4) class differences between the Regulators and their opponents.

(1) *Economy and Demography.* An analysis of white and black populations (not taxables) in North Carolina around 1767 demonstrates that contrasting the coastal and piedmont areas alone overlooks important variations within the east and within the west, as well as trends which are similar in the two regions.[17] The economy and demography of the Lower Cape Fear region in the southeast (New Hanover and Brunswick counties), for example, were unlike those in the rest of the colony with the limited exception of the Upper Cape Fear (Bladen County). Adequate transportation facilities and capital accumulation in the Lower Cape Fear resulted in a large slave population concentrated in the hands of a relatively large number of wealthy landowners who produced naval stores and lumber for export. Sixty-two percent of the population in the region was black, representing 12 percent of the province's black population. The region's white population, however, comprised only 2 percent of the colony's white population.

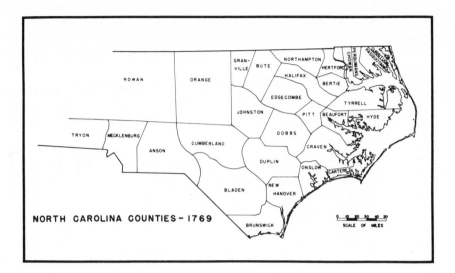

NORTH CAROLINA COUNTIES - 1769

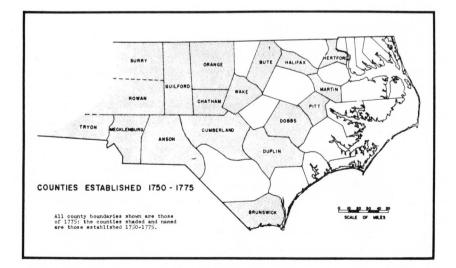

COUNTIES ESTABLISHED 1750 - 1775

All county boundaries shown are those
of 1775: the counties shaded and named
are those established 1750-1775.

Elsewhere, the highest concentration of blacks was in the tobacco, lumber, and commodities-producing Albemarle Sound region (the seven northeastern coastal counties) where they comprised 35 percent of the population. This area had relatively few large slaveholdings, a condition true throughout North Carolina except in the Lower and Upper Cape Fear regions. Thus, the range of slave ownership in the Albermarle was 87 and the percentage of slaves living in households with 20 or more slaves was 21.1 percent; comparable figures for the Lower Cape Fear were 242 and 72.9 percent, and for the Upper Cape Fear, 93 and 47.5 percent.[18]

The slaveholding patterns of the Cape Fear region contrast most strongly with those of the western counties of Orange, Rowan, Anson, Mecklenburg, and Tryon. This is piedmont country, generally 500 to 1,000 feet above sea level, rising gradually westward; swift flowing rivers, unsuitable for navigation, necessitated dependence upon overland wagon routes for inland transportation.[19] Western counties grew rapidly from their political organization in 1750s through the Regulation. The taxable population grew from about 2,000 in 1754 to approximately 10,500 in 1767. During these years black taxables grew even more rapidly, from about 50 to 730 in Orange County, for example.[20] Towns also developed during this period. In Orange, Childsburg was established in 1759 (it became Hillsborough in 1766), and Salisbury was formed in Rowan about 1755. By 1760 the towns were commercially viable. Stores preceded towns, but multiplied as towns developed.[21]

Equally important as the late settlement of this region and its rapid population growth, therefore, was an early establishment of stores to handle the marketing, supply, and credit needs of the backcountry. Along with commerce came a political and a juridical development, which meant a rapid movement of lawyers into the area.

Despite this development, in the sample western county of Anson, in 1763, slaveholdings averaged less than .5 among all households. Only 11.4 percent of all households owned slaves, and those households held an average of slightly more than four slaves. By comparison, in the Lower Cape Fear slaveholdings averaged 9.6, 50 percent of the households owned slaves, and the average number of slaves among slaveholding households was 19.

(2) *Wealth Distribution in the Western Counties Where the Regulators Were Organized.* While there were only a small number of slaves and slaveowners in the western counties, a small number of large owners held

most of the slaves. Thus, in 1763, in the sample western county of Anson, 41 percent of the slaves were owned by less than 2 percent of the households, each of whom owned five or more slaves. The largest owner had seventeen slaves.[22] Moreover, the larger owners plus a few others followed multiple economic pursuits which enabled them to accumulate considerable wealth, resulting in an inequitable distribution of wealth within the region.

The extent of the unequal distribution of wealth in the western counties can be better demonstrated by using more data than slaves alone. To do so, I studied the estate records of a sample county (Orange County's 121 inventories) for the years 1762–1772.[23] The results indicate that the lower 30 percent of the free population owned 6 percent of the wealth, the middle 30 percent owned 15 percent, the upper 30 percent owned 36 percent, and the wealthiest 10 percent owned 43 percent. (See Appendix, table I). This distribution reflected the early, if incomplete, development of commercial farming in the region. Thus, although wealth distribution in the western counties was inequitable when compared with many colonial farming communities, it was not as inequitably distributed as in the more economically mature eastern counties of North Carolina.[24]

(3) *The Pattern of Political Power in the Regulator Counties.* An analysis of officeholders in the western counties (the assemblymen, major militia officers, clerks, registers, sheriffs, and justices of the peace) shows they were drawn from the upper class (the most affluent and prestigious members of society). Three sets of statistics presented in tables II, III, and V verify this for the sample counties of Anson and Orange.

Using slaveholdings in Anson County in 1763 as one gauge (table II), we can see that whereas the mean slaveholding among the county's household heads was 0.61, the average holding among the top 10 percent of the county's slaveholders was 4.62, and among the officers 3.64.

In order to measure the total wealth of the officers it was necessary to use tax lists compiled eight to eleven years after the period in question. The historian working with quantitative data often does not have the luxury of choice: the 1779 to 1782 tax lists are the *best* complete records available to evaluate the total wealth of the western county officials. Use of records from a later period exaggerates the wealth of the officers as compared with the wealth of the remainder of the inhabitants. Very likely, however, the resulting bias is not important. This view is supported by the fact that when we trace Anson

officers to a tax list of 1782 for Montgomery County (formed from
Anson in 1779) we find almost identical slaveholding figures as those
gleaned from the 1763 list for Anson. (See tables II and IV). Also supporting this view is impressionistic evidence and a multiple regression analysis that I have done of class and mobility in North Carolina
for the years 1748 to 1772, using slaveholding as a measure of
wealth.[25]

In any case, in Montgomery County the wealth of the officers
averaged slightly higher than that of the wealthiest 10 percent of the
county (table IV), while in counties formed largely from Orange
County, the officers' wealth averaged about twice that of the wealthiest
10 percent of the population (table V). That officer affluence is even
greater when total wealth is measured than when only slaveholdings
are considered probably indicates the importance of nonagricultural
wealth among the officers.

(4) *Class Differences Between the Regulators and Their Opponents.* Statistical evidence also supports the Regulators' class descriptions of themselves and their antagonists. To demonstrate this, I traced on available
tax lists the names of all known Regulators and anti-Regulators.[26]
Thus, using slave ownership in 1763 as the gauge of wealth, table VI
shows that in Anson County a slightly smaller percentage of the Regulators owned slaves than was the case in the county at large, and that
the mean number of slaves held by the Regulators was also slightly less
than that of the county. On the other hand, somewhat over 71 percent
of Regulator antagonists owned slaves, in comparison with about 17
percent of the county's householders, and the mean number of slaves
they held was six times larger than the average in the county.

The findings are similar when we investigate the total wealth of
the Regulators and their opponents (table III). Tax lists compiled
eight to eleven years after the Regulation are the best and earliest data
available to compare the wealth of Regulators and known anti-Regulators. Such data very likely exaggerates the wealth of both groups, with
this exaggeration greatest among Regulators. Thus, use of these later
tax lists to discern the wealth of the Regulators results in a conservative
bias.[27] The tendency to exaggerate the wealth of both groups was
additionally caused by the records used to compile the lists of Regulators and their opponents. This once again resulted in an acceptable
conservative bias—that is, an overestimate—in measuring Regulator
wealth. On the other hand, poorer westerners who opposed the Regulators cannot be identified. We know they were there; the number of
western militiamen who mustered against the Regulators in 1768 and

1771 is proof, despite the fact that the vast majority of the poorer folk in Anson, Orange, and Rowan counties supported or joined the Regulators. A consequence of this incapacity to identify the poorer anti-Regulators is that our analyses only demonstrate the affluence of the most outspoken and influential anti-Regulators. Nevertheless, the fact is that *almost all wealthy westerners have been identified as being opposed to the Regulators,* although many of them could not be traced on the available tax lists. Thus, the emphasis on the wealth of the opponents of the Regulators is not seriously questioned by the limits of our data. The data in table III from both counties argue that the Regulators were poorer than average while their antagonists were an affluent group. This last is strikingly illustrated in Orange County where the traceable anti-Regulators comprised most of the wealthiest 1 percent of the population.

Other evidence supports the Regulators' understanding of the class differences between themselves and their adversaries. A partial check of land records, for example, reveals that Regulators were landowners, squatters, tenants, or dependents of various kinds. Very few were affluent.[28] On the other hand, of the twelve merchants operating in Orange County whose affiliations can be traced, eight of whom also held important offices, all were antagonists of the Regulators. Similarly, of the twelve persons who have been identified as Orange County sheriffs, clerks, registers, coroners, and Hillsborough commissioners during the period, none became Regulators. Of the twelve attorneys who practiced law in Orange County whose affiliations can be traced, all opposed the Regulation. Of the twenty-three militia officers serving between 1768 and 1771, none became Regulators, and of the fifty-nine justices of the peace who served between 1766 and 1771 only three became Regulators. In Rowan County, sixty-two officers and lawyers were traced; only one, a justice of the peace, was a known Regulator.[29] Anson County, however, had a somewhat higher Regulator representation among militia officers (one captain and five junior officers out of thirty). Among justices of the peace, five out of twenty-six were Regulators, and in a sample of county court officers, one out of nine were Regulators. Almost all the known anti-Regulators, on the other hand, were officers either during or close to the Regulator period.

The exceptions to these generalizations should not be lost. Some Regulators were affluent. Leaders or spokesmen, whether they ever formally joined the movement or not, such as Hermon Husband of Orange County, Charles Robinson of Anson County, and Christopher

Nation of Rowan County, were relatively well-to-do farmers. But the leaders of rebellions and revolutions have frequently been more affluent than the rank and file. And the presence of a handful of such men does not indicate that an important section of the western elite joined the western rebels; the elite of the west showed a remarkable unity in the face of the threat to their interests.

The quantitative evidence does not permit us to generalize precisely about the allegiances of those at the other end of the social structure, namely dependents—that is, propertyless sons of farmers, indentured servants, or apprentices. However, an analysis of the Anson County tax list of 1763 gives us conservative estimates concerning the number of Regulators and anti-Regulators who were dependents: 22.5 percent of the Regulators and none among the anti-Regulators. The number of dependents who were apprentices and servants is unclear; certainly they were no more than one-third of the total. More traditional sources buttress the view that servants were of minor importance among the Regulators; Regulators never expressed servant grievances. Lastly, neither quantitative nor traditional evidence has revealed the participation of blacks, slave or free, in the uprising.

II

Discord during the 1750s and 1760s over land problems preceded and influenced the Regulators. For example, settlers on the lands of Henry McCulloh and his associates (including Governor Arthur Dobbs), who had received grants totaling 1,386,000 acres, resisted attempts by the speculators to eject those who refused to pay exorbitant rents and land prices. Resistance led to violence in 1765 in the Sugar Creek uprising in Anson and Mecklenburg counties.[30] There were other land-related disturbances in the Granville district which encompassed the entire northern half of North Carolina. The land and quitrents in this district were distributed and collected by the agents of the proprietor, Lord Granville. Disturbances provoked by the corrupt practices of the earl's land agents began in the 1750s, peaking in Halifax, Edgecombe, Johnston, and Granville counties between 1758 and 1760. These disturbances led to the closing of Lord Granville's land office in 1763, which forced new settlers in the western counties to squat on the lands they settled, a fact which generated squatter fears about unpaid quitrents and the future disposition of their improved lands.[31] Both fears continued to nag at the Regulators, and in 1769 they proposed the passage of preemption laws to protect their unpatented lands.

In the more immediate background were the grievances articulated by George Sims in 1765 in "An Address to the People of Granville County."[32] Sims condemned the exorbitant and fraudulent fees collected by the county court officers, especially the sheriffs and clerks, and the "damned lawyers who practiced numberless . . . devilish devices to rob you of your livings in a manner diametrically opposite to the policy of our State and the intention of our legislature." He excoriated the collusion between these corrupt officers and grasping merchants who precipitately instituted suits against the indebted and moneyless farmers, who would then not only be swindled by corrupt officers but also be forced to pay off their indebtedness to the merchants in the form of distrained property "sold at one tenth its value." If unable to meet these obligations with their personal property, the farmers would be ordered by the court to work off their indebtedness to the merchants, lawyers, and public officials. This often led to the debtor's loss of his farm, since he had no time to care for it.

Pointing to the possibility that some statutes were "private acts . . . that favour [the officers] in these devilish practices," Sims argued that the people were "bound by no authority to submit to them" since they were "consequently derogatory from the System of the laws of England"—a higher law argument to nullify "unconstitutional" legislation. In a less radical vein, he argued that the problem was neither "our mode or form of government nor yet the body of our laws that we are quarrelling with." Consequently, he proposed that the inhabitants refuse to pay illegal fees, petition the governor for redress, and appeal to the courts to suspend business until the governor could correct the prevailing abuses.

Although the inhabitants of Granville responded to these proposals by no more than petitioning the legislature, Sims's ideas outraged county officers. Corrupt, intransigent, and insistent upon their constitutional prerogatives, they promptly filed libel suits against Sims and the petitioners. This neutralized Sims and apparently stymied organized farmer resistance in Granville County. Yet complaints about abuses continued there and elsewhere. In 1766, for instance, opposition to tax payments—"great levies were raised from the people and no accounts given for what use"—occurred in such disparate counties as Granville, Cumberland, and Brunswick. That same year the focus of resistance moved westward.[33]

The precursor of the Regulators in Orange County was the Sandy Creek Association, organized in the summer of 1766. It voiced grievances similar to those Sims had articulated: burgeoning suits by creditors against indebted farmers, extortionate fees collected by court officers, unfair and corrupt distraining practices and sales of debtor property at public auction, high taxes, and suspicions about the necessity and lawful application of these taxes. After having expended much time, effort, and money in attempting to redress their grievances in the courts, and having gotten nowhere and believing they would accomplish little by petitioning the governor or legislature, the Orange County protesters decided to address their "public officers," including their assemblymen, directly.

Direct access to and control over county officers and elected representatives through instructions given in regularly scheduled meetings had far-reaching democratic ramifications. If successful, this innovation would have challenged both upper-class notions of virtual representation and their control over local and provincial government.

Demands of the Sandy Creek Association were clothed in the general appeal of opposition to the Stamp Act promoted by the Sons of Liberty in the previous year in seaboard North Carolina. Adapting the Whig arguments to democratic ones, the Association ironically called for direct control by the people over local government to prevent "Officers under" the Sons of Liberty from carrying on "unjust oppression in our own Province." All men were corruptible unless directly accountable to their constituencies.

Through at least 10 October 1766, the Association tried to meet with their representatives and local officials. Led by Edmund Fanning (Hillsborough lawyer and merchant, assemblyman, militia colonel, town commissioner, and county register), they refused to meet, contending that to do so would give credence to the Association's grievances and enable the people to set up a "jurisdiction" among themselves. To Fanning this was "more like an insurrection than a settlement." Unable to gain direct access to their officers, the Association reluctantly turned to the courts. When this failed, the Association died.[34]

The officers, in turn, were emboldened by their capacity to withstand reform and continued to abuse the public. The grievances that prompted the Sandy Creek Association mounted until the state of mind that prevailed among many Orange County residents could be depicted as follows:

Thus were the People of Orange insulted by the Sheriff, robbed and plundered by the Bombs, neglected and condemned by the Representatives and abused by the Magistracy; obliged to pay Fees regulated only by the Avarice of the officer; obliged to pay a Tax which they believed went to inrich and aggrandise a few, who lorded it over them continually; and from all these Evils they saw no way to escape; for the Men in Power, and Legislation were the Men whose interest it was to oppress, and make gain of the Labourer.[35]

It was, therefore, just a matter of time before organized resistance resumed, triggered by the introduction of a new tax collection method in Orange County and, more important, by a rumor, later verified, that £15,000 had been granted the governor to construct a dwelling that would significantly raise tax levels. According to Hermon Husband, early in 1768 a "new Association" was formed on the "West Side of the Haw River commonly called the Mob; which in little time altered to that of the Regulators."[36]

The new association was concentrated in the southwestern part of Orange County, an area encompassing Sandy Creek. Its founders were moved by the same grievances which led to the first organization, but believed as well that persons in Orange County paid higher taxes than did taxpayers in the adjoining counties. The new movement was also more militant. Complaining that county officials had rudely rejected meeting with the people and asserting their right as Englishmen not to be taxed without knowing "what use its for," members pledged not to pay further taxes until their grievances were directly redressed.[37]

Because their militancy alarmed the erstwhile supporters of the old Sandy Creek Association, whose allegiance was needed, the new association was reorganized on 4 April 1768 to regulate "publick Grievances and abuses of Power." Assuming the name "Regulators," they now couched their concerns in moderate language and prescribed noncompliance with the law only up to the point of confrontation; but they still advocated direct control over representatives and local officials. They vowed to advise their assemblymen about necessary legislation and elect more suitable vestrymen, and proposed a meeting with officials to discuss how tax monies had been spent and the legality of fees.

Until 3 May 1768, the Orange County Regulators tried to set up local meetings and to prevent the collection of taxes or the distrainment of the properties of tax delinquents. This led to limited acts of violence. Sixty to a hundred Regulators, for instance, recaptured a distrained mare and shot two or three bullets into the house of their most hated enemy, Col. Edmund Fanning.[38]

County officials, both elected and appointed, carried on a frantic, revealing correspondence among themselves and with Governor Tryon.[39] They knew that the Regulators lacked power, and this they meant to deny to them at all costs. Thus, while encouraging the Regulators to believe that they meant to negotiate, the officers were plotting together, and with Tryon and the council, to repress the "insurrection" by raising the militia to arrest its leaders. The officers branded Regulator attempts at direct control over officers as seditious attacks upon government and an insult to their class position. To submit would have them "be arraigned at the Bar of [the lower classes'] Shallow Understanding and...be punished and regulated at their Will, and in a word, for them to become sovereign arbiters of right and wrong."[40] Defining Regulator acts of violence as either riotous, insurrectionary, or, at times, treasonous, the officers urged quick repression with all necessary force.

The officers could not mount a direct assault on the Regulators because most Orange County militiamen were sympathetic to the Regulators and refused to muster. Fanning warned Tryon that the "traiterous Dogs" were also powerful in four other counties. Anxious to break the movement, Fanning proposed arresting its leaders immediately or "nobly die" in the effort. More realistically, he requested permission to call upon the militia of neighboring counties to suppress the uprising.[41]

Tryon and the council, deciding that "an absolute Insurrection of a dangerous tendency has broke out in Orange County," issued a proclamation ordering all "Riotous and disorderly persons" to disperse and to cease committing "outrages in open Violation of the Laws of their Country." Commanders in eight other counties were ordered to be prepared to march their units to Orange.[42]

Heartened by this support and the arrival of the governor's private secretary, Isaac Edwards, bearing the proclamation, Fanning arrested two Regulator spokesmen, Hermon Husband and William Butler, on 2 May 1768. When 700 armed farmers assembled near Hillsborough, however, the frightened officers released the two. On that same day Edwards read the governor's proclamation to the farmers and delivered a message from Tryon, which promised action if the people petitioned him to deal with their grievances. "No sooner was the Word spoke, but the whole multitude, as with one Voice cried out, Agreed. That is all we want; Liberty to Make our grievances Known."[43]

This promise by Tryon moved the Regulators into the second phase of the movement, which lasted from early May 1768 to late September 1768. During this period, the Regulators frequently corresponded with the governor and council, but also continued to disrupt the collection of taxes and tried to set up regular meetings to control their county representatives and officers. In addition, they began to organize a regional response.

The officers immediately attempted to co-opt the Regulators. In fact, they threatened the Regulators with charges of treason if they did not submit to a petition, drafted by Fanning, which laid the blame for what had occurred on their own "illegal and unwarrantable conduct ...infinitely more criminal than we apprehended or imagined...." The Regulators rejected this invitation to destroy their movement and sent a copy of all their papers to the governor along with an apology for their past transgressions, a petition for a redress of their grievances, and a detailed narrative of events from 1766 on. This history cited as the basic cause of their many problems "the unequal chances the poor and the weak have in contentions with the rich and powerful."[44]

In answer to the Regulators' request that he correct the imbalance of power, Tryon, on 20 June, accused the hopeful farmers of "assuming to themselves Powers and Authorities unknown to the Constitution of calling Publick Officers to a settlement." Backed by a unanimous council, Tryon condemned the Regulators' unlawful acts and ordered them to hold no more meetings, drop the titles "Regulators or Associators," allow all officers to execute their duties, and submit to process of law all "Breakers of the peace against His Majesty's Government." The Regulators, he stressed, could expect further clemency only if they adhered to all his demands. At the same time Tryon promised to order the attorney general to prosecute all officers upon application by the injured parties, and offered his services to rectify any other abuses which might be demonstrated.[45]

Prior to receiving Tryon's letter, the Orange County Regulators had become aware of official corruption in other counties. They had also learned of gross abuses in the collection and disbursement of public tax monies: though £20,000 to £30,000 had been collected beyond the amount necessary to sink some currency emissions, £60,000 remained in circulation.

> Either our Assembly have been deficient in burning the Monies returned into the Treasury—or, the Officers, in the Treasury have been deficient in accounting for it, or the Sheriffs have been faulty in the payment of the Money into the Treasury—or, some counties must be in arrears—for they knew that Orange had paid in full.[46]

All of these explanations were correct: corruption and inefficiency typified tax collections and disbursements as well as accounting and auditing procedures.[47] But when the Regulators voiced their suspicions, their adversaries warned against hurling slanderous accusations at "Men of *such credit*" and that it was "criminal even to suppose such things." Despite this advice, the Regulators pressed their assemblymen to check into the accounts of the Orange County officers and the treasurers of the province, vowing to call for an election if the assemblymen refused to cooperate.[48]

The Regulators were further angered by Tryon's letter, which "multiplied all our faults" while lauding "the discreet Behaviour of the Officers." Their petition a failure, unable to meet with their county officials or obtain relief in the courts, directed by Tryon not to assemble, and beleaguered by the persistence of extortionate fees, the Orange County Regulators appeared to have few options left.[49]

Meanwhile, farmers were organizing in other counties, particularly Anson and Rowan. Of the two movements, that in Anson is most fully documented. Anson Regulators organized some time prior to 28 April 1768, prompting Col. Samuel Spencer to complain to Tryon of "the unparalleled tumults, Insurrections, and Commotions which at present distract this County." Vexed by high taxes, the currency shortage, and damaging court suits, the Anson Regulators, like those in Orange, resisted paying taxes, distrainments, and consequent jailings. Violence peaked when 100 men temporarily disrupted the proceedings of the county court. After the Orange Regulators advised them not to act rashly but to petition the governor, the Anson Regulators changed their tactics. They adopted a petition complaining of exorbitant county taxes, the collection of illegal taxes and extortionate fees, illegal and abusive distraining practices, and the corruption of the court system by the three most powerful men in the county. The

Regulators urged Tryon to end these practices, discharge the county clerk and all justices of the peace, and allow constituents to nominate new officers. Ignoring the latter request as unconstitutional, Tryon tendered palliatives similar to those in Orange, but promised lenient treatment if the Anson Regulators ceased their unlawful activities. The priority of stifling the insurgency in Orange—to Tryon, the fount of disturbances—dictated this relatively moderate response.[50]

And so he went to Hillsborough in July 1768 to observe the situation in Orange County firsthand, to end all Regulator meetings, and to force them to allow the courts to meet and taxes to be collected. On 1 August 1768 he sent a letter to assembled Regulators, reminding them of his proclamation of 21 July prohibiting the collection of illegal fees and his orders to the attorney general to prosecute officers upon the receipt of complaints; he concluded by directing the Regulators to be law-abiding and, most important, to pay their taxes.[51]

In their reply the Regulators defiantly argued that the officers had ignored the governor's proclamation, were more extortionate than ever, and that individuals would be ruined by attempts at redress in the courts. Condemning Tryon for placing their petition before only a part of his council, they refused to pay their taxes and pledged to seek relief from the "Assembly and the Whole Council." But the Regulators were also alarmed at rumors that Tryon meant to attack them with frontier Indians and the militia. On 11 August, 1,000 men, a majority from Orange joined probably by some from Anson and Rowan counties, assembled twenty miles from Hillsborough. Tryon, fearful that they intended to burn the town, mustered 400 Orange County militia and agreed to parley with eight Regulator leaders. The meeting allayed immediate fears of attack, and both forces disbanded.[52]

Determined to restore law and order, Tryon, two days later, received approval from his council to raise the militia. He then wrote to the Regulators demanding that they pay their taxes, cease acting unlawfully, and post £1,000 bond that they would not interfere with the superior court trials of Husband and Butler for their roles in the mare incident. Without waiting for a reply, Tryon left for Rowan and Mecklenburg counties to raise troops and pacify the people. In response, the Regulators' leaders simply promised to try to use their influence to end unlawful acts by Regulators, but they refused to post bond and added a new demand: that Tryon call for elections.[53]

Through a liberal use of rhetoric, ceremonial display, liquor, and the appeals of dissenting ministers (especially Presbyterians), Tryon managed to raise a total of 1,419 troops (195 in Rowan, 310 in Mecklenburg, 126 from Granville, 699 from Orange, and 89 complementary officers and men from other counties). Although a disproportionate number of these were officers (many of them members of the assembly and council) and only about three-fourths were privates, Tryon was able to muster more than twice as many westerners at this time than he would be able to do in 1771, during the climatic struggle with the Regulators.[54]

Estimates concerning the number of Regulators who gathered near Hillsborough from Orange, Rowan, and Anson counties to oppose the militia vary from 800 to 3,700. Whatever their number, Tryon's show of force intimidated them. After brief negotiations with Tryon, who was barely restrained from force by his advisory council, the Regulators disbanded on 23 September, promising to use their influence to end unlawful behavior and to submit themselves to the clemency of the governor. They refused, however, to surrender their arms or deliver nine leaders for trial.[55]

A third phase of the Regulation had begun—a peaceful phase in which Regulators paid their taxes and resorted only to legal tactics: petitions to the legislature and political campaigns to elect sympathetic farmer assemblymen. This phase lasted from 23 September 1768 until the dissolution of the assembly on 2 November 1769. In this period, Husband, Butler, and thirteen other Regulators submitted to trials; three were convicted, but all were pardoned by Tryon.[56] And Regulators in Orange and Rowan counties again sought relief in the courts, but were stymied by stacked juries, hostile and manipulated justices, and countersuits.[57]

Petitions now articulated grievances in much greater detail and with sharper rhetoric. In October 1768, Orange and Rowan Regulators jointly pleaded their inability to obtain relief from officers who "continually Squez'd and oppressed poor...families" by collecting extortionate fees and unlawful taxes. Unable to pay the high taxes because of their poverty and the scarcity of currency, they urged the legislature to investigate the sinking fund, end all taxes that had served their purposes, not build the governor's palace, and establish small-claims courts to limit court costs. They concluded with a wistful appeal to the assembly to "Exert yourself this once in our favour."[58]

The assembly, acting within the limits of a somewhat enlightened upper-class self-interest, focused on fiscal and monetary matters. It passed an appropriation act which emitted £20,000 in treasury notes to cover the £4,844 cost of the recent military expedition and other expenditures, and levied a sinking tax of 2s. per poll to begin in 1771, but provided that all taxes, except those for the sinking fund, could be paid in inspectors' notes for six rated commodities. The Regulators were hurt by the new levy, but benefited from the increase in the currency supply resulting both from the emission and from allowing commodity payments for taxes. The immediate effect of the currency increase for the Regulators, however, was minimal because there were no inspection warehouses in the west.[59] Members of the ruling class supported both provisions. Commodity payments ensured the eventual establishment of western warehouses, eagerly sought by the elite in the region.[60] And all members of the provincial ruling class, especially those from the Cape Fear region, would benefit from some increase in the currency supply.[61]

The legislature also resolved to cease collecting 3s. in poll taxes levied to sink two currency emissions totaling £32,000. Here the main interest may have been to supplement the currency supply (many of the bills remained in circulation), but the assemblymen were not averse to lowering taxes and recognized that the Regulators supported both effects of the resolution, especially the tax cut that nearly halved the provincial poll tax for 1768.

Tryon, though long sympathetic to provincial attempts to alleviate the currency shortage, followed British instructions to the Currency Act of 1764 and vetoed the resolution because many of the bills in question were still circulating.[62] As a result, tax levies were probably little affected by the assembly's resolution. In summary, the positive actions of the assembly had little immediate effect upon the Regulators, while the new tax levy to pay for the military expedition hurt and enfuriated them. The session demonstrated the vitality of the alliance between the ruling classes of the east and west.

On 6 May 1769 Tryon dissolved the assembly.[63] Whatever his reasons, the Regulators made the most of it. In the election campaign that followed, Orange, Rowan, and Anson County Regulators collaborated in an effort to elect farmer legislators. Their appeals were primarily to class. One extant campaign document asserted

> that a majority of our assembly is composed of Lawyers, Clerks, and others in Connection with them, while by our own Voice we have excluded the Planter.—Is it not evident their own private Interest is, designed in the whole Train of our Laws?—We have not the least Reason to expect the Good of the Farmer, and consequently of the Community, will be consulted, by those who

hang on Favors, or depend on the Intricacies of the Laws.—What can be expected from those who have ever discovered a Want of good Principles and whose highest Study is the Promotion of their wealth; and with whom the Interest of the Public, when it comes in Competition with their private Advantages, is suffered to sink?—nothing less than the Ruin of the Publick.[64]

The same appeal then called upon citizens "for once [to] assert your Liberty and maintain your Rights" and resist all strategems (including plying them with liquor) by incumbents who, if elected again, would "draw from you the last Farthing."[65]

In the 1770 campaign that followed the dissolution of the 1769 assembly, Husband, in his *Impartial Relation,* once again urged the farmers to elect either farmers or those who would support farmers' needs. Especially to be shunned were the

clerk[s], lawyer[s], or Scotch merchant[s], or any sect who are connected with certain companies, callings and combinations, whose interests jar with the interest of the public good.—And when they come to solicit you with invitations to entertainments, etc., shun them as you would a pestilence.—Send a man who is the choice of the country, and not one who sets up himself, and is the choice of a party; whose interest clashes with the good of the publick.[66]

The Regulators' opponents were no less class-conscious. In supporting Edmund Fanning for the assembly, they stressed his "considerable" property, which ostensibly ensured that "the interest of the public must be his interest." Those who questioned Fanning's "attachment to the welfare and interest of his constituents" were both "assassin[s] who...stab in the dark" and "persons courting the voice of popularity." This was a classic appeal to the masses to defer to their "betters," who, in turn, would act benevolently to promote the interests of all their constituents.[67]

One result of the October 1769 assembly elections was an abnormally high turnover: of the 84 men elected, 38 had not served previously and displaced incumbents. This was a turnover of 45.24 percent as compared with the turnover in November 1766 of 25.61 percent. Very likely there was some relationship between the unusual turnover in 1769 and the Regulation, but exactly what must be explained.[68]

It is not enough, as is invariably done, to state that two Regulator spokesmen (Hermon Husband of Orange County and Christopher Nation of Rowan County) and some sympathizers were elected in

1769, but that there were some reversals in the 1770 election. A more precise and meaningful statement can be made by analyzing changes in the class composition of the assembly. This can be done by tracing fluctuations in the election of those types the Regulators abhorred most: the first economic (merchants, lawyers, placemen, and physicians) and the other political (clerks, registers, sheriffs, and coroners), two overlapping groups.

Such an analysis supports the hypothesis that it was precisely where the Regulators were most active politically that the only significant change in the class character of assemblymen occurred. In the 1766 election the Regulator counties (Orange, Rowan, and Anson plus neighboring Granville) returned four freshman assemblymen. Three of them were merchants, lawyers, or placemen, and three also held major county offices in addition to the office of justice of the peace. In the 1769 elections there was a dramatic change. Only one of eight newly elected assemblymen was of the commercial elite, and only two held important county offices. Six of the eight incumbents who were defeated were of the commercial elite, and five were important county officeholders. Some reversals occurred in the 1770 elections; one of the four freshman was of the commercial elite, and two of the four were important officeholders.[69]

After their limited successes in the 1769 elections, the Regulators concentrated on sending petitions to their spokesmen in the assembly. Calling themselves "poor Inhabitants," "poor Petitioners," "poor Industrious peasant[s]," and "honest industrious familys," they proposed legislative remedies to old and new grievances. Anson County Regulators asked that the chief justice receive a salary instead of fees; Orange and Rowan Regulators in a joint petition asked that all clerks be paid in the same way. Both petitions urged an end to the collection of unlawful fees, but the Orange-Rowan petition also called upon the legislature to cashier all clerks, prohibit clerks and lawyers from serving in the assembly, and freeze the fees of lawyers.[70]

To cut court costs further, Orange and Rowan advocated a small-claims court with a single magistrate who would handle cases to £6, with six-man juries, if either litigant so requested. Anson suggested that cases involving 40s. to £10 should be tried without lawyers by a six-man jury empaneled by a single magistrate whose judgement could not be appealed. It was in the context of such proposals that the Regulators *first* formally proposed that large counties be divided because it was so expensive to travel to court.

Orange and Rowan demanded that sheriffs be replaced as tax collectors, called for reforms in the clearing of accounts, and urged that the corrupt handling of public monies and the "mystery" of the sinking fund be investigated. Both petitions mentioned the currency shortage, and Anson County demanded that no further taxes be levied until a sufficient money supply was emitted and that currency should be backed by land and not be "call'd in by a Tax." Moreover, to enable westerners to pay their taxes in "the produce of the country," Anson proposed constructing inspection warehouses in the west. The Orange and Rowan Regulators requested a more inclusive law to make inspectors' notes for "imperishable commodities" *legal tender* for *all* payments throughout the province.

The petitions went beyond elaborating upon prior grievances. The Regulators now perceived the regressive nature of the tax system and argued that the poor in the province were disproportionately taxed. Since western farmers were "generally in mean circumstances," the Anson Regulators argued that they were particularly oppressed. They urged that each person "pay in proportion to the profits arising from his Estate."

Orange and Rowan counties proposed the same reform, but for somewhat different reasons.

And may it please you to consider of and pass an Act to Tax everyone in proportion to his Estates; however equitable the law as it now stands, may appear to the inhabitants of the Maritime parts of the province, where estates consist chiefly in slaves; yet to us in the frontier, where very few are possessed of slaves, tho' their estates are in proportion (in many instances) as of one Thousand to one, for all to pay equal, is with submission, very grievious and oppressive.[71]

While many read this as a protest against a tax system that favored the east, the Regulators were actually saying just the reverse. They admitted the possibility that easterners paid their share of taxes, because a large portion of their wealth, slaves and servants, was taxed. But the petition protested that *westerners* who were rich in property other than slaves paid no more taxes than their poorer western neighbors. The petitioners attacked the poll tax and called for an equitable levy on all forms of wealth (although in so doing they underestimated or ignored the wealth of easterners in property other than slaves and the degree to which easterners were being subsidized by the province).[72]

Anson Regulators also, for the first time, raised the land-related grievances of pre-Regulator dissidents. They complained of court suits over delinquent quitrents and charged that corrupt administration by the governor and council resulted in favorites engrossing the best lands. To relieve the fears of squatters, Anson proposed that the assembly pass a preemption law guaranteeing squatters with improved lands in the Granville District first choice in purchasing their farms.

The Regulators now moved from reforms to redress particular grievances to proposals to achieve more democratic elections, more open legislative procedures, and representatives who would serve the needs of the farming community. Orange and Rowan demanded that lawyers and clerks be prohibited from the house because

> ...intent on making their own fortunes [they] are blind to, & solely Regardless of their Country's Interest are ever planning such schemes or projecting such Laws, as may best Effect their wicked purposes, witness the Summons and Petition Act calculated purely to enrich themselves, and Creatures at the expense of the poor Industrious peasant.[73]

Anson asked that the viva voce method of voting, so subject to pressures and abuses, be replaced by voting by "Ticket and Ballot." And Orange and Rowan called for recording the votes in the legislative journal, with copies to be sent to each justice of the peace so that constituents might "have an Opportunity to Distinguish our friends, from our foes among you, and to act accordingly at any future choice."

During the 1770 election campaign Hermon Husband raised still another significant new issue, arguing that people spent, on the average, fully *one twelfth of the year* at militia musters or working the roads. Work levies were severely regressive taxes because they took from the poor the time equal to or greater than that required from the rich; this regressive bias was compounded by the fact that the poor could least afford the loss of their labor time on their own farms. No specific reforms were recommended to alleviate these problems other than to suggest that the militia question might be made more tolerable if the officers were elected by the people.[74]

Husband also appealed for the abolition of a tax-supported church establishment, probably as much a fiscal as a religious reform.[75] The only previous religious reform proposed by the Regulators was that all sects be allowed to marry "according to their respective Mode ...after due publication or License." This was urged in both 1769 petitions.

Tryon, in his opening remarks to the 1769 assembly, was not able to devote his attention solely to Regulator problems; he had to contend with a strong Whig reaction, among the elite, to his failure to obtain relief for North Carolina from the British Currency Act of 1764. He attempted to pacify the assembly by stressing the imminent repeal of most Townshend duties and by inviting it to pass laws encompassing the resolves he had vetoed in 1768. Lastly, he sought reforms in the keeping and auditing of public accounts.[76]

The assembly made no attempt to effect the last reform. But this so-called Regulator assembly demonstrated that it could distinguish between "legitimate" (its own) and "illegitimate"(Regulator) threats to authority. Hope of gaining currency relief from the Crown had previously moderated the assembly's reactions to the Townshend duties. With this hope negated, the assembly passed Virginia's resolves against the Townshend Acts. Tryon promptly dissolved the assembly and severely condemned its members for denying his assurances that all Townshend duties except those on tea would be repealed.[77]

The assembly reacted meekly to Tryon's outburst, begging him not to take personally its passage of the Virginia resolves and lauding "the Benefits this Province received from" his administration. In this atmosphere of opera bouffe, Tryon in his final address praised the assembly for its high opinion of him. Then he attacked its unwillingness to reform the accounting of public funds, claiming its recalcitrance was dictated by the control the treasurers, sheriffs, and their sureties exerted over it.[78]

The Regulators were unable to exploit either the governor's conflict with the assembly or the factionalism within the body; all factions feared the farmer dissidents more than each other. But the Regulators reacted angrily to the assembly's performance and, on its dissolution, moved into what can be identified as the fourth phase of their movement. They refused to pay taxes and committed their most violent acts while intensifying their attempts at local solutions to their county grievances, writing petitions, and participating in another political campaign.

Regulators participated in the elections of 12 March 1770 with minimal expectations, high frustrations, and a commitment to disobedience. Their loss of seats in the election undoubtedly added to their frustration. In Orange the Regulators were in an angry mood when they again sought relief in the courts. They petitioned the superior court justices to select unprejudiced juries, to bring to "fair Tryals" extortionate officers, lawyers, and clerks, and to force sheriffs to settle their accounts. Arguing for these reforms in the name of higher and positive law, they warned that if the judges could not protect the people's properties against enemies whose crimes were worse than "open robbery," then they would have to bear the consequences.[79]

That fall the Regulators carried out their threat in a large-scale riot directed against lawyers, merchants, and powerful officials, whatever their source of wealth. In late September Regulators disrupted the Hillsborough Superior Court and forced the despised Judge Richard Henderson to flee. They beat and abused three lawyers, John Williams, William Hooper, and Alexander Martin, and damaged the house of another, John Cooke, after he fled. Merchants Thomas Hart and Michael Holt were also beaten, while most of Hillsborough's stores were broken into, rifled, and their windows broken. Important Orange County officials escaped beatings only because they fled, among them John Gray, Thomas Lloyd, Francis Nash (also a merchant), and Tyree Harris. It was Edmund Fanning, however, who received the harshest treatment. An affluent lawyer, merchant, and powerful official, he had long been the leading object of Regulator hatred. He was severely beaten and forced to flee for his life, and his house and personal property were destroyed, as well as a bell worth £60 to £70 which he had donated to the Anglican Church.

Of the ten Hillsborough residents who wrote Tryon or signed depositions requesting intervention, six were merchants, and all but two held important county or provincial offices. In one letter, seven merchants and/or wealthy officials wrote, "We think Ourselves Hourly in the most iminent Danger not only of losing our Lives and Fortune, but of every connection which we esteem Valuable."[80]

On 7 October Tryon promised relief for the petitioners and punishment for the chief offenders. On 16 October the council had the governor direct militia colonels to muster their regiments to determine the reliability of the men. On 18 October Tryon ordered justices of the peace to start taking depositions on the riot, and on 20 November he wrote the commander of Fort Johnston for most of his military hardware. Fears escalated as rumors spread that the Regulators intended to march on Newbern to intimidate the assembly and prevent Fanning from taking his seat. On 5 December, when the assembly finally met, one regiment was stationed in the capital and another placed on the alert.[81]

In his address to the legislature Tryon gave a consummate performance. He called for reforms to ensure an honest handling and auditing of public monies and accounts and an end to the collection of unlawful fees, thanked the assembly for the "palace," and asked it to set up a Presbyterian school in the backcountry. But his heart was most involved in his denunciation of the Regulators, and, to avert the spread of their sedition, he implored the legislature to raise an army. Thus, he beseeched the Whig elite to join with him to put down those who would insult the "honor and dignity of His Majesty's sacred person and Government" and deny the rights of the assembly and the people.[82]

Following the governor's lead, the assembly passed mild reform legislation which left essentially untouched the power of the provincial and county elite and placated the least angry of the farmers. To forestall Regulator overtures to Mecklenburg and Tryon counties and to meet the demands of significant numbers of the elite as well, ameliorative legislation was passed for the Presbyterians. This done, the assembly expelled Hermon Husband from the house for allegedly libeling Associate Justice Maurice Moore, and authorized the governor to use the courts and militia to suppress the Regulators.[83]

Tryon was delighted with the assembly's passage of laws that were both co-optive and repressive, and wrote approvingly to Lord Hillsborough of the expulsion of Husband and of his (Tryon's) own collusion with the chief justice to have him jailed.[84] Tryon's solution to the Regulator problem, however, would be military, and the chief vehicle that would enable him to do this was an act "to prevent riots and tumults," passed on 15 January 1771, which was so severe that it was later repealed by the Crown. The act contained ex post facto provisions (to take care of the Hillsborough riot) and defined riots as felonies without benefit of clergy. It even equated riots, under certain conditions, with treason and stipulated that indicted rioters who did not surrender themselves within sixty days would be declared outlaws who could be killed on sight. To insure convictions, the act authorized the attorney general to try rioters in any court in the province. Finally, the law enabled Tryon to raise the militia and call for financial support for any necessary military measures.[85]

The reform legislation did not impress the Regulators. Four new counties had been formed (Chatham, Guilford, Surry, and Wake), but this was low on the list of Regulator priorities, as were the reforms setting up a Presbyterian school and authorizing Presbyterian ministers to perform marriages. It had never occurred to the Regulators to ask for such a school. Of greater importance, the fees authorized for clerks and lawyers by new legislation probably increased the legal fees of these officers. The new fee laws, however, were less open to misapplication than the old statutes and did incorporate more adequate legal redress for the collection of extortionate fees. Laws were also passed granting a salary to the chief justice, ending the taxes referred to in the 1768 resolves, and establishing a small-claims court. But provincial tax levels remained steady and the small claims act fell far short of Regulator demands.[86]

While the reform laws changed conditions in the Regulator counties very little, the Riot Act enraged them. Furthermore, the Rowan Regulators, who had finally succeeded, five years after the formation of the Sandy Creek Association, in forcing their officers to arbitrate differences, now saw Tryon negate the agreement. It is not surprising, therefore, that Regulators continued to refuse to pay their taxes, submit to distrainments, or allow the courts to operate.

Tryon, aware of the Regulators' intransigence, insured a military confrontation by pursuing it relentlessly. He was infuriated by the release of Husband from jail on 2 February 1771 and blamed the failure of the grand jury to indict him on the composition of the jury. Husband had been in jail in Newbern since his arrest on 20 December 1770. To insure indictments when charges were brought against other Regulators under the Riot Act (mainly for actions at Hillsborough), Tryon ordered sheriffs to send as jurymen to the March court only "gentlemen of the first rank, property, and probity in their respective counties." Tryon's efforts, as he later observed, "had their desired effect": the grand jury handed down sixty-two indictments against thirty-four persons, pledged support for Tryon's intended military expedition, and signed an oath to help suppress the rebellion.[87]

Armed with these indictments, and the signatures of other men of "first rank" to the oath, Tryon sought council approval for a march against the Regulators. An intercepted Regulator letter that defiantly predicted the spread of the movement to Halifax, Edgecombe, Bute, and Northampton counties provided whatever additional incentive might have been needed. On 18 March 1771 Tryon received the council's unanimous approval to use military force. On the following day Tryon proceeded to attempt to raise 2,500 militiamen from twenty-nine counties, including a prospective 800 men from the five westernmost counties. He would have to settle for far less.[88]

Not all members of the provincial establishment supported Tryon's military solution. The Albermarle region refused to contribute either troops or money. Their leaders may have agreed with Samuel Johnston, wealthy Whig leader and author of the Riot Act, that severe application of the act was sufficient to quell the uprisings without a military expedition. On the other hand, other elite leaders berated the assembly and governor for passing ill-advised reform laws and for not suppressing the Regulators quickly enough. Whatever difference existed among the elite, all agreed it was necessary to end the uprising and punish its leaders. And those proposing a military solution to do this were in a position to achieve it.[89]

While Tryon was readying military confrontation, Regulators in Rowan finally were winning from frightened officers an agreement to meet with a countywide committee of Regulators to arbitrate outstanding grievances. Two of the officers, Alexander Martin (attorney and justice of the peace) and the leading atagonist of the Regulators in Rowan, Col. John Frohock (representative of Henry McCulloh, assemblyman, and county court clerk), reported this agreement to Tryon.[90] Tryon was furious. Denouncing them both in scathing terms for their weakness, he relieved Frohock of his command of the Rowan militia regiment and informed them that he had decided "to raise Forces to march into the settlements of the Insurgents in order to restore peace to the country upon honourable Terms and constitutional principles."[91]

Thus, when Tryon, on 23 April, began his march from Newbern against the rebellious backcountry, the Regulators were pursuing their long-standing goals as militantly as ever. Still, they wanted to prevent bloodshed. The mood of conciliation is apparent in the Regulator letter to Tryon written in March or April while rumors were rife that he would lead an army against them. They appealed to him not to do so.

> But if your Excellencys designs contrary to the public Interest of the Country are to force us to submit to that Tyranny which has so long been Premeditated by some Officers of the Province we will contend for our just rights and Humbly Intreat you Sir to return with your men where there may be more need of them— our civil liberties are certainly more dear to us than the good opinion of a ruler tho' both are desirable.[92]

As late as 15 May 1771, the day before the Battle of the Alamance, the Orange County Regulators again beseeched Tryon to redress their grievances,

> which happy Change would yield such Alacrity, and promulgate such Harmony..., that the sad presaged Tragedy of the warlike

Troops marching with Ardour to meet each other, may by the happy Conduct of our Leaders on each side be prevented.[93]

Tryon was deaf to such appeals. No negotiations were possible. The Regulators refused to submit, but, not completely aware of Tryon's implacability, tried to the end to negotiate. In this sense they "wandered" or "stumbled" into battle. Nevertheless, since they were no longer willing in 1771, in contrast with 1768, to submit to a show of governmental military strength, a battle became inevitable when some 3,000 to 5,000 Regulators assembled to oppose Tryon's marching into their country.

Tryon, therefore, in May 1771, was confronted by a population in the three Regulator counties that was almost solidly united in opposition to the local and provincial ruling class. While reluctant to fight, they would do so rather than submit. They displayed remarkable solidarity, with from 50 to 83 percent of the total number of Regulators mustering to resist Tryon's forces.[94]

In the first confrontation of Regulator and government troops a battle was avoided. A body of 286 government troops from Rowan, Anson, Mecklenburg, and Tryon counties under the command of Gen. Hugh Waddell met as many as 2,000 Regulators just across the Yadkin River from Salisbury, Rowan County. Tryon noted that given the great numerical superiority of the insurgents and their threat "to cut [Waddell's forces] to pieces," Waddell and his officers decided to "retreat back to Salisbury." A later account recorded that Waddell's western troops did not want to fight. Whatever the reason, his troops did not join the main government army under Tryon until after the Battle of Alamance.[95]

On 11 May Tryon's forces moved from Hillsborough, possibly to relieve Waddell's troops.[96] He had under him about 1,185 men (less than 200 were from the west—Orange County), an army comparatively well disciplined and well equipped, with two cannon from General Gage and smaller pieces from Fort Johnston. Before making contact with Waddell, he confronted 2,000 to 3,000 undisciplined, poorly armed Regulators. On 16 May he deployed his troops for battle at Alamance. It was at this time that Tryon answered the Regulators' petition of 15 May calling on him to avoid a battle by redressing their grievances. He demanded that the Regulators "lay down your Arms, surrender up the outlawed Ringleaders and submit yourselves to the Laws of your Country," and gave them one hour to comply.[97] A half hour after the first shots the Regulators retreated to some trees and continued to return the fire. Two hours after the battle began a remnant of their army was finally driven from the trees. Official government casualty figures were 9 killed, 61 wounded. Regulator casualties are more uncertain: perhaps 17 to 20 were killed and over 100 wounded.

Immediately after the battle, Tryon summarily hanged a Regulator and destroyed a considerable amount of Regulator property. A month later, on 19 June, in accordance with the Riot Act, fourteen Regulator prisoners were tried: two were acquitted, twelve found guilty—six of whom were hanged and six pardoned. Eventually, in response to various gubernatorial proclamations of amnesty, over 6,000 Regulators or supporters signed oaths of allegiance.[98] An indeterminate number of Regulators left the colony.[99] As an organized movement, the Regulation was over.

III

In the wake of the Battle of the Alamance, Regulators and their adversaries turned to a war of words. Regulator spokesmen, unable to use North Carolina's newspapers, used popular Whig northern newspapers such as the *Boston Gazette,* the *Massachusetts Spy,* the *Pennsylvania Gazette,* and the *Pennsylvania Journal.* Articles in these papers endorsed the Regulators' accounts, certified the validity of their complaints, and condemned Tryon as a "Patron of Pettifoggers," notable for his "Avarice, Ambition, Injustices, Perjury, Perfidy, and Murder." When they editorialized, the printers partially embraced the Regulators' views that while they were aggrieved against the Sons of Liberty, they were contending for similar reforms. In so doing the printers linked the Regulator uprising to revolutionary events, thus implicitly condemning Tryon's Whig allies in the North Carolina elite as upholders of British tyranny.[100]

In response, North Carolina's elite advanced its views in provincial newspapers and the *Virginia Gazette.* Though stung by northern attacks, most Whigs in 1771 still proclaimed their alliance with provincial defenders of the royal prerogative, praised Tryon, and defended their joint onslaught on the Regulators in the name of the British Constitution and liberty.[101]

Other Carolina Whigs, chiefly it seems in the northern tier of counties, from Albemarle Sound to Granville County, outlined an alternative Whig position. The arguments were publicly stated by "Atticus" in a letter to the *Virginia Gazette,* 7 November 1771. Historians have misinterpreted this letter because they have not placed it within the context of Whig factionalism; it tried to clear Whigs of the charge that they were, with the representatives of royal prerogative, the corrupt oppressors of defenders of American liberties. "Atticus" followed most other North Carolina Whig leaders in reading the Regulators out of the American resistance movement by labeling them licentious and misguided malcontents who had used violence to attack legitimate laws and institutions. Yet, while commending Tryon for defeating a "Host of Scoundrels" at Alamance, he accused the governor of magnifying the uprising by insisting upon building an expensive and unnecessary "palace," intransigently supporting western officials, and resorting to military solutions for political problems. Proper reforms and limited repression of rioters, "Atticus" suggested, would have avoided two expensive military expeditions. The eastern Whigs, in this view, were innocent bystanders to an unfortunate event.[102]

During this controversy a new royal governor, Josiah Martin, took office. The restoration of order, Whig factionalism, growing revolutionary controversies, and Martin's lack of personal ties with western county leaders all enabled him to follow a sympathetic bent for the poor and gradually develop a position independent of Tryon's. Thus, during the summer of 1772 when Martin visited Regulator country, he concluded that insolent, mercenary, and dishonest officers and lawyers had taken advantage of the people's ignorance to subject them to "every sort of rapine and extortion." The local officers by misrepresenting affairs to the provincial authorities, Martin decided, had driven the people to rebel. He, therefore, did his best to obtain royal pardons for the Regulators and end the collection of exorbitant fees and the corrupt handling of public funds. To achieve these reforms he publicized the extent of corruption in the province and ordered clerks to send him a copy of their fee tables and to display them in their offices. He also convinced Edward Fanning to withdraw his suits to recover property losses. However, the assembly, true to form, refused to pass sufficient reform legislation, while most clerks refused to obey the governor's orders.[103]

Many historians, following John S. Bassett's account of 1894, have argued that Regulator dissaffection to the Revolution represented a reaction against the large number of their old antagonists who led the revolutionary movement.[104] This was certainly true, although it should be noted that many of their adversaries, including Fanning and Tryon, remained loyal to Great Britain. But equally important was the continued inadequate response of the Whig elite to Regulator grievances after Alamance, compared with genuine attempts at reform by Governor Martin.

The old Regulator leader James Hunter pointed to this difference. The governor has "given us every satisfaction" that could be expected of him, he wrote William Butler. "I think our officers [that is, county officials] hate him as bad as we did Tryon, only they don't speak so freely." On the other hand, Hunter derisively noted that Maurice Moore and Abner Nash (two old antagonists, both wealthy Whig leaders) had visited him "to try to get me in favor again . . . and I think they are more afraid than ever."[105]

More recently, other historians have challenged the argument that most Regulators opposed the Revolution. Elmer D. Johnson, for example, traced 883 Regulator names and indentified 34 Tories and 289 patriots; 560 could not be traced.[106] His method of determining revolutionary loyalties, however, was heavily biased towards the patriots: he identified as patriots all who were members of the Continental army or state militia, while he counted as Tories only those who were positively identified as such. Since North Carolina from 1776 to 1780 was controlled by the Whigs, militia lists are a poor gauge for determining loyalties. Johnson's figures, therefore, are unreliable.[107]

Though, unfortunately, I have not been able to develop a full set of statistics on the revolutionary loyalties of the Regulators, some isolated figures are suggestive. For example, it has been estimated that from 100 to 200 Regulators fought on the side of the Tories at the Battle of Moore's Creek Bridge in February 1776, and that many more Regulators went home prior to the battle when they learned that the British reinforcements they expected were not forthcoming.[108] This faintheartedness of many of the Regulator Tories perhaps is a clue to understanding the loyalties of most of the Regulators.

Possibly the largest number of Regulators remained neutral. Such an interpretation would be further supported by the fact that the impressionistic evidence is contradictory and by the fact that the great majority of known Regulators cannot be traced on the militia lists.[109] The hypothesis is appealing for many reasons. It may be assumed that after Alamance many Regulators would have been battle shy and that they were not enamored of the democratic possibilities offered by either the Whig or Tory elite. After all, it was a coalition of Whigs and Tories that had originally suppressed the Regulators. And *if* neutralism was the response of most Regulators to the Revolution, it would have been similar to the response of a large number of democratically-inclined farmers in other colonies, New York being one, with Maryland another.[110]

Further evidence of the uncertainty of Regulator sympathies is that they were equally in question in 1775 when Governor Martin and the Whigs vied with each other for Regulator support. Once hostilities began, the British-Loyalist ability to rally the Regulators to the royal standard was limited by the fact that the Whigs as a rule controlled the countryside from 1775 to 1780. Unable to communicate effectively with the Regulators, who were subjected to more direct and continuous pressure by the patriots, Martin had to rely upon his past good relationship with the Regulators, the countervailing pressures applied by backcountry Tories, his securing a pardon in June 1775 for all Regulators (except Hermon Husband), and the rhetoric of loyalism combined with promises of future military aid. On the other hand, the patriots, in control all over the countryside, could promise and deliver more. For example, the Third Provincial Congress that met in Hillsborough in late summer of 1775 promised the Regulators that Congress would protect them against any punishment for past transgressions. More important, in its resolutions of 10 September the Provincial Congress took the first steps to legitimize squatter holdings in the Granville District. Lastly, Congress sent a committee to the Regulators to convince them to join the revolutionary movement.[111] The Continental Congress also got into the act, using Presbyterian ministers to argue that Romans 13:1–2, formerly used to condemn the Regulator movement, only commanded that the "just" demands of authority be obeyed.[112] One wishes to be able to record the growls of the old Regulators, but the records are silent.

If both sides attempted to placate the Regulators, there was also, especially in the west, increasing advocacy of many old Regulator reforms. Indeed, Regulator ideas appear to have become dominant in the western counties as a whole. This does not mean that during the years 1773–1776 the officers were predominantly Regulators; this was not the case. Rather, the western officers, normally dependent upon provincial support to maintain their power against concerted opposition from their constituents, during a period of heightened revolutionary tensions when they were forced to rely more than ever upon their own power resources, were probably more vulnerable to democratic pressures. Instructions to their representatives, adopted by the constituents of western counties from 1773 on, reflect an acceptance of Regulator class-assumptions and democratic reforms. Regulator attempts to institute direct participation by constituents in the legislative processes, for instance, were incorporated in Orange County's instructions to its representatives in 1773: "You will speak our Sense in every case when we shall expressly declare it, or when you can by an other means discover it. . . ."[113] Similarly, the Mecklenburg County resolves of 31 May 1775 echoed Regulator abhorrence of plural officeholding as well as their demands that lawyers, clerks, and sheriffs be prohibited from serving in the legislature.[114]

Instructions to delegates to the state constitutional convention of 1776 showed a further debt to the Regulators. The admonition to the Mecklenburg representatives to "oppose everything that leans to aristocracy or power in the hands of the rich and chief men exercised to the oppression of the poor," bespoke the Regulator spirit, as did the call for voter selection of clerks and sheriffs. Orange County's instructions argued for the abolition of plural officeholding, taxation in proportion to wealth, salaried justices in the county courts, changes in attachment laws, lowered court fees, and elections by ballot—all reforms dear to the Regulators. Even the acceptance of suffrage qualifications in Orange County's instructions and Mecklenburg's silence on the issue along with the silence of both about an equitable apportionment of representation smacks of Regulator lack of concern (or lack of sophistication) in these areas.[115]

North Carolina's 1776 Constitution reflected in only a few ways such western concerns. The Whig elite, as always, kept reform to a minimum. They incorporated election by ballot, denied past or future receivers of public monies and treasurers a seat in the legislature (until they had settled their accounts), remunerated all supreme court justices by salary instead of fees, abolished imprisonment for debt, and disestablished the church.[116] It is hard to believe that the constitution co-opted many Regulators to the ranks of the patriots. Many Regulator reforms and their philosophy of the relationships between constituents and government were still awaiting fulfillment in the 1790s, when the Democratic-Republican societies revived similar ideas.[117]

Historians who argue that class consciousness and class conflict were denied in the colonies by the equitable distribution of wealth and social mobility, as compared with England, are merely prescribing shibboleths to replace hard analysis.[118] The Regulation in North Carolina took place in counties where over 40 percent of the wealth was controlled by the upper 10 percent of society, where class mobility was slight, where class consciousness was a normal, preferred condition, and where class exploitation was great. The Regulation took place when and where it did because of past disturbances in the area, the exaggeration of certain traditional grievances resulting from commercial growth, a ruling class that was new and not firmly entrenched in a recently settled and fast growing west, the end of the French threat, and sensitivities heightened by increasing revolutionary tensions. The movement grew among a numerous class of poor farmers who saw nothing wrong in either using the term "peasants" or in asserting that they were farmers/laborers. Their class consciousness was a sign of their times; their class conflict was a manifestation of their particular situation and opportunities. They proposed democratic reforms to implement class rule. And their legacy has been lost amidst the "liberal paradoxes" proposed by contemporary historians and the heedless reassertions of older shibboleths that reduce their struggle to "west" versus "east."

Appendix

TABLE I

Distribution of Wealth in Orange County 1762–1772[1]

Percentile	N	Total Assessments	X̄	% of Total Wealth
Lower 30%	36.3	£ 1,297	£ 35:14	6%
Middle 30%	36.3	£ 3,352	£ 92:7	15%
Top 30%	36.3	£ 7,826	£ 215:12	36%
Top 10%	12.1	£ 9,388	£ 775:18	43%
Totals	121	£ 21,865	£ 180:14	100%
Top 1%	1.21	£ 2,407	£ 1989:5	9%

[1] See Raleigh Archives: Orange County Estates, 1758–1785 (this is a bound volume of estate records).

TABLE II

Wealth of Anson County Officers Compared with County Totals and Those of Top Ten Percent of County Household Heads as Measured by Slaveholdings in 1763[1]

Group or County	N	Total Number of Slaves	X̄
Anson County	291	177	0.61
Top 10% of County Household Heads	29	134	4.62
Anson County Officers[1]	11	40	3.64

[1] Officers' names for Anson County during the Regulator period were obtained from Raleigh Archives—Anson County, Minute Docket County Court, July 1771–July 1777; Minutes, County Court of Pleas and Quarter Sessions, 1771–1777; Governor's Office, Lists of Taxables, Militia, and Magistrates, 1754–1770, Undated; Governor's Office, Council Papers, 1761–1779; Military Collection, Troop Returns (1747–1859) Militia and Continental Returns, 1770–1778. In addition, see Clark, ed., *State Records of N.C.*, 22: 381–82: Saunders, ed., *N.C. Colonial Records*, 4:889, 951; 6:779. For 1763 slaveholdings and 1782 wealth totals, see Raleigh Archives, Secretary of State Tax Lists, 1720–1839; Legislative Papers, Tax Lists. Also see table IV.

TABLE III

Total Wealth of Regulators Compared With That of
Anti-Regulators and the Entire County's Population
in Select Western Counties

Group or County-Years of Survey	N	Total Wealth Assessments Within the Group or County- £	X Assessment of the Group or County- £
Orange (1779), Randolph (1779), and Caldwell (1780) Counties- Combined[1] (Orange County)	2,607	4,038,856	1,549:4
Regulators in these three Counties[2]	146	180,105	1,233:12
Anti-Regulators in these three Counties[3]	47	460,733	9,802:16
Montgomery County-1782[4] (Anson County)	455	62,254	136:16
Regulators in Montgomery County[5]	35	2,715	77:12
Anti-Regulators in Montgomery County[6]	7	2,759	394:2

[1] See Raleigh Archives: Legislative Papers, Tax Lists; Secretary of State, Tax Lists, 1720–1839.

[2] Four hundred and forty-five Regulators were uncovered for Orange County, 320 for Anson County, 19 for Rowan County, and 67 who resided in one of the three counties for a total of 851 names. An additional 72 names that were not used were gathered from Granville and Halifax County petitions concerning problems similar to those that bothered the Regulators. The 851 names were checked off against each of the above four tax lists.

Range of Assessments of the Group or County- £	Group's Percentage of County's Population	Group's Percentage of County's Assessed Wealth	Proportion Between Wealth and Population
21–70,431	100	100	1
100–17,038	5.60	4.45	0.79
100–70,431	1.80	11.41	6.33
1–1,975	100	100	1
4–280	7.69	4.36	0.57
17–1,187	1.54	4.44	2.89

[3] One hundred and twenty-nine Anti-Regulators were uncovered in Orange County, 61 in Rowan County, and 42 in Anson County for a total of 232. They were treated in the same manner as were the Regulator names.

[4] See Raleigh Archives, Legislative Papers, Tax Lists.

[5] See footnotes 2 and 3 for this table.

[6] Ibid. For a published list of 883 Regulator names that I have corrected in developing my own list, see Johnson, *The War of the Regulation,* pp. 155-73.

TABLE IV

Wealth of Anson County Officers Compared with County Totals and Those of Top Ten Percent of Taxables as Measured by Slaveholdings and Total Assessments in Montgomery County in 1782

Group or County	N	Total Number of Slaves and $\overline{X}$	Total Assessed Wealth and $\overline{X}$
Montgomery County	455	474; $\overline{X} = 1.04$	62,254; $\overline{X} = 136:16$
Top 10% of Montgomery County Taxables	45.5	377.8; $\overline{X} = 8.3$	32,328; $\overline{X} = 712$
Anson County Officers	5	33; $\overline{X} = 6.6$	2,980; $\overline{X} = 745$

TABLE V

Wealth of Orange County Officers Compared with County Totals and Those of Top Ten Percent of Taxables as Measured by Total Assessments in Orange County (1779), Randolph County (1779), and Caldwell County (1780)[2]

Group or County	N	Total Assessed Wealth	$\overline{X}$
Orange Randolph, and Caldwell Counties	2,607	4,038,856	1,549:4:8
Top 10% of Above Counties' Taxables	261	2,038,451	7,810:3:2
Orange County Officers[2]	27	336,952	13,395:13:4
Leading Orange County Officers	7	109,352	15,621:14:3

[2] Officers' names for Orange County during the Regulator period were obtained from Raleigh Archives, Orange County Court Minutes, 1752-1766; Governor's Office, Lists of Taxables, Militia, and Magistrates, 1754-1770, Undated; Governor's Office, Council Papers, 1761-1779; Hillsboro District Minute Docket, 1768-1788, part I. In addition, see Saunders, ed., *N.C. Colonial Records,* 5:320, 365, 835; 6:340, 573, 798, 1016; 7:91, 821, 827, 832, 833, 863-64, 888; 8:574-600, 659-77. Leading Orange County officers included only assemblymen, sheriffs, clerks, registers, and militia colonels, lieutenant colonels, majors, and adjutants. All other citations of officers in this table included the above leading officers plus justices of the peace and militia captains. For 1779 and 1780 wealth totals, see Raleigh Archives, Legislative Papers, Tax Lists; Secretary of State Tax Lists, 1720-1839.

TABLE VI

Slaveholdings of Regulators Compared With Those of Anti-Regulators and the Entire County's Population Anson County, 1763[1]

Group or County	Total Number of Slaves Owned Within Group or County	N and Number of Households in Group or County That Owned Slaves	Percent of Households in Group or County That Owned Slaves	X̄ Slave-holdings in County or Group	Group's Percentage of County's Population	Group's Percentage of County's Slaves	Proportion Between Slave-holdings and Population
Anson County	177	291 49	16.84	0.61	100	100	1
Regulators in Anson County[2]	36	62 9	14.52	0.58	21.31	18.34	0.95
Anti-Regulators in Anson County[3]	49	13 9	69.23	3.77	4.47	27.68	6.19

[1] Raleigh Archives: Secretary of State, Tax Lists, 1720–1839.

[2] Three hundred and twenty Regulators were uncovered for Anson County and traced in the 1763 Anson County tax list. To obtain these Regulator names, I used all available Regulator petitions, advertisements, court records, pamphlets, letters, and statements along with comments of other contemporaries. Identical techniques were used to uncover Regulator names for other counties.

[3] Forty two Anti-Regulators were uncovered for Anson County and traced in the 1763 Anson County tax list. Documents similar to those used to identify the Regulators, but also including official correspondence among officers, were used to obtain the names of the Anti-Regulators for Anson County as well as the other counties.

1. For help in writing this essay, I wish to thank, in addition to the individuals I have acknowledged in the preface, Mark Jones (graduate student at Northern Illinois University), Ronald Hoffman (University of Maryland), and Philip Foner (Lincoln University). Alfred Young did service beyond the normal call of duty for editors. All administrators and personnel of the North Carolina Department of Cultural Resources, Divison of Archives and History, have constantly and thoughtfully aided my research in their excellent archives. A warm thanks to them all.

2. James Hasell wrote to Lord Hillsborough on 4 July 1771, that "above six thousand of them ["Rebels"] have submitted to Government and taken the oaths prescribed." Governor Josiah Martin, on 26 December 1771, stated that 6,409 men had taken the oath. Probably some Regulators and sympathizers did not sign the oaths, while a few who did had not been active in the movement. Thus, the above estimate of the number of Regulators is reasonable.

Estimates concerning the white taxable population may be found in State Department of Archives and History, Raleigh, North Carolina: Secretary of State Tax Lists, 1720–1839; Governor's Office, Lists of Taxables, Militia, and Magistrates, 1754–1770; William L. Saunders, ed., *Colonial Records of North Carolina* (Raleigh, Printer to the State, 1886–1890), 7:145–46, 288–89, 539; Evarts B. Greene and Virginia D. Harrington, *American Population Before the Federal Census of 1790* (Gloucester, Mass.: Peter Smith, 1966), pp. 166–69; Marvin L. Michael Kay, "The Institutional Background to the Regulation in Colonial North Carolina" (Ph.D. diss., University of Minnesota, 1962), pp. 21–33.

For evidence of the movement's expansion, see, for example, William K. Boyd, ed., *Some Eighteenth Century Tracts Concerning North Carolina* (Raleigh: Edwards and Broughton Co., 1927), pp. 256, 257, 348; Saunders, ed., *N.C. Colonial Records,* 7:715; 8:537.

3. In this introduction I will normally only footnote statements concerning the Regulators that are not footnoted in the detailed analysis that follows the introduction. However, it is desirable at this time to analyze the major sources of Regulator statements. Two pamphlets were issued by the Regulators prior to the Battle of Alamance: Hermon Husband's *An Impartial Relation,* 1770, and his *A Continuation of the Impartial Relation,* 1770. A third pamphlet, *A Fan for Fanning and a Touchstone to Tryon,* 1771, the author of which remains unknown, was printed after the Battle of Alamance. *An Impartial Relation* and *A Fan for Fanning* have both been reprinted in Boyd, ed., *Eighteenth Century Tracts,* pp. 251–333, 339–92, while *A Continuation of the Impartial Relation* is reprinted in Archibald Henderson, ed., *North Carolina Historical Review* 18 (1941): 48–81. A fourth pamphlet, a statement of grievances by the Granville County farmer spokesman, George Sims, was issued one year prior to the formation of the Sandy Creek Association, the immediate precursor of the Regulators in Orange County. Sims's pamphlet was partially reprinted in Husband's *Impartial Relation* and had an important effect upon the Regulators. It has been reprinted in its entirety in Boyd, ed., *Eighteenth Century Tracts,* pp. 182–92.

Most extant Regulator letters, petitions, minutes, agreements, and appeals made prior to the Battle of Alamance (eleven are recorded as "Advertisements") are reprinted in Saunders, ed., *N.C. Colonial Records,* 7:249–52, 671–72, 699–700, 702–3, 716, 726, 731–37, 758–67, 801–3, 806–9, 810–13, 847–48; 8:68–70, 75–80, 81–84, 231–34, 260, 536–37, 543–44, 640–41. The October 1768 joint petition of the Regulators from Orange and Rowan counties may be found in David L. Corbitt, ed., "Historical Notes," *North Carolina Historical Review* 8 (1931): 342–44. James Hunter's open letter to Maurice Moore (23 November 1770) may be found in Rind's *Virginia Gazette,* 10 January 1771.

For post-Alamance Regulator statements see the above cited *A Fan for Fanning* and citations in nn. 100, 101, and 105 below. See also Walter Clark, ed., *The State Records of North Carolina* (Goldsboro, N.C., 1894–1914), 22:891.

4. For recent blatant examples of this genre, see Hugh Talmage Lefler and Albert Ray Newsome, *The History of a Southern State: North Carolina* (Chapel Hill: University of North Carolina Press, 1973), pp. 173–90; Hugh T. Lefler and William S. Powell, *Colonial North Carolina, A History* (New York: Charles Scribner's Sons, 1973), pp. 217–39; and, in sweeping fashion, Edmund S. Morgan, "Conflict and Consensus in the American Revolution," in Stephen G. Kurtz and James H. Hutson, eds., *Essays on the American Revolution* (Chapel Hill: University of North Carolina Press, 1973), pp. 297–302.

5. An intelligent, concise discussion of the role of deference in eighteenth-century America may be found in J. R. Pole, "Historians and the Problem of Early American Democracy," *American Historical Review* 67, no. 3 (1962): 622–46. For a recent analysis that questions a liberal interpretation of the colonies prior to the Revolution and thereby lends support to the above class analysis, see Rowland Berthoff and John M. Murrin "Feudalism, Communalism, and the Yeoman Freeholder: The American Revolution Considered as a Social Accident," in Kurtz and Hutson, eds., *Essays on the American Revolution*, pp. 256–88. I struggled with the themes of class deference, class consciousness, and class conflict in an earlier essay: M. L. M. Kay, "An Analysis of a British Colony in Late Eighteenth Century America in the Light of Current American Historiographical Controversy," *Australian Journal of Politics and History* 11, no. 2 (1965): 170–84.

6. See n. 2 concerning population estimates, plus Saunders, ed., *N.C. Colonial Records*, 5:320, 575, 603; Green and Harrington, *American Population*, pp. 157–69. For the development of commerce and wealth, see Kay, "Regulation in North Carolina," pp. 444–590; Kay, "Analysis of a British Colony," *Australian Journal of Politics and History* 11, no. 2 (1965): 174–75; Raleigh Archives: Orange County Court Minutes, 1752–1766; Rowan Court of Pleas and Quarter Sessions Minutes, 1753–1772.

7. See n. 5 above. For Regulator descriptions of themselves, see a narrative of events through May 1768 sent to Tryon and written by a committee of eight Orange County Regulators (John Low, James Hunter, Rednap Howell, Harmon Cox, John Marshel, William Cox, William Moffitt, and George Hendry), in Saunders, ed., *N.C. Colonial Records*, 7:759–66; a letter written to Tryon by the Regulators at the beginning of August 1768 and signed by eight Regulators (Francis Dorset, William Paine, Peter Craven, Peter Julian, Jacob Fudge, Richard Cheek, Charles Saxon, and Ninian Hamilton), in Saunders, ed., *N.C. Colonial Records*, 7:802–3; the October 1768 petition to the assembly from the Orange and Rowan County Regulators (signed by thirty Regulators), in Corbitt, ed., "Historical Notes," *North Carolina Historical Review* 8 (1931): 342–44; the 1769 petition to the legislature by the Orange and Rowan County Regulators, in Corbitt, ed., "Historical Notes," *North Carolina Historical Review* 8:81–84; Hermon Husband's *An Impartial Relation*, in Boyd, ed., *Eighteenth Century Tracts*, pp. 302–3; and *A Fan For Fanning*, in Boyd, ed., *Eighteenth Century Tracts*, p. 360.

8. See, for example, Hermon Husband's *An Impartial Relation*, in Boyd, ed., *Eighteenth Century Tracts*, pp. 301–4; *A Fan For Fanning*, ibid., p. 360; the Regulators' narrative of events sent to Tryon in May 1768, in Saunders, ed., *N.C. Colonial Records*, 7:760–61; the Orange and Rowan petition of 1769 to the legislature in ibid., p. 81; and the October 1768 petition to the assembly from the Orange and Rowan County Regulators (signed by thirty Regulators), in Corbitt, ed., "Historical Notes," *North Carolina Historical Review* 8 (1931): 342–44.

9. Boyd, ed., *Eighteenth Century Tracts*, p. 303.

10. Marvin L. Michael Kay, "The Payment of Provincial and Local Taxes in North Carolina, 1748–1771," *William and Mary Quarterly*, 3d ser. 26, no. 2 (1969): 227–30. I developed this theme in "Some Economic Developments in the North Carolina Piedmont During the Late Colonial Period," an unpublished paper delivered before the Organization of American Historians in Los Angeles, in 1970.

11. I will discuss all these themes in detail below, but have also discussed them in the following works: "Payment of Provincial and Local Taxes in N.C.," *William and Mary Quarterly*, 3d ser. 26, no. 2 (1969): 218–39, and passim; "Provincial Taxes in North Carolina During the Administrations of Dobbs and Tryon," *North Carolina Historical Review* 42 (1965): 440–53; "Regulation in North Carolina" pp. 200–441, and passim.

12. A review of the Orange County Court Minutes (in the Raleigh Archives) from 1752 to 1766 (omitting the first and last years because of sparse records) reveals that during the years 1753–1756, 1757–1761, 1762–1763, and 1764–1765 there were respectively 180, 358, 223, and 576 civil cases. This means, taking population into account, that there were 36.53 cases per year for each 1,000 taxables during the period 1753–1756. Cases per year for each 1,000 taxables for the three succeeding periods were: 36.29, 42.88, and 94.55. Thus, in Orange County there was a discernible increase in court cases during the years 1762–1763, but very likely it was not enough to alarm the county's inhabitants. The sharp increase during the years of 1764–1765 (and undoubtedly continuing in 1766) was certainly known among the inhabitants of Orange County

and helped to precipitate the organization of the Sandy Creek Association during the summer of 1766. Inadequate court records prevent an analysis of Anson County, but Rowan County's records reveal a similar but considerably more moderate and later developing trend. Thus, analyzing the periods 1755–1758 and 1761, 1762–1763, 1764–1765, and 1766–1769, we find 133, 54, 55, and 143 cases respectively. This equals for each period 26.6, 27, 27.5, and 35.75 cases per year respectively for each 1,000 taxables. Perhaps the increase during the years 1766–1769 agitated Rowan's inhabitants. See Raleigh Archives: Orange County Court Minutes, 1752–1766; Rowan Court of Pleas and Quarter Sessions Minutes, 1753–1772.

13. See n. 11 above.

14. See Clark, ed., *State Records of North Carolina,* 23: 565–68 for appropriate clauses dealing with Inferior Court procedures for small claims during the Regulator period. See also an inadequate reform law passed during the height of the Regulation, January 1771, in ibid., pp. 846–49. With respect to the imprecision and inadequacy of fee laws, see John S. Bassett, "The Regulators of North Carolina (1765–1771)," *Annual Report of the American Historical Association* (1894), pp. 181–82; Kay, "Payment of Provincial and Local Taxes in N.C.," *William and Mary Quarterly,* 3d ser. 26, no. 2 (1969): 231–35; and Clark, ed., *State Records of N.C.,* 23, pp. 275–84. The last is a copy of the basic law in effect concerning fees for the period under review. See ibid., pp. 814–18, 859–62 for acts passed towards the end of and after the Regulation.

15. Saunders, ed., *N.C. Colonial Records,* 8:83.

16. In addition to the works cited in n. 4 see the following for examples of these weaknesses: Elmer D. Johnson, "The War of the Regulation: Its Place in History" (Master's thesis, University of North Carolina, Chapel Hill, 1942), pp. 1–13, and passim; James Loy Walker, "The Regulator Movement: Sectional Controversy in North Carolina" (Master's thesis, Louisiana State University, Baton Rouge, 1962), pp. 1–11, 111–15, and passim; Lawrence F. London, "Sectionalism in the Colony of North Carolina" (Master's thesis, University of North Carolina, 1933), passim; Hugh Lefler and Paul Wager, eds., *Orange County: 1752–1952* (Chapel Hill, N.C.: Orange Print Shop, 1953), pp. 24–40.

17. Multipliers of 4.1017 and 1.8868 were respectively used for whites and blacks to convert taxables to population. For data and aids used to develop these multipliers and the demographic analysis in the text, see Raleigh Archives—Secretary of State Tax Lists, 1720–1839; Legislative Papers, Tax Lists; Governor's Office, Lists of Taxables, Militia, and Magistrates, 1754–1770 and Undated; Treasurer's and Comptroller's Papers, County Settlements with the State, Tax Lists; County Records, Bertie County Taxables; Kay, "Regulation in North Carolina," pp. 23–43; Greene and Harrington, *American Population,* pp. 157–72; Harry Roy Merrens, *Colonial North Carolina in the Eighteenth Century* (Chapel Hill: University of North Carolina Press, 1964), pp. 53–81, and passim.

18. The range equals the difference between the number of slaves owned by the largest slave owner and zero. For a more extensive development of all the statistical points made in this essay, see "Class, Mobility, and Conflict in North Carolina on the Eve of the Revolution," a paper I read at North Carolina State University, Raleigh, on 2 October 1975. The conference at Raleigh was jointly sponsored by the North Carolina Bicentennial Commission and the Institute of Early American History and Culture. My paper (jointly authored with Calman Winegarden and Lorin Lee Cary) will be published, together with eight other North Carolina Bicentennial Symposium papers, in book form very shortly.

19. See Merrens, *Colonial North Carolina in the Eighteenth Century,* pp. 37–49.

20. See nn. 2 and 6 above. Anson, Orange, and Rowan were formed in 1750, 1752, and 1753 respectively, while Mecklenburg was formed in 1762 from Anson, and Tryon was formed in 1768 from Mecklenburg. David Leroy Corbitt, *The Formation of the North Carolina Counties, 1663–1943,* (Raleigh: State Department of Archives and History, 1950), pp. 8–11, 147–49, 167–69, 185–88, 205–6, 296.

21. See n. 29 below. See also Merrens, *Colonial North Carolina in the Eighteenth Century,* pp. 162–72; Corbitt, *Formation of North Carolina Counties,* pp. 167, 185; Kay, "Regulation in North Carolina," pp. 442–81; Kay, "Analysis of a British Colony," *Australian Journal of Politics and History* 11, no. 2 (1965): 174–75.

22. Raleigh Archives: Secretary of State, Tax Lists, 1720–1839.

23. See notes to table I.

24. The above analysis is supported by Jackson Turner Main's analysis in *The Sovereign States, 1775–1783* (New York: Franklin Watts, 1973), especially pp. 17–36. See n. 18 above.

25. A recent study of other colonies that supports my above statement is Main, *The Sovereign States*, especially pp. 318–48. See "Class, Mobility, and Conflict in North Carolina on the Eve of the Revolution," a paper presented at the North Carolina Bicentennial Symposium, North Carolina State University, Raleigh, October 1975. Using slaveholding as our measure of wealth, we found that in relatively mature regions ownership of slaves powerfully predicted future ownership and that the relative position of the wealthy over the years remained stable. In less developed regions fluctuations were greater, but increased mobility patterns in these regions reflected minor variations in slave ownership. Moreover, the wealthy in these regions, in the midst of fluctuations, appear to have held their relative position of affluence.

26. For the sources and methods I used to compile the names of the Regulators and their opponents, see notes to tables III and VI.

27. I do not, at present, know of a way to correct for this bias.

28. Raleigh Archives: County Records—Rowan County, Record of Deeds—1753–1800 (vols. 1, 2), 1755–1762 (vols. 3, 4), 1762–1798 (vols. 5, 6, 7). County Records—Orange County, Record of Deeds, 1755–1785 (vols. 1, 2); County Records—Anson County, Record of Deeds (vols. 1, 3, 5, 6–7, B, C–1, H–1, K 1–294). The traditional sources I used to determine this were primarily the Regulators' statements. These will not be listed here because they are cited in detail below.

29. Names of merchants and lawyers for Orange, Rowan, and Anson counties were obtained from the following sources: Johnston and Bennehan Account and Invoice Book, 1769–1775, Snow Hill, N.C., Cameron Papers, 1700–1921, Southern Historical Collection, University of North Carolina, Chapel Hill; Lefler and Wager, eds., *Orange County, 1752–1952*, pp. 24, 323–25, 328–29, 332, 337, 340; Kay, "Regulation in North Carolina," pp. 442–590, and passim; Charles Crittenden, *The Commerce of North Carolina, 1763–1789* (New Haven: Yale University Press, 1936), pp. 97–98; Francis Nash, "Hillsboro, Colonial and Revolutionary," *North Carolina Booklet,* 3, no. 4 (1903): 6–8; Saunders, ed., *N.C. Colonial Records,* 7, pp. 506–7; 8, pp. 241–47, 273–75; Clark, *State Records of N.C.,* 22, pp. 425, 442, 454–55, 458–59, 475, 478, 870–76, 878–89; David L. Corbitt, ed., "Historical Notes," *North Carolina Historical Review* 4 (1927): 111–12; Purdie and Dixon's *Virginia Gazette,* 25 October 1770; *Annual Register* London, 1770; William S. Powell, James K. Huhta, and Thomas J. Farnham, eds., *The Regulators in North Carolina, A Documentary History* (Raleigh: State Department of Archives and History, 1971), pp. 253–55; Raleigh Archives: Orange County Court Minutes, 1752–1766; Hillsboro District Minute Docket, 1768–1788, part I; Rowan, Court of Pleas and Quarter Sessions Minutes, 1753–1772; Salisbury District, Minute Docket Superior Court, 1756–1770; Anson County, Minute Docket County Court, July 1771–July 1777; Minutes, Anson County Court of Pleas and Quarter Sessions, 1771–1777.

30. Saunders, *N.C. Colonial Records,* 4:156, 162–63, 212, 215, 253–54, 640, 664–65, 668–772, 684–99, 742–43, 1076–1152; 5:80–81, 121–22, 355–57, 493–94, 574, 621–22, 624–27, 641–43, 739–40, 762, 769, 964; 6:7, 532–36, 568–78, 625, 718–20, 773–75, 779–96, 993–94, 996–98, 1025, 1046–47, 1069–70; 7:6, 10–38, 140–41, 275, 451–54, 455, 529–30, 676–77, 752–55, 783; 8:52–53, 220, 223–25; 9:46–47, 368–70; Desmond Clarke, *Arthur Dobbs Esquire 1689–1765* (Chapel Hill: University of North Carolina Press, 1957), pp. 71–78, 123, 151–52, 184–86; Charles G. Sellers, Jr., "Private Profits and British Colonial Policy: The Speculations of Henry McCulloh," *William and Mary Quarterly,* 3d ser. 8 (1951): 535–51; Marvin Lucien Skaggs, "Progress in the North Carolina–South Carolina Boundary Dispute," *North Carolina Historical Review* 15 (1938): 347–50; Southern Historical Collection, Chapel Hill: Fanning McCulloh Papers; Cameron Papers; Joshua Sharpe Papers, 1747–1761; Raleigh Archives: Fanning-McCulloh Papers; English Records, Colonial Office Papers, Letters from the Governors, Dobbs to Martin with Enclosures, 1767–1768.

31. See the following concerning the Granville District and the closing of the office in 1763: Saunders, ed., *N.C. Colonial Records,* 7:157; Beverly W. Bond, *The Quit Rent System*

in the American Colonies (New Haven: Yale University Press, 1919), p. 81; E. Merton Coulter, "The Granville District," *The James Sprunt Studies in History and Political Science* 13 (1913): 33–56, especially p. 52; C. B. Alexander, "Richard Caswell's Military and Later Public Services," *North Carolina Historical Review* 23 (1946): 18–21; David L. Corbitt, ed., "Historical Notes," *North Carolina Historical Review* 5 (1928): 339–41.

32. Boyd, ed., *Eighteenth Century Tracts,* pp. 182–92.

33. Ibid., pp. 254–57, 345–48.

34. Ibid., pp. 257–61, 348–59; Saunders, ed., *N.C. Colonial Records,* 7: 249–52.

35. Boyd, ed., *Eighteenth Century Tracts,* p. 360. "Bombs" was a contemptuous term for the sheriff's deputies. It is a diminutive form for "Bumbailiff," who was a bailiff of the meanest kind—one who was employed in arrests. Scorn was dripping from the diminutive "Bombs," for this word literally meant a person's rump ("bum"; "bom").

36. Ibid., pp. 262–63, 359–61.

37. Ibid., pp. 264–66, 362, 363; Saunders, ed., *N.C. Colonial Records,* 7:699–700.

38. Boyd, ed., *Eighteenth Century Tracts,* pp. 263–64, 266–67, 363–65; Saunders, ed., *N.C. Colonial Records,* 7:702–3, 716, 732–33; Powell, Huhta, and Farnham, eds., *The Regulators in North Carolina, A Documentary History,* p. 80.

39. The county officals referred to above were Col. Edmund Fanning (Hillsborough lawyer and merchant, assemblyman, militia colonel, town commissioner, and county register), Lt. Col. John Gray (former and future assemblyman, sheriff, and justice of the peace), Major Thomas Lloyd (assemblyman, justice of the peace, chairman of the county court, member of the parish vestry, and coroner), Adjutant of the militia Francis Nash (merchant, former and future assemblyman, justice of the peace, building commissioner, and county court clerk), and Thomas Hart (merchant, mill owner, justice of the peace, former sheriff, and future assemblyman and lieutenant colonel of the militia). For their correspondence, see Saunders, ed., *N.C. Colonial Records,* 7:705–7, 710–12, 713–16, 717–20.

40. Saunders, ed., *N.C. Colonial Records,* 7:713.

41. Ibid., pp. 705–7, 710–16.

42. Ibid., pp. 717–22.

43. Ibid., pp. 739–45, 750–51; Boyd, ed., *Eighteenth Century Tracts,* pp. 267–68, 365–67.

44. Boyd, ed., *Eighteenth Century Tracts,* pp. 268–71, 368–70; Saunders, ed., *N.C. Colonial Records,* 7:758–71.

45. Saunders, ed., *N.C. Colonial Records,* 7:791–96; Boyd, ed., *Eighteenth Century Tracts,* pp. 271–73, 370–72.

46. Boyd, ed., *Eighteenth Century Tracts,* p. 374.

47. See Kay, "Regulation in North Carolina," pp. 164–68, 286–424; Kay, "Taxes During Administrations of Dobbs and Tryon," *North Carolina Historical Review* 42 (1965): 440–53.

48. Boyd, ed., *Eighteenth Century Tracts,* pp. 273–74, 374.

49. Ibid., pp. 274, 375–77.

50. Ibid. pp. 270–71, 370; Saunders, ed., *N.C. Colonial Records,* 7:722–28, 750–52, 806–10.

51. Saunders, ed., *N.C. Colonial Records,* 7:801.

52. Ibid., pp. 798–99, 801–4, 819–21; Boyd, ed., *Eighteenth Century Tracts,* pp. 275–76, 378–81.

53. Boyd, ed., *Eighteenth Century Tracts,* pp. 276–80, 381–85; Saunders, ed., *N.C. Colonial Records,* 7:800–806, 810–11, 821.

54. Saunders, ed., *N.C. Colonial Records,* 7:811–17, 819–42, 887–89; Boyd, ed., *Eighteenth Century Tracts,* pp. 280–82, 385–86; Raleigh Archives, Governor's Papers, William Tryon, 1765–1771. For 1771 figures, see n. 98.

55. See n. 54.

56. Saunders, ed., *N.C. Colonial Records,* 7:842–48, 850–51, 863–64, 884–86, 934; 8:17, 32, 67; Archibald Henderson, ed., "Hermon Husband's Continuation of the Impartial Relation," *North Carolina Historical Review* 34 (January 1941): 48–81; Boyd, ed., *Eighteenth Century Tracts,* pp. 281–93, 386–412; Raleigh Archives, Governor's Papers, William Tryon, 1765–1771.

57. Saunders, ed., *N.C. Colonial Records,* 7:847, 884–85; 8:27–29, 33–36, 68–70,

223–26; Boyd, ed., *Eighteenth Century Tracts*, pp. 292–300.

58. Raleigh Archives, Legislative Papers, 1768–1769; David L. Corbitt, ed., "Historical Notes," *North Carolina Historical Review* 8 (July 1931): 342–48.

59. A sinking tax was levied to liquidate currency emitted to pay for a specific appropration of public funds. See Clark, ed., *State Records of N.C.*, 23:781–82; Kay, "Payment of Provincial and Local Taxes in N.C.," *William and Mary Quarterly*, 3d ser. 26, no. 2 (1969): 218–40.

60. Saunders, ed., *N.C. Colonial Records*, 8:80a.

61. The best analysis of the attitudes of eastern North Carolinians toward currency emissions may be found in James B. Schick, "Regionalism and the Revolutionary Movement in North Carolina, 1765–1776: The Administrations of Governor William Tryon and Governor Josiah Martin" (Master's thesis, University of Wisconsin, Madison, 1963), pp. 20–38.

62. For the history of this resolution through the passage of a law in 1771 to implement the resolution, see Saunders, ed., *N.C. Colonial Records*, 7:922–23, 983, 986; 8:478–79; Clark, ed., *State Records of N.C.* 23:840–41. See also Kay, "Regulation in Colonial North Carolina," p. 325; Saunders, ed., *N.C. Colonial Records*, 8:9.

63. Saunders, ed., *N.C. Colonial Records*, 8:38.

64. Boyd, ed., *Eighteenth Century Tracts*, pp. 302–3.

65. Ibid., pp. 301–4.

66. Ibid., p. 323.

67. Raleigh Archives, War of the Regulation, 1768–1773, printed in Saunders, ed., *N.C. Colonial Records*, 8:230–31.

68. The Raleigh Archives has compiled a list of assemblymen for each county and session. These lists were used to identify assemblymen. The backgrounds of these assemblymen were checked in the records cited in notes 2, 6, 12, 17, 22, 28, 29. See also tables I-VI and their footnotes.

69. See n. 68.

70. The petition of the Anson County Regulators is printed in Saunders, ed., *N.C. Colonial Records*, 8:75–80. The joint petition of the Orange and Rowan County Regulators is in ibid., pp. 81–84.

71. Ibid., p. 83.

72. I have analyzed the regressive nature of North Carolina's tax system in "Payment of Provincial and Local Taxes in N.C.," *William and Mary Quarterly*, 3d ser. 26, no. 2 (1969): 218–39, and passim. In so doing I underestimated the regressiveness of the system in two ways. First, I was not aware of the important financial role played by the grisly practice of compensating owners for their executed slaves: about 25 percent of the yearly provincial budget was allocated to do this. Since a disproportionate amount of these compensations went to large eastern slaveholders, they, on the average, were repaid all their tax payments through this large tax subsidy. Second, although I recognized the importance of work levies, I could not quantify them. Since writing the article, however, it has come to my attention that Hermon Husband in his "Impartial Relation" (Boyd, ed., *Eighteenth Century Tracts*, p. 319) estimated that the inhabitants spent one-twelfth of each year working on roads and mustering for militia duty. See below for a further discussion of this last point. See Marvin L. Michael Kay and Lorin Lee Cary, "The Planters Suffer Little or Nothing: North Carolina Compensations for Executed Slaves, 1748–1772," *Science and Society* (forthcoming), for an analysis of compensations made by the province to masters for their executed slaves.

73. Saunders, ed., *N.C. Colonial Records*, p. 81.

74. Boyd, ed., *Eighteenth Century Tracts*, p. 319. Thus far I have not been able to cross-check the validity of Hermon Husband's assertion that inhabitants spent one-twelfth of each year on road and militia duty. However, it can be done. William Price of the Raleigh Archives and I are planning a joint investigation of this problem in the near future. We both believe, given past research, that Husband's assertion is close to the mark. If so, this means that work levies equalled £3 (North Carolina currency) yearly tax per taxable or nearly three times the yearly money taxes and fees paid by or for each taxable.

75. Ibid., pp. 319–21.

76. Saunders, ed., *N.C. Colonial Records*, 8:86–89.

77. Ibid., pp. 86–141.

78. Ibid., pp. 93–97, 104–5, 134, 135, 140–41. Ronald Hoffman has suggested that the November 1768 South Carolina assembly, when confronted with a simultaneous challenge from the backcountry Regulators and the Charleston "mechanics," enthusiastically acknowledged the Massachusetts circular letter in eager anticipation of dissolution. Perhaps, in an analogous move, the North Carolina assembly in 1770 passed the Townshend Resolutions, partially as a pretext to have the assembly dissolved. Such a view would not necessarily clash with the interpretation expressed in the text. Thus, the assembly's tendency to pass the Townshend Resolutions because of Britain's failure to lift the burden of the Currency Act would be reinforced by the assembly's desire to be dissolved. The assemblymen wanted dissolution for two reasons. One, as Tryon noted, they did not wish to pass reform legislation, and they hoped thereby to enflame the Regulators into committing illegal acts which would enable them to use repressive measures.

79. Ibid., pp. 231–34.

80. Raleigh Archives, Hillsboro District Minute Docket, 1768–1788, part I; War of Regulation; Saunders, ed., *N.C. Colonial Records*, 8: 235–47, 257–58, 260; Powell, Huhta, and Farnham, eds., *The Regulators in North Carolina, A Documentary History*, pp. 250–58; Purdie and Dixon's *Virginia Gazette*, 25 October 1770; 28 March 1771.

81. Saunders, ed., *N.C. Colonial Records*, 8:248–49, 251–54, 258–60, 262, 678–82; Clark, ed., *State Records of N.C.*, 22:408–10; Raleigh Archives, Governor's Papers, William Tryon, 1765–1771 (October 1770).

82. Saunders, ed., *N.C. Colonial Records*, 8:282–86.

83. Ibid., pp. 282–479. I explain in the text why the Regulation occurred primarily in Orange, Rowan, and Anson counties, but never explain why it only weakly developed in the far-western county of Mecklenburg. Perhaps the best explanation is that Mecklenburg was less developed commercially than the other three counties during the Regulator period. This meant that the grievances that precipitated the Regulation were less severe in Mecklenburg and its farmers were less politically aware and less capable of organizing than those who lived in Orange, Rowan, or Anson. Parenthetically, since class passions were comparatively unaroused in Mecklenburg, it is likely that religious factors played a more important role there than in the other three counties. Thus, Tryon's and the assembly's religious appeals, which were meant to co-opt wavering dissenters during the Regulation, probably were more effective in Mecklenburg than in the three counties that had effective Regulator organizations.

84. Ibid., pp. 494–95.

85. For Johnston's Riot Act, see ibid., pp. 348, 390, 411, 428–29, 481–86, 516; 9:237–38, 284–89, 366; Clark, ed., *State Records of N.C.*, 25:519a–519d.

86. For reform laws discussed above, see Clark, ed., *State Records of N.C.*, 23:787–849, and passim; 25:519d–519f.

87. Saunders, ed., *N.C. Colonial Records*, 8:269, 450, 462, 471–73, 494–95, 498–99, 501–2, 507–11, 528–32, 546–49, 686–91, 693–97; Clark, *State Records of N.C.*, 22:428.

88. Saunders, ed., *N.C. Colonial Records*, 8:536–42, 546–49, 697.

89. Saunders, *N.C. Colonial Records*, 8:257–58; 270–71; 9:12–13; Raleigh Archives: Samuel Johnston Papers, 1763–1803; War of Regulation; Hayes Collection, 1748–1806; Southern Collection, Chapel Hill, Edenton Papers, 1717–1937 (1770).

90. Saunders, ed., *N.C. Colonial Records*, 8:519–21, 533–36.

91. Ibid., p. 545. Tryon's removal of Frohock from command of Rowan regiment on p. 701.

92. Ibid., pp. 543–44.

93. Ibid., p. 641.

94. See n. 98.

95. Tryon's account is in Saunders, ed., *N.C. Colonial Records*, 8:610. The later account is reprinted in ibid., p. 608.

96. Bassett, "Regulators of North Carolina," *Annual Report of American Historical Association*, p. 202; Saunders, ed., *N.C. Colonial Records*, 8:580; Raleigh Archives, English Records, Colonial Office, Extract of Letter from Mr. Samuel Cornell to Mr. Elias Debrosses Merchant in New York, Newbern, 6 June 1771.

97. Saunders, ed., *N.C. Colonial Records*, 8:642.

98. Ibid., pp. 574–611, 634, 638–639, 641–43, 646–47, 664–77, 712–27; Clark, ed., *State Records of N.C.*, 19:840–41, 843–45, 849, 853; David L. Corbitt, ed., "Historical Notes," *North Carolina Historical Review* (1926), pp. 482–83, 487–89, 492–501; Purdie and Dixon's *Virginia Gazette*, 30 May 1771, 6 June 1771, 13 June 1771, 10 June 1771, 27 June 1771, 4 July 1771, 25 July 1771, 15 August 1771, 7 November 1771; Rind's *Virginia Gazette*, 15 August 1771; *Gentleman's Magazine*, June 1771, p. 290; Raleigh Archives, English Records, Colonial Office, Extract of Letter from Mr. Samuel Cornell to Mr. Elias Debrosses Merchant in New York, Newbern, 6 June 1771; War of the Regulation; Powell, Huhta, and Farnham, eds., *The Regulators in North Carolina, A Documentary History*, pp. 469, 490–91, 492, 493–97, 506.

99. One contemporary, Morgan Edwards, a Baptist minister, estimated that 1,500 families fled. I have not been able to corroborate this figure, nor can I determine with exactness the causes of such migration as did take place. The best account of the effects of the Regulation on emigration is in Johnson, "The War of the Regulation," pp. 117–23.

100. Pauline Maier's *From Resistance to Revolution* (New York: Alfred A. Knopf, 1972), pp. 196–97, is the best short account of the northern popular press's handling of the North Carolina Regulation and the latter colony's Whig response to northern attacks. Footnotes 57–59 have a good bibliography of northern newspaper accounts of the Regulation. In addition, see Purdie and Dixon's *Virginia Gazette*, 25 July 1771; Saunders, ed., *N.C. Colonial Records*, 8:618–19, 635–48.

101. An exception to this trend was a letter that appeared in the *Boston Gazette* shortly after the Battle of Alamance (July 1771). It was written by Samuel Cornell, a staunch opponent of the Regulators, and is reprinted in Saunders, ed., *N.C. Colonial Records*, 8:615–16. See the following accounts in Purdie and Dixon's *Virginia Gazette* that were antagonistic to the Regulators: 28 March 1771, 2 May 1771, 23 May 1771, 6 June 1771, 4 July 1771, 15 August 1771, 29 August 1771, 17 September 1771, 26 September 1771, and 5 December 1771. An account in Rind's *Virginia Gazette* of 15 August 1771, however, is sympathetic to the Regulators. One account in Purdie and Dixon's *Gazette*, the famous Leonidas letter in the 25 July 1771 number, was copied from the *Massachusetts Spy* and supports the Regulators. Another, Atticus's letter in Purdie and Dixon's 7 November 1771 *Virginia Gazette*, attacked both the Regulators and Tryon. See n. 102.

102. Purdie and Dixon's *Virginia Gazette*, 7 November 1771. The Atticus letter has often been attributed to the rich Cape Fear planter, assemblyman, and associate justice of the superior court, Maurice Moore. William Price of the Raleigh Archives agrees with me that Moore, in all likelihood, was not the author. Price, who has read all of Moore's extant manuscripts, believes that Atticus's writing style definitely is not Moore's. Perhaps a more likely prospect is Samuel Johnston, author of the Riot Act. His conservative but staunch Whiggism together with his coolness towards Tryon and his opposition to a military expedition all make this Whig leader from the Albermarle a leading possibility. See n. 89.

103. Saunders, ed., *N.C. Colonial Records*, 9:1–3, 15–20, 24–25, 36–37, 55, 75–78, 101–4, 245, 263–70, 274–75, 278–79, 311–14, 329–30, 348–50, 357–60, 362, 364–65, 377–78, 425, 433, 548, 551–52, 560–62, 620–21, 972, 1157–58, 1228, 1258; Raleigh Archives: Dartmouth Manuscripts, 1720–1783 (Letter from Issak Edwards to Governor Tryon of New York, 3 April 1774; Alexander Schaw's letter to Lord Dartmouth, 31 October 1775); English Records, Colonial Office Papers (Dartmouth Letters, 6 May 1775; Royal Pardon of all Regulators but Husband, 1 June 1775).

104. Bassett, "Regulators of North Carolina," *Annual Report of American Historical Association*, pp. 209–10.

105. 6 November 1772. Southern Historical Collection, Chapel Hill, Regulator Papers.

106. Johnson, *The War of the Regulation*, pp. 98–116, appendix 3.

107. "Control," as used above, simply means that from Moores Creek Bridge to 1780 the Rebels controlled local and provincial government. This does not mean that such control enabled the officials to act as they pleased. Nor were they able to make over most North Carolinians into patriots. It did mean, however, that Tories *normally* were not open in their opposition. Thus, the tendency of neutrals and even Tories in such

a situation, was nominally to join the militia. However, to fight for the patriots was quite another story.

Jeff Crow, in "Tory Plots and Anglican Loyalty: The Llewelyn Conspiracy of 1777," points out that even during the period 1776–1780 there was some overt Tory resistance. It, however, took hardy souls to operate in the fashion of the Martin County conspirators, for the Llewelyn conspiracy was broken up and some of the conspirators were tried for treason. I wish to thank Dr. Crow for sharing his article with me prior to its publication.

108. Saunders, ed., *N.C. Colonial Records*, 10:468. Robert M. Calhoon, *The Loyalists in Revolutionary America*, 1760–1781 (New York: Harcourt Brace Jovanovich, 1973), pp. 439–46.

109. Evidence that Regulators were Tory sympathizers may be found in *Annual Register*, 1776, pp. 156–58; Evangeline W. and Charles McClean Andrews, *Journal of a Lady of Quality* (Chapel Hill: University of North Carolina Press, 1939), p. 281; Purdie and Dixon's *Virginia Gazette*, 1 March 1776, 22 March 1776; Raleigh Archives: Dartmouth Manuscripts, 1720–1783 (Letter from Isaak Edwards to Governor Tryon of New York, 3 April 1774; Alexander Schaw's letter to Lord Dartmouth, 31 October 1775); Saunders, ed., *N.C. Colonial Records*, 9:1155, 1162, 1166–67, 1228, 1256, 1258; 10:146. Counter evidence is slimmer: Dixon and Hunter's *Virginia Gazette*, 21 October 1775; Saunders, ed., *N.C. Colonial Records*, 10:243.

110. Elisha P. Douglass's "A Three-Fold American Revolution" stresses the above position. It may be found in John Parker and Carol Urness, eds., *The American Revolution: A Heritage of Change* (Minneapolis: Associates of the James Ford Bell Library, 1975), pp. 69–83. Also see Staughton Lynd, *Class Conflict, Slavery, and the United States Constitution* (Indianapolis, 1967), especially pp. 33–34, and Ronald Hoffman's and Edward Countryman's articles in this volume.

111. Saunders, ed., *N.C. Colonial Records*, 10:169, 211.

112. Ibid., pp. 222–28, 338; Elisha P. Douglass, *Rebels and Democrats* (Chicago: Quadrangle Books, 1955), pp. 109–10.

113. Saunders, ed., *N.C. Colonial Records*, 10:700.

114. Ibid., pp. 239–42.

115. "Instructions to the Delegates from Mecklenburg to the Provincial Congress at Halifax in November, 1776" are in ibid., pp. 870a–870f. The Orange County instructions are in ibid., pp. 870f–870h. Douglass's *Rebels and Democrats*, pp. 125–29, has a good summary of these instructions.

116. Saunders, ed., *N.C. Colonial Records*, 10:1006–13.

117. Philip Foner, who is collecting all the extant documents for the Democratic-Republican societies, was kind enough to let me see the documents he has collected for North and South Carolina. Documents from the latter state and others were the basis for the above statement.

118. See Morgan, "Conflict and Consensus," in Kurtz and Hutson, eds., *Essays on the American Revolution*, p. 292.

Preachers and Patriots: Popular Culture and the Revolution in Virginia

Rhys Isaac

A blacksmith preaching to an open-air Methodist revival meeting in Virginia. The sketch, the earliest of its kind in existence, is from the Diary of Benjamin La Trobe, 1809. The Papers of Benjamin Henry La Trobe, Maryland Historical Society.

This essay originated from a larger project still in progress. I have been working on a series of linked studies of specific episodes, seeking to identify certain sociocultural patterns in eighteenth-century Virginia. The book, which I hope to bring out soon, will deal with transformations (and continuities) in religion and authority, values and beliefs in the period before and during the Revolution. My particular concern is with the changing relationships between the ideologies and life-styles characteristic of the gentry and those of humbler ranks. It seems worthwhile to try to understand the Revolution's movements in terms of the nature of authority customarily exercised by the educated elite from which leadership was drawn, and in terms of the interaction of the leaders' "higher" literary culture with more generally diffused forms of popular culture. Media of "communication" in that preindustrial world have become for me matters of central concern.

Formerly a student of European history, I became interested in early America through its relation to the wider context of the Atlantic Revolution. Embarking on a study of that Atlantic-world man, Thomas Jefferson, I set out to discover the contemporary social meaning of the lapidary phrases in which he enunciated his timeless declarations of principle. The search for the sources of the shared passions that stirred Jefferson's generation of Virginians has long since become a more absorbing question for me than the interpretation of Thomas Jefferson and the Atlantic Revolution per se. Although I have come to feel an intimate involvement with eighteenth-century Virginians of all ranks, races, and opinions, I would nevertheless define the ultimate objectives of my work less in terms of a country and a time-period than in terms of that "new history" which, while studying each past society in its own unique cultural context, seeks at the same time to contribute to the enlargement of our understanding of what people are.

Rhys Isaac was educated at the University of Cape Town, South Africa, and Balliol College, Oxford. He is now an Australian, teaching at La Trobe University in Melbourne. In 1974 he held a fellowship from the American Council of Learned Societies' American Studies Program, and in 1975 he was visiting professor at Johns Hopkins University.

An itinerant evangelist, John Leland, reported the following encounter that took place in central Virginia sometime in the 1780s:

> As I was returning from Fredericksburg, in the lower part of Orange, a young man had married and brought his bride to his father's where there was music and dancing. I stopped in the road, and the groom came out and wished me to drink sling with him. I asked him what noise it was that I heard in the house? He answered it was a fiddle. As he was going to the house, I requested him to bring the fiddle to me. But as this was not done, I lighted off my horse and went into the house. By the time I got in, the fiddle was hidden and all was still. I told them, if fiddling and dancing was serving God, to proceed on, and if I could gain conviction of it I would join them. As they did not proceed I told them I would attempt to serve God in my own way. I then prayed among them and took my leave. The next week I was sent for to come and preach at the same house. The power of the Lord was present to heal. In the course of a few weeks, numbers were converted and turned to the Lord, whom I baptised in a stream of water near the house.[1]

The last part of this account reveals Leland as a Baptist. For the rest, the account could as well have been written by a Methodist itinerant, for the two movements were alike in their condemnation of gaiety and their consecration of a different mode of fellowship founded on the shared experience of conversion. At the time of this confrontation, Baptists and Methodists, though comparative newcomers to the Virginia religious scene, had already come to dominate it. Encapsulated in Leland's account is a miniature of the evangelical revolution that was working in Virginia's rural society. In the decades before and after 1776, many individuals and family units were "turned to the Lord" and their lives profoundly altered thereby. They decisively rejected a traditional social world, in which the convivial taking of "sling" and "fiddling and dancing" constituted important bonds; they entered another—the world of "vital religion," which had very different conformations and characteristic activities.

The evangelical reorientation in popular values, styles, and forms of association had begun slowly in the 1740s under the leadership of New Light Presbyterians from the North. The movement, however, only began to turn into a landslide in the decade after 1765, when native Virginian Separate Baptist preachers became active in forming congregations in the southwest and central parts of the province. By 1775 the Baptist adherents may have numbered 15, or even 20, percent of the white population. Their rate of growth had been startling (from close to zero in 1765), and the forms of their mass meetings of up to 5,000 for preaching and processions to the rivers for baptism had aroused intense hostility amongst many gentry leaders of traditional society and their adherents, so that violence, riot, arrest, and imprisonment were not infrequent occurrences.[2] By 1775, leadership in the evangelical movement was passing to the Methodists. For the time being the Baptists experienced "cold times," while John Wesley's itinerants, working nominally (until 1784) as missionaries within the established Episcopal Church, were able in the early years of the war with Great Britain to attract a vast following (especially in southern Virginia) to their form of radical evangelicalism.

The same decade that saw the spread of the Separate Baptists saw the rise of the movement of patriotic resistance to Parliament in Virginia. The first great upsurge of Methodist evangelism came in the years that produced the patriot movement's rebellious climax.[3]

In an attempt to interpret this double ideological eruption, this essay will offer, and then attempt to draw together, a number of distinct approaches: 1. Illustrations of the tone and structure of the traditional society upon which the evangelical and the patriotic ideologies burst. 2. A descriptive analysis of the two contemporaneous movements, seeking, above all, to reveal something of *what each meant to its participants.* 3. An attempt, from the viewpoint of a twentieth-century ethnographic historian, at a comparative interpretation of the relationship of both movements to the traditional Virginian culture. 4. A brief concluding sketch of the most prominent Virginian, who seemed to combine in himself elements of the appeal of both movements.

In seeking to identify the meaning of the movements for their

participants, the historian is confronted by familiar difficulties, since
the great majority, even of the more educated actors, have left no
personal record of their views. In our search for an understanding of
the nature of their engagement, it will be necessary to rely on the close
analysis of descriptions (which we do have) of the meetings for collective action, which constituted the principal medium for the growth and
power of the movements. Analysis will be concentrated on the dramaturgical structure of formal and informal gatherings—on the socially
important body language communications that are an integral part of
such transactions.[4] Similarly, in reviewing the characteristic forms and
styles of the traditional Virginian culture our attention will be directed
primarily to the focal points of collective action. A great deal is to be
learned about a way of life from a close study of those events within
it that engender shared excitement.

I

The social world of eighteenth-century Virginia must be viewed
in its own distinctive landscape. Then, as now, the Old Dominion was
a forested country, well-watered, and dissected by many rivers which
formed convenient and ready-made highways deep into the backcountry. Settlement was scattered; there were no towns to speak of. Physically, Virginia was divided into three regions. There was the Tidewater
—a flat, often swampy terrain bordering on the Chesapeake and the
estuaries of the broad rivers that run into it. Here the oak and pine
forests came down literally to the arms and fingers of the sea. It had
been discovered early in the seventeenth century that tobacco would
thrive for a few harvests after first planting, after which it was time to
clear a new field. Thus Virginia got both its staple crop and its land-
greedy expansionism. A line of falls on the rivers (from Petersburg to
Alexandria) checked further navigation from the sea and bounded the
Tidewater region. To the west, between the fall line and the Blue
Ridge Mountains, lay the Piedmont, where there stretched out gentle
rolling hill country and good tobacco land, which had been taken up
rapidly in the second quarter of the eighteenth century. Here Patrick
Henry was born, raised, and settled. Contrary to legend, this region
had a social structure similar to that of the Tidewater from which it had
grown. Beyond the Blue Ridge lay the broad Shenandoah Valley—
wheat and corn lands, settled largely by German Protestants and

Scotch-Irish Presbyterians who had come through Pennsylvania. This area was culturally and socially distinct, and it shall not be dealt with in this essay.[5]

A common Church of England heritage and a common concentration on the tobacco staple were shared by the Tidewater and Piedmont regions. The evangelical and patriot movements will need to be understood in relation to the folk culture of these older settled parts—the social world where the fiddler, disapproved of by Leland, was such a significant figure.

A Virginian of humble origin, whose life was reshaped by the religious revolt, has left us in his autobiography a richly evocative account of the traditional world of neighborhood conviviality, out of which, in travail, he passed into the world of evangelical fervor. We cannot better discover some of the characteristic forms of the two worlds and the relationship between them than by taking Devereux Jarratt as our guide.

Jarratt was born in tidewater New Kent County in 1733, the youngest child in the family. His father "was brought up to the trade of a carpenter, at which he wrought till the very day before he died." He also owned a modest farm on which the family lived, and "always had plenty of plain food and raiment, wholesome and good, suitable to their humble station...altogether the produce of the farm, except a little sugar, which was rarely used...." Jarratt further recalled that "we made no use of *tea* or *coffee*... nor did I know a single family that made any use of them." These and other "luxuries" were distinguishing marks of the gentry. The circumstances of the boy's father gave him a sturdy yeoman independence, and since the parents "neither sought nor expected any titles, honors, or great things, either for themselves or children," they were able to live "in credit among their neighbors,...and above the frowns of the world." Nevertheless, the young Jarratt grew up with a profound awareness that there were in his world "what were called *gentle folks*... beings of a superior order," distinguished by their dress. The figure of a periwigged gentleman riding down the road near his home created such awesome impressions of authority that he would run off, as for his life. He recalled: "Such ideas of the difference between *gentle* and *simple*, were, I believe, universal among all of my rank and age."[6]

The young Jarratt probably had no direct experience with the political system, little occasion to observe the concentration of gentry power in the county court, and no concern with the House of Bur-

gesses, whose elected members were almost invariably drawn from
leading county families. Nevertheless, over this fearful boy there
loomed, vaguely but powerfully, the Virginia squirearchy. This was a
society in which considerable importance attached to rank and precedence. At the top stood the gentry: perhaps fewer than 10 percent of
the white males could lay claim to this station. Below the gentry were
the freeholders, varying in degrees of wealth and independence—the
yeomen; beneath them were the landless poorer whites (about 30
percent of all white males); and then there were the slaves, who were
estimated at about 40 percent of Virginia's population.[7]

Contented with farmer-artisan status, Devereux Jarratt's parents'
"higest ambition was to teach their children to read, write, and understand the fundamental rules of arithmetic. They wished us all to be
brought up in some honest calling, that we might earn our bread, by
the sweat of our brow, as they did." However, the boy, it seems, was
more apt at learning to master the spoken word: "The number of
songs I could repeat and sing, when but a child, might seem incredible
to relate. The old song of *Chevy Chase. . .* I learned to repeat and sing,
by hearing it a few times only, though it contained near a hundred
stanzas." Similarly, he relates: "Before I knew the letters of the alphabet, I could repeat a whole chapter of the Bible, at a few times hearing
it read, especially if the subject of it struck my fancy." With a keen ear,
and encouraged by finding he had a "voice remarkably tuneable. . .
soft, or sonorous; as the case required," he early became steeped in
the oral culture of his people. Thus, long before he studied Latin and
theology, there was prepared in this boy the foundation of the preaching which was deeply to stir the simple farming people of southern
Virginia, who had little to do with letters and book learning. Small
wonder, too, that the young man found in himself no inclination to
attend church, where the parson, "preaching wholly by a written
copy," delivered sermons in the style of formal literary prose that
"seemed rather addrest to the cushion, than to the congregation."[8]

The distinctness of oral and literary culture is a very significant
aspect of premodern agrarian social structure. Country gentlemen
were, of course, included in the folk culture of the neighborhoods and
counties over which they presided, but they alone had ready access to
the literary world and the written medium through which higher authority was more largely communicated. Jarratt's account of his formal
education is illuminating in relation to this important theme. At the
age of eight or nine the boy was sent to an "English" neighborhood

school—that is, not a Latin one. He "continued to go to one teacher and other...(though not without great interruptions)" until he was twelve or thirteen. He learned some arithmetic "and to write a sorry scrawl," but chiefly the boy, whose ear and voice had been so apt to master the chapters he heard read aloud, now "learned to read in the Bible, (though but indifferently)." Few, if any, of Jarratt's fellow farm-boys can have attained sufficient mastery of reading to enable them to gain ready access to books and literary culture. About half of them would fail to master the most elementary skills of literacy.[9]

By the time Jarratt was thirteen both his father and mother were dead. All schooling ceased and he went to his elder brother's to be introduced to the business of earning his bread by the sweat of his brow. He was most constantly employed "in ploughing, harrowing and other plantation work," which he found "very irksome." His brother was "exceeding kind to him," not strict concerning his conduct, and encouraged him to enjoy such pleasures as this country life afforded. Indeed, the youngster was given the "keeping and exercising race-horses for the turf...[and the] taking care of, and preparing game-cocks for a match." In this way began an introduction to the world of contest pastimes. "*Cards, racing, dancing &c...* were then much in vogue. In these I partook, as far as my time and circumstances would permit, as well on Sundays as any other day." Jarratt noted that in this he "only copied the example" of his elders and superiors, and that "the example of such has great influence." Exciting activities of this kind were a vital part of initiation into the social world beyond family and farm. They were a very significant aspect of the socialization process.[10]

The independence of the simple yeoman, which Jarratt celebrated in his father, is only attainable if one has a farm, and if, free of ambition, one is "above the frowns of the world." A younger son with a twenty-five pound patrimony must earn favors, if he is to achieve even modest self-sufficiency—and more so if he aspires higher. The young Devereux "was not contented with the small degree of learning" he had acquired. Since a knowledge of arithmetic was, in that rustic society, "reckoned the height of learning," the young plowman borrowed a manuscript manual on the subject, and while the horse grazed at midday, he "frequently spent the time in application to that book." Diligence soon had its reward: "I was so well skilled," he recalled, "in the *Division of Crops,* the *Rule of Three,* and *Practice,* that, you may be sure, the fame of my learning sounded far." Such was the extension of the bonds of neighborhood and kin connection in this rural world, that one Jacob Moon, who lived in Albermarle County, a hundred miles away, "heard how learned I was... [and] being a native of New Kent... prejudiced in favour of his old county folk, sent me word, that he should be glad to employ me as a schoolmaster..." The eighteen-year old lad set off with all his belongings—a suit of coarse clothes and a spare osnaburg shirt; and, since he aspired to cut more of a figure, he took also a cast-off wig (purchased from the slave to whom his master had given it), and a horse borrowed from his brother.[11]

Away from home, the poor young schoolmaster came in time under the influence of a pious gentlewoman who began his conversion to evangelical "vital religion." He was moved to impose upon himself the strict code of forbearances enjoined by this faith—the forswearing of cards, gaming, sporting pastime, and dancing. Later, when his economic circumstances were somewhat improved, he paid a visit back home, and there a revealing confrontation took place. Jarratt's account is richly evocative of the warmth and inclusiveness that familial and neighborhood ties often had in old Virginia, and of the way the new evangelical code was perceived as a threat to the traditional community:

> My brothers and their wives, and all the black people on the plantation, seemed overjoyed at my coming. The pleasure of seeing each other was mutual.... Nothing was thought too good for me, which their houses afforded.... The *cellars*... were generally stored with good, sound cider. *These* were set open with great liberality... they knew I had been very fond of company and merriment, and wished to entertain me with frolic and dance. This proposal I rejected, and told them my reason... that my mind was turned to religion. This put some damp on their spirits, though they allowed that all people ought to be better than they were—but they thought I had overshot the mark... "We all ought to be good, say they, but sure there can be no harm in *innocent mirth*, such as dancing, drinking, and making merry."[12]

Their determination to win him back to the old way of life soon proved too strong. When Jarratt returned from visiting an uncle, he found that a stratagem had been devised. His brother "had contrived to gather a considerable company of people, of different sexes and ages, for the purpose of drinking cider and dancing, as liked them best." Jarratt describes the test of strength and its outcome:

> I was surprised when I rode up, to see such numbers, both within and without doors. Without, the tankard went briskly round,

while the sound of music and dancing, was heard within. I was
strongly solicited to join the company within—but I held back for
some time. But too soon. . .here was I drawn in, once more, to
join those vanities. . . .At first I joined with reluctance—but I
soon found myself shorn of all my strength. . . .[Thereafter] I
thought it vain for me to attempt a religious life any more. . . .I
might as well. . .get what little happiness I could in sports and
sensual gratifications.[13]

Now that the once gentry-shy plowboy had something of polite
manners, wore linen in place of osnaburg, and had a mount of his own,
he discovered that virtuosity in the traditional convivial style could be
a way to advancement, "as I possesst a great degree of vivacity, and
was extremely jocose, my company was very acceptable. . .and courted
by persons much my superior, in family and fortune."[14]

After a time, however, Jarratt returned to the house of his evangelical benefactress (as a tutor at fifteen pounds a year). His pious resolutions were renewed; he experienced conversion, and began the
arduous training in Latin and Greek required for the Presbyterian
ministry. A number of considerations, including the example of those
great evangelical Church of England ministers, the Wesleys and
George Whitefield, led him, however, to change his allegiance and to
go to London to take Anglican orders. It was as rector of a parish of
the established church in southern Virginia that he was able to prepare
for and take part in the spectacular Methodist evangelical upsurge that
developed within the legally established Church of England in 1775–
1776.[15]

Jarratt's account conveys vividly the ethos of the traditional society and the context of the resistance that the spreading evangelical
culture was to meet. In order to bring out more fully the subversive
character of the new movement, it is necessary to offer an overview of
some of the customary forms of social interaction in old Virginia. This
may best be done by sketching a "map" of the centers of collective
activity. We live now in a society whose structures are known and
maintained to a large extent through impersonal media. In the face-to-
face society of the Old Dominion it was different. Settlement was thinly
spread across a forested, river-dissected landscape. For the existence
of community in these circumstances special importance necessarily
attached to the places and occasions where the inhabitants came together for common purposes; on these occasions their scattered society would become visibly present to them. A people's sense of what is

dramatic profoundly shapes its experience of life. It is important to understand the shared interests and excitements that related the members of this society to each other at times of their coming together.[16]

The most generally distributed centers for regular assembly were the parish churches. The Church of England was established in Virginia; it was supported by taxes, and dissenters from it were few in the Tidewater and Piedmont before the evangelical upsurge of the 1760s and 1770s. An ideal of community was expressed in the law—sporadically enforced—making attendance at Sunday worship compulsory. The predominant tone was not grave piety. An acerbic Scots observer thought the country folk attended "only to make bargains, hear and rehearse news, fix horse races & cock matches, and learn if there are any barbecued Hogs to be offered...Gratis to satisfy a voracious appetite." The occasion also served to represent vividly the rank structure of society. The most prominent pews at the front of the church were owned by the leading families. A contemporary diary entry gives a vivid impression of the proud display that would occur: "It is not the Custom for Gentlemen to go into Church til Service is beginning, when they enter in a Body, in the same manner as they come out . . . "[17]

An even more important local center for the display of rank and dignity was the county courthouse. There the gentlemen-justices—the elite of the region—presided once a month, with all the ceremonial of authority, over a wide range of the affairs of the community. The display was not without spectators, for court day was also the occasion for a regular country fair, with persons gathered from far and near for both business and pleasure.[18]

Another notable center of public action was the muster field. The militia was, in many ways, a little microcosm of the white male society of Virginia, for although it mustered infrequently, it embodied important continuing social structures. Patronage, in face-to-face society, is the necessary return for deference. In old Virginia the militia served as a channel for both. The deference to which the gentry aspired was figured in the identification with titles of militia rank. The use of these titles was as continuous as the musters were intermittent. A stranger exclaimed: "Wherever you travel...your Ears are constantly astonished at the Number of Colonels, Majors and Captains that you hear mentioned: In short the whole Country seems at first to you a Retreat of Heroes." The same observer, however, noted (in the words of Dryden) that at the muster itself, another aspect of the institution was revealed: "Of seeming arms, they make a short essay, Then hasten to get drunk, the bus'ness of the day." The patronage of the gentlemen officers would be extended in the supply of liquor—a customary return for deference. The whole merging of social authority with male warrior fraternity is clearly seen in the case of Captain Wager, who "at the Muster of his Company, after the Exercise was over . . . usually treated them with Punch, and they would after that come before his door and fire Guns in Token of their Gratitude, and then he would give them Punch 'til they dispersed." Numerous records make it clear that "treating" the militia was especially important in establishing "an interest" for election purposes.[19]

Court days and muster days not only served as opportunities for the plentiful taking of liquor, with the customary accompaniment of gay banter, swearing, fighting, fiddling, and dancing; but they also provided occasions for more formal expressions of socially approved aggression. Such was the quarter-mile horse race—a contest between two men in which "jostling was customary. . . . and riders used whip and knee to unseat opponents or drive their mounts off the track," amid the exultation of the spectators. Horse racing (and other forms of gambling sports) had once been reserved by statute to gentlemen. The law was, of course, unenforceable; but whether the events took place at courthouse, muster field, or on gala occasions specially appointed for the purpose, it was usually the gentry who presided over these contest pastimes. Intensely shared interests of this kind, crossing but not obliterating distinctions of rank, have powerful effects in transmitting the style, and so confirming the leadership, or hegemony, of the ruling group that regulates proceedings and dominates in the display.[20]

Through all the collective activities in which the folk culture found expression, we may trace certain dominant values. Pride expressed in constant self-assertion stands foremost. It is evident that the overt proving of prowess perpetually obtruded, even through the convivial gaiety, which was also highly valued. This was certainly so in dancing —a deeply absorbing pastime. "*Virginians* are of genuine Blood—They will dance or die!" The preferred form was the jig—a solo performance (by partners of opposite sex) whose competitive character was reflected in the close scrutiny, appraisal, and comments of the company. (The allure of the dance is a recurrent theme in the evangelical autobiographical literature. Clearly it came to symbolize worldly attachment. More even than the gaiety, it was the proud display of the body that gave offense.)[21]

Convivial occasions and contests played an important part in the formation and maintenance of personal relationships and assessments of "worth" in the face-to-face communities of old Virginia. Dominant values were thus communicated, and the same process served to reinforce the hegemony of the gentry whose life-style represented the highest expression in rural society of proud self-assertion.

II

The evangelical movement represented a sharp challenge to the style and values of the traditional society over which the proud gentry presided. The religious revolt inculcated radically opposed ideals of what life should be like, and how members of society should relate to each other. In a face-to-face society with a customary framework of authority, such a proclamation of an alternative way of life must be highly subversive. The nature of the implicit conflict may best be seen by an analysis of the forms of collective action, and of the modes of association and conduct of the emergent counterculture. Attention will be concentrated on the Methodist phase of the evangelical upsurge, because it coincided in time with the climax of the Virginia patriot movement, as resistance became rebellion.

In June 1776, when Thomas Rankin, John Wesley's assistant in America, came to Virginia, he found the outbursting of piety, which had been building up for some years (partly under Jarratt's nurture), nearing its climax. He tells in his narrative:

Sunday, 30. . . .in the afternoon I preached again, from "I set before thee an open door and none can shut it." I had gone through about two-thirds of my discourse, and was bringing the words home to the present—Now, when such power descended, that hundreds fell to the ground, and the house seemed to shake with the presence of God. The chapel was full of white and black, and many were without that could not get in. Look wherever we would, we saw nothing but. . .faces bathed in tears. . . .My voice was drowned amidst the groans and the prayers of the congregation. I then sat down in the pulpit; and both Mr. Shadford and I were so filled with the divine presence, that we could only say, This is none other than the house of God! This is the gate of heaven!. . .those who were happy in God themselves, were for bringing all their friends to Him in their arms. This mighty effusion of the Spirit continued for above an hour, in which time many were awakened. . . .[22]

After such occasions, "the multitudes that attended. . .returning home all alive to God [would] spread the flame through their respective neighbourhoods. . .from family to family." The intensity of the movement, reported Jarratt, was such that "scarce any conversation was to be heard. . .but concerning the things of God. . . .The unhappy disputes between England and her colonies, which just before had engrossed all our conversation, seemed now in most companies to be forgot, while things of far greater importance lay so near the heart."[23]

"Conversion" is the central term for understanding both the subjective meaning of the movement shared by the participants, and its objective relationship to the traditional culture upon which it burst.

Paradoxically, conversion was both a set of intense, intimate experiences, and a pattern shaped by the experiences and expectations of others. Characteristically, candidates would be "awakened" to a sense of sin during a sermon, and then, still "under preaching," but also attending "classes," they would be guided through the desolate quest for a sense of total self-abnegation before God. The bitter experience of despair that God's mercy could ever reach the vile self would be followed by a blissful release when "the Lord. . .spoke peace to their souls. This he usually did in one moment. . .so that all their griefs and anxieties vanished away, and they were filled with joy and peace in believing." Thus came the precious moment of ecstatic conversion.[24]

Ample testimony exists as to the intensity that was usual in this experience; yet it was not in itself sufficient to confirm the convert in a radically new way of life, for it was almost invariably succeeded by doubt. Had God really extended His pardon, and given that "present salvation" which came to true Christians? Much of the organizational structure of the evangelical movement—Baptist and Methodist—was devoted to the creation of social contexts in which this final anguish could be alleviated by the collective validation of the experience. Both groups provided for the solemn "hearing of experience," whether in "class" or church meetings. An opportunity was thus afforded for the humblest members to seek and secure a deeply meaningful acceptance. In the emotional response of the auditors, the initiate was reassured, while the established believers might in the same process relive and reconfirm their own experiences. The converts were proffered some escape from the harsh realities of disease, debt, overindulgence, deprivation, violence, and sudden death, which were the common lot of small farmers. They could seek refuge in a close, supportive, orderly community, where there was a resonance for profound emotions. The search for the deep fellow-feeling which characterized popular evangelicalism must be set in contrast to the formal distance and rivalry in the conventional social exchanges of the traditional system. A concomitant of fellowship in deep emotions was comparative equality.

Preaching was the "ordinance" central to the movement and its cult of conversion. Under preaching, persons became awakened; by it, candidates were guided through the stages of conversion; and in its message the faith of the converts was periodically renewed. The text was always an introduction to the theme of rebirth, the need for "present" salvation. The preaching therefore was extempore, and the preachers sought a sense of inspiration in themselves, and a response, or "liveliness," from the people. The phrase that recurs again and again in the preachers' writings concerning their strivings was a pregnant one in this time of political revolution—"had liberty," "had not as much liberty as at some other times . . ." The search was for a collective, emancipating sense of divine power.[25]

Through extempore preaching in search of "liberty" the oral culture of the people was surfacing in a form of rebellion against the dominance of the literary culture of the gentry. In the eighteenth century the Bible was still generally conceived of as the highest arbiter of ultimate truth. Custody of this precious deposit was therefore required to be vested in those whose mastery of the ancient languages enabled them both to interpret Holy Writ soundly, and to make informed judgments concerning the learned arguments surrounding the many disputed points. The assumption by unlearned farmers and mechanics of authority to expound the Scripture as they felt moved by a "gift" of the Spirit was an offense against the twin hierachies of nature and society. The pre-Revolution antievangelical riots and arrests can partly be understood in terms of the contention that a breach of order was inherent in unauthorized preaching. The ironic term "New Light," by which the evangelicals were designated in common speech, suggests a general perception that what was at stake was the proper authority of ancient learning.[26]

As the conversion experience lay at the heart of the beliefs and organization of the evangelical movement, so a conviction of guilt lay at the heart of the conversion experience. The rapid spread of evangelical religion shows that many were coming to see customary society as a disordered abomination. It seems that a social process was at work by which popular perceptions of disorder in society—and hence in the

self—came to be expressed in the metaphor of "sin." The stern code
of forbearances imposed upon the candidates for evangelical conversion expressed this new perception, and asserted the distance intended
to be set between the new way and the old. Strictly forbidden were the
enjoyments that Jarratt's New Kent family had taken for granted as
"innocent mirth. . .dancing, drinking and making merry."

Order was symbolized in this new strict code of conduct, and, in
the close groups for the sharing and confirmation of religious experience, there existed a means for controlling behavior—a new focus of
authority that operated at a popular level, and far tighter than any that
had previously existed in Virginia's scattered rural communities.
These controls were exerted in support of a set of values diametrically
opposite to those of the customary society over which the gentry presided. Against the gay conviviality of proud contest and self-assertion
was set solemn brotherhood, commenced in denial of the flesh, confirmed in shared self-abnegation, and consecrated in a release into
joy-through-tears.

Meanwhile, throughout Virginia a different, more general form of
excitement had been building up. The patriot movement had originated effectively during the Stamp Act crisis of 1765–1766, and had
had an erratic continuance since then. With the news of the closing and
impending occupation of the port of Boston in the summer of 1774,
it began a sustained crescendo, which continued through 1776. In a
search for the meanings that the movement of resistance to British
authority assumed for its participants, the forms of action and communication that were developed must be described and analyzed.

The leaders of the patriot movement had a very clear notion about
what was at stake. It was: all that makes life worth living. At that time,
"virtue" was the word that (as "democracy" does now) encompassed
within itself the most cherished ideals of Americans. A letter to the
Virginia Gazette in June 1769 is eloquent on this point:

> The prevailing principle of our government is *virtue*. . . . We must
> be more attentive to it than we hitherto have been: By that only
> can liberty be preserved. . .By *virtue,* I here mean a love for our
> country, which makes us pursue, with alacrity, such measures as
> tend to its preservation, and chearfully resist the temptations of
> ease and luxury with which liberty is incompatible.[27]

"Patriot" was the name adopted by men who were inspired by this
vision to make a stand against the corrupt tyranny of Parliament.

The problem in the analysis of the patriot movement and its relationship to popular culture lies not in the lack of a record of transactions but in the formal character of such records. Minutes of many patriot meetings survive, but resolutions drafted in a gentleman's library and brought to the meeting for adoption may not faithfully reflect the sources of excitement that were at work in the popular gatherings. For present purposes, it is more important to seek traces of the oral-aural messages actually transmitted to the unlettered farming folk. In the dramatic structure of the assemblies, indications must be sought of the mutual postures and body language communications that passed both ways between leaders and people.

Among the patriots there was no equivalent of the often lonely anguish of conversion. In its essence, the patriot movement was collective: at its heart lay the meeting of the county community at the courthouse, where certain characteristic patterns of action developed early.

The patriot movement, although resonating deeply-felt aspirations within Virginia society, was in its rise occasioned by external pressures—by new policies for the continental empire formulated in Great Britain. Much of the outward course of the movement was thus directed to negative response. It is appropriate to deal first with what may be termed "rituals of detestation." In many of the American colonies, the execution of symbolic figures in effigy—usually Crown ministers who were leaders in Parliament, or their hated American agents—formed a prominent part of the rituals of detestation. In Virginia, it seems that ceremonies of this kind were imitative, unconvincing, and infrequent. The recurrent form of ritual of detestation was rather the singling out for exemplary denunciation (or reclamation by public penance) of individuals deemed disloyal to the patriot cause. The nature of such enactment may be seen in the newspaper report of a case in Accomac County in July 1775, where at a meeting of the vigilance committee at the courthouse, "it was found necessary to hold up to publick contempt a certain John Sharlock...for having expressed himself...in the most daring and insulting manner against the good people who have proved themselves...friends to American liberty." Since Sharlock defied the committee, the next day "part of the Independent [Militia] Company...went to his house, took, and carried him to the courthouse, and, after a solemn trial, received from him, under the Liberty Pole, his recantation...." Sharlock, in order, as he now pleaded, "to retrieve [his] character with [his] countrymen," had to make abject submission. He had to repeat his own intemperate words concerning the "rebels," and from the Independent Company he had, "in the most humble manner [to] ask . . . pardon . . . application being made to each member of the said Company respectively." The recantation had to be total. He had to declare his opinion altered and heartily to "wish success to this my native country in her present honest struggle for liberty with the mother country." His humiliation was sealed with a declaration that his exacted "confession" was "freely and voluntarily made"—a very secular version of evangelical repentance![28]

The striving for solidarity, which is evident in the enforced conformity of Sharlock, was the very essence of the enactment in the "rituals of affirmation" that predominated in the Virginia patriot movement. The scenario of such rituals is clearly indicated in many reports, of which one (from Princess Anne County) many serve as an illustration. First, at the courthouse, in July 1774, there was a "meeting of a respectable body of Freeholders . . . for the purpose of choosing Deputies . . . and of entering into resolutions expressive of the sentiments of the County in support of their just rights and privileges." A man named Saunders alone "obstinately refused [to sign the resolves] though particularly solicited by some of the principal gentlemen then present." The printed minutes, however, pass over this unwelcome dissent and tell how: "The above resolutions being unanimously agreed to, and signed . . . they then repaired to a place prepared for the occasion, and there drank. . . . [some sixteen named] TOASTS." The affirmation of solidarity was thus concluded in the then traditional Virginia fashion, with bumpers raised to a succesion of unifying sentiments.[29]

Three weeks later the freeholders gathered again to reinforce the bonds that linked them to each other as a county community, and those that joined them to the province at large. The Virginia Convention's "Association" for the boycott of British manufactures "was read and offered to the people that they might express their approbation by signing it. . . ." The centrality of formal resolutions in rituals of affirmation of this kind raises a general problem in relation to our concern for an understanding of the processes of communication. The Association declaration was conceived not as an oral address but as a written statement, cast in the language of the literary-legal culture of the higher elite of this society. Its appeal, and even its meaning, can scarcely have been directly available to common folk raised in an oral culture tradition. The dramatic symbolic significance of the solemn reading aloud of the printed word—and the handing about of texts for signature—could not have been clearer, but we have yet to search out more fully the actual communication achieved. It is essential to explore the concepts and understandings held in common between the gentry and the simple folk.[30]

Professor Bernard Bailyn has shown conclusively how the gentry who gave form and expression to the American Revolution had come to be in the grip of a dark and fearful world view. They discerned a plan to commence in America the overthrow of the last haven of an ancient teutonic liberty, believed once to have prevailed throughout the Western world. If American virtue—which included martial valor —were not proof against the insidious assault, liberty "and everything that is held dear among men" would have no further home on the earth.[31] For an instant—a dizzy moment—Virginia (to which America looked as Great Britain seized Boston) felt itself to stand at the center of the world's stage. That very awareness of the awesome character of their role could not but give a certain charisma to the leaders—a sense of power that in turn inspired respect in their followers.

The patriot world view had a rich and varied intellectual ancestry, but its outline was stark and communicable. One did not have to be familiar with the history of the Roman Republic to be receptive to the grim fear that "corruption" had attained an almost total sway over the high and the mighty in Great Britain, and that the "arm of despotism" was raised against America. Little sophistication was required to comprehend the argument that if Boston was not supported, the colonies might be reduced one by one to a state of "slavery."

Virginians needed no literary image to teach them the degradations of slavery, but we must seek to identify the specific themes through which the fear of enslavement and the meaning of the patriot cause were communicated to men for whom written statements were obscured by the high-flown Latinate prose-style characteristic of this age of literary self-consciousness. The great bulk of newspaper and pamphlet statements were clearly directed toward the persuasion and inspiration of the educated gentry. Nevertheless, there do survive a few accounts of meetings and specimens of written addresses which indicate some of the verbal forms of persuasion adopted to enlist the common freeholders in the cause.

Persuasion, it seems, was a matter of urgency in some parts. Philip Fithian, an observer in the Northern Neck, made an entry in his diary

for 31 May 1774 which suggests an anxiety on the part of poor farmers
not to be involved in the fate of the Yankees: "The lower Class of
People here are in tumult on account of Reports from Boston, many
of them expect to be press'd & compell'd to go and fight the Brit-
ains!"[32]

We have the text of one "address delivered to the inhabitants of
a certain county...assembled for...choosing deputies," which (so
the gentleman who sent it to be printed explained) was "adapted to
the understandings, and intended for the information of, the middling
and lower classes of people...." The mode of argumentation adopted
deserves analysis. The speech begins with an appeal to the pride of
Virginians as free men, and as leaders in the cause of liberty at the time
of the Stamp Act, but now in danger of lagging behind other colonies.
The address proceeds through a lengthy resumé of the oppressions
worked by Parliament upon America, climaxing with a denunciation of
the violent injustice against Boston:

> Many more things, of like tendency, are they [the Parliament]
> now preparing for all North America. To you then, my country-
> men...does it belong to...prevent their wicked designs.... On
> the virtue and courage of the people of these colonies does it
> depend whether we shall be happy or miserable in this world, and
> enjoy, in peace and quietness, the fruits of our labour.

Allaying immediate panic, the speaker discountenanced "Rashness
and violence," held up the Association boycott as a peaceful measure,
but nevertheless concluded by urging preparations for invasion and
war.

There recurred within the speech an anxious reassurance that the
conflict with the British government was not to be disregarded as an
affair concerning the gentry only. Of the property-violating Post Office
Act, the speaker stressed that it oppressed all commerce, although his
hearers might not feel it, "because your circumstances in life are such
that you have but little to do with *letters.*" Dwelling on the occupation
of Boston, he anticipated that, as it was a dispute about the duty on
tea, "some of you may now tell me it is a dispute with which you have
nothing to do, as you do not make use of that commodity...." In this
connection he felt impelled to contend with the opinion "that the
high-minded gentlemen are the occasion of the present confusion" and
that they were bringing common folk "into difficulties to support their
extravagance and ambition." The speaker's rejoinder was to ask:

Are not the *gentlemen* made of the same materials as the lowest
and poorest amongst you?...Have you found...that the *gentlemen...* are so very frugal and saving of their money as to bring
themselves into the smallest difficulty for so small an advantage
[as saving the tea tax]?... Listen to no doctrines which may tend
to divide us, but let us go hand in hand, as brothers...firmly
united to defend our rights and liberty, and to preserve freedom
to our posterity.

In "the detestable STAMP ACT" the courthouse orator discovered "proof of the injustice and tyranny they prepared for us," and
found cause to declare:

I thank the God of heaven and earth, who permits the wicked
sometimes to provide torments for themselves; that of his
gracious mercy to us he suffered that act to be passed, which
opened our eyes, and made us behold the *slavery* intended
for three millions of people. Let us return thanks to HIM, my
countrymen....[33]

Devotional piety or appeal to the Scriptures—at the center of the
education of the comparatively unschooled—was more usual in addresses to the people than in the classical republican writings of the
newspapers. Related to this appeal was the evocation of the popish
peril—a bogey which lurked deep in Anglo-Saxon popular culture by
this time. The Parliament's 1774 Quebec Act, establishing the Roman
Catholic Church in Canada, served to give the alarm that the ministry
designed to impose popery on America.

Putting this full address together with other more fragmentary
indications, it appears that the gentry, themselves alarmed by the
prospect of the forceful subjection of the American colonies, laid
heavy stress in their communications to the common people on the
violence done to Boston, and the prospect that this violence would be
extended generally. The resulting enslavement would destroy all
moral values—a destiny symbolized in the dreaded replacement of
"our pure Religion" by popery, that compound of superstitions fit only
for men without virtue.[34]

Liberty, virtue, and pure Protestant religion were all inextricably
intertwined. Here lay a nagging source of anxiety, a strain that was to
be felt throughout the patriotic exhortations both of the gentry to each
other and to the people generally. What if America—if Virginia—
already was found deficient in virtue? Corruption and the designs of

the overmighty corrupt could be readily discerned and denounced in Great Britain, but were there not signs that the same disorder was spreading to the colonies? This anxiety had a powerful resonance with the abhorrence (at a popular level) with which converts to the evangelical culture were suddenly induced to see the ways of their society. In the terms of the agreement signed by the upholders of the patriotic cause, there were imposed forbearances similar to those obligatory for the adherents to "vital religion." Article eight of the Association, adopted by the Continental Congress on 20 October 1774, and enforced in Virginia, engaged signatories to "discountenance and discourage every species of extravagance and dissipation, especially all horse-racing, and all kinds of gaming, cock-fighting . . . and other expensive diversions and entertainments." In parts of Virginia even dancing (not specifically listed) was taken to be forbidden.[35]

Readiness to proscribe such important forms of social exchange and prestige-confirming contest was radical enough, but behind the alarm at "extravagance" there lurked in Virginian patriots other anxieties. There was the concern over indebtedness, which vented itself in part in attacks on the Scots merchants, but which also led to the expression of deep misgivings about the shape that society had assumed. The indebtedness was only partly attributed to extravagant living; it was seen to be more deeply linked to the absence of manufacturing in Virginia; this in turn was attributed to the large importation of African slaves in place of free farmers and artisans.[36]

Judged from the standpoint of Anglo-Saxon liberties—or of evangelical Christianity—colonial Virginian slavery was an anomaly in the moral order. As the imperial crisis brought questions about the nature and destiny of Virginian society more clearly into consciousness, it necessarily sharpened long-standing uneasiness concerning slavery into explicit anxiety. The popular evangelical movement could begin to resolve the problem by extending membership to the blacks, incorporating as many as possible in the more restrictive moral community that was being generated. The patriot movement, however, was dedicated to the propagation of an ideal of "virtue," which required as its very foundation the moral autonomy of the free man. The patriots' remedy for the evils of the times could *not*, therefore, be extended (as could "conversion" by the grace of God) to include and to obligate slaves. A vain longing for the exclusion and even removal of the blacks was the only expression the Virginia patriots could give to their uneasiness at the morals of a society that depended upon hereditary servitude for much of its work force.

Since the imperial crisis imposed on Virginians a reassessment of their own virtue, and intensified old anxieties concerning such intractable realities of colonial life as slavery and indebtedness, there was a necessity within the patriot movement for the affirmation of the purity of American society. The celebration of manly virtue was as central to the patriot rituals as the confirmation of conversion was among those of the evangelicals. A similar reassurance against the oppression of focussed anxieties was sought in both cases. At first, the patriots' need for appropriate forms of ritual found its most striking expression in the way some elections were staged. Later, the focus came to be more directly upon martial virtue and the militia.

The potential of the public election as a ritual for the affirmation of community virtue is clearly revealed in a document drawn up in 1771 (by one who signed himself NO PARTY MAN) for the guidance of the ordinary freeholder-voter. The portrait of the ideal candidate is revealing. He must be a "Gentleman" of "penetrating Judgement," otherwise he will be "unable to strip every Measure of...Disguise... and penetrate through all the sinister Designs and secret Machinations of the Enemies of Freedom, the Slaves of Interest." Further, "it is absolutely necessary that he be a Man of Probity and Integrity.... One who regards *Measures*, not Men...." To this end it is imperative that he have "that Fortitude...which enables a Man, in a good Cause, to bear up against all Opposition, and meet the Frowns of Power unmoved." The portrait of a true Roman! Of no less importance, of course, was the virtue by which the "Countrymen" addressed were to be able to recognize and elect thoroughly patriotic gentlemen. First they were to be uplifted by a reverential sense of privilege:

> It is your greatest Glory...that you give Being to your Legislature, that from you they receive their political Existence. This renders an American Planter [i.e., farmer] superiour to the first Minister of an arbitrary Monarch, whose glittering Robes serve but to veil from vulgar Eyes the Chains of Slavery. Guard it then, as the most precious Pledge committed to you by the Deity. Let every Gentleman's true Merit determine his Place in the Scale of your Interest.

There follow commands which catalog the considerations that normally influenced voting in old Virginia: "Say not that he is my Neighbour.... Say not I am too much in his Power, I shall experience his

Resentment unless I give him my Vote.... Say not he is my Friend.
... Say not I am under Obligations to him: You are under still greater
to your Country...." The whole represents an affecting tableau: a free
yeomanry with fearless honesty elevating to trust and authority the
wisest and firmest of the "Gentlemen" to "meet the Frowns of Power
unmoved."[37]

As the imperial crisis heightened and the fervor of the patriots
mounted, a ritual enactment of this scene could be most strikingly
achieved in the unanimous election. The customary strenuous competition among the gentry for the honor of being a county representative
was frequently set aside. A single example serves to illustrate the
idealization that was involved. In the election that followed the dissolution of the House of Burgesses in 1769, the freeholders of Elizabeth
City County,

> being truly sensible of the spirited and patriotick behaviour of
> their late members ... unanimously determined to re-elect them;
> and to convince Administration in England, as well as all man-
> kind, that their notions of *Virtue* and *Freedom,* are exalted, they
> would not suffer their new elected representatives to be at any
> *expense,* giving orders for a genteel entertainment to be provided
> at Mr. Younghusband's, where they dined with those Gentlemen.
> After dinner... many patriotick toasts, were drank.[38]

The display of genteel liberality in the supplying of the voters with
liquor was too ingrained to be eliminated by the austerity to which the
patriots ideally aspired. Even the stoic Roman NO PARTY MAN despaired of the speedy elimination of "treating." In the case cited, and
in others, the custom was, however, inverted, so that the candidates no
longer appeared to make a self-interested return for the votes of the
community. Instead the community proclaimed the disinterested virtue of both electors and the elected by standing the charges. Patriotic
unanimity could then be celebrated and sealed in customary fashion
by the communal taking of liquor. The calling of toasts provided an
ideal medium for the oral and dramaturgical communication of the
beliefs, symbols, and values of the movement.

The collective enactment expressed in the "treating" of the
county representatives had its apogee in the feting of the leaders of
Virginia and America at large. In the public honoring of the outstanding patriots, and in the identification with them that such ceremonies
communicated, their own and the people's virtue were at once
affirmed. It was reported in Pinkney's *Virginia Gazette* of 1 June 1775:

Last Monday morning, about 10 o'clock, the WILLIAMSBURG
TROOP OF HORSE left this city, well accoutred, in order to
meet our good and worthy speaker [Peyton Randolph] on his
return from the continental congress. Notwithstanding the in-
clemency of the weather, these hardy friends and supporters of
American liberty pursued their journey with the utmost eager-
ness, whilst the most unfeigned joy diffused itself in every countenance.

For order, good discipline, and regularity, this company was
greatly applauded. Ruffen's ferry was the place where they met the
object of their wishes, whom, after giving three hearty cheers, they
conducted until they arrived within about two miles of the city, when
they were joined by the COMPANY OF FOOT, who also gave three
cheers, and shewed every other mark of decency and respect. The
pleasing deportment of the speaker, on account of this peculiar honour done him, animated, in the highest degree, every person that
attended; and on Tuesday, about 5 o'clock in the afternoon, the whole
body arrived here, surrounding the FATHER of his COUNTRY,
whom they attended to his house, amidst repeated acclamations, and
then respectfully retired.

The above *tableau vivant* reveals the patriots for the first time in
martial array. This was, in terms of the movement's own idealizations,
its necessary and highest form. The ultimate test of true virtue was the
readiness to sacrifice one's life for one's country.[39] Time and again,
assembled Virginia freeholders proclaimed loyalty to the king and
determination to uphold the constitution "at the hazard of our lives
and fortunes." One of the most powerful recurrent themes in the
declarations of the period was the warm identification with the "good
old cause" of English liberty, and the invocation of the "ancestors
[who] have liberally shed their blood to secure to us the rights we now
contend for." All of this directed attention to the warrior who should
be within every free man, and it may thus be associated not only with
the gentry's ideal of Roman republicanism, but also with the robust
tradition of English "roast-beef" patriotism. Since the English were
then emerging as the enemy, we may note the boast in a song—that
"our peach-brandy fellows can never be beat"—and style this rising
strain of assertive pride as "Virginia peach-brandy patriotism!"
Bravado of this kind was a prominent feature of the toast-drinking that
had so important a place in the patriotic ceremonial.[40] The emergence

of the warrior band as a dominant form of the expression of patriotism began in late 1774, with the organization of Independent Companies of gentlemen volunteers. This movement became a landslide in 1775. By 1776 the initial excitement had died down, and the newly formed Commonwealth had to replace spontaneous action by governmental direction through conscription and requisitioning.

III

The gentry had long denounced the evangelical "New Lights" as a set of ignorant "enthusiasts"—a term which had then the connotation of excess implicit in the word "fanatic" nowadays. By 1775, the passionate involvement of gentlemen and their followers in the patriot movement had reached the pitch where it could be aptly designated by a critical participant as "political enthusiasm,"[41] and there were indeed certain common features between the movements. Most notable was the use in both cases of popular assemblies for communication, emotional sharing, and the intensification of the involvement of common people. Contrasts were also very much apparent.

The meetings of the patriot movement (typically to elect genteel delegates or to adopt resolutions cast in literary prose) were less participatory than those of the "vital religionists." Furthermore, they were less inclusive, since freeholders not of the gentry elite had a rather limited role, the landless white inhabitants were on the fringe only, and the blacks had no role at all. In the evangelical movement even the slaves participated vocally. The same contrast was reflected in the leadership of the two movements. For the patriots it was exclusively genteel, whereas many of the foremost evangelical preachers were self-taught men of humble origin. The characteristic tone of the meetings again was very different. We may compare the sermonic striving to achieve "liberty"—a state of ecstatic release—with the celebration of order and deference figured and emphasized in the feting of Peyton Randolph on his return from Congress.

The most important contrast between the two movements lies in their relationship to the old way of life. The evangelical movement constituted a radical rejection of it, with the introduction of a strikingly new set of models for moral conduct and moral authority. The patriot movement must be seen in its initial conception as an apotheosis of customary ways. Its immediate tendency was to reinforce with a new sense of meaning and purpose the traditional styles and values. The forms of its action—meetings at the courthouse, elections, committees, and their resolutions—coincided with and, for a short-lived moment, reinforced the traditional structures of gentry-dominated local authority. The independent companies were a barely popularized form of the old militia, while the ceremonies of the toasts and the feting were but adaptations of the customary conviviality. With aggressions for the moment turned outwards, all of these forms figured and reinforced the style and values of pride, gaiety, and self-assertion which we have seen as the principal currency of social exchange in the geographically scattered, gentry-dominated society of old Virginia. It was these same values that the evangelicals, with their shared emotions of guilt, suffering, and joy-through-tears, most profoundly negated.[42]

Fundamental shifts in values and organization that occur outside and against established structures are highly subversive in tendency. As the movement of vital religion worked to weaken the hegemony of the gentry, so the patriot movement contained a vigorous reassertion of the cultural dominance of the elite. A view of the diametrically opposed tendencies of the two movements raises the important question of whether the patriot movement in Virginia may be understood as in part a defensive response from the traditional order to the transformations in popular orientation toward authority manifested in the spread of evangelicalism. An answer to this question, however, would go well beyond the scope of the descriptive analysis undertaken in this essay.

IV

In conclusion, it must be asked: Was the contrast between the movements really so extreme? Must we not expect to find common elements in two powerful popular movements at work in the same society at the same time?

Considered as social forms and as cultural expressions, the contrast and opposition between the evangelical and patriot movements is striking. But at a deeper level—the need for psychic relief from the oppression of guilt, anxiety, and perceived disorder—the two ideologies struck a common chord. The resonance between the two movements may most clearly be sensed by turning attention, in a concluding sketch, to the man most universally celebrated in the troubled Virginia of his day. What was the secret of Patrick Henry's popularity? Full treatment of this question would be impossible and inappropriate here, but the reason why the answer to it has proved so elusive is easy to find, and leads in turn to that aspect of the man which concerns us most. Patrick Henry's surviving writings are few and give no clue as to his powers. He was a master of the *spoken word*—the spoken word in a form which did not derive, as did the Latinate oratory of Richard Henry Lee, from the language of writing. His genius lay instead in the exploitation of the possibilities of the oral culture of his society. For this reason, there could scarcely be drafts of his speeches, and their distance from the forms of literary culture must have made it seem inappropriate even to attempt to take notes upon them. What has been passed on to us in writing, however, are vivid accounts of the *impressions* created by his oratory.

It is clear that when, some two or three decades later, Edmund Randolph wrote the history of his own times, he could still vividly see and hear Patrick Henry speaking. The memoirist, trained in letters, could not retain the verbal content of even the greatest of these speeches, but the style, manner of delivery, and even the thematic traits of Henry's performances were indelibly impressed upon Randolph's memory. Constant recurrence to the subject indicates a virtual obsession with the conflict between Henry's style of oratory and that of his colleagues in the leadership of Virginia. Henry annihilated the classical rules of rhetoric to which, as a gentleman, he should have adhered. There was "an irregularity in his language, a certain home-spun pronunciation..."; yet Henry entered public life "regardless of that criticism which was profusely bestowed on his language, pronunciation and gesture," for he soon discovered that "a pronunciation which might disgust in a drawingroom may yet find access to the hearts of a popular assembly."

In his memory Randolph followed the orator through a powerful performance: "In Henry's exordium there was a simplicity and even carelessness.... A formal division of his intended discourse he never made." His eyes "fixed upon the moderator of the assembly addressed without straying in quest of applause, he contrived to be the focus to which every person present was directed.... He transfused into the breast[s] of others the earnestness depicted in his own features, which ever forbade a doubt of sincerity." The memoir then drops the most revealing clue concerning the source and power of Henry's mode of oratory ("His was the only monotony which I ever heard reconcilable with true eloquence. . . .'')—a form of sermonic chant, directed primarily toward affect! Most of the remaining traits fall into place around this core:

> [the] chief note was melodious, but the sameness was diversified by a mixture of sensations which a dramatic versatility of countenance produced. His pauses, which for their length might sometimes be feared to dispel the attention, riveted it the more by raising the expectation. . . . His style . . . was vehement, without transporting him beyond the power of self-command. . . . His figures of speech . . . were often borrowed from the Scriptures. The prototypes of others were the sublime scenes and objects of nature. . . . His lightning consisted in quick successive flashes, which rested only to alarm the more.[43]

Henry had brought into the politics of the gentry world an adaption of that popular oral form, the extempore sermon, which had been setting different parts of Virginia ablaze ever since the coming of the New Side Presybterians in the 1740s. The success of this mode with the country squires, who formed the great majority of the legislatures that Henry addressed, and on whose reported impressions his popularity must largely have rested, is striking evidence of fundamental cultural continuities between "gentle" and "simple" folk in the Virginia countryside. Living closely integrated in rural society, the squires could respond heartily to this style of oratory, when it was introduced in the service of their own cause, and not in condemnation of their life-style.

Throughout his career Patrick Henry remained firmly attached to the world of the gentry. His mastery of the convivial mode of that world is suggested by some of the earliest recollections of him as "an excellent performer on the violin," whose "passion was music, dancing and pleasantry." This essay began with John Leland setting his face against "fiddling and dancing" at the wedding feast. It shall conclude with a view of Patrick Henry, the fiddler who came to be universally revered in the Virginia of his day. Henry never made the dramatic renunciations characteristic of evangelical converts, but his life-style developed with profound sensitivity to the popular moral concerns of the time, and achieved a harmony above the clashing discords of the old traditional culture and the new evangelical counterculture. The great patriot retained always the easy affability of the gentleman, yet he adopted a sober manner of dress, and became deeply preoccupied with the fostering of Christian virtue in his society.[44] Supremely, what enabled Patrick Henry to tower above his generation—in its general estimation—was his ability to communicate in popular style that passion for a world reshaped in truly moral order, which lay at the heart of both the revolutionary evangelical and the revolutionary patriot movements.

I would like to acknowledge the generosity of the American Council of Learned Societies whose American Studies Fellowship program made this work possible. The following have patiently read drafts and given me helpful advice: Richard Beeman, Richard Bushman, Philip Greven, Emory Evans, Allan Kulikoff, and Thad Tate.

1. L. F. Greene, ed., *The Writings of John Leland* (New York: Arno Press, 1969), p. 28.

2. For a fuller statement concerning the social conflicts unleashed by the rising Separate Baptist movement, see Rhys Isaac, "Evangelical Revolt: The Nature of the Baptists' Challenge to the Traditional Order in Virginia, 1765–1775," *William and Mary Quarterly*, 3d ser. 31 (1974): 345–68. A number of interpretive themes summarized in the present essay are treated more fully there.

3. For an excellent narrative account of the triumph of evangelicalism in Virginia, see Wesley M. Gewehr, *The Great Awakening in Virginia, 1740–1790* (Durham, N.C.: Duke University Press, 1930).

4. My use of the term "body language" has met with objections. I retain it because the concept is essential to the interpretation of modes of communication that were most important in the society studied—proud self-presentation, respectful deference, ecstatic religious seizure. Striking evidence that such forms may be accessible to the historian can be seen below in Thomas Rankin's descriptions of revival meetings (p. 138) and in the account of the return of Peyton Randolph to Williamsburg (pp. 149–50).

5. For a rich description of the regions and their characteristics, see Carl Bridenbaugh, *Myths and Realities: Societies of the Colonial South* (New York: Atheneum Publishers, 1963).

6. *The Life of the Reverend Devereux Jarratt* (New York: Arno Press, 1969), pp. 13–15. The main part of these memoirs was reprinted earlier in "The Autobiography of the Reverend Devereux Jarratt, 1732–1763," ed. Douglass Adair, *William and Mary Quarterly* 3rd ser. 9 (1952): 346–93.

7. For the interlocking system of local and central gentry authority, see Charles Sydnor, *American Revolutionaries in the Making: Political Practices in Washington's Virginia*, 2d ed. (New York: Free Press, 1965). On the proportions of the population in different status categories, see D. Alan Williams, "The Small Farmer in Eighteenth Century Virginia Politics," *Agricultural History* 43 (1969): 92–93, where estimates reached in a number of studies are drawn together.

8. Jarratt, *Life*, pp. 15–22. For a profoundly illuminating discussion of the relationship of oral to literary culture, see Walter J. Ong, *The Presence of the Word: Some Prolegomena for Cultural and Religious History* (New Haven: Yale University Press, 1967). Close attention to the issues raised and discussed in this work will be essential if the history of popular culture, and of the so-called inarticulate, is to advance satisfactorily. I am deeply indebted to Dr. Norman Fiering for this reference, as well as for much valuable discussion and encouragement.

9. Jarratt, *Life*, pp. 19–20. A subtle, sophisticated attempt at estimating literacy comparatively in America and Europe has been made in Kenneth A. Lockridge, *Literacy in Colonial New England: An Enquiry into the Social Context of Literacy in the Early Modern West* (New York: W. W. Norton & Co, 1974). Lockridge finds an overall white male literacy rate in Virginia of about 60 percent throughout the eighteenth century. The figure for humble farmers would be around 50 percent; for women, much lower again. (See pp. 77–81.)

10. Jarratt, *Life,* pp. 16–23.
11. Ibid., pp. 13, 24, 25, 26.
12. Ibid., pp. 42–43.
13. Ibid., pp. 43–44.
14. Ibid., p. 45.
15. Ibid., pp. 45–59, 79, 86–109.
16. See Rhys Isaac, "Evangelical Revolt," *William and Mary Quarterly* 3d ser. 31 (1974): 348–53. The stress placed here upon public occasions is not intended to deny the importance of ongoing neighborhood association at stores, taverns, etc. A most illuminating study of the frequency of such activity has been made by Dr. Allan Kulikoff —a personal communication, for which I am most grateful.
17. James Reid, "The Religion of the Bible and Religion of King William County Compared," in Richard Beale Davis, "The Colonial Virginia Satirist: Mid-Eighteenth-Century Commentaries on Politics, Religion, and Society," American Philosophical Society, *Transactions,* N.S. 57, pt. 1 (Philadelphia, 1967), p. 50; H. D. Farish, ed., *Journal and Letters of Philip Vickers Fithian 1773–1774: A Plantation Tutor of the Old Dominion* (Charlottesville, Va.: University of Virginia Press, 1968), p. 29.
18. See Sydnor, *American Revolutionaries,* pp. 74–85.
19. Anonymous, "Observations in Several Voyages and Travels in America," *London Magazine,* July 1746, reprinted in *William and Mary College Quarterly,* 1st ser. 16 (1906): 5–6; H. R. McIlwaine and John P. Kennedy, eds., *Journals of the House of Burgesses of Virginia* (Richmond, Va.: Colonial Press, E. Waddey Co., 1905–1915), *1752–1755; 1756–1758,* pp. 360–61. For an account of treating at elections, see Sydnor, *American Revolutionaries,* pp. 44–59.
20. Jane Carson, *Colonial Virginians at Play* (Williamsburg, Va.: Colonial Williamsburg, 1965) pp. 109–12, 130.
21. Farish, ed., *Fithian's Journal,* pp. 56–58, 154–55, 177. Andrew Burnaby, *Travels Through the Middle Settlements in North America in the Years 1759 and 1760. . .* (Ithaca, N.Y.: Cornell University Press, 1960), p. 26, suggests that African dance forms were considered by contemporaries to have influenced the Virginia "jig."
22. Thomas Rankin to John Wesley, 24 June 1776, in Elmer T. Clark et al., eds., *The Journal and Letters of Francis Asbury,* 3 vols. (London and Nashville: Abingdon Press, 1958), 1:221. The text is from *Revelations,* 3:8. Its inaccurate citation reveals its passage from literary to oral culture.
23. Devereux Jarratt to Thomas Rankin, 10 September 1776, in ibid., 1:211.
24. Ibid., p. 217.
25. Ibid., pp. 351, 354, and passim; John Williams, "Journal, 1771." (MS in the collection of the Virginia Baptist Historical Society, Richmond, Va.), passim.
26. For a superbly articulated statement of the conventional view by a Virginia gentleman, see Robert Carter Nicholas, in *Virginia Gazette* (Purdie and Dixon), 3 June 1773.
27. "Brutus" in *Virginia Gazette* (Rind), 1 June 1769. For a profound, illuminating analysis of the theme of "virtue" and of the social values of the patriots, see Gordon S. Wood, *The Creation of the American Republic, 1776–1787* (Chapel Hill, N.C.: University of North Carolina Press, 1969), part 1.
28. *Virginia Gazette* (Pinkney), 20 July 1775.
29. Peter Force, ed., *American Archives,* 4th ser. (Washington, D.C., 1837–1853), 2:76–77; William J. Van Schreeven and Robert L. Scribner, eds., *Revolutionary Virginia: The Road to Independence;* Vol. 1, *Forming Thunderclouds. . .* (Charlottesville, Va.: Virginia Independence Bicentennial Commission, 1973), pp. 153–55.
30. Force, *American Archives,* 4th ser. 2:76; Van Schreeven and Scribner, *Revolutionary Virginia* 1:231–35.
31. Bernard Bailyn, *The Ideological Origins of the American Revolution* (Cambridge: Harvard University Press, 1967); *Virginia Gazette* (Rind), 30 June 1774.
32. Farish, ed., *Fithian's Journal,* p. 111; see also Jack P. Greene, ed., *The Diary of Landon Carter of Sabine Hall* (Charlottesville, Va.: University Press of Virginia, 1965), 2:821–22.
33. *Virginia Gazette* (Purdie), 14 July 1775.
34. "D.C." in *Virginia Gazette* (Purdie and Dixon), 22 December 1774. See also an

antiministerial song to a popular tune, *Virginia Gazette* (Rind), 12 January 1775, and Thomas Adams to Thomas Hill, November 1774, in *Virginia Magazine of History and Biography*, 23 (1915): 178.

35. Force, *American Archives*, 4th ser., 1:915; for analyses of this aspect of the American Revolution, see Wood, *Creation of the American Republic*, pp. 107–24, and Edmund S. Morgan, "The Puritan Ethic and the American Revolution," *William and Mary Quarterly*, 3d. ser. 24 (1967): 3–43.

36. Van Schreeven and Scribner, eds., *Revolutionary Virginia* 1:87, 23. "Associator Humanus" in *Virginia Gazette* (Purdie and Dixon), 18 July 1771.

37. *Virginia Gazette* (Purdie and Dixon), 11 April 1771.

38. *Virginia Gazette* (Purdie and Dixon), 14 September 1769. See also *Virginia Gazette* (Rind), 7, 14 July 1774; ibid (Pinkey), 8 June 1775; ibid. (Dixon and Hunter) 20 May 1775; ibid. (Purdie), 24 February and 5 May 1775, supplement.

39. The central importance of martial valor in eighteenth-century Anglo-Saxon social and political values has been decisively demonstrated in J. G. A. Pocock, "Machiavelli, Harrington, and English Political Ideologies in the Eighteenth Century," *William and Mary Quarterly*, 3d ser. 22(1965): 549–83.

40. Force, *American Archives*, 4th ser. 1:685, 2:578; "Proposals . . ." in *Virginia Gazette* (Rind), 6 April 1769; "B.D." in ibid. (Rind), 4 August 1774; Courtlandt Canby, ed., "Robert Munford's *The Patriots,*" *William and Mary Quarterly*, 3d ser. 6 (1949): 466.

41. Canby, ed., "Munford's *Patriots,*" *William and Mary Quarterly*, 3d ser. 6 (1949): 497.

42. It is not suggested here that these aspirations which the gentry infused into the patriot movement were in the long run realized. All the evidence suggests the contrary. By drawing the freeholders more actively into politics, and by reorienting the fundamental conceptions of authority to focus on the sovereignty of the people, the patriot gentry inaugurated an era of more popular participatory politics. The unanimous elections were a short-lived phenomenon, and when they passed, it was found that the grip of the old social hierarchy upon power was for the moment loosened. See Jackson T. Main, "Government by the People: The American Revolution and the Democratization of the Legislatures," *William and Mary Quarterly*, 3d ser. 23 (1966): 401–7.

43. Arthur H. Shaffer, ed., *Edmund Randolph: History of Virginia* (Charlottesville, Va.: 1970), pp. 168, 179–81. William Wirt Henry, *Patrick Henry: Life, Correspondence and Speeches*, 3 vols. (New York: Charles Scribners', 1891), 1:13–16, stressed the influence of the Reverend Samuel Davies upon Henry's oratorical style.

44. W. W. Henry, *Patrick Henry*, 1:9, 18. Henry's gentry attachments as well as his preoccupation with Christian virtue are admirably described in Richard R. Beeman, *Patrick Henry: A Biography* (New York: McGraw-Hill, 1974), pp. 53, 57, 60, 67, 89, 92, 103, 110–16. I am deeply indebted to Professor Beeman for sharing his interests with me and for valuable discussions concerning Patrick Henry's career.

Patriots and Radicals

"Ideology" and
an Economic Interpretation
of the Revolution

Joseph Ernst

Shipbuilding, the largest single industry of revolutionary America, as portrayed in a late eighteenth-century engraving of a Philadelphia ship-yard by William Birch. Courtesy Library Company of Philadelphia.

I have always been fascinated by a tendency among historians of the American Revolution to read history backwards. One gathers that, because the colonies declared their independence in July 1776, the revolutionary movement that emerged in the decade following the end of the French and Indian War must also have been a movement for independence. But the Revolution and independence seem to me to be two aspects of a far more chaotic and intractable reality. The events and ideas of a revolutionary decade do not, I believe, simply add up to an escalating crisis that manifestly led to an independent United States.

Another matter that interests me is that there is too much analysis of the Revolution's superstructure—ideas, principles, politics, and culture—and too little of its substructure—political economy. As for the connections and interrelations between the two, there is virtually nothing. My research suggests that not only do such connections exist, but also that they were central to the dynamics of the revolutionary movement. Specifically, in my work on *Money and Politics in America, 1755–1775: A Study in the Currency Act of 1764 and the Political Economy of Revolution,* I tried to indicate the fundamental importance of economic considerations in understanding colonial resistance to imperial policies in the 1760s and 1770s. In addition, I noted the existence of a direct conflict of interest between the British and American political nations, which helps explain the American desire for independence.

More recently, in "An Economic Interpretation of the American Revolution," *William and Mary Quarterly,* 3d ser. 29 (1972): 3–32, a joint article written with my colleague, Marc Egnal, I explored further the accumulating economic pressures and policies after the middle eighteenth century that led both to important new political activity on the part of a traditional colonial elite of merchants and planters who dominated the provincial assemblies and to the active involvement of the "lower orders" in the revolutionary movement. I am currently extending this analysis of the revolutionary substructure. My present aim is to show how the contest for the protection of interests in a changing economy might have shaped the American perception of empire on the eve of independence.

Joseph Ernst (Ph.D., University of Wisconsin, 1962) teaches history at York University, Ontario, Canada.

There is nothing new about the connection between ideas and the "real" condition of life. The precise nature of this relationship remains undetermined, of course, and is probably indeterminable. Still, the question has inspired numerous speculative works and prompted modern scholars from Karl Mannheim to Clifford Geertz to try their hand at unraveling the complex ties between thought and social circumstances. Contemporary historians have also investigated this problem in various empirical studies.[1] Despite this wealth of suggestive literature, the exploration of ideas during the era of the American Revolution often has divorced thought from social reality. There seem to be several reasons for this lapse. One is the persistence of an "idealist" tradition in which thought is viewed as an autonomous construct.[2] Another is the despair, more recently expressed, of finding a rational and conscious link between the sentiments of the revolutionaries and their social experiences. Writers of this persuasion call for an examination of subjective and even unconscious tendencies that may have led to independence.[3]

More troublesome than the question of why some historians have neglected to consider the interplay of ideas and "reality" in the American Revolution is why historians who have explored this relationship arrive at such contradictory conclusions. A major difficulty seems to center on the definition and use of the concept of "Ideology." Defined broadly, Ideology refers to the general process of mediation between ideas and social circumstances. Used more narrowly, it is associated with the result of that process, with some particular set of beliefs. Whether or not this confusion might be cleared up by speaking of Ideology in one way only could be debated at length. But the dual usage is so well established that it would be pedantic to insist on a single meaning. More important is that the term be clear in context.[4] Important, too, is the recognition that ideological interpretations of the Revolution occur on at least three different levels of explanation, or abstraction. They are *Weltanschauung* (or world view), *mentality,* and *ideology* (used here in the narrow sense). In the following sketch, I shall also use this tripartite taxonomy that I find in the writings of others; but I will argue that all three levels are interrelated, and that all are necessary to an understanding of the interlacing of economic events during the Revolution and the circumstances, interests, speculations, and actions of economic classes in America.

The present paper grew out of my concern with this question of the meaning of Ideology, and with a related problem, that of political economy. It rejects, therefore, "materialism" as well as "idealism." It rejects also the subjectivist adage that "situations are real if people think so" and the belief in subjective and unconscious motivation where perception is always blurry, defective, and warped by psychological mechanisms. This essay argues that the crucial level of "reality" is that of ordinary human consciousness with all its limits and distortions; that the American Revolution was both rational and necessary; and that the outlook and actions of colonial economic classes were inextricably linked to economic change during the decade bracketed by the credit and commercial crises of 1762 and 1772. This last point, the association of the Revolution with the decade 1762–1772, is important. In 1762 the collapse of the Atlantic economy ushered in the worst colonial economic depression to that time. The collapse in 1772 produced an even greater crisis, which, it may be argued, marked the end of the revolutionary movement.

The suggestion that historians might usefully distinguish a revolutionary movement characteristic of the years 1762–1772 from what might be called an independence movement in the years 1772–1776 rests on the belief in a shift in revolutionary consciousness and the discontinuity of events. Between 1762 and 1772 the conception of empire among colonial leaders was based upon a feeling that the British mercantile system was beneficial to the colonies as well as to the mother country; that metropolitan regulation of trade, money, and manufacturing was necessary for the well-being of all economic classes operating within the Atlantic economy; and that control by local assemblies over the remaining areas of economic concern (taxes, land, etc.) was a vital principle of colonial self-government. But the economic disorders after 1762 had their effect. The severity of trade and credit problems led the colonial elite to put aside "party" differences and to unite in the adoption of a policy of economic reform and retrenchment based on self-interest. During the debate over the means for solving these problems, the larger question arose concerning the place of the colonies within the imperial trading system and the need for greater economic sovereignty. The crisis of 1772 shattered this illusion of the possibility of reform. It became evident that the real problem was the empire itself; the periodic and increasingly disruptive credit and trade crises were too high a price for remaining within the British mercantile system.

The distinction between revolution and independence rests on another consideration: that the change in consciousness after 1772 involved several new issues. Whatever disruptions accompanied the revolutionary movement in the decade after 1763, their force was contained by the existing structures of empire. Furthermore, the sudden entry of the farmers into the fray in 1774 posed a new social and political problem. The thought of independence now had to be weighed against the likelihood of social and political upheaval.

Like any new explanation, the thesis to be explored here is tentative and subject to the findings of future scholarship. Meanwhile, it may serve to raise questions and to open areas of inquiry that others might wish to follow up. But the present essay also leans heavily on existing scholarhip, and it is useful briefly to review the literature.

I

In their discussion of the American Revolution, both the progressive and neo-Whig schools of history have probed the question of the relationship of ideas to external circumstances. The progressives disputed the older Whig view of a movement carried forward in defense of the great constitutional ideals of freedom, justice, and liberty, and offered in its place a broad if complex political and social explanation against the backdrop of economic events.[5] They evinced little interest in articulating any general theory of ideology. While some narrow "economic-determinist" thinking about the importance of ideas in politics marred the writings of Charles Beard, for the most part the progressives stood aloof from debate on theoretical propositions.[6] Rather they indulged themselves in arguing that whenever "consciousness" and "existence," ideas and realities, interact, "real" life was the determining factor.

But the progressives did credit the idea of "democracy" with a measurable effect on revolutionary events. For instance, in discussing the rise of the "lower orders" to the leadership of the revolutionary movement after 1770, Carl Becker and Arthur Schlesinger, Sr., readily identified democracy with the interests of the people (in the eighteenth century as well as in their own times), and they viewed it as a class expression of artisans, mechanics, and plain farmers.[7] Nor did the assertion that democracy played an important role die out with the first generation of progressive historians. This aspect of the work of Beard, Becker, Schlesinger, and Vernon Parrington received its most elaborate treatment in the writing of Merrill Jensen. Jensen argued cautiously that "in spite of the paradoxes involved one may still maintain that the Revolution was essentially, though relatively, a democratic movement."[8]

In short, the progressive school of historians was of two minds in dealing with ideas. From one angle, the progressives saw a cluster of ideas—the traditional Whig ideals of freedom, justice, and liberty—as subordinate to, even irrelevant to, more basic human experiences. It was the political, social, and economic imperatives of the age to which the colonists were responding, not Whig constitutional ideals. These they manipulated according to the needs of the moment. At the same time, the progressives could not escape the feeling that democracy was, if not a primary, then a "proximate" cause of a Revolution fought "not for home rule alone" but for the "democratization of American society as well."[9] To the progressives, however, democracy was not simply an idea that existed in some realm of mental constructs. Democracy was an ideology, a manifestation of deeper-seated political-economic interests and class oppression. Still, the contemporary uses of the term were never fully considered or related to other thought that was current at the time.

Ambiguity also characterizes the approach of the neo-Whig school to the problem of ideas and of Ideology. Neo-Whig scholars commonly are depicted as "idealists." Theirs, it is said, is an American Revolution seen as an "intellectual movement" wherein the colonists acted because of a set of beliefs. But it is worth noting that while all neo-Whigs hold to the importance of the intellectual origins of the Revolution, some conceive of ideas as essentially autonomous. Others share with the progressive defenders of democracy a notion that ideas have some connection with social circumstance. And at least one neo-Whig, Edmund Morgan, has attempted to sustain both conceptions. Morgan's dilemma is both interesting and instructive.[10]

In *The Stamp Act Crisis,* coauthored by Edmund and Helen Morgan, the colonists are depicted as coming together in 1765 on the common ground of constitutional rights. Acknowledging Parliament's authority over the empire as a whole, they nonetheless steadfastly denied its right to tax them, a position they continued to hold until 1776 when they "stood Bluff." This time when England refused to back down, they fought. In short, the Morgans affirmed that values shaped behavior. Americans were moved to revolutionary action primarily by abstract ideals.[11]

In discovering a dogged adherence by patriotic Americans to fundamental principles in the critical years of 1765 and 1766, the Morgans threatened to reduce the revolutionary movement to a static and conservative defense of existing ideals and traditions. The notion of a revolution charged with transforming qualities, with a significance that outlived the event itself, appeared about to be swept aside in the effort to discount social conflict, the play of economic forces, political interests, and indeed any of those issues that distinguished the writings of the progressives. A few years later, Edmund Morgan shifted his position and explicitly rejected the autonomy of ideas after 1765 in favor of quite a different intellectual explanation.

Morgan's *The Birth of the Republic* was a popular and polemical work. Reviewers had little trouble in recognizing its anti-progressive and specifically anti-Beardian tones. Less obvious was the fact that the author now found that the patriot leaders had surrendered themselves to a developing awareness of a zeitgeist: the principle of "human equality." Not traditions, not the disembodied abstractions of political and constitutional theories, but the processes of revolution itself had shaped consciousness; and not simply shaped consciousness, but radicalized it. While clinging to old ways, the patriots now appeared to Morgan actually to be moving away from them. The entire course of their resistance to Parliament after the repeal of the Stamp Act led them to embrace the new, radical, and transforming doctrine of the equality of rights, a doctrine "still reverberating among us."[12]

Whatever his intentions, Morgan's insistence that men of action, not beliefs, shaped revolutionary consciousness invoked an alternative view of the play of ideas in history. This view had little in common with simple idealism. Ideas were now looked upon as the result of the interpenetration of historical awareness, or the thoughts and theorizing of the revolutionaries, and the actions of the period. Yet a glaring deficiency remained. Despite his new emphasis on active men, Morgan offered no clear-cut explanation of the basis of action. The links between the concrete social, political, and economic realities of the day were not made clear. Moreover, Morgan had reduced causation to a "mono-causal" emphasis on the equality of rights at a time when the literature describing the mental world of eighteenth-century Americans was beginning to reveal a landscape of great complexity.[13] It was left to writers like Bernard Bailyn to attempt a sophisticated, dynamic explanation of the intellectual causes and nature of the Revolution.

In his introduction to the *Pamphlets of the American Revolution*,[14] Bailyn described an elaborate realm of ideas and perceptions which derived from the writings of radical English publicists and opposition politicians of early eighteenth-century England. As true believers in these abstractions, the colonists were propelled into revolution by the fear engendered by such ideas, the fear of conspiracy directed against colonial liberty and nourished by the corruption of the British political nation. Herein lay the origins of that swirl of ideas, pressures, and constraints that Bailyn found at the center of the Revolution. At first glance this interpretation of the critical role of subjective, dynamic elements appears idealistic. The perceptions and anxieties of the revolutionaries have few ties with social circumstances—at least they did not in the decade after 1763.

In his more recent work, *The Origins of American Politics*, Bailyn made his thesis more attractive by establishing a structural foundation for his system of revolutionary political thought. In this work, Commonwealth ideas are rooted in the political environment of colonial America: "For political life in America, while similar to England's in important respects, was yet significantly different in ways that would give a heightened meaning and a sharper relevance to—would make more obvious, more vital, and more necessary—the libertarian doctrines of coffeehouse radicals and the rancor of the anti-'Robinarchs'."[15] These Commonwealth doctrines are said to have exerted great force in the colonial political arena long after they had lost much of their vigor back home. And it was these ideas that the colonists conjured up to describe and to judge their world and their actions at the time of the Revolution.

In short, Bailyn's interpretation of the ideological nature of the American Revolution comprises two contrasting parts. First, Bailyn does not hold an "idealist" view of ideas; rather there is the assertion of a relationship between subjective and objective, rational and irrational, elements in the formation of a colonial political ideology. Early in the eighteenth century, according to his argument, a body of political beliefs began to find acceptance in America because these beliefs seemed to offer an accurate rendering of the realities of colonial political life. Second, Bailyn suggests that the elaborations upon these doctrines (as well as the changes in them) that took place after 1763 were no longer determined by objective links between ideas and "real" life. Rather the dialectical process was located in the subjective. Fears of British tyranny and corruption seemed everywhere to be confirmed by events which were misconceived; hence these fears only called forth new and more advanced ideas, and caused further misconception. In the end, this explosive and increasingly irrational outlook drove Americans to independence.

Scholars have rightly taken issue with Bailyn's reasoning. Some critics have pointed out that his insistence on the primacy of Commonwealth ideas denies a causative role to other political beliefs current at the time, such as the familiar concerns about parliamentary rights and privileges.[16] Others have argued that Bailyn overlooks the fact that beliefs about such abstract notions as "power," "virtue," "tyranny," and "corruption," concepts central to Commonwealth thinking, were susceptible to a variety of interpretations.[17]

But Bailyn's thesis also leaves unanswered a more important question: Which Americans, or groups of Americans, subscribe to which interpretations, and why? Bailyn's failure to deal with this problem means that not only varying political beliefs and feelings but also personal motives, group interests, class values, and disruptive social change[18] are subsumed by this all-encompassing Commonwealth view. Like any widely spread set of ideas, the Commonwealth tradition is useless in explaining differences in conduct, and Bailyn's assumption that it provided the basis of ordinary discourse about politics results in a too-simplistic consensus view of colonial behavior.[19] It is not surprising that in his most recent comments on the Revolution Bailyn continues to reject economic discontent or conflict as a cause of crisis.[20]

In sum, both the progressive and neo-Whig discussions of the relation of thought to "reality" in the era of the American Revolution have serious shortcomings. Some of the difficulty can be ascribed to conceptual crudeness and to polemical writing. Much is inherent in the two approaches to ideas. While the progressives tended to dismiss the Whig ideals of freedom, liberty, and justice as rationalizations or propaganda, they took more seriously the ideology of democracy, a belief they associated with the specific interests of the artisan and mechanic classes. But even here they failed to undertake a serious investigation of the term and to spell out its many uses and definitions. Many of the neo-Whigs, on the other hand, thought of ideas in the Revolution as composing an independent and elaborate realm of mental constructs to be comprehended only after careful scrutiny and subtle reading. And when, as in the case of Morgan or Bailyn, they considered the possiblity of a dialectical tension between thought and experience, they handled the matter on a highly abstracted and homogenized plane.

Another modern school of interpretation, the New Left, has also had its difficulties with the concept of Ideology.[21] One tendency of these scholars—William Appleman Williams, for example—is to discuss economic beliefs on the same high level of abstraction employed by Bailyn in his treatment of political beliefs, that of Weltanschauung. Studies on this level of interaction between such grand ideas as "mercantilism" and external reality show that Americans were at least as anxious about theories of empire and economic exploitation by the mother country as they were concerned with political views and the question of the corrupting influence of the English government. But precisely because Weltanschauung as a tool of analysis "cuts across and subsumes personal motives, group interests, and class ideologies," as Williams puts it, these works remain of limited use in examining the dynamic connections between a changing economy and revolutionary behavior and ideas.[22] Williams, for instance, simply ignores the changes in the Atlantic economy after the middle-eighteenth century and their impact on planters, merchants, mechanics, and farmers. Moreover, shifts in world view of such large ideas as "mercantilism" normally occur at a snail's pace and are unaffected by specific crises such as the economic collapses in 1762 and 1772. Therefore this ideological model seems not useful in explaining so brief a period of history as that traced by the American Revolution.[23]

Another conceptual level of explanation that has caused difficulties among New Left scholars is mentality. Mentality may be said to encompass those attitudes, aspirations, and prejudices that affect the behavior of all social groups. Like Weltanschauung, mentality also falls within the rubric of Ideology, defined in the broadest possible sense as the process of mediation between social thought and social experience. Groups engaged in common activities presumably share common interests and beliefs. Unlike Weltanschauung, mentalities are not highly abstracted theories, but the opposite. Mentality owes more to immediate feeling than to intellectualization, more to attitudes than to speculation. Consequently, historians have argued that mentality is better used to explain the behavior of the humbler and less literate classes than of the wealthy and powerful. For example, an historian like Richard Cobb, concerned with the psychosociological dimension prominent in mentality, has discovered in the habits and activities of the common people of France a state of mind that cuts across other currents of the 1789 Revolution.[24]

Students of the American Revolution, by contrast, have dealt with the concept of mentality only rarely, and then in a confused manner. The progressives, for instance, in interpreting lower-class motivation, posited a "radical" movement based on the "democratic aspirations of a denied population."[25] Yet in describing behavior, progressive historians not only failed to explain in any depth the origins of this democratic feeling, or mentality, among the lower classes, but also tended to fall back on curbstone psychology and a crude interpretation of a riotous mob manipulated by the propaganda and deceptions of both gentry and popular leaders. In their effort to rework the progressive conception of the revolutionary lower classes, recent scholars of the "lower classes" have largely abandoned mentality and a psychosociological view of popular beliefs and behavior. Scholars of such diverse views as Jesse Lemisch, Staughton Lynd, and Alfred Young rely not on the French school's explanation of popular conduct but on the English Marxist traditions of E. P. Thompson, Eric Hobsbawm, George Rudé, and Christopher Hill.[26] Here, despite their different approaches, ideas and action are securely rooted in lower- or working-class interests.

II

The following pages sketch in barest outline the interlacing of Weltanschauung, ideology, and mentality against a background of the economic events of the Revolution. It must be emphasized at the outset that economic problems and issues perceived by colonial merchants, planters, farmers, and artisans on one level of abstraction, or explanation, were often discussed and analyzed on another level—or on two levels at the same time. An example was the tendency to translate matters of self-interest into questions of common interest.[27] Self-interest as a rationale for conduct was still suspect in colonial America. Self-styled community spokesmen were likely to condemn "selfish" economic activity, as in the case of the merchant class. Social values—not economic considerations—were thought to provide the best guidelines for behavior. The public interest defined not only the end of good government but the ideal basis of the common life of the good society. On the other hand, matters of self-interest were not always and invariably elevated to the level of social ethics. The colonists, as F. Scott Fitzgerald said of another period, demonstrated a very human "ability to hold two opposed ideas in the mind at the same time, and still retain the ability to function." If "economic man" was not the social ideal, he was nonetheless a necessary and acceptable member of society. Americans then as now could be guided by market considerations without worrying too much about higher values and the loss of virtue.[28]

On the eve of the Revolution, the American Weltanschauung of empire—or of the place of the colonies in the British mercantile system —drew upon two different sources. The first was the conventional wisdom in Britain that held that the essential utility of the American colonies depended upon a monopoly of their trade, or upon their role as suppliers of raw materials and customers for finished products. This monopoly was widely defended in the name of the national or "general" interest of the mother country. For instance, Thomas Pownall, writing in 1768, could argue confidently in his work on *The Administration of the Colonies* that:

> The view of trade in general, as well as of manufactures in particular, terminates in securing an extensive and permanent vent; or to speak more precisely (in the same manner as shopkeeping does,) in having many and good customers: the wisdom, therefore, of a trading nation, is to gain, and to create, as many as possible. Those whom we gain in foreign trade we possess under restrictions and difficulties, and many lose in the rivalship of commerce: those that a trading nation can create within itself, it deals with under its own regulations, and makes its own, and cannot lose.[29]

A more succinct view of this matter was aired that same year by the Lords Commissioners for Trade and Plantations. "The great object of colonizing upon the continent of North America," the Commissioners confirmed, "has been to improve and extend the commerce, navigation, and manufacturing of this kingdom, upon which its strength and security depend."[30] And like most British commentators at the time, Pownall and the Commissioners for Trade felt that this "great object" was being thwarted by the independent-minded colonies and by imperial administrative structures that badly needed both reform and tightening up.[31]

Critics of this theory of colonial subordination formed a second British source for the American Weltanschauung of empire. The most important of these critics was Adam Smith, who expressed the misgivings of a small but growing body of anticolonialists with the terse remark that, "To found a great empire for the sole purpose of raising up a people of customers, may at first sight appear a project fit only for a nation of shopkeepers. It is, however, a project altogether unfit for a nation of shopkeepers; but extremely fit for a nation whose government is influenced by shopkeepers."[32] Proponents of the conventional wisdom, Smith felt, exhibited a noticeable tendency to confuse class interest with the national interest.

In America this Weltanschauung was compounded of the wisdom of both the Pownall and Smith version of an empire of trade. To begin with, there was the shared belief in a British "mercantile system" designed to protect and encourage the commerce and manufactures of the mother country through the creation of a system of metropolitan economic controls that would produce a favorable balance of trade with America. This economic calculus was seen to be part of the natural course of things. But if prior to the Revolution the colonists seemed ready to acquiesce in their "exploitation" and to accept their inferior role, it was because they profited from the system. Not only were they beneficiaries of a rich flow of credit, capital, and cheap manufacturers from the most rapidly developing commercial-industrial economy of the Atlantic world, they also enjoyed the security and protection of their property and lives under the umbrella of the British army and navy. Furthermore, the colonists believed that this was as it should be, and they constantly stressed the reciprocal obligation of the mother country to "nourish and cultivate, to protect and govern" her offspring.[33]

This experience of the tangible benefits of empire was the major reason for accepting the principles and practices of British regulation. In the half-century following Queen Anne's War, the colonists shared in the relatively uneven but continuous long-run development of the

Atlantic economy.[34] Not everyone in America would wax as enthusiastic as Benjamin Franklin in surveying conditions at mid-century—"What an accession of power to the British empire by sea as well as land! What increase of trade and navigation!"[35]—but all could take comfort in the fact that the empire was indeed expanding in size and prosperity, that centralized controls over shipping, commerce, and manufacturing, whatever their deficiencies, had at least not interfered with the well-being of the dominant economic classes on either side of the Atlantic.[36]

On the other hand, the colonists had also experienced the justice of Adam Smith's remarks. They knew well enough that the definitions of the economic system, like the very cloth and hardware they were buying in ever increasing amounts, were products of a commercial-industrial society, and that the interest-group demands of the British merchant and manufacturing classes lay barely hidden beneath the surface rhetoric of mercantilist theory. As the major colonial interest groups, merchants and planters in America did what they could within the institutional structures of empire to protect their property and to advance their concerns by achieving some control in the sensitive areas of land, labor, marketing, credit, and currency. The familiar struggles of the colonial assemblies for their rights and prerogatives against Crown and Parliament reflected, therefore, not merely the rise of the assemblies but also the ascent of economic leaders in America to a measure of political power and sovereignty. Whatever else it may have meant, this growth of the assemblies became the essential means of accomodating colonial interest groups to the shifting demands of a nation of mercantilists and shopkeepers.[37]

These perceptions of a relatively prosperous commercial empire in which Americans exercised a degree of control over their own economic destinies helped shape the Weltanschauung of the vast majority of colonists. And before 1763 most Americans rested content. British challenges to this conception were remarkably unsuccessful. With the Molasses Act of 1733, and again in the early 1740s, Britain did launch a number of assaults against the self-government and economic independence of the colonies. But war and the rumors of war brought about the defeat or emasculation of these initiatives, as the mother country compromised a felt need for tighter controls in the interest of enlisting American aid in her war efforts.[38]

The conclusion of the Seven Years War radically altered the situation. Collapse of the wartime economy after 1762; the sudden tightening of metropolitan controls over money and trade; the desire of the

Grenville ministry, acting on behalf of Britain's heavily-taxed squire-archy, to make the colonies pay a major share of their administration; and a renewed attack by Crown and Parliament against American autonomy raised anew the question of the place of the colonies within the empire. In word and deed, Americans began to challenge the structures and policies of imperial control. Is it fair? Is it reasonable? These were the queries raised with growing frequency following the Treaty of Paris.

The basic changes in the Atlantic economy after the middle of the eighteenth century that affected the outlook of the colonial economic classes during the revolutionary decade, 1762–1772, may usefully be discussed on the level of ideology. Shifts in ideology can then be viewed as responses to changing conditions, responses that took the form of short-run solutions and immediate programs for relief—as well as some longer-term reforms—and that drew support from the various economic classes according to their interests. This ideology of relief and reform, and the programs inspired by it, at first fell within the general framework of the existing mercantile system. Ultimately it altered the colonial Weltanschauung of empire.

A surge in British exports to the American colonies after mid-century paralleled the rapid growth of the British economy and was made possible in large part by an accompanying expansion of credit. British suppliers helped boost sales by increasing colonial credit through a number of devices. Most important were lengthening the terms and enlarging the amount of credit available to large and estab-lished merchants everywhere in America; opening a new and equally liberal line of credit to smaller and marginal merchants in the commer-cial colonies—or colonies dominated by a large urban center—; and building an extensive chain of British "stores," or credit outlets, in the Staple colonies. The predictable result of this rapid growth was an eventual glut of British goods of unprecedented proportions, a widen-ing depression, and frequent bankruptcies among colonial merchants. Only the onset of the Seven Years War and of wartime prosperity that continued through the middle of 1760 saved the colonies from further distress. But while a generally strong wartime demand helped clear the overstocked dry-goods market, it did little to resolve the larger struc-tural problems created by the expansion of commercial credit.[39]

A major problem of this kind in the Staple colonies concerned the currency system, and it quickly touched off a bitter ideological contro-versy over paper money as a cure for the many economic ills that afflicted the colonial economy. One of the difficulties lay in the fact that the sharp rise in British credit shipments to the southern colonies after mid-century narrowed trade balances with the mother country. Short-run abatements in credit flows or a decline in the price of staple tobacco effectively raised the cost of sterling bills of exchange and lowered the value of British assets in the colonies. These relationships were not well understood at the time. Thus at the beginning of the Seven Years War, when exchange rates in Virginia spiraled upwards, British merchant-creditors and Scottish factors falsely attributed the condition to the newly-created paper currency system.[40]

This view of paper money as a defective and disruptive medium of exchange was held by most British leaders in trade and politics.[41] American attitudes were not very different. The planting and trading classes of the South also preferred specie to paper.[42] Still, it must be understood that the debate over the uses and abuses of paper money in America did not center on matters of principle but on conflicts over interest. In the absence of an adequate supply of specie, and in the face of an increasing demand for a source of military funds, Virginia, for instance, like many another colony at an earlier time, reluctantly and belatedly turned to a system of "currency finance" in the spring of 1755. Within a few years, continuing wartime appropriations boosted the volume of paper in circulation to the point where it played a major role in meeting local transaction and liquidity demands for money. By the late 1750s the controversy in Virginia revolved around the apparent usefulness of paper in meeting these monetary demands of the planter class. Thereafter, the ideology of interest prompted the planter-dominated assembly to rebuff vigorously attempts by British creditors working through the Board of Trade either to eliminate or otherwise to assert effective control over Virginia's currency system.[43]

The intent of the British merchants was to lower sterling exchange rates in order to defend their property and profits. The manipulation of the currency by the planters was similarly motivated. That the planter class should have identified its needs with the interest of the country in the ensuing struggle—as in the nicely honed remarks of the Virginia Committee of Correspondence in the summer of 1764: "Our only Solicitude proceeded from an Apprehension, that the overbearing Dispositions of the Merchants might have had weight enough to effect their purpose, which would inevitably have involved the Country in the greatest Difficulties and Distresses"—was only to be expected.[44]

The heavy inflow of commercial credit in the decade after King George's War was not restricted to the Staple colonies, however, and there was a rapid expansion of the credit system to every part of colonial America. With classes in all regions thereby increasingly exposed to the play of market forces, Americans everywhere became more vulnerable to economic change. One example is the financial and credit crisis of 1762–1764, whose devastating effects John Dickinson so accurately characterized. "Trade is decaying," Dickinson observed in his famous pamphlet on economic affairs, *The Late Regulations*, published late in 1765: "All credit is expiring. Money is become so extremely scarce, that reputable freeholders find it impossible to pay debts which are trifling in comparison to their estates. If creditors sue and take out executions, the lands and personal estates, as the sale must be for ready money, are sold for a small part of what they are worth when the debts were contracted. The debtors are ruined. The creditors get but part of their debts, and that ruins them. Thus the consumers break the shopkeepers; they break the merchants; and the shock must be felt as far as London."[45]

Preoccupied with "visible" money, past historians have tended to treat this widespread cry of a scarcity of money, alluded to by Dickinson, as a simple reflex to the rapid contraction of paper notes following passage of the Currency Act of 1764. But contrary to the view long held by most scholars, the difficulty following the credit crisis of 1762–1765 was the contraction of the *total* money supply. In part, this meant paper, coin, and other forms of "visible" money in America. Far more importantly, it meant the contraction of book credit, or credit in the form of debt carried on the ledgers or books of colonial merchants.[46] In a credit squeeze, paper money promised a "solution." To all classes in the commercial colonies—merchants, farmers, artisans—it seemed a useful source of liquidity and an alternative source of "loans." It held out the same advantages to the embattled planter-debtors in the Staple colonies. Even Virginia's merchants came to look with a less jaundiced eye on paper money as they, too, began to balance out their need for liquidity, credit, and a medium of local exchange against expected losses from shifts in the sterling exchange rate. Likewise many of the British merchants responsible for passage of the Currency Act of 1764 in the first place felt that whatever its deficiencies paper money helped to facilitate their American sales and to repatriate their assets. In the years after 1764 they actively united their interest with the interests of all economic groups in America to repeal or revise the Currency Act. It was only a short while before the Act was repealed.[47]

However complicated the credit problem became after mid-century, and however great the political force exerted in efforts at currency manipulation designed to ease this problem, new infusions of paper money did not seem to be "the sovereign remedy" after all for the many economic ailments plaguing colonial interests throughout the 1760s. Economic and political leaders in America soon turned to other specifics.

In the ideological debate over proper treatment for a weakened economy during the early years of the revolutionary movement, another "popular" remedy was redressing the balance of trade. The colonies would be expected to buy less and sell more. Every remedy had its advocate, and newspaper writers went to a great length to advertise the respective benefits of their favorite cure. Apologists for a balance of trade solution tended to develop and use in combination two lines of argument. The first was economic. It dwelled on familiar mercantilist propositions concerning the good effects of retrenchment and a favorable trade balance on fluctuating exchange rates, the glut of British goods in American markets, the swelling volume of colonial debt, and the growing threat of a "general bankruptcy." Broadly speaking, the second was moral. It, too, represented a reworking of traditional and accepted principles, in this case Puritan and Republican, concerning the personal evil and public immorality of excessive spending and avidity. Industry and frugality were deemed the only suitable virtues for the American farmer and artisan to practice. As for avarice, it was a vice of the merchants who, "actuated by selfish views and motives," seemed more unwilling than most to sacrifice "private interest and emolument to that of the public."[48]

Proposals for best achieving this favorable balance of trade varied. They ranged from liberalizing British trade laws, encouraging production of raw materials for sale to Britain, nonimportation, nonconsumption and local manufacturing in the commerical colonies to economic diversification, urban development, and cooperative stores in the Staple colonies. Because they appealed to the short-run as well as the long-run interests of many of the colonial economic classes, these were popular policies. For example, merchants threatened by a mounting flood of British goods and anxious to sell off inventories at good prices, clear debts, catch up on remittances, and generally straighten out finances found nonimportation much to their liking. "You will have a good price for all your dead goods which have always been unprofitable," a supporter of nonimportation, writing in the *Pennsylvania Gazette* in November 1767, reminded merchants: "You will collect your debts and bring your debts in England to a close, so that balances would hereby be brought about in your favour, which without some such method would forever be against you."[49] In addition, nonimportation offered established merchants a way of eliminating shopkeepers who, in increasing numbers, were being set up in the import trade by enterprising British firms interested in expanding their colonial business.[50]

Merchants in the commercial colonies were also among the strongest proponents of plans for production of raw materials for the British market and the encouragement of local manufactures. These were sound policies, and they mirrored an actual economic trend. Exports of commodities and manufactures from New York to Britain, for instance, rose 30 percent between 1752 and 1767. Meanwhile, falling profits among dry-goods merchants helped stimulate investment in such domestic colonial industries as hats, shoes, finished ironware, and furniture, which openly competed with British imports in both North America and the West Indies.[51]

Merchants and those artisans who competed with imported goods normally made natural enemies. American merchants served as the advance agents of the British manufacturing and mercantile firms that supplied—and oversupplied—the colonies with a growing stream of relatively cheap finished wares sold on favorable credit terms. Accordingly, the colonial artisans worked their way into a tight market in whatever way possible. Seldom able to undersell their rivals, local artisans counted on superior craftsmanship and their ability to offer extra services to win them customers. But the going was rough. Stephen Paschall, for instance, advertised in the *Pennsylvania Gazette,* in June 1770, that some Philadelphia merchants had "for these five or six years past, imported from Great Britain large quantities of sickles, stamped *S. Paschal,* in imitation (as I apprehend) of my stamp, which is *S. Paschall,* and in the credit thereof have sold great quantities." "The workmanship," he emphasized, "is by no means equal."[52]

This enmity between merchants and such mechanics was temporarily set aside during the business slump in 1765–1766, and again in 1768–1769. Policies like nonimportation and domestic manufacturing not only helped artisans meet the competition of British goods in local markets, but also helped merchants dispose of their surplus stocks.

Self-interest, not constitutional principle, brought the merchants and mechanics together in a common cause. And interest, not abstract principle, also separated them again. Consequently, nonconsumption of British goods received full support from the mechanics, and virtually none from the merchant classes. And when a majority of merchants, having sold off their inventory, moved to abandon nonimportation in 1770, artisans in Philadelphia quickly called a meeting of "Artificers, Manufacturers, Tradesmen, Mechanics, and others" to advertise their position and to help keep the merchants in line. Even after the merchants successfully rescinded their nonimportation agreements, Philadelphia's artisan community refused to accept defeat. After holding another meeting, spokesmen for the community called upon all citizens to boycott the offending merchants and to reinforce efforts at domestic manufacturing. "The protection of the American market and the promotion of home manufactures had clearly emerged as a cardinal article of artisan economic thinking."[53]

But the difficulty of securing a home market for their products was not simply, or even fundamentally, a matter of the mechanics' relationship with the merchants. The promotion of American manufacturers ran counter to the very intent of the British mercantile system, and it was this question that in the end both mechanics and merchants had to look at. "It is sincerely to be lamented," remarked an anonymous correspondent to the readers of the *Pennsylvania Gazette* in the summer of 1771, "that the mechanic arts and manufactures cannot be encouraged by our Legislature with the same Propriety that they promote the liberal Arts and Sciences; but it happens somehow, that our Mother Country apprehends she has a right to manufacture every article we consume, except Bread and Meat." In these circumstances, the writer continued, "it cannot be doubted, that she would take great and insuperable offense at any Colony Legislature that should attempt to encourage domestic manufactures; . . . were it not for this impediment, we might expect to see the mechanic Arts soon arrive at great Perfection in this Province."[54]

In the Staple colonies, as I have argued elsewhere,[55] the various policies for redressing trade balances also met the immediate needs of economic classes to contract their British purchases and achieve liquidity. And, by the late 1760s, these efforts at retrenchment in both commercial and Staple colonies seemed to have some positive results. Trade stratagems adopted after 1763, plus an upturn in the Atlantic economy in the late 1760s, eased the most pressing of the economic problems.[56] But fundamental questions of Weltanschauung and ideology concerning the enduring ability of Britain's trading empire to satisfy the needs and ambitions of economic classes in America had been raised and continued to be raised.

Many of the same fundamental changes in the Atlantic economy after the middle eighteenth century that affected the ideology of Americans may also be said to have affected their mentality. Mentality is the most difficult of the three ideological concepts to deal with. If social and political historians have barely begun to explore this problem in their area of the Revolution, it must be admitted that students of political economy have ignored the matter altogether. It is impossible, then, to do much more than to suggest some ways of looking at the issue.

The urban lower classes in the Revolution—the artisans, mechanics, and day laborers that made up the bulk of the population of the major colonial ports—have often been cited, sometimes favorably, more recently less favorably, for their violent behavior during the Stamp Act and Townshend Act crises. Yet their passionate response at such moments, like their antipathy to wealth and privilege on both sides of the Atlantic, might be explained otherwise than as irrationality or, more commonly, as an emerging class consciousness. That such a consciousness did arise out of involvement in programs of nonconsumption, nonimportation, and domestic manufacturing seems plain, and goes a long way in explaining their desire to strike out against those forces and individuals who exploited them. But might not questions of interest be overlaid with other pressing fears among the lower classes, fears of a darker reality of poverty, hunger, and unemployment? This question of the mentality of the urban poor, the jobless, and the hungry in the Revolution clearly needs to be distinguished from the problem of the ideology of the mechanic and laboring classes.

At issue here are two related considerations: the stratification or layering of colonial society along economic lines, and the impact of economic change on social stratification.[57] Economic classes, as sociologists use that term today, not only existed in colonial America but also were recognized as such by contemporaries. These subdivisions of society were usually called "ranks" or "orders," although the word "class" was sometimes used. Contemporaries handled the concept of economic class in two different ways. One way was to define class according to occupation. Thus mechanic or artisan was a term for a group of men whose function in the economy set them apart from other occupational classes, like merchants and farmers, and gave them, it appeared, a separate identity, interest, and ideology. A second and more obvious way was to rank men according to their wealth.

In an age intensely concerned with the connection between property and social position, wealth, not occupation, was the most important economic class distinction. To be sure, the more desirable form of wealth was land, and in the colonies, as in England, a rich man was careful to establish his mark as a gentleman through land ownership. In the northern cities land was less important a measure of social standing, naturally, than was mercantile wealth. Mechanics, therefore, ordinarily found themselves relegated to the "middling ranks," as they were called, although mechanics "of the poorer sort" could easily become members of the so-called lower orders. But wherever their share in the distribution of wealth placed them in the social scale, the laboring classes of the cities at least had a stake and a role in a society which took for granted some sharing of power and authority among men of different social positions and economic standing. Poverty and unemployment cut across these economic and social lines based on occupation and the division of wealth. It threw a mechanic into the ranks of the "propertyless rabble," whose very existence was perceived as a threat to good order and social stability. It also altered one's outlook on things, and one's actions.

The second consideration concerning the question of the mentality of the urban poor, the jobless, and the hungry is the impact of economic change on social stratification and division in the Revolution. The relatively few studies of colonial economic development suggest that by the middle-eighteenth century long-run patterns of secular growth in America had already laid the basis for the emergence of a relatively complex commercial-agricultural society. In the process, colonial ports like Philadelphia drew frequent comments from English travelers about their likeness to the great English cities. But if the growth and rising opulence of American cities fascinated contemporary visitors, it was the more disturbing reality of widespread unemployment and poverty that excited the inhabitants, especially during the 1760s when members of the urban lower class suffered grievously from the added burdens of short-run economic disorders.[58]

As British and southern European demands for American wheat, bread, and flour rapidly escalated after 1765, article after article appeared in the colonial newspapers decrying the plight of the urban poor. A writer in New York, in late 1766, for example, echoed a familiar cry about farmers becoming rich at the expense of the poor. In New York the price of food was too much for the poor, and "to call upon the charity of the rich and affluent, is disagreeable to many of the most deserving, and in general but a cold comfort. In the present state of things here, scarce any but of opulent fortune can keep up with the world." More desperate was a Philadelphian who remarked on the condition of the poor of his city early in 1767: "One half of the world are ignorant how the other half lives...while the slightest incoveniences of the great are magnified into calamities, while tragedy mouths out their sufferings in all the strains of eloquence, the miseries of the poor are disregarded; and yet some of the lower rank of people undergo more real hardships in one day than those of a more exalted station suffer in their whole lives." More direct were the queries in 1767 of another New Yorker, a "tradesman": "Are our circumstances altered? Is money grown more plenty? Have our tradesmen full employment? Is grain cheaper?" Nor is this darker perception of things confined solely to a few contemporary observers of the urban scene; recent scholarship has also begun to reveal a growing specialization of economic function and an accompanying increase of social stratification, joblessness, and poverty.[59]

In sum, the ideology of the artisan should not be confused with the mentality of the "lower orders." Doubtless the lower the social strata and the greater the economic hardship in the colonial cities, the more likely the appearance of a mentality of rising hatred directed against wealth and privilege on both sides of the Atlantic. But unlike the ideology of the colonial economic classes, which fueled the revolutionary movement for economic reform and relief in the decade after 1762, the mentality of popular protest against poverty, hunger, and unemployment appears to have been counterproductive. If the economic elite in America disliked the politicizing of the mechanic and laboring classes and the demands of these classes for the further democratization of colonial society during the Revolution, they did not fear the ideology of class interest. Here, as has been shown, an alliance, or at least accommodation, was possible. What the elite feared was social disorder of a propertyless rabble.

Colonial expectations of continuing growth and prosperity following the successful conclusion of the French and Indian War were an exciting vision. The economic crisis in 1762 did not destroy it. Most

Americans believed that the postwar depression was a temporary disorder, that the British mercantile system was essentially sound, and that centralized metropolitan control over colonial money, trade, and manufacturing was a practical necessity. But, as the depression deepened and lengthened, the colonial economic classes felt a need for a program of relief and reform aimed at easing trade and credit pressures, and at convincing the British political nation to replace economic legislation like the Revenue and Currency Acts with new and enlightened measures more suitable to the realities of economic conditions in America. It was this ideological concern with economic realities that gave rise to a passionate debate, largely carried on in the colonial newspapers, about the best means to remedy the situation and to serve American interest. The favored cures—an increase of colonial currency and credit and the adoption of a program of retrenchment associated with the boycott of British goods—may not have worked as well as the colonists expected, but what the colonists said and did about their economic problems provided the essential impetus for what is commonly called the "revolutionary movement." Nonimportation was, after all, the chief means of protest against excessive importation of British goods at the time of both the Stamp Act and the Townshend Acts.

It was predictable that during the course of the long debate over the most suitable means for solving their problems, the Americans should reconsider the larger question of the place of the colonies within the empire, and of the need for a greater degree of economic sovereignty. Predictable, too, was the fact that men like Christopher Gadsden and Benjamin Franklin, who had already begun to doubt the desirability of metropolitan control of American economy in the mid-1760s, found it easier to get a hearing for their views.[60] Still, it was not until the final collapse of the economy in 1772 that American leaders generally discussed not the long-run benefits of empire as against immediate need for practical reform but the possibility of having to break with imperial economic and political structures altogether in the effort to protect colonial interests. The ideological debate arising out of that situation has yet fully to be described and analyzed.

The author wishes to thank his colleague Marc Egnal for his critical reading of the present article and his useful suggestions on points of analysis. He also wishes to thank The American Council of Learned Societies for financial assistance.

1. See, for example, Karl Mannheim, *Ideology and Utopia, An Introduction to the Sociology of Knowledge* (New York: Harcourt, Brace & World, 1936); Clifford Geertz, "Ideology as a Cultural System," in David E. Apter, ed., *Ideology and Discontent* (Glencoe, Ill.; Free Press, 1964), pp. 47–76; and Norman Birnbaum, "The Sociological Study of Ideology (1940–60): A Trend Report and Bibliography," *Current Sociology* 9 (1960): 91–172.

2. See the analysis of this difficulty by Gordon S. Wood, "Rhetoric and Reality in the American Revolution," *William and Mary Quarterly*, 3d ser. 23 (1966): 3–32.

3. Robert E. Shalhope, "Towards a Republican Synthesis: The Emergence of an Understanding of Republicanism in American Historiography," *William and Mary Quarterly*, 3d ser. 29 (1972): 79.

4. I shall employ the simple device of using Ideology with a capital "I" when referring to the process and ideology with a small "i" when referring to some particular result of the process.

5. For a more extensive analysis of the progressive viewpoint, see Marc Egnal and Joseph A. Ernst, "An Economic Interpretation of the American Revolution," *William and Mary Quarterly*, 3d ser. 29 (1972): 3–36.

6. The best essay on Beard remains Lee Benson, *Turner and Beard, American Historical Writing Reconsidered* (Glencoe, Ill.: Free Press, 1960), pp. 95–233.

7. Carl L. Becker, *The History of Political Parties in the Province of New York, 1760–1776* (Madison: University of Wisconsin Press, 1909), and Arthur M. Schlesinger, Sr., *The Colonial Merchants and the American Revolution 1763–1776* (New York: Columbia University Press, 1917). For an interesting and recent discussion of this problem, see Bernard Friedman, "Shaping of the Radical Consciousness in Provincial New York," *Journal of American History* 56 (1970): 781–881.

8. The quote is from "Democracy and the American Revolution," *Huntington Library Quarterly* 20 (1957): 321, where Jensen elaborates on a point made in a reprint of *The Articles of Confederation: An Interpretation of the Social-Constitutional History of the American Revolution, 1774–1781* (Madison: University of Wisconsin Press, 1948) p. 15. Cf. Jensen, "The American People and the American Revolution," *Journal of American History* 57 (1970): 5–35.

9. Carl L. Becker, *Beginnings of the American People* (Cambridge, Mass.: Houghton Mifflin, 1915), p. 240.

10. The following analysis of the neo-Whigs is drawn from my review-essay, "Ideology and the Political Economy of Revolution," *Canadian Review of American Studies* 4 (1973): 137–48.

11. Edmund S. and Helen M. Morgan, *The Stamp Act Crisis, Prologue to Revolution* (Chapel Hill: University of North Carolina Press, 1953).

12. Edmund S. Morgan, *The Birth of the Republic, 1763–1789* (Chicago: University of Chicago Press, 1956), p. 67. David S. Lovejoy, a Morgan student, attempts to work out this idea in *Rhode Island Politics and the American Revolution, 1760–1776* (Providence: Brown University Press, 1958).

13. Shalhope, "Toward a Republican Synthesis," pp. 60–71.

14. Bernard G. Bailyn, *Pamphlets of the American Revolution 1750–1773*, vol. 1 (Cambridge: Harvard University Press, Belknap Press, 1965).

15. Bernard G. Bailyn, *Origins of American Politics* (New York: Random House, Vintage Books, 1967), p. 58.

16. See Jack P. Greene, "Political Nemesis: A Consideration of the Historical and Cultural Roots of Legislative Behavior in the British Colonies in the Eighteenth Century," "A Comment" by Bailyn, and a "Reply" by Greene in *American Historical Review* 75 (1969–1970): 337–67; and J. G. A. Pocock, "Virtue and Commerce in the Eighteenth Century," *Journal of Interdisciplinary History* 3 (1972): 119–34.

17. See, for example, Shalhope, "Toward a Republican Synthesis," pp. 65–80, and John Howe, Jr., "Republican Thought and the Political Violence of the 1790s," *American Quarterly* 19 (1967): 147–65.

18. On the question of social change and the Revolution, see Jack P. Greene, "The Social Origins of the American Revolution," *Political Science Quarterly* 88 (1973): 1–22; Kenneth A. Lockridge, "Social Change and the Meaning of the American Revolution," *Journal of Social History* 6 (1973): 403–39; Thomas A. Archdeacon and Maris A. Vinovskis,

"Ideology and Social Structure in the Coming of the American Revolution: A Critique of the Bailyn Thesis," paper presented at the meeting of the Organization of American Historians, Denver, Colorado, April 1974.

19. Alfred Young has made this point in a comment, "The Bailyn Thesis and the Problem of 'Popular' Ideology," delivered at the meeting of the Organization of American Historians, Denver, Colorado, April 1974.

20. See Bailyn, "The Central Themes of the American Revolution, An Interpretation," in *Essays on the American Revolution* (Chapel Hill: University of North Carolina Press, 1973), and the comments in Ernst, "Ideology and the Political Economy of Revolution," p. 141.

21. A useful bibliography and introduction to some of the concerns and special insights of the New Left school may be found in Jesse Lemisch and John K. Alexander, "The White Oaks, Jack Tar, and the Concept of the Inarticulate," *William and Mary Quarterly*, 3d ser. 19 (1972): 109–134.

22. William Appleman Williams, *The Contours of American History* (Cleveland: World Publishing Co., 1961), p. 20.

23. See William A. Williams, "The Age of Mercantilism: An Interpretation of the American Political Economy, 1763–1828," *William and Mary Quarterly* 15 (1958): 419–37, and "Samuel Adams: Calvinist, Mercantilist, Revolutionary," *Studies on the Left* 2 (1960). See also Egnal and Ernst, "Economic Interpretation of the Revolution," pp. 11–28.

24. See Richard Cobb, *The Police and the People; French Popular Protest, 1789–1820* (Oxford: Oxford University Press, 1970), and *Reactions to the French Revolution* (London, Oxford University Press, 1972).

25. See the discussion by Friedman, "Shaping of Radical Consciousness," pp. 781–801. For a discussion of the "mob" in more recent works, see Edward Countryman, "The Problem of the Early American Crowd," *Journal of American Studies* 7 (1973): 77–90.

26. Cf. 22 n. above and the interesting discussion of this kind of history in E. J. Hobsbawn, "From Social History to the History of Society," *Daedalus* 100 (1971): 20–45.

27. See the discussion of this point in J. E. Crowley, *This Sheba Self: The Conceptualization of Economic Life in Eighteenth-Century America* (Baltimore: Johns Hopkins University Press, 1974).

28. Crowley, *This Sheba Self*, chap. 1.

29. Thomas Pownall, *The Administration of the Colonies*, 4th ed. (London, printed for J. Walter, 1768), p. 38. The best general discussion of contemporary British views of the colonies is Klauss Knorr, *British Colonial Theories, 1570–1850* (Toronto: University of Toronto Press, 1944); see also Richard Koebner, *Empire* (London: Cambridge University Press, 1961). The best discussion of the colonial view of empire is James Louis Cooper, "Interests, Ideas and Empires: The Roots of American Foreign Policy, 1763–1779" (Ph.D. diss., University of Wisconsin, 1964), chaps. 1–7.

30. John Bigelow, ed., *Complete Works of Benjamin Franklin*, vol. 5 (New York: G. P. Putnam's Sons, 1887), p. 414.

31. See the discussion by J. M. Bumsted, " 'Things in the Womb of Time': Ideas of American Independence, 1633 to 1763," *William and Mary Quarterly*, 3d ser. 31 (1974): 533–64.

32. Adam Smith, *An Inquiry into the Nature and Causes of the Wealth of Nations*, xx, Edwin Cannan, ed., (New York: Modern Library, 1937), p. 579. For a discussion of the "Anti-colonialists," see Knorr, *British Colonial Theories*.

33. See Joseph A. Ernst, *Money and Politics in America 1755–1775, A Study in the Currency Act of 1764 and the Political Economy of Revolution* (Chapel Hill: University of North Carolina Press, 1973), pp. 18–19ff.

34. See Egnal and Ernst, "Economic Interpretation of the American Revolution," pp. 11–28. An extended discussion of the subject appears in Marc Egnal, "The Economic Development of the Thirteen Continental Colonies, 1720 to 1775," *William and Mary Quarterly*, 3d ser. 32 (1975): 191–222.

35. "Observations concerning the Increase of Mankind, Peopling of Countries, etc.," in Leonard W. Labaree, ed., *The Papers of Benjamin Franklin*, vol. 4 (New Haven: Yale University Press, 1961), p. 233.

36. See 34 n. above and the essay in this book by Gary Nash for a discussion of the impact of economic growth on other economic classes at the time.

37. On this point compare, for instance, Jack P. Greene's essentially institutional history of the rise of the assemblies, *The Quest for Power: The Lower Houses of Assembly in the Southern Royal Colonies 1689–1776* (Chapel Hill: University of North Carolina Press, 1963), with John M. Hemphill's, "Virginia and the English Commercial System, 1689–1733: Studies in the Development and Fluctuations of a Colonial Economy under Imperial Control" (Ph.D. diss., Princeton University, 1964).

38. Ernst, *Money and Politics*, pp. 32–39.

39. For an extended discussion of these matters, see Egnal and Ernst, "Economic Interpretation of the American Revolution," pp. 15–16 and Ernst, *Money and Politics*, chap. 3.

40. See Ernst, *Money and Politics*, chap. 3.

41. See Ernst, *Money and Politics*, chaps. 2 and 3.

42. See Ernst, *Money and Politics*, pp. 86–87.

43. See Ernst, *Money and Politics*, chap. 3.

44. Quoted in Ernst, *Money and Politics*, pp. 86–87.

45. Paul Leicester Ford, ed., *The Writings of John Dickinson* (Philadelphia: Historical Society of Pennsylvania, 1895), pp. 227–28.

46. See the discussion of this in Egnal and Ernst, "Economic Interpretation of the Revolution," pp. 17–19, 24–27, and in Ernst, *Money and Politics*, chap. 1.

47. See Ernst, *Money and Politics*, chaps. 4–8.

48. This moral argument is discussed in Crowley, *This Sheba Self*, especially in pp. 125–46, and Edmund S. Morgan, "The Puritan Ethic and the American Revolution," *William and Mary Quarterly*, 3d ser. 24 (1967): 3–43. See especially the older and suggestive discussion by Jacob Viner, *Studies in the Theory of International Trade* (New York: Harper & Bros., 1937), pp. 26–30, which makes explicit the connection between the moral and economic dimensions. The quote is from the *New-York Journal or General Advertiser*, 24 December 1767.

49. Quoted in Egnal and Ernst, "Economic Interpretation of the American Revolution," p. 21.

50. See the discussion in Egnal and Ernst, "Economic Interpretation of the American Revolution," pp. 21–23.

51. William S. Sachs, "The Business Outlook in the Northern Colonies, 1750–1775" (Ph.D. diss., Columbia University, 1957), p. 81, and Egnal and Ernst, "Economic Interpretation of the American Revolution," pp. 19–20.

52. The quote is from Charles S. Olton, "Philadelphia Artisans and the American Revolution" (Ph.D. diss, University of California, Berkeley, 1969), chap. 2, p. 37. See also the general discussion of these points in ibid., chap. 2.

53. The quote is from Olton, "Philadelphia Artisans," chap. 2, p. 64. See also the general discussion in ibid., chap. 2. Not all mechanics were in competition with importers of British goods. Butchers and bakers, like those in the building trades, produced for a naturally protected market, while the fortunes of those in the shipbuilding and related trades might be tied more generally to commerce—points brought out by Alfred Young in "Some Thoughts on Mechanic Participation in the American Revolution," MS., Conference on Early American History, Newberry Library, Chicago, October 1974.

54. Quoted in Olton, "Philadelphia Artisans," chap. 2, pp. 49–50.

55. Ernst, *Money and Politics*, pp. 236–39.

56. These are suggestions based on the author's work in progress, but see the discussion in Ernst, *Money and Politics*, and Egnal and Ernst, "Economic Interpretation of the American Revolution."

57. The following page is based on the author's work in progress, my discussions with colleagues and friends, especially Professor Alfred Young, and my reading of much of the recent studies in the social history of the colonial period.

58. See the suggestive discussion by Gary Nash in this same collection.

59. The quotes are all from Sachs, "Business Depression in the Northern Colonies, 1763–1770" (Masters thesis, University of Wisconsin, 1950), pp. 206–7.

60. On Franklin, see Albert Henry Smyth, ed., *The Writings of Benjamin Franklin*, vol. 5 (New York: Macmillan & Co., 1905), pp. 114–15; on Gadsden, see Robert M. Weir, ed., "Two Letters by Christopher Gadsden, Feb., 1766," *South Carolina Magazine of History* 75 (1974): 169–76.

Tom Paine's Republic:
Radical Ideology and Social Change

Eric Foner

A public procession in Philadelphia, September 1780, depicting, in giant effigies, the treason of Benedict Arnold, who is being prompted by the Devil. The engraving by Charles W. Peale appeared on a contemporary broadside. Courtesy **Historical Pictures Service, Inc.**

My interest in Thomas Paine stems from my work on a larger project—a study of nineteenth-century American radicalism, tracing the interrelationship between changes in the nature of American society and the development of radical ideologies and programs. This study itself reflects the changes in my own intellectual interests over the past few years. My first book, *Free Soil, Free Labor, Free Men: The Ideology of the Republican Party Before the Civil War* (my doctoral dissertation at Columbia University), examined a particular ideology within the context of antebellum American history, but devoted far more attention to the political than to the social dimensions of that history. Since the publication of that book, like other contributors to the present volume, I have become convinced of the necessity of integrating ideological, political, social, and economic history far more fully and comprehensively. This belief has been strongly influenced by my reading of such European scholars as Edward Thompson, Eric Hobsbawm, and Albert Soboul, and American historians like Eugene Genovese, David Montgomery, Herbert Gutman, and Alfred Young (not to mention that superb historian Karl Marx.)

At any rate, as a dominant figure in the history of radical thought in the Age of Revolution, Thomas Paine seemed a natural starting point for a study of American radicalism. Like many others who have attempted to probe Paine's career, however, I soon found myself fascinated by this enigmatic personality. I also found that not only did Paine's career abound in unanswered questions, but that, despite the growing body of literature on eighteenth-century American society, much of the social context with which Paine lived still remained to be investigated. In the end, I found myself devoting as much attention to exploring the English roots of Paine's thought, the nature of Philadelphia society at the time of his residence there and the enormous changes it underwent during the Revolution, the artisan community with which Paine developed a special tie, and the reasons for the enormous influence of Paine's writings, as to Paine himself. The results of this work will appear in a forthcoming book, *Tom Paine and Revolutionary America,* relating Paine's career to the political and social life of revolutionary Philadelphia, and using Paine as a vehicle for exploring early American radicalism. The present essay is a preliminary summary of some of my conclusions.

Eric Foner (Ph.D., Columbia University, 1969) held a fellowship in 1972–73 from the American Council of Learned Societies for the study of nineteenth-century American radicalism. He teaches at the City College, City University of New York.

Of the men who made the American Revolution, none had a more remarkable career, or suffered a more peculiar fate, than Thomas Paine.[1] While his friends Thomas Jefferson and George Washington, and his ideological antagonist John Adams, came from middle and upper-class families long established on American soil, Paine's origins lay among the "lower orders" of eighteenth-century England, and he did not arrive in America until the very eve of the war for independence. Adams, who disliked Paine intensely, still could write in 1805: "I know not whether any man in the world has had more influence on its inhabitants or affairs for the last thirty years than Paine."[2] But after his death—indeed, even before it—Paine was excluded from the list of leaders of the Revolution canonized in American popular culture, his memory kept alive only by succeeding generations of radicals and freethinkers, who rediscovered him as a symbol of revolutionary internationalism, free thought, and defiance of existing institutions.

Paine's biographers have always faced an unenviable task. To depict Paine in his entirety requires a knowledge not only of the history of America, England, and France, but of eighteenth-century science, theology, political philosophy, and radical movements. Paine's connections must be traced among the powerful in Europe and America, and also in the tavern-centered world of politically-conscious artisans and workingmen in London and Philadelphia. In fact, the questions central to an understanding of Paine's career lie well beyond the confines of conventional biography. It is perhaps not surprising that while several fine lives of Paine now exist, a great deal of mystery still surrounds his career. Paine's ideas have never been grasped in their full complexity, nor have they been successfully located in the social context of Paine's age. Some writers have isolated individual strands of Paine's thought—Newtonian science, deism, political egalitarianism, the defense of private property and business enterprise—as the "key" to Paine's thought, but no one has shown how, why, and when these various strands became integrated into the coherent ideology of which, for Paine at least, they were component parts. Others have attempted to portray Paine as a radical in a modern sense, without paying sufficient attention to the profound differences between the radicalism of the eighteenth century and radical thought after the industrial revolution.[3]

A study of Paine's career during the American Revolution may enable us to begin the process of reexamining the meaning of Paine's life and of resolving some of the unanswered questions about his career. What were the roots of Paine's thought? How can the immense impact of his writings in America and Europe be explained? How did Paine's conception of government and society change as a result of his participation in the American Revolution? What was Paine's exact relationship to the upsurge of egalitarian and republican thought on both sides of the Atlantic in the late eighteenth century? How can the apparent contradiction be explained between Paine's democratic republicanism, which led him to defend the highly democratic Pennsylvania Constitution of 1776, and his support of the Bank of North America and the federal Constitution of 1787? By addressing these questions in the context of the vast political and social changes which the nation underwent in the era of the American Revolution, it should be possible to achieve a fuller understanding of Paine himself, and of his America.

I

The first thirty-seven years of Paine's life (1737–1774), spent in England, gave no indication of the prominence he would later achieve. He was born in the village of Thetford, a small Norfolk market town seventy miles northeast of London. Paine's family was humble but by no means impoverished. His father, a Quaker and a master staymaker (i.e. corset maker), and his mother, an Anglican and the daughter of a local attorney, were able, although not without sacrifice, to send Paine to the local grammar school. Paine received several years of formal education, and at age thirteen left school to apprentice himself to his father's craft.

Paine served as a journeyman staymaker in London in 1758, and later as a master artisan in Sandwich and Dover, but he seems to have been unhappy in the trade. He left staymaking for good in the 1760s, obtaining a position as an excise tax officer in Lincolnshire and, after he was dismissed for falsifying a report, working as a teacher in a London school. In 1768, Paine was reinstated as excise officer in Lewes, Sussex, a town fifty miles due south of London. In Lewes, he married for the second time (his first wife had died within a year of their wedding) and ran his father-in-law's tobacconist shop. Paine spent the winter of 1772–1773 in London, unsuccessfully attempting to win the Excise Board's approval for a salary increase for excise collectors, his only experience in England in political pamphleteering. Within the next year, his life virtually disintegrated: he was again dismissed from his excise position, his Lewes shop failed, and Paine and his wife separated. At the age of thirty-seven, in 1774, Paine decided to seek a new beginning in America.[4]

Paine was well into middle age before his talents received any recognition, but it is not unreasonable to assume that many of his ideas were fixed by the time he arrived in America. He later attributed the success of his early writings to the fact that he had "brought a knowledge of England with me to America." What had life taught Paine in England? What were the formative influences on his thought? Because so little is known of Paine's early career, the answers must be somewhat tentative. Certainly, his father's Quakerism influenced Paine's later humanitarianism, his rejection of hierarchies in church and state, and his support for reforms ranging from antislavery to the abolition of dueling. Paine, moreover, had lived in Thetford, Dover, Sandwich, and Lewes, all of which were examples of the inequities of the system of parliamentary representation and the dominance of the landed aristocracy in political life. Each of these tiny towns sent two representatives to Parliament—the members from Lewes chosen by a closed coporation of thirty-two voters who followed the orders of the Duke of Grafton—while the metropolis of Manchester had no representation at all.[5]

Certainly, too, Paine had traveled widely in England, and as he later declared, the job of revenue officer put him a unique position "to see into the numerous and various distresses which the weight of taxes even at that time of day occasioned." Paine could hardly have escaped the signs of economic distress and decay which abounded in southeastern England in the mid-eighteenth century; and he lived in or near

London in the 1760s and 1770s, a period of food riots and industrial disputes. This was also the period of the popular movement for "Wilkes and Liberty," an agitation in which Paine probably took no part, but which developed new kinds of political appeals aimed at the world of artisans, shopkeepers, and humbler professional men in which Paine moved.[6]

In recalling his years in England, Paine later wrote, "the natural bent of my mind was to science." During one of his stays in London, Paine purchased some scientific equipment and attended the lectures of Benjamin Martin and James Ferguson, two of the itinerant lecturers who helped bring scientific knowledge to audiences with little opportunity for advanced education. There was no overt political content to these lectures, but the audiences were composed largely of religious dissenters and self-educated artisans, many of whom leaned to deism and political radicalism. Paine remained something of a scientist for the rest of his life, and it was through his scientific interests that he became acquainted with Benjamin Franklin in London. More important, Newtonian science became one of the major influences that shaped Paine's intellectual outlook.[7]

Undoubtedly referring to his own experience, Paine once wrote that it was the study of science that lifted the "soul of the islander" beyond the concerns of everyday life to questions of universality. Like so many other Enlightenment figures, Paine viewed the Newtonian universe as one of natural harmony and order, guided by universal laws. Just as Newton had laid bare the laws of the natural world, men also could create a science of society. The point was that every human institution could and should be brought to the bar of reason for judgment. It was this critical attitude that made popular Newtonianism a breeding ground for radical political ideas in Paine's England.[8]

There was another tradition of criticism in eighteenth-century England, more dangerous than popular science, that may have influenced Paine. This was the underground tradition of antimonarchial, prorepublican belief inherited from the days of the Civil War of the 1640s and 1650s. One contemporary critic claimed that Paine's attack on monarchy in *Common Sense* was simply a restatement of the arguments of the Cromwellian writer John Hall, whose antimonarchial pamphlet of the 1650s was republished in London in 1771.[9]

If Paine was touched by radical ideas stemming from the seventeenth century, this exposure is likely to have taken place in London and Lewes, where he spent the six years before his departure for

America. London was notorious as a center of opposition to the government, and Lewes had been a center of republicanism in the 1640s and 1650s and retained in the eighteenth century a strong tradition of antipopery. The Lewes celebration of Guy Fawkes Day, for example, was famous throughout Sussex for its elaborate pageantry, anti-Catholic speeches, and carnival atmosphere. Although Paine later wrote that during his years at Lewes he "had no disposition for what is called politics," he did take part in political debates at the White Hart Evening Club, and his name appears in the town records of local government meetings and of church vestry activities, distributing poor relief. The people of Lewes seem to have been a rather recalcitrant lot during the time of Paine's residence there. When John Wilkes visited the town in 1770, "vast crowds of people" assembled to see him. The town was a stronghold of the Pelham-Newcastle family, whose agents included local officials, innkeepers, and clergy, but in a heated election campaign shortly before Paine's arrival, the Duke of Newcastle's hand-picked parliamentary candidate was defeated, a result which prompted the astonished Duke to order his stewards to evict tenants who had voted the wrong way, and to "call in the bills of such tradesmen at Lewes, who have been usually employed by me, and did not vote as above, and not employ them again on my account."[10]

That Lewes was a center of disaffection seems clear, although the precise effect on Paine of his residence there must remain problematical. The only evidence of his political beliefs before his arrival in America is the *Case of the Officers of Excise.* Four thousand copies were printed of the *Case,* and the pamphlet contains in embryo many of Paine's later ideas. Paine complained of "the voice of general want" in England, the ever-increasing prices which made it impossible for excise officers to make ends meet, and the fear that impoverishment would affect the morals of the petitioners. "Nothing tends to a greater corruption of manners and principles than a too great distress of circumstances," Paine wrote; and he warned that low salaries were an inducement to corruption in the excise service ("poverty and opportunity corrupt many an honest man."). Paine blamed "the increase of money in the kingdom" as one cause of rising prices, but he displayed a certain hostility, which seems out of place in a "humble" petition, toward "the rich, in ease and affluence," whose wealth was "the misfortune of others." Paine spent the winter of 1771–1773 in London, attempting to gain support for the petition, but Parliament ignored it, while increasing the appropriation for the King's expenses.[11]

It is not unreasonable to assume that when he left for America in 1774, Paine brought with him resentments against the English system of government nourished both by personal disappointment and by exposure to political disaffection and radicalism. In the new environment of America, this latent radicalism would suddenly blossom forth.

II

The Philadelphia that Paine entered late in 1774 was "the capital of the new world." With a population of some 30,000, it was the largest city in English America, and its polyglot citizenry included Anglicans, Quakers, Catholics, Germans, and Scotch-Irish, many of them recent immigrants. It was the financial and commercial center of the colonies, as well as the home of science, the arts, the theater, and educational and philanthropic institutions. The busiest port in America, its tonnage of shipping was exceeded only by London and Liverpool among English cities, and wealthy merchants, mostly Quakers and Anglicans, dominated the political, social, and economic life of the city.[12]

A majority of Philadelphia's population probably consisted of artisans or mechanics, a broad and indeterminate stratum which ranged from master mechanics in highly-skilled trades like instrument making and silversmithing, to such "inferior craftsmen" as coopers, tailors, and weavers, many of whom were quite poor. But most artisans apparently were able to escape want, acquire some property, educate their children, and take part in politics. Despite the diversity of the master artisans, they were clearly differentiated from the journeymen and apprentices who worked for them and from the preindustrial, pre-proletariat lower class of sailors and unskilled laborers who lived solely by manual work, did not own their own tools, moved readily from job to job (and often from city to city), were excluded from craft organizations, and, in general, could not vote.[13]

Paine's experiences in revolutionary Philadelphia cannot be understood apart from the vast political changes that occurred in the city during the era of the Revolution. The most important political development in Philadelphia in the decade before Paine's arrival was the emergence of the artisans as a self-conscious political group, with its own organizations and demands. Provincial Pennsylvania, a recent student has written, "was ruled by a narrow, privileged minority, whose power and policies were maintained in a political structure that had changed little since 1701." But the opposition to British taxation policies of the 1760s, initiated by members of the ruling elite, had awakened the artisans to a sense of political consciousness. The first political meeting specifically restricted to mechanics was held in 1770, and two years later, master craftsmen formed a permanent political organization, the Patriotic Society, to promote artisan candidates and policies, especially protection against competition from the importation of British manufactured goods. By 1774, when the Tea and Intolerable Acts sparked a new round of popular protests and non-importation agreements, a group of young merchants and lawyers, mostly Presbyterian, backed by lesser merchants and a majority of the artisan community, had taken control of the resistance movement in the city.[14]

In the late eighteenth century, artisans on both sides of the Atlantic awakened to political consciousness and, more than any other group, became the nursery and carriers of egalitarian ideas. Throughout the revolutionary period, they denounced the pretensions of men of wealth, who had "the impudence to assert that Mechanics are men of no consequence," who "make no scruples to say that the mechanics . . . have no right to be consulted in matters of government." They insisted on sharing political power with these men of "greatness and opulency."[15]

In the year or two preceding independence, hundreds, indeed thousands, of men were for the first time brought into organized political life in Philadelphia. For master artisans, the vehicles were the numerous committees that were established to conduct public affairs and police nonimportation agreements. This was in itself a new thing in Pennsylvania politics, but even more revolutionary was the politicization of poorer artisans, journeymen, apprentices, and laborers, as a result of mobilization into the militia. Representing a very different constituency from the master craftsmen who comprised the "mechanical interest" in the politics of the early 1770s, the militia, by 1776, had become an active force in Pennsylvania politics, and remained so throughout the Revolution.

Contemporary evidence indicates that the Philadelphia militia was drawn most heavily from the ranks of poorer artisans and laborers, and included "a great many apprentices" and minors as well. Aristocratic Whigs described the militia privates as "in general damn'd riff-raff— dirty, mutinous, and disaffected." The militia described themselves as "composed of tradesmen, and others, who earn their living by their industry," and who had left behind families "destitute of every means of acquiring an honest living." It is not surprising that a constant refrain in militia petitions in 1776 was that many privates were "not entitled to the privileges of freeman electors," because they could not meet the property requirements.[16]

Such men had traditionally expressed their grievances and discontents in sporadic crowd activity, rather than sustained political organization. For many in Philadelphia's lower classes, participation in the militia was the first step in the transition from the crowd to organized politics. Like the New Model Army of the English Civil War, the militia was "a school of political democracy." It became a center of intense political debate and discussion, in which privates were drawn into contact with radical artisans and intellectuals.[17]

The demands of the militia privates, as they emerged in late 1775 and 1776, were fairly simple. First, they insisted upon the right to elect all their officers—not simply the junior officers, as provided by the Pennsylvania Assembly—sometimes even suggesting that all officers should be elected annually by ballot, "for annual Election is so essentially necessary to the Liberty of Freemen." Second, they demanded the right of every associator to vote, regardless of whether he met property or age qualifications. Third, they insisted that militia service be made truly universal, or at least that significant financial sacrifice be asked of the men of wealth who avoided service. The legal fine of fifty shillings for nonservice was insultingly low, and offered "the lazy, the timid, and disaffected," an easy way to avoid service and to "ridicule those whose patriotism" led them to enlist. Non-associators, the militia's Committee of Privates declared, included "some of the most considerable estates in the Province." Fines should be levied on them "proportioned to each man's property," and the proceeds used to support the families of associators, "as no man, who is able, by his industry, to support his wife and children, could ever consent to have them treated, by the Overseers of the Poor, as the law directs."[18]

The emergence of the militia as a significant force in Philadelphia's political life was the most striking example of the politicization of the city's artisan and lower-class communities during the era of the Revolution. The comment that the perceptive conservative Gouverneur Morris made about a mass meeting in New York was also pertinent to Philadelphia: "The mob begin to think and reason."[19] The conflicts that inevitably arose as a result of this transformation would shape Paine's first years in America.

III

Thomas Paine arrived in Philadelphia on 30 November 1774. He bore letters of recommendation from Franklin, which secured him a job as editor of a new journal, the *Pennsylvania Magazine.* In 1775, through his connection with the magazine, Paine made the acquaintance of the young physician Benjamin Rush, himself a friend of John Adams and other members of Congress, who were already discussing in private the idea of American independence. Through friendships like this, and in the electrically-charged political atmosphere of Philadelphia, Paine's ideas expanded and deepened. By the end of his first year in America, he was familiar with the issues and arguments in the conflict with Great Britain, and with some of the sterner realities of American society.

The political situation at the close of 1775 was confused and ironic. War between British troops and Americans had broken out in Massachusetts in April, and in May the Second Continental Congress gathered in Philadelphia. Through the summer, as Pennsylvania, like the other provinces, actively enlisted troops, debate raged in Congress between advocates of vigorous opposition to the mother country and friends of reconciliation, led by Pennsylvania's Joseph Galloway and John Dickinson. In November, Britain virtually declared war on the colonies, and announced a naval blockade and the intention of sending German mercenaries to fight beside her own soldiers. At the same time, as popular participation in political life expanded rapidly, voices were beginning to be heard challenging the political and economic prerogatives of Philadelphia's merchant elite. All these developments weakened the prospects of a peaceful settlement. But, as yet, few men were calling publicly either for independence or for the establishment of republican government in America. It was Paine's *Common Sense,* published in January 1776, which not only gave articulate expression to the growing sense that reconciliation was impossible, but changed the terms of debate from the colonists' rights within the British Empire to the new issues of the future: independence and republican government.

Like the Newtonian lecturers, whose talks he attended in his youth, Paine's aim was to bring modern ideas to a new mass audience. His phenomenal success in this endeavor perhaps stemmed from the fact that Paine (almost alone among colonial pamphleteers) had sprung from that same mass audience. *Common Sense* announced a new style of political writing, a style Paine would perfect in *The Rights of Man* and *The Age of Reason,* each of which would have the same astonishing circulation as his first work.

"My motive and object in all my political works, beginning with *Common Sense,*" Paine recalled thirty years later, "...have been to rescue man from tyranny and false systems of government, and enable him to be free." Paine began *Common Sense* not with a discussion of America's relations with Great Britain but with an analysis of the principles of government, an attack on hereditary rule, and on the validity of monarchy itself. Paine always considered the republican argument of *Common Sense* more important than the call for independence. Before Paine, "republic" had been used in political discourse primarily as a term of abuse; he transformed it into a living political issue.[20]

Paine's savage attack on "the so much boasted Constitution of England" contains the most striking passages in *Common Sense:* "Male and female are the distinctions of nature, good and bad the distinctions of heaven, but how a race of men came into the world so exalted above the rest, and distinguished like some new species, is worth enquiring into." He denounced the whole notion of the historical legitimacy of the monarchy: "A French bastard landed with an armed banditti and establishing himself king of England against the consent of the natives, is in plain terms a very paltry rascally original.... The plain truth is that the antiquity of the English monarchy will not bear looking into."

Paine was the first writer in America to attack the English constitution so completely; he also differed from contemporary radicals, both in America and England, in not looking back to some mythical Saxon past for an ideal of government. Instead, he simply called for the institution of republican government in America, although he gave only a few hints as to its structure. Paine was always more interested in principles than structures of government, but he did call for frequent elections with a broad suffrage, and the creation of a continental legislature, as well as new unicameral state assemblies.

Common Sense then turned to a discussion of independence, a subject which had been mentioned sporadically in the press in 1775, but which most colonists still refused to confront. Paine's arguments again departed from those of previous pamphleteers, whose attacks on British policy had stressed the danger to colonial liberties. Paine gave more emphasis both to economic self-interest and to a vision of the future greatness of America, once freed from England. He denounced

British mercantilism as hostile to the economic growth and prosperity of the colonies and responsible for "many material injuries," insisted that "no nation in a state of foreign dependence" could ever achieve "material eminence" or political greatness, and painted a picture of an American empire, trading freely with the entire world. An independent America would "steer clear of European connections," but would pursue a policy of friendship and free trade with all nations, promoted by a strong continental government, complete with a national debt to serve as a national bond.

The most lyrical passages in *Common Sense* are couched in the language of an impending millenium: republicanism was for Paine a secular vision of utopia. "We have it in our power to begin the world over again," he declared, ". . . the birthday of a new world is at hand." Paine transformed a struggle over the rights of Englishmen into a contest with meaning for all mankind:[21]

> O! Ye that love mankind! Ye that dare oppose not only tyranny but the tyrant, stand forth! Every spot of the old world is overrun with oppression. Freedom hath been hunted round the globe. Asia and Africa have long expelled her. Europe regards her as a stranger, and England hath given her warning to depart. O! receive the fugitive, and prepare in time an asylum for mankind.

The immediate success and impact of *Common Sense* was nothing less than astounding, as every scholar of the Revolution has agreed. At a time when the average political pamphlet was printed in one or two editions, *Common Sense* went through twenty-five editions and reached literally hundreds of thousands of readers in the single year 1776. If the era of the Revolution witnessed "the massive politicization of American society," *Common Sense* was central to the explosion of political argument beyond the confines of a narrow, educated elite to "all ranks" of Americans. From up and down the colonies in the spring of 1776 came reports that the pamphlet was read by "all sorts of people" and that it had made "innumerable converts" to independence. A Connecticut man announced, "You have declared the sentiments of millions. Your production may justly be compared to a land-flood that sweeps all before it. We were blind, but on reading these enlightening words the scales have fallen from our eyes." And from Philadelphia itself, a writer, in February, commented on "the progress of the idea of Colonial Independency in three weeks or a month," adding, "surely thousands and tens of thousands of common farmers and tradesmen must be better reasoners than some of our untrammeled *juris consultores,* who to this hour feel a reluctance to part with the abominable chain."[22]

John Adams always resented the idea that *Common Sense* contributed much to the movement for independence. Its discussion of that subject, he insisted, was "a tolerable summary of the arguments which I had been repeating again and again in Congress for nine months." Nothing in it was new, with the exception of "the phrases, suitable for an emigrant from New Gate, or one who had chiefly associated with such company, such as 'the royal brute of England,' 'the blood upon his soul,' and a few others of equal delicacy." Adams may have been ungrateful, but to some extent he was right. *Common Sense* did express ideas that were becoming fixed parts of American ideology: the separateness of America from Europe, the corruption of the Old World and the innocence of the new, the virtues of republican government, the absurdity of hereditary privilege, none of which were original with Paine. What set *Common Sense* apart was not only that Paine combined these elements in a new way but that he did so in a new tone and style. Its tone, which contemporaries described as "daring impudence" and "uncommon frenzy," was far removed from the legalistic, logical arguments of other political pamphlets. The phrases that offended Adams, "those indecent expressions" that shocked Henry Laurens of South Carolina, were meant to show that Paine had absolutely no deference for existing institutions. He minced no words in his assaults on hereditary privilege: the House of Lords was "the remains of aristocratic tyranny," and as for monarchy, "Of more worth is one honest man to society, and in the sight of God, than all the crowned ruffians that ever lived."[23]

But there was more to Paine's appeal than these assaults. He was the conscious pioneer of a new style of political writing, aimed at extending political discussion beyond the narrow bounds of the eighteenth century's "political nation." "As it is my design to make those than can scarcely read understand," he once wrote, "I shall therefore avoid every literary ornament and it put in language as plain as the alphabet." Paine was capable, to be sure, of creating brilliant metaphors, such as in his reply in *The Rights of Man* to Burke's sympathy for the fate of Marie Antoinette: "He pities the plumage, but forgets the dying bird." But the hallmarks of his writing were clarity, directness, and forcefulness. He assumed knowledge of no authority but the Bible, employed no Latin phrases—or when he did, immediately provided translations—and avoided florid language designed to impress more cultivated readers. He ridiculed other writers for their reliance on precedents and obscure authorities. "In this part of the debate," he wrote, in the spring of 1776, of a newspaper antagonist, "Cato shelters himself chiefly in quotations from other authors, without reasoning on the matter himself; in answer to which, I present him with a string of maxims and recollections, drawn from the nature of things, without borrowing from any one."[24]

To his critics, Paine was as guilty of degrading the language as of attacking the government. Gouverneur Morris scoffed at him as "a mere adventurer...without fortune, without family or connections, ignorant even of grammar." But Paine was indeed a conscious artist. He was aware that he was creating a style of writing "hitherto unknown on this side of the Atlantic," according to Virginia's Edmund Randolph.[25] Most writers of the eighteenth century believed that to write for a mass audience meant to sacrifice refinement for coarseness and triviality. Before Paine, most American pamphleteers consciously aimed their works at the educated classes. Paine's literary style, his rejection of deference, and his political egalitarianism were all interrelated. For him, the medium, in effect, was of one piece with the message.

IV

Common Sense not only propelled Americans along the path to independence, it also generated an intense debate over the nature of government within America. The very success of the pamphlet plunged Paine into an intense involvement in the tangled and divisive politics of Philadelphia and Pennsylvania. For several months, in the spring and summer of 1776, he would play a leading role in the struggle that began as a movement to commit Pennsylvania to independence and broadened into an assault upon the state's government. Paine's vision of republican government strongly influenced a group of radical intellectuals, professionals, and artisans who emerged to sudden political prominence in 1776, playing a leading role in overturning the established government and drafting a new state constitution which reflected many of the demands and social resentments of the newly politicized artisans and militia of Philadelphia. The bitter debate over the merits of the constitution which ensued would lead Paine to define for the first time his conception of the limits of political participation and the proper extent of voting rights under republican government.

The heated nature of political debate in Philadelphia stemmed from a unique combination of circumstances. In almost every other colony the established political leadership either stepped wholesale onto the Whig side by the spring of 1776, or at least split into Tory and Whig factions. But in Pennsylvania, the old elite obstinately opposed independence, and the Whig leaders of the early 1770s—men like Charles Thomson, Joseph Reed, and John Dickinson—were either drawn off into national affairs or lapsed into silence, as the movement for independence accelerated.[26]

It was this vacuum of political leadership that opened the door for the sudden emergence of a new radical party in Philadelphia politics. Along with Paine and Benjamin Rush, the Philadelphia radicals included Dr. Thomas Young, Christopher Marshall, Timothy Matlack, David Rittenhouse, and Charles Willson Peale. As a group, these were men of modest wealth who stood outside the merchant elite, and who, prior to 1776, had exerted little political influence in Philadelphia. Many were outsiders of one kind or another; Young and Peale, like Paine, were recent arrivals in the city, and Marshall and Matlack had been disowned by their Quaker meetings. Together, they reflected the various ideological strands and political styles that made up the radical wing of the revolutionary movement in Philadelphia. The Philadelphia radicals, to be sure, shared many of the assumptions about colonial virtue and English corruption which were common among all American Whigs. But there were other political strands as well, which made this group more akin to the radical artisans and professionals of a city like London than to the cultured Whig merchants and planters who populated the Continental Congress. Matlack brought to the Philadelphia radicals immense popularity in the popular culture of lower-class Philadelphia; Rush reflected the evangelical roots of popular republican thought; and Paine himself, along with Cannon, Young, Rittenhouse, and Peale, were men whose roots lay among the rationalist, politically-conscious artisans.

Timothy Matlack, the son of a Quaker brewer who had fallen into debt and been "torn to pieces" by his creditors, had himself been disowned by the Philadelphia Quakers in 1765 for neglecting his hardware store business and for failing to pay his debts. His greatest claim to fame, before he rose to political prominence during the Revolution, was his penchant for gambling, horse racing, bullbaiting, and especially the popular sport of cockfighting. His popularity among Philadelphia's lower classes was assured in 1770 when his prize bantam cocks engaged in a celebrated match with those of James Delancey, a New York aristocrat who had traveled to Philadelphia for the contest.[27]

Far different from Matlack's life-style was the austere Presbyterianism of Benjamin Rush, whose life illustrated how the evangelical religious fundamentalism which flowed from the Great Awakening of the 1740s was a potent source of republican social and political ideology. "It is perhaps impossible," one historian has recently written, "for the modern secular mind to grasp the revolutionary implications of an imminent millennium." But the Awakening inspired countless Americans with this very vision. Religious enthusiasm, contemporaries declared, appealed most strongly to poorer colonists, and the evangelical ministry often combined an attack upon the dissipation, luxury, and corruption of English life, with a critique of increasing selfishness, extravagance, and lack of social concern among colonial men of wealth. They also implied that separation from England would be only the prelude to a social and moral transformation within America itself, eventually coming to identify the millennium with the establishment of governments that derived their authority from the people, and which were free from the great disparities of wealth that characterized the old world.[28]

Evangelicalism had been a major continuing element of Philadelphia life ever since Reverend George Whitefield attracted throngs of listeners, mostly of the "lower orders," to his sermons in the city in 1739. It was among the Scotch-Irish Presbyterians, a majority of whom were artisans, laborers, or servants, that the revivalism of the Great Awakening struck deepest roots in the city. It is well known that the Revolution led to a transition from Anglicans and Quakers to Presbyterians in Pennsylvania office-holding. But the Presbyterian contribution to the revolutionary movement was far deeper than this. Contemporaries believed that the Scotch-Irish of Pennsylvania were the "most God-provoking Democrats on this side of Hell." Many, it was said, looked back fondly to the days of Cromwell, and were of "republican principles." As one Philadelphian explained to a London friend in 1776, "The Scotch, in the Province of Pennsylvania, act like and speak like their Ancestors. They covenanted against the tyranny of a Stewart, their own countryman; and they are determined with us never to become the slaves of any Parliament or Potentate on earth . . . they are here the very warmest advocates for liberty."[29]

When Benjamin Rush equated "a pope in religion and a king in power," he was speaking for many Pennsylvania Presbyterians. Rush, though born an Anglican, was converted to evangelical Presbyterianism as a youth and attended the College of New Jersey, the bulwark of colonial Presbyterianism. Religion and politics were always closely intertwined for him; he considered republicanism the natural consequence of true Christianity, and believed the American Revolution heralded the millennial reign of Christ on earth. Rush moved easily among the artisan and poor communities of Philadelphia—his medical practice, until well into the 1770s, was confined to the lower classes of Philadelphia, whom he often treated free of charge. He was a leader in the drive for home manufacturing, arguing that this would provide for the poor of Philadelphia, while lessening American dependence on England. And like so many other Presbyterians, Rush equated the movement for independence with the spirit of the English Civil War, and often invoked the memory of his "great ancestor," John Rush, who had served in Cromwell's army against "the minions of arbitrary power."[30]

Rush thus represents a strand of radicalism far different from the measured arguments of the "radical Whig" publicists in England and America. The "lower class" Philadelphia Presbyterians, who as early as 1765 exclaimed, "no King but King Jesus," also contributed something to the ideological origins of the American Revolution.[31]

Despite his friendship with Rush, Paine's political outlook had much more in common with the rationalism and deism of professionals like James Cannon and Thomas Young, and such skilled artisans as Rittenhouse and Peale. Cannon, who aside from Paine was the radical group's leading political thinker, was a mathematician and student of science who had emigrated from his native Edinburgh in 1765, and whose first involvement in public affairs came in March 1775, when he became a manager of the United Company for Promoting American Manufactures.[32] Thomas Young, a self-educated physician whom John Adams called "an eternal fisher in troubled waters," was a peripatetic revolutionary who had already lived in Albany, Boston, and Newport, before moving to Philadelphia in 1775. The son of a Scotch-Irish immigrant, Young had been hauled into court for abusing the name of Jesus Christ in the 1750s, and he remained a lifelong deist. He was involved with the Sons of Liberty in Albany, and was closely associated with Sam Adams as an organizer of Boston crowds. Young considered artisans "the most worthy members of society," and counted on them to inspire "the other ranks of citizens" to resist Great Britain.[33]

Rittenhouse and Peale were artisans of great skill who achieved intellectual distinction in other areas as well. Rittenhouse was a watch-maker, one of the most difficult and prestigious of colonial crafts, who had followed the common route from watchmaking to science. He was widely regarded as America's leading scientist after Franklin, and, like Franklin, had a wide following among Philadelphia mechanics, who chose him in 1774 as a member of an eleven-man committee to repre-sent their political interests. Peale rose from poverty to artisan status as a silversmith and then a clockmaker, and later became America's leading portrait painter. Since the Stamp Act crisis, Peale had been a republican, who "would never pull off his Hat as the King passed by." He was an early advocate of independence and home manufacturing.[34]

In some ways, the cooperation between the evangelical and ratio-nalist republicans may seem surprising. There was a seemingly impass-able gulf between the universe of the deists, in which God had been relegated to the status of prime mover, and that of the evangelicals, who believed in continuing divine intervention in worldly affairs. De-ists like Paine believed that man was inherently good, and substituted for the fall of man his corruption by tyrannical governments. The evangelicals, of course, could not abandon the idea that sin was inher-ent in all men.

Nevertheless, evangelical and rationalist republicanism had more in common in the era of the American Revolution than they would a generation later, after the French Revolution had weakened the link between them. Both groups were early converts to independence and republicanism, and both had strong links to the Philadelphia artisan community, via the movement for home manufacturing, and to the militia—Cannon served as secretary of the Committee of Privates, and Matlack, Peale, and Young were militia officers. All the Philadelphia radicals came to envision an internal transformation in American soci-ety as a desirable, even necessary, counterpart to separation from England.

Indeed, much of Paineite rationalist thought can be viewed as an expression in secular terms of ideas which the evangelicals viewed through the lens of religion. Paine and the Calvinist ministers both used the language of millennialism—Paine in his description of repub-lican government, the clergy in identifying such government with the reign of Christ on earth. Paine's doctrine of common sense—that every man was capable of judging political institutions for himself, without any special learning—could be equated with the Quaker notion of the inner light and the Protestant emphasis on the primacy of the individual conscience. Benjamin Rush may well have summed up the sources of radical thought—and he saw no contradiction between them—in the symbols he designed as a seal for a new college after the end of the revolutionary war: a Bible, a telescope, and a cap of liberty.[35]

V

It was the success of *Common Sense* that transformed the nature of colonial political debate and created the opportunity for the Philadelphia radicals to emerge as a major force in the city's politics. Between January and July 1776, scarcely a week went by without a lengthy article in the Philadelphia press that attacked or defended Paine's ideas, or extended and refined them, and the same was true in other cities as well. Nothing reveals the revolutionary aspects of the struggle for independence better than the swiftness with which established institutions were attacked and overturned, and established authorities called into question. In this atmosphere, old ideas were transformed, and new ones entered the political arena with great suddenness. "It seems as if everything was to be altered," came a report from Massachusetts. "Scarcely a newspaper but teems with new projects."

In the Philadelphia press, the leading radical propagandists were Paine himself, writing under the name "The Forester," and Cannon, Rush, Young, Rittenhouse, and Christopher Marshall. The newspaper debate dealt not only with the pros and cons of independence but with the meaning of republican government. On this question, the old leaders of resistance to Great Britain had little to say in common. As John Adams observed, a republic might mean "anything, everything, or nothing." Everyone agreed that republican government must involve the representation of the people through frequent elections, but beyond this there was no consensus. *Common Sense* may have introduced "a new system of politics as widely different from the old system of politics as the Copernican system is from the Ptolemaic" (a compliment Paine must certainly have cherished), but the precise meaning of republicanism in America remained to be worked out.[36]

Common Sense catalyzed conservatives as well as radicals; defenders of the connection with England, and of balanced government, rushed into print to dispute Paine's ideas. Loyalist writers defended the British Constitution—"the admiration of mankind"—and denounced Paine as "a crack-brained zealot for democracy" and a "violent republican." One Loyalist revealed a fear of the growing radicalism within the militia, when he warned that "the soldiers" would find an "Agrarian law" dividing property "very agreeable."[37]

There were also many who were convinced of the necessity of independence, but felt it necessary to combat Paine's views of government. Foremost among these was John Adams, who applauded Paine's arguments for a separation from England, but considered his ideas of government "too democratical." "Indeed," Adams informed his wife Abigail, "this writer has a better hand in pulling down than building up." In order to counteract Paine's pamphlet and give the American people a lesson in "the science of government," Adams quickly composed *Thoughts on Government,* which was widely circulated in the spring and summer of 1776. In *Common Sense,* Paine had leaned toward unicameral legislatures, but Adams insisted on the virtues of balanced government. His arguments were more appealing to the Whig elite in the various colonies than Paine's, for it was only in Pennsylvania, Georgia, and Vermont that single-house legislatures were established.[38]

Adams was no less of a republican than Paine, but his republicanism had an unmistakable elitist bias. He was alarmed by and sought to counteract the leveling spirit that *Common Sense* had both articulated and intensified. The "one thing" absolutely essential in the new republican governments, he informed one correspondent, was "a decency, and respect, and veneration introduced for persons in authority." And he opposed demands for an extension of the franchise: "It is dangerous to alter the qualifications of voters. . . . It tends to confound and destroy all distinctions and prostrate all ranks to one common level."[39]

Yet it was precisely the demand that Americans be reduced to "one common level" that seemed to animate much of the egalitarian outpouring. What was new in the debate of the spring of 1776 was the sudden emergence of "equality" as the great rallying cry of Philadelphia radicals. To be sure, the notion of equality, like many slogans of the revolutionary era, was an idea whose meaning lay in the eye of the beholder. There was a respectable tradition of thought that viewed equality of property as an essential prerequisite for republican government. It was an axiom, dating back to James Harrington, that "power follows property"; hence, it was only where property was widely distributed that political power could be as well. Some writers in 1776 used the idea of equality to argue that America was indeed uniquely suited for republicanism. "America," declared one writer in the Philadelphia press, "is the only country in the world wholly free from all political impediments at the very time it is laid under the necessity of framing a civil constitution. Having no rank above that of freeman she has but one interest to consult."[40]

Other writers, however, used "equality" as a weapon of attack against the emergence of an American aristrocracy which threatened the basis of republican politics, not as grounds for self-congratulation. Paine, in fact, was not one of these writers. His impudent attacks on established institutions had helped others break out of traditional habits of deference, but he was less alarmed than others at the increasing social stratification and gap between rich and poor which characterized revolutionary Philadelphia.[41] Paine compared the city with London, not with the Philadelphia of 1750. It was left to others to take the lead in 1776 and to introduce an incipient class consciousness— or at least a vocal hostility to the rich—into Philadelphia politics. "Candidus" denounced Pennsylvania's men of wealth for being "petty tyrants" who opposed independence because they dreamed of creating "millions of acres of tenanted soil." James Cannon, as "Cassandra" and the anonymous author of a broadside entitled "The Alarm," issued similar warnings about "an aristocratical junto" who were "straining every nerve to frustrate our virtuous endeavours and to make the common and middle class of people their *beasts of burden.*" And Dr. Thomas Young wrote that "men of some rank" desired to establish in America "the system of Lord and Vassal, or *principal and dependent,* common in Europe."[42]

In one sense, what Cannon and Young were describing was only a tendency toward inequality—they seemed to be expressing concern more about the future than the present. But for them, the notion of equality became an argument for a radical reformation in the principles of government of Pennsylvania, especially a wide expansion of the right to vote, and an end to the monopoly of political power by "the *profligate* and *corrupt.*"[43] Seizing the opportunities created by the vacuum of political leadership in the state and the movement for independence, the Philadelphia radicals played a leading role in the movement that overthrew the provincial government and established a new constitution strongly influenced by the ideas of Paine and James Cannon.

The tangled story of Philadelphia politics in 1776 needs no retelling here.[44] After a turbulent spring and summer, a constitutional convention established a new frame of government, widely regarded as the most radical constitution created during the American Revolution. The overthrow of the government of provincial Pennsylvania was the work of a coalition of western farmers and Philadelphia artisans, not of any single social class. Numerically, the agrarians dominated the coalition, but at the constitutional convention, the urban radicals took the lead—James Cannon seems to have had the leading hand in drafting the document, and Matlack, Rittenhouse, and Young were all present at the convention. As for Paine, he was out of the city, having taken a position as secretary to Daniel Roberdeau, brigadier-general of the militia. He later insisted that he "had no hand in forming any part of it, nor knew anything of its contents." Yet his political ideas were now essentially the same as Cannon's, and the constitution as adopted was in line with the governmental structure outlined in *Common Sense.*[45]

The Pennsylvania Constitution of 1776 was a culmination of both the ideological and political developments of the preceding year. It incorporated many of the specific ideas of government and general warnings about aristocratic influence that had held a prominent place in the political debates of the spring, and by creating a taxpayer suffrage, it formalized the vast expansion of political participation that had occurred in the preceding years. It also rejected the notion of balanced government, by providing for an all-powerful single-house legislature and a vetoless plural executive. It contained strict provisions for rotation of officeholders, annual elections, and keeping legislative debates always open to the public. And despite the fact that the delegates rejected a proposal by Cannon to declare explicitly the principle that large accumulations of property should be discouraged by state action, it reflected an antiaristocratic outlook in provisions attacking the practice of entail, affirming the right of Pennsylvanians to "fowl and hunt" on all unenclosed land, and disqualifying candidates who sought to bribe electors with food or money. And its provisions for inexpensive state schools and a limitation on imprisonment for debt spoke directly to the needs of many urban artisans.[46]

The Constitution of 1776, wrote one contemporary, "split the Whigs to pieces." Soon after the convention adjourned and announced the promulgation of the constitution without a popular referendum, moderate Whigs called a mass meeting in Philadelphia, which adopted resolutions denouncing the "strange innovations" in the doc-

ument, and calling for amendments to create balanced government
and a two-house legislature. The debate over the constitution divided
Pennsylvania politics for the next decade. It was conducted in the same
rhetoric of class antagonism that had emerged in the spring of 1776.
Opponents of the constitution, condemning their foes as "coffeehouse demagogues" and "political upstarts," attributed the document's flaws to a broadside, written by Cannon, which had circulated
among "the unthinking many, that men of property . . . men of experience and knowledge" were not to be trusted as delegates to the convention. The constitution's defenders characterized their opponents
as "all the rich great men and the wise men," who did not consider that
they had "a common interest with the body of the people." The demand for the creation of an upper legislative body was characterized
as an attempt to introduce a House of Lords, "consisting of a small
number of grandees" anxious to increase their wealth and power.[47]

How did Paine react to the fracturing of the Whigs? As we have
seen, he was not in Philadelphia when the Constitutional Convention
met, and for much of 1777 and 1778 was engaged in the national war
effort and in writing the *Crisis* papers to mobilize public support for
the war. Yet with the exception of Benjamin Rush, Paine's former
Philadelphia associates were fully committed to the new constitution.
Despite Paine's absence from state affairs, it is not surprising that when
he finally entered the debate on the merits of the new frame of government, he defended the constitution, but not in a spirt of class hostility.
In a series of letters to the Philadelphia press in March and June 1777,
and again in December 1778, Paine attempted to unite Pennsylvanians
behind the new government. Rather than pleading the cause of the
poor against the rich, he wrote, "I am clearly convinced that the true
interest of one is the real interest of both." The closest Paine would
come to identifying himself with a specific class was to praise the
attributes of the middle of the social spectrum. "There is an extent of
riches, as well as an extreme of poverty, which, by narrowing the circles
of a man's acquaintance, lessens his opportunities of general knowledge." It was "in the practical world," in "business," that men acquired the knowledge appropriate for governmental service.

His letters on the Pennsylvania constitution included Paine's fullest elaboration of his views on equality of political rights. In *Common
Sense,* he had referred vaguely to the utility of a wide suffrage; now he
broke explicitly and decisively with the tradition that linked the right
of voting with ownership of property. Yet he still remained tied to the

idea that some sort of guarantee of personal independence was necessary in voters. "I consider freedom as personal property," Paine declared, insisting "wherever I use the words *freedom* or *rights,* I desire to be understood to mean a perfect equality of them." Yet Paine allowed that freedom could be temporarily forfeited by criminality, or "servitude." By "servitude," he explained, he meant both offices of profit under the state, and

> all servants in families; because their interest is in their master, and depending upon him in sickness and in health, and voluntarily withdrawing from taxation and public service of all kinds, they stand detached by choice from the common floor; but the instant they reassume their original character of a man and encounter the world in their own persons, they repossess the full share of freedom appertaining to that character.[48]

Paine was here arguing for what he viewed as the broadest possible suffrage. He insisted that property qualifications were inherently unfair, since property "makes scarce any, or no difference, in the value of the man to the community." It seems clear that in line with his general antideferential attitudes, it was *personal* rather than economic independence which he perceived as a necessary qualification for voting. The key to Paine's argument is that servants had "voluntarily" relinquished their independence—an assumption logical enough when applied to indentured servants or apprentices who in most cases freely entered their contracts, but one which also seemed to assume a degree of abundance and economic opportunity that forced no one to give up his personal independence against his own wishes.

From 1778 onward, Paine would always condemn property qualifications for voting. But it was not until the 1790s that he would unequivocally embrace universal manhood suffrage and its principle that it was wrong "to disfranchise any class of men." Even in 1778, however, his definition of suffrage, which presumably would allow men too poor to pay taxes, but not employed as servants, to cast ballots, was significantly wider than that in the constitution he was defending.

VI

From 1776 to the end of 1778, two issues had framed Paine's career: the struggle for independence, and the working out of new political arrangements in Pennsylvania. Beginning in 1779, Paine

would become involved in a new series of disputes, which were a
consequence of the economic effects on Philadelphia and the nation
of the revolutionary war. The 1770s and 1780s witnessed a vast expansion of market relations and capitalist institutions in America.[49] In the
debates that arose as a result of these changes, Paine would find himself forming new and unusual alliances, and realizing for the first time
the full dimensions of his attitudes toward the development of the
American economy.

The immediate issues agitating Philadelphia in 1779, the year
which saw Paine's greatest involvement in local affairs since 1776,
arose from the tremendous rise in prices. The economic crisis spawned
by inflation led to the formation of committees throughout the colonies to set prices and regulate commercial activities. It also generated
an intense debate over the meaning of the republican concepts of
"virtue" and "luxury" at a time of immense profits for some colonists
and terrible hardships for others, forcing Americans to confront the
issue of whether property rights were absolute and inviolable or
should be controlled for the benefit of the entire community. Like
many other Americans in this period of economic transition, Paine was
caught between traditional ideas of economic regulation and the new
philosophy of laissez-faire. He shared assumptions with both economic outlooks, and, in 1779, found it difficult to maintain a consistent
position with regard to an increasingly militant extralegal popular
movement for economic controls. But in view of the overall cast of his
mind, his rejection of tradition, and his affinity for new ideas, it should
not be surprising that Paine eventually found he had more sympathy
with the emerging "modern" doctrine of laissez-faire.

In the past two decades, historians of England and France who
have reexamined food riots as a major form of eighteenth century
crowd activity, have drawn attention to the legitimating ideas of
"moral economy" which animated such actions. The urban poor, and
many artisans, believed that the operations of the free market worked
against their own economic interests. They rejected the emerging
doctrine of free trade, so far as it applied to grain, bread, and meat,
denying the right of the farmer, merchant, or shopkeeper to an absolute property right in the necessities of life. Instead, they affirmed the
traditional idea of a "just price" for bread, which viewed millers and
bakers as servants of the entire community. On occasion, they resorted
to "taxation populaire"—the seizure of food supplies and their sale at
a traditional price in times of inflation or dearth. And they tended to

blame increases in food prices not on the inexorable operation of impersonal market forces but on the greedy activities of forestallers, engrossers, and monopolizing merchants and farmers.[50]

Colonial Americans, like their European contemporaries, lived with a wide range of governmental economic regulations. The nonimportation agreements of the 1760s and early 1770s clearly infringed on the freedom of trade, and usually included provisions to prevent merchants from profiting from the scarcity of British goods. Increasingly, however, such measures inspired opposition from merchants and other adherents of the newer doctrines of laissez-faire. The philosophical underpinning for these beliefs came from the new economics of Adam Smith. Smith's *Wealth of Nations* was not published until 1776, but it expressed ideas that had been widely circulated in preceding years. The world of Smith was not the corporate commonwealth of a previous age, but a collection of self-interested individuals whose very competing ambitions produced, through the operations of the natural order of society (the "invisible hand"), the greatest public benefit.[51]

There were some essential points of the new outlook with which Paine could not agree. His republicanism still embraced the older view of a society that comprised a uniform general interest, rather than competing individual ambitions. The world of Smith seemed to leave little room for a general good which could be consciously perceived and pursued by all members of society. Nonetheless, there was much in Smith's universe that must have appealed to Paine. Paine's Newtonian emphasis on the natural order in society went hand in hand with Smith's assertion of a natural harmony in the economic world. Unlike many colonists, Paine did not view commercial motives with distaste. "In all my publications," he would later observe, "..."I have been an advocate for commerce." In *Common Sense* he had specifically tied the economic hopes of the new nation to the kite of commercial freedom. And in the *Crisis* papers of 1777 and 1778, Paine had reiterated the merchants' belief that "trade flourishes best when it is free," attributing rising prices to an excess of paper money, rather than to the machinations of monopolizers.[52]

Paine thus stood midway between the new doctrine of commercial freedom and the older view of public virtue and an undifferentiated public good as the animating spirit of a republic. In the turbulent year of 1779, it was a specific political situation that determined at the outset Paine's reaction to the issue of price controls. In December 1778 and January 1779, Paine found himself in the midst of an acrimonious congressional controversy involving the conduct of Silas Deane, the Connecticut merchant who had been sent to France early in the war to purchase supplies for the army. The immediate issue was whether a shipment of supplies was a gift from the French government, or a commercial transaction on which Deane could claim a commission. But behind the Deane affair lay far larger issues. One was a growing disgust over war profiteering and the questionable ethical standards of merchants like Robert Morris, who served both the government and their own private gain at the same time, often purchasing supplies from their own companies or business partners at inflated prices. Then there was the perennial question of inflation and the renewed tendency of many in and out of Congress to blame it on "engrossers and monopolizers." Uniting these and other issues were traditional ideas: that "luxury" and "corruption" were incompatible with republicanism, and that "virtue" and self-sacrifice should take precedence over private interest and profit.[53]

Paine's involvement in the Deane affair led him to abandon temporarily his high regard for men of commerce, and launch an attack on "monopolizers." (The two were not, however, incompatible—the Smithian free market was based on the assumption that no one merchant or group could consciously control the price level.) A close associate of the anti-Deane faction in Congress, Paine rushed into print to defend their side of the Deane controversy, only to find himself under attack for indiscreetly using secret government correspondence in his writings. In January 1779, he was forced to resign his position as secretary to the Committee on Foreign Affairs (a post he had held since 1777), and was denounced in the press as a "stranger, without either connections or apparent property in this country." The newspaper debate continued well into the spring—as late as May, Paine was still denouncing Deane as an embezzler, and his business partner, Robert Morris, as corrupt.[54]

This prolonged controversy temporarily ended Paine's association with the national war effort and brought him back into Pennsylvania politics. His popularity in Congress waned, but "out of doors" it increased, while, according to contemporaries, Deane and his supporters "lasped into general contempt" in Philadelphia. The situation was complicated by the continuing rapid price spiral—in one month, early in 1779, prices rose by the astonishing rate of 45 percent.[55] As state and congressional measures failed to halt inflation, increasing numbers of Philadelphians came to the conclusion that only extralegal direct action could resolve the economic crisis. As early as December 1778, a writer, who styled himself "Mobility," had issued a "Hint" in the Philadelphia press, reminding readers that in Europe "the People have always done themselves justice when the scarcity of bread has arisen from the avarice of forestallers. They have broken open magazines—appropriated stores to their own use without paying for them —and in some instances have hung up the culprits who created their distress. . . ." In May 1779, as in 1776, it was the militia who took the lead. The First Company of Philadelphia Artillery presented a lengthy memorial to the Assembly, detailing the plight of "the midling and poor" and threatening violent action against "those who are avariciously intent upon amassing wealth by the destruction of the more virtuous part of the community." The result of this and other popular outcries was a mass meeting in May, the most important extralegal gathering in Philadelphia since preindependence days. The meeting adopted a plan that called for a gradual reduction of prices. Two committees were appointed, one to investigate the affairs of Robert Morris, who was accused of holding food from the market, and another to carry out the price reductions. To both committees, were appointed such radicals of 1776 as Matlack, Rittenhouse, and Peale—and Thomas Paine.[56]

The price-control committee functioned through June and July 1779, as did similar committees in countless localities in and out of the state. Not suprisingly, as the extralegal movement expanded, so did vocal opposition. The loudest criticism came from Philadelphia merchants, who generally believed that trade should be "free as air" and that the private interest of the merchant and the good of the public went "hand in hand." This was expected; more worrisome to the Philadelphia committee was that many master artisans became disillusioned with price controls as the summer of 1779 wore on. The militia who had inspired the movement in the first place were, after all, primarily laborers and poorer artisans—urban consumers. But the masters were as much businessmen as the merchants, and often stood to lose by price controls. In July, a committee of master tanners and shoemakers attacked the price schedules established for leather crafts, echoing the merchants' belief that "trade should be free as air, uninterrupted as the tide."[57]

The developing opposition to controls not only posed a serious dilemma for the committee but also for Paine. In May, June, and July, he was closely identified with the price-control movement. He served on the committee investigating the conduct of Robert Morris, and drafted a report which, while admitting that there was no specific evidence of engrossing, declared, "we are at a loss to find any other name" for Morris's business conduct. At the same time, Paine continued his involvement in the newspaper war against Silas Deane and his supporters. At the end of July, a crowd of several hundred "of the lower orders" descended on the house of Whitehead Humphreys, who had attacked Paine in the press. At a mass meeting a few days later, General John Cadwalader, who rose to denounce this "riot," was prevented from speaking by a group of armed men. The meeting unanimously resolved "that Mr. Thomas Paine is considered by this meeting as a friend to the American cause."[58]

Nonetheless, Paine, and probably others among his radical friends, were not happy with the turbulent atmosphere and class hostility that pervaded Philadelphia in the summer of 1779. Peale sought to disperse the crowd at Humphreys's house. And Paine, as always, sought a means of uniting the entire community for the common good. In July, he helped to devise a "Citizen's Plan" for reducing prices, which would unite "public and private interest" in support of the war effort. Paine had always believed that paper money was the primary cause of inflation. His plan called for a commitment on the part of Congress to stop emitting paper currency and to establish a subscription list, to which men could voluntarily contribute funds to support the war, their contributions credited against their next three years' state taxes. Presumably, stopping the printing presses would restore confidence in the currency and reduce prices, while the public subscription would both finance the government and enable men of wealth to prove their loyalty to the cause.

The Citizen's Plan was, in effect, an alternative to price controls, but Paine continued to be involved in the committee movement. At the beginning of August, he was one of 120 members elected to an expanded city committee. But the enlarged group proved extremely unwieldy, and at the end of September it suspended operations, attributing its failure to lower prices to its inability to regulate the prices of country produce and of goods in neighboring states.[59]

It was the failure of the city committee to end inflation and the reluctance of the state government to take effective action that produced the so-called "Fort Wilson riot" of early October. On 4 October 1779, a militia group began to march into the city, eventually making their way to the house of James Wilson. Wilson had long since "become obnoxious to a large portion of the community" because of his opposition to price controls and his strenuous opposition to the Constitution of 1776. With him in the house were some twenty political allies, including Robert Morris. Someone fired a shot, the militia attacked the house, and within a few minutes a troop of the City Light Horse, the aristocratic "silk stocking brigade," arrived, the militia were driven off, and many were arrested.[60] Benjamin Rush, who believed the militia "were enraged chiefly by liquor," said their objects were "unknown," but it seems clear that while the battle at the house was not premeditated, the purpose of the march was to demonstrate support for "the Constitution, the laws and the Committee of Trade" and to oppose "their internal enemies" and "Tories," who were held responsible for inflation. Rush was perceptive, however, when he wrote of the crowd, "their leaders abandoned them." Charles W. Peale had refused to lead the march, and Timothy Matlack headed the brigade that helped to break it up. As for Paine, he published a gloomy letter in the press, attributing the militia march to misguided patriotism. Paine seemed to place primary blame for the incident on the men gathered within Wilson's house, but he insisted it would be wrong to condemn them as Tories: "The difference is exceedingly great, between not being in favor and being considered as an enemy." And Paine revealed his alienation from the militia action by writing, "Those whose talent it is to act, are seldom much devoted to deliberate thinking."[61]

VII

The "Fort Wilson riot" was a major turning point in the history of popular radicalism in revolutionary Philadelphia. It was the culmination of a year of increasingly militant popular action against inflation, but it also marked the beginning of a decade in which such activity would be sporadic and ineffectual. The Wilson incident had irrevocably split the artisan-intelligensia radical leadership from mass crowd activities. What remained of the popular radicalism of the 1770s was a set of stubbornly egalitarian ideas, which lacked both articulate leadership and organized political expression. And at the same time, the artisans of Philadelphia found that neither of the state's two political parties gave much heed to their demands. The Constitutionalist party, to be sure, continued to employ the egalitarian rhetoric of the 1770s, but as a party dominated by backcountry farmers, merchants, land speculators, and up-and-coming small town capitalists, it took little notice of the artisan demand for tariff protection against the influx of British manufactured goods which flooded the city after the Peace of Paris of 1783.[62]

This political situation is essential for understanding one of the most controversial and, perhaps, not entirely explicable episodes of Paine's career: his alliance with Robert Morris and his defense of Morris's fiscal creation, the Bank of North America. During the 1780s Paine seemed to find his former political enemies increasingly congenial, and some of his former allies in disagreement. Yet his activities in that decade did not represent a complete break with his previous political and economic outlook. Paine had long been a proponent of strong central government, a critic of paper money, and a defender of institutions like the Bank of North America as essential props of American economic development. In 1779, he had seen the inability of older notions of "moral economy" to regulate the capitalist market. Moreover, Paine's alliance with Morris did not represent a full break with his artisan constituency, the majority of whom had allied themselves with Philadelphia merchants in opposition to a repetition of price controls and in support of Morris's financial program of the early 1780s.[63] A large portion of the artisans would side with Paine and Morris against the agrarians who led the attack on the Bank of Pennsylvania. On the other hand, the Bank war would also lead Paine to rethink some of his assumptions about the nature of republican government.

The Paine-Morris alliance was formalized in February 1782, when Paine entered into a secret agreement with Morris, Robert R. Livingston, and George Washington, to write "in support of the measures of Congress and their ministers." He was paid from a secret fund under Morris's control as superintendent of finance. In some ways, the wealthy merchant and Paine were strange bedfellows. Morris was an elitist in politics—his private correspondence reveals only contempt for the common people. The movement to strengthen the Continental government, which he spearheaded between 1781 and 1783, was motivated to some extent by the belief that a firm central government could "restrain the democratic spirit." But on certain basic questions, Paine had more in common with Morris than with the agrarian opponents of strong central government in Pennsylvania and other states. The politics of the agrarians was locally-oriented; their leaders were generally state politicians who had seen little or no service in Congress or the Continental army during the war. Paine, as a recent immigrant and a man who had devoted much of his time to the army and congressional affairs, had more in common with cosmopolitans like Morris than with agrarian localists. Morris looked forward to an American empire of "power, consequence and grandeur"—and such a vision of the future had been implicit in *Common Sense.* Paine had never seen any contradiction between business enterprise and "virture," and he agreed with Morris on the necessity of a stable currency and the evils of paper money. For Paine, in summary, there was no contradiction between an egalitarian political outlook and a nationalism coupled with free enterprise, commercial expansion, and economic development.[64]

Paine's major effort for the Morris group in 1782 and 1783 was a series of public letters on the 5 percent tariff on imported goods, which Congress had adopted as a means of providing a permanent revenue for the Continental government. Paine believed, as did Morris, that the nation's economic problems were "ascribable to the loose and almost disjointed condition of the Union," and he hoped that the impost would be the first step in strengthening the federal government. The union of the states, Paine wrote, was "our Magna Carta—our anchor in the world of empires.... It is on our undivided sovereignty, that our greatness and safety, and the security of our foreign commerce, rest." And he warned opponents of the Congressional measure that their opposition "serves only to unhinge the public mind, even in their own state, from every obligation of civil and moral society, and from all the necessary duties of good government; and to promote a profligacy, that may in time think all property common." This was the closest Paine would come to the Morris group's belief that a stronger central government was a barrier to dangerous radical tendencies in the states; it was an appeal specifically directed to Rhode Island, which opposed the impost.

With Rhode Island's veto of the impost and the end of the revolutionary war, much of the steam went out of the nationalist movement of the early 1780s. Paine continued to pen appeals for a stronger central government, but when Morris fell from his post as director of finances, Paine's secret salary was discontinued, and he more or less withdrew from political to personal concerns.[65]

Paine did not reenter politics until the end of 1785. The issue was the Bank of North America, the nation's first bank, established late in 1781 by Morris and his associates. In 1785, the rural Constitutionalists, who dominated the state legislature, moved to undermine Morris's financial policies. The legislature authorized a new issue of state paper money and assumed the federal debts owing to citizens of Pennsylvania—a direct challenge to the nationalists' intention to use the federal debt as a means of strengthening the central government. When the bank refused to accept the new state money at par, the legislature, in September 1785, repealed the bank's charter.[66]

The bank was a major subject of debate for most of 1785 and 1786. To its foes, it was an instrument of special privilege, a closed corporation established under authority of the state, which by its very nature threatened the republican ideal of equality. In the legislature the attack was led by a triumvirate of western Constitutionalist leaders, William Findlay, John Smilie, and Robert Whitehill. The Bank of North America, Findlay declared, was "inconsistent with our laws—our habits—our manners." The essence of republicanism was equality "of wealth and power," and "enormous wealth, possessed by individuals, has always had its influence and danger in free states." The sole purpose of the bank charter, he added, was to "give a special law to enable monied men to increase their gain," since "none but men of wealth have money to spare to be bankers."[67]

The arguments of the anti-bank legislators anticipated strikingly the rhetoric employed against the Bank of the United States during the Bank War of Andrew Jackson's presidency. And, as in the 1830s, the enemies of the Bank of North America represented a coalition of diverse economic and social groups. They ranged from opponents of all banks and all legislative grants of corporate charters, to business competitors of Morris, usurers who resented the low interest rates established by the bank, speculators in public securities who supported the state's assumption of Continental debts, agrarians who favored an extensive state issue of paper money, and farmers and artisans who believed themselves excluded from credit by Morris's bank. As in the 1830s, this coalition found it much easier to agree on the negative proposition of eliminating the bank, than on a positive fiscal program to replace it. For the agrarian Constitutionalists, the alternative to the bank was the creation of a state land bank, issuing paper money and making loans at low interest rates to farmers, with land as security.

The Philadelphia artisan community was divided on the bank question. The artisans, after all, owned no land and would be unlikely to benefit from a state land bank. On the other hand, some artisans charged that "a few wealthy merchants and those of good credit" monopolized loans from the Bank of North America. Many mechanics responded to the Constitutionalists' antiaristocratic appeal and hoped the destruction of the bank would result in easier credit, but many others feared it would unleash a flood of paper money and a new round of inflation.[68]

Paine was not particularly anxious to enter the Bank of North America controversy, or to differ publicly with his friends in the Constitutionalist party. But, in December 1785, he began a series of newspaper letters, added a widely-circulated pamphlet the next February, and continued to press the issue in a series of articles in the fall of 1786. In some respects, Paine, in his writings on the bank, simply restated long-established beliefs. His hostility to government-issued paper money had never been expressed more strongly, but it was hardly new. Paine sent to the press an article by a Rhode Island merchant who protested that state's legislation in making it illegal to refuse to accept paper money. This, Paine said, was "one of the most vile and arbitrary acts" in any of the states, and a threat to both "liberty and property." As the historian Bray Hammond observes, Paine seemed to assume that all issues of paper money were automatically legal tender. "Gold and silver are the emissions of nature; paper is the emission of art," Paine wrote, arguing that paper money "cannot stand on the principles of civil government," because it was inconsistent with personal liberty and the rights of property. He even said that any legislator proposing a law for legal tender paper money should be sentenced to death. (This Hammond notes, was "going pretty far.")[69]

To Paine, the bank was a bulwark against paper money and a promoter of the prosperity of the entire community, which was to play an essential role in his vision of an American republican empire. The "great improvements and undertakings" that the nation required—internal improvements, roads, and bridges—could not be undertaken in the atmosphere produced by the repeal of the bank charter. In a departure in his thinking, Paine distinguished between laws and legislative contracts; the first could be repealed at any time, the latter had to be respected by succeeding legislatures. In a sense, Paine anticipated the later contract theory of John Marshall, holding that the state stood as a "private citizen" in a contract like the bank charter. But Paine also declared that no act of a legislature could exist "forever." In this respect, the bank charter was faulty. Since no generation could rightfully bind a future one, all acts of legislation and contract should automatically go out of existence every thirty years. Yet, in a sense, the historian Louis Hartz is right in noting that "Paine on popular sovereignty did not get along easily with Paine on charter contracts." For, as one contemporary opponent of the bank asked, "Where is the benefit of annual election if the wisdom of one asembly may not be extended to correct the errors of a former?"[70]

Paine also objected to the idea that the Bank of Pennsylvania constituted some kind of aristocracy. Far from being an engine of privilege, it was really an egalitarian institution, for if the bank were destroyed, "a few monied men"—the only ones with personal wealth sufficient to finance commercial enterprises—would monopolize the commerce of the state. By providing credit at nonusurious rates, the bank allowed other entrepreneurs to challenge these wealthy merchants. The bank, moreover, could hardly be charged with serving the interests of only one class. Paine still viewed commerce and economic enterprise as serving the public good, and so would the bank, by establishing the "credit and confidence among individuals, which for many years was lost, and without which agriculture, commerce, and every species of business, must decline and languish." Significantly, Paine added that those who had the most to lose from repeal of the bank charter were the "manufacturers and mechanics," because they were the groups "against whose immediate interest paper money operates the strongest." Not only did it reduce their real income, but paper money banished "all the hard money which the exports of the country brought in," sending it abroad "to purchase foreign manufactures and trinkets." Banning paper money would therefore be "the most effectual encouragement" to American manufacturers.[71]

In one important respect, the ideas expressed in the bank controversy differed markedly from Paine's previous writings. He was shocked by the intensity of party conflict in Pennsylvania. In the bank writings, he voiced his displeasure at the political situation—a state "rent into factions," legislation conducted under the influence of "vehemence of party spirit and rancorous prejudice." Laws "founded in party"—like the repeal of the bank charter—were quite different from republican laws motivated only by the general good. This disillusionment led Paine to reconsider his advocacy of a unicameral legislature. "My idea of a single legislature," he explained, "was always founded on a hope, that whatever personal parties there might be in a state, they would all unite and agree in the general principles of good government . . . and that the general good, or the good of the whole, would be the governing principle of the legislature." But experience had shown that this classic vision of a republican utopia had been overwhelmed by party feeling. Paine concluded that a single house, when under the control of one party, "is capable of being made a compleat aristocracy for the time it exists." For a unicameral legislature to function properly, "it was absolutely necessary that the prejudices of party should have no operation within the walls of government." Without quite saying so, Paine seemed to be moving toward the conservative view that a two-house legislature was the only check on the passions and rash proceedings of the people. This was the closest Paine would come in his entire career to the political, as opposed to the economic, outlook of a John Adams or Robert Morris. In the 1790s he would revert to his prior position of unicameralism, although in *The Rights of Man* he proposed that the single house be divided into two parts, with each debating legislation in turn, to prevent over-hasty action.[72]

The party conflict of the 1780s also led Paine to rethink his vision of a republican America free from the conflict of class interests. Paine for the first time announced the principle that "a man's ideas are generally produced in him by his present situation and condition." He attributed opposition to the bank to agrarians whose circumstances limited their views and who had no material interest in the welfare of Pennsylvania. The backwoods farmers who formed the heart of the Constitutionalist party were men who "from their remote situation feel themselves very little, if at all, interested in the prosperity of the more settled and improved areas of the state." They were vastly different from commercial farmers:

> Their ideas of government, agriculture, and commerce, are drawn from and limited to their own frontier habitations. . . . A settler is not yet a farmer. . . . In the stage of a settler, his thoughts are engrossed and taken up in making a settlement. If he can raise produce enough for the support of his family, it is the utmost of his present hopes. He has none to bring to market, or to sell, and therefore commerce appears nothing to him; and he cries out, that a Bank is of no use.

Moreover, Paine insisted, what exports did emanate from the back-country areas were carried down the Susquehanna River to Baltimore rather than to Philadelphia and its surrounding counties.[73]

Paine's defense of the bank certainly cost him whatever popularity he had maintained in the Constitutionalist party. But Paine still retained his following among the artisans of Philadelphia, who by and large were abandoning the Constitutionalists. At the height of the bank controversy, in January 1786, a "numerous company of printers" assembled at a tavern in the city to celebrate the eighty-first birthday of Benjamin Franklin. Their toasts included praise of the printer's craft, freedom of the press, George Washington—and Thomas Paine.

The pro-bank Republican party swept the 1786 elections, including Philadelphia, and the bank was rechartered the following year. Paine, by this time, was working on a series of scientific interests, from smokeless candles to his design for an iron bridge. In April 1787, he sailed from New York for Europe, hoping to promote the bridge and to return within a year. No one, least of all Paine himself, could foresee the turbulent career that lay ahead of him in the 1790s. He believed he had "closed my political career" and could devote himself to "the quiet field of science."[74]

It was typical of the international notoriety Paine had achieved that in 1788 he followed the debates on the federal Constitution with Jefferson and Lafayette in Paris. And it was not surprising that Paine, long an advocate of stronger continental government, favored the new document, although he quite possibly shared Jefferson's concern over the absence of a bill of rights. Later, he also criticized the single executive and "the long duration of the Senate." In his support for the Constitution, Paine's views once again coincided with those of the great majority of America's urban artisans, who viewed the campaign for the Constitution as "a direct continuation of the independence struggle," and hoped a stronger federal government would encourage commerce and provide protection for American manufactures. Like the artisans, Paine saw no contradiction between his support for the Constitution and a continuing belief in egalitarian politics.[75]

VIII

The writings of Thomas Paine, one historian has recently written, contain the voice of "the intelligent artisan come into his own at last." Paine, of course, had begun life as an artisan, and throughout his life he retained a manual agility with tools as well as his interests in applied science. There was much in Paine's political outlook to which politically-enlightened artisans on both sides of the Atlantic responded with enthusiasm. But it would be wrong to consider Paine the exclusive spokesman of any single group within American society. Paine's personal and political associations were limited to no one group; in both Europe and America they spanned the worlds of the upper-class salon and tavern political debates. His writings, one contemporary declared, were read in "all ranks," and this was precisely as Paine intended. As he wrote in 1787, "I defend the cause of the poor, of the manufacturers, of the tradesmen, of the farmers...but above all, I defend the cause of humanity." Despite his prolonged involvement in Pennsylvania politics, Paine always considered himself a man above party, whose interest was simply "the general good, the happiness of the whole."[76]

Nor was Paine in any sense a critic of existing rights of property, although his views on this subject underwent change during his lifetime. In *Agrarian Justice,* written during the French Revolution, Paine did insist that "a revolution in the state of civilization is the necessary companion of revolutions in the system of government." Then, for the first time, he blamed poverty on the oppression of the poor by the rich, and called for a government program of direct payments to every citizen at age twenty-one, as compensation for the loss of the natural right to land which private property in land entailed. Even then, however, Paine rejected an "agrarian law" dividing existing property.

In *Common Sense,* by contrast, Paine took a typical Lockean view of private property, attributing economic distinctions and inequalities of wealth to differences in talent, industry, and frugality among individuals. "The distinctions of rich and poor," he declared, "may in a great measure be accounted for, and that without recourse to the harsh ill-sounding names of oppression and avarice. Oppression is often the *consequence,* but seldom or never the *means* of riches." Indeed, like many European commentators, what impressed Paine about America was its egalitarian distribution of property and high standard of living compared to the Old World. "There are not three millions of people in any part of the universe," Paine wrote in 1782, "who live so well, or have such a fund of ability, as in America. The income of a common laborer, who is industrious, is equal to that of the generality of tradesmen in England.... In America, almost every farmer lives on his own lands, and in England not one in a hundred does."[77]

"I see in America," Paine wrote in 1791, in *The Rights of Man,* "the generality of the people living in a style of plenty unknown in monarchial countries; and I see that the principle of its government, which is that of the *equal rights of Man,* is making rapid progress in the world." This association between America's economic abundance and its republican form of government was a crucial element in Paine's social outlook and helps explain why he did not attribute inequalities of wealth to economic oppression. Indeed, Paine's republican utopianism had little room for class or social conflict of any kind. What distinguished republican government for Paine was not the "particular form" of government, but its object: "the public good." Both class and party conflict were, in a sense, incompatible with republican government, which, by its very nature, Paine believed, "does not admit of an interest distinct from that of the nation." Unlike Madison and other republican thinkers, who viewed men as motivated basically by selfish interests and believed the only way to preserve liberty was to create a governmental structure balancing competing ambitions (a political analogue to Adam Smith's vision of the economy and marketplace), Paine was utterly optimistic about human nature. "Man," he wrote, "were he not corrupted by governments, is naturally the friend of man, and . . . human nature is not of itself vicious.[78]

For Madison, representative government was not simply a utopian experiment, but also an organizational device to prevent self-interested factionalism from destroying the state. For Paine, it was a means of insuring that the unitary interest of a homogeneous people was reflected in governmental decisions. Obviously, such a view left little room for any notion of class conflict, or even of competing class interests. To be sure, Paine was an eloquent and scathing critic of the social order of Europe. But the cause of the "mass of wretchedness" in English society was political, not economic: the existence of poverty implied that "something must be wrong in the system of government."[79]

Paine thus saw no reason for inevitable antagonism between rich and poor, or employer and employee. Harmony, not conflict, would characterize social relations under republican government. Yet, by the same token, Paine had no use for paternalisitc, deferential relationships of any sort. His aim was to wean the lower classes from a respect for elites into self-respect and sustained involvement in political life. As a result, Paine had little use for mob activity. "I never did, nor never would, encourage what may properly be called a mob," he wrote, "when any legal mode of redress can be had." Paine knew, moreover, that in England, mobs as often rallied to the cause of church and king as to Wilkes and liberty, and too often were motivated by "prejudices, which the government itself had encouraged."[80]

The cause of mobs, for Paine, was poverty, and the cause of poverty, bad government; both would disappear under republican government. As a man who had known poverty and pulled himself out of it, Paine did not romanticize want. As early as 1772, in the *Case of the Officers of Excise,* he had written that "poverty, in defiance of principle, begets a degree of meanness that will stoop to anything." Yet Paine was not content simply to condemn the poor for idleness, like so many other writers of the eighteenth century. His writings are filled with expressions of genuine compassion for "the hordes of miserable poor" in Europe. He despised not the poor, but poverty. The establishment of republican government, coupled (in Europe) with the social welfare plans he outlined in *The Rights of Man*—the abolition of poor rates, aid to the unemployed, free public education—would not only eliminate poverty and end "riots and tumults," but would destroy an entire pattern of oppressive legislation and deferential relationships which prevented the poor from participating in the mainstream of the life of society.[81]

Paine's republicanism, therefore, looked forward to a future of political egalitarianism and economic well-being that would embrace all members of the social order. He did not share the fears of Americans in the agrarian "country party" tradition, who viewed economic growth and the expansion of commerce and urbanization as elements of national decay. Paine "was always a city man at heart." Jefferson may have hoped America could insulate itself against the industrial revolution, but Paine was enchanted by the cotton mills, potteries, and steel furnaces of England in the 1780s, and hoped such enterprises could be "carried on in America as well."[82] He was an urbanite, a cosmopolitan, and a proponent of economic growth and commerical intercourse, as well as a republican and a democrat. In *Common Sense,* these various strands of thought had seemed fully compatible. At other times during his American career, one belief took precedence over the others. In the price control movement of 1779, the implications of republicanism for a time overshadowed Paine's commitment to commercial freedom. In the bank war, his economic values pushed his political egalitarianism into the background.

There would always be important tensions and ambiguities in Paine's thought; such tensions were inevitable in an age of rapid change. But, in general, Paine embraced the key social transformations of his era—the emergence of mass political involvement and the development of the free market—as agents of progress and equality. What makes Paine's radicalism relevant for later generations is not the specific tenets of his belief, but his essential cast of mind: his impatience with the past, his utter contempt for institutions that could not stand the test of reason, and his belief that men could shape their own destinies. In neither America nor Europe was Paine's the most radical voice in the Age of Revolution. On both sides of the Atlantic, men would take Paineite republicanism and, unlike Paine, forge it into an aggressive weapon against the existing distribution of property. But it was precisely because he raised the possibility of total change that Paine's ideas could be extended in this way. He expressed the political and social resentments of men outside the eighteenth century's "political nation" and gave them a political language they could utilize themselves. His lasting legacy was what John Adams derisively called "Paine's yellow fever"—the spread of egalitarianism and political consciousness on both sides of the Atlantic in the Age of Revolution.[83]

1. The author wishes to thank the American Council of Learned Societies and the Faculty Research Award Program of the City University of New York for financial assistance. He also expresses gratitude to David F. Hawke, John Alexander, Gary Nash, and Stephen J. Rosswurm, for allowing him to read in manuscript writings relating to the subject of this essay, and to Mark Hirsch, who served as research assistant in the summer of 1974. A special debt of thanks is owed to Alfred Young, who has shared his unrivaled knowledge of the revolutionary period and offered encouragement and advice on numerous occasions over the past few years.

2. David Freeman Hawke, *Paine* (New York: Harper & Row, 1974), p. 24.

3. Among useful works that isolate one aspect of Paine's thought are: Joseph Dorfman, "The Economic Philosophy of Thomas Paine," *Political Science Quarterly* 53 (September 1938): 372–86; Howard Penniman, "Thomas Paine—Democrat," *American Political Science Review* 37 (April 1943): 244–62; Harry Hayden Clark, "Toward a Reinterpretation of Thomas Paine," *American Literature* 5 (May 1933): 133–45. Staughton Lynd, in *Intellectual Origins of American Radicalism* (New York: Pantheon Books, 1968), deals with eighteenth-century radicalism as much the same thing as twentieth-century radicalism. Hawke's is now the best one-volume biography, but Moncure D. Conway, *The Life of Thomas Paine*, 2 vols. (New York: G.P. Putnam's Sons, 1892) is still useful.

4. The best treatment of Paine's early life in England is contained in Audrey Williamson, *Thomas Paine, His Life, Work and Times* (London: Allen & Unwin, 1973), pp. 11–59.

5. Philip S. Foner, ed., *The Complete Writings of Thomas Paine*, 2 vols. (New York: Citadel Press, 1945), 2:1189; Williamson, *Paine*, pp. 19–20.

6. Foner, *Complete Writings*, 2:464; T. S. Ashton, *An Economic History of England: The Eighteenth Century* (London: Methuen, 1955); George Rudé, *Wilkes and Liberty* (Oxford: Oxford University Press, 1962).

7. Foner, *Complete Writings*, 1:496; F. W. Gibbs, "Itinerant Lecturers in Natural Philosophy," *Ambix* 8 (1960): 111–17; Nicholas Hans, *New Trends in Education in the Eighteenth Century* (London: Routledge & Kegan Paul, 1951), pp. 145–46, 152–53, 160–61.

8. Foner, *Complete Writings*, 1:164, 387; J. H. Plumb, *In the Light of History* (London: Allen Lane, 1972), pp. 9, 13–21.

9. Charles Inglis, *The True Interest of America* (Philadelphia, 1776), p.22; John Hall "The Grounds and Reasons of Monarchy Considered . . .," in *The Oceana and Other Works of James Harrington* (London, 1771), pp. 3–30.

10. Lucy Sutherland, "The City of London in Eighteenth-Century Politics," in

Richard Pares and A. J. P. Taylor, eds., *Essays Presented to Sir Lewis Namier* (London, Macmillan and Co., 1956), pp. 49–74; Jacqueline Simpson, *The Folklore of Lewes* (London, Batsford, 1973), pp. 134–36; Foner, *Complete Writings*, 1:496; Walter H. Godfrey, *At the Sign of the Bull, Lewes...* (London, 1924); Williamson, *Paine*, pp. 37–39; *Sussex Weekly Advertiser, or Lewes Journal,* 27 August 1770; William Page, ed., *The Victoria County History of the County of Sussex* (London: Constable, 1905–)1:530–31; Basil Williams, *Carteret and Newcastle* (Cambridge: Cambridge University Press, 1943), pp. 32–34, 223.

11. Foner, *Complete Writings,* 2:4–11, 1129; 1:441.

12. L. H. Butterfield, ed., *Letters of Benjamin Rush,* 2 vols. (Philadelphia: American Philosophical Society, 1951) 1:450; David Freeman Hawke, *In the Midst of a Revolution* (Philadelphia: University of Pennsylvania Press, 1961); Arthur L. Jensen, *The Maritime Commerce of Colonial Philadelphia* (Madison: State Historical Society of Wisconsin, 1963), p. 5.

13. Charles S. Olton, "Phildelphia Artisans and the American Revolution" (Ph.D. diss., University of California, Berkeley, 1967); Jackson Turner Main, *The Sovereign States, 1775–1783* (New York: New Viewpoints, 1973), pp. 71–80; Carl Bridenbaugh, *The Colonial Craftsman* (New York: New York University Press, 1950), passim; David Montgomery, "The Working Classes of the Pre-Industrial City," *Labor History* 9 (Winter 1968): 13–16.

14. William S. Hanna, *Benjamin Franklin and Pennsylvania Politics* (Stanford: Stanford University Press, 1964), pp. 2–3; Olton, "Philadelphia Artisans," pp. 141–48, 161–64; Charles H. Lincoln *The Revolutionary Movement in Pennsylvania, 1760–1776* (Philadelphia: University of Pennsylvania Press, 1901), pp. 159–90.

15. Gwyn Williams, *Artisans and Sans-Culottes* (New York: W. W. Norton & Co., 1969); *To the Free and Patriotic Inhabitants of the City of Philadelphia,* Broadside, 31 May 1770; "A Lover of Liberty and a Mechanics' Friend," *Pennsylvania Gazette,* 27 September 1770; Lincoln, *Revolutionary Movement,* p. 80 n.

16. R. A. Ryerson, "Political Mobilization and the American Revolution: The Revolutionary Movement in Philadelphia, 1765 to 1776," *William and Mary Quarterly,* 3d ser. 31 (October 1974): 565–88; *Pennsylvania Gazette,* 14 February, 1 May, 28 August 1776; "The Lee Papers," New-York Historical Society *Collections,* 4 vols. (1871–74), 1:212; *Pennsylvania Archives,* 8th ser. 8:7406–8.

17. *Pennsylvania Evening Post,* 30 July 1776; H. N. Brailsford, *The Levellers and the English Revolution* (Stanford: Stanford University Press, 1961), pp. 148–51.

18. *Pennsylvania Archives,* 8th ser. 8:7397–7405, 7409, 7422, 7438–39; *Pennsylvania Gazette,* 11 October 1775, 6 March 1776; Elisha P. Douglass, *Rebels and Democrats* (Chapel Hill: University of North Carolina Press, 1955), p. 252.

19. Peter Force, ed., *American Archives,* 4th ser. 1:342.

20. Foner, *Complete Writings,* 2:1480; Gordon S. Wood, *The Creation of the American Republic, 1776–1789* (Chapel Hill: University of North Carolina Press, 1969), pp. 199–200, 223; W. Paul Adams, "Republicanism in Political Rhetoric Before 1776," *Political Science Quarterly* 85 (September 1970): 398–404; Pauline Maier, *From Resistance to Revolution* (New York: Alfred A. Knopf, 1972), pp. 288–95.

21. Foner, *Complete Writings,* 1:3–46.

22. Thomas R. Adams, *American Independence, The Growth of an Idea* (Providence: Brown University Press, 1965), pp. xi–xii; John R. Howe, *From the Revolution Through the Age of Jackson* (Englewood Cliffs, N.J.: Prentice-Hall, 1973), pp. 28–31; *Pennsylvania Evening Post,* 13 February, 26 March 1776; Winthrop D. Jordan, "Familial Politics: Thomas Paine and the Killing of the King," *Journal of American History* 60 (September 1973): 295; *Pennsylvania Packet,* 12 February 1776.

23. Lyman H. Butterfield, ed., *Diary and Autobiography of John Adams,* 4 vols. (Cambridge: Harvard University Press, 1961), 3:333; Bernard Bailyn, "Common Sense," *American Heritage* 25 (December 1973): 36–39; Douglass, *Rebels and Democrats,* p. 21; Bernard Bailyn, *The Ideological Origins of the American Revolution* (Cambridge: Harvard University Press, 1967), pp. 12–19; Inglis, *True Interest,* p. 34; Foner, *Complete Writings,* 1:7, 16.

24. Foner, *Complete Writings,* 2:111, 78; 1:260.

25. Foner, *Complete Writings,* 1:xviii; "Edmund Randolph's Essay," *Virginia Magazine of History and Biography* 43 (1935): 306. See also the excellent discussion of Paine's

literary style in James T. Boulton, *The Language of Politics* (London: Routledge & Kegan Paul, 1963), pp. 134–50.

26. Merrill Jensen, *The Founding of a Nation* (New York: Oxford University Press, 1968), p. 687; Theodore Thayer, *Pennsylvania Politics and the Growth of Democracy 1740–1776* (Harrisburg: Pennsylvania Historical and Museum Commission, 1953), pp. 170–77.

27. A. M. Stackhouse, *Col. Timothy Matlack* (n. p., 1910).

28. David Brion Davis, *The Problem of Slavery in the Age of Revolution* (Ithaca, N.Y.: Cornell University Press, 1975), pp. 288–89; Alan Heimert, *Religion and the American Mind, From the Great Awakening to the Revolution* (Cambridge: Harvard University Press, 1966), pp. 12–14, 59–60, 460–63, and passim.

29. Thomas J. Scharf and Thompson Westcott, *History of Philadelphia 1609–1884*, 3 vols. (Philadelphia, 1884), 1:261; Carl and Jessica Bridenbaugh, *Rebels and Gentlemen* (New York: Reynal and Hitchcock, 1942), p. 19; Thayer, *Pennsylvania Politics*, pp. 134–35, 185; Margaret W. Willard, ed., *Letters on the American Revolution 1774–1776* (Boston, 1928), p. 315.

30. Butterfield, ed., *Letters of Rush*, 1:18, 265;2:825–26; Donald D'Elia, "The Republican Theology of Benjamin Rush," *Pennsylvania History* 33 (April, 1966): 187–203; David Freeman Hawke, *Benjamin Rush: Revolutionary Gadfly* (Indianapolis and New York: Bobbs-Merrill, 1971), pp. 12–14, 73, 157–58; John A. Woods, "The Correspondence of Benjamin Rush and Granville Sharp, 1773–1809," *Journal of American Studies* 1 (1967): 9.

31. John Hughes to Lords Commissioners of His Majesty's Treasury, 13 January 1766, Treasury Papers, Class One, 452:218, Public Record Office (Library of Congress Transcripts).

32. *Pennsylvania Packet*, 7 February 1782; Hawke, *In the Midst*, p. 105.

33. David Freeman Hawke, "Dr. Thomas Young—'Eternal Fisher in Troubled Waters': Notes for a Biography," *New-York Historical Society Quarterly* 54 (January 1970): 7–29; John C. Miller, *Sam Adams, Pioneer in Propaganda* (Boston: Little, Brown and Co., 1936), pp. 84–87, 198; Isaac Q. Leake, *Memoir of the Life and Times of General John Lamb* (Albany, 1850), p. 89.

34. Brooke Hindle, *David Rittenhouse* (Princeton: Princeton University Press, 1964); Charles Coleman Sellers, *Charles Willson Peale* (New York: Charles Scribner's Sons, 1969); Daniel J. Boorstin, *The Lost World of Thomas Jefferson* (New York: Holt, 1948), pp. 13–22; Charles Willson Peale Autobiography, typescript copy, p. 40, Peale Papers, American Philosophical Society.

35. Heimert, *Religion and the American Mind*, pp. 74–76, 479, 493, 538–39; Butterfield, ed., *Letters of Rush*, 1:335.

36. Page Smith, *John Adams, 1735–1826*, 2 vols. (Garden City, N.Y.: Doubleday & Co., 1962), 1:245; Howe, *From the Revolution*, p. 2; Adams "Republicanism," pp. 397–98; New York *Constitutional Gazette*, 24 February 1776.

37. Inglis, *The True Interest*, pp. vii, 10, 49–53, 79; [William Smith], *Plain Truth* (Philadelphia, 1776), pp. 2, 8–12, 34–36.

38. Charles Francis Adams, ed., *Familiar Letters of John Adams and His Wife Abigail Adams* (New York, 1876), p. 146; *The Warren-Adams Letters*, 2 vols. (Boston, 1917–25), 1:234; Butterfield, ed., *Diary and Autobiography of Adams*, 3:331–33; Charles Francis Adams, ed., *The Works of John Adams*, 20 vols. (Boston, 1856), 9:616–18.

39. *Warren-Adams Letters*, 1:234, 339; Adams, ed., *Adams Works*, 9:376–78.

40. Wood, *Creation*, p. 482; "Salus Populi," *Pennsylvania Journal*, 13 March 1776; "Eudoxus," *Pennsylvania Packet*, 22 April 1776.

41. See the essay by Gary B. Nash in this volume.

42. "Candidus," *Pennsylvania Gazette*, 6 March 1776; "Cassandra," *Pennsylvania Ledger*, 13 April 1776; *The Alarm*, Broadside, May 1776; "Elector," *Pennsylvania Gazette*, 15 May 1776.

43. "Elector," *Pennsylvania Packet*, 29 April 1776; "Elector," *Pennsylvania Gazette*, 15 May 1776; "To the Worthy Inhabitants," *Pennsylvania Packet*, 20 May 1776; "Eudoxus," *Pennsylvania Packet*, 22 April 1776.

44. The best surveys of the complex chronology of events are in Hawke, *In the Midst*, and Richard A. Ryerson, "Leadership in Crisis, The Radical Committees of

Philadelphia and the Coming of the Revolution in Pennsylvania, 1765–1776: A Study in the Revolutionary Process" (Ph. D. diss., Johns Hopkins University, 1972).

45. Butterfield, ed., *Letters of Rush,* 1:336; Hawke, *In the Midst,* pp. 183–86; Foner, *Complete Writings,* 2:269–72.

46. *The Proceedings Relative to Calling the Conventions of 1776 and 1790...* (Harrisburg, Pa., 1825), pp. 54–55; *An Essay of a Declaration of Rights,* Broadside, 1776.

47. "Diary of James Allen," *Pennsylvania Magazine of History and Biography* 9 (1885): 177; *At a Meeting, Held at the Philosophical Society Hall, 17 October 1776,* Broadside; *Pennsylvania Packet,* 29 October 1776; "Agricola," *Pennsylvania Packet,* 29 October 1776; "John Trusshoop," *Pennsylvania Gazette,* 13 November 1776; *To the Free and Independent Electors of the City of Philadelphia,* Broadside, 5 November 1776; "The Considerate Freeman," *Pennsylvania Packet,* 26 November 1776.

48. Foner, *Complete Writings,* 2:278, 283–87, 399, 578–80; 1:330.

49. The best introduction to this subject is still Robert A. East, *Business Enterprise in the American Revolutionary Era* (New York: Columbia University Press, 1938).

50. George Rudé, *The Crowd in History, 1738–1848* (New York: Oxford University Press, 1964), pp. 21–45, 108–21, 228; E. P. Thompson, "The Moral Economy of the English Crowd in the Eighteenth Century," *Past and Present* 50 (February 1971): 76–136.

51. Richard B. Morris, "Labor and Mercantilism in the Revolutionary Era," in Morris, ed., *The Era of the American Revolution* (New York: Columbia University Press, 1939), pp. 76–91; Arthur M. Schlesinger, *The Colonial Merchants and the American Revolution 1763–1776* (New York: Frederic Ungar, 1957), pp. 211, 498–99, 554–55, 584–85; Adam Smith, *The Wealth of Nations* (Penguin Books, London, 1970).

52. Foner, *Complete Writings,* 1:20, 36, 80, 98–99, 153, 157, 400.

53. Hawke, *Paine,* chap. 6; Edmund Burnett, ed., *Letters of Members of the Continental Congress,* 8 vols. (Washington, D.C.: Carnegie Institute, 1921–1936), 2:401; 3:437, 490–92; E. James Ferguson, *The Power of the Purse* (Chapel Hill, N. C. : University of North Carolina Press, 1961), pp. 71–81, 92–102; Clarence L. Ver Steeg, *Robert Morris: Revolutionary Financier* (Philadelphia: University of Pennsylvania Press, 1954), pp. 13, 25.

54. Foner, *Complete Writings,* 2:136, 141, 1176; Hawke, *Paine,* pp. 89–94.

55. Burnett, ed., *Letters,* 3:545; 4:110; Paine to Henry Laurens, 9 Janaury 1779, Gimbel Collection, American Philosophical Society; Anne Bezanson, *Prices and Inflation During the American Revolution: Pennsylvania, 1770–1790* (Philadelphia: University of Pennsylvania Press, 1951).

56. "A Hint," *Pennsylvania Packet,* 10 December 1778; *Pennsylvania Archives,* 1st ser. 7:392–94; *At a General Meeting of the Citizens of Philadelphia,* Broadside, May 1779.

57. Ver Steeg, *Morris,* p. 38; Pelatiah Webster, *Political Essays* (Philadelphia, 1791), pp. 9–20, 30–46; *Pennsylvania Packet,* 10 September 1779; *Pennsylvania Packet,* 15 July 1779.

58. Burnett, ed., *Letters,* 4:236; H. James Henderson, "Constitutionalists and Republicans in the Continental Congress, 1778–1786," *Pennsylvania History* 36 (April 1969): 133–34; Foner, *Complete Writings,* 2:188, 193, 202–3; "Letter of Silas Deane to His Brother Simeon Deane," *Pennsylvania Magazine of History and Biography* 17 (1893): 350; *Pennsylvania Evening Post,* 2 August 1779; *Pennsylvania Packet,* 29 July 1779.

59. Charles Willson Peale Autobiography, p. 71, typescript copy, Peale Papers; *Pennsylvania Packet,* 10, 29 July, 5, 14, 28 August, 11 September 1779; *Pennsylvania Gazette,* 27 September 1779.

60. The most recent and best published account is John Alexander, "The Fort Wilson Incident of 1779: A Case Study of the Revolutionary Crowd," *William and Mary Quarterly,* 3d ser. 31 (October 1974): 589–612.

61. Butterfield, ed., *Letters of Rush,* 1:240; William B. Reed, *Life and Correspondence of Joseph B. Reed,* 2 vols. (Philadelphia, 1847), 2:151; Charles Willson Peale Autobiography, typescript copy, pp. 71–75, Peale Papers; "C——. S——.," *Pennsylvania Packet,* 16 October 1779.

62. Edwin G. Burrows, "Albert Gallatin and the Political Economy of Republicanism," (Ph. D. diss., Columbia University, 1973), pp. 176–79; Robert L. Brunhouse, *The Counter-Revolution in Pennsylvania 1776–1790* (Philadelphia: Pennsylvania Historical Commission, 1942), pp. 63, 82, 149, 157–58; Olton, "Philadelphia Artisans," pp. 284–97.

63. Brunhouse, *Counter-Revolution*, pp. 83–84, 94–95; Olton, "Philadelphia Artisans," pp. 245–47.

64. Memorandum, 10 February 1782 (photostat of original in Library of Congress), Gimbel Collection; Ferguson, *Power of the Purse*, pp. 120–21; E. James Ferguson, "The Nationalists of 1781–1783 and the Economic Interpretation of the Constitution," *Journal of American History* 56 (September 1969): 241–61; Wood, *Creation*, pp. 403–5; Foner, *Complete Writings*, 1:185; 2:228–29.

65. Foner, *Complete Writings*, 1:232–34, 333–47, 364; 2:1213–14; Hawke, *Paine*, pp. 137–47.

66. Janet Wilson, "The Bank of North America and Pennsylvania Politics, 1781–1787," *Pennsylvania Magazine of History and Biography* 66 (January 1942): 3–28, M. L. Bradbury, "Legal Privilege and the Bank of North America," ibid., 96 (April 1972): 139–66; Bray Hammond, *Banks and Politics in America* (Princeton: Princeton University Press, 1957), pp. 42–52.

67. Matthew Carey, ed., *Debates and Proceedings of the General Assembly of Pennsylvania* . . . (Philadelphia, 1786), pp. 52–57, 62–69, 79, 130; Bradbury, "Legal Privilege," pp. 148–49.

68. Forrest McDonald, *E Pluribus Unum* (Boston: Houghton Mifflin Co., 1965), pp. 48–51; Olton, "Philadelphia Artisans," pp. 273–80, 302, 318–23; *Pennsylvania Packet*, 31 March 1785, 29 March 1786.

69. "Common Sense," *Pennsylvania Packet*, 7 November 1786; "Common Sense," *Pennsylvania Packet*, 21 August 1786; Hammond, *Banks and Politics*, pp. 60–61; Foner, *Complete Writings*, 2:382, 404–6.

70. Foner, *Complete Writings*, 2:413–16; *Pennsylvania Gazette*, 20 September 1786; Hawke, *Paine*, p. 154; Louis Hartz, *Economic Policy and Democratic Thought* (Cambridge: Harvard University Press, 1948), pp. 250, 304; "Atticus," *Pennsylvania Packet*, 8 May 1786.

71. Foner, *Complete Writings*, 2:391, 424, 428; *Pennsylvania Gazette*, 21 December 1785, 20 September 1786.

72. Foner, *Complete Writings*, 1:390; 2:390, 409, 1247, 1255; "Common Sense," *Pennsylvania Gazette*, 20 September 1786.

73. Foner, *Complete Writings*, 2:426, 1256.

74. *Pennsylvania Gazette*, 25 January 1786; Paine to George Clymer, 13 December 1786, Paine to Edmund Burke, 7 August 1788, Gimbel Collection; Foner, *Complete Writings*, 2:909.

75. Hawke, *Paine*, pp. 185–86; Foner, *Complete Writings*, 2:691–93, 1390–91; Staughton Lynd, *Class Conflict, Slavery, and the United States Constitution* (Indianapolis and New York: Bobbs-Merrill, 1967), pp. 123–26; Olton, "Philadelphia Artisans," pp. 309–11, 342–57.

76. Gwyn Williams, "Tom Paine," *New Society*, 6 August 1970, p. 236; "The Lee Papers," 1:312–14; Hawke, *Paine*, p. 47; Foner, *Complete Writings*, 1:413–14; 2:362, 621, 1228.

77. Foner, *Complete Writings*, 1:9, 203, 618–20; Hawke, *Paine*, pp. 327–29.

78. Foner, *Complete Writings*, 1:326, 343, 369, 397; 2:294; Arthur O. Lovejoy, *Reflections on Human Nature* (Baltimore: Johns Hopkins University Press, 1961), pp. 50–65.

79. Wood, *Creation*, pp. 55–62; Foner, *Complete Writings*, 1:90, 175, 341, 404–5, 412, 421–24; 2:191.

80. Foner, *Complete Writings*, 1:63, 359; 2:289, 369, 1296.

81. Foner, *Complete Writings*, 1:355, 360, 405, 424, 431, 446–47.

82. Foner, *Complete Writings*, 2:90, 202, 241–42, 1292; Hawke, *Paine*, p. 71.

83. Smith, *John Adams*, 2: 845.

Boston Leaders and Boston Crowds, 1765-1776

Dirk Hoerder

A Boston crowd that got out of hand: the demonstration, in February 1770, outside the shop of T. Lilly, violator of the nonimportation agreement. A pro-British official is depicted firing from the second-story window, mortally wounding Christopher Seider, an eleven-year-old boy, who lies dying, to the right, while a woman, at the door, looks on, aghast. From a broadside, "The Life and Humble Confessions of Richardson, the Informer," Pennsylvania Historical Society.

My interests in the role of the "little guy" in making the history of a society began with what I learned in school in Germany about German fascism. When I came to study the German resistance movement, I discovered that historians had concentrated on resistance among the social elite, while there was almost a conspiracy of silence about resistance in the trade unions and left-wing parties. I also discovered that research about resistance was encouraged and financed, with intention to draw away attention from fascism and, to overstate the case, make the Third Reich appear as a hothouse of resistance, particularly among the leaders.

About the same time, I read George Rudé's book on the crowd in the French Revolution. Both disgust with the way the history of the Third Reich was being remade and admiration for the stimulating results yielded by Rudé's approach led me to the decision to examine the role of the common people in a period of accelerated social change. A seminar at the Free University of Berlin, with Gerald Stourzh, on de Tocqueville's *Democracy in America,* and the unusually good research facilities of the department for interdisciplinary studies on the United States, led me to select the American Revolution as the object of my research.

As a graduate student of John Howe, at the University of Minnesota, I examined the possibilities the lower classes had in colonial Massachusetts to express grievances within the system of the town meeting and provincial legislature. My findings, put down in 1968 in a brief thesis, "Society and Government, 1760–1780: The Power Structure in Massachusetts Townships," were quite different from Robert E. Brown's middle-class democracy. The crop of township studies of recent years, I might add, was not yet available at that time. My next logical step was to examine extra-institutional action, which resulted in a doctoral dissertation, in 1971, about the revolutionary crowd in Massachusetts and its colonial antecedents. I found that "my" crowds did not have the mind of Whig pamphleteers, especially if they were from the bottom of society. Their relationship with the Boston leadership is the theme of this essay. Their ideology, especially its Protestant, common-law traditions, and the molding of these traditions into a rudimentary class consciousness, will have to be refined by future studies.

I am currently working on the economic thought of artisans and workers as part of a larger project on class consciousness and nationalism among these groups, from the revolutionary period to the depression of 1837.

Dirk Hoerder (Dr. phil., Free University of Berlin, 1971), spent the 1974–1975 academic year at Harvard on fellowships at the Charles Warren Center and the John F. Kennedy School of Government. He is currently in Berlin, where he has been on the faculty of the Kennedy Institute for American Studies at the Free University.

"The Boston Mob, raised first by the Instigation of Many of the Principal Inhabitants, Allured by Plunder, rose shortly after of their own Accord, attacked, robbed, and destroyed, several Houses, and amongst others, that of the Lieutenant Governor; and only spared the Governor's, because his Effects had been removed. People then began to be terrified at the Spirit they had raised, to perceive that popular Fury was not to be guided, and each individual feared he might be the next Victim to their Rapacity. The same Fears spread thro' the other Provinces, and there has been as much Pains taken since, to prevent Insurrections, of the People, as before to excite them."[1] This assessment of the anti-Stamp Act riots was given by Gen. Thomas Gage, commander of the British forces in the North American colonies, at the end of September 1765. Crowd action had begun by the middle of August, and when Gage surveyed the situation, there was little doubt that the Stamp Act could not be put into execution. Obviously, too, the colonists had other problems to deal with than stamps. What was the character of the "popular fury"? What were its causes? If town meetings achieved consensus, if property were widely distributed, why were there "plundering poor" and "terrified rich"? If the "mob" could defy guidance and act on its "own accord," why had Boston's "principal inhabitants" "instigated" crowd action in the first place? Or was it so simple? What was the relationship between "the principal inhabitants" and "the people" in the crowds? Were the former in fact the leaders, as Gage and historians have claimed ever since? Or did they follow the crowd? In this essay an attempt will be made to explore the relationships between the crowd and the town leaders in Boston.

Riots in defiance of established authorities had a long tradition in the colonies, especially in Boston, the leading port of Massachusetts.

So had crowd action in support of authority. The latter has been thoroughly treated by Pauline Maier, whose research has focussed on crowd action which "used extralegal means to implement official demands," "to enforce laws not otherwise enforceable," or to extend "the law in urgent situations beyond its technical limits." In the eighteenth-century colonies, law enforcement was not yet vested solely with authorities, whether elected or appointed. Part of the enforcement was still the responsibility of the society at large. One of the societal means was crowd action, originally directed against outsiders, high-handed magistrates, or influential community members whose powers placed them beyond the reach of the authorities.[2]

Later, with increasing diversification and stratification, different social strata developed an understanding of the laws, norms, and traditions, including those regulating direct action, at variance with those of other classes. With the changing character of society and the stress to which corporate ideology was subjected, the nature of crowd action changed, as did the attitudes of some social groups toward it. What once was and still could be, in Maier's phrase, "quasi-institutional" action became after the 1740s more and more often an expression of social discontent, of group and class interests. These changes have not received adequate attention by scholars of crowd action. In this essay my concern will be with the clash of the tradition of crowd action and the postulates or expectations of policy-making groups about what it should achieve against British policies; with the interaction between leadership and crowd; and with the development of these relationships under the impact of new imperial policies on local issues and interests.

All strata of society, whether the "lower classes," the "middling interest," or the "better sort," to use the then contemporary terms, agreed that under certain conditions crowd action was justified, but they disagreed what these conditions were. In the first decades of the eighteenth century, food riots against wealthy merchants, individuals who conducted their business to the detriment of the inhabitants' interests, were condoned by many magistrates. By the 1730's, interest groups opposed each other over the sale of provisions. When large merchants pushed their views, crowd action destroyed the centralized markets and "civil war" was threatened by disenfranchised men as well as by voters disappointed with the town leaders' inability to reverse Boston's economic decline. In the 1740s, sailors and laborers from the waterfront resorted to anti-impressment riots, after town leaders proved unable to curb the violence of the British press-gangs. When

Governor William Shirley, in 1747, ordered the crowd to disperse, he was interrogated instead by self-conscious rioters about his role in granting impressment permission to the Royal Navy.[3]

In these decades the currency controversies and the increasingly ostentatious display of wealth and luxury contributed further to the separation of social classes. Sharp debates in the public prints resulted from such antagonisms. Mechanics continued to use crowd action, a community activity against outsiders, to assert their interest and to express their ideology against the increasing domination of the "better sort." Considering this increased stratification, did mechanics represent the public interest, for which riots were justified according to contemporary ideology? Upper-class Bostonians felt that the rioters were wrong in opposing hard money and the display of wealth. Claiming to represent the public interest, the provincial legislature opposed the crowds of the hard money episode; but the authorities then opposed the wealthy, whose display of luxury provoked other Bostonians to riot.

Justifiable riots received ex post facto sanction by legislative action to redress grievances. In this line of reasoning the test of public interest was no longer support by the whole community but leadership support. For the rioters, on the other hand, public interest was defined by traditions of equity and relative equality stemming in part from Puritan concepts about "just" dealings among community members. "Let no man seek his own, but every man another's wealth." Those who broke these biblical-traditional commands were to be "cut off." In the early decades of the century, this was done to individuals who transgressed community norms. By the middle of the century a whole class had to be opposed.[4]

The tradition of crowd action developed in a sociopolitical system that can best be described as combining participatory and hierarchical elements. In the 1760s Boston was a town of about 15,000 inhabitants. Adult free-white males, about a quarter of the population, were entitled to vote in town meeting provided they met the property qualification. This was the participatory component (sometimes mistakenly called "democratic"). The ownership of property suggests a stratified society: the lowest 30 percent of the taxpaying population paid only the poll tax and had no taxable property at all. The second lowest 30 percent owned 8.5 percent, the third 25.6 percent, while the top 10 percent of the taxpayers held two-thirds (65.9 percent) of Boston's taxable wealth. This meant that while probably all of the merchants and professional people and most of the poorer self-employed artisans and journeymen could vote, probably none of the sailors, and certainly no laborers, apprentices, or indentured servants could vote. Even the most optimistic scholarly estimate is that only 56 percent of the adult white males (or about 1,500) were enfranchised. What some historians have called the lax admission policies of the Boston town meeting were sufficiently exclusive that Whig leaders, when they wanted to broaden support against British policies, had to call separate meetings without property qualifications. And, in 1780, when the draft constitution was debated and the town permitted (1) all white adult males over twenty-one to participate and (2) asked that all shops and workshops be closed during the meeting, attendance increased fourfold over the previous meeting on the constitution from about 200 to 850.

The hierarchical elements of political life developed from these factors. The middling sort usually filled the large number of town offices concerned with supervision of internal trade regulations, by preventing fraud, short weight, and the like. But the leading town officials—the selectmen, overseers of the poor, assessors, auditors, and town meeting moderators—were chosen only from the ranks of prominent merchants and professional men. Social restrictions and procedural factors further limited the participation of enfranchised males. The meetings were held during the day, making attendance difficult for those dependent on their daily labor for subsistence, or for those who had to obtain leave from their employers. Furthermore, in the caucus system developed in the 1760s, politicians associated with men from the middling interest—master craftsmen, keepers of reputable taverns, small merchants, and shopkeepers. Here was the stronghold of Samuel Adams, the arena where issues of the town meeting agenda were debated, slates decided, and voting slips prepared for distribution among the inhabitants. Such preconcerted plans made *independent* articulation of interests by those journeymen mechanics who were enfranchised even more difficult—men from the middling interest employed most of the men of the lower classes.[5]

This raises the question as to whether social distinction and economic position continued to command respect and provide authority and influence by the middle of the eighteenth century. They did, contrary to the assertions of some consensus historians and bards of early American democracy. In a legal writ the omission of the designation "gentleman" was sufficient cause to declare it invalid. The Suffolk County sheriff did not dare to bother John Hancock, "a Gentleman of his great superiority," with a court summons. Church pews were assigned according to rank or, in Boston, sold to those who could pay for the best seats. Boston's town meeting participants were spoken of by contemporaries as either "gentlemen" or "populace" (or "rabble"). The conservative Lt. Gov. Thomas Hutchinson refused to talk to mechanics in 1765, politics not being their business. An influential Whig official, faced in 1770 with a petition by dozens of mechanics, simply destroyed it because it did not fit into the policies of the Whig leadership. In the same year, Whig politicians railed against the coercion of "standing armies," but the owner of a ropewalk dismissed one of his ropemakers for allegedly starting a quarrel with a British soldier about labor competition. Spontaneous action from below was unwanted, deference was to remain the foundation of political action.[6]

Within the framework of this societal structure, crowd action passed several different stages during the years from 1765 to 1776. As will be argued on the basis of the examples that follow, these factors shaped the following developments: (1) After the passage of the Stamp Act in 1765 the leadership had to turn to extralegal crowd action, because traditional institutions and procedures proved insufficient. The resort to direct action was neither preceded by the development of an ideology of resistance that filled the void between mere petitioning and open rebellion, nor was it accompanied by a systematic inquiry into the role of different social groups in the opposition policies.[7] (2) The patterns of crowd action were adapted from the symbolic rituals and practices—sometimes nonviolent, sometimes violent—of popular holidays, foremost among them Pope's Day, as well as from the traditions of intrasocietal direct action and of anti-British crowds, limited before the 1760s to action against impressment, customs regulations, and mast-pine laws. (3) Among the rioters, the increased frequency of action and the new targets—high-level officials who were men of wealth—led to an increase in political awareness and social consciousness. Moreover, differences between social strata in Boston were accentuated during the struggles with Great Britain because imperial policies influenced internal socioeconomic relationships; because the policies adopted by the Whig leaders seriously hurt the lower classes, including shopkeepers and many master craftsmen; and because the interaction between the colonial elite, whether Whig or pro-Crown, and those sections of the population from which the crowd members were recruited became more intense. Thus, reasons for crowd action, precipitating incidents, and opportunities for action multiplied. (4)

Among Whig leaders—the Sons of Liberty type drawn from the middling interest and well-to-do merchants—the Commonwealth ideology with which they were imbued meant reckoning with differences between Crown supporters and Whigs. It did not, however, prepare them adequately for internal dissensions among themselves, and even less for taking into account shifting concepts about the relations between social groups and differing economic interests within one class and between classes. (5) Under these circumstances the leaders were hardly ever certain what the next step should be. They were divided as to tactics and strategy, oscillating between initiating riots and controlling the impulses from below, torn between class interest and ideology. They were a hesitant leadership, "radical" toward Great Britain, "conservative" about concepts of internal social relations and deference. (6) Analysis of the crowds reveals no single pattern. There were determined, self-led, and goal-directed crowds on many occasions, baffled or gagged crowds on others. Sometimes, rioters needed better-placed leaders to articulate concepts to make communication possible with the well-educated target of a riot. More often the rioters themselves explained what they intended and demanded. Sometimes imperial issues dominated crowd action, and sometimes local issues dominated, ranging from economic conflict to law enforcement to opposition to whorehouses. The imperial issue riots were influenced to a considerable degree by the leaders, the local issue riots only when the problems touched the economic interests of the merchants. When imperial and local issues were closely entwined, the leaders led and the crowds acted, but ended up miles apart in spirit, and sometimes geographically.

Over the entire period, from 1765 to 1776, several distinct trends of crowd action can be discerned and, in a schematic way, described as follows: The Stamp Act period (1765–66) was one of leadership-initiated action that quickly turned into spontaneous riots over local social and economic grievances. After 1767, in shocked reaction, the town elite called for "no mobs" and popular deference to the new customs commissioners. Merchants dominated the opposition to the Townshend duties. But they soon needed the crowd again to enforce nonimportation. In response, British army units were quartered in Boston in 1768. Mechanics, suffering from nonimportation and the presence of the soldiers, rioted against the troops and forced reluctant leaders to support them. By the tea crisis of 1773, the "radical" leadership had gained experience and was capable of using the Boston crowds as agents for its policies of orderly destruction of the dutied tea.

I

In the Stamp Act crisis of 1765—the first phase of opposition—the leadership was caught unprepared, with no ideology of gradually escalating resistance at hand to fill the gap between mere petitioning and rebellion. Confident about their hold over the lower clases, some Boston leaders decided on symbolic crowd action. They were in for some surprises. *Passive* resistance, as practiced against the Sugar Act, would be inadequate. Trade would come to a standstill and government would be paralyzed. To Whigs, moderates, and supporters of the administration alike, the latter was synonymous with chaos, while the former meant unemployment and the danger of social disorder. *Active* opposition was therefore necessary. Since Parliament could not be touched directly, the tangible local representatives of the Act, the stamp distributors, had to be prevented from executing their office. The lucrative positions had been offered to well-placed colonials by the British ministry in a conscious move to minimize opposition to the tax. By accepting the employment, by profiting from a tax which hurt almost everybody else, the distributors "betrayed," (stressed again and again) their fellow colonials. They had become placemen (political appointees) of an outside power. Betrayal of the community (action from private interest), by tradition, justified exhortation, public condemnation, or direct community action.[8]

In Boston, a political club, with good connections to the town officialdom, organized the opposition. The "Loyal Nine," whose members came from the socially conservative and economically hurting middling interest, were small merchants, distillers, part owners of ships, and master craftsmen. Where established institutions had temporized, they took the step toward action.[9] They made plans to force the stamp "master" to resign, but decided to rely almost exclusively on symbolic action. They contacted master craftsmen, who were to march in a solid bloc of about fifty men at the head of a procession, probably mixed with some "gentlemen" disguised as artisans.[10] The main actors were to be men from Boston's poorest quarter, the Northend, where artisans from the shipbuilding and outfitting trades predominated, and the Southend, ranking second lowest in property ownership per inhabitant. These people would be able to draw on their experience from the annual celebration of Pope's Day—Guy Fawkes Day in England. The existing rivalry between both sections receded into the background when the Loyal Nine brought together the men who had emerged as ringleaders in their neighborhoods—most prominently a shoemaker and a ship carpenter—and brought about an agreement to cooperate. The Pope's Day crowds followed old customs and had a rudimentary lore: "a tradition of patriotic anti-Stuart Protestantism, the Puritan's seventeenth-century heritage"; a popular ritual, already politicized in England, including effigies, pageantry, mummery ("street theatre"), bonfires, effigy burning; a practice of reversal of social roles, by posing as arrogant "better sort," and by levying contributions from social superiors. The annual celebration provided experience in self-organization for the lower classes; a training ground for direct action; an occasion for expression of "ill-defined feelings of class and defiance of authority." On this day, interference by officials who belonged to a different social class was fought off by the crowd members, mainly poorer mechanics and apprentices.[11]

On 14 August 1765, the day of the first demonstration, everything seemed to follow the carefully laid plans of the Loyal Nine. Effigies were suspended early in the morning. Later, a guard of Southend men first told the sheriff (sent by Crown officials) to keep off, then "stamped" the goods of in- and outgoing teamsters in an exaggerated display of the stamp master's powers. Soon thousands from the town and surrounding areas participated. In the evening, men from the Northend took over and carried the effigies through town. Anybody (except Negroes) could join the procession, and two or three thousand did, as many more watched. Property damage was limited to pulling down a half-finished building that belonged to the stamp distributor Oliver and was reported to be his future stamp office. To make clear to Oliver that a stamp master was not wanted, the effigy was beheaded in front of his house and then burnt on the adjoining hill. The Loyal Nine intended the day's activities to stop here. At this point, the "gentlemen" present left.[12]

The crowd, however, showed an independence of action and a rudimentary class feeling that carried it beyond the goals set by the Whig leadership. After the departure of the "gentlemen," they destroyed some of Oliver's property and proclaimed a "union" between Northenders and Southenders. On the next day, 15 August, the "amazingly inflamed people," as one of the Loyal Nine reported, reassembled to get clarification on Oliver's ambiguous promise to resign and to question Lieutenant Governor Hutchinson about his role in the preparation of the Stamp Act.[13]

The direct action in Oliver's sumptuously furnished house lifted latent misgivings about the rich and the powerful to a level of acute awareness. From the rioters' viewpoint, the officials "rioted in luxury," as the contemporary expression went. Their wrath was no longer directed only against Oliver, the stamp master, or Hutchinson, the lieutenant governor, but against them as high-handed officials and men of wealth whose arrogant conduct and use of economic power was resented. Moreover, the opposition against one placeman-official-merchant led to the realization that other obnoxious officials-merchants could be opposed, too. The Loyal Nine, by social position and political concepts different from the rioters, had not taken into account that crowd action during the first half of the eighteenth century was frequently motivated by economic grievances.

Ten days later, on 26 August, the crowd attacked the houses of the lieutenant governor, a clerk of the Court of Vice-Admiralty, and two customs officials, all men of wealth. The patterns of action suggest the prevalence of the rudimentary class feeling. As in earlier decades, the rioters damaged window panes, which were expensive because they had to be imported. They also damaged coaches and coach-houses, which only a few wealthy could afford. The mansion of customs official Hallowell, which was partly destroyed, had just been built at the expense of £2000 sterling (at a time when laborers and journeymen had to support their families on an annual income from £30 to £60). These workers had often criticized officials who lived from fees and who accumulated public offices for the sake of private gain. Hutchinson's mansion, which was completely gutted on 26 August, was probably the finest residence in the province. Hutchinson was so arrogant that he did not even condescend to explain to his troubled neighbors his position on the Stamp Act. To appear at a window and talk to the multitude, he considered an "indignity, to which he would not submit."[14]

Grievances against specific conduct in office were also behind the crowd's selection of targets. All officials knew well why they had incurred the displeasure of their fellow townsmen and admitted as much: support for or connection with the Stamp Act, malpractice in office, arrogance, pride about their wealth, ostentatious display of luxury.[15] The rioters seem to have preceded their actions with debates about the selection of targets. Several inhabitants, in fact, heard beforehand that they were being considered. They or their friends sometimes talked to the prospective crowd and were able to head off some violence.[16] Even during the riot the crowd members stopped occasionally to discuss further proceedings. But nobody could *talk* them out of their basic intentions.

For a century and a half, ministers had preached against the sins of pride, ambition, and covetousness, whether for possessions or for offices. On the day before the 26 August action, the Reverend Jonathan Mayhew had preached on the text: "I would they were even cut off which trouble you. For brethren, ye have been called unto liberty; only use not liberty for an occasion to the flesh, but by love serve one another." One rioter who had heard the sermon later declared that he felt he had done God service. A newspaper account called the burning of Oliver's effigy an "Offering for the Sins of the People." Almost all effigies prepared during the Stamp Act period in Boston contained a devil prompting evil thoughts and deeds to the corrupted officials. In the next ten years other Boston crowds continued to speak in terms of Mayhew and the Bible.[17]

The rudimentary class feeling that had found expression in the action against five wealthy officials, 14 and 26 August, threatened to escalate to a more generalized attack on the upper classes, the dominant elite. "For, it seems," reported the governor, "the Mob had set down no less then fifteen Houses in or near the Town to be attacked the next Night [i.e., 27 August], among which was the Customhouse and the houses of some of the most respectable persons in the Government. It was now become a War of Plunder, of general levelling and taking away the Distinction of rich and poor."[18]

That the governor's analysis was not the overreaction of a distraught official is suggested by the fact that the wealthy and powerful took to guns. Their violent reactions testify that they perceived the class character of the 26 August events. Their political influence, economic power, and social position were at stake. A military unit of the town elite, used normally for ceremonial duties only, mustered and was beefed up by "gentlemen-volunteers." Rewards were offered for information, rioters were arrested, and the town's selectmen ordered out guards. The provincial Council threatened to march in militia units from country towns. For several weeks armed gentlemen patrolled the town each night. On one occasion, on 17 August, they lowered their guns to disperse a group of lower-class men. They did not trust the local militiamen to protect their property, since many of these had been among the rioters.

In a hurriedly called town meeting the leaders denounced violence and the meeting formally disavowed it.[19] The rioters probably were not present. The meeting did succeed in calling into line a number of wealthy lawbreakers, who had used the crowd action as a screen to send hired men to achieve their private aims, unconnected with the Stamp Act or lower-class grievances.[20]

By armed patrols and arrests, the Loyal Nine and higher echelons of the Whig leadership reimposed their position on the crowds, which for further opposition to the Stamp Act were still needed. Accordingly, "gentlemen" interposed when the county sheriff arrested Ebenezer Mackintosh, neighborhood leader of the Southend men. Thus no officials opposed a crowd that forcibly rescued from prison those few rioters arrested. But when extensive symbolic crowd action was planned for 1 November, the day the Stamp Act went into effect, and as Pope's Day (5 November) drew near, the selectmen called out the military watch again. At the same time, the Whig leaders made it clear to the governor and other crown officials that they had lost command over the Boston militia; the men refused to obey the governor's orders.[21] To secure their control over the lower classes, Whig leaders and merchants attempted to bribe crowd members, particularly the local leaders. They furnished Mackintosh and others with pompous militia uniforms and insignia and addressed them with titles, trying to tie them to men of top social rank. They provided a feast at a local tavern, ostensibly to further the union between Northenders and Southenders. But only a select group of rioters was admitted, and to impress them with notions of hierarchy, the managers divided the diners into five different classes according to rank.[22]

All these efforts notwithstanding, the propertied sections of Boston remained uneasy. Pressure from below was too strong to abandon opposition to the Stamp Act, as some suggested. But if, after 1 November, no business requiring stamps would be transacted, shipping and trade would practically come to a standstill. Then the poorer sort would suffer most and large numbers of seamen would be unemployed. Fearing "Great uneasiness and Tumults," the leadership pressed for open defiance of the act and asked the port officers to clear ships on unstamped papers. When the officials were reluctant to do so, the merchants proved equally reluctant to turn to their unwanted allies, the crowd: the officials who had to be opposed resembled Oliver. The placeman-wealthy merchant equation might be set off again.[23] Whig merchants therefore informed the customs officers about a "rumor" of impending crowd action against them—obligingly, the Crown officials felt forced to act without stamps. It seems that by consent the rioters were not let in on this "rumor" of action.[24]

The consequences of these crowd actions were twofold. The people began to develop an awareness of their power as a political crowd against the officials. The upper groups in Boston developed a full-fledged fear of spontaneous action, as did those of other towns, if General Gage's assessment, quoted at the beginning of this essay, was correct. Once the Stamp Act was repealed all connections with the rioters were cut. Boston Whigs reportedly threatened Ebenezer MacIntosh, the lowly shoemaker, to remain silent about their role.[25] To them, economic discontent at home was licentiousness, and they suppressed memories of 26 August, when class feeling (in their words a "war of plunder" or "general levelling") reached its height. To monopolize the tradition of opposition, the leaders staged an annual celebration of the controlled symbolic action of 14 August against Oliver which glossed over the violence, and developed both a mythology about this event and a valid theory of constitutional opposition. They invited mainly upper- and middle-class Bostonians, who traveled in coaches and carriages to Roxbury or Dorchester for opulent feasts. The rioters were not invited.[26] They probably would not have been able to pay for the admission tickets, and they probably would also have seen the similarity of this ostentation, pomp, and reveling to that which they had opposed on commencement days and on 26 August.

II

Passive resistance, a means rejected as insufficient in 1765, was advocated again when news of the Townshend duties arrived in the fall of 1767. Nonimportation and nonconsumption by the whole community became the means of opposition. Thus the Whigs committed the same error as in 1765: they assumed a leadership-articulated interest common to all. Since important segments of the population were adversely affected by nonimportation, the differences in interest were soon to come into the open again. But for the moment, no crowd action seemed necessary, and lest anybody had not gotten the message, the town leaders mounted a concerted effort to drive the lesson home. "No Mobs or Tumults, let the Persons and Properties of your most inveterate Enemies be safe—Save your Money and you save your Country," exhorted the *Gazette.* "No Mobs—No Confusions—No Tumults," urged Samuel Adams. "But, let our burthens be ever so heavy, or our grievances ever so great," pleaded James Otis, "no possible circumstances, though ever so oppressive, could be supposed sufficient to justify private tumults and disorders, either to our consciences before God or legally before men."

Otis equated the leadership and its interests with the public. This was the antithesis of the rioters' understanding of the tradition of a Christian commonwealth expounded by Mayhew in 1765 and in innumerable sermons before him. Otis only repudiated *private* disorders, that is, the opposite of public action supported by the whole community. It is reasonable to argue that the opposition to the new duties was sufficiently widespread to call it public. Thus, Otis implied, nonleadership-sponsored action was private. The explanation for this stand is that Boston's elite had replaced the notion of a corporate community, still current in many of the smaller agricultural towns and seemingly among Boston's lower classes, by the notion of a leadership over an unenlightened multitude. Secondly, it implies a consciousness that the bulk of the rioters, even in a widely supported riot, came from a different section or class of the community with separate interests.[27]

These groups were adversely affected by nonimportation. Small traders and shopkeepers were faced with the alternative of continuing their business, that is, violating the agreements, or of joining the policy and suffering a serious, sometimes irreversible deterioration of their economic status. They were also aware that some large-scale importers refused to sign the agreement for political (and possibly economic) reasons. Mechanics experienced similar economic hardships. Since British merchants paid for ships built or repaired in Boston by their exports to the colonies, they placed no further orders for ships, which was a kind of involuntary counter-boycott. Among mechanics, unemployment rose steeply, and with it Boston's budget for poor relief. On the other hand, well-stocked or overstocked merchants were hardly touched.

For still other reasons, a considerable potential for direct action built up among those directly afflicted by the new British regulations. Higher duties and stricter enforcement of the regulations meant increased seizures by the revenue officers, who received rewards for justified seizures, but who incurred no liabilities in case of unjustified ones. The deputizing of officers as customs agents increased the opportunities for friction between them and sailors, who, because of the navy's impressment practices, never had a particular liking for them. The crackdown on petty smuggling by sailors made them even more bitter against the customs service. Wealthy Whig merchants, often overstocked, who saw profits go to importing Loyalists, soon reverted to threats of violence to enforce nonimportation. The customary means of opposition, aside from smuggling and bribes, were intimidation of informers, or rescue riots after the event. Both relied on the willingness of sailors and dockworkers to use force.[28]

For a time, the Whig, moderate, and conservative leaderships' fear of direct action prevented advocacy of open resistance. But on Pope's Day the united Northenders and Southenders, in addition to their old customs, paraded politicized slogans: "Liberty & Property & no Commissioners."[29] On 20 November 1767, the day the act took effect, active inhabitants posted a number of papers advocating violent resistance in different parts of the town. In anticipation of this, the selectmen had called a town meeting, and those present disavowed the "scandalous and threatening Papers."[30] They again prevented action on the anniversary of the Stamp Act repeal, 18 March 1768. When crowds hung two customs officers in effigy, they were taken down by the Loyal Nine even before town or provincial magistrates could step in. The selectmen also wanted a flagpole in the town's center removed, but the men who assembled there balked and self-consciously argued with the officials. They wanted to celebrate, and no unruly crowds would assemble; any fears were unjustified. The men decided that the pole should remain, and so it did. Later a crowd paraded through town. While the Sons of Liberty had been unsuccessful in their attempts to prevent any and all crowds, they did control the public reports about the crowds. The "great number of people of all Kinds, Sexes, and ages," reported by Governor Bernard, became in Whig accounts "a few disorderly persons mostly boys," or "sailors and apprentices."[31]

However, by spring 1768, some merchants were ready to defy the "no crowd" policy. They did not want to lose their goods by seizures, just because most of the better sort had so much fear of waterfront social unrest that they considered riots to rescue goods from customs officials dangerous. First, Daniel Malcom, of the middling interest and very active among the merchant-captains, was aided by a crowd of "stout fellows" in unloading a ship clandestinely. Next, a wealthy merchant, John Hancock, spoke up. Laborers, beginning to unload one of his ships, were harassed by officials. While it took little trouble to solve the problem with the officials, Hancock had to use all his influence to prevent a noisy crowd of dockworkers from celebrating this victory.[32] Finally, small coasters entering the harbor were harassed by HMS *Hope*. Along wharves and in taverns, sailors whose ships had been boarded and searched told how they had been treated in the most insulting manner. Dockworkers got restless whenever one of the *Hope*'s boats came close to shore. In May 1768, a town meeting, rejecting all calls for politeness, passed a vote insulting the customs commissioners and any government official who associated with them. That included governor, high officials, councillors, and a host of other "gentlemen."[33]

In this situation HMS *Romney* arrived, and shortly afterwards sent out a pressgang for seamen. Sailors, whose liberty was endangered, fled ashore and were aided in their escape. When the pursuing pressgang came within throwing range for stones, bricks, and the like, they realized that they were unwelcome. A crowd prevented them from landing.[34] The next day was quiet, even though Artillery Election, a local celebration, as usual, drew thousands of spectators. Although this underlines the significance of internal restraints in the tradition of rioting, all preconditions for crowd action were present nevertheless. The town leaders stood by complacently. They could or would not interfere with the merchant-initiated direct action in opposition to the trade regulations. Nor would they bother about impressment, which hurt primarily the lower classes.

III

On 10 June 1768, the famous *Liberty* incident illustrated the revival of independent crowd action and a successful effort by the suddenly active Whig leaders to divert such action into safe channels. The name for the incident, which refers only to the seizure of the ship, is actually a misnomer, since the impressment grievances of the lower classes figured as prominently as John Hancock's conflict with the customs commissioners. Reportedly, his men had unloaded part of the *Liberty*'s cargo in secret. After the first anti-impressment riot, the captain of the *Romney* sent out further pressgangs, breaking legal rules by taking sailors from outgoing vessels, violating tradition by refusing to accept substitutes, and breaking biblical commands by impressing on Sundays. Once reports of the impressment would spread along the coast, small vessels with provisions and firewood would shun the harbor, and prices would rise. Thus not only sailors and dockworkers, but particularly low-income households would suffer. In the midst of this agitated state of affairs the news spread that customs officals were on their way to seize the *Liberty*. The customs tidewaiters, at first intimidated by threats, had now admitted that they had witnessed the clandestine landing of undutied goods. For the seizure, customs officials and the navy cooperated, thus provoking a long evening of crowd action.

People assembled immediately, in particular merchant-captains, who felt the procedure a breach of law—the sun was setting and the warrant was valid only till sunset—and sailors, who on seeing the navy boats, were "suspicious of an Intention to put them on board the Ship," that is, to impress them.[35] The crowd could not prevent the seizure, although it certainly tried, because the *Romney* sent reinforcements faster than the townspeople could assemble. But they beat up several of the officers involved. The crowd, numbering about 2,000, made the rounds of the town and visited three customs officials. Each time they were informed that their target was out. Each time they refrained from violence (with the exception of some window-breaking) and left. This march through town also brought the rioters a lesson in civics. The town leaders, who had taken no action to redress the rioters' grievances, impressment and the danger of rising prices, were busily protecting their avowed enemies, the customs officials, from their supposed allies, the inhabitants. Whenever the rioters arrived at an official's house, "gentlemen" were already there to discountenance the rioting, by announcing that a meeting would be called where all problems could be discussed and solved by legal measures. The rioters, intent on making their point their own way, returned to the waterfront and searched for boats of the *Romney*. Finding none, they took the pleasure boat of a customs official, dragged it to Liberty Tree, and from there to the Common, where they burnt it.

Once the crowd had dispersed on Friday night, the Whig leaders lapsed into internal dissension during the ensuing weekend. As to the *Liberty*, should a compromise be struck with the customs officials, or a hard stand be taken? The weakness of the officials' case weighted the scales in favor of the latter. As to impressment, the officials consulted the lawbooks and found what sailors had always claimed: ships in

American trade were exempted from impressment. Did they act to stop impressment? No, they merely informed other officials about the law. As to the crowd and the promised meeting about the grievances, the leaders vacillated. The strength of the rioters weighted the scales in favor of activity. But what? The leaders spread stories about the gentlemanly behavior of the *Romney*'s captain to quiet the people. To quiet the customs officials, one of the leading Whigs expressed regrets about the rioters "Frensey," explaining that "Such Sort of People Inhabit Every Great City Perhaps in the World."[36]

On Monday, the lower-class Bostonians "were in great agitation" about the situation; the better placed leaders were still undecided. Then, "least any tumult might arise at Night, the Consequences whereof would be very prejudical," as was darkly intimated, the Sons of Liberty called a meeting for Tuesday. This was a successful device to prevent rioting, "the expectation of this Meeting kept the Town in Peace," since one of the traditional restraints on crowd action was that all legal means had to be exhausted before extralegal steps could be taken. Meanwhile the councillors refused to take strong precautionary measures against further riots for the simple reason "that they did not desire to be knocked on the Head."

At the appointed time on Tuesday "vast numbers" appeared at Liberty Tree, but no substantial action was taken, except a vote to call a regular town meeting for the afternoon. At the meeting Otis was chosen moderator, and then the thousands present adjourned to the more spacious Old South meetinghouse.[37] After this slow start, which nevertheless consumed energy, the inhabitants got down to business. "After very cool and deliberate Debates upon the distressed Circumstances of the Town, and the present critical Situation of their Affairs," a petition to the governor was accepted and a committee elected to deliver it. Taken in by the governor's good wine, the committeemen accepted an absolutely noncommittal answer. In town meeting the next day, they steered clear of the cliffs of opposition by "acquaint[ing] the Town with the manner in which they had been received." This did not stop the navy from impressing, nor prices from rising.

While the top leaders were being wined by the governor and could not supervise the proceedings, the voters, probably expecting such foot-dragging by the moderate leadership, had elected a number of more flexible men into important committees. From this time on, Whigs of the type of Samuel Adams more and more replaced the men from the Merchants' Club, who all too often had been willing to compromise with Crown officials over the heads of their constituents. These men, often called "radical," were in fact merely more responsive to popular grievances, if not from genuine sympathy or understanding, then because they needed popular support.

Two years later, in 1770, the last of the moderates lost their influence in town committees, when the town suffered badly from the presence of British troops. Rioters and voters thus did not simply act on the basis of abstract principles or theories of government. They acted when imperial policies and practices had a local impact and became issues in their daily lives. Impressment and the quartering of troops affected them directly. It was then that they acted faster and more decisively than the leadership.[38]

Just as the impressment and the seizure of the *Liberty* had shown the inability of the leadership to find solutions for popular grievances, an incident four weeks later, in July 1768, showed the limitations of the rioters' abilities. John Williams, a customs inspector who had become particularly obnoxious, had been hung in effigy in 1767, and had had his house surrounded after the *Liberty* seizure. At that time the crowd had left when informed that he was out of town, promising to come again. On 15 July the fire-bells signaled Williams's return, and the crowd, in no mood for negotiations, ordered him to appear under Liberty Tree, to resign his office and swear never to resume it. Three years earlier, Oliver, the stamp agent, had done so, and the customs commissioners lived in constant fear that they would have to submit to the same fate. But Williams first refused to resign, then talked with the rioters, and finally announced that he would be on the Exchange in the center of the town the following day and answer any charge against him.

At the appointed time, probably as many as 1,500 men assembled at the townhouse. Williams stuck to his promise, with one change. Instead of facing the crowd members on the same level, he looked down on them from the balcony of the Council chamber. He offered to answer any objection against him, but no charges were brought forward. Williams repeated his offer. "Again Nothing was said." The crowd was unable to articulate grievances and general principles on a level adequate for the atmosphere of the townhouse, which contained better educated onlookers. It seems that their access to pamphlets expounding counstitutional theories and the thought of the British "Commonwealthmen" was limited. Boston's Whig leaders, under their customary name of "Sons of Liberty," publicly disavowed the proceedings and ordered the printers not to mention the affair. Privately they told Williams to resign. But Williams refused again, and during the following days was assured by members of the crowd, "particularly the[ir] Captain," that he was safe. This was their way of disavowing in turn the Whig leaders who, though agreeing with the intent of the action, had deserted them at the townhouse for fear of prosecution.[39]

IV

The presence of about 2,000 soldiers in Boston from October 1768 on introduced a new element that further divided the leadership from the crowd. The troops were sent in response to the incessant and rather frantic calls of customs officials for protection from crowds and to enforce the trade laws. While many of the merchants curried favor with the British, the ordinary citizen came into increasing friction with the troops. The first problems arose over making provisions for quartering and supplying the soldiers. Only the elected representatives, dissolved by order from the British government, could appropriate funds for supplies. Only the Boston selectmen could provide quarters according to the law. Bostonians neither wanted to have soldiers about town nor pay for their presence. Quartering in private houses was permissible only if all barracks in town were filled. This, argued the selectmen, was not the case, since the barracks in Castle William, on a harbor island, provided space seven miles away from the center of the town. The framers of the act had overlooked the difference between an English town and a New England township.[40]

The commanding officer, Dalrymple, finally began to make provision at Crown expense; he began to build barracks. The frames had hardly been erected when overnight a crowd of Boston men tore the edifice down. But, certainly to the surprise of Loyalist Bostonians, leading Whigs, who had advocated resistance a few weeks earlier, sharply reproved this action. This time the motivating force was not primarily fear of spontaneous direct action by the lower clases. Supplying and quartering troops meant profits. While, under the guise of darkness, some Bostonians continued their opposition to the troops, many a wealthy merchant in open daylight solicited the friendship of the officers. The tools of British tyranny were recognized as a source of contracts. "I am much in fashion, visited by Otis, Hancock, &c., who

cry peccavi, and offer exhortations for the public service," noted the
commanding officer proudly. The "Journal of the Times," probably
authored by William Cooper, town clerk and supporter of mercantile
views, openly suggested that attitudes to troops and to liberty were
governed by commercial considerations. It noted that in Halifax, Nova
Scotia, from where the troops had come, "patriots were about erecting
a liberty pole, and *employing* some boys to sing the Liberty Song
through the streets, in hopes it may procure the return of those ships
and forces or a larger number from Britain, in order to quell such
disturbances," and in order to bring back lucrative army and navy
contracts.[41]

Lower-class Bostonians meanwhile were experiencing an increasing number of grievances. Unemployment, as stated above, was widespread because of the nonimportation policies. Now the soldiers in
their off-hours provided a formidable pool of labor, willing to work at
low wages. At the same time there was the danger of rising taxes. By
law, the province had to pay for quarters and supplies as well as for
the numerous poor persons following the army. Standing armies had
always been considered a danger to the liberties of a free people, and
the army in town provided excellent illustration for this maxim. There
were constant annoyances. The elaborate guard system, partly for
ceremonious reasons, partly to prevent desertion, constantly challenged civilians. Military music on Sundays during public worship
attracted idle spectators. The troops were careless about safety measures to protect the inhabitants from smallpox, and often the poor
could not afford inoculation. Robberies and assaults increased, broth-
els and liquor shops multiplied, and daily life was interrupted. Expected to show deference to magistrates, Bostonians now witnessed
frequent obstruction of civil officers by the military, which particularly
in the case of officers went unpunished. While most affrays with soldiers remained limited to small crowds, hundreds and sometimes as
many as 2,000 of the townsmen attended hearings and trials of soldiers
to see that they were properly punished. Under such circumstances the
soldiers soon complained that justice was not meted out impartially.
Too lenient at the beginning, many justices, afraid of becoming the
target of riots, now were too harsh. As a final grievance, desertions
from the many war and transport ships in the harbor led to further
sweeping impressments.[42]

The friction with the troops occurred in a context of a steadily
worsening economic position of the laboring population and division

among leaders about how to handle poor relief. The ranks of the indigent were swelled by mechanics and shopkeepers who had lost employment or business because of nonimportation. This was officially acknowledged in March 1769, when the town elected a committee "to Consider of some Suitable Methods [of] employing the Poor of the Town, whose Numbers and distresses are dayly increasing by the loss of its Trade and Commerce." Two years earlier, when the first nonconsumption agreement had been introduced, a similar committee had been elected to employ the poor in the manufacture of linen. The majority of this committee established itself as private manufacturers, gained access to the town's tax-funds for the support of the poor (more than 50 percent of the town's total budget), and, as a public committee, asked the town for additional money. The inhabitants, perceiving the duplicity, refused further funds. One of the manufacturers felt forced to assert publicly: "Our design in pursuing this Business is not to enrich ourselves, but for employing the many Poor." The committee of 1769, consisting partly of the same men, reported 230 persons in the almshouse and another 40 in the workhouse. Hundreds more were on outrelief. These people and children, the "proper Objects of such Charity," according to the committee, should be made to work in a spinning factory. The committee volunteered the services of a "responsible gentleman," who was willing to take the risk of this undertaking. The gentleman turned out to be a committeeman again. He did not have access to the poor funds, so he asked the town for £500. This time the inhabitants appropriated the money, though part of it as a loan only, and later had difficulty getting repaid. The available evidence suggests that the two plans for employing the poor were made by a few well-to-do men on the rise who wanted to line their own pockets. The "responsible gentleman" of the second plan, an ardent Whig, had also rented a warehouse to the British troops at a rate that some considered exorbitant. Why then, did the inhabitants provide him with financial support?[43]

The precarious social and economic situation again prompted fears among the well-to-do of an uprising. Demands for work were raised among artisans and journeymen. Support for nonimportation and its advocates slumped further and brought something akin to class alignments into the open. A petition was passed around in Boston, demanding that certain goods for the shipbuilding trade be exempted from the agreement. More than seventy artisans in these trades signed within a few hours. But then John Ruddock, justice of the peace, selectman, and Whig, arrived on the scene with some of his colleagues. He seized the petition and destroyed it, telling the artisans that they were the ruin of their country. A fortnight later, the Whig committee rejected another application.[44] Unlike the artisans, Whig merchants could get exceptions from the agreement upon application. Small shopkeepers were also hurting. Miss Cummings and her sister, non-subscribers to the nonimportation agreement, were visited and threatened by the committee. Miss Cummings explained that "it was verry trifling, owr Business, but that littil we must do to enabel us to Suport owr family," and accused the committee of trying "to injur two industrious Girls who ware Striving in an honest way to Get there Bread." Many small shopkeepers in a similar position, according to the Tory Andrew Oliver, were "to be sacrificed to the Interest of a few who were overstocked." However, they began to perceive these manipulations: "the Advanced price put upon the old Stock begins to open the eyes of some." One opponent noted that the Whig committee became aware of the suffering and discontent, too, and began "to talk of selling . . . [the stored goods taken from nonsubscribing importers at auction] and distributeing the money to the poor," in order to stop the clamor for jobs and subsistence, and to weld the suffering people to the cause.[45]

V

By the fall of 1769, it was clear to merchants, leading politicians, and lower classes that the position of mere passive resistance to the customs service and the stationing of troops had accomplished almost nothing. There was a lack of enthusiasm, particularly among the hardest-hit sections of the people, for continuing this policy. In addition, the motives of the merchants' committee enforcing nonimportation, as well as those of William Molineux, a most active Whig leader, were ambivalent. Nonimportation often seemed to be not so much opposition to British regulations as a local fight between business rivals for the markets in which small shopkeepers were the losers. The friction between inhabitants and soldiers had also escalated. The refusal of the leaders to support the rioters who had destroyed the frame of the guardhouse at Boston Neck brought about the first large-scale incident. The tenant of the land, Robert Pierpoint, together with twenty or thirty others, appeared at the guardhouse and threatened the soldiers, who, on the next day, were assaulted again by hundreds of townsmen. Whigs tried to calm such crowds.[46]

But the Whigs were willing to enforce nonimportation by whatever means necessary. Sometimes they mobilized crowds. The Whig leaders themselves riotously assaulted John Mein, publisher of a pro-administration newspaper, which printed the customhouse entries, showing the duplicity of importing Whig merchants, who had violated the agreement. Mein issued separate broadsides of these lists for distribution in other colonies, causing innumerable disputes among Whig merchants. Just after the Neckguard riot he published a devastating attack on the principal Whigs. They, who had preached "no mobs, no tumults," now accosted Mein on the street in an attempt to beat him up. A spectator reported "a larg croud of those who Call themselves Gentelman" and heard them cry "Kill him, Kill him." While lower-class crowds usually were unarmed, or armed with sticks only, one of the gentlemen aimed a blow at Mein with an iron shovel. They considered him so dangerous that they were willing to get him out of the way by any means. Clearly this was not a traditional riot with community support as well as restraints, but a full-scale "*private* mob." On the day of the anti-Mein riot a lower-class crowd tarred and feathered a customs informer. Passing Mein's house, they merely smashed a few windows. These rioters had grievances different from those of the leaders. Some of the lower-class rioters were arrested, while none of the Whig leaders was ever brought to justice. The latter in fact even got a man indicted who had condemned their riot.[47]

Enforcement of nonimportation remained complicated even after Mein had been forced to flee Boston. Not only did nonsubscribing merchants try to continue importing, but, clandestinely, Whig merchants did so, too, seemingly in large numbers. They charged and countercharged each other with violation of the agreement and then denied any breaches to the public. In a letter to a friend, one of the Boston Sons of Liberty, Thomas Young, admitted that proscribed goods had been carried in the vessels of the chief Whig merchants. Taking the acquisitiveness of the merchants for granted, as did other Whig politicians, he shrugged these violations off, stating that if they had not carried them, others would have. When the original agreement ended in January 1770, several importers who had been forced to store their goods, decided to sell. Instead of defending the agreement, the merchants committee merely complained that others should be given reasonable time to import, too. When the importers rejected this demand, a mass meeting was called. The merchants extended invitations to small shopkeepers to broaden the base and to weld them to the cause, an unprecedented measure in this deferential society.

To force submission of the importers, a march to their stores was organized. Josiah Quincy, Jr., Whig lawyer and radical opponent of British policies as well as of crowd action, declared that such a march would amount to high treason. The sons of the acting governor, Hutchinson, were among the nonsubscribing importers, and the house where he and his sons lived would be one of the targets. This dampened the spirits of the leadership so much that, as in the case of the action against customs official Williams, none of them dared to lead the crowd. This time the crowd did not act on its own. The potential rioters, shopkeepers for the most part, were dependent on the merchants for credit and their supply of goods. They also knew that some of the "biggest shops in Town," Whig shops, were selling imported goods. Once the leadership had regained its composure after Quincy's attack, the marches were finally organized. Immediately after most of the nonsigning importers gave in, the merchants began to meet separately again, no longer inviting the shopkeepers. At the last common meeting, however, it was resolved that importers should be excluded from all common civility, and, secondly, that all business connections with them should be severed.[48]

As a result, the stores of some importers were picketed on market days. On this day, countrymen were in town and, schools being closed, boys could participate. On these, and not on the self-conscious artisans or laborers from the Northend and Southend, the Whig merchants relied. Boys could be manipulated more easily. Since they lacked the internal restraints of intra-community crowd action—boys could not participate in politics and countrymen were from a different community—the practices became more violent. In addition, importers were intimidated by attempted arson, personal abuse, and besmearing of their houses with "Hillsborough paint," a combination of excrement and urine. All this was done at night by small groups, perhaps even individuals. One of the picketing incidents, however, took on a larger significance. A number of boys paraded a carved wooden head in front of an importers' store, suggesting perhaps that he should be beheaded. Ebenezer Richardson, a particularly disliked customs informer, attempted to take down the image, but, pelted and abused, he retreated to his house. In the course of the action the crowd grew, broke his windows, and threatened more violence. Richardson fired a gun into the crowd, killing a boy. The crowd then stormed his house. Only at this point did the Whig leader, William Molineux, who had been standing by with other gentlemen, interpose to get Richardson safely into jail. About 1,000 people attended his examination, held before the justices of the peace, and roughly handled supporters of the customs establishment.[49]

A few days later, an incident about labor competition between ropemakers and soldiers, on top of the numerous other grievances, provided the spark for the lower classes to fight the soldiers, who for their part were bent on subduing the hostile inhabitants. On 5 March 1770 men from the Northend and Southend united again for crowd action. Importers, the leaders' primary targets, were hardly mentioned the whole evening. Men assembled around the gate of the barracks in the center of the town and declared that "if the soldiers did not come out and fight them, they would set fire to the four corners of the barracks, and burn every damned soul of them." Elsewhere, a bleeding oysterman graphically described how soldiers had assaulted him. A deckhand, who began to tell his story to the other sailors of his vessel, all at once found himself without an audience. The fire-bells had begun to ring to collect the people. In King Street, sailors, dockworkers, and mechanics pressed around the reinforced customhouse sentry, suggesting in waterfront jargon, "let us burn the sentry box, let us heave it over-board." Among them was the ropemaker who had been fired, after his employer conferred with the military commander, for being involved in a quarrel with a soldier who had been looking for a job. In front of the customhouse, the soldiers, provoked beyond endurance, fired. The crowd began to throw lines of defense over the adjoining streets and sent others to get guns.

It is not necessary to recount the complex details of the crowd action, since termed the "Boston Massacre," in the context we have established for the relation of leaders and crowds. In general, it can be said that the leaders stepped in only after the firing, when the lower-class men went to get their guns. They knew that they needed the people, and urged the crowd to stay around the townhouse until they had negotiated concessions from governor and military commander. On the one hand, they protected the governor from the crowd, while on the other, they were trying to get back control over crowds and events. In Council on the next day, councillor Royal Tyler did this so strongly and openly that Crown officials tried to pin him down on admitting treasonous conduct of the Boston Whig leaders.

But these were already busy taking depositions to prove to Great Britain the exclusive guilt of the soldiers, to clear themselves from any active involvement, and to prove to the crowds that they were active on their side. But the fact remains that it was the rioters who achieved their goal: removal of the troops from town.[50]

In the aftermath the leadership also had to reverse its position on refusing employment opportunities to mechanics, because it would allegedly hurt nonimportation. One of the committeemen for this purpose was John Ruddock, who a few months earlier had torn up the petition of the mechanics who demanded work. By giving permission for shipbuilding, hundreds of mechanics began to provide again for the support of their families, although the town still had to keep its poor-relief budget high.[51]

Having thus contained lower-class discontent, the Whig leaders helped the soldiers who had fired into the crowd to hire John Adams and Josiah Quincy, Jr., as their lawyers. These two were among the strongest opponents of crowd action in the Boston Whig elite. The acquittals or merely token punishments of the "murderers" as a result of the trial with a packed jury, were another sign for many Bostonians that justice could not be expected from courts and leaders. This discontent, too, was contained. A new resistance mythology was developed, by means different from that of the opulent feasts of 14 August. The orations in memory of the Massacre, open to all, became a political forum attended annually by four or five thousand persons. Whigs thundered against the dangers of standing armies and submission to unlimited authority. They also pointed out the glory of dying for one's liberty and country. Resistance in the practice of the rioters and in the orations and theory of the leaders had reached a new level.[52]

VI

Acting swiftly after the riot in King Street, the Boston leadership was able to shape the direction of the policies in response to and as a result of the riot. Three years later, in December 1773, they controlled the crowd action against the tea from the start. For months they had tried to foster a spirit of resistance in the country towns. The Boston Committee of Correspondence, created in November 1772, had begun to establish contacts all over the province. When news of the shipment of dutied tea to specific consignees arrived, Boston no longer acted on its own. There was constant communication with neighborhood towns. The assemblies that were called to debate the issues were extended from town meetings to nonrestricted meetings of townsmen, and finally to "provincial meetings." At the beginning of the anti-tea agitation, a broadside was distributed in Boston—"The Tradesmens Protest against the Proceedings of the Merchants"—arguing that the earlier nonconsumption and nonimportation agreements had been forced on the tradesmen, who, consequently, had incurred heavy losses. Under the watchful eyes of the leadership, the tradesmen were asked at a town meeting to collect in one corner and express their sentiments about the broadside. They disavowed it. But doubts about the honesty of the merchants lingered. It was common knowledge that for three years all merchants, Whig or Loyalist, had imported tea, duties notwithstanding.[53]

During the several mass meetings held to debate the political and constitutional consequences of submission to the duties and of the possible means of opposition, none of the leaders except Thomas Young mentioned the possibility of destroying the tea, though shouts from the audience occasionally suggested it. Instead two groups of about sixty men were organized by the Whig leaders to do the work. On 16 December they went to the wharf before the mass meeting was dissolved. Though joined by a 100 or more on the spur of the moment, most of the 2,000 men who came from the meeting remained spectators. The "activists" divided into three groups, one for each ship, and once on board quickly distributed the different tasks between themselves. Armed guards watched so that nobody came too close. The swiftness of the destruction and accounts by contemporaries make clear that the participants were men with experience in unloading ships, handling winches, opening chests—men from the waterfront community who acted in well-organized groups.[54] Three months later, when an additional shipment of tea arrived, a spontaneous crowd had the load overboard even before the Committee of Correspondence could meet to consider the situation. But it, too, did not go beyond the confines for action set by the leaders.[55] By 1773, the Boston crowd, at least in part, had been weaned from its own tradition and won over to exclusively anti-British action, most of the instigation for which came from the top down.

VII

After July 1774 crowd action declined in Boston, because the large number of troops sent to punish the town for the Tea Party made riotous resistance difficult. Henceforth, the Boston patriot leadership was confronted with the radicalism of rural crowds—a challenge it was unprepared for.

The so-called Coercive Acts, changing the structure of Massachusetts provincial and town government, made it difficult or impossible to use regular institutions: the General Court, town meetings, or juries. But if Bostonians could do little, inhabitants in the country soon realized that the troops could not garrison each and every town. Accordingly, town meetings were soon operating again, and three weeks of crowd action all over Massachusetts, from 20 August to 10 September, prevented the execution of the other clauses of the Coercive Acts. The new councillors appointed by the Crown were forced to resign in front of thousands. Judges were ordered to stop any court proceedings until the Administration-of-Justice Act was repealed. Sometimes the crowds elected leaders, frequently militia officers. When several towns cooperated in crowd action, each town's contingent elected one or a few men as speakers who would concert measures with crowds from other towns. The groups were usually armed, but to prevent bloodshed they stacked their guns outside of the town where their target lived and, leaving only a guard behind, entered, if not unarmed at least without firearms.[56]

The Boston Committee of Correspondence had promoted country participation in the opposition since 1772. But after the successful destruction of the tea, the Committee became bossy and overconfident of its influence. Disregarding town meeting instructions, the members were strongly criticized by Bostonians and rebuked by the country towns for attempting to dictate to them. Nevertheless, the Whig committeemen did not reexamine their position, and at times were as incapable as Governor Hutchinson of understanding and responding to spontaneous direct action.[57] After the British troops had seized the provincial powder supply at Cambridge, reports were received in Boston that irate countrymen, 30,000 strong, were on the march to Boston to teach the British a lesson. Boston's selectmen hurriedly sent out messengers to prevent the armed men from coming into Boston. However, before the selectmen's messengers could stop them, units within

a 140-mile radius were converging on the town.[58] While most returned
when told that no active fighting had taken place, some 4,000 men
from the neighboring towns assembled in Cambridge, where a number
of wealthy officials had their "suburban" homes. The crowd, partly
consisting of militia units, ordered them to resign, and they did so.
While even Loyalists commented positively on the discipline and good
order shown by the crowd, mainly farmers, Whig leaders were appre-
hensive. The Cambridge and Charlestown Committees of Correspondence first tried to send the crowd home, then urgently demanded that
the Boston Committee come over to help contain the spontaneous
movement. The chairman of the Boston Committee, probably afraid
of the reaction of Boston crowds to this news, did not even dare to
state the reason when he sent out messengers to call the members into
emergency session. At Cambridge the militia crowds had received
most of the resignations they had demanded, when the Boston Whigs
arrived: Warren, Cooper, Young, Molineux, Bradford, Greenleaf. Unlike the elected ad-hoc committeemen of the companies, they took
their place on the elevated steps of the courthouse, and William
Cooper addressed the people. In the name of the Committee and the
town of Boston, he thanked them "for their Readiness to serve the
Caus of the Country. . .[and] for discovering such a Spirit of Jealousy
over their Rights and Priviledges." Having thus complimented them,
he began to show his real concern: their spontaneous and determined
action. As he had attempted to hush up the discontent about the tea
importation by Whig merchants in 1773, he now hushed up the powder seizure: the Captain General and military Governor of the Province, Gage, had a right to take the powder and therefore should not
be opposed. Besides, he added, the powder was old and wet. Then
Molineux spoke to the same effect. When Captain Bradford began to
pull Cooper on the sleeve to stop him, he was in turn told to keep
quiet. Nevertheless, he stepped up when Molineux had ended: the
seizure was illegal, because it was done without the advice of the legal,
that is, the elected, Council. Mr. Devans, of Charlestown, a committeeman who early in the morning had attempted to persuade the companies to return to their towns, contradicted Bradford: "His Excellency
had a Right to take it and by that Charter which they [the crowd] were
constantly striving to preserve and defend." The "state of nature,"
often referred to even by as moderate man as Boston merchant John
Andrews, was not once mentioned. Either Young or Cooper then put
an end to the haggling by proposing that the men vote "that they

abhorred and detested all petty Mobs, Riots, Breaking Windows, and destroying private Property." The vote passed unanimously; the men had said so earlier, anyway. Cooper, revealing his total lack of understanding, suggested that the crowd go to the Common, while the Boston Committee would retire to an inn. He "would be very glad if they chose a Committee (1 or 2 from each Company)" to come to the tavern "to confer about the situation." He was drily informed that that had been done long ago.[59]

This surprising failure to establish contact and understanding with the "fine body of respectable freemen"—Warren's phrase—can be explained only by the lack of radicalism of the Boston leadership with Cooper as its spokesman. Bradford, from the merchant-captains, and Young, sympathetic to western agrarian thinking and unusually open-minded, did grasp the implications and the potential of such mass movement. But, in general, their "radical" stand merely concerned constitutional doctrines about imperial relations that were further developed than those of Crown officials; but the stratification and deferential character of Boston's society made them blind to the social implications which the theory of popular sovereignty held. They acted as they were accustomed to at public celebrations: the gentlemen drank toasts inside the town hall, and the people acclaimed from the outside. Now in Cambridge the action had been done by the people; leaders had been elected and had acted for several hours, but the Boston men literally did not see them, and wanted to get inside the tavern—the day was extremely hot—and have the people wait outside. They sustained their enemy—the military governor and Coercive Acts —rather than accept the spontaneous action of the Massachusetts farmers.

In addition to the Cambridge crowd action, country towns prodded Bostonians to refuse to work for the British troops, and a political strike was called. Next, an embargo of supplies was vigorously enforced by crowd action against merchants or farmers who attempted to break it. At the same time, Boston mechanics promoted desertion among soldiers (210 men left within 10 weeks) and organized an intelligence-gathering operation. The result of the latter was the early warning given to the militia units of Lexington and Concord on 18 April 1775.[60] Only after the British had evacuated Boston, did internal popular grievances again lead to direct action. Merchants who used the scarcity of provisions to monopolize the market or to extract extortionate prices were forced to sell at prices acceptable to those dependent on wages or small daily earnings.[61]

To sum up, from 1765 to 1770 crowd action propelled Boston along the way to independence. Initiated by the leadership in 1765, the crowd immediately turned to their own traditions of voicing economic and social discontent and opposition to authorities. It achieved a momentum of its own that forced socially conservative leaders to take into account the popular radicalism, spurred by the negative impact of British policies and Whig countermeasures on the economic standing of the lower clases. In 1765 armed military units, manned by the better sort only, reinstituted what from their viewpoint was order. In 1768, town meetings, the rhetoric of resistance, and a seeming responsiveness to impressment grievances curtailed the trend toward direct action. In the course of this the all too compromising old merchant elite met defeat in town meeting and was replaced by seemingly more responsive political leaders.

Between October 1769 and March 1770, Whig leaders, still afraid of mechanic consciousness, relied on a motley mixture of people, ranging from schoolboys to country people to shopkeepers, and on acts of individual terror to enforce nonimportation policies. The end of this period was marked by the largely spontaneous King Street riot ("The Boston Massacre"), arising in good part from labor competition between artisans and soldiers. With a flexibility unimaginable for the elevated gentry of Hutchinson's type, the Whig leadership responded quickly and reestablished its control over the crowd. They negotiated the withdrawal of the troops under crowd pressure, and accepted demands by the lower classes for employment.

By the 1773 tea action, control over the crowd was sufficiently well-established, so that the whole riot became a "party," with no danger to internal social cohesion. Master mechanics acting as intermediaries between higher leadership echelons and crowds, the willingness of some Whig leaders to respond to lower-class grievances, and their capacity of (1) fusing the local impact of British regulations on the lower classes to constitutional theories concerning imperial problems and of (2) presenting victories in the latter as solution to the former blunted the further development of the rudimentary and often submerged class consciousness that had reached a momentary high point of expression in August 1765. From 1774 on, the suffering mechanics did not turn against profiteering merchants or imperious Whig politicians, increasing instead pressure on Crown officials, locust-like "placemen." By sanctioning some of the spontaneous rioting ex post facto, the Whig elite appeared as leadership even when it was trying to catch up with the crowds. At the same time it thereby could

continue to demand deference in local society for its successful imperial policy.

Some Whig politicians and the crowd had struggled for a virtuous
republic, but in the years after 1774, the leaders, with few exceptions,
deserted the common goal, concerned about their own dignity and
power, and demanding deference again. They thus ended up in the
socially conservative camp, which some of them had opposed earlier,
but which they had left only temporarily in search of support from the
people. They were as much opposed to the demands of "the people
out of doors" as to British regulations and taxes. Peaceful coexistence
with the people would have meant compromises, but popular demands
were deflected by rhetoric about united interests and by the conde-
scension of leaders. It seems that the established social structures in
Boston and Whig ideology hampered the development of a separate
lower-class ideology, and that the mechanics' social consciousness, if
not their political thinking, was kept down to its rudimentary pre-1765
levels. But lower-class radicalism had brought about the change from
the compromising cautious merchant leadership to politicians who
were outspoken, perhaps radical, in their opposition to further domination by and dependence on Great Britain.

On 18 July 1776, the Declaration of Independence was proclaimed in Boston. It was read from the town hall's balcony by Thomas
Crafts, a member of the Loyal Nine, who had repeatedly been accused
of acting like a Tory, who had been willing to sacrifice specific resistance policies for concessions from the British military governor, and
who had been reading a book on class war in the Roman Empire and
the necessity of containing the "many" in favor of the well-versed few.
Four days later the Boston Committee of Correspondence, as auto-
cratic as ever since its tea-party success, ordered the townsmen to
appear on the Common for a military draft. Just as in 1765, when
gentlemen-volunteers had guarded the property of the wealthy, a similar unit now surrounded the draft-age population with lowered guns.
Gentlemen, subject to the draft, bought substitutes when their members were drawn by lot to join the army. Incensed by this show of class
or money-based differences, the people rioted against the gentlemen
and the Whig committee, shouting, "Tyranny is Tyranny let it come
from whom it may."[62]

I want to thank the Charles Warren Center, Harvard University, for providing support for the preparation of this essay. The Center's fellows of the academic year 1974–1975, particularly Pauline Maier, commented on an earlier version and helped me to sharpen my points of argument. Alfred Young, a very demanding taskmaster, was always willing to help me clarify my concepts and the expression of them. His thorough criticism helped more than anything else or any other person to make my argument as clear as possible. I have profited immensely from his comments. But, of course, not all criticism and suggestions have been taken, so the shortcomings of the essay are my responsibility.

1. Gage to Conway, 23 September 1765, in *Correspondence of General Thomas Gage with the Secretaries of State, 1763–1775,* Clarence E. Carter, ed., 2 vols. (New Haven: Yale University Press, 1931), 1:67–68.

2. Pauline Maier, "Popular Uprisings and Civil Authority in Eighteenth-Century America," *William and Mary Quarterly,* 3d ser. 27 (1970): 3–35, especially p. 4. In addition to Maier, see Gordon S. Wood, "A Note on Mobs in the American Revolution," ibid., 3d ser. 23 (1966): 635–42; Arthur M. Schlesinger, Sr., "Political Mobs in the American Revolution, 1765–1776," *Proceedings of the American Philosophical Society* 99 (1955): 244–50.

3. For further literature and a more extensive treatment of the tradition of rioting in Massachusetts, see chap. 3 of Dirk Hoerder, "People and Mobs: Crowd Action in Massachusetts During the American Revolution, 1765–1780" (diss., Free University of Berlin: photoprint 1971). See also Merrill Jensen, "The American People and the American Revolution," *Journal of American History* 57(1970): 5–35.

4. Massachusetts crowds in 1765 and 1775 quoted the Bible in justification of their deeds. Thomas Hutchinson, *The History of the Colony and Province of Massachusetts-Bay,* Lawrence Shaw Mayo, ed., 3 vols. (Cambridge: Harvard University Press, 1936), 3:89; *Boston Evening Post,* 13 March 1775; *Massachusetts Spy,* 17 March 1775. Rioters from New Jersey to Maine claimed that they acted against offending community members who were sinners and that property was not destroyed but sacrificed to the Gods of the world. See Countryman's "Out of the Bounds of the Law" in this anthology. For a suggestive essay on Puritan concepts during the revolutionary period, see Edmund S. Morgan, "The Puritan Ethic and the American Revolution," *William and Mary Quarterly,* 3d ser. 24 (1967): 3–43. See also the introductory chapter of Stephen E. Patterson's *Political Parties in Revolutionary Massachusetts* (Madison: University of Wisconsin Press, 1973), and Richard D. Brown, *Revolutionary Politics in Massachusetts. The Boston Committee of Correspondence and the Towns, 1772–1774* (Cambridge: Harvard University Press, 1970), pp. 10, 119–20, and passim. Alfred F. Young in an unpublished paper, "Pope's Day, Tar and Feathers, and 'Cornet Joyce, jun.': From Ritual to Rebellion in Boston, 1745–1775," has explored the Protestant traditions of Boston crowds. But a thoroughgoing study of the ideological origins of revolutionary lower-class action, particularly the adaptation of religious tenets and of political concepts of the Whig leadership, remains to be written.

5. James Henretta, "Economic Development and Social Structure in Colonial Boston," *William and Mary Quarterly,* 3d ser. 22 (1965): 75–92; Alan and Katherine Day, "Another Look at the Boston Caucus," *Journal of American Studies (GB)* 5 (1971): 19–45; Richard Buel, Jr., "Democracy and the American Revolution: A Frame of Reference," *William and Mary Quarterly,* 3d ser. 21 (1964): 165–90; Jack R. Pole, "Historians and the Problem of Early American Democracy," *American Historical Review* 67 (1962): 626–46; Hoerder, *Crowd Action,* chap. 2, and *Society and Government 1760–1780: The Power Structure in Massachusetts Townships* (West Berlin: John F. Kennedy-Institute, 1972), pp. 41–49 and passim. *Boston Town Records,* 26:127.

6. Josiah Quincy, Jr., *Reports of Cases Argued and Abjudged in the Superior Court of Judicature of the Province of Massachusetts Bay, between 1761 and 1772,* Samuel M. Quincy, ed. (Boston: Little, Brown & Co., 1865), pp. 237–38. Greenleaf to Murray, 4 May 1770, in *Legal Papers of John Adams,* L. K. Wroth and H. B. Zobel, eds., 3 vols. (Cambridge: Harvard University Press, 1965), 1:217–18; Robert J. Dinkin, "Seating the Meeting House in Early Massachusetts," *New England Quarterly* 43 (1970): 450–64; *Letters and Diary of John Rowe, Boston Merchant,* ed. Annie Rowe Cunningham (Boston: W. B. Clarke Co., 1903), p. 157. On mechanics: Hutchinson, *History,* 3:88; Journal of Transactions at Boston, Sparks MSS., 10.3:55–56, Houghton Library, Harvard University; *Advertisement*

[Brds. about building of ships] (Boston, 1769); reversal of the Whig policies after large-scale mechanic and sailor-dominated rioting, *Boston Town Records*, 18:20. Deposition of John Gray, Frederic Kidder, ed., *History of the Boston Massacre, March 5, 1770* (Albany: J. Munsell, 1870), p. 51.

7. The political ideology of the Whig leadership, as Bernard Bailyn and others have emphasized, grew as a reasoned reaction to the changes in British policies based on the suppositions of Locke and the Commonwealthmen. Beginning with the Stamp Act, each issue compelled a redefinition of imperial relations and, viewed from the writings of Whig leaders, the movement toward independence flowed steadily and logically from the political assumptions. But the translation of ideological principles into action on the local level was much more complex and far less steady and well-reasoned.

8. For the genesis of the Stamp Act and the developments in the colonies, see Edmund S. and Helen M. Morgan, *The Stamp Act Crisis: Prologue to Revolution* (Chapel Hill: University of North Carolina Press, 1953). For the betrayal motif see, for example, *Liberty, Property, and No Excise. A Poem* (Boston, 1765).

9. William Gordon, *The History of the Rise, Progress and Establishment of the Independence of the United States of America*, 4 vols. (London: privately printed 1788), 1:175; *Diary and Autobiography of John Adams*, Lyman H. Butterfield, ed., 4 vols. (Cambridge: Harvard University Press, 1961–1966), 1:294, 2:73.

10. Hutchinson, *History*, 3:87; Bernard to Earl of Halifax, 15 August 1765, Sparks MSS., 4.4:142, Houghton Library, Harvard University.

11. I am grateful to Alfred F. Young for permission to paraphrase his findings about the Pope's Day crowds from his unpublished paper "Pope's Day," section II, p. 20.

12. *Boston Evening Post*, 19 August 1765; *Boston Newsletter*, 22 August 1765; *Boston Gazette*, 19 August 1765, Supplement; Hutchinson, *Diary* 1:67; Samuel Mather to his son, 17 August 1765, Letterbook, Massachusetts Historical Society.

13. John Avery to John Collins, 19 August 1765, in *Extracts from Itineraries and Other Miscellanies of Ezra Stiles*, F. B. Dexter, ed. (New Haven, Conn.: Yale University Press, 1916), pp. 435–37. Morgan, *Stamp Act Crisis*, pp. 124–29.

14. Bernard to Halifax, 22 August 1765, Sparks MSS. 4.4:144–48; Hutchinson, *History* 3:88.

15. Gordon, *History of the Revolution*, 1:176–80; William Story's petition to the governor, Massachusetts Archives, 44:604–6, Massachusetts State House, Archives; Benjamin Hallowell's account, 7 September 1765, House of Lords MSS. 209:199–203, transcripts, Library of Congress; Ebenezer Parkman, Diary, 26 August 1765, photostats, Massachusetts Historical Society; Hutchinson, *History* 3:89–90, *Diary* 1:67. Display of wealth had motivated crowd action on Harvard Commencement days, when the wealthy feasters returned via Boston's Northend. Hoerder, *Crowd Action*, pp. 78–79.

16. For example, customs collector Benjamin Hallowell, and the owner of the house rented by the surveyor of the port, Charles Paxton.

17. Charles W. Akers, *Called unto Liberty. A Life of Jonathan Mayhew, 1720–1766* (Cambridge: Harvard University Press, 1964), p. 198, passim; Hutchinson, *History*, 3:89; *Boston Evening Post*, 19 August 1765.

18. Bernard to Halifax, 31 August 1765, Sparks MSS. 4.4:153; see also Lloyd to Butler, 29 August 1765, Letterbook, pp. 151–52, Harvard Business School; Powell to Champlin, 2 September 1765, Letters of Boston Merchants, 1732–1766, 4 vols., Harvard Business School, 1:72; John Hancock, Letterbook, 10 September 1765 and later, Hancock Papers, Harvard Business School.

19. Council Records, 16:37–39, Massachusetts State House, Archives; *Boston Town Records*, 16:152, 20:174; *Boston Evening Post*, 2 September 1765; Gordon to Smith, 10 September 1765, *Massachusett Historical Society Proceedings*, 2nd ser. 13 (1900): 393; Bernard to Halifax, 31 August 1765, Sparks MSS. 4.4:153.

20. Gordon, *History of the Revolution*, 1:180. Hutchinson had taken depositions about merchants whose wealth was at least partly based on smuggling. As chief justice he was known to have evidence among his papers refuting claims of a land company whose suit was just then pending in court. This evidence was destroyed. The amount of property damaged and the amount of liquor consumed were not only alien to the tradition of crowd action. Both also occurred only after the first customarily restrained

stage of the riot, lending further credibility to the contemporary assertion that "secret influences" hid behind the Pope's Day people.

21. Morgan, *Stamp Act Crisis,* pp. 129–43; *Boston Town Records* 16:158, 20:183; Bernard to Pownall, 1 November 1765, Sparks MSS. 10.1:95–96; Council Records, 16:66, 68–69.

22. *Boston Newsletter,* 31 October, 7 November, 14 November, 1765; *Boston Evening Post,* 11 November 1765; Bernard to Pownall, 1 November, 26 November 1765, Sparks MSS., 4.5:16–21, 10.1:97; Hutchinson to———, 1 November 1765, to Franklin, 18 November 1765, Massachusetts Archives, 26:173–75, transcripts, Massachusetts Historical Society; "Reminiscences by General William H. Sumner," *New England Historical and Genealogical Register* 8(1854): 187–91, especially p. 191; Herbert S. Allan, *John Hancock, Patriot in Purple* (New York: Macmillan Co., 1948), pp. 91–92.

23. Oliver to Whately, 20 August 1765, House of Lords MSS. 209:104–6; Bernard to Board of Trade, 7 September 1765, Sparks MSS. 4.4:158–61; *Boston Gazette,* 23 September 1765, Supplement. See also Jesse Lemisch, "Jack Tar in the Streets: Merchant Seamen in the Politics of Revolutionary America," *William and Mary Quarterly,* 3d. ser. 25 (1968): 371–407, especially pp. 397–400.

24. Council Records, 16:74–75; Hutchinson to Pownall, 8 March 1766, Massachusetts Archives, 26:207–14.

25. George P. Anderson, "Ebenezer Mackintosh," *Colonial Society of Massachusetts Publications* 26(1924–1926):15–64, 348–61, especially pp. 360–61.

26. The development of the middle class celebrations has been treated more extensively in Hoerder, *Crowd Action,* pp. 230–33.

27. *Boston Gazette,* 9 November 1767, 14 March 1768; Otis's speech reported in *Boston Evening Post,* 23 November 1767. For opposition to and fear of crowd action of other Whig leaders, see John R. Howe, Jr., *The Changing Political Thought of John Adams* (Princeton: Princeton University Press, 1966), and George H. Nash, III, "From Radicalism to Revolution: The Political Career of Josiah Quincy, Jr.," *American Antiquarian Society Proceedings* 79 (1969): 253–90. For Samuel Adams's differently motivated negative attitude to crowd action, see his article signed "Determinatus," in the *Boston Gazette,* 8 August 1768 (reprinted in *Writings of Samuel Adams,* H. A. Cushing, ed., 4 vols. (New York: G. P. Putnam's Sons, 1904–1908), 1:236–240 in conjunction with the excerpts of a debate in Parliament, 1737, reprinted in *The Conduct of the Paxton Men* (Philadelphia, 1764), pp. 278–79, in *The Paxton Papers,* John R. Dunbar, ed. (The Hague: 1957). For the Puritan and Protestant traditions, see note 4 above.

28. Oliver M. Dickerson, *The Navigation Acts and the American Revolution* (Philadelphia: University of Pennsylvania Press, 1951); Charles M. Andrews, "The Boston Merchants and the Non-Importation Movement," *Colonial Society of Massachusetts Publications* 19 (1916–1917): 159–259; Hoerder, *Crowd Action,* chaps. 5 and 7.

29. "[John] Boyle's Journal of Occurrences in Boston, 1759–1778," *New England Historical and Genealogical Register* 84 (1930): 253; Anne Hulton, *Letters of a Loyalist Lady* (Cambridge: Harvard University Press, 1927) p. 8.

30. *Boston Town Records,* 16:225; *Boston Gazette,* 16, 23 November 1767; *Boston Evening Post,* 23 November 1767.

31. *Boston Gazette,* 21 March 1768; *Letters and Diary of John Rowe,* pp. 156–57; Hutchinson, *History,* 3:136; Hutchinson to Jackson, 23 March 1768, Massachusetts Archives, 26:295–96; Bernard to Shelburne, 19 March 1768, Sparks MSS. 10.2:74; *The Writings of Samuel Adams,* 1:241–47; *Boston Newsletter,* 24 March 1768.

32. Hutchinson, *History,* 3:136; Allan, *Hancock,* pp. 102–4; G. G. Wolkins, "The Seizure of John Hancock's Sloop *Liberty,*" *Massachusetts Historical Society Proceedings* 55 (1921–1922): 239–84; D. H. Watson, ed., "Joseph Harrison and the *Liberty* Incident," *William and Mary Quarterly,* 3d ser. 20 (1963): 385–95.

33. Dawson v. *The Dolphin, Legal Papers of John Adams,* 2:223–237, cf. ibid. 237–42; *Boston Town Records* 16:250, 253, 20:292.

34. Hiller B. Zobel *The Boston Massacre* (New York: W. W. Norton & Co., 1970), pp. 73–74.

35. Deposition of Benjamin Goodwin, House of Lords MSS., 252:288–90. *Boston Evening Post,* 20 June 1768.

36. Council Records 16:319–20, 333–45; Misc. Unbound Papers, 1768, Boston

City Hall; *Boston Newsletter,* 23 June 1768; *Boston Gazette,* 4 July 1768; Molineux to Harrison, 15 June 1768, Sparks MSS. 10.3:1.

37. *Boston Evening Post,* 20 June 1768; Hutchinson to Jackson, 16 June 1768, *Massachusetts Historical Society Proceedings* 55 (1921–1922): 282–83; Bernard to Hillsborough, 12 December 1768, Sparks MSS. 10.3:3.

38. *Boston Town Records* 16:253, passim; for a more detailed analysis of the change in leadership, see Hoerder, *Crowd Action,* pp. 273–80.

39. Bernard to Hillsborough, 18 July 1768, Sparks MSS. 4.7:8–10; *Letters and Diary of John Rowe,* p. 170.

40. Council Records, 16:354; *Boston Town Records,* 20:309–11; Gage to Hillsborough, 10 October 1768, *Correspondence of General Thomas Gage,* 1:200–201.

41. Council Records, in Massachusetts Archives 85:752; *Letters and Diary of John Rowe,* p. 177; Oliver to Spooner, 28 October 1768, Andrew Oliver, Letterbook, 1:41–45, Massachusetts Historical Society; *Boston Under Military Rule,* O. M. Dickerson, ed. (Boston: Chapman & Grimes, 1936), hereafter cited as *Journal of the Times,* pp. 5, 19; Dalrymple to Hood, 4 October 1768, House of Lords MSS., 253:12–14; "Journals of Capt. John Montresor, 1757–1778," G. D. Scull, ed., *New York Historical Society Collections 1881* (New York, 1882), pp. 402.

42. *Journal of the Times,* p. 7, passim; *Boston Town Records* 23:19; *Boston Gazette,* 26 December 1768; depositions by the soldiers, Gay Transcripts, State Papers, vol. 12, Massachusetts Historical Society.

43. *Boston Town Records,* 16:222, 226–27, 230–31, 239, 249–50, 273, 275–77, 18:70–73, 138–39; Thomas Mewse to ?, 23 September 1770, Daniel Brooke to Joseph Otis, 24 November 1768, Otis Papers 3:7ff, Massachusetts Historical Society.

44. Journal of Transactions at Boston, Sparks MSS., 10.3:55–56.

45. Cummings to Smith, 20 November 1769, James Murray Robbins Papers, vol. 2, 1769–1770, Massachusetts Historical Society; Oliver to Bernard, 10 January 1770, Letterbook, 1:119, 135–36; Powell to Champlin, 23 October 1769, *Massachusetts Historical Society Collections* 69:294; *Letters of James Murray, Loyalist,* N. M. Tiffany and S. I. Leslay, eds. (Boston: privately printed 1901), pp. 132–33, 176–79.

46. *Boston Town Records,* 18:51, 23:39–40, 42, 45–46; soldiers' depositions, Gay Transcripts, State Papers, 12:54–70.

47. John E. Alden, "John Mein: Scrouge of Patriots," *Colonial Society of Massachusetts Publications* 34 (1942): 571–99; [John Mein], *A State of the Importation from Great Britain* (Boston 1769, 1770); vindications by the merchants' committee, *Boston Evening Post,* 28 August, 4 September 1769; "The Boston Patriots Characterized," *Boston Chronicle,* 23–26 October 1769, and "Key to a certain publication," Sparks MSS. 10.3:45–47. *Letters and Diary of John Rowe,* p. 194; Cummings to ?, 28 October 1769, James Murray Robbins Papers, vol. 2 (1769–1770); *Boston Evening Post,* 30 October 1769.

48. Hutchinson, *History* 3:191–93; Eliot to Hollis, 25 December 1769, *Massachusetts Historical Society Collections,* 4th ser. 4(1858): 446; Journal of Transactions at Boston, letter from George Mason, 24 January 1770, Narrative of Proceedings at Boston, Sparks MSS. 10.3:55–56, 63, 70–71; *Letters and Diary of John Rowe,* pp. 196–97; Cooper to Pownall, 30 January 1770, *American Historical Review* 8:314–16. Whig merchants violating the agreement reportedly exchanged their merchandise for bricks before publicly agreeing to reship.

49. Rex v. Richardson, 1770–1772, case 59, *Legal Papers of John Adams* 2:396–430; Hutchinson to Gage, 25 February 1770, Massachusetts Archives 26:445–448; Palfrey to Wilkes, 5 March 1770, *Colonial Society of Massachusetts Publications* 34 (1937–1942): 415–17; Cooper to Pownall, 26 March 1770, *American Historical Review* 8:316–18; Gordon, *History of the Revolution* 1:276–77.

50. Frederic Kidder, ed., *History of the Boston Massacre* (Albany: J. Munsell, 1870), pp. 195, 202, 209, 217; *Legal Papers of John Adams,* vol. 3; Hiller B. Zobel, *The Boston Massacre.* Cf. Jesse Lemisch, "Radical Plot in Boston (1770): A Study in the Use of Evidence [review]," *Harvard Law Review* 84 (1970–1971): 485–504; and Pauline Maier, "Revolutionary Violence and the Relevance of History [review]," *Journal of Interdisciplinary History* 2 (1971–1972): 119–34, for Zobel's Tory bias. Council action: Council Records, 16:457–61 and depositions on the meetings, Massachusetts Archives 50:360–67.

51. *Boston Town Records,* 18:12–20; Anne Hulton, *Letters,* p. 26.
52. *Legal Papers of John Adams,* vol. 3; John R. Howe, Jr., *The Changing Political Thought of John Adams,* pp. 11–14, 28, 106–7; George H. Nash, III, "Josiah Quincy, Jr.," *American Antiquarian Society Proceedings* 79 (1969): 258–59, 286.
53. Richard D. Brown, *Revolutionary Politics,* pp. 92–93, passim; Benjamin W. Labaree, *The Boston Tea Party* (New York: Oxford University Press, 1964); Tradesmen's protest, in *Massachusetts Historical Society Collections* 71:203; *Boston Town Records* 18:141–44; *Diary of John Adams,* 1:351; "Proceedings of Ye Body Respecting the Tea," L. F. S. Upton, *William and Mary Quarterly,* 3d ser. 22 (1965): 295–96.
54. Labaree, *Tea Party,* pp. 126–45.
55. *Boston Evening Post,* 14 March 1774; Committee of Correspondence, Minute Book, 9:726–28, New York Public Library.
56. Hoerder, *Crowd Action,* chaps. 8 and 9.
57. Brown, *Revolutionary Politics,* pp. 191–99; for other criticism directed at Boston's leaders, cf. Hoerder, *Crowd Action,* pp. 542–47.
58. Robert P. Richmond, *Powder Alarm 1774* (Princeton, N. J., etc.: Auerbach Publications, 1971); *The Literary Diary of Ezra Stiles,* F. B. Dexter, ed., 3 vols. (New York: Charles Scribner's Sons, 1901), 1:479–85; "Letters of John Andrews, Esq., Boston 1772–1776," Winthrop Sargent, ed., *Massachusetts Historical Society Proceedings* 8 (1864–1865): 352; Tea Notes, 1774, in: Sewell Papers, Public Archives of Canada; Tudor to Adams, 3 September 1774, *Adams Family Correspondence* 1:149; Edward Hill's report, ibid.; *Letters and Diary of John Rowe,* p. 284.
59. Tea Notes, 1774, Sewell Papers, 7630–34; Lee to Gage, 1 September 1774, *Colonial Society of Massachusetts Publications* 32 (1933–1937):483.
60. *Boston Town Records* 23:229; Committee of Correspondence, Minute Books 11:853–54, 861–65, New York Public Library; "Letters of John Andrews," *Massachusetts Historical Society Proceedings,* 8:366–69, 370–71, 384–85; *Memoir and Letters of Capt. W. Glanville Evelyn,* G. D. Scull, ed. (Oxford: J. Parker & Co., 1879), p. 39; *Boston Gazette,* 3 October 1774; *Boston Evening Post,* 26 September 1774; Force, ed., *American Archives,* 4.1:780–83, 802, 810, 4.2:283; Gage to Dartmouth, 25 September 1774, *Correspondence,* 1:376; John Shy, *Towards Lexington. The Role of the British Army in the Coming of the American Revolution* (Princeton: Princeton University Press, 1965), pp. 413–14; Noyes to Henshaw, n.d., *New England Historical and Genealogical Register* 43 (1889): 144–45; deposition of Samuel Dyer, 30 July 1774, Admiralty Papers, Sec. Department 1:484, 535–38, transcripts, Library of Congress.
61. Hoerder, *Crowd Action,* chap. 13.
62. *Letters and Diary of John Rowe,* p. 313; Abigail Adams to John Adams, 21 July 1776, *Family Correspondence* 2:55–57; William Knox to Henry Knox, 24 July 1776, Knox Papers, 2:173, Massachusetts Historical Society.

The "Disaffected" in the Revolutionary South

Ronald Hoffman

A flag adopted by numerous patriot military units. The slogan "Dont Tread on Me" was equally symbolic of the spirit of those who refused to be conscripted by either side. No original flag or contemporary drawing seems to have survived. The above is from a recent drawing for an exhibit in the Library of Congress.

One central conviction more than any other has guided my research—an understanding that the War for Independence was a revolution. The dissension, chaos, and social anarchy spawned by the war interacted with egalitarian tendencies and attitudes inherent in colonial society to transform the value structure of American life. Nowhere was this change more evident than in the South. Confronted by the varied patterns of disintegrating social control and a lack of vigorous broad-based support for the Revolution, southern Whig leaders in the late 1770s and early 1780s governed tenuously. The possibility that a ferocious internal struggle may have occurred simultaneously with the war has been perceived by only a few sensitive scholars: Don Higginbotham, John Shy, Paul Smith, and Franklin and Mary Wickwire. The contribution of their work lies not just in its military character but more importantly in its appreciation of the social and political dimensions of the conflict. Their examinations have provided a needed corrective to the pejorative bias which surrounds military history and suggest directions of exploration into some of the era's richest history.

My study, *A Spirit of Dissension: Economics, Politics, and the Revolution in Maryland* (Baltimore: Johns Hopkins University Press, 1973), investigated the pattern of wartime dissidence in the upper Chesapeake. One of the most salient aspects of revolutionary Maryland was the wide degree of civil strife that accompanied independence. In the war's early years, waves of discontent and social violence seriously undermined and eroded the dominant position of the political leadership. The experience in Maryland—the causes of the discontent and the elite's successful retention of authority—encouraged my interest in other regions, especially the Lower South, where social and regional divisions ran deeper than in any area of colonial society, and where, during the war, near anarchy prevailed.

In exploring the revolutionary South, I have discovered that most historians have no understanding of the civil struggle that shattered most of that region during the war years, and that little serious thought has been given to how the rather unpopular Whig elites managed to retain their authority during the period's incredible turmoil. None of the relevant interpretations—progressive, neo-Whig, or New Left—are very helpful in explaining either the pattern of wartime social disruption or political behavior. In my judgment, we must develop a new synthesis to interpret the dissension and anarchy unleashed by the Revolution and the ultimate restoration of social control by the Whig elite.

Ronald Hoffman (Ph.D., University of Wisconsin, 1969), is Associate Professor of History at the University of Maryland.

The profound disaffection that took place during the War for Independence poses one of the most challenging questions of the revolutionary era. Violent clashes erupted throughout the breadth of America, with the most intense disruptions occurring in the South where the military struggle contained critical social dimensions. The prevalence of this civil dissension raises a number of fundamental questions about the maintenance of social order in the revolutionary South. To be precise, how did southern political elites, usually wealthy and responsible for policies branded unjust, manage to retain their authoritative positions amid the shattering turmoil? Why did their Whig ideology persuade some of the "meaner sort," (the bulk of the population) but fail to rouse others? Why did some of the people resist the revolutionary governments? Why did others resist the British? And why did still others continually waffle from side to side? With unusual insight, one scholar has recently commented that "Of the many dilemmas in understanding the American Revolution probably the deepest still remains: how could a long and difficult revolution fought on liberal principles and led by a social elite, at once unleash many forms of serious social discontent without the unrest essentially disrupting the elite's moderate but flexibly responsive social vision?"[1]

One conventional explanation for problems of this character is that colonial society was deferential. All accepted the hierarchy of the better, middling, and meaner sort, and the vast majority of people unconsciously internalized the expected forms of behavior. During the war these models of deportment presumably endured, providing the social cohesion exploited by various revolutionary leaderships in their difficult but ultimately successful quest to retain power.

Many students of early America have impressively developed this eminently reasonable explanation, relying especially on the writings of conservative spokesmen, their behavioral forms, and their exercise of power.[2] Yet the conservative portrayal of American society must always be viewed with caution and not confused with actual conditions. No automatic extrapolations about the hierarchical character of society can be made because an elite exercised authority. Such things as monopoly of office, manner of dress and address, pew in church, or position in a receiving line may be of great significance to the constricted elite community, but they possess marginal importance for the wider social order. Indeed, the elites' self-characterizations and their arrogant or paternalistic attitudes in the late colonial era may well have reflected uncertainty about their status and security.[3] From recently developed quantitative evidence, no one could reasonably dispute that wealth was unevenly divided in colonial America, with the upper elite controlling close to three-fourths of the wealth.[4] Nevertheless, direct correlations cannot be mechanically assumed between inert tables and cultural values.[5] Certainly, the social disorder unleashed by the war suggests that serious conflicts existed within the value structure of revolutionary America. Similarly, the elite's ultimate success in maintaining control of this violence implies some modifications in its cultural attitudes.

I

The Revolution plunged the states of Delaware, Maryland, North Carolina, South Carolina, Georgia, and, to a much lesser degree, Virginia into divisive civil conflicts that persisted during the entire period of struggle. Delaware and Maryland began to experience serious disorders in late 1775. Earlier, the imperial protest movement had demanded little sacrifice. Basically, the opposition to England had occurred in the urban areas. Nonimportation, the principle means of colonial resistance, had only slightly inconvenienced the pattern of community life. As a method of protest, it also possessed the virtue of being simple to enforce. One or two leaders and a well-disciplined crowd could easily shut down a port, whether or not the merchants agreed. Many of the traders who had willingly adopted nonimportation in 1765, but reversed their stand in the late 1760s, found themselves as vulnerable to concerted intimidation and violence as the resident royal or proprietary officials.[6] Still, the wider society, over 90 percent of which lived outside the urban confines, experienced minimal inconvenience. The basic rhythm of agricultural and commerical life remained unmolested.

All that had changed by 1775. In 1774, the First Continental Congress authorized a program of orchestrated economic pressure to protest Parliament's punishment of Massachusetts. When Massachusetts petitioned for an immediate policy of nonimportation, nonexportation, and nonconsumption, the South vehemently objected to nonexportation as a threat to the region's entire commercial economy. The compromise reached called for immediate nonimportation, with nonexportation to follow a year later. Most of the delegates probably never expected that nonexportation would ever be put into effect, nor was any action taken toward establishing enforcement apparatus until the crisis intensified with the battles at Lexington and Concord in April 1775. Yet the summer's news from England indicated a determination to compel obedience. Clearly, the confrontation would be serious. Within the colonies, those who had led the protest and others who believed in opposition, though not in independence, closed ranks and formed provisional governments to expand their base of support and engage the participation of the broader community.[7]

From the beginning these efforts to secure popular cooperation stimulated a diverse pattern of resistance. In the Upper South, the struggle, especially on the eastern shores of Maryland and Virginia and in Delaware's southern counties—the Delmarva Peninsula—created confusion, civil strife, and frequent outbursts of violence. But the Lower South ultimately endured a much more lethal form of civil war, as marauding, pillaging, and wanton murder verged on permanency. In both regions the particular form of dissension and response depended upon the preceding political, economic, and social realities.

II

Revolution came to most southerners, including those Whigs who were to lead it, as an unwelcome development. Drawn from the same class as were the upper echelons of their Tory opponents—in many instances wealthy, educated, and slave owning—they comprised one of the many shifting factions that competed for power and award in the colonies. Both limiting circumstances and limited commitments had led them to oppose the royal forces in the years after 1763, when

England tried to exert greater control over the colonies. Yet they operated securely in the old colonial context of struggle for influence between competing elites, and down to the eve of the war, they did not clearly recognize what would result from the various colonial protests. Had they known where their actions against certain British policies were to lead, it is questionable whether many would have long supported them. Given their social and economic position and the structures of the societies the revolutionary leaders presumed to lead, there was hardly anything Great Britain could do that would prove so threatening to them as did the Revolution itself. Its dislocations and demands raised the popular political consciousness to an unprecedented level. Never before had any political elite, imperial or provincial, requested so much from the people. And, while some of the "meaner sort" responded positively, others, in many instances the majority, resisted with actions that ranged from passive refusal to fierce opposition.

The men who guided Maryland during the Revolution were fundamentally conservative. Known by their contemporaries as the "popular" party, they had coalesced as a leadership group in 1773. By skillfully exploiting two related antiproprietary issues concerning the proper salaries for public officials and clerics, they had acquired control of the assembly's lower house. Elated with their ascension to power, these men—Charles Carroll of Carrollton, Samuel Chase, Matthew Tilghman, Thomas Johnson, and William Paca—anticipated the enjoyment of the traditional benefits of power—money, prestige, and influence within the existing society. The strain in Anglo-American relations had not been a direct or immediate cause in their rise, although Great Britain's indifference to the colony's political sensitivities and economic problems certainly enhanced their appeal. Still, with the exception of Chase and Tilghman, their attitudes on the imperial dispute with Parliament were not widely known. Chase deservedly enjoyed the reputation of an incendiary, while Tilghman's conduct as a leader in the lower house was steady and cautious. The feelings of Johnson and Carroll toward England were not matters of public record, and, although Paca was close to the proprietary governor, Robert Eden, all three men were regarded as warm friends of the reform cause.

Prior to the popular party's rise to power, the imperial protest movement within Maryland had been composed of a narrow coalition of two wings, one in Baltimore, the other in Annapolis. Samuel Chase, personally ambitious and the only popular party member to play an active role in decrying Parliament's conduct, led the Annapolis component. The Baltimore wing was led by various figures, the most prominent of which were William Lux and Samuel Purviance. The merchants had joined with Chase primarily because of England's insensitivity to the economic blight that afflicted the trading community in the late 1750s and early 1760s. Though going through several stages of formation and disintegration, the Baltimore-Annapolis alliance accurately reflected the basic goals adopted and widely expressed by the popular party in 1773: greater political power at home and control over the colony's economic destiny.

Once in power, the popular leaders encountered a series of increasingly severe challenges, all of which were related to the Anglo-American conflict. Basically, most of them were anxious to seek a reconciliation, but events beyond their control forced them to adopt stands they privately lamented. Because of the worsening crisis and the structure of politics, they soon developed those apprehensions shared by other elite elements throughout the South: the fear that the tension of the rebellion would unleash those convulsive social forces previously restrained by the old system. Within all of the southern colonies a host of potential dissensions existed—the uneven distribution of wealth, the clash of varied cultures, the potential of servile insurrection, and division within the church. From each of these factors deep-seated animosities had developed. Equally threatening was the existence of radical political factions that were ambitious for power and which attempted to manipulate and exploit the imperial controversy, thus continually placing the Whig leaders on the defensive. By 1776, the southern Whigs faced an increasingly desperate situation, as the traditional sanctions of authority and conduct weakened. With the threat of slave resistance and violence by the common sort becoming more pronounced, they clearly recognized the need for stability and a new system of authority.

In Maryland, the Whigs moved forcefully to achieve a measure of security through the establishment of strong institutional controls soon after the decision for separation, a step almost universally regretted by the province's leadership, which had voted unanimously on 21 May 1776 not to seek independence. At the constitutional convention, held that summer and fall, they designed and enacted a charter which made the possession of extensive property the fundamental basis of government. No one could participate in public life without large amounts of material wealth. To qualify for membership in the lower house, a man had to own a minimum of £500 real or personal property, and in the upper house, a minimum of £1000. The governor's position was to go only to a man holding an estate valued at £5000 or more. Also, eligibility for the governor's executive council, the position of congressional delegate, and the strategic local office of county sheriff required an estate of £1000. Complementing these prerequisites, the constitution outlined an election method that was structured to insure the selection of an aristocratically oriented government. Voters could directly elect individuals to only two positions: the lower house and county sheriff. The election of sheriff constituted something of a reform, since prior to this time he had been appointed. Yet, with a property qualification of £1000 attached to the office, the concession to popular rule seems hardly dramatic. Senate members were to be selected by an electoral college. The voters could choose only electors who had estates valued at a minimum of £500. These electors, in turn, selected the senate. Nine members of that body were to come from the Western Shore and six from the Eastern Shore. An election was to be held every five years. Lastly, the governor of the state was to be selected annually by the legislature.

The property requirements contained in the Maryland constitution excluded almost 90 percent of Maryland's male taxpaying population from holding provincial office. Because of these restrictions, only 10 percent could qualify for the lower house and 7 percent for the upper. The elite's dominance of the constitution accurately reflected the class structure of the society. In Maryland, as elsewhere in the colonial South, the wealthiest 20 percent of the population controlled approximately 75 percent of all wealth, with the upper 10 percent holding well over 50 percent alone. By contrast the remaining 80 percent shared only 25 percent of the wealth, with the bottom 60 percent—the meaner sort, or common sort—possessing less than 8 percent. Physically, their lot was not pleasant, although they managed a crude and, for their culture, acceptable living. But their frustrations were sharp, and during the war these people—the ubiquitous small slave holders, nonslaveholding planters, tenants, renters, and casual day laborers—posed a serious problem of social control for the Whig elite.

In essence, the architects of the Maryland Constitution intended the charter to establish a foundation for the performance of two related functions: the restoration of order and the prevention of further social disintegration. Since late 1775 and early 1776, disorder within the province had included Loyalist resistance, defiance by independent-minded whites (nonassociators), militia insubordination, and black unrest. All of these elements were visible, though blended together, making the dissension difficult to interpret clearly or to channel politically. Robert Eden, Maryland's last colonial governor, helped initiate the resistance through the formation of a private paramilitary association in late 1775. How large the organization became is unknown, though after the war a Maryland Loyalist claimed that including the branches in Virginia and Pennsylvania, it numbered 1,900 men capable of bearing arms. The association contained members throughout the province, but enjoyed especially wide acceptance on the Delmarva Peninsula, where its efforts were linked with those of Lord Dunmore, the Royal Governor of Virginia, who planned to retake his colony by forming a slave-manned force, the Ethiopian Regiment. Bolstered by Dunmore's support, Eden's association developed a number of elaborate schemes, including nocturnal kidnappings of prominent Whig spokesmen. In some cases, this opposition was open. Isaac Atkinson, a partisan of Eden's and Dunmore's, appeared before the patriot Somerset County Committee of Observation in late 1775, but refused to back down. A witness to the meeting recorded that about thirty men accompanied Atkinson to "the court house of Somerset County where the committee sat, with short clubs in their hands, and that when Atkinson came out of the court house, near fifty people crowded around him and the said Atkinson said a day must be appointed and they must fight it out."[8]

The reputed willingness of whites to encourage slave resistance especially unnerved the political authorities. Reports of insurrectionist plots circulated everywhere, and several were uncovered by grand jury investigations. Negro slaves made up some 25 percent of the population and were most heavily concentrated on the southern part of the Western Shore. In Calvert, Prince George's, Charles, Anne Arundel, and St. Mary's counties they made up close to 50 percent of the population. On the Eastern Shore, in Queen Anne's, Kent, and Somerset counties, slaves made up 40 to 45 percent of the population. These concentrated centers of black population were severe sources of worry and strain during the Anglo-American conflict. A Whig minister angrily wrote his friend that "the governor of Virginia, the captains of the men of war, and mariners have been tampering with our Negroes; and have nightly meetings with them; and all for the glorious purpose of enticing them to cut their masters' throats while they are asleep. Gracious God! that men noble by birth and fortune should descend to such ignoble base servility." The minister's remarks proved his state of anxiety more than any real conspiratorial organization, but his fears were widely shared. Robert Eden recounted the impact of Dunmore's activities in Maryland. The "minds of the people," he wrote to the British colonial secretary, Lord George Germain, "were extremely agitated by Lord Dunmore's proclamation giving freedom to the slaves in Virginia; our proximity to which colony and our similar circumstances with respect to Negroes augmenting the general alarm induced them to prohibit all correspondence with Virginia by land or water." If Dunmore's activities were frightening, worse still for the Whig leaders were the actions of his Maryland admirers. From Dorchester County came the following dispatch that fall: "The insolence of the Negroes in this county is come to such a height, that we are under a necessity of disarming them which we affected on Saturday last. We took about eighty guns, some bayonets, swords, etc. The malicious and imprudent speeches of some among the lower classes of whites have induced them to believe that their freedom depended on the success of the King's troops. We cannot therefore be too vigilant nor too rigorous with those who promote and encourage this disposition in our slaves."[9]

Problems and fears of this character largely explain Maryland's reluctance to accept independence. Throughout 1776, conditions within the province continued to deteriorate. The Tory insurgents along the Eastern Shore, their numbers swelling rapidly, commenced a full-scale insurrection, as British supplies were funneled to them and fears of black unrest continued. In July, Thomas Johnson, a prominent Whig, who would later become the state's first governor, informed the Council of Safety from the Eastern Shore that men "reluctantly leave their own neighbourhoods unhappily full of Negroes who might, it is likely on any misfortune to our militia, become very dangerous."[10]

Worse still, men in the militia were also being adversely affected by the chaos that swirled around them. Indeed, they were emerging as a threatening part of the resistance pattern. Some units had already been prevailed upon to "lay down their arms," while others, often sympathetic or indifferent to the insurrectionists, refused to follow the orders issued by Whig officers of whom they disapproved. From Queen Anne's County, a militia colonel, Thomas Wright, apprised the Annapolis officials that "the people have been induced to believe they ought not to submit to any appointments but those made by themselves." Similarly, a Caroline County colonel reported in May 1777, that when he called muster "two-thirds of the people remain at home abusing and ridiculing the honest few who think it their duty to attend." On the Delmarva Peninsula, local military personnel favored the British as much as the Annapolis government, although the Crown's recruiters also had no real success in enlisting these people. Wanting mainly to survive with minimal suffering, the people conveniently signed whatever loyalty oath was handy, but as one of them said, it meant nothing "more than a blank piece of paper." George Dashiell, colonel of the Somerset militia, understood the depth of the disaffection. He could not order out the men of his command, "there being more than three to one disaffected." Dashiell did not even dare issue arms, knowing "it is a fact not to be controverted that three-fourths of the Somerset militia are unfriendly to our cause." Other militias rebelled further by actively encouraging rioters, and rioting themselves. Because of erosion within militia ranks, local Whig officials openly admitted their inability to suppress the endemic disorder: "We are unanimously of the opinion," wrote the Dorchester County Committee of Observation, "that it is very improbable there can be in General Hooper's brigade a sufficient number of militia raised who would on the present occasion take up arms to suppress and stop the progress of these rioters and their adherents and bring the offenders to justice; and we therefore think it most prudent to decline making the attempt as a failure would be very detrimental to our cause and give strength and spirits to their party and friends."[11]

Local Whig officials were bothered not only by the rioting but by the targets of the violence. Frequently, the attacks were directed against leading Whig families suspected of engrossing needed commodities, and were led by rioters who sometimes expressed a sincere attachment to the Revolution. This type of protest raised for the elite the possibility that the Revolution might unleash either violent or legal attacks on privilege, which would threaten their own position. In Caroline County, a mob raided the storehouse of James Murray, a convention delegate; in Talbot County, James Lloyd Chamberlain, another convention delegate, and also a brigadier general of the militia, had his storehouse sacked. John Gibson, one of those involved in appropriating Chamberlain's salt supply, bluntly stated that the mob were better Whigs than their victims. Gibson only hoped that the Council of Safety would "not think them men of seditious principles who might be desirous of stirring up party faction. They are by no means such. I know several of the leading men to be men of reputation...I could only wish our leading gentlemen on this side of the bay was as little inclined to party designs and self interest as Colston, who was their leader of the salt company. They have been sincere in their country's cause and have acted like men of spirit and principle ever since these distressing times commenced, which is more than can be said of any engrossers of salt here." Shortly after the incident, Brig. Gen. Chamberlain resigned his commission, explaining that conditions precluded his ability to command. "Many of us," he averred, are "rather disposed to quarrel with his neighbor than face the enemy." As a result, "a general discontent prevails," which produces an "unwillingness in the people to do any duty," or to obey "any sort of order."[12]

Conditions on Maryland's Western Shore were calmer, though there, too, rioting and disorder were common during much of 1776 and 1777. Some of the most serious fighting occurred in the patriot strongholds around Baltimore, and black resistance and militia insubordination were reported throughout the region. Col. Richard Barnes noted, typically, that St. Mary's County was exposed, inadequately defended, and weakened by internecine conflict. "No part of the state, I am satisfied," he maintained, "is worse armed than this county, added to our internal weakness, the Negroes who, I am informed in the lower part of the county are beginning to be very insolent." And beyond that, the militia men under his command were openly threatening "that they will shoot several of their field officers. It really begins to be high time," he pressed, "to put our government in full force and some examples made or nothing but anarchy and destruction must ensue." Yet, in intensity or duration, the Western Shore's violence never approached that of the Delmarva Peninsula, nor was it as difficult to control, since Whig support was especially well-organized in the zone surrounding Annapolis. Still, the division in that sector is particularly interesting because of the recorded role played by the nonassociators.[13]

During the war, there existed throughout Maryland a category of persons known variously as nonassociators or nonjurors who represented that large part of the population labeled by Whigs as "disaffected." The nonassociators provide a strategic barometer for assessing some of the broadly held attitudes that underlay much of the civil dissension. Legally, they were people who refused to sign loyalty oaths and were placed under certain restrictions which were rarely enforced.[14] Although numerous, they cannot be accurately counted; yet they shared many of the emotions and anxieties of the disaffected or indifferent population, people who clearly opposed making an appreciable sacrifice for either belligerent.

Surviving court records about the nonassociators offer some key to that least known segment of the wartime citizenry—persons who were on neither side. As a group, especially in the South, they were probably more numerous than either Whigs or Loyalists. Robert Davis of Anne Arundel County expressed the frustration of many who contested the heavy hand of the new authorities. According to the county committee, Davis had said that "he looked on the Americans to be exceedingly wrong in their present pursuit," and "therefore he would support freedom by keeping clear." Moreover, he warned that "if the poor of the province would raise and take the Congress, he would head or back them and confine them and all our leading men." For these remarks, Davis received a summons, but, as the Whig officer serving the warrant approached the fence, "Davis came out to his yard gate with a gun in his hand and said stand off you damned rebel sons of bitches—I will shoot you if you come any nearer and declared he would not attend the committee." When Robert Gassaway, of Frederick County, who was an equally feisty character, was pressed, he declared that "it was better for the poor people to lay down their arms and pay the duties and taxes laid upon them by King and Parliament than to be brought into slavery and to be commanded and ordered about as they were." Another nonassociator, Alexander Magee, of Baltimore County, argued that "the American opposition to Great Britain is not calculated or designed for the defence of American liberty or property, but for the purpose of enslaving the poor people thereof." Magee's reasoning made good sense to many people, since the leading Whigs were invariably the dominant local creditors. Magee added shrewdly that "signing a paper did not alter the heart and he knew there was thousands among us who enrolled that was still of his way of thinking."[15]

The public authorities usually urged gentle treatment of the nonassociators, despite the restrictive measures adopted to control them. No one wished to chance their joining the more violent resistance. And when vexed or threatened, they could successfully retaliate. The case of Vincent Trapnell and James Bosley is instructive in this

regard. In mid-November 1776, Bosley traveled to Trapnell's Baltimore County farm, hoping to collect a small fine. Trapnell ran him off
by brandishing "a large stick, swearing, and cursing." According to
Bosley, when he threatened to inform the patriot committee, Trapnell
said to him that "the committee and I might kiss his arse and be
damned pulling his coat apart behind." In Trapnell's opinion, they
were all "a parcel of roguish damned sons of bitches." Later, another
man told Bosley that he "had better quit collecting fines and if he did
not he would be as surely killed as he was born." Henry Guyton,
another Baltimore County nonassociator, scatologically outdid Trapnell. When threatened with legal action, he told the courier that "he
would wipe his ass with his law," and then directed the official "to go
about his business and seek his recompense and then turned up his ass
and said a fart for them that will give it to you."[16]

Quite clearly, the Revolution widened some cracks in the deferential society. Local Whig authorities, in short, struggled with what were
often paralyzing conditions. As one committee man aptly stated, "It
was out of their power to help." Luther Martin, a rising personality in
the Whig party, was dispatched by Governor Thomas Johnson to in-
spect the Eastern Shore in the spring of 1778. He traveled much and
saw nothing he liked. The disaffected inhabitants "have arrived to so
daring heights of insolence and villainy," he observed, "that there
appears but little security for the lives or property of any person who
from political or other reasons are obnoxious to them. Bodies of
armed men pass unhampered and disaffected leaders openly recruit
followers." Anyone who opposes them, especially Whig officials, continued Martin, puts his own life in jeopardy. To survive, he concluded,
Whigs had always to be on the alert, moving only in certain areas and
avoiding large sections nominally under their jurisdiction.[17]

Revolutionary Maryland thus provided great dangers to its Whig
leaders who found themselves, rather against their intentions and will,
pursuing independence. Old political rivals were now free to use new
methods to manipulate the various grievances of the "meaner" sort,
perhaps even to foment attack by the slave population. New demands
had to be put on the population that had operated largely outside the
old political process, while, at the same time, those disinterested in the
cause had to be placated or treated gingerly so they didn't become
opponents. And there always existed the fear that the Whigs' rhetoric
about liberty and their attacks on royal privilege might come to be used
on themselves.

III

The problems of the Maryland Whigs during the Revolution were, to a greater or lesser degree, those of the entire South. Nathaniel Potter, a militia officer on Maryland's Eastern Shore, blamed the lower counties of Delaware for many of the problems he encountered: "I am fully satisfied if something is not done with that petty insignificant state of Delaware they will poison the minds of the greatest part of our people." This was so because the "infernal tory party" of that province "carries everything before them and I believe deters many of our country from doing their duty." Potter told the truth. The Tory faction in Delaware, even more than its Maryland counterpart, lived freely and safely. Even the Chesapeake's most notorious Tory partisan, China Clow, a middling planter whose followers wore a queue as a symbol of defiance, moved openly in Delaware, and no serious efforts were taken to apprehend him until the early 1780s. But most of Delaware's disaffected elements were not committed Loyalists. Few demonstrated any real intention of making meaningful sacrifices for the Crown. Whenever a majority of them, like their associates in Maryland, voiced support of the king, it was because he demanded less than the Whig leadership.[18]

Prior to independence, little Whig sentiment had developed in Delaware. Some protest to British policy resulted from the actions taken by a small faction headed by Caesar and Thomas Rodney, James Tilton, and Charles Ridgely. Drawing their support from northern New Castle County, these men, during the war years, gradually acquired tentative acceptance in Delaware's other two counties, Kent and Sussex, where a majority of the people and leadership remained disaffected to independence. Possibly the province's maritime character and its obvious sensitivity to British power accounted for the sharp split, but whatever the reasons, revolutionary Delaware contained a divided elite and populace that lived together uneasily and waited for the deadlock to be broken by the fortunes of war elsewhere.

All of Delaware experienced civil conflict during the Revolution, but the most concentrated resistance took place in the lower counties, Kent and Sussex, which shared a common border with Maryland's Eastern Shore. Though clashes were reported in late 1775 and early 1776, the first designated "insurrection" took place on "Black Monday," in mid-June 1776. Details about the incident remain unclear. Essentially, it involved an abortive coup staged by local Tories to occupy the town of Dover in Kent County. The participants, angered by recent political actions, wanted to punish the "imperious" resident Whigs, but quick action by the rebels forced a stand off. Several days later serious civil fighting began in neighboring Sussex County, where it remained common throughout the rest of the the 1770s. A notation penned in a Sussex County family Bible provides an apt commentary: "1777, Friday, September 7 at one o'clock in the morning was born John Clowes and was baptized by the Reverend Samuel Tingley on Saturday, May 28, 1778 at our home. The reason why he was so long unbaptized was the times. Toryism prevailed and it was dangerous to go to church and the parson seldom called on us."[19]

As in Maryland, local officials were unable to restore order; indeed they seldom tried, in part because many of Delaware's officers were as disaffected as those they were to control. William Richardson, a Continental officer who labored to consolidate support for the Revolution in both states, declared angrily that in Delaware dissidents were rarely imprisoned, and then secured their freedom almost immediately from disaffected judges. Richardson, having finally arrested several leading Tories, who were "as wild as deer and run almost as fast," decided to send his prisoners to the Congress in Philadelphia: "As there is no great probability that tory judges [in Delaware] will punish tory offenders however atrocious their offense. I have sent Messrs. Peter and Burton Robinson under guard to Congress (where they will be properly dealt with) rather than to the civil powers of this county or state."[20]

Richardson clearly found the defiance of these "rascals" insufferable. The scion of a wealthy family, Richardson expected deference, and this attitude he found in short supply: "They are a set of poor ignorant illiterate people, yet they are artful and cunning as foxes; 'tis hardly possible to detect the most open offenders, yet they are almost every day offending. I have had several of the most open and daring before me but upon examination nothing has been proved against them that would justify my keeping them prisoners."[21] Joseph Dashiell, a contemporary of Richardson's, charged with securing Maryland's Worcester County, wrote similarly of the meaner sort's behavior. Also a member of a leading family, Dashiell's sympathy for the poor curdled because of their intransigent independence from him and his cause: "Humanity can scarce forbear to drop a tear on reflecting on the circumstances of many of them. With a poor wretched hut crowded with children, naked, hungry and miserable without bread or a penny of money to buy any; in short they appear as objects almost too contemptible to excite the public resentment: yet these are the wretches, who set up to be the arbiters of government; to knock down independence and restore the authority of the British King in Parliament which by testimony taken by us was the avowed design of some of the principles although they have sworn directly the reverse. Yet, despicable as these creatures really are, they have their influence within their own peculiar sphere."[22] Each day, Dashiell better appreciated how pitifully few were his powers over such people.

Unlike Dashiell, Richardson perceptively recognized that there were limits beyond which the peninsula's disaffected elements would not go: "It appears that a majority of the inhabitants," he informed the Board of War, "are disaffected; and would I believe afford the enemy every aid in their power except service in the field which the greater part want spirit to do." The same general attitude held true for the rebel cause. Thomas Robinson, a leader of the disaffected, contended that much of the discord had resulted from fears of the government's intentions. Similarly, William Perry, a local Whig official in southern Delaware, ascribed the disruption of elections in 1777 to misgivings about the rebel authorities. Obviously, the strongest desire of many Delaware citizens was to avoid serving either side: "For some time before the election," wrote Perry, "various stories were circulated throughout the county to enflame the minds of the disaffected multitude here, one of which was that if the whigs got into the Assembly the militia would be drafted and obliged to go to camp, in consequence of which the disaffected came out almost to a man. As soon as they had collected, they began in their usual strain of drinking prosperity to King George and damning the whigs and swearing there was not rebel enough in town to take them up." Angered by the demonstrators, Perry "ordered some of them under guard" and requested that the sheriff attend the poll and administer the loyalty oath before allowing the people to vote. A scene of curious chaos followed, as the disaffected advised the sheriff he would "be thrown neck and heels out of the court house if he tendered any such oath." Wisely, the sheriff demurred, and only after the arrival of some Whig militia were the Tories obliged "to fly to their houses with all possible speed jumping out of the court house windows and getting off as fast as they could." The soldiers pursued, "firing their guns," concluded Perry, but were soon restrained by their concern about touching off a wider conflagration.[23]

In sum, a sharp and intense civil conflict plagued Delaware as well as Maryland—danger and animosity were always present, the violence occurring in cycles. A modicum of order existed, largely because the Whig leaders, recognizing their weakness, tolerated widespread indifference to their cause, and handled most forms of opposition cautiously, or, in the case of Delaware, not at all. The war created an abnormal social situation where institutions lost substantial credibility. And yet, unlike the Lower South, these institutions were not totally destroyed. Though often inactive, they existed. Some courts managed to meet, some elections were held, and in certain zones—northern Delaware and Maryland's Western Shore—a visible, if rather undemanding, authority stood. Though terribly frail, this shadow government functioned as a symbol of some continuity and hope of things to come.

IV

In the Carolinas and Georgia, vast regions were left without the slightest apparition of authority. Within the Lower South the structure of power had long shown a deep estrangement between two regional cultures, one concentrated in the eastern sector along the low country, the other in the piedmont uplands. Though important differences existed among the various eastern Whig elites—North Carolina's was severely factionalized, South Carolina's unified, and Georgia's immature and barely formed—they shared a common desire to restrict backcountry participation in both the governing process and the imperial protest campaign. They saw the piedmont's residents as a crude and unlettered lot, too much addicted to democracy.

By the end of the French and Indian War, the piedmont zones within the Carolinas contained substantial populations which, if equitably represented, would have threatened domination of the various lower houses. In fact, many parts of the backcountry were much more densely settled than the older coastal regions, a factor of considerable importance in the Regulator conflicts. Reverend Charles Woodmason recorded in the 1760s that the country was "most surprisingly thick settled beyond any spot in England of its like extent." Josiah Martin, North Carolina's last royal governor, found settlement in the area "beyond belief."

Confronted with this extensive population, the Carolina assemblies deliberately stunted backcountry participation in government at both the provincial and local levels. In North Carolina a pattern developed of county corruption directed and exploited by the assembly, while in South Carolina the lowland elite adamantly refused to establish any form of county government in the backcountry, despite repeated appeals to cope with anarchic conditions. The story of the Regulator conflicts that resulted is familiar. In North Carolina the Regulators seized control of their courts and drove out those officials, lawyers, and other persons they opposed. At the urging of the assembly, the colony's royal governor, William Tryon, organized a small army which triumphed decisively over the Regulators at Alamance Creek in May 1771, executing one backcountry leader on the spot and six more soon after. In South Carolina the Regulators formed associations in the mid-1760s which, in vigilante fashion, brought a semblance of security and order to the piedmont. Following this success, they threatened to invade the lowland and Charleston itself, unless the assembly established a viable court system for the backcountry. At first intimidated, the legislature agreed, but when the immediate danger passed, the delegates procrastinated and refused to accord the backcountry any meaningful representation until 1776. Charles Woodmason, the itinerant Anglican minister, summed up well the eastern attitude: "They would fetter and chain the backcountry inhabitants could they get them in their clutches. And deprive them equally of their civil concerns as they do their spiritual. These are the Sons of Liberty!"

With the coming of the war, the piedmont's population naturally viewed the low country's cry of liberty and natural rights as hypocrisy, and made clear their unwillingness to sacrifice for the Whig cause. At the same time, the Carolina leadership, while clearly recognizing the need for the area's support, refused to discard those restrictive attitudes that underlay its prewar policies. Some concessions were made, but the overtures amounted to little. In South Carolina the constitutions written during the war years admitted western representation, but the bulk of power remained concentrated where it always had been, in the east, with Charleston alone sending half as many delegates to the assembly as the entire west. The high property qualifications for office holding—£1000 for the lower house, £2000 for the senate—and the system of appointive county offices similarly were designed to perpetuate the elite's dominance. Although the North Carolina constitution made more gestures to popular rule, including the election of some local offices, there, too, power remained the prerogative of the prewar elite. Only in Georgia, a weak and exposed colony without a history of deep east-west antagonisms, did the Whigs make a serious bid for support by adopting a very democratic constitution, which included a one-house legislature, minimal property requirements for office, and the popular election of most county officials.[24]

Actually, by the end of 1776 these constitutions made little difference, because the authorities exercised by the central governments in the backcountry had vanished. In the Carolinas a pattern developed of hostile defiance, punctuated by a few large uprisings and frequent low-level insurgent violence. Georgia's condition was even more precarious, as factionalism among the Whigs, dangerous threats from Florida, fears of slave and Indian uprisings, and fiscal bankruptcy eroded the revolutionary leaders' ability to act. After the British invasion in 1778, extensive civil fighting erupted throughout the state, and for the next four years Whig authorities struggled to survive, not rule. The situation was little different in the Carolinas after the British invasion of 1780. Indeed, governments there almost disappeared, with bewildered military officers often having no idea how they might even contact their civilian superiors. The British did not expand their authority effectively either. Although plans were drawn up and assignments made, the program failed, partially for lack of vigor, but mainly because of the disrupted conditions which made the task insurmountable.[25]

No more chaotic a situation can be imagined than that of the Lower South in the years from 1780 to 1783. The readiest vantage point for viewing this situation is that of the military antagonists, especially Gen. Nathanael Greene and his British adversaries. The descriptions of these men, based on a steady and fairly voluminous flow of intelligence, showed some social insight. This is particularly true of Greene, who early understood that political rather than military solutions were required to secure the South.

During the war years, the long-standing split in the Carolinas between the lowland gentry and the piedmont up-country Regulators directly influenced English strategy. The British command, clearly believing the region's inhabitants to be furiously opposed to the revolutionary leadership, initially structured their strategy on the basis of this social and regional antagonism. The reasons for British failure are intricate. Historians have given some thought to the causes for the British military defeat, but not enough to the area's peculiar social context, where a rather unpopular Whig elite managed to emerge from a near anarchic revolutionary situation with much of its authority still intact.[26]

With the fall of Charleston, in the spring of 1780, a total civil war engulfed the Lower South. From that time until the war's end, the region experienced social anarchy. Murder and banditry, brutal intimidation, and retaliation became a way of life. In this situation both belligerents attempted to consolidate support. Each occasionally succeeded—at various times and in different areas—but stability remained elusive. Lt. Col. Alexander Innes, the Cornwallis aide responsible for organizing the sector along the Congaree River in South Carolina, reported his experiences in June 1780. The area had been "drained" both of men—"drove off or dragooned"—and supplies for the ill-fated rebel army at Charleston. Because of this, he found the country's condition "favorable," as even "the most violent rebels are candid enough to allow the game is up." Still, several security problems remained, the most troublesome of which "was the violence of the people toward the whigs." The people called for their hanging, and "it was necessary to secure those men to save their lives from the just resentment of the people they have persecuted." Other officers fowarded similar accounts. From Cheraw Hills, Cornwallis was told that "the country people in general seem desirous to return to their allegiance and form a militia as the only means to prevent plunder from the banditti that are robbing indiscriminately." For this reason, Major Archibald McArthur happily observed, "the lower class are all desirous of being enrolled."[27]

The Whigs had similar complaints. They, too, suffered from persecution, plunder, and murder. Thomas Brandon informed General Thomas Sumter of one such incident in December 1780: "Colonel Moore and a strong party of tories marched through my settlement and robbed and plundered many people and myself among the rest." Soon after, Brandon "heard of a party of tories on the Sandy River—I proceeded after them and fell in with a small party—we killed three and wounded three most notorious villains."[28] So the struggle proceeded in scores of unrecorded skirmishes.

When General Nathanael Greene took command of the shattered southern Continental Army, after its disastrous defeat at Camden, South Carolina, he expected some adversity, but was aghast at what he saw. Greene was a former Quaker, born in Rhode Island, and this was his introduction to the South. He joined the Continental Army early, and his wide reading in military history helped his rapid advancement.

Greene had performed a number of assignments well and had done a
superb job with the quartermaster department. After Gen. Horatio
Gates's humiliation at Camden, Washington's selection of Greene received a rare tribute—quick approval by Congress. He proved to be
brilliant.[29] Without ever winning a decisive engagement, he demonstrated one central fact to the British: that even in the South they could
not win. And if they could not fashion a permanent victory there,
abetted by severe social tensions and a lack of enthusiasm for the Whig
cause or its elite leadership, where in all of the rebel colonies could
they hope to triumph?

At first Greene despaired. To his friend, Gen. Robert Howe, he
confided near the end of December 1780: "When I left the Northern
Army I expected to find in this department a thousand difficulties to
which I was a stranger in the northern service but the embarrassments
far exceed my utmost apprehension nor can I find a clue to guide me
through the complicated scene of difficulties." To another close companion, Gen. Henry Knox, Greene wrote: "The word difficulty when
applied to the state of things here as it is used to the northward is
almost without meaning, it falls so far short of the real state of things."
He possessed only the shadow of an army; his troops, he grimly reported, "are almost naked and we subsist by daily collections and in
a country that has been ravaged and plundered by both friends and
enemies." Because of this condition, "it is impracticable to preserve
discipline when troops are in want of everything," Greene explained
to Virginia's governor, Thomas Jefferson, "and to attempt severity will
only thin the ranks by more hasty desertions." With similar emphasis,
Greene instructed Governor Nash of North Carolina, "it is natural for
an army in distress to lose its discipline and invalidate rights and
property of the citizens."[30] But these troubles, though exceptionally
severe, he had anticipated.

What struck Greene most was the manner with which "the whigs
and tories pursue one another with the most relentless fury killing and
destroying each other whenever they meet. Indeed, a great part of this
country is already laid waste and in the utmost danger of becoming a
desert. The great bodies of militia that have been in service this year
employed against the enemy and in quelling the tories have almost laid
waste the country and so corrupted the principles of the people that
they think of nothing but plundering one another." "With the militia,"
he lamented, "everybody is a general and the powers of government
are so feeble that it is with the utmost difficulty you can restrain them

from plundering one another." As Greene told his friend, Chevalier de la Luzerne, the French minister, "The country is full of little armed parties who follow their resentments with little less than savage fury." The southern army, Greene concluded, was "without discipline and so addicted to plundering that the utmost exertions of the officers cannot restrain the soldiers. Nor are the inhabitants a whit behind them."[31]

This civil struggle continued unabated through 1781. It was almost as if the momentous military contests at Cowpens, Guilford Court House, Hobkirk's Hill, Eutaw Springs, Cornwallis's surrender at Yorktown, and even Greene's recapture of the British-held backcountry forts, constituted but one discrete level of conflict, in many ways distantly removed from the raging civil strife. Whatever "shock waves" the major engagements unleashed, the civil warfare persisted unchanged. As Greene reported to Robert Morris, the superintendent of finances, in March 1782, the South remained in the greatest state of confusion imaginable, with all of the provinces "still torn to pieces by little parties of disaffected who elude all search and conceal themselves in the thickets and swamps from the most diligent pursuit and issue forth from these hidden recesses committing the most horrid murders and plunder and lay waste the country."[32]

The account of the southern situation by an opponent of Greene's paralleled the Continental general's description almost exactly. Early in 1782 Col. Robert Gray, a South Carolinian who fought with a British provincial regiment, believed, as did Greene, that the war was far from over. Since the last large battle at Eutaw Springs, in September, the partisan clashes within the area had not slackened significantly. Instead, the province "resembled a piece of patchwork, the inhabitants of every settlement when united in sentiment being in arms for the side they liked best and making continual inroads into one another's settlements . . . the tories in many places would neither submit nor go to Charleston, they hid themselves in the swamps from whence they made frequent incursions upon their enemies. When opposed by a superior force they dispersed, when the storm blew over they embodied and recommenced their operation. A petty partisan started up in every settlement and headed the whigs or tories both parties equally afraid of the other dared not sleep in their houses but concealed themselves in swamps. This is called lying out. Both parties were in this condition in general all over Ninety-Six District and every other part of the province wherever it was checquered by the intersection of whig and tory settlements."[33]

Still fearing a British offensive in 1782 because the ongoing civil conflict debilitated his position, Greene urged Gen. Anthony Wayne, operating in Georgia, to "Try by every means in your power to soften the malignity and deadly resentments subsisting between the whigs and tories and put a stop as much as possible to the cruel custom of putting people to death after they surrender themselves prisoners."[34] Naturally, the bulk of the populace caught in this vortex wished principally for order or escape. By 1781, the majority would have supported any side that could insure stability, or so both Greene and his adversaries believed. But neither belligerent could guarantee security, and many on both sides thrived on the turmoil. Plunder and murder had become a way of life with its own peculiar rewards.

One of the most vexing problems for military commanders in the South involved the transitory allegiances of military personnel. Greene's finest troops, his Maryland and Delaware lines, contained many of the "disaffected" persons who had been responsible for the disorder along the Chesapeake and Delaware. By 1780, after the Whigs in those states managed to restore their authority, the disaffected were frequently persuaded to join the southern army rather than face possible retribution from the government or their neighbors. Ironically, these were the lines whose tenacious fighting in the decisive battles of 1781 caused Cornwallis to abandon the Lower South. Greene's Carolina recruits were even more suspect, and contained numbers of Tory partisans who entered the Continental service for protection from the civil strife. Conversely, the British forces of Lord Francis Rawdon and Lt. Col. Alexander Stewart contained many defectors from Gates's defeated Camden army, who nonetheless served the British bravely at both Hobkirk's Hill and at Eutaw Springs. In the strange configuration of the southern war, this eddying from one side to another of many a fighting man stopped only with his hanging.

Some shifted for mercenary reasons. "Colonel Thomson," wrote one Cornwallis aide, "is the leading man here and I am informed although active on the other side, yet he has not been harsh nor oppressive, and from a good many reasons I believe he may be made useful in taking the other side—especially as he is fond of money." Others changed because of social discrimination. Capt. Jesse Barefield, second in command of the notorious Little Pedee Loyalists, served out his term with the South Carolina Continentals and then took up Tory arms because of the supercilious treatment he received from the low-country gentry patriot officers. Col. Robert Gray of the

Loyalist Provincial Regiment also remarked on the social factor after Charleston's fall: "The loyal part of the inhabitants being in number about one half of the whole and those by no means the wealthiest readily took up arms." Many of course embraced whichever side seemed to be winning. After the British triumphs of 1780, Gray recounted how "the whigs and tories seemed to vie with each other in giving proof of their submission." Yet protestations of this sort were always fleeting. As Cornwallis informed Clinton in the late summer of 1780, he had started to disarm "in the most rigid manner the country between the Santee and Pedee and to punish severely all those who submitted or pretended to live peaceably under His Majesty's Government since the reduction of Charleston . . . I have myself ordered several militia men to be executed who had voluntarily enrolled themselves and borne arms with us and afterwards revolted to the enemy."[35]

The rebels confronted the same problems, and, like the British, they variously exploited and decried the conditions. Colonel Francis Marion, of "swampfox" fame, complained in November 1780: "Many of my people have left me and gone over to the enemy for they think that we have no army coming on and have been deceived." Yet Greene and his subordinates also took advantage of the deranged situation. After Camden, when a number of Continental veterans left for British lines, the angry retribution of partisan bands drove others into the rebel ranks. "Many of the tories seem disposed to return to their allegiance," wrote Gen. William Smallwood in October 1780, and "I understand numbers have offered to enter for a term in the Continental Army." That fall Maj. Mark Armstrong also informed his superiors that "the tory prisoners have all enlisted into the continental service excepting a small number."[36]

Making this his official policy, Greene eventually convinced Governor John Rutledge of South Carolina to issue a total pardon in September 1781 to all those who had taken up British arms, provided they would join the patriot militia.[37] Many did, and some of the Tory partisans even negotiated agreements to support the Whig cause. Francis Marion worked out such an arrangement with Maj. Micajah Ganey's followers in 1781, and, though intermittent fighting occurred, they renewed the pact in 1782 and later that year fought together against a corps of British Black Dragoons.[38] Nevertheless, Greene always kept in mind the fragile character of southern allegiances. Greene reported of Sumter's and Marion's troops that some were men "whose cases are desperate being driven from their dwellings." Yet others were only "allied by the hopes of plunder. The first are the best of citizens and the best of soldiers; the last are the dregs of the community and can be kept no longer than there is a prospect of gain."[39] In both cases, the commitment to the Whig cause was seemingly more personal than political.

Both Cornwallis and Greene understood how this "fever of plunder" and policy of terror could serve their ends, but neither wholeheartedly endorsed the strategy. Greene's reason was more than moral. In his mind, southern conditions had already degenerated beyond the point where a policy of this sort could be effectively employed. First, there had to be some order. No side could win by merely defeating its military opposite: uncontrolled social violence was an equally dangerous enemy. To construct a victory in the Lower South without reestablishing order, Greene wrote Washington, was "really making bricks without straw."[40]

V

Those areas of the South which experienced the deepest civil conflict, the Delmarva Peninsula and the Carolina Piedmont, superficially had little in common; yet they shared a crucial historic experience. Since mid-century, their patterns of trade and settlement had greatly changed, and these alterations produced a temperament that was resentful toward those more secure. More important, in the decade prior to the Revolution the two regions suddenly experienced a period of unusual prosperity, only to have it paralyzed by the outbreak of fighting. The war wrenched away the newfound good fortune of these areas.

The southern part of the Delmarva Peninsula had long had economic difficulties. Because of the area's poor soil—a sandy, wet, low-lying plain better suited for shallow rooted grains than the deeper-rooted tobacco plant—the quality of tobacco raised could be profitably sold only in heavy-demand markets. Lumber products were produced in abundance in its ubiquitous swamp-like lands. Generally the returns for these forest commodities had not been substantial, until the early 1770s, when conditions improved because of increased English bounties. Other crops were also grown, the most profitable of which was wheat. Before mid-century the shift to grain production had proceeded at a steady, if gradual, pace. The French and Indian War, by disrupting commercial patterns, had depressed the trade, but after hostilities ended, the wheat market first stirred and then took off in an unprecedented manner. Because of disastrous European harvests and increased demographic pressures, the Atlantic trading area started to run short of food, and the price of colonial grain soared to all-time high levels. With the added convergence of good prices for tobacco and lumber, the Delmarva region experienced unprecedented prosperity.[41]

The Carolina Piedmont people shared an economic heritage similar in many of its broad characteristics to that of the Delmarva Peninsula residents. They, too, emerged from a state of uncertainty and great anxiety to experience unaccustomed prosperity from the mid-1760s on. Entering into an area without established institutions, these people unexpectedly discovered an element that afforded them coherence and stability. Almost immediately they began to earn exceptionally fine profits for their grain crops. By the mid-1760s, commodities, headed by wheat, poured out of the backcountry, and the region's trade centers grew in size and number. Charleston's considerable expansion on the eve of the Revolution attested graphically to the backcountry's prosperity. At the junction of the Ashley and Cooper rivers, Charleston received the vast bulk of the piedmont's exports, which came down the region's many rivers. This trade allowed Charleston to grow after two decades of stagnation. By the Revolution, its wharves so teemed with piedmont grain that British officials believed a blockade of the port would strangle the backcountry and bring the region to its knees. To a large degree they were right.[42]

The grain shortage in the Atlantic areas, beginning in the late 1750s, affected all of the south, but most dramatically the Delmarva Peninsula, the lower James River Valley in Virginia, and the piedmont. Each committed itself extensively to this market and enjoyed unusual prosperity. Urban clusters, reflecting the new commerce, proliferated in each zone because of new demands for services and greater disposable income. For a brief period, during the 1772–1773 depression, the market collapsed, but it soon rebounded, partly in response to an artificial stimulant, the Continental Congress's threat of nonexportation in 1774. By that time, Europe's bad harvest years had finally passed, inevitably lessening the profits from American grain. Still, the common planters and farmers in the colonies rarely understood this.

In a vague way they blamed the British leadership's mercantile policies and/or their native leadership class—men who were viewed suspiciously in the Chesapeake and despised in the Carolinas—for their loss of profitable markets. And at this point, both sides were asking them to make great sacrifices in the name of abstract principles. Often in debt, angered over losing their limited affluence, and resentful of their superiors who were frequently their creditors, they were not given to concerns about individual liberties and natural rights. What they wanted most seemed little enough: modest good fortune and some security in their lives. And the Revolution interfered with both of these wishes.[43]

The war forced individuals to make extremely difficult choices. Authoritative personages on both sides demanded that common people supply material, reduce consumption, leave their families, and even risk their lives. Forced to make hard decisions, many flailed out in frustration or evaded and defied first one side, then the other, each contender's popularity fluctuating in rough accord with the seeming balance of power, or the balance of demand upon them. In any social system, feelings of dissatisfaction inhere in classes of subordinate people, but, except in periods of marked social disorder, these attitudes are controlled by established institutions and rarely find societal expression. The Revolution, however, created an exceedingly abnormal condition in which most institutions and sanctions were impaired or inoperative. Simultaneously, the Revolution brought popular anger to a boil, so that it took on the appearance of a spasmodic social convulsion essentially hostile to any rigid political direction. These convulsions offered no coherent political or social alternative but, in places like the Carolinas where traditions were weakest, threatened something approaching Thomas Hobbes's sordid vision of a state of nature.

Yet, through the welter of conflict, one configuration seems clear. The incompatibility of two major values, equality and deference, which had been developing during the colonial era, reached the point of critical confrontation during the Revolution. By that time, the rough value or social attitude, best conceptualized as an equality of respect, rubbed abrasively with the elite notion of deference. Consequently, when the revolutionary leadership placed heavy demands on the people—demands in many ways more oppressive than the comparatively mild tyranny of Parliament—many men, especially those with limited involvement in their political culture, resented and resisted them.

Possibly Charles Sydnor's description of Virginia's election practices, when the "gentlemen of long-tailed families treated the great vulgar" with liquor and food, offers some insight into why that state experienced considerably less discontent than its neighbors. It is conceivable that had these election rites been ritualized on the Delmarva Peninsula or in the Carolina backcountry as a central and active ingredient of political culture, less contention would have developed. Certainly to the Virginia gentry who were running for office, such a practice was paternalistic, but the "meaner sort" undoubtedly saw the "swilling of bumbo" differently. To them, the custom constituted an important behavioral obligation when the gentlemen attested to the need for "treating" the people with respect and not only liquor.[44] Year after year Virginia's leaders recognized the importance of this concession to the popular will. A wealthy planter might strut and sneer at the common herd, but, if so, he paid a price for this luxury—he would not be elected to public office. The people, in other words, did not easily brook contempt in Virginia or elsewhere. Maryland's Charles Carroll of Carrollton, soon after returning from his English studies, caught this point well: "There is a mean low dirty envy which creeps thro all ranks and cannot suffer a man a superiority of fortune, of merit, or of understanding in fellow citizens—either of these are sure to entail a general ill will and dislike upon the owner."[45]

Carroll, however, could not account for this attitude, nor could other commentators who noted how gentlemen were frequently addressed irreverently by their social inferiors, indeed sometimes by their slaves. Carroll himself soon learned how his lordly family, possibly the richest in the colonies, sometimes had to bargain aggressively with "mean tenants" lest someone else should acquire their labor. The roots of this attitude—this notion of respect or esteem—lay principally in the difficulty of transferring institutions and values formulated in a society where land was scarce to an area where it abounded. Many complex efforts were made, both royal and proprietary, but all failed to restrain the egalitarian impulses unleashed by the land's visibly overpowering existence. Physically, the man-land ratio by the mid-eighteenth century had greatly decreased, and in many older settled areas upwards of 30 percent of the population lived as tenants. But the conceptual vision, rather than the legal reality, had the more significant impact on the structure of values. In England, the recognized scarcity of land afforded commanding power to those who controlled it; in the New World the endless territorial expanses precluded the development of a value system that could support an elite with an authority of like extent. Beginning in the 1740s, four decades of intense struggle brought the principle of hierarchy under heavy challenge. Symptomatic of this confrontation, the Great Awakening laid down an especially direct frontal assault to the basic operational law of superiority and subordination. Each man, it was in essence said, could individually interpret God's will without the assistance of corporate intermediaries. Politically, socially, and theologically, the belief emerged that each man was entitled to be esteemed worthy, since in Carroll's words, he would not "suffer" otherwise. With the onset of the Revolution, the old expectations and patterns had to accommodate themselves more completely to new psychological attitudes long in the making. The war and the violent discord it spawned created the needed pressure for change.[46]

VI

Two very different types of revolutionary elites attempted to subdue the South's disorders. In the Upper South an indigenous political leadership struggled to survive the discord by developing political programs designed to secure popular acceptance within existing, if much weakened, institutions. In the Lower South, with the native governments helpless, military commanders from outside of the region labored to restore order by employing strategies to acquire political support, sometimes even at the expense of military advantage. In every case, Whig leaders had to devise strategies in response to local conditions so that neither the battle for independence nor the larger one for the restoration of authority was lost.

In those southern colonies, like Georgia and Delaware, where Whigs were weakest and where control was least necessary to the larger war effort, the policy followed was one of nonactivity, to prevent the disaffected from becoming the opposition. Georgia's Whigs had little alternative after the arrival of British troops in 1778. Retreating out of danger, the Whig leaders simply promulgated a popular program to give them a basis of support, should the war be won elsewhere. In Delaware, Whigs followed a similar policy of nonaggressive, watchful waiting. Even men who openly proclaimed their opposition to the Revolution were allowed to hold offices in those sections of sharp civil strife. About this matter, Thomas Rodney wrote to Caesar Rodney in August 1776, informing him of the Tory efforts in Kent County to secure, by election, control of the delegation to the constitutional convention: "The tories are exerting themselves to get in the convention...but they seem at a loss how to contrive it for they have put out several tickets to see I believe how they would be relished."[47] Much to the Rodneys' dismay, the Tory ticket won, a proof of revolutionary necessities rather than Whig tolerance.

During the first years of the war the situation in Delaware remained largely a standoff, with the Whig forces making some gains in 1777 and 1778. Essentially, each side tolerated the other, their coexistence occasionally punctuated by sharp, brief fighting. Tory partisans under China Clow periodically raided and pillaged, as did their counterparts in the Whig militias, but there was none of the confusion or savage bloodletting that characterized the Lower South. Few people were ever imprisoned, because judges of the respective persuasions would invariably see to their associates' release. Strong advocates found this situation irritating, to say the least. Matthew Wilson of Lewes, Delaware, a Whig Presbyterian clergyman, appealed, in July 1778, to the Board of War in Philadelphia to destroy Delaware—that being the only way to save it. Correctly pointing out that "a score of the leading men" were both disaffected and likely to be reelected, Wilson irritably offered two possible congressional solutions: "Either disfranchise the Delaware state, and divide it between Maryland and Pennsylvania," or "exclude all tories and disaffected persons from holding any office in the state during the generation at least."[48] Congress, as the Whig leadership of Delaware wanted, wisely neglected Wilson's advice. As the conflict wore on, most people in Delaware accommodated themselves to the changes over which they had no real control. But neither side ever really backed down, and the repercussions of divided sentiments influenced Delaware politics into the Federal Age. The diary of William Adair, a Whig who lived in the heartland of the resistance, Sussex County, graphically captured the temper of those years:

> (1776) Tories are pushing on the poor church to kill Presbyterians...Tories are joining Dunmore...Independence declared at Lewes, three cannons discharged and three toasts—unhappy quarrel about ducking a Whig...Election, Tories cut down the Liberty Pole...(1777) English men of war, Negroes gone aboard ...Tory election prevailed though not half the Whigs came in— They had persuaded nay sworn to cut down the Liberty Pole today, as they had last fall at another election...intimidated

them...only a few drank health and success to the King of England etc. at Tory Davy's Tavern etc....At election Whigs and Tories battle...(1778) Whigs beat and drove off the tories... Whig election—Tories affrighted came not to vote...Tory insurrection and alarm Capt. Kirkwood hangs one Tory in arms. John Whiltbank and Negroes gone to English...(1780) Election, Whigs prevailed...Election peaceable, few Tories...(1781) Thanksgiving for the capture of Lord Cornwallis...Lewes Tories met the English on the Cape and got drunk.[49]

Adair's diary concluded with the following entry of October 1783: "Tories made a great struggle at election but are conquered and intimidated by the Whigs. Had they prevailed the Whigs might have fled from their oppression to some other state, possibly over the mountains."[50] Delaware's Tories—a hard breed—were not easily discouraged; Delaware's Whigs were probably wise to apply as little force against them as possible during the revolutionary struggle.

In Maryland the revolutionary leadership demonstrated similar flexibility and intelligence in controlling civil discontent, but because of the comparative significance of the state, they had to develop a more active authority and political structure. Maryland's leaders, frightened and divided over impending independence, procrastinated as long as possible. They reluctantly accepted separation, and their worst fears were confirmed, as dissension mounted within the province. Persuaded by late 1776 that a revolution without serious anarchy was impossible, most yearned for a return to the British Empire. Yet regrets over past decisions settled nothing. Desperately hoping to stabilize the situation, the revolutionary leaders instituted a variety of control measures and composed an extremely conservative constitution that insured the rule of a propertied elite. But the unrestrained deterioration they witnessed soon convinced them of the need to go much further, and, in fact, to reverse the elitist philosophy of the constitution.[51]

During the new government's first assembly session in early 1777, the state's leaders anxiously sought to save both their class and the Revolution by popularizing the movement for independence. Believing these elements to be mutually entwined, the political elite designed a fiscal program aimed at subduing the class antagonisms that underlay much of the internal protest. Two major measures were enacted. The new tax system shifted the burden of assessment from polls to land and slaves, in essence from the majority to the planter elite. The tender law was even more radical. Its purpose was plain—by authorizing the pay-

ment of all prewar debts, including sterling obligations, with depreciated paper money, the legislation voided the bulk of all internal credit
obligations. For the revolutionary leaders, these measures constituted
an extreme financial sacrifice in order to maintain power. Practically
all of them were large creditors, and they now faced the prospect of
seeing as much as one-third of their fortunes wiped out. A few who
were debtors would benefit, but the majority would suffer considerably. Yet they unanimously endorsed the proposal as a fundamental
prerequisite to save their class and the Revolution. In short, they were
frightened, though sensible, men who recognized what the "temper of
the times" demanded, and they accepted reality with sorrow but without dissent. They designed a radical fiscal policy and adroitly managed
their new court system to achieve popularity, acceptance, and a sense
of legitimacy. By making certain visible concessions, these men detached the estranged, the aggrieved, and the disgruntled from the
hard-core resisters. They were ultimately successful, and their policy
of enlightened self-interest reflected their comprehension of the
changing demands placed on those who wished to occupy positions of
command in American society.

The experience of Charles Carroll of Carrollton during these
years is especially instructive. Unlike some of his allies, Carroll possessed a reformist streak, despised corruption, and because of his
extraordinary wealth, was somewhat detached about the financial
losses entailed. But Carroll's wartime analysis correlated exactly with
the Whig elites' pattern of legislative action. Year after year the assembly votes paralleled his writings, which urged severe sacrifices upon the
elite in order to insure its long-run survival. Presumably, his contemporaries, neither perverse nor philanthropic enough to want to give
away their money, understood the crisis in a similar manner.

At first Carroll enthusiastically embraced the movement for independence. Having entered the political arena in 1773, he was swept up
in the imperial protest. He was still a young man of thirty-six, but his
Catholic religion had precluded his holding public office. Now the
movement for imperial reform offered him an exciting role which
included his diplomatic mission to Canada for the Continental Congress. Leaving Maryland in March 1776, he did not return until mid-
June to argue for independence. But his euphoria was shattered, as he
came to appreciate the immense proportions of the civil conflict and
the way "factious and designing men" intended to exploit it. In words
laced with horror and anger, he condemned the Revolution. Nothing

but a return to the British Empire, he contended, could bring stability and prevent the onset of social upheaval. Should reconciliation not take place, he warned, the colonies "would be ruined not so much by the calamities of war as by the intestine divisions and the bad governments which I foresee will take place in most of these united states: they will be simple Democracies, of all governments, the worst, and will end as all other democracies have in despotism."

The fall and winter of 1776–1777 were difficult for Carroll. Reluctantly, he acknowledged that rapprochement with England was not imminent. And so, with the faint hope of some institutional authority established by the constitution, he lobbied hard during the first assembly session for the popular fiscal program. His political colleagues agreed with its necessity, but not his testy seventy-six year-old father, Charles Carroll of Annapolis, who single-handedly had built an immense fortune, much of it based on usury, and who now railed at the financial sacrifices occasioned by the impending flood of worthless money. For the next several years hundreds of letters were exchanged between the two as they strenuously argued their points in private, with total honesty. They loved each other deeply, but their words often rang with anger in one paragraph and affection in the next. The elder Carroll regularly censured his son as a "panderer" of popularity, a "courter" of the rabble, and challenged him to cast off his "meekness of temper." And yet he would also implore "Charley" to "drudge not since nothing is dearer to me than your health." The younger Carroll, while castigating his father's behavior as "meddlesome" and certainly "out of season," would simultaneously plead with the old man to forego his long walks in the "chill" winter air.[52]

The younger Carroll tried to convince his father that the act was an essential concession demanded by a popular revolution; the elder Carroll saw nothing but dangerous leveling in the measure: if the assembly could pass such a bill, what was to stop them from deciding "that no man shall hold above 500 acres of land—that he shall sell all above that quantity at the rate of £100 current per thousand? Why should not the landholder be obliged to part with his land as well as the sterling money holder be obliged to part with his sterling?" Admitting both the personal cost and the unjust effect of the bill, the son repeatedly tried to educate his father about revolutionary necessities: "The law suits the multitudes, individuals must submit to partial losses; no great revolutions can happen in a state without revolutions or mutations of private property." "There is a time when it is wisdom to yield to injustice and to popular heresies and delusions," the son instructed the father; if the populace was not legislatively placated in revolutionary times, "they commonly have recourse to violence and greater injustice towards all such as have the temerity to oppose them, particularly when their unjust proceedings are popular." Carroll and his legislative colleagues reasoned well, even though he could never convince his father, who vowed, "I will not let the tender law sleep, nor the rogues who have taken advantage of it, nor the men who ought to repeal it."

Only in late 1780, with the state's convulsions markedly diminishing, did the assembly repeal the tender act. For Charles Carroll of Carrollton, the return of stability constituted a great political triumph. He and his allies in a very real sense were the architects of a successful campaign to win legitimacy, support, and popular approval in a very trying and dangerous situation. Also aiding a restoration of order were the fading of Britain's military fortunes in the Chesapeake and the cautious methods by which the Whig courts gradually reasserted their judicial authority. But, basically, the Maryland Whig elite believed they had prevailed by acquiescing in those sacrifices necessary to appease the "revengeful democracy" that had been unleashed by the Revolution. "No great revolution can happen in a state without revolutions or mutations of private property," Carroll had written to his father. So, too, he might have added, no revolutions can occur without mutations in the conception and appearance of authority.[53]

VII

In the Carolinas, Gen. Nathanael Greene faced much greater civil conflict. And yet from the beginning, he pursued a strategy similar in broad outline to the one Carroll and his contemporaries followed in the Chesapeake. Greene and Carroll had little in common in their backgrounds. Carroll enjoyed great wealth and a fine continental education, while Greene had mediocre schooling and middling means. Although neither found religion especially compelling, Carroll was Catholic and Greene a former Quaker. Carroll, frail and forever worried over his health, would on occasion display real fortitude, but he generally disliked violence and had to work at building his courage. Greene, stocky and heavily muscled, relished the rigors of the martial life, though not the killing and suffering it brought. Yet, despite these differences, had they met and spoken at length, the two would have discovered much in common. Both possessed acute insight into the social impact exerted by the war. Similarly, the two fully appreciated the need for making the goals they desired a matter of self-interest to the people. And most important perhaps, they realized that the war's dislocation required the leadership class to bend if it were to remain in power.

Greene recognized clearly that military actions had political repercussions, and based his strategy largely on the goal of winning over public opinion. Often allowing political considerations rather than short-run military advantages to dictate his actions, he strove to popularize the Revolution by politicizing the South. Shortly after arriving in the Carolinas, Greene explained to Knox the context that would guide his moves: "Everything here depends upon opinion and it is equally dangerous to go forward as to stand still for if you lose the confidence of the people you lose all support and if you rush into danger you hazard everything."[54]

Because of the South's convulsed political and military situation, Greene early decided to pursue what he called a "partisan" or "fugitive" war. To retain support, an image of resistance had to be maintained, and yet his resources left few options. "Until a more permanent army can be collected than is in the field at present," he wrote Francis Marion, "we must endeavor to keep up a partisan war and preserve the tide of sentiment among the people as much as possible in our favor."[55]

Greene's first major strategic decision—to divide his small army and dispatch Gen. Daniel Morgan to operate west of the Catawba—proceeded directly from his desire to influence public sentiment. He told the departing Morgan that "the object of this detachment is to give protection to that part of the country and to spirit up the people." His letters reiterated his basic strategy: all action must be designed to "keep up the spirit of the people." Besides improving the morale of the well-affected, Greene designed his partisans' tactics sometimes to frighten, sometimes to attract those less supportive. Concerning one successful Whig raid, he told Thomas Jefferson that "They made a dreadful carnage of them, upwards of one-hundred were killed and most of the rest cut to pieces. It has had a very happy effect on those disaffected persons of which there are too many in this country." Greene similarly told Gen. Thomas Sumter, the notorious "Carolina Gamecock," that partisans were "to strike terror into our enemies and give spirit to our friends."[56]

Still, Greene realized fully the social dangers of terrorism in the Carolina context. Only a regular, well-appointed army could, in the long run, properly engage the majority's respect and allegiance. He tried delicately to quiet Sumter's punishing raids in early 1781: "Partisan strokes in a war are like the garnishing of a table—they give splendor to the army and reputation to the officers but they afford no substantial national security...there is no mortal more fond of enterprise than myself but this is not the basis on which the fate of this country depends. It is not a war for posts but a contest for states dependent upon opinion." Racing to avoid Cornwallis that winter, Greene similarly pointed out to a militia general: "While there is an army left in the field the hopes of the people are kept alive but disperse that and their spirits will sink at once."[57]

Cornwallis's situation and strategy enjoyed a curious symmetry with those of Greene. After Charleston's fall, the British constructed a functional occupational authority in South Carolina by organizing Tory militias supported by sizable British posts scattered throughout the interior. But the British command discovered that in the context of a civil conflict, even after victories such as Camden, complete security could not be established. Greene's army, reasoned Cornwallis, constituted the key disruptive element. As long as the rebel force existed as a symbol of willful defiance, the partisans would bedevil all occupation programs. The answer seemed clear—Greene had to be destroyed. At Guilford Court House, North Carolina, in March 1781, Cornwallis missed his major opportunity. Greene's force, having recently been expanded by a large complement of militia, stood to battle. The British, outnumbered two to one, drove the Americans from the field, but at a price that exhausted the victors. Greene's force left in good order and camped nearby, knowing that the British were too debilitated to pursue. Cornwallis wrote that he camped "near part of the country where the greatest number of our friends were supposed to reside. Many of the inhabitants rode into camp, shook me by the hand, said they were glad to see us and to hear we had beat Greene and then rode home again; for I could not get one-hundred men in all the regulator's country to stay with us even as militia."[58]

Greene's strongly preferred strategy of avoiding any decisive struggle was the military equivalent of the Whig political actions in Delaware and Georgia; but because the fate of the Carolinas mattered much to the whole cause of independence, he knew that his army need not win but did need to survive to prevent the disaffected from becoming the opposition. In addition, Greene, well aware of the need to maintain popular support, invariably stressed to his subordinates the importance of observing "strict discipline" and of preventing "your people from plundering and abusing the inhabitants." One could not be too cautious, he explained to Colonel Few of Georgia, in late 1780, when "people are halting between two opinions." He repeatedly ordered his officers, when impressment could not be avoided, "to treat the inhabitants with tenderness, to inform them of the urgency of this measure," for this "business must be conducted with the greatest delicacy." Receipts were always to be given, whether material was taken "from whig or tory." No matter what his fortunes on the field, Greene clung to this policy until the close of hostilities. Late in the war, he summed up the essential concept to Gen. Anthony Wayne: "The modes of subsisting your troops you will also concert with the magistrates of the state and let the manner be as little oppressive to the people as possible."[59]

By late 1781 the British had withdrawn their forces inside Charleston. Though Greene had accomplished much, he considered his position extremely tenuous, and he worked feverishly that fall and winter to subdue the civil conflict and consolidate support for the rebel cause. Convinced that the internecine struggle dangerously impaired his capacity to resist, Greene ordered his subordinates to follow a policy of pacification through forgiveness. Beginning in November, he outlined his new strategy. Thomas Sumter surely read his commander's letter of 28 November 1781 with amazement. Three days earlier Greene had hinted about drawing "off" the Tory partisans "from the enemies interest." He now elaborated: "Don't spare any pains to take off the tories from the British interest for tho we have great reason to hate them and vengeance would dictate one universal slaughter yet when we consider how many of our good people must fall a sacrifice in doing it we shall find it will be more for our interest to forgive than to persecute. This was always my opinion and if the war continues in this country, unless we can detach the people from the British interest we shall feel more incoveniences from them than from all the British Army. Indeed we do now."[60] Greene's other commanders, including Gen. Anthony Wayne, operating in Georgia, received similar instructions: "When you get in the lower country you will invite all the people to join you and such as shall engage in the service under your command afford them your protection and security. Try by every means in your power to soften the malignity and deadly resentments subsisting between the whigs and tories." Present and future safety demanded that old hostilities be quieted, that those masses formerly opposed or indifferent to the cause be placated rather than persecuted.[61]

Greene urged the same philosophy on the Whig authorities who were working on the difficult task of reestablishing political control. Strife and confusion accompanied the entire process, including a brief capture of the governor and council of North Carolina by Tory partisans in late 1781. Yet, this agitated context made clear to Greene the need for his conciliatory strategy. In early 1782 he advised Governor John Martin of Georgia "to open a door for the disaffected of your state to come in with particular exceptions. It is better to save than destroy especially when we are obliged to expose good men to destroy bad. It is always dangerous to put people in a state of desperation and the satisfaction of revenge has but a momentary existence and is commonly succeeded by pity and remorse." When Martin replied that it was against human "nature" to do what Greene recommended, the General retorted: "You say nature would not be nature if you forgave them—legislators should follow policy not their own private resentments. A man in his legislative capacity is not at liberty to consult his own private feelings in determining upon measures but how they will affect the interests of his country."[62] Thus Greene, in the Carolinas, like Carroll in Maryland, saw that the revolutionary situation required not always following policies that the Whig elite might consider abstractly just or desirable. Tact and conciliation were the essential elements to insure that the partially alienated "public opinion" be won to the cause of independence and order.

From this survey of the war years in large sections of the Upper and Lower South, several common factors seem clear. First, the War of Independence irrevocably altered the value structure and behavioral pattern of the late eighteenth-century South. The dislocative forces unleashed during this period raised the political sensibilities of both participants and nonbelligerents, most especially those of the meaner sort, who, with loyalty and support sought by both sides, could demand an equality of respect at least partially denied under the old colonial system. These people, their recent prosperity shattered by the war, vigorously resisted Whig demands—demands in many ways more oppressive than the comparatively mild tyranny of Parliament. They did so largely because the war created a political and social situation in which established standards of conduct lost their hold. Conscious that a unique condition was present, most felt secure in expressing and acting upon emotions long suppressed. With the uncertainty of authority evident, and with the broader community sharing their hostility, they believed themselves protected from any real punishment. All of these forms of disorder—civil conflict, Loyalist action, murder, plunder, militia insubordination, unrest among blacks, defiance by independent-minded whites, opportunism—shared one common trait: an undisciplined resentment of authority. Hate, greed, anger, envy, fear, and memories of old injustices accounted for the pattern of dissension, which cannot be explained by the traditional categories of patriot and Loyalist but requires instead a more comprehensive understanding of social behavior within a revolutionary context.

For the region's leadership, the violence of the war years forced a related transformation in cultural attitudes. No longer could political control be exercised on the basis of class prerogative or rightful privilege. That notion, already under heavy attack, especially in Virginia before the Revolution, was now largely abandoned. To maintain power, all the elites—whether political leaders in the Chesapeake or military commanders in the Lower South—realized the need for catering to opinion to seek accommodation and acceptability. No longer could they rule without serious regard to their image. Recognizing the seriousness of the internal violence, they sought to surmount the challenge by avoiding heavy demands on the populace and by implementing political programs specifically intended to secure popularity. On the Delmarva Peninsula, Whig leaders bided their time and struggled to contain the animosity to Whig power among the poor and the disaffected whom they could not hope to repress. In Georgia they retreated and, while waiting for the British to leave, labored to attract popular support. In Maryland, Carroll and his colleagues, appreciating that governing institutions could not secure their class's authority, manipulated fiscal policies as the "price of Revolution." And in the Carolinas, Greene, convinced of his inability to restore meaningful order by force, labored to subdue the "division of sentiment" by an artful blending of military policy and conciliation. Stating the fundamental concept of his strategy in 1782, he emphasized: "I have always observed both in religion and politics moderation answers the most valuable purposes. Persecution either in the one case or the other but too commonly established the interest it meant to destroy."[63] In reality rather than through rhetoric, both Carroll and Greene and many of their Whig contemporaries understood that the Revolution could only be saved by directly channeling the popular will into the republic's creation. By so doing, they established the order and stability necessary for the continued growth of the new nation and the power of the revolutionary elite.

My friend and colleague at the University of Maryland, David Grimsted, provided detailed criticism for several drafts of this essay. I am most indebted to him for his valuable assistance. Peter Albert, Joanne Giza, Rhys Isaac, Sally Mason, Whitman Ridgway, and Alfred Young also read the manuscript and offered useful comments.

1. David Grimsted, "The American Revolution: Old Problems and New Research," paper presented at the Institute of General History, American Sector, Moscow, U.S.S.R.

2. The clearest presentation of the historical literature devoted to this subject remains Jack P. Greene, "Changing Interpretations of Early American Politics," in Ray A. Billington, ed., *The Reinterpretation of Early American History* (San Marino, Calif.: Huntington Library, 1966), pp. 151–77.

3. For a suggestive essay on this, see Rhys Isaac, "Evangelical Revolt: The Nature of the Baptists' Challenge to Traditional Order in Virginia, 1765 to 1775," *William and Mary Quarterly*, 3d. ser. 30 (July 1974): 345–68; also of interest is Kenneth A. Lockridge, "Social Change and the Meaning of the American Revolution," *Journal of Social History* 6 (Summer 1973): 403–39.

4. The most technically sophisticated examinations of wealth distribution for the eighteenth century include Carville V. Earle, *The Evolution of a Tidewater System: All Hallow's Parish Maryland, 1650–1783* (Chicago: University of Chicago, Department of Geography, 1975), chap. 5; James A. Henretta, "Economic Development and Social Structure in Colonial Boston," *William and Mary Quarterly*, 3d ser. 22 (January 1965): 75–92; Allan Kulikoff, "The Progress of Inequality in Revolutionary Boston," *William and Mary Quarterly*, 3d ser. 28 (July 1971): 375–412; James T. Lemon and Gary B. Nash, "The Distribution of Wealth in Eighteenth Century America: A Century of Changes in Chester County, Pennsylvania," *Journal of Social History* 2 (Fall 1968): 1–24; Russell R. Menard, P. M. G. Harris, Lois Green Carr, "Opportunity and Inequality: The Distribution of Wealth on the Lower Western Shore of Maryland, 1638–1705," *Maryland Historical Magazine* 69 (Summer 1974): 169–84; also informative is Jackson Turner Main, *The Social Structure of Revolutionary America* (Princeton: Princeton University Press, 1965).

5. Two older monographs are especially revealing in this regard: Max Savelle, *Seeds of Liberty: The Genesis of the American Mind* (New York: Alfred A. Knopf, 1948); Charles S. Sydnor, *Gentlemen Freeholders: Political Practices in Washington's Virginia* (Chapel Hill: University of North Carolina Press, 1952).

6. An unsurpassed account of prerevolutionary politics is Merrill Jensen, *The Founding of a Nation: A History of the American Revolution, 1763–1776* (New York: Oxford University Press, 1968).

7. An extremely helpful survey that reconstructs the period at the state level is Jackson Turner Main, *The Sovereign States, 1775–1783* (New York: Franklin Watts, 1973); also useful are Robert McCluer Calhoon, *The Loyalists in Revolutionary America, 1760–1781* (New York: Harcourt Brace Jovanovich, 1973); Arthur M. Schlesinger, Sr., *The Colonial Merchants and the American Revolution* (New York: Columbia University Press, 1918).

8. Ronald Hoffman, *A Spirit of Dissension: Economics, Politics and the Revolution in Maryland* (Baltimore: Johns Hopkins University Press, 1973), p. 146. My study of revolutionary Maryland should be consulted by those interested in the themes developed in this essay. Although all of the Maryland references are contained in that study, I have generally repeated the primary citations. Two convenient guides to studies for the eighteenth-century South are Jack P. Greene, *The American Colonies in the Eighteenth Century*

(Northbrook, Ill.: AHM Publishing Corp., 1972); John Shy, *The American Revolution* (Northbrook, Ill.: AHM Publishing Corp., 1973).

9. "Extracts of a Letter from a Clergyman in Maryland to His Friend in England," 2 August 1775, in Peter Force, ed., *American Archives*, 4th ser., 6 vols. (Washington, D.C., 1837–1846), 3:10; Robert Eden to Lord George Germain, 25 January 1776, Fisher Transcripts, Maryland Historical Society, Baltimore, Md. (cited hereafter as MHS); Report of the Dorchester County Committee of Inspection, Fall 1775, Gilmor Papers, MHS.

10. Thomas Johnson to Council of Safety, 22 July 1776, *Archives of Maryland,* ed. William H. Browne et al., 71 vols. (Baltimore, 1883–) 12:92.

11. Col. Thomas Wright to Council of Safety, 20 September 1776, ibid., pp. 288–89; William Whitely to Gov. Thomas Johnson, 19 May 1777, Maryland State Papers, Red Books (cited hereafter as *Red Books*), Maryland Hall of Records, Annapolis, Md. (cited hereafter as MHR), 18:68; Col. George Dashiell to Gov. Thomas Johnson, 12 March 1778, Executive Papers, portfolio 4, folder 60 Y, MHR; Dorchester County Committee of Observation to the Council of Safety, 15 November 1776, *Archives of Maryland,* 11:449–51; for some interesting material on the Maryland militia, see David Curtis Skaggs, *Roots of Maryland Democracy, 1753–1776* (Westport, Conn.: Greenwood Press, 1973).

12. John Gibson to Council of Safety, 4 January 1777, *Archives of Maryland,* 16:16–18; James Lloyd Chamberlain to Daniel of St. Thomas Jenifer, 26 December 1776, ibid; 12:552–53.

13. Col. Richard Barnes to Gov. Thomas Johnson, 15 September 1777, *Red Books,* 17:177; Col. Richard Barnes to Gov. Thomas Johnson, 20 December 1777, *Red Books,* 17:192.

14. *Proceedings of the Conventions of the Province of Maryland* (Annapolis, 1836), p. 18.

15. Case of Robert Davis, Executive Papers, box 1, MHR; Proceedings of the Council of Safety, 4 April 1776, *Archives of Maryland,* 11:309; Baltimore County Committee of Observation to Council of Safety, 7 May 1776, ibid., 11:415–16.

16. Testimony of James Bosley before Committee of Observation, 14 November 1776, ibid., 16:87–88; charge against Henry Guyton, ibid., 16:76–77.

17. Luther Martin to Gov. Thomas Johnson, 18 March 1778, Executive Papers, portfolio 4, folder 60Z, MHR.

18. Nathaniel Potter to Gov. Thomas Johnson, 9 March 1778, Maryland State Papers, Blue Books (cited hereafter as *Blue Books*), MHR, 4:912.

19. Nelson Waite Rightmyer, *The Anglican Church in Delaware* (Philadelphia: Church Historical Society, 1947), p. 91. Revolutionary Delaware has not received the attention it deserves from historians. Fortunately some very thorough research has been accomplished by Harold B. Hancock, whose monograph and articles in *Delaware History* contain interesting material; see especially Harold B. Hancock, *The Delaware Loyalists* (Wilmington: Historical Society of Delaware, 1940); "Thomas Robinson: Delaware's Most Prominent Loyalist," *Delaware History* 4 (1950–1951): 1–36; "The New Castle County Loyalists," *Delaware History* 4 (1951); "The Kent County Loyalists," *Delaware History* 6 (1954); "Letters to and from Caesar Rodney," *Delaware History* 12 (1966–1967); "The Revolutionary War Diary of William Adair," *Delaware History* 13 (1968).

20. Col. William Richardson to the Commissioners of the Board of War, Philadelphia, 9 August 1777, in George Herbert Ryden, *Letters to and from Caesar Rodney 1756–1784* (Philadelphia: University of Pennsylvania Press, 1933), pp. 210–12.

21. Ibid.

22. Joseph Dashiell to Gov. Thomas Johnson, 12 April 1777, *Red Books,* 14:71.

23. Col. William Richardson to the Commissioners of the Board of War, Philadelphia, 9 August 1777; William Perry to Caesar Rodney, 3 October 1777, Ryden, *Letters to and from Caesar Rodney,* 3 October 1777, pp. 210–12, 238–40.

24. For a basic introduction to conditions in the immediate years of the prewar South, see Jensen, *The Founding of a Nation;* Main, *The Sovereign States;* Richard M. Brown, *The South Carolina Regulators* (Cambridge: Harvard University Press, 1963).

25. British strategy during the southern campaigns has been authoritatively explored by a number of rich book-length studies including: Piers Mackesy, *The War for America, 1775–1783* (London: Harvard University Press, 1964); Paul H. Smith, *Loyalists*

and Redcoats: A Study in British Revolutionary Policy (Chapel Hill: University of North Carolina Press, 1964); Franklin and Mary Wickwire, *Cornwallis: The American Adventure* (Boston: Houghton Mifflin Co, 1970); William B. Willcox, *Portrait of a General: Sir Henry Clinton in the War of Independence* (New York: Alfred A. Knopf, 1964). For a perceptive analysis of the implications of these studies, see John Shy, "The American Revolution: The Military Conflict Considered as a Revolutionary War," in Stephen G. Kurtz and James H. Hutson, eds., *Essays on the American Revolution* (Chapel Hill: University of North Carolina Press, 1973), pp. 121–56. Professor Shy's excellent investigation establishes a number of original dimensions, some of which are explored in my essay.

26. For an interesting analysis of the factors responsible for the British defeat, see Wickwires' *Cornwallis*, especially chaps. 8 and 9.

27. Lt. Alexander Innes to Gen. Charles Cornwallis, June 1780, Cornwallis Papers (P.R.O. 30/11, vols. 1–6, 58, Library of Congress microfilm) Library of Congress, Washington, D.C. (cited hereafter as LC); Maj. Archibald McArthur to Gen. Charles Cornwallis, 13 June 1780, Cornwallis Papers, LC.

28. Thomas Brandon to Brig. Gen. Thomas Sumter, 4 December 1780, Thomas Sumter Papers, LC.

29. The best writing on Greene includes the following: George W. Greene, *The Life of Nathanael Greene, Major-General in the Army of the Revolution*, 3 vols. (New York, 1867–1871); Theodore Thayer, *Nathanael Greene: Strategist of the American Revolution* (New York: Twayne Publishers, 1960); M. F. Treacy, *Prelude to Yorktown: The Southern Campaign of Nathanael Greene, 1780–1781* (Chapel Hill: University of North Carolina Press, 1963); Russell F. Weigley, *The Partisan War; The South Carolina Campaign* (Columbia: University of South Carolina Press, 1970).

30. Gen. Nathanael Greene to Gen. Robert Howe, 29 December 1780; to Gen. Henry Knox, 7 December 1780; to Gov. Thomas Jefferson, 6 December 1780; to Gov. Abner Nash, 6 December 1780, Greene Papers, LC.

31. Gen. Nathanael Greene to Gen. Robert Howe, 29 December 1780; to Gen. Henry Knox, 7 December 1780; to Chevalier de la Luzerne, 9 January 1781, Greene Papers, LC.

32. Gen. Nathanael Greene to Robert Morris, 7 March 1782, Greene Papers, LC; for the impact created by the movement of troops, see Shy "The American Revolution," pp. 144–45.

33. "Col. Robert Gray's Observations on the War in Carolina," *South Carolina Historical and Genealogical Magazine* 11 (1910): 153–54.

34. Gen. Nathanael Greene to Gen. Anthony Wayne, 9 January 1782, and 6 March 1782, Greene Papers, LC.

35. Lt. Nesbitt Balfour to Gen. Charles Cornwallis, June 1780, Cornwallis Papers, LC; Hugh Rankin, *Francis Marion: the Swamp Fox* (New York: Thomas Y. Crowell, 1973), p. 69; "Gray's Observations on the War in Carolina," p. 140; Gen. Charles Cornwallis to Gen. Henry Clinton, 29 August 1780, in Benjamin F. Stevens, ed., *The Campaign in Virginia, 1781: The Clinton-Cornwallis Controversy*, 2 vols. (London, 1888), p. 261.

36. Col. Francis Marion to Gen. Horatio Gates, 21 November 1780; Gen. William Smallwood to Gen. Horatio Gates, 27 October 1780; Maj. Mark Armstrong to Gen. Horatio Gates, 7 November 1780, all in Walter Clark, ed., *The State Records of North Carolina*, 26 vols. (Goldsboro, N.C., 1886–1907) 14:746, 712, 727–28.

37. Proclamation of Gov. John Rutledge issued from Gen. Nathanael Greene's camp at the High Hills of the Santee, 27 September 1781, Thomas Sumter Papers, LC.

38. Rankin, *Francis Marion*, pp. 280–87.

39. Gen. Nathanael Greene to Samuel Huntington, President of the Continental Congress, 7 December 1780, Greene Papers, LC.

40. Gen. Nathanael Greene to Gen. George Washington, 28 December 1780, Greene Papers, LC.

41. Carville Earle and Ronald Hoffman, "Urbanization in the Early South: The First Two Centuries," essay presented at the Eastern Historical Geography Association Conference, spring 1975; for information on economic conditions during this period see Hoffman, *A Spirit of Dissension*, chaps. 1–5; Joseph A. Ernst, *Money and Politics in America 1755–1775: A Study in the Currency Act of 1764 and the Political Economy of Revolution* (Chapel Hill: University of North Carolina Press, 1973).

42. Earle and Hoffman, "Urbanization in the Early South."

43. Hoffman, *A Spirit of Dissension*, chap. 6.

44. Sydnor, *Gentlemen Freeholders*, chaps. 2–5.

45. Charles Carroll of Carrollton to Edmund Jennings, 23 November 1765, Charles Carroll of Carrollton Letterbook, 1766–1769, MHS.

46. For the Great Awakening's impact on the Revolution see the essay by Rhys Isaac in this collection; also see Richard L. Bushman, *From Puritan to Yankee: Character and Social Order in Connecticut, 1690–1765* (Cambridge: Harvard University Press, 1967); Alan Heimert, *Religion and the American Mind from the Great Awakening to the Revolution* (Cambridge: Harvard University Press, 1966); William G. McLoughlin, "The Role of Religion in the Revolution: Liberty of Conscience and Cultural Cohesion in the New Nation," in Kurtz and Hutson, *Essays on the American Revolution*, pp. 197–255; Rhys Isaac, "Religion and Authority: Problems of the Anglican Establishment in Virginia in the Era of the Great Awakening and the Parson's Cause," *William and Mary Quarterly*, 3d ser. 30 (January 1973): 3–36. For an especially acute discussion of conflicting cultural values, see Rowland Berthoff and John M. Murrin, "Feudalism, Communalism, and the Yeoman Freeholder: The American Revolution Considered as a Social Accident," in Kurtz and Hutson, *Essays on the American Revolution*, pp. 256–88. A broader discussion of these values and their place within the political culture of the eighteenth century can be found in Bernard Bailyn, *The Ideological Origins of the Eighteenth Century* (Cambridge, Mass.: Harvard University Press, 1967); Pauline Maier, *From Resistance to Revolution: Colonial Radicals and the Development of American Opposition to Britain, 1765–1776* (N.Y.: Alfred A. Knopf, 1972); and Gordon S. Wood, *The Creation of the American Republic, 1776–1787* (Chapel Hill: University of North Carolina Press, 1969).

47. Thomas Rodney to Caesar Rodney, 5 August 1776, Ryden, *Letters to and from Caesar Rodney*, pp. 101–2.

48. Matthew Wilson, D.D. of Lewes, Delaware, to the Board of War in Philadelphia, 29 July 1778, in Rev. E. E. Neill, "Matthew Wilson, D.D. of Lewes, Delaware," *Pennsylvania Magazine of History and Biography* (November 1884), pp. 52–53.

49. Hancock, "The Diary of William Adair," pp. 151–65.

50. Ibid.

51. Hoffman, *A Spirit of Dissension*, chaps. 7–10.

52. Ibid., especially chaps. 8, 9.

53. Ibid.

54. Gen. Nathanael Greene to Gen. Henry Knox, 7 December 1780, Greene Papers, LC.

55. Gen. Nathanael Greene to Col. Francis Marion, 4 December 1780; also to George Washington, 30 October 1780; Samuel Huntington, 2 November 1780, Greene Papers, LC.

56. Gen. Nathanael Greene to Gen. Daniel Morgan, 16 December 1780, and 19 January 1781; see also to Colonel Few, 16 December 1780; Samuel Huntington, 28 December 1780; Gov. Thomas Jefferson, 29 February 1781, Greene Papers, LC; Gen. Nathanael Greene to Gen. Thomas Sumter, 6 May 1781, Thomas Sumter Papers, LC.

57. Gen. Nathanael Greene to Gen. Thomas Sumter, 8 January 1781; to Gen. Richard Caswell, 16 February 1781, Greene Papers, LC.

58. Gen. Charles Cornwallis to Gen. Henry Clinton, 10 April 1781, Stevens, *Clinton-Cornwallis Controversy*, pp. 396–97.

59. Gen. Nathanael Greene to Colonel Few, 16 December 1780; also to Lt. Clement Reed, 14 December 1780; Lt. Col. William Washington, 16 February 1781; Gen. Anthony Wayne, 9 January 1782, Greene Papers, LC.

60. Gen. Nathanael Greene to Gen. Thomas Sumter, 25 November 1781, and 28 November 1781, 12 December 1781, Thomas Sumter Papers, LC.

61. Gen. Nathanael Greene to Gen. Anthony Wayne, 9 January 1782, and 28 January 1782, 4 February 1782, Greene Papers, LC.

62. Gen. Nathanael Greene to Gov. John Martin, 9 January 1782 and 12 March 1782, Greene Papers, LC.

63. Gen. Nathanael Greene to General Rutherford, 28 January 1782, Greene Papers, LC.

Outsiders

The Indians' Revolution

Francis Jennings

A cartouche decorating the testimonial certificate distributed to friendly Indians by the British. The figure, devised by Superintendent of Indian Affairs Sir William Johnson, symbolizes, in terms of Indian metaphor, the Covenant Chain confederation, binding Great Britain and its colonies to the Iroquois League and its tributaries. Engraving by Henry Dawkins, 1770. New York Historical Society.

A long tradition in American historiography treats the formative era of American society as a time of collision between "civilization" and "savagery," which means, in objective terms, Europeans and Indians. Whether presented in the melodrama of Francis Parkman's multivolume *France and England in North America* or in the theorizing of Frederick Jackson Turner's *The Frontier in American History,* the identification of Indians as savages has served as a convenient way of transforming them to nonpersons and thus to justify their subjection and dispossession.

In reaction against this tradition, some modern revisionists have attempted to restore humanity to Indians by directing attention to the internal evolution of tribal society. Robert F. Berkhofer, Jr., has made an explicit case for this approach in "The Political Context of a New Indian History," in *Pacific Historical Review* 40 (August 1971): 357–82. Anthropologists generally have tended to skirt political issues by referring to the acculturation of whole societies and cultures, but their admirably neutral terminology is not very informative about what happened when particular Europeans met particular Indians.

My own work rests on the revisionists' assumption that Indians were indeed human beings with recognizable emotions and rational processes, and I have guided myself by the acculturation theories of the anthropologists' ethnohistory. My primary aim is to explore the interplay of the politico-legal institutions of specific European and Indian communities in contact. "Frontier theory" denies even the existence of such a subject by denying that Indian tribes had governments "worthy the name." I find, on the contrary, that the meshing of governmental sanction systems between tribe and nation is evidenced by huge masses of source materials that the frontier mythologists simply refuse to examine.

I am now at work on a long history of a complex bicultural political institution called the Covenant Chain. This was an alliance of Indian tribes under Iroquois leadership on the one hand, with English colonies and the British Crown on the other. Its origins, and the cultural matrices from which it emerged, are explored at length in my book, *The Invasion of America: Indians, Colonialism, and the Cant of Conquest,* published for the Institute of Early American History and Culture (Chapel Hill: University of North Carolina Press, 1975).

Francis Jennings (Ph.D., University of Pennsylvania, 1965) is past president of the American Society for Ethnohistory. He teaches history at Cedar Crest College, Allentown, Pennsylvania.

There were more than two sides in the American Revolution. The British Crown and the Continental Congress formulated general strategies and policies that became distorted and sometimes negated when they were put into effect by officers who served themselves as well as their governments. There were thirteen separate and individually sovereign states, which had bitter quarrels among themselves, which they sometimes settled by force of arms even while they jointly engaged in struggle against the Crown.[1] There were colonies in the West Indies and Canada that did not rebel. Though the revolutionaries solicited Quebec to join them, and invaded that province to make persuasion stronger, the French-speaking Catholic inhabitants preferred the liberties and religious toleration guaranteed by the Crown to the more doubtful prospects of subordination to the English-speaking Protestants of the Continental Congress.[2]

Still other affiliates of the Crown that did not rebel were the tribal governments that exerted jurisdiction over lands "reserved" for Indian use. Multiple ambiguities and semantic distortions have excluded tribal governments—as distinct from Indian "auxiliaries"—from recognition as political participants in the revolutionary struggle. The so-called international law created to serve the purposes of governments in the state form does not recognize a parity between bureaucratic states and kin-ordered tribes.[3] A large literature purports to describe Indian communities as congregations of wild men—savages bereft of "real" government, existing in a condition of chronic anarchy. On such convenient assumptions, there had been agreement between Crown and colonist, until 1776, that the country west of the Appalachian Mountains was under British sovereignty. Disputes never challenged that basic agreement; disputes centered upon the competition of particular jurisdictions within the empire to administer the sovereignty. The Indians, however, did not agree that they lived in Crown lands that had merely been reserved for them. They conceived themselves as living in their own territories under their own free and independent governments, and they started fighting well before 1776 to maintain as much as circumstances would permit of political independence.

The situation was not novel. As is usual in history on the grand scale, details of time and place were unique, and some fresh changes were rung on old tunes, but a familiar theme emerges from the variations. The colonists were the lineal descendants of the conquerors and colonizers of Wales and Ireland, those lords marcher who had created England's first empire. When England invaded America—what we usually call "settling" it—the Crown lawyers had consulted their only precedents to rationalize the position of the new American outposts in the structure of the empire. Each colony became in legal theory a collective lord analogous to the barons who had marched into Ireland.[4] When the Americans turned against the Crown they continued an ancient tradition of lords who have marched too far and grown too powerful to accept royal orders gladly. In this perspective the American Revolution was a barons' revolt. Geography determined that these rebels could not follow the tradition to its logical conclusion of seizure of the throne—Washingtons were rather more distant than Tudors—so they fought for the more limited objective of elevating their baronies into sovereignties. Sweet are the uses of sovereignty. In Ireland the "Old English" colonizers had struggled to win sovereignty for themselves in order to dominate the "mere" Irish to greater advantage.[5] So also in America. As Irish peasants strove against king and baron alike to preserve native lands and independence, the Indian natives of North America fought also. When cultural actualities are substituted for the myths of savagery, the Indians' revolution appears analytically as a series of peasants' wars.[6]

This paper argues that the American revolutionaries fought for empire over the west as well as for their own freedom in the east.[7] While the colony-states fought for independence from the Crown, the tribes had to fight for independence from the states. It makes a huge embarrassment to ideology that the Revolution wore one face looking eastward across the Atlantic and another looking westward into the continent, but Indians have always obtruded awkwardly from the smooth symmetry of historical rationalization.

Indian trade and Indian land had first brought Europeans to the shores of America. In one sense, the Indian struggle for independence had started with Jamestown, but natives and colonists had managed to accommodate erratically with each other in the symbiotic community of trade. In spite of occasional wars of particular tribes against particular colonies, there had never been a universal conflict of red against white. Some tribes—notably in Virginia and New England—had been subjected by force, but until 1750 most Indians continued to live in "free" tribes allied by treaty to one or more English colony. Crisis came then because of the accelerated growth of colonial population with a concomitant demand for expansion into the Indian territories west of the Appalachians.

Had Great Britain been the only European power colonizing North America, perhaps the pace of colonization might have been regulated and arrangements made to give the Indians alternatives other than desperate war; but France had planted colonies in Canada and Louisiana, and France was determined to halt British expansion beyond the Appalachians by establishing a long chain of Indian protectorates controlled from strategically placed French forts. The British Crown and colonies were equally determined to destroy the French barrier and to seize all the territory between the Atlantic and Pacific oceans. Competition accelerated the plans of both powers, and they raced to confront each other at the strategic junction of waters where the Ohio River begins. Here they set in motion the events that resulted in the first world war of modern times, the vast imperial conflict called the Seven Years War.

The Ohio region and its resident Indians will be constantly at or near the center of attention in this essay. Although southern tribes, especially the Cherokees, faced much the same problems as the Ohio Indians, they lay in a separate theater of action, with a distinct history.[8]

The events to be discussed mark a period when many Indian tribes joined together in great confederations to fight for their territorial integrity. These struggles began with diplomatic maneuvers in 1750 and continued through tribal war on the largest scale ever known in this country, intermixed with the imperial and secessionist conflicts of Great Britain with France and the revolutionary United States. The era ended with the Treaty of Greenville that followed the Battle of Fallen Timbers, twelve years after the official conclusion of the American colonists' war for independence. In this dramatic and turbulent era, the attention of historians has fastened chiefly upon the motives and initiatives of Europeans and Euramericans with regard to each other; Indians have been treated, usually in afterthoughts, as appendages to the "important" persons and issues. These Indians are presented as robot-like characters who respond reflexively to stimuli and commands from the real people. I propose to show that this attitude is fallacious. Not only did the tribes undertake initiatives for their own reasons, but their independent actions caused colonies and empires to respond, sometimes even reflexively, by drastically revising plans and policies. The tribes' independence, power, and possessions were central issues of what we see only as the American Revolution. Blended in with that familiar process was a tribal revolution conducted by governments effective enough to wage devastating war and to enforce recognition through formal diplomatic protocol by Crown, colonies, and the United States.

The tribes of the upper Ohio in 1750 were Delawares, Shawnees, and "Mingo" Iroquois, confederated in a complex multiple alliance called the Covenant Chain. (The name is specific: there were many alliance "chains" in colonial times, and many "covenants," but only one Covenant Chain.)[9] In this confederation the Ohio Indians were not only "brothers" of the British, but also "nephews" of the Iroquois Six Nations, whose grand council met at Onondaga (where Syracuse, New York, now stands). That is to say, all the Indians were allied by treaty to certain British colonies that diplomatically recognized the Iroquois as responsible spokesmen for the other tribes, and because of this favored status the Iroquois had been able to assume a degree of authority, symbolized by the deferential "uncle" form of address, over the tributary tribes. It was an uneasy relationship in which the tributary Delawares and Shawnees often paid more heed to the ceremony than the substance of deference, but it held together as long as Iroquois diplomacy seemed to preserve the Ohio from European intrusion. Also consequential were guarantees of protection against attack by English colonial forces, and continuing participation in trade with English merchants for such necessities as cloth, tools, and guns. Englishmen gained reciprocally in the trade, and they valued the Covenant Chain also as a barrier against the French and as a stabilizing instrument of order in the "back country."

In 1751 the Covenant Chain was suddenly strained when an advance agent of the Ohio Company of Virginia appeared at the Ohio.

This agent, Christopher Gist, stirred suspicion immediately because he carried no stock of goods like the traders who traveled normally in Indian country. Gist's real purpose, of course, was to scout the land for his employing company in preparation for the planting of a new colony under Virginia's auspices, and his errand transformed the Ohio region into a cockpit of imperial and revolutionary wars.[10]

An astonishing number of conflicting parties engaged very quickly. The traders then plying through the region were mostly based in Pennsylvania and antagonistic to new competition from Virginia. Pennsylvania's Proprietary, Thomas Penn, claimed the Ohio's headwaters as within his chartered bounds, disputed Virginia's right to assume jurisdiction there, and attempted to hamper the Ohio Company by influence in London and diplomacy among the tribes. The government of Canada, backed by the French crown, determined to forestall all English expansion west of the Appalachians by enforting and garrisoning the Ohio. Iroquois statesmen, accompanied by tributary chiefs, rushed from treaty to treaty in frantic vain attempts to stop the advance of all Europeans.[11]

The Iroquois nuclear League of Six Nations was having its own troubles farther east. Shrewd New Yorkers had contrived swindling schemes for seizing vast tracts of Indian territory, the most notorious of which (called the Kayaderosseras patent) embraced 800,000 acres of land belonging to the Mohawk tribe of the Six Nations.[12] Though the Mohawks had been New York's most faithful allies since the colony's foundation, their friendship departed with their territory. On 16 June 1753, Chief Hendrick stood up in conference with the provincial council of New York, faced Governor George Clinton squarely, and poured out his bitter anger:

> Brother when we came here to relate our Grievances about our Lands, we expected to have something done for us, and we have told you that the Covenant Chain of our Forefathers was like to be broken, and brother you tell us that we shall be redressed at Albany, but we know them so well, we will not trust to them, for they [the Albany merchants] are no people but Devils, so we rather desire that you'll say, Nothing shall be done for us; Brother By and By you'll expect to see the Nations [of Indians] down [here in New York City] which you shall not see, for as soon as we come home we will send up a Belt of Wampum to our Brothers the [other] 5 Nations to acquaint them the Covenant Chain is broken between you and us. So brother you are not to expect to hear of me any more, and Brother we desire to hear no more of you.[13]

This was the Indians' declaration of independence, instantly recognized as such by the Yorkers. Its significance is somewhat blurred
for modern students by the biases of terminology in histories written
to serve political ends. A famous example of such conquest propaganda is the *History of the Five Indian Nations Depending on the Province of
New-York in America,* written by Cadwallader Colden, lieutenant governor of the state. Even Colden's title asserts that the jurisdiction of New
York took in the native neighbors of England's emigrants as well as the
colonists themselves. It was literally legal double-talk intended to bol-
ster English diplomats contending with the French over claims of
territorial sovereignty. The actual status of the Iroquois was confessed
more candidly by Sir William Johnson in a confidential summary for
officialdom. The Iroquois "called themselves a free people," wrote
Johnson, "who had an independent Lands, which were their ancient
possessions . . . so that whatever words are usually made use of respecting submission, etc., are only to be understood as in compliance with
form and custom . . . and whoever should undertake to go further on
the subject with them must have a good army at his back to protect him
from their resentment."[14]

Though Johnson's remark was made years after the Mohawk declaration, it faithfully echoed the private understandings of British officials in 1753, and the Mohawk action was interpreted in accordance
with that knowledge. The experienced members of the Crown's Board
of Trade in London immediately recognized the Mohawk declaration
as a diplomatic event "of a very serious nature." The board saw that
"the Indians . . . considered the alliance and friendship between them
and the Province of New York to be dissolved," and this was most
alarming because "the steady adherence of these Indians to the British
interest" had been vital to the security of all the northern colonies
"from the fatal effects of the encroachments of a foreign power"—that
is, France. Without the Indians, "all our efforts to check and disappoint
the present view of this power may prove ineffectual."[15] It was curious
language from a government that claimed, when treating with the
French, to hold a protectorate over the Iroquois, but it was not a
blindingly new revelation. Half a century earlier, Pennsylvania's Secretary James Logan had known that "if we lose the Iroquois we are gone
by land."[16]

With what was lightning speed for that sluggish body, the Board
of Trade moved to remedy the situation. It instructed the colonial

governors to assemble the most impressive joint treaty with the Indians of the Covenant Chain that had yet been held, and to treat in the king's own name rather than in behalf of the individual colonial governments that the Indians so distrusted. Thus was born the famous Albany Congress of 1754.[17]

The gentlemen of Virginia had their own notions of how to deal with that foreign power at the Ohio, and they did not intend to let the Crown hinder their own encroachments. Virginia "excused" itself from attendance at Albany and the possible restrictions that attendance might have entailed;[18] and Virginia continued its rash, calamitous adventuring. The colony fielded troops under young George Washington to attack the French forces on their march. The French were experienced, intelligent, and brave. Washington was self-confident and brave. The headstrong young Virginian disregarded the advice given by his experienced Iroquois ally and succeeded in getting himself completely surrounded, and surrendered.[19] The French chased English traders and Iroquois chieftains out of the region and built Fort Duquesne at the strategic forks of the Ohio.[20] Delaware and Shawnee tributaries of the Covenant Chain found themselves, alone and without resource, living in a country occupied by enemy troops. While the Mohawks had severed the Chain's links with New York, the French had smashed its links with the western tributaries.

At Albany the Indians were angry and suspicious. "Never were so few Indians seen at any public meeting," mourned one colonial observer.[21] The colonial delegates made the Congress a vehicle for the very abuses that the Crown was trying to correct. Connecticut speculators of the Susquehannah Company poured rum down some Indians outside the council chamber to get signatures on a "deed" for an enormous tract of land that these Indians had no authority to convey.[22] The clandestine methods of the Susquehannah Company were rendered more necessary because Pennsylvania claimed the same territory and was using much the same methods. The mood of its representatives was expressed by veteran interpreter Conrad Weiser, who had approached the Congress with the thought that "I may fall in with some greedy fellows for money." His wish was fulfilled. The fellows greedy for land found the fellows greedy for money, and Thomas Penn got another deed.[23] It did not simplify the Crown's problems, nor assuage the Indians' grievances, that Penn's new deed for the region at the forks of the Ohio conflicted with the claims of Virginia.

In the midst of this welter of intrigue and conspiracy, the Albany conferees produced an edifice of dreams—the Plan of Union that the mythology of the frontier characterizes as a foreshadowing of the federal union of the United States.[24] Such hindsight is willful illusion. No colony ratified the Albany Plan, and the Crown rejected it, and they all had good reasons.[25] Albany, in 1754, was the last gasp of an old system rather than a precursor of the new. Intercolonial Indian treaties had been held at Albany since 1677, and the Crown had followed custom in ordering the Congress to assemble there in 1754, but the system had deteriorated so badly that even the delegates recognized the need for change in a time of crisis. They recommended—the one positive result of the Congress, and it was probably a maneuver of Pennsylvania to outflank absent Virginia—that the Crown take over the management of Indian affairs directly. This the Crown soon did, at great expense. The only intercolonial cooperation to be evidenced at Albany was an agreement to abdicate the separate regulation of Indian affairs previously exercised by the colonies.[26]

In response, the Crown gradually created a Department of Indian Affairs. It started, without much thought to constitutional issues, as a function of the military. To eject the French from the Ohio, the Crown dispatched two regiments of regular troops under Major General Edward Braddock. On 15 April 1755, Braddock commissioned the New York merchant and public official William Johnson "to have the sole Management and direction of the Affairs of the Six Nations of Indians and their Allies, to the end that the said Indians may be heartily engaged in and attached to the British Interest." There was not even a name for the new office; Johnson acquired effective authority by supplementary commissions of command over provincial troops, and his primary responsibility was to lead an expedition against the French. His duties with the Indians were simply to round up as many as he could to join the expedition. In his supplementary instructions, however, were the seeds of his office's growth into a powerful institution. He was authorized to attract Indian recruits by making a large promise: "You are to acquaint the Indians of the Six Nations . . . with his Majesties design to Recover their Lands at Niagara, and upon the River Ohio, out of the hands of the French, and to protect them against future Incroachments, for the benefitt of their Tribes." It will be observed that His Majesty's expressed design was not to recover his own lands, but the Six Nations'. That sentence, with its ambiguities and seeming commitments, became the center of attention and hope for all the Indians. Though the Crown wavered, vacillated, and reneged, the tribes constantly forced the issue.[27]

Certainly the sentence meant nothing to Johnson's superior officer, General Braddock. After commissioning Johnson, Braddock sent him off to the north, while he himself began his march westward toward Fort Duquesne. On his way he met with chiefs of the Ohio tribes who wished to negotiate terms for their help in evicting the French. Braddock not only failed to assure the Indians of protection against future encroachments, he guaranteed that the encroachment would take place. It was inconceivable to this powerful, haughty man that he should thereby pronounce his own death sentence.

Here is the conversation and its consequences as given in the only surviving report—a description narrated by Delaware chief Shingas to an English colonial prisoner of war.

> He [Shingas] with 5 other Chiefs of the Delaware, Shawnee, and Mingo Nations (Being 2 from Each Nation) had applied to General Braddock and Enquired what he intended to do with the Land if he Could drive the French and their Indians away. To which General Braddock replied that the English Should Inhabit and Inherit the Land. On which Shingas asked General Braddock whether the Indians that were Friends to the English might not be Permitted to Live and Trade Among the English and have Hunting Ground sufficient to Support themselves and Familys as they had no where to Flee too But into the Hands of the French and their Indians who were their Enemies (that is, Shingas' Enemies). On which General Braddock said that No Savage Should Inherit the Land. On receiving which answer Shingas and the other Chiefs went that night to their own People—To whom they communicated General Braddock's Answer And the Next Morning Returned to General Braddock again in hopes he might have Changed his Sentiments and then repeated their Former Questions to General Braddock again and General Braddock made the same reply as Formerly. On which Shingas and the other Chiefs answered That if they might not have Liberty To Live on the Land they would not Fight for it. To which General Braddock answered that he did not need their Help.

Shingas remarked that his tribesmen were "very much Enraged" by Braddock,

and a Party of them went Immediately . . . and Join'd the French,

But the Greater Part remained neuter till they saw How Things
would go...And they made it their Business to draw nigh the
Place where the Engagement Happened that they might see what
Passed at it, and were still in hopes that the English would be
Victorious, But after the French had ruined Braddocks Army they
immediately compelled the Indians To join them and let them
know that if they refused they would Immediately cut them off.
On which the Indians Joined the French for their Own Safety.[28]

The last sentence of Shingas's narration is a little on the self-
serving side. Certainly the French had the Delawares in an awkward
position, because the Indians depended largely for subsistence on the
trade which the French now controlled absolutely, but subsequent
events show that a number of the Ohio Indians—temporarily, at least
—accepted their new necessity with some enthusiasm. The targets
chosen for their raids were scenes of old grievances. In bowing to the
French yoke, the Ohio Indians paid off many an old score.

Braddock's beaten army, though it still greatly outnumbered the
French force at Fort Duquesne, retreated all the way to the coast,
leaving the backcountry wide open to the Indian raids. Colonists and
Indians alike observed that a fully equipped army, as good as any in
the empire, could be beaten by an opposing force less than half its
number and made up mostly of poorly armed "savages." What the
Indians had concluded from this observation was demonstrated in
flames and blood. The entire system of management of Indian affairs
lay in ruins. What the Albany Congress had suggested about provincial
blundering was now plainly proved. Individual tribes in isolation could
be mastered and directed by individual colonies, but tribes collected
and supported by a hostile empire could only be resisted by the resources of the Crown. In 1756 the Board of Trade began salvage
operations with a new commission to Sir William Johnson. It greatly
increased his authority and proceeded directly from the Crown. Johnson had already been elevated to the status of baronet; now he was
given large new titles: "Colonel of Our Faithfull Subjects, and Allies,
the Six united Nations of Indians, and their Confederates, in the
Northern Parts of North America" and "Our Sole Agent and Superin-
tendant of the said Indians and their Affairs."[29]

The royal pomp bore little relation to real circumstance. Johnson's was a commission of potentiality, rather like those of the Lords
Lieutenant of medieval Ireland whose writ ran as far as the castle walls
surrounding them. It was noticeably equivocal in declaring the Iro-

quois to be subjects *and* allies, and at that historical moment the Iroquois left much to be desired in either capacity. We have already seen Johnson's own recognition of them as a self-consciously "free" people, and in 1756 a large proportion of them were ostentatiously demonstrating their freedom by maintaining neutrality between the warring French and British. Their "confederates" at the Ohio had taken up the hatchet *against* the king's loving subjects in his colonies and were devastating the back settlements of Pennsylvania, Maryland, and Virginia.

The Crown's ministers understood as well as their new colonel that he was in no position to issue commands to his disorderly regiment. Board of Trade Secretary John Pownall disregarded the formal bombast of Johnson's commission when he sent notification of its issuance. Pownall wrote nothing about "subjects." He instructed Johnson that the "great end" of the appointment was to establish the Indians "steadily in our Interest" and to "engage them in the service." Johnson was to find means (unspecified) to "remove those difficulties and doubts in their minds which have hitherto operated as an obstruction to their heartily engaging with us, and have induced some to enter into engagement with the French." And he was to attend carefully to "redressing the grievances complained of by the Indians, with respect to the Lands which have been fraudulently taken from them."[30]

Since the statesmen understood so well the distinction between their legal pretenses and the actuality, it seems sensible for historians to take note of some of the implications of the situation. The Crown claimed sovereign jurisdiction over the Indians and their territories, but it admitted (privately) to de facto tribal independence and (publicly) to a "natural law" right of property of the Indians in their lands. The property right would be enforced by the Crown, even against British colonial subjects, as inducement for the Indians to formally accept British sovereignty. (It would have created considerable difficulty in Europe if the chiefs were to proclaim French sovereignty instead.) The form would be sufficient. The Indians would not be required to obey statute law of any British jurisdiction. They could continue to order their own customs and councils, and to negotiate their obedience to their "sovereign" by treaties with his representatives. The royal agent for persuading the Indians to accept this bargain would become their "superintendent." Johnson was expected to gain the homage of the tribes—the vassalage of their chiefs—and if he succeeded he would have the status and prerogatives of a great lord capable of mustering an armed host at his liege's summons. Johnson spent the rest of his life pursuing that goal.

Johnson's appointment signified more than an effort to manage Indian affairs with greater competence; it was the beginning of substantial change in the constitution of the empire. Previously the colonies had been under the Crown's protection and the Indians under the colonies' protection—or at their mercy. Johnson represented not only the Crown's assumption of administration over Indian affairs, but also the extension of the Crown's protection directly to the tribes. His instruction to redress the Indians' grievances was an exertion of the Crown's protection *against* the colonies, for the grievances in question had been created by colonial governments as well as private persons.[31]

With his new authority, Johnson championed the Mohawks against the shareholders in the Kayaderosseras grant (in New York), and finally, after many years, achieved a settlement acceptable to the Indians. Meanwhile, as the Mohawks' friend, he found a way through the maze of Pennsylvania's incredibly complex political struggles. Though it would be a mistake to credit him with the achievement of peace in Pennsylvania—which was accomplished primarily by tribal diplomacy, with an assist from the Quakers—Johnson cooperated through his deputy in the crucial treaties at Easton, Pennsylvania, in 1757 and 1758, when Delawares and Iroquois negotiated to restore the Covenant Chain. In the murk of intrigue at Easton, Johnson's goal was clear: all the tribes must once more become tributary to the Iroquois, the Iroquois would be responsible solely to him, and he would be responsible solely to the Crown. To attain this great goal, Johnson proposed a policy to stand on three legs: (1) an alliance cemented by trade with the Indians on fair terms; (2) redress of Indian complaints about land transactions; and (3) "by a solemn public Treaty to agree upon clear and fixed Boundaries between our Settlements and their Hunting Grounds, so that each Party may know their own and be a mutual Protection to each other of their respective Possessions."[32]

The complex and controverted history of the Easton Treaty of 1758 need not be recited here. Many clashing interests and personalities were involved. To whomever the credit may be due, the outcome of the treaty showed a distinct resemblance to Johnson's goal and Johnson's policy. The Covenant Chain was reestablished in the east, and an Iroquois delegation accompanied the Delaware emissary from the Ohio when he carried word of the treaty back to his people. The

Iroquois immediately assumed their former position of superiority. They told the Ohio council, "We desire you would lay hold of the covenant we have made with our brethren the English... We likewise take the tomahawk out of your hands...it is the white people's; let them use it among themselves." Delaware spokesman Beaver agreed, and expressed the renewal of his tribe's tributary status in conventional metaphor: "I have not made myself a king. My uncles [the Iroquois] have made me like a queen, that I always should mind what is good and right."[33]

The Delawares abandoned the French, the French abandoned Fort Duquesne, and the Ohio opened up to the British army that had until then been halted in its approach. Late in 1758 the war turned around for Great Britain where it had begun, at the forks of the Ohio. A few months later, in 1759, the reinvigorated Iroquois under Johnson's command captured Fort Niagara, the key to the Canadian west.

But the western Indians discovered that it was harder to get rid of the British than the French. On 4 December 1758, shortly after the fall of Fort Duquesne, the Delawares were summoned to a treaty on the site. Two substantially discrepant reports of the treaty survive: one was recorded by a French officer as the description carried to him by the Delaware chief, Custaloga; the other was dutifully sent to Britain as the official minutes of the occasion. Custaloga noted that the Indians (Delawares and Iroquois alike) had asked the English to withdraw from the smoking ruins. No such disturbance of harmony found its way into the English minutes, though it seems apparent from Colonel Henry Bouquet's speech to the Indians that he was responding defensively to Indian suggestions. "I return you hearty Thanks for the Speech you made," he remarked; but he did not record that speech. He went on, "We are not come here to take Possession of your hunting Country in a hostile Manner, as the French did when they came amongst you, but to open a large and extensive Trade with you and all the other Nations of Indians to the Westward who chuse to live in friendship with us." In these official minutes, the Delawares have become happy that 200 soldiers are to be left by the British "to support and defend the Traders."[34]

One of the Pittsburgh traders told a different tale six months later. Quaker James Kenny confided to his journal, "how that I have observ'd that the Indians are very Jealous of the English comeing here with an Army. They seem Jealous of thire Lands being settled...old [Delaware chief] Pisquitomen, the Beaver's Brother, and some others Came to our Houses and the Old Man put it Closely to me to tell what the English or the General Meant by Coming here with a Great Army."[35]

Discontent grew stronger among the Indians as British troops marched west to seize and garrison Detroit, and as Virginia (ignoring all promises to Indians) sent officials and settlers to occupy western lands. The Iroquois Six Nations split amongst themselves; though the Mohawks held to their alliance with Sir William Johnson, the Senecas circulated a war belt among the western tribes to solicit a general uprising against the British garrisons. The Ohio Delawares gradually developed a new political strategy for achieving total independence. As against the British, they adopted a new nativist religion that required boys to hunt with bow and arrow and abstain from the use of firearms.[36] After seven years of such training, the Delawares calculated, it would be possible for them to do without European trade and thus to maintain their political positions without suffering corrosion from economic and technological dependence. As against their Iroquois "uncles," the Delawares cemented friendship alliances in a confederation of western tribes strong enough to resist Iroquois pretensions to dominate. Johnson and his deputy, George Croghan, kept well informed of the unrest. They rushed about from one council fire to another, showing favor where friendship seemed strongest, and menacing those elsewhere.[37]

All came to crisis in 1763 when France ceded all of Canada's territorial claims to Great Britain in the treaty that ended the two empires' long war. The news that the the trans-Appalachian west had been ceded stunned the Indians. In their view, as reported by Croghan, "the French had no Right to give away their Country; as, they Say, they were never Conquered by any Nation."[38] To make things worse, the British commander-in-chief General Jeffrey Amherst decided to discipline the tribes by withholding from them the trade in arms and ammunition which was still essential to their way of making a living.[39]

The tribes rose in May 1763 in the liberation war for independence, miscalled Pontiac's Conspiracy. It acquired the name because Ottawa chief Pontiac launched the first attack, against Fort Detroit, but Pontiac was a minor figure in the tribal diplomacy that brought the war into being. The Senecas and Delawares had been circulating war belts among the tribes for about two years before combat began, and the French traders of the backcountry obviously played a conspiratorial role. When news of Pontiac's initiative reached the Delawares, they were ready to act upon the grievances they had been voicing for five years; they immediately laid siege to Fort Pitt.[40]

The rising failed. Although the Indians won minor successes, both major forts held out until the sieges were lifted. Secret advance intelligence enabled Fort Detroit's commander to thwart Pontiac's intended surprise. At Fort Pitt, under orders from General Amherst, the fort commander parleyed with the besieging Indian chiefs and presented them with blankets from the smallpox hospital. The epidemic that subsequently raged among the warriors made easier the task of Colonel Henry Bouquet when he marched to the fort's relief.[41]

Though the Indians had not won, they had not fully lost. They sued for peace because they could not overwhelm the British, and because they wanted to forestall punitive destruction of their villages. Under strong urging from Sir William Johnson, the British came to terms because they could not overwhelm the Indians. Though they could burn villages and inflict suffering, experience had long shown (and would again) that such measures were not necessarily sufficient to destroy the Indians' will to continue fighting guerrilla war. In short, the peace that followed the liberation war named for Pontiac reflected a military stalemate.[42] Nevertheless, it left the British with the strategic advantage: their forts and garrisons remained to become a permanent occupation establishment. The price for that advantage was financially and politically extravagant. For an empire already burdened with the unprecedented debt acquired during the recently completed Seven Years War, the cost of the western garrisons was an intolerable extra load. Politically, the military establishment would ultimately aggrieve the empire's colonists as much as the Indians.

Naturally, the empire ministers could not foresee all the future consequences of the western occupation, but they understood budgets, and they recognized that the Indians, though subdued, were not submissive. Naturally, also, the ministers resorted to political action to reduce the necessity for maintaining military action; but the harder they worked to mollify the tribes, the more they exacerbated quarrels with their colonies. The Indians were wooed with the Royal Proclamation of 1763, with which the Crown offered them a bargain that advanced the Crown's interests by sacrificing what the colonists regarded as their own interests. A frontier line of separation was decreed, and the territory west of it was declared an Indian sanctuary in which no more colonial settlements would be permitted. Thus, if the Indians would accept a few widely scattered garrisons, the Crown would preserve them from the tide of civilians. The only civil jurisdictions allowed to operate validly beyond the Proclamation Line were those of British appointed Indian superintendents.[43]

The Board of Trade was not satisfied, however, with merely letting the Indians go their own way. To integrate the tribes into the political fabric of the empire, the board proposed a "Plan for the future management of Indian affairs" that provided for extensive administrative machinery for governing the west and enforcing the Proclamation Line. What the board intended was to convert the tribes themselves into "colonies," in one of the senses of that unfortunately ambiguous word—that is, to make the tribes into native "dependencies" linked directly to the Crown instead of being responsible to the intermediate jurisdictions of the Crown's Euramerican provinces. Indeed the provisions of the Board of Trade's plan suggest strongly that the board envisioned a process through which the Indian governments would gradually be transformed from tribes to state-form provinces, through an intermediate feudal form. Superintendents William Johnson and John Stuart, in their respective Northern and Southern districts of the Indian territory, would preside over the transition as lords of the west and protectors of its people.[44]

Apparently, because the process would entail great expense, and further expense was precisely what the Crown was trying to avoid, the board's plan was shelved.[45] Though the Proclamation Line and the superintendents' offices continued in force, it would seem that nobody but the Indians believed that the line could be anything but a temporary measure. Neither the great land speculators nor the penniless squatters got very excited about the line, partly perhaps because the superintendents were so accommodating. The speculators made certain arrangements to the benefit of the superintendents, and the superintendents surveyed the line with gratifyingly large bulges at spots where the speculators had plans for imminent development. Lobbyists besieged ministers in London and made them partners in great schemes for new inland colonies that would, among other things, preclude the possibility of tribal territory evolving into native provinces. Squatters continued to squat beyond the line, and the protesting Indians were merely advised not to disturb the peace so that all could be made well eventually.[46]

If the Indians had just agreed to roll over and play dead, no doubt the Crown and colonies would have worked out an arrangement convenient for all, but the tribes expressed their discontent in word and deed. Because of the Crown's vacillating approach to a political solution of the problem of western stability, the military solution had to be maintained—and paid for. The payment was what finally tore the empire apart. It seemed reasonable to His Majesty's ministers that the colonists should bear some part of the charge for their own defense. It seemed reasonable to the colonists that, since the lands beyond the line had been proclaimed to be outside colonial jurisdictions, the policing of such Crown lands should be wholly at the Crown's expense. Two such conflicting assumptions might have produced an eternal wrangle if submitted to the judgment of the courts, but the Crown's ministers submitted the issue to Parliament instead, and Parliament chose to command rather than negotiate. In 1765 Parliament enacted the Stamp Tax.[47] The colonists challenged Parliament's right to tax them, on the grounds that their own legislatures held that right exclusively, and to underscore their point they rioted a bit. Parliament avoided immediate confrontation by rescinding the Stamp Tax, but in 1767 it declared its own supremacy in principle over any and all legislatures subject to the Crown of England. The colonists correctly perceived this declaration as a restructuring of sovereignty that threatened their liberties and interests, and rioted some more. In a comparatively short time, the Crown concluded that the violence of the eastern colonies was more dangerous than the violence of the western tribes, and the troops whose cost had precipitated the crisis were gradually moved east to restore authority where the need was greater. As the troops continued to require upkeep, Parliament enacted more taxes. Then, indeed, the colonists' grievances became indisputably genuine. Taxes that once had been levied ostensibly to protect them from the French and Indians had become quite plainly taxes levied to suppress their civil liberties.[48]

Meantime, the land speculators had discovered that the Proclamation Line could be bent but not broken. The Virginians of the Ohio Company especially were frustrated. By virtue of its ancient sea-to-sea charter, Virginia claimed jurisdiction over an immense western domain which included, to begin with, the Ohio country; but the Crown viewed Virginia as a royal province subject to the royal pleasure in such matters as boundaries. Ministers seriously considered establishing alternative new colonial jurisdictions where Virginia made its claims, and they disregarded the Ohio Company's grant as legally lapsed. Some of the richest and most important Virginians saw their future in the west, and they would not be denied it. Their anger and determina-

tion mounted simultaneously with the general colonial resentment
against Parliament's taxes and the Crown's measures of repression.[49]

Virginia's way out of the impasse was Lord Dunmore's War. After
the evacuation of Fort Pitt by the royal garrison in 1772, a band of
Virginia militiamen occupied the fort and used it as a base from which
to terrorize the Ohio Indians. In 1774 Virginia's Governor Dunmore
climaxed the process by fomenting a war with the Shawnees to force
them to cede land rights to Virginia, apparently hoping thereby to
compel the Crown to recognize a *fait accompli.* Had he succeeded,
Virginia would have acquired permanent possession of the whole Ohio
region. Dunmore did not succeed in his ultimate objective, though by
creating an either-them-or-us situation, he forced the cooperation of
the Indian superintendents in his war.[50] The quality of that war, and
the effect it created among the Indians, is illustrated by what happened
to Cayuga chief James Logan. Logan, like his father, the celebrated
Shickellamy, had been a strong adherent of the British all his life; but
without any provocation Virginia's frontier ruffians massacred his entire family. Logan stopped being an adherent of the British. He took
thirty scalps in revenge, according to tradition, before he succumbed
to depression and drink. His lament has become classic: "I appeal to
any white man to say if ever he entered Logan's cabin hungry and he
gave him not meat; if ever he came cold and naked, and he clothed him
not.... [But now] there runs not a drop of my blood in the veins of any
living creature.... Who is there to mourn for Logan?—Not one!"[51]

The news of these doings aroused strong feeling in Iroquoia
where angry Iroquois chiefs confronted Sir William Johnson to demand that the frontiersmen be brought under control. They attributed
their own anger to their young men, in a diplomatic device to permit
the continuation of speaking terms with Johnson, but their intent was
clear. The young men, they said, were "much affected and exasperated
at the cruel murders" committed by the "lawless people" of the British
colonies. It was a strange complaint to come from a "savage" people,
but it was not a slip of the tongue. The Iroquois questioned seriously
whether the British were capable of making responsible contracts and
living up to their terms. "Brother," they addressed Johnson,

> We are sorry to observe to you that your people are as ungovern-
> able, or rather more so, than ours. You must remember that it
> was most solemnly, and publicly settled, and agreed at the Gen-
> eral Congress held at Fort Stanwix in 1768 on behalf of the great
> King of England our Father, and the Governors, and Commis-

sioners of the several Provinces then assembled there, that the Line then pointed out and fixed between the Whites and Indians should forever after be looked upon as a barrier between us, and that the White People were not to go beyond it. —It seems, Brother, that your People entirely disregard, and despise the settlement agreed upon by their Superiors and us; for we find that they, notwithstanding that settlement, are come in vast numbers to the Ohio, and gave our people to understand that they wou'd settle wherever they pleas'd. If this is the case we must look upon every engagement you made with us as void and of no effect.[52]

Having made their point, the Iroquois pleaded for a peaceable solution:

. . . but we hope it is not so, and that you will restrain your people over whom you say you have authority, and make them lay aside their ill designs, and encroachments, . . . and we must beg that if your people insist upon settling so near ours, they may be made subject to some authority that can keep them in order."[53]

By a curious coincidence, the same thought was in the minds of the members of Parliament. To make the rebels of Massachusetts Bay subject to some authority, Parliament, in 1774, enacted four Coercive Acts. Then Parliament added an act for the government of Quebec which, by extending Quebec's boundaries to the Ohio River, nullified the land seizures made by Virginia in Lord Dunmore's War. For various reasons, the colonists promptly identified the Quebec Act with the Coercive Acts and called them all "Intolerable."[54] Although the initial outcry against the Quebec Act stressed the horrors of "Papacy," because it permitted Canada's Catholics to worship without disturbance, something more than toleration made it intolerable. A Jesuit scholar has noted that when the First Continental Congress appointed a committee to draw up an address of protest to the king, "the cancelling of the political arrangements effected by the Quebec Bill was included among the conditions essential to a restoration of commerce and good will; of the religious arrangements there was no mention whatever."[55]

The issue was land. The territorial pretensions of the colonies with sea-to-sea charters extending through the Ohio country—Virginia, Connecticut, and Massachusetts—were now nullified by an act of Parliament which, unlike the merely administrative Royal Proclamation of 1763, could only be reversed by another, most improbable, act of Parliament.[56] To obtain and develop a new tract of territory, a company speculating in land above the north bank of the Ohio River would have multiple barriers to hurdle—the Crown's, the superintendent's, the Indians', and that of the almost inaccessible governor of Quebec. Remote geographically, the governor ruled with the support of a permanent garrison under his direct command, and was unhampered by the pressures of a representative assembly.

Colonial reaction to the Quebec Act was swift and strong, but not as unanimous or evenly distributed as appears in formal documents. In the first Continental Congress, which met in the fall of 1774, a seemingly improbable combination of Virginia and Massachusetts delegates demanded the inclusion of the Quebec Act in the list of grievances necessitating a boycott of British trade. New York's delegates at first opposed such inclusion, but were overruled. Their defeat has been dryly and illuminatingly described by a nineteenth-century biographer of New York's James Duane:

> Among the subjects of debate before this committee was the question whether the Quebec bill should be reported as a grievance, and Mr. Duane was against including it in the report, but Mr. Lee, from Virginia, on territorial considerations, the eastern [New England] members, under pretence of religious uses, and others, because it would be popular to insert it both in England and America, having united, formed a great majority against him and he acquiesced in its being reported unanimously.[57]

The full Congress then resolved unanimously "that these his majesty's colonies were . . . entitled to all the immunities and privileges granted and confirmed to them by royal charters," among which privileges (though not literally detailed by the Congress) were the rights to extend jurisdiction and patent real property within their chartered bounds.[58]

After the battles of Lexington and Concord, the Second Continental Congress made an address to "the oppressed inhabitants of Canada," in which the Congress "perceived the fate of the protestant and catholic colonies to be strongly linked together"—so much for the popish menace—and appealed to the Canadians to overthrow the yoke of their "present form of tyranny." A few months later, the Congress's armies invaded Quebec to confer the boon of liberty upon those poor, deserving Catholics. Had the enterprise succeeded, the Ohio country would certainly have been liberated back into the jurisdictions of the invaders; but Quebec held out, a British fleet arrived with thousands of reinforcements, and the invaders fell back to the enforced protection of their own liberties in their own lands.[59] (There may be significance in the fact that not until then did Congress declare independence.)

In the war that followed, Indians were drawn in by active recruiting on both sides, in spite of their strongly expressed desires to stay neutral; and it should not be forgotten that their peaceful inclinations were overcome, in some part, by the machinations of Protestant missionaries.[60] At first divided and vacillating, the bulk of the Indians were eventually driven by events to fight for their "ancient protector and friend" the king of England.

It is not neccessary to follow the military history of the Indians in the American war for independence. Iroquois and Delaware warriors fought fiercely and with considerable success until Great Britain was defeated. Then came the diplomats and lawyers to the treaty tables, and Britain ceded sovereignty to the United States of all the territory west from the Atlantic Coast to the Mississippi River. The rationale was that Great Britain had acquired sovereignty from France, which had claimed it in the first instance because the French King was Christian and his subjects had "discovered" the place. Neither France nor Great Britain had discovered North America before the people who greeted the European "discoverers" at the Atlantic shores, and neither European power had ever succeeded in imposing rule on the native inhabitants of that vast area between the mountains and the Mississippi. Neither had been able to dissolve the tribes or to enact and enforce laws regulating the conduct of individual Indian persons in their own country. Neither had been able to do more than station tiny islands of garrisons in order to preserve a presence through trade and treaty. But the game called international law is played with legal fictions, and at Paris in 1783 Britain passed the card called sovereignty to the United States. The British ambassadors did not even try to get some consideration for the property of their Indian allies, as they did for property of loyalists of European descent. Except for refuge permitted in Canada, the tribes and all they possessed were abandoned.[61]

The governments of the united states were not themselves very sure about what sovereignty meant for them, besides relief from Britain. Though confederated for mutual support, each state claimed sovereignty for itself, and Virginia maintained its claims to the west as part of itself. Virginia had offered Congress a conditional cession of its claims in 1781, but the conditions forestalled acceptance. After the peace with Great Britain in 1783, Congress failed to seek treaties with the Indian tribes, and the reason seems to have been indecision as to whether Congress or Virginia held jurisdiction. While the bargaining continued over the terms for Congress's acceptance of Virginia's cession offer, Pennsylvania forced the issue. Pennsylvania wanted no more trouble with Indians at Pittsburgh, and was equally intent on having no more trouble there with Virginians. The simplest means to acquire undisputed authority in the trouble spot was to follow the ancient practice of the Colony's founder, William Penn—to recognize the Indian property right and negotiate a purchase on terms satisfactory to the Indians; then, with possession of the Indian right backing up Pennsylvania's own charter right, Pennsylvania would be one up on Virginia. But, unless Congress first made formal peace with the Indians, Pennsylvania would have to make its own peace with tribes who would then remain in a state of enmity with the other states. What, then, would be left of Congress's supposed monopoly of the conduct of Indian affairs?

On 12 September 1783, Pennsylvania did Congress the courtesy of requesting approval of its intended Indian purchase. Congress stalled, being still enmeshed in its difficulties with Virginia; so Pennsylvania decided to proceed with its treaty and purchase the property regardless of Congress's approval. Congress faced the ridiculous possibility of losing any role in Indian affairs, for the other states would not have been slow in following Pennsylvania's precedent. At the point of crisis, Congress capitulated to Virginia's demands for concessions in order to avoid the total loss of its own authority in the west. On 23 February 1784, Pennsylvania appointed its commissioners to treat with the Indians. On 1 March 1784, Congress accepted Virginia's cession and the national domain came into being.[62] On 4 March 1784, Congress appointed its own commissioners to treat with the Indians, and they assumed political control of the subsequent treaty conference. Speaking for the United States, they made the peace, allotting time to the Pennsylvanians only for the specific purpose of purchasing property within what were now Pennsylvania's unchallenged bounds.[63]

The irony of this first American treaty with the tribes—the Treaty of Fort Stanwix of 1784—was that Pennsylvania's subordinate land purchase was accepted by the Indians as valid, and it lasted, but the general peace with the United States was regarded as invalid, and did not last. The distinction is clear. The validity of the purchase resulted from a fair and acceptable bargain, while the invalidity of the peace was a direct function of its being the product of duress. The commissioners of the United States were accompanied by a body of troops. The commissioners dictated the treaty terms as an ultimatum, and seized hostages to enforce compliance. Looking down the gun barrels, the Indians signed where told; but a treaty made under duress was no more valid in Indian custom than a contract made under duress was valid in American law. The western Indians, far out of range of the guns at Fort Stanwix, simply ignored the treaty dictated there.[64]

The theory of the United States commissioners was that the victory over Great Britain had been simultaneously a conquest of the Indians, and that it made the Indians' lands forfeit to their conquerors. The commissioners therefore *assigned* boundaries of lands reserved for the Indians at the pleasure of the United States government, instead of negotiating cessions of territory from the Indians on agreed terms of purchase. The trouble with this theory was that the Indians did not agree that they had been conquered, and they subsequently defeated two United States expeditionary forces to demonstrate their point— Harmar's Humiliation, 1790, and St. Clair's Shame, 1791.[65]

Fighting continued until General Anthony Wayne defeated the Indians' western confederation at the Battle of Fallen Timbers in 1794. It is always called a "decisive" battle, but Wayne was too intelligent to regard it as conquest. In August 1795 he *negotiated* the Treaty of Greenville as an agreement between peers. In return for specific "cessions and relinquishments of lands" made by the Indian tribes, and "as the great means of rendering this peace strong and perpetual," Wayne agreed that the United States would relinquish claims "to all other Indian lands, northward of the river Ohio, eastward of the Mississippi, and westward and southward of the Great Lakes, and the waters uniting them, according to the boundary line agreed on by the United States and the King of Great Britain."

The meaning of the agreement was spelled out precisely and unambiguously: "The Indian tribes who have a right to those lands, are quietly to enjoy them, hunting, planting, and dwelling thereon, so long as they please, without any molestation from the United States; but when those tribes, or any of them, shall be disposed to sell their lands, or any part of them, they are to be sold only to the United States; and until such sale, the United States will protect all the said Indian tribes in the quiet enjoyment of their lands, against all citizens of the United States, and against all other white persons who intrude upon the same. And the said Indian tribes again acknowledge themselves to be under

the protection of the said United States, and no other Power whatever."

The consequence of this treaty for the United States was peace in
the Northwest Territory, a new flood of immigration into the territory,
and the creation of the State of Ohio in 1803. The consequence for
the Indians was the firm establishment of the practice by the United
States of dealing with the Indian tribes as "nations," a practice continued until 1871. That the treaties so made were often fraudulent and
always violated is another matter.

Current theories of history do not fit well on data such as have
been recited above. Nationalist and racist doctrines suppress the facts
of tribal government in myths about savagery. Theories of history
based on class conflict, whether of socialist or capitalist orientation, do
not provide for the hybrid relationships that occur when societies with
different systems of social organization adjust to each other on terms
other than quick assimilation of the one by the other. The romantic
theory of revolution, in which all the lowly unite to rise against their
oppressors, is embarrassed by the American Revolution's multiplicity
of variously oppressed and exploited peoples who preyed upon each
other; what most aggrieved the poor frontiersman was his sovereign's
ban on robbing the even poorer native, and the first target of the
Indian's hatchet was the frontiersman's skull. But realism must also
contemplate the disparity between upper class rhetoric and conduct.
The gentry cried out passionately for liberty in general, but itemized
it as rights for themselves to hold slaves and attack Indians.

Heedless of theories, Americans began the building of their empire with an inheritance of ethnocentric semantics that made logic
valid to themselves out of the strange proposition that invasion, conquest, and dispossession of other peoples support the principle that
all men are created equal.

1. An example is the Yankee-Pennamite "wars." See .Philip S. Klein and Ari Hoo-
genbaum, *A History of Pennsylvania* (New York: McGraw-Hill Book Co., 1973), p. 171.
    2. See Gustave Lanctot, *Canada and the American Revolution, 1774–1783,* trans.
Margaret M. Cameron (Cambridge: Harvard University Press, 1967).
    3. Howard H. Peckham, *Pontiac and the Indian Uprising* (1947; reprint ed., Chicago:
University of Chicago Press, Phoenix Books, 1961), p. 104.

4. See Julius Goebel, Jr., "The Matrix of Empire," introduction to Joseph Henry Smith, *Appeals to the Privy Council from the American Plantations* (New York: Columbia University Press, 1950), pp.xiii–lxi. By an act of 8 April 1702, the Privy Council recognized the American colonies as tenants in chief of the king, thereby confirming the language of the royal charters, all of which have the grantees "holding" as of one or other royal manor. The Privy Council's Act classed corporate Massachusetts and Connecticut (as well as other colonies) together with proprietary Pennsylvania and Maryland as not only "proprietors of the soil and Lands comprehended within the said places but also Lords and Governors thereof." MSS. in Public Record Office, Proprieties, Board of Trade, vol. 6, 1:16, printed facsmile in *Records in the British Public Record Office Relating to South Carolina*, 1701–1710 (Columbia, S.C.: Historical Commission of South Carolina, 1947), p. 72.

5. J. F. Lydon, *The Lordship of Ireland in the Middle Ages* (Toronto: University of Toronto Press, 1972), pp. 270–78.

6. I have discussed at length the cultural traits that justify classing Indians as peasants in *The Invasion of America; Indians, Colonialism, and the Cant of Conquest* (Chapel Hill: University of North Carolina Press, 1975), chap. 5.

7. See Richard W. Van Alstyne, *The Rising American Empire* (1960; reprint ed., New York: W. W. Norton and Co., The Norton Library, 1974), chap. 1, "The Conception of an American Empire."

8. See James H. O'Donnell, III, *Southern Indians in the American Revolution* (Knoxville: University of Tennessee Press, 1973).

9. Francis Jennings, "The Constitutional Evolution of the Covenant Chain," *Proceedings of the American Philosophical Society* 115 (1971): 88–96.

10. Gist's instructions and journals in *George Mercer Papers Relating to the Ohio Company of Virginia*, ed. Lois Mulkearn (Pittsburgh: University of Pittsburgh Press, 1954), pp. 1–39.

11. Nicholas B. Wainwright, *George Croghan: Wilderness Diplomat*, published for the Institute of Early American History and Culture (Chapel Hill: University of North Carolina Press, 1959), p. 30; Lawrence Henry Gipson, *The British Empire Before the American Revolution*, 15 vols. (New York: Alfred A. Knopf, 1939–1970), 4, chaps. 8, 9; R. Peters to T. Penn, Philadelphia [1750], MSS., Penn Papers, Official Correspondence, 6:107; Penn to Peters, London, 10 October 1754, MSS., Penn Letter Books, 4:4–11. MSS. in Historical Society of Pennsylvania, Philadelphia, Pa.

12. Georgiana C. Nammack, *Fraud, Politics, and the Dispossession of the Indians*, Civilization of the American Indian Series (Norman: University of Oklahoma Press, 1969), pp. 53–57.

13. Treaty minutes, 16 June 1753, in Edmund B. O'Callaghan and Berthold Fernow, eds., *Documents Relating to the Colonial History of the State of New York*, 15 vols. (Albany: Weed, Parsons and Co., 1856–1887), 6:788. Hereinafter abbreviated to *N.Y. Col. Docs.*

14. "Review of the Trade and Affairs of the Indians in the Northern District of America," [22 Sep 1767], in *N.Y. Col. Docs.*, 7:958.

15. Lords of Trade to the Earl of Holdernesse, 18 Sep 1753, in *N.Y. Col. Docs.*, 6:799; Lords of Trade to Lt. Gov. De Lancey, 5 July 1754, in ibid., 6:845–46.

16. Logan to W. Penn, 2 May 1702, in Edward Armstrong, ed., *Correspondence between William Penn and James Logan...*, 2 vols., Memoirs of the Historical Society of Pennsylvania, 9, 10 (Philadelphia: J. B. Lippincott and Co., 1870–1872), 1:88.

17. Lords of Trade to Sir Danvers Osborn, 18 September 1753, in *N.Y. Col. Docs.*, 6:855–56.

18. Congress minutes, 27 June 1754, in *N.Y. Col. Docs.*, 6:861.

19. Gipson, *British Empire*, 6, chap. 2. George Washington, *Diaries*, edited by John C. Fitzpatrick, 4 vols. (Boston: Houghton Mifflin Co., 1925), 1:102n.; Journal of Conrad Weiser, in *Minutes of the Provincial Council of Pennsylvania* [Colonial Records], ed. Samuel Hazard, 16 Vols. (Philadelphia and Harrisburg, 1838–1853), 6:151–52. The Iroquois "Half King" Tanacharisson complained that Washington "would by no means take Advice from the Indians; that he lay at one Place from one full Moon to the other and made no Fortifications at all, but that little thing upon the Meadow [Fort Necessity], where he thought the French would come up to him in open Field; that had he taken the Half King's advice and made such Fortifications as the Half King advised him to make

he would certainly have beat the French off."
    20. Wainwright, *George Croghan*, chap. 3.
    21. Peter Wraxall, "Some Thoughts Upon the British Interest in North America,"
9 January 1756, in *N.Y. Col. Docs.*, 7:20.
    22. C. A. Weslager, *The Delaware Indians: A History* (New Brunswick, N.J.: Rutgers
University Press, 1972), pp. 211–16; Paul A. W. Wallace, *Conrad Weiser, 1696–1760,
Friend of Colonist and Mohawk* (Philadelphia: University of Pennsylvania Press, 1945), pp.
361–63.
    23. P. Wallace, *Conrad Weiser*, p. 353; Gipson, *British Empire*, 5:121–22; Sir William
Johnson to the Lords of Trade, 10 September 1756, in Edmund B. O'Callaghan, ed.,
The Documentary History of the State of New York, 4 vols. (Albany: Weed, Parsons, and Co.,
1849–1851), 2:736–37.
    24. The Plan of Union, in *N.Y. Col. Docs.*, 6:889–91. In the world of Frederick
Jackson Turner's imagination the Albany Congress became evidence that "the unifying
tendencies of the Revolutionary period were facilitated by the previous cooperation in
the regulation of the frontier." Indeed the Albany Congress was Turner's only cited
evidence for that strange fantasy. In the world of fact, however, the Albany Congress
was evidence of the need for the Crown to take control of relations with the Indians
precisely because the squabbling colonies could not cooperate, and the Congress failed
of its intended purposes because neither the Indians nor the colonies tried to make it
work. F. J. Turner, *The Frontier in American History* (1920; reprint ed. New York: Holt,
Rinehart and Winston, 1962), p. 15; Gipson, *British Empire*, 5:347–48.
    25. Gipson, *British Empire*, 5, chap. 5.
    26. *N.Y. Col. Docs.*, 6:888, 890; Gipson, *British Empire*, 5:133–37, esp. n. 69 at p. 137.
    27. Commissions and instructions in James Sullivan et al., eds., *The Papers of Sir
William Johnson*, 14 vols. (Albany: University of the State of New York, 1921–1965),
1:465–75. It should be noted that the cited instructions concerning Indian lands were
not from Braddock. See also T. Pownall to W. Johnson, New York, 16 August 1755, in
ibid., pp. 854–55. (Hereinafter abbreviated as *Johnson Papers*.)
    28. Beverley W. Bond, Jr., ed., "The Captivity of Charles Stuart," *Mississippi Valley
Historical Review* 13 (1926): 63–64.
    29. Royal commission, 17 February 1756, in *Johnson Papers*, 2:434–35.
    30. J. Pownall to W. Johnson, Whitehall, 5 March 1756, in *N.Y. Col. Docs.*, 7:40–41.
    31. Report of the Lords of Trade, 1 June 1759, in O'Callaghan, ed., *Documentary
History of New York*, 2:775.
    32. W. Johnson to W. Denny, 21 July 1758 in *Johnson Papers*, 2:879.
    33. Francis Jennings, "A Vanishing Indian: Francis Parkman Versus His Sources,"
Pennsylvania Magazine of History and Biography 87 (1963): 306–23. Quotes at 322–23.
    34. S. K. Stevens et al., eds., *The Papers of Henry Bouquet* (Harrisburg: Pennsylvania
Historical and Museum Commission, 1951–), 2:621–26.
    35. James Kenny's Journal, MSS., entry of 24 July 1759: Historical Society of
Pennsylvania.
    36. Ibid., entries of 15 and 18 October 1762; Peckham, *Pontiac*, pp. 98–101.
    37. See Johnson's journal, 4 July–30 October 1761, in *Johnson Papers*, 13:215–74.
    38. Gipson, *British Empire*, 9:105.
    39. Peckham, *Pontiac*, pp. 71–73, 101.
    40. Ibid., pp. 106–11, 166.
    41. Ibid., p. 170; Amherst-Bouquet correspondence quoted in Francis Parkman,
The Conspiracy of Pontiac . . ., New Library ed., 2 vols. (Boston: Little, Brown & Co., 1909),
2:44–45. See also Bernhard Knollenberg, "General Amherst and Germ Warfare," *Mississippi Valley Historical Review* 41 (December 1954): 489–94; and the additional evidence
provided by Donald H. Kent, together with Knollenberg's retraction, in "Communications," ibid., 41 (March 1955): 762–63.
    42. Peckham, *Pontiac*, chaps. 19, 20, especially pp. 282–86; Thomas Elliott Norton,
The Fur Trade in Colonial New York, 1686–1776 (Madison: University of Wisconsin Press,
1974), pp. 211–12.
    43. Proclamation, 7 October 1763, in Adam Shortt and Arthur G. Doughty, eds.,
Documents Relating to the Constitutional History of Canada, 1759–1791, Canadian Archives
Sessional Paper No. 18, 6–7 Edward VII (Ottawa, 1907), pp. 119–23.

44. Ibid., pp. 433–37. There is much contemporary discussion of the Board of Trade plan in *Johnson Papers* and *N.Y. Col. Docs.* Consult indexes.

45. Norton, *Fur Trade*, pp. 212–13.

46. See Jack M. Sosin, *The Revolutionary Frontier, 1763–1783*, Histories of the American Frontier edited by Ray Allen Billington (New York: Holt, Rinehart and Winston, 1967), chaps. 3, 4; Louis De Vorsey, Jr., *The Indian Boundary in the Southern Colonies, 1763–1775* (Chapel Hill: University of North Carolina Press, 1966); Merrill Jensen, *The Founding of a Nation: A History of the American Revolution, 1763–1776* (New York: Oxford University Press, 1968), pp. 387–91.

47. Jack M. Sosin, *Whitehall and the Wilderness: The Middle West in British Colonial Policy, 1760–1775* (Lincoln: University of Nebraska Press, 1961), pp. 4–5. Sosin demonstrates that the Stamp Tax was levied to finance a continuing program rather than to defray the debt left by the Seven Years War.

48. Sosin, *Whitehall and the Wilderness*, pp. 79–80, 220; Jensen, *Founding of a Nation*, pp. 288–89.

49. Thomas Perkins Abernethy, *Western Lands and the American Revolution* (1937; reprint ed., New York: Russell and Russell, 1959), chap. 4; Jensen, *Founding of a Nation*, pp. 386, 391–92.

50. Jack M. Sosin, "The British Indian Department and Dunmore's War," *Virginia Magazine of History and Biography* 74 (1966): 34–50; Abernethy, *Western Lands*, chap. 6.

51. Variants of Logan's speech are given critically in Brantz Mayer, *Tah-Gah-Jute; or Logan and Cresap* (Albany: Joel Munsell, 1867), pp. 98–104, 120–23. Mayer wrote with heavily biased rhetoric as an apologist for the frontiersmen, but even he expressed shock and horror at what he acknowledged to be their "massacre" of the Indians. Sosin's "British Indian Department" (preceding note) puts Mayer's data in perspective. See also Randolph C. Downes, *Council Fires on the Upper Ohio: A Narrative of Indian Affairs in the Upper Ohio Valley until 1795* (Pittsburgh: University of Pittsburgh Press, 1940), chap. 7.

52. The Treaty of Fort Stanwix of 1768 made an adjustment in the boundary line set by the Royal Proclamation of 1763. It provided by solemn agreement that Euramericans would not cross the Ohio River from southeast to northwest. This was exactly what Dunmore's Virginians were doing.

53. Seneca chief Serihowane, treaty minutes, Johnson Hall, 9 July 1774, in *N.Y. Col. Docs.*, 8:476. Two days later, in the midst of the conference, Johnson died suddenly.

54. Sosin, *Whitehall and the Wilderness*, chap 10, esp. p. 240. The Quebec Act's text is in Shortt and Doughty, *Documents Relating to Canada*, pp. 401–5, together with early drafts and other documents discussing the ministers' considerations. Ibid., pp. 123–401.

55. Charles H. Metzger, S.J., *The Quebec Act: A Primary Cause of the American Revolution*, United States Catholic Historical Society Monograph Series, 16 (New York: U.S. Catholic Historical Society, 1936), pp. 149–50.

56. I differ here from Lawrence Henry Gipson who held that Parliament intended only a "tentative" boundary in the Quebec Act. Gipson cited the act's provision that it should not "in anywise affect the Boundaries of any other Colony." This was a clause intended to safeguard Pennsylvania and New York, with precedent in the administration of the Proclamation of 1763. The pretensions of the colonies with sea-to-sea charters had already been nullified by the Proclamation, so far as the British government was concerned, before the Quebec Act was passed. In debate, while the act was under consideration, Solicitor General Alexander Wedderburn advocated the enlargement of Quebec's boundary explicitly to command the seaboard colonies; "This is the border, beyond which, for the advantage of the whole empire, you shall not extend yourselves." The land speculators understood this; their outcry against Catholicism was a smoke screen, as their subsequent actions demonstrated. Gipson, *British Empire*, 13:163; Sosin, *Whitehall and the Wilderness*, p. 245; Abernethy, *Western Lands*, pp. 101, 104.

57. Samuel W. Jones, "Memoir of the Hon. James Duane," in *Doc. Hist. N.Y.*, ed. O'Callaghan, 4:1071.

58. Henry Steele Commager, ed., *Documents of American History*, 7th ed., 1 (New York: Appleton-Century-Crofts, 1963), p. 83.

59. Lanctot, *Canada and the American Revolution*, pp. 46–48, 126–28, 244–45, 255. In England, Dr. Samuel Johnson observed that, "After representing the Canadians as a nation of blood-thirsty bigots, highly dangerous to the freedom of the Protestant

province, we see the Congress flattering those bigots as they call them into rebellion."
Quoted in Metzger, *Quebec Act*, p. 159.

60. Barbara Graymont, *The Iroquois in the American Revolution* (Syracuse, N.Y.: Syracuse University Press, 1972), chaps. 2, 3. See also Downes, *Council Fires on the Upper Ohio*, pp. 181–82.

61. Sosin, *Revolutionary Frontier*, pp. 146–50; Graymont, *Iroquois in the Revolution*, pp. 260–62.

62. Donald H. Kent, *History of Pennsylvania Purchases from the Indians*, The Garland American Indian Ethnohistory Series: Iroquois Indians, 1 (New York: Garland Publishing Co., 1974), pp. 67–81; Merrill Jensen, *The New Nation: A History of the United States During the Confederation, 1781–1789* (New York: Alfred A Knopf, 1950), pp. 350–53.

63. Kent, *Pennsylvania Purchases*, pp. 83–114.

64. Anthony F. C. Wallace, *The Death and Rebirth of the Seneca* (New York: Alfred A. Knopf, 1970), pp. 151–52; Kent, *Pennsylvania Purchases*, pp. 72, 115, 124; Graymont, *Iroquois in the Revolution*, pp. 276–84; John Heckewelder, *History, Manners, and Customs of the Indian Nations Who Once Inhabited Pennsylvania and the Neighbouring States* (1819), rev. ed., ed. William C. Reichel, Memoirs of the Historical Society of Pennsylvania, 12 (Philadelphia, 1876): 57. Graymont notes (p. 283) that some Iroquois chiefs complained in 1890 about even the Pennsylvania purchase.

65. Both campaigns were sloppily conducted by commanders overwhelmingly aware of their own importance and contemptuous of the fighting ability of naked savages. General Josiah Harmar lost two battles at or near modern Fort Wayne, 18 and 22 October 1790. Northwest Territory Governor Arthur St. Clair was routed at modern Fort Recovery, 4 November 1791.

66. The process by which the Treaty of Greenville came into being was long and tortuous. Source materials trace it in Thomas C. Cochran, ed., *The New American State Papers: Indian Affairs*, 4 (Wilmington, Del.: Scholarly Resources, 1972), pp. 13–177; and some comment of importance is to be found in Wilcomb E. Washburn, *Red Man's Land / White Man's Law: A Study of the Past and Present Status of the American Indian* (New York: Charles Scribner's Sons, 1971), pp. 52–58. The treaty terms are in *State Papers*, 4:150–52, followed by the minutes of the treaty conference.

The Revolution in Black Life
Ira Berlin

The title page of the almanack issued by Benjamin Bannaker, a free black of Maryland, a self-taught mathematician and astronomer, born in 1731, the son of an African-born slave freed by his master. The almanack appeared in twenty-eight editions between 1792 and 1797. Maryland Historical Society.

Most historians of black life in the United States have concentrated their attention on a comparatively short period between 1830 and 1880—years of an extended debate over slavery, a bloody civil war, and a largely unsuccessful attempt to remold the racial structure of American society. Their work, especially during the last two decades, has greatly enlarged our understanding of the complex nature of slave life, the wrenching transit of a people from slavery to freedom, and the limits of black liberty before and after 1863. Still, the disproportionate attention given these few years has badly misshapened knowledge of black life and blinded scholars to the origins of Afro-American culture and its complex chronology. More recently, the search for the roots of black life has sent historians back to the seventeenth and eighteenth centuries, first to investigate the transformation of a free people into slaves—the question of status—and then to study the transformation of Africans into Afro-Americans—the question of culture.

This essay evinces an interest in black culture and status at a time when both changed rapidly. My understanding of the importance of the revolutionary years grew out of a study of southern free blacks, *Slaves Without Masters: The Free Negro in the Antebellum South* (New York: Pantheon Books, 1974). Originally, I had projected that work to begin in 1790, the starting point for earlier studies of free black life. But the cataclysmic changes in the structure of free black society in the late eighteenth century made no sense from that vantage point. Unwittingly, I had barged into the middle of a society undergoing a profound transformation. Only by backtracking to the beginning of the revolutionary period could the nature and magnitude of the changes underway in the 1790s be fully comprehended.

In writing this essay, I have drawn upon my ongoing research into slave and northern free black life during the last third of the eighteenth century as well as my published studies of southern freemen. Eventually, they will be brought together as part of a larger study of Afro-American society—free and slave, North and South—during the revolutionary era.

Ira Berlin (Ph.D., University of Wisconsin, 1970) won the Distinguished Teaching Award at the University of Wisconsin and a Younger Humanist Fellowship from the National Endowment for the Humanities. He teaches at the University of Maryland and is presently a fellow at the Shelby Collum Davis Center for Historical Studies at Princeton University.

The years between 1770 and 1810 were a formative period for Afro-American culture. The confluence of three events—freedom for large numbers of blacks with the abolition of slavery in the North and large-scale manumission in parts of the South; the maturation of a native-born Afro-American population after more than a century of American captivity; and a new, if short-lived, flexibility in white racial attitudes—made these years the pivot point in the development of black life in the United States. The social patterns and institutions established during the revolutionary era simultaneously confirmed the cultural transformation of the preceding century and shaped black life well into the twentieth century. In many ways, the revolutionary era, far more than the much studied Reconstruction period, laid the foundation for modern Afro-American life.

The events and ideas of the revolutionary years radically altered the structure of black society and the substance of Afro-American culture. The number of blacks enjoying freedom swelled under the pressure of revolutionary change, from a few thousand in the 1760s to almost two-hundred thousand by the end of the first decade of the nineteenth century. Freedom, even within the limited bounds of white domination, enhanced black opportunities by creating new needs and allowing blacks a chance to draw on the rapidly maturing Afro-American culture to fulfill them. But the revolution in black life was not confined to those legally free. The forces unleashed by the American Revolution soon reached beyond the bounds of free black society and deeply influenced the course of slave life in the critical years before the great migration to the Lower South. Most importantly, the revolution in black life created new and enlarged older regional distinctions between the black populations, free and slave, of the North, the Upper

South, and the Lower South. In each of these regions, differences in the size, character, and dynamics of development of the free and slave black populations bred distinctive patterns of relations with whites and among blacks, shaping the development of black life and American race relations during the nineteenth century and beyond.

I

The growth of the free Negro population was one of the most far reaching events of the revolutionary era. Before the Revolution only a tiny fraction of the black population enjoyed liberty in English mainland North America. A 1755 Maryland census, one of the few enumerations of colonial freemen, counted slightly more than 1,800 free Negroes, who composed about 4 percent of the colony's black population and less than 2 percent of its free population. Moreover, over 80 percent of these freemen were of mixed racial origin, and more than one-fifth were cripples or old folk deemed "past labour." Few full-blooded Africans found their way to freedom. Maryland's tiny free Negro population was composed almost entirely of the descendants of mixed racial unions—freed after a term of service if their mothers were white, or perhaps liberated by their white fathers—and bondsmen who, through age or circumstance, had become liabilities to their masters. Although colonial freemen demand further study, it appears that Maryland's free Negroes typified those found throughout the mainland English colonies. In 1805, Virginians recalled that "less than thirty years ago, the number of free negroes was so small that they were seldom to be met with." Some years later, William Gaston, the chief justice of North Carolina, investigated the subject and found "that previous to the Revolution there were scarely any emancipated Slaves in this State; and that the few free men of color that were here at that time, were chiefly Mulattoes, the children of white women." Unsure of his judgment, Gaston queried "some aged persons"; they too confirmed that before the 1770s "scarcely an instance could be found at that time, either in Virginia or this State of an emancipated Slave."[1]

Although few in number and much like whites in appearance, free Negroes raised white fears of subversion. During the colonial years, lawmakers steadily gnawed at the freemen's liberty, taxing them with numerous proscriptions on their civil, political, and social rights.[2] On the eve of the Revolution, few whites, even those who opposed slavery, showed any inclination to increase the number of Negro freemen. But the events of the revolutionary years moved in unpredictable and uncontrollable ways. As the war dragged on, military necessity forced the British and then, more reluctantly, Americans to muster black slaves into their armies by offering them freedom in exchange for their services.

The British, who had no direct interest in slavery, first offered the exchange. In November 1775, Lord Dunmore, the royal governor of Virginia, declared martial law and freed all slaves that were able and willing to bear arms in His Majesty's service. Even though this declaration shook colonial Virginians, it came as no surprise. Dunmore and other British officials had been threatening such action for several months. Slaves, ever alive to the possibilities of liberty, quickly picked up these first rumblings of freedom. Some months earlier, a group of blacks had visited Dunmore and offered to join him and take up arms. At that time, Dunmore brusquely dismissed them. But the blacks would not be put off, and when Dunmore officially tendered the promise of liberty, they flocked to British headquarters in Norfolk harbor.

Defeat deflated Dunmore's promise of liberty. In December, about a month after his proclamation, patriot troops routed Loyalist forces, including a large number of blacks wearing sashes emblazoned with the words "Liberty to Slaves." The loss broke the back of Dunmore's attempt to discipline rebellious Virginians, and thereafter the colonials limited him to foraging raids from his seaborne headquarters. Despite military defeat and patriot propaganda that he would sell his black followers to the West Indies, Dunmore's promise stirred slaves throughout the Chesapeake region. Whenever his flotilla neared the coast, slaves, as one dejected master put it, began "flying to Dunmore." Slaveholders became so desperate to stop their flight that they addressed an article directly to their slaves in the *Virginia Gazette,* in which they alternately denied complicity in the slave trade, threatened death to runaways, and enjoined slaves to "be content with their situation, and expect a better condition in the next world."

Dunmore used his black recruits to raid the Virginia coast; and in August 1776, when he retreated to Bermuda, 300 blacks sailed north for future military service and freedom. All told, perhaps 800 slaves escaped to join Dunmore, and more important, hundreds more heard of his promise of freedom and were infected with the dream of liberty.[3]

The manpower shortage that forced Dunmore to use black troops worsened as the war dragged on. British commanders, despite popular opposition in England, increasingly followed Dunmore's lead and recruited slaves. When the war turned south in 1778, thousands of blacks flocked to the British standard. General Henry Clinton, the British commander-in-chief, officially promised liberty to all slaves who deserted their masters for British service. In the years that followed, British reliance on black manpower increased, and the proponents of utilizing black military might on a massive scale grew ever more vocal. Dunmore, now in Charleston, South Carolina, urged the formation of a black army of ten thousand men to end the rebellion swiftly, and other British officers dickered over the creation of a southeastern sanctuary for black Loyalists. No attempt was made to implement these proposals or even give them a full hearing, but their continued presence during the last years of the war suggests the mode of warfare that the British might have adopted had they continued to prosecute the rebellion.[4]

Colonial commanders and policymakers were considerably more chary about accepting slave recruits. Many were large slaveholders who had much to lose from any disruption of slavery. Most feared that a servile revolt or a mass defection of slaveholders would follow the arming of blacks. Although blacks had occasionally served in colonial militias and distinguished themselves in the first battles of the Revolution, the Continental Congress, at South Carolina's instigation, barred them from the Continental army. But patriots proved no more immune to the exigencies of war than the British. As the struggle for independence lengthened and manpower grew critically short, the patriot policy shifted. The northern states, led by New England, began to solicit black recruits, and Rhode Island created a black regiment. When the war moved south, Upper South states grudgingly adopted a similar course of action, in spite of their larger black populations and greater dependence on slave labor. Maryland authorized slave enlistments and eventually subjected free Negroes to the draft. Virginia allowed black freemen to serve in its army and navy, and Delaware and North Carolina, following Virginia, occasionally permitted slaves to stand as substitutes for their masters. In the Lower South, however, white resistance to arming blacks stiffened. The numerical superiority of blacks in the lowland rice swamps, the large numbers of newly arrived African slaves, and the commonplace absenteeism bred an overpowering fear of slave rebellion. Despite the pleas of the Continental Congress and the urgings of commanders in the field, South Carolina and Georgia rejected the hesitant measures adopted in the Upper South. Yet, even in the Lower South, the pressures of the war produced at least one native son, John Laurens, who argued eloquently for a black soldiery as the only means of securing independence. The "howlings of a triple-headed monster, in which prejudice, avarice, and pusillanimity were united," easily defeated Laurens's proposal, but its presence suggests the potential transforming force of revolutionary warfare on slavery—even where it was most deeply entrenched.[5]

Almost everywhere, the war widened opportunities for blacks to gain their liberty. When the British left America at the end of the war, they carried thousands of blacks to freedom in Great Britain, the West Indies, Canada, and, eventually, Africa. Hundreds, perhaps thousands, of others that were freed by British wartime policy eluded their masters and remained in the United States. There is "reason to believe," petitioned angry white Virginians in 1781, "that a great number of slaves which were taken by the British Army are now passing in this Country as free men." Many blacks who fought with the patriots also secured their liberty. Some grateful masters freed their slaves, and occasionally state legislatures liberated individual bondsmen by special enactment. Most whites seemed to think this was right. The Virginia General Assembly drew back in horror at reports that slaveholders had reenslaved black military substitutes, and ordered their emancipation. In other states, a slave who served in his master's place had only a verbal promise of freedom. Some masters kept their word, others did not. Doubtless most bondsmen did not wait around long enough to find out.[6]

Whatever the effects of official British and American policy, the chaos created by rampaging armies did even more to expand a slave's chances for liberty. The actions of soldiers of both belligerents, and the often violent disputes between patriot and Tory militiamen, created near anarchic conditions, revealed the limits of slaveholder authority, and encouraged slaves to take their freedom. Runaways, previously few in number, increased rapidly in the confusion of the war. This was especially true in the Upper South, where the nature of agriculture had allowed second and third generation Afro-Americans to gain broad familiarity with the countryside.[7] At war's end, these fugitives also passed into the growing free black population.

II

The war did not last long enough to destroy slavery, but the libertarian ideology that patriots used to justify their rebellion continued to challenge it when the war ended. If all men were created equal, why were some men still slaves? Lockean ideology protected slavery, even as it commended universal liberty, and that duality allowed slaveowners to fashion a defense of chattel bondage out of America's first principles. But, in the context of the Revolution, the impetus to universal liberty could not be easily ignored. "How is it," asked Samuel Johnson, "that we hear the loudest *yelps* for liberty among the drivers of negroes?" Those stinging words, like similar indigenous charges of hypocrisy, made it impossible for Americans to escape the confrontation between their ideology and their reality. However narrow its bounds, and whatever its internal flaws and ambiguities, revolutionary equalitarianism forced large numbers of men and women to question slavery for the first time, thereby subverting slavery throughout the new republic. Some of these men and women freed their slaves, and others, taking the ideology of the Revolution to heart, demanded liberty for all and pushed for a general emancipation. Even more important, the persistent questioning of slavery allowed blacks and white emancipationists to push slavery on to the defensive. Plantation slavery expanded greatly during the postrevolutionary years, and there were many more enslaved blacks in 1800 than in 1776; but slavery was no longer a national institution, and its routine acceptance could no longer be taken for granted. By the beginning of the nineteenth century, chattel bondage had become the South's "peculiar institution."[8]

Slavery fell first in New England, where blacks were few in number and never an important part of the labor force or a threat to white dominance. In the Middle Atlantic states, where blacks were more numerous and bondage more deeply entrenched than in New England, slavery proved more resistant to revolutionary change. But an influx of white immigrant workers assured employers of an adequate supply of labor, and undermined the most persuasive argument against abolition. By 1804, every northern state had provided for eventual emancipation.[9]

Still, slavery died hard. In 1810, almost 30,000 blacks—almost a quarter of the region's black population—remained in chattel bondage. Although that number fell dramatically in succeeding decades, slavery continued. There were over 1,000 bondsmen in the "free" states in 1840. Moreover, in many of the new northern states, slave-holders and their allies tried to overthrow the antislavery provisions of the Northwest Ordinance and reinstate the peculiar institution. Failing that, they enacted various forms of long-term indentureships, which allowed chattel bondage to flourish covertly until the Civil War.[10] Nevertheless, slavery was doomed, and the mass of Northern black people had been freed.

South of Pennsylvania, emancipation faced still greater obstacles, and, in the long run, these difficulties proved insuperable. But the Christian equalitarianism unleashed by the evangelical revivals of the mid-eighteenth century complemented and strengthened the idealism of the Revolution in many parts of the South. Like revolutionary ideology, the religious awakenings transcended sectional boundaries. Methodists and Baptist evangelicals crisscrossed the southern states and, in hundreds of camp meetings, made thousands of converts. Propelled by the revolutionary idea that all men were equal in the sight of God, they frequently accepted black and white converts with equal enthusiasm. The equality of the communion table proved contagious, and some evangelicals broke the confines of other-worldly concerns to make the connection between spiritual and secular equality. Methodists, Baptists, and other evangelical sectarians joined with Quakers to become the mainstays of the southern antislavery movement. Like their northern counterparts, they organized antislavery societies, petitioned legislatures, and aided freedom suits.[11]

Economic changes in the Upper South, especially in Maryland, Delaware, and northern Virginia, offered emancipationists an opening wedge. Beginning in the 1760s, the increased worldwide demand for foodstuff encouraged planters to expand cereal production. Dislocations in mercantile ties, resulting from the war and the depression that accompanied independence, further speeded the shift from tobacco to cereal agriculture in many parts of the Chesapeake region. This change reduced the demand for slaves, since wheat culture on small units under the existing technology thrived on free labor. Many farmers found themselves burdened with a surplus of slaves. Moreover, the agricultural transformation and the resultant establishment of new methods of processing and development of new patterns of marketing quickened the pace of commerce, stimulated the growth of light industry, and swelled urban centers. Baltimore, Richmond, Fredericksburg, and Petersburg grew as never before. In all, changes in the agricultural landscape increased commercial activity, and nascent urbanization and industrialization profoundly altered the region. Many Americans believed that the Upper South would follow the pattern of development exemplified by Pennsylvania, and not the states farther south. As the price of slaves sagged under the weight of these changes, the future of slavery became an open question.[12]

The combined force of revolutionary and Christian equalitarianism pressed on slavery in the Upper South and allowed abolitionists to score impressive, if fleeting, gains. Legislatures and courts, under emancipationist pressure, liberalized manumission codes and relaxed strictures against freedom suits, greatly increasing the slave's opportunity for liberty. Emancipationist principles also profited from the drop in slave prices and the general insecurity of slave property. Although most slaveowners profitably sold their excess slaves to the South, masters burdened with surplus bondsmen were susceptible to abolitionist rhetoric. Throughout the region, the number of manumissions rose sharply. Moreover, since most manumitters were motivated by ideological and economic concerns, they tended to free their slaves relatively indiscriminately. Field hands as well as house servants, unskilled laborers as well as skilled artisans, and blacks as well as mulattoes passed from slavery to freedom.[13]

Economic changes in the Upper South affected the nature of slavery as well as its future. The seasonal demands of wheat farming, especially when compared to the year-long routine necessitated by tobacco cultivation, made it profitable for farmers to hire their slaves out to the growing industrial and commercial enterprises in the region.[14] Hiring out greatly enlarged the slaves' occupational opportunities and widened their knowledge of the world. Some slaves, encouraged by the self-esteem that accompanied their new skills, reached beyond their new status as artisans and saved enough money to buy their way out of bondage. Masters, sympathetic to the libertarian spirit of the age, but unwilling to free their slaves outright, encouraged self-purchase because it satisfied their conscience as well as their purse. But as slave artisans passed from job to job and town to town, their confidence grew and their tolerance for slavery waned. Many eschewed the onerous task of buying liberty. More than a few used their sanctioned time away from their masters' homesteads to make good their escape.[15]

The economic transformation of the Upper South supported freedom in other less direct ways. The growing number of tenant farmers and independent tradesmen in the region, often in need of an extra hand and rarely in a position to purchase slaves, frequently employed blacks, with few questions asked. The ability to find a safe haven, even for a few days, could make the difference between a successful flight and a return to bondage. The success of many fugitives, like relatively indiscriminate manumission, not only enlarged the free black population, but darkened it as well.[16] The larger, darker-skinned free Negro population camouflaged fugitives, increased their chances of success, and encouraged still other blacks to make their way from slavery to freedom. The increase in runaways begun during the tumult of the Revolution continued into the postwar years.

Slavery easily survived the increase of manumissions and runaways, recovered its balance, and in most places continued to grow. But the social changes of the revolutionary era profoundly altered the size and character of the free Negro population in the Upper South, and sent reverberations of liberty into the region's slave quarters.

The growth of the free Negro population can be most clearly viewed in Maryland. Between 1755 and 1790, the number of free Negroes in that state increased almost 350 percent, to about 8,000, and in the following decade it again more than doubled. By 1810, almost a quarter of Maryland's blacks were free, numbering nearly 34,000.[17] Although not immediately apparent, slavery in Maryland had been dealt a mortal blow.

Free Negroes registered similar gains throughout the Upper South. In 1782, the year Virginia legalized private manumissions, St. George Tucker estimated the number of freemen in his state at about 2,000.[18] By 1790, Virginia's free Negroes had increased to 12,000. Ten years later, Negro freemen numbered 20,000, and by 1810, the total

Free Negro Population, 1790–1810

	1790	1800	1810
United States	59,466	108,395	186,466
North	27,109	47,154	78,181
South	32,357	61,241	108,265
Upper South	30,158	56,855	94,085
Lower South	2,199	4,386	14,180

* Increase in the Lower South between 1800 and 1810 is largely due to the accession of Louisiana.

Source: *Population of the United States in 1860* (Washington, D.C., 1864), pp. 600–601.

stood at over 30,000. During the twenty years between 1790 and 1810, the free Negro population of Virginia more than doubled. In all, the number of Negro freemen in the Upper South grew almost 90 percent between 1790 and 1800, and another 65 percent in the following decade, so that freemen now composed more than 10 percent of the region's black population.

In 1810, the nearly 100,000 freemen were the fastest growing element in the Upper South's population. Although the number of whites and slaves also grew rapidly during the early years of the republic, the growth of the free Negro population outstripped both. In Virginia, for example, the number of free Negroes doubled between 1790 and 1810, while whites increased 24 percent, and slaves 31 percent. Maryland during the same period presented an even more startling comparison. Maryland's free Negroes increased fourfold, while the white population grew 12 percent, and the slave population a mere 8 percent. In Delaware, the expansion of freedom undermined slavery. In 1790 there were 4,000 free Negroes in Delaware, a smaller total than the state's slave population. Twenty years later, that state's 13,000 free Negroes outnumbered slaves more than three to one, and Delaware slavery was permanently impaired. Moreover, relatively indiscriminate manumission and the increase of successful fugitives added large numbers of blacks—as opposed to mulattoes—and young folk to the free Negro population. Free Negroes, whose thin ranks had previously been filled largely by mulattoes and a disproportionate number of cripples and old people, were now a considerably larger, darker, and more vigorous group.

The social forces that transformed black society in the North and in the Upper South met stern resistance in the Lower South. There, economic and demographic considerations countered the ideology of the Revolution and the great revivals. During the war, Lower South whites had rejected the pleas of the Continental Congress to arm slaves in the patriot cause. With independence, no antislavery societies appeared, and few masters freed their slaves. Instead, the increased demand for slaves caused by enormous wartime losses, the expansion of rice production in the low country, and the spread of cotton culture in the up-country hardened the Lower South's commitment to slavery. Under such circumstances, abolition, as one Savannah, Georgia, newspaper observed, was simply "not a prudent subject for discussion." Following the war, Lower South whites imported thousands of slaves from the states to the north and, in 1803, South Carolina reopened the slave trade with Africa.[19] Not until the 1790s, when the successful black revolution in Saint Domingue sent hundreds of light-skinned *gens de couleur* fleeing for American shores, did the number of free Negroes increase significantly in the Lower South.[20] Thus, unlike northern and Upper South freemen, Lower South free people of color remained a tiny mulatto fragment of the larger black population.

In transforming the structure of black society, the events of the revolutionary years created new, and enlarged older, regional distinctions between the black populations of the North, the Upper South, and the Lower South. By the end of the century, northern whites had committed themselves to emancipation, and the great majority of blacks enjoyed freedom. Upper South slavery, on the other hand, withstood the challenges of the revolutionary years, but its free black population expanded rapidly during the period, so that better than one black in ten was free by 1800. Slavery in the Lower South, although greatly disrupted by the war, never faced the direct emancipationist pressures present in the North or even the Upper South. It stood almost unchallenged throughout the postwar period, quickly recouped its wartime losses, and entered into a period of its greatest expansion. Lower South free people of color remained as they had been in the colonial era, a small appendage to a rapidly increasing slave population. While the northern and Upper South free Negro population grew darker in color with emancipation and relatively indiscriminate manumission, most Lower South freemen continued to display the somatic attributes of their mixed racial origins. An influx of West Indian coloreds following the Haitian Revolution reinforced the mulatto bias of the Lower South free Negro population, without significantly altering its share of the black population. These regional distinctions in the structure of both slave and free black societies reflected and influenced white racial attitudes and shaped the development of black life in the years to come.

III

It was not only the structure of black society that changed during the revolutionary era. By the eve of the American Revolution, black people had been living in English mainland North America for more than 150 years. After a century of American captivity, they were not the same people whom John Rolfe had watched march down the gang-

plank at Jamestown in 1619. The transplanted Africans were no longer
an alien people whose minds were befogged by the horrors of the
Middle Passage, whose tongues were muted by the strange language
of their enslavers, and whose senses were confused by the unfamiliar
landscape that everywhere surrounded them. By the 1770s, if not
earlier, the vast majority of blacks were native Americans with no
firsthand knowledge of Africa. Increasingly, secondhand accounts of
the "great land across the sea" were losing their meaning to new
generations of American-born blacks—just as the fading memories of
English life were losing their meaning for new generations of American-born whites. Beyond their master's eyes many tried to maintain the
ways of the old country, difficult though that was. But since adapting
to the conditions of the New World was literally a life and death matter,
most of them changed. Slowly, almost imperceptibly, transplanted
Africans became a new people. They spoke English, worked with English tools, and ate foods prepared in the English manner. On the eve
of the Revolution, many blacks had done so for two or three generations, and sometimes more.

But black acculturation was more than a leeching process whereby
an English culture, modified by New World conditions, replaced an
African one. To the emerging Anglo-American culture, transplanted
Africans added their own heritage, a way of thinking and acting that
had survived the Middle Passage. And this was not just a single African
heritage. A melange of African cultures, some compatible, some antagonistic, had been thrown together in the barracoons of Africa, and
continued to blend under the pressures of New World enslavement.
The African melting pot—unlike the European one—melted. The diverse heritage of Africa and the dominant Anglo-American culture, in
turn, were molded and shaped by the peculiar status and circumstances of black people to create a new cultural type: the Afro-American.[21] The maturation of Afro-American culture gave added force to
the transformation of black society during the revolutionary era,
deeply affecting those who slipped out of slavery as well as those who
remained locked in bondage.

Structural and cultural changes in black society profoundly influenced white attitudes and behavior. In the long run, they stiffened
white racism. With so many blacks in possession of freedom, whites
could no longer rely on their status alone to distinguish themselves
from a people they despised. They began to grope for new ways to
subordinate Negro freemen and set themselves apart from all blacks.
Thus as the free Negro population grew, whites curbed their mobility,

limited their economic opportunities, all but obliterated many of their political rights, and schemed to deport freemen from the country. Yet, the Revolution, with its emphasis on equality, forced whites to reconsider their racial values. This reconsideration produced a new flexibility in the racial attitudes of some whites and a brief recession in the color line. The liberalization of manumission codes, the passage of antikidnapping laws, the increased number of free Negroes, and the challenge to slavery all reflected small, but real, changes in white racial attitudes. These changes allowed blacks some room to maneuver in a society that was often hostile to their very being. Nevertheless, racism remained a potent force in revolutionary America.[22] The society and culture that emerged from this first attempt to remake black life in America represented an easing of white racial hostility within a system of continued racial oppression.

IV

The cumulative impact of freedom, cultural maturation, and the new flexibility in white attitudes unleashed the creative energies of black people. Newly freed blacks moved at once to give meaning to their freshly won liberty and form to the cultural transformation of black life in America. They took new names, established new residential and occupational patterns, reconstructed their family life, chose the first recognizable leadership class, and developed new institutions and modes of social action.

Blacks commonly celebrated emancipation by taking new names. A new name was both a symbol of personal liberation and an act of political defiance; it reversed the enslavement process and confirmed the freemen's newly won liberty, just as the loss of an African name had earlier symbolized enslavement. Emancipation also gave blacks the opportunity to strip themselves of the comic classical names that had dogged them in slavery, and to adopt common Anglo-American names. Few Caesars, Pompeys, and Catos remained among the new freemen. In bondage, most blacks had but a single name; freedom also allowed them the opportunity to take another. Robert Freeman, Landon Freeland, and Robin Justice chose names that celebrated their new status. Many, like Tom, who took the name "Toogood" when he ran off, flaunted the increased self-esteem that accompanied liberty. Others, following an ancient tradition, borrowed names from their trades or skills: James Carter was a drayman, Henry Mason a bricklayer,

Charles Green a gardener, and Jacob Bishop a preacher with obvious aspirations. Similarly, James Cook took his name "from his being skilled in the art of cooking and house service," and the origins of Jockey Wheeler's cognomen can be safely surmised. More significantly, some identified themselves by their pigment and origin and took names like "Brown," "Coal," "Africa," and "Guinea." But slave society, which identified wealth, power, and authority with whites, was not easily denied. Some blacks called themselves "White," and others borrowed the name of some local notable, more often than not a slaveholder. But only a few took the name of their emancipator.[23]

Newly manumitted bondsmen also tried to escape the stigma of bondage by deserting the site of their enslavement. Runaways did it as a matter of course, and some newly liberated freemen were no longer welcome on their masters' homesteads. But even when invited to stay, many free blacks gladly left. The expectations generated by emancipation encouraged freemen to venture out on their own. Bondage had limited the physical mobility of blacks, and now many seemed determined to compensate for their confinement. "Negro Soloman," one manumitter ruefully observed, "now free, prefers to mould bricks than serve me." In snubbing their former masters, free Negroes demonstrated their liberty. Some freemen seemingly went out of their way to break the bonds of dependence that weighed so heavily in slavery. Much to the displeasure of one Delaware mistress, her former servant ignored her offer of a "a good place" with a Philadelphia friend and found a job on her own. "I cannot help thinking," complained the rejected aristocrat, that "it is too generally the case with all those of colour to be ungrateful."[24] Throughout the South, emancipated blacks tested their liberty by asserting it.

Fleeing the memory of servitude, looking for new opportunities, searching for loved ones, freemen moved in all directions. Many went north, some to Canada, and some to Haiti, and a few found their way back to Africa. Yet most of those who abandoned the place of their enslavement remained in the United States. Friendless and fearful, some doubtless returned to their old neighborhoods where they had friends and relatives. A few, however, continued to wander aimlessly, living off the land while searching for a new life. As a result, every state had a transient group of free Negroes that encouraged "dangerous" thoughts among restless slaves and frightened, edgy whites. In 1786, for instance, whites in Sussex County, Delaware, complained that large numbers of wandering blacks "under the name and Character of Free

Negroes" were residing "thoughout this Country [and] stroll thro' the same."[25] Such bands of freemen were a magnet for runaways and occasionally grew so large that officials called upon the militia to disperse them.

But most migrating free Negroes chose their destination with care. Many sought out loved ones, hoping to reconstruct their shattered families or simply to share the exhilaration of liberty. Some freemen, like whites, searched for new opportunities in the West, but more often free blacks turned to the urban frontier. Cities, where the relative anonymity of urban life provided an additional measure of liberty, were the most important refuges from the memory of plantation slavery. Throughout the nation, municipal officials joined the mayor of Petersburg, Virginia, in lamenting that "large numbers of free blacks flock from the country to the towns. . . ." Although cities added police and passed special ordinances to curb this migration, urban freemen throughout the South increased in numbers more rapidly than did the free Negroes generally. While the free Negro population of Virginia more than doubled between 1790 and 1810, that of Richmond increased fourfold, and of Norfolk tenfold. Similar patterns of growth could be observed in New York, Philadelphia, and Charleston.[26] Most freemen, like most whites and slaves, resided in the countryside, but, by the beginning of the nineteenth century, cities had become centers of free black life.

Migration, no matter how tempting, was never easy. For many newly freed blacks, it meant abandoning enslaved loved ones. Although many free blacks would later attempt to improve their status by distinguishing themselves from slaves, in the formative years free and slave blacks stood together to a large degree.[27] Changes in free black life had a deep and lasting impact on slave society. The extent of this relationship has yet to be fully explored, but it is important to emphasize the close ties between freemen and bondsmen during the revolutionary era. It could hardly be otherwise, with so many free Negroes just a step away from bondage, and so many slaves hopeful of freedom, especially in the North and Upper South. Abolition and relatively indiscriminate manumission in those regions eliminated many of the differences in social origins and color that had existed between freemen and slaves during the colonial era. Free and slave blacks were perhaps closer than they were at any time in the past, and perhaps than they had been at any time in the future. Bonds of friendship and kinship, rooted in common experience and sealed by common expectations, made freemen reluctant to leave their old homes without family and friends.

As a result, the era witnessed a major reconstruction of black family life. Although traditional West African society rested on a powerful familial base, the trauma of the Middle Passage, the diversity of their African heritage, the sexual imbalance of the colonial slave population, and the physical isolation of life on colonial plantations prevented the first generation of enslaved blacks from reconstituting family life as they had known it in Africa. Often these forbidding circumstances subverted the development of stable family relationships of any kind. Not until the second decade of the eighteenth century in many colonies, and still later in others, did the emergence of a more favorable sexual balance and a larger plantation unit allow first generation Afro-Americans to build the family life that had been destroyed by enslavement. That process, which entailed shaping new marital roles, molding new familial structures, and defining anew the relationship between family and society in accordance with the diverse heritage of Africa and the circumstances of American slavery, is little understood at this point. It was influenced by the cultural origins of the first Africans in a particular area, the number and origins of new slaves later brought into that area, the size of the plantation unit, the kind of labor demanded of blacks, the master's example, as well as other factors. Yet whatever the process, it had been completed in most places by the 1770s. By the time of the Revolution, blacks had shaped the most important instrument of their survival in slavery: the family. Yet the master's whim continually threatened the slave family. The forces unleashed by the Revolution offered blacks the opportunity to place their family life on a stronger base, and they quickly took advantage of it.[28]

Many freemen, themselves fresh from bondage, helped family and friends purchase their liberty, and thus rebuilt families separated by slavery. Since most freemen were poor, buying the freedom of a loved one took years of austere living. It was not unusual for a free Negro to save for five to ten years in order to liberate a single bondsman. Despite these obstacles, some free blacks dedicated much of their lives and fortunes to help others escape bondage. Graham Bell, a Petersburg freeman, purchased and freed nine slaves between 1792 and 1805. In 1792, Bell emancipated five slave children (probably his own) whom he had bought three years earlier. In 1801 he purchased and freed a slave woman, who later paid him £15 for the service. The following year, noting "that God created all men equally free," he emancipated two more slaves, and in 1805 he manumitted his brother. Bell's persistence was exceptional, but not unique. In New Bern, North Carolina, John C. Stanly, a successful free Negro barber, purchased and emancipated his wife and children in 1805, and two years later freed his brother-in-law. During the next eleven years, Stanly freed another eighteen slaves. Aletha Tanner of Washington equalled Stanly's benevolence. After purchasing her own freedom, she bought and liberated twenty-two friends and relatives.[29]

Other free Negroes, anxious to reunite their families or friends, had not the patience, money, or inclination to buy liberty. Instead, they plotted to aid fugitives from bondage. So often did newly freed blacks rescue their families from servitude, that masters looked first to them when their slaves ran off. When Jonathan fled slavery, his owner noted he was "related to a family of negroes, who lately obtained their freedom"; Bet's mistress believed she "went off in company with a mulatto free fellow name Tom Turner, who follows the water for a living and calls her his wife"; and Sam's master thought he would go to Baltimore where he had "several relations (manumitted blacks), who will conceal and assist him to make his escape." Little wonder that slaveholders, determined to stop the growing number of fugitives, demanded legislative restraints on free blacks because of the "great number of relations and acquaintances they still have among us, and from the harbours and houses such manumitted Negroes" afford runaways. Although slaveowners found freemen easy scapegoats for slave unrest, their presumption proved true often enough to sustain their generalized suspicions.[30] Once liberated from bondage, free blacks did not forget those left behind.

Yet even more important than a fast horse or a forged pass, freemen provided fugitives with the example that blacks could be free. The rapid growth of the free Negro population swelled the expectations of those still in bondage. Many who saw their friends and relatives shed the shackles of slavery began thinking about what previously seemed unattainable. "Henny," noted a Maryland slaveholder in 1783, "will try to pass for a free woman as several have lately been set free in this neighbourhood."[31] The increase of successful fugitives not only added to the free Negro population but provided just one more measure of the close ties between freemen and bondsmen during the formative postrevolutionary years.

Selecting a new name and address or helping a friend from slavery to freedom were symbolically important. These acts marked a clean break with bondage and an effort to begin life anew. But whatever psychic satisfaction a freeman received from his new name, address, or reunited family, they provided little of the substance of liberty. Newly emancipated blacks were still black in a society that presumed only whites to be free, and propertyless in a society that measured status mainly in dollars.

Some blacks moved from slavery to freedom in relative comfort. Their masters, partly from necessity and partly out of foresight, provided for them after emancipation. George Washington and Robert Carter, both of whom manumitted several hundred slaves, composed elaborate plans to support their former bondsmen and ensure that they would not burden the community. Washington provided for apprenticeship and tenancy for the able-bodied and lodging and pensions for the aged. But only a few slaveowners furnished their former bondsmen with a means of making a living. Occasionally, some masters gave them small gifts of clothing, a few sticks of furniture, or a little money; rarely did they give more than this.[32] Since most manumitters were motivated by the ideology of the Revolution and since that ideology required nothing more than the bestowal of freedom, slaveholders saw little reason to go beyond emancipation. Certainly there was never a hint of compensation for the long years of bondage. Slaveholders might be compensated, but not slaves. Thus for most blacks, slavery was a poor school for freedom, and emancipation at first added nothing to their inheritance. Once free, they usually found themselves without property or steady work.

Newly freed blacks frequently suffered a sharp decline in occupational status. As slaves, blacks had been the artisans who did much of the skilled labor in colonial society. Indeed, the proportion of slaves engaged in skilled labor had increased during the second half of the eighteenth century. Yet, once freed, blacks found themselves proscribed from many of the trades at which they excelled. The decline of free Negro occupational status took place at an uneven pace during the pre-Civil War years, speeded by competition from newly arrived immigrant workers and retarded by the general demand for labor and the refusal of whites, especially in the slave states, to work at trades deemed "nigger work." But from the outset, whites objected to working alongside blacks, especially free ones. Similarly, many white employers gave preference to white workers, and those who wanted blacks usually preferred slaves, over whose labor they had greater control. Thus freemen were driven from certain jobs because they were black, and they were excluded from others because they were free. This dual proscription allowed whites to limit free Negroes to an ever shrinking range of menial occupations, increasing tensions between white and black workers, and sometimes between freemen and bondsmen as well.[33]

Although accompanied by proscription and exclusion, freedom also created new opportunities, often for slaves as well as freemen. It allowed some blacks to attain postions from which all blacks previously had been barred. Suddenly blacks took the role of a painter, poet, author, astronomer, minister, and merchant. The almanacs of Benjamin Banneker, the poems of Phillis Wheatly and Jupiter Hammon, and the portraits of Joshua Johnston stand not only as tributes to the achievements of talented men and women, but also as symbols of the cultural transformation of the revolutionary era.[34]

The new opportunities of freedom also allowed some freemen to accumulate property and achieve a modicum of economic security. William Flora, a revolutionary veteran, purchased several lots in Portsmouth, Virginia, soon after his discharge from the army. Later he opened a livery stable, served Portsmouth for thirty years, and willed his property to his son. In 1783, James McHenry, a Maryland shoemaker, purchased his freedom, and four years later rented a farm for £35 a year and had "a house and other stock more than sufficient for his farm." Henry Carter, a Virginia freeman, was similarly successful. He was emancipated in 1811, and within six years not only had "funds sufficient to purchase his wife Priscilla but some other property, personal & real." Throughout the nation the growth of a black propertyholding class followed the growth of the free Negro population. In some places, freemen controlled sizable businesses. The striking success of sea captain Paul Cuffee of New Bedford, Massachusetts, sail manufacturer James Forten of Philadelphia, and merchant Robert Sheridan of Wilmington, North Carolina, suggests how quickly blacks took advantage of the expanding, if still limited, opportunities created by freedom.[35] Although most blacks remained, as in slavery, poor and propertyless, some freemen rose to modest wealth and respectability.

Slowly, a new black elite emerged: Prince Hall in Boston, Richard Allen in Philadelphia, Daniel Coker in Baltimore, Christopher McPherson in Richmond, Andrew Bryan in Savannah, and a host of others in black communities throughout the new republic. Born in the decade before the Revolution, these men came of age with the emergence of the free Negro population and the maturation of Afro-American culture. Many of them owed their liberty to the changes unleashed by the

American Revolution, and they shared the optimism and enthusiasm that accompanied freedom. Wealthier and better educated than most blacks, they moved easily into positions of leadership within the black community and pressed whites to expand black liberty. Pointing to the ideas of the Declaration of Independence, the new black elite provided the leadership in petitioning Congress and state legislatures to abolish slavery and relieve free blacks of the disabilities that prevented them from enjoying their full rights as citizens. Norfolk freemen, in a typical action, requested that they be allowed to testify in court against whites so they could prove their accounts. Boston blacks demanded an equal share of the city's school fund so they might educate their children. South Carolina's free Negroes petitioned for relief from a special head tax that pushed them into a condition "but small removed from Slavery." And from Nashville, Tennessee, came a plea that free Negroes "ought to have the same opportunities of doing well that any Person being a citizen & free...would have, and that the door ought not be kept shut against them more than any other of the Human race." In the North, blacks, themselves but recently liberated, urged an end to the slave trade and the establishment of a universal emancipation. Occasionally, a few bold southern freemen like Baltimore's Daniel Coker added their voices to this public condemnation of slavery.[36]

These freemen protested in vain. Even the most restrained pleas led to harsher repression, further anchoring them to the bottom of free society. The experience of Charleston's free Negroes indicates how vehemently whites opposed any improvement in the status of blacks. In 1791, Peter Mathews, a free Negro butcher, along with several other free black artisans and tradesmen, petitioned the state legislature to expand their rights. The law barred them from testifying in court against whites—"for which cause many Culprits have escaped punishments," made it difficult and sometimes impossible for them to collect their debts, and subjected them to numerous frauds. At the same time, they were tried without a jury in courts that permitted slaves to testify against them. For many years, according to Mathews, Negro freemen had supported the government, paid their taxes, and upheld the peace. "Your memorialists," he tactfully concluded, "do not presume to hope that they shall be put on an equal footing with free White Citizens of the State in general [but] humbly solicit such dictates in their favor" by repealing the offending laws. Although Mathews measured his words carefully and tailored his request to avoid threatening white dominance in any way, his petition received no hearing from the legislature. Yet it may not have gone unnoticed. Three years later, when fears of insurrection ran high, white vigilantes broke into Mathews's house to search for a cache of arms. Mathews, a substantial tradesman of good repute, had little choice but to try and explain publicly that an "old pistol without flint, a broken sword, and an old cutlass" he kept in his attic were not the beginning of a revolution.[37] Perhaps he convinced Charleston vigilantes, perhaps not; in any case the lot of Peter Mathews was just further proof that whites would tolerate no alteration of their standards of race relations.

V

Frustrated by unyeilding white hostility, freemen took two divergent courses. Some turned away from slaves in an effort to ingratiate themselves with whites, by trying to demonstrate they were more free than black. This strategy was especially evident in—although not limited to—the Lower South, where ties between freemen and slaves had never been strong and where many of the newly arrived *gens de couleur* had suffered heavy losses at the hands of the Haitian slave rebels. During the 1790s, the free people of color in Charleston established the Brown Fellowship Society, an organization limited to free brown people, and one which remained a symbol of mulatto exclusiveness throughout the antebellum period.[38]

Most freemen, especially in the North and Upper South, took a different course. Increasingly, they turned inward and worked to strengthen the black community—free and slave. Freemen, frequently joined by slaves, established institutions where blacks might pray, educate their children, entertain, and protect themselves. African churches, schools, and fraternal societies not only served the new needs of the much expanded free Negro population and gave meaning to black liberty, but they also symbolized the emergence of Afro-American culture and represented the strongest effort to unite the black community.

Yet, even while they shouldered the new responsibilities of freedom, blacks did not immediately form separate institutions. The development of the African church, for example, was not merely a product of the emergence of the free Negro population. At first, most blacks looked to the white-dominated evangelical churches, which made acceptance of the gospel the only criteria for salvation and welcomed blacks into the fold. Free Negroes, along with slaves and poor whites, found this open membership policy, the emotional sermons, and the generous grants of self-expression an appealing contrast to the icy restrictiveness of the older, more staid denominations. Although racially mixed congregations were often forced to meet at odd hours to avoid hostile sheriffs and slave patrols, black membership in these churches grew rapidly. By the end of the eighteenth century, thousands of blacks, free and slave, had joined Methodist and Baptist churches.

The newness of the evangelical denominations together with their Christian equalitarianism fostered new racial patterns. In many such churches, blacks and whites seated themselves indiscriminately. It was not unusual for black churchmen to attend synods and association meetings with whites. In 1794, when one Virginia church called this practice into question, the Portsmouth Baptist Association firmly announced that "it saw nothing in the Word of God nor anything contrary to the rules of decency to prohibit a church from sending as a delegate, any male member they shall choose." Sometimes blacks served as preachers to a mixed congregation. John Chavis, a black Presbyterian circuit rider, enjoyed his greatest success among whites; Fayetteville whites regarded Henry Evans, a black Methodist, as the "best preacher of his time in that quarter"; and when Richard Allen looked down from his Philadelphia pulpit he saw "Nearly . . . as many Whites as Blacks."[39]

Yet the old racial patterns had remarkable resilience. Christian equalitarianism momentarily bent the color line, but could not break it. In most churches, membership did not assure blacks of equal participation. Indeed, whites usually placed blacks in a distant corner or gallery and barred them from most of the rights of church members. One Virginia congregation painted some of its benches black to avoid any possibility of confusion.[40]

As blacks found themselves proscribed from white churches or discriminated against in mixed churches, they attempted the difficult task of forming their own religious institutions. In doing so, blacks not only lacked the capital and organizational experience, but they frequently faced fierce white opposition. This was especially true in the South, where whites identified freemen with slaves and seemed to see every meeting of free blacks, no matter how innocuous, as an insurrectionary plot.[41] The abolition of slavery in the North, in large measure, had freed whites from this fear, allowing blacks greater organizational opportunities. Northern whites frequently took a benign view of black institutions and believed, along with Benjamin Rush, that it would "be much cheaper to build churches for them than jails."[42]

Regional differences in white attitudes allowed blacks to act more openly in the North. While nórthern freemen quickly established their own churches and schools, southern free blacks, frequently joined by slaves, continued to meet intense opposition. The difficulties faced by blacks in Williamsburg, Virginia, typified the problems that confronted blacks throughout the South. In the 1780s, when Moses organized a group of Williamsburg Baptists "composed, almost, if not altogether, of people of colour," he was seized and whipped. Gowan Pamphlet, who succeeded Moses as church leader, also encountered stiff opposition. The local Baptist Association refused to recognize the church, and when Pamphlet persisted, they excommunicated him and some of his congregation. Still, Pamphlet's church continued to meet and expand. In 1791, announcing that they numbered over 500, blacks again petitioned the Dover Baptist Association for membership, and two years later the Association grudgingly received the church, with Pamphlet as its minister. Even then the Association could not resist one last slap. In 1793 Pamphlet was accepted as a delegate from the Williamsburg African Church only "as they could not have done better under the circumstances."[43]

Despite the rising pitch of white opposition, the number of black churches increased steadily throughout the 1780s and 1790s. Whites, who monopolized all the important ecclesiastical offices, controlled church finances, and regulated church discipline, increasingly found themselves confronted by blacks who demanded autonomy or a greater share of power within the church organization. Visiting Baltimore in 1795, Methodist Bishop Francis Asbury issued the common lament of many white churchmen: "The Africans of this town desire a church, which in temporals, shall be altogether under their own direction, and ask greater privileges than the white stewards and trustees ever had the right to claim."[44] When their demands were not met, blacks usually seceded from the white-dominated organizations. In some places, they left after a violent confrontation, as when whites physically removed Absalom Jones from his pew in Philadelphia's St. George Methodist Church.[45] More often, blacks quietly withdrew when it became obvious that their pleas for greater equality would never be satisfactorily answered.[46] The rank discrimination of white-dominated churches fostered black separatism, but some blacks welcomed the split. It allowed them, for the first time, full control over their own religious life. By the end of the century, black communities from Boston to Savannah boasted their own African churches.[47]

The equalitarian moment had not lasted long, but it was crucial nonetheless. Anglo-American and Afro-American religious styles mixed freely during these years, and when whites and blacks retreated to their separate segregated organizations, they carried much of the other's culture with them. The West African call-response pattern, for example, became a regular part of early Baptist and Methodist services, and the polity and theology of the evangelical denominations became central to the development of the African Baptist and African Methodist Church. The full dimensions of these cultural exchanges have not been fully studied, but it is important to observe that they were part of a larger cultural transformation at a time of relatively easy racial intermingling, especially among the lower classes.[48]

During the early years of the nineteenth century, blacks continued to establish new African churches in the northern and border slave states. In 1816, leading black churchmen from various parts of these regions joined together to form the first independent black denomination, the African Methodist Episcopal (AME) Church.[49] But if the African church flourished in the North, it fell upon hard times in the South. While the abolition of slavery had freed northern whites from the fear of insurrection, those anxieties grew among white southerners. In 1800, when Gabriel Prosser's aborted insurrection in Virginia nearly transformed the worst fears of southern whites into a dreadful reality, the African church came under still greater pressure. Hysterical whites shut many black churches and forced black ministers to flee the South. Even white churchmen found themselves under attack for proselytizing blacks. When a white circuit rider tried to preach to a mixed congregation in Richmond in 1802, he was threatened with the lash and driven out of the city. Charleston Methodists similarly found themselves "watched, ridiculed, and openly assailed" for allowing blacks to attend their meetings. The growth of the African church in the South was abruptly halted during the first years of the nineteenth century.[50] Later it would revive under very different conditions.[51]

The early development of African schools followed the same tortuous path as that of the independent black churches. In the years immediately following the Revolutionary War, the momentary respite in racial hostility encouraged some freemen and sympathetic whites to establish integrated academies throughout the North and even in some border states. But the emotions and ideals that united poor whites and blacks in evangelical churches were absent from the founding of schools. Schools were middle- and upper-class institutions, and class distinctions alone doubtless excluded most free blacks. Handicapped by a lack of funds and surrounded by increasingly hostile whites, integrated schools languished. By the turn of the century, the ebbing of revolutionary equalitarianism forced those few remaining integrated schools to close their doors or segregate their classrooms. The support of black schools fell largely on black communities. African schools, usually attached to black churches, continued to meet in the North, and in some places increased in size and number. But in the South, they faced intense opposition from whites, who viewed them as nurseries of subversion.[52]

The destruction of the Richmond African school suggests the depth of white hostility to any attempt blacks might make to secure their liberty and improve themselves. In 1811, Christopher McPherson, a free Negro of considerable talent and modest wealth who also styled himself "Pherson, the first son of Christ," hired Herbert H. Hughes, a white schoolmaster, and established a night school for free Negroes and slaves who had obtained the consent of their masters. Classes began at dusk and ran until nine-thirty, and Hughes taught "the English language grammatically, Writing, Arithmetic, Geography, Astronomy, &c.&c." for a fee of about $.25 per month. Slaves and freemen flocked to Hughes's classroom. The school opened with twenty-five pupils, and McPherson noted "from frequent applications since, 'tis expected the number will shortly be doubled." McPherson was so pleased with his initial success that he boasted of the school in the *Richmond Argus,* and recommended "to the people of colour throughout the United States (who do not have it in their power to attend day schools) to establish similar institutions in their neighbourhoods." Excited over the new possibilities, he hoped "that everyone who loves his Country, and has it in his power will generously further and foster every institution of the kind that may be established throughout this happy Union."[53]

Richmond whites were less enthusiastic. The following day, "several citizens...whose opinions we highly respect" confronted Samuel Pleasants, the editor of the *Argus,* and demanded that McPherson's advertisement be withdrawn. "They deem it," Pleasants reported, "impolitic and highly improper that such an institution should exist in this City." Pleasants dissented, but dutifully withdrew the advertisement. Herbert Hughes, the white schoolmaster, was made of sterner stuff. He took space in the *Argus,* defended the school, and attacked the idea that it was impolitic to educate blacks as Rousseauian sophistry. Reiterating his commitment to the school, Hughes declared that

"without Education in some degree *they are* in a state of bastard civilization," and he pledged to teach until "a verdict from a proper tribunal"
closed the school.[54]

That apparently was not long in coming, for soon after Hughes
made his appeal, Richmond officials summoned McPherson to court
to show why his school should not be declared a nuisance. The case
was delayed, but the police continued to harass McPherson, and probably drove Hughes out of town. Despite the greater threat implicit in
the police action, in April, when the court again delayed his case,
McPherson advertised his desire to establish "a seminary of learning
of the arts and sciences" as soon as he could find a "proper tutor." But
before he could act, police jailed McPherson and then shipped him to
the Williamsburg Lunatic Asylum. McPherson doubtless had religious
delusions, but these had not prevented him from functioning for years
in a manner acceptable to Richmond whites; only when he established
a school was he clapped into a madhouse.[55] His lesson was obvious:
any black who would attempt to found a school was "crazy."

The dismantling of African churches and schools suggests the
intensity of white opposition to the development of independent black
institutions wherever slavery continued to exist. Yet, even as whites
closed black churches and schools and slapped new proscriptions on
black liberty in order to freeze blacks into a place of permanent social
inferiority, they could not erase all the gains made in the first flush of
freedom. In the North, African churches and schools continued to
grow and occasionally flourish, and even in the South some of these
institutions limped on, although often forced to accept white supervision or meet clandestinely.

On the surface, African churches and schools and allied benevolent and fraternal societies were but a weak imitation of those of the
larger society. Often they reflected white values and mimicked the
structure of their white counterparts. But, on closer inspection, they
embodied an Afro-American culture that was over a century in the
making. Whites who visited black church meetings or attended black
funerals almost uniformly observed the striking difference between
them and their own somber rituals.[56] It was no accident that blacks
called their churches African churches, their schools African schools,
and their benevolent societies African benevolent societies.

These organizations provided an institutional core for black life
throughout the nineteenth century and well into the twentieth. In
African churches and schools, black people baptized their children,

educated their youth, and provided for the sick, aged, and disabled. African churches strengthened black family life by insisting that marriages be solemnized, by punishing adulterers, and occasionally by reuniting separated couples. Leaders of these institutions, especially ministers, moved into dominant positions in the black community, and African churches, in turn, provided a means of advancement for ambitious black youth. More than this, these institutions gave the black community a sense of solidarity and common purpose. At no time was this more evident than in the postrevolutionary era, when slaves and freemen joined together to re-form black society and give shape to the cultural transformation of the preceding century. Later, free Negroes and slaves would drift apart, and many of the institutions formed during this earlier era would become identified with the free blacks and urban slave artisans who placed them at the center of black life in the North and urban South. But the new social and institutional forms established during the years after the Revolution were not lost for the mass of enslaved black people. The changes set in motion by the Revolution permeated slave life in ways that are only barely recognized now. The new occupational, religious, and familial patterns and the new social roles and modes of social action established by the convergence of changes in Afro-American and Anglo-American life during the revolutionary era continued to inform slave society, as the great cotton boom pulled slaves out of the seaboard states and into the Lower South. The revolution in black life spread across the continent. On the rich, loamy soils of the cotton South, slaves reshaped the cultural legacy of the revolutionary era to meet the new needs of plantation life. And with the Civil War, the Emancipation Proclamation, and the Thirteenth Amendment, the transformed institutional and cultural legacy of the revolutionary era emerged once again and stood at the center of black life.

1. *Gentlemen's Magazine and Historical Chronicle* 34 (1764): 261; Petition from Petersburg, 11 December 1805, Virginia Legislative Papers, Virginia State Library, Richmond; *Proceedings and Debates of the Convention of North-Carolina Called to Amend the Constitution of the State* (Raleigh, N.C.: J. Gales and Son, 1835), p. 351; [John S. Tyson], *Life of Elisha Tyson* (Baltimore: B. Lundy, 1825), p. 7.

2. Winthrop D. Jordan, *White Over Black: American Attitudes Toward the Negro, 1550–1812* (Chapel Hill, N.C.: University of North Carolina Press, 1968), pp. 122–28; Edgar J. McManus, *Black Bondage in the North* (Syracuse, N.Y.: Syracuse University Press, 1973), pp. 67–70, 122, 161–62; Lorenzo J. Greene, *The Negro in Colonial New England* (New York: Columbia University Press, 1942), pp. 298–304.

3. Benjamin Quarles, *The Negro in the American Revolution* (Chapel Hill, N.C.: University of North Carolina Press, 1961), pp. 19–32; *Williamsburg Virginia Gazette* (Purdie), 17 November 1775, (Dixon & Nicholson) 2 December 1775. For an enlightening comparative perspective on war and slavery, see David Brion Davis, *The Problem of Slavery in the Age of Revolution, 1770–1823* (Ithaca, N.Y.: Cornell University Press, 1975), pp. 72–82.

4. Quarles, *Negro in the American Revolution*, pp. 111–57; Donald L. Robinson, *Slavery in the Structure of American Politics, 1765–1820* (New York: Harcourt Brace Jovanovich, 1971), pp. 98–113.

5. Quarles, *Negro in the American Revolution*, pp. 3–18, 51–67; Robinson, *Slavery in the Structure of American Politics*, pp. 113–22, quote pp. 120–21; Pete Maslowski, "National Policy toward the Use of Black Troops in the Revolution," *South Carolina Historical Magazine* 73 (1972): 1–17.

6. Quarles, *Negro in the American Revolution*, pp. 68–93, 111–57; Petition from Henrico County, 1784, Virginia Legislative Papers, Virginia State Library, Richmond; Luther P. Jackson, "Virginia Negro Soldiers and Seamen in the American Revolution," *Journal of Negro History* 27 (1942): 274–75; William W. Hening, comp., *The Statutes at Large; Being a Collection of All the Laws of Virginia*, 13 vols. (Richmond, New York, Philadelphia: Samuel Pleasants et al., 1809–1823), 8:103, 9:308–9.

7. Complaints about the loss of slave property and the growing number of fugitives were rife throughout the war years. For example, see Walter Clark, ed., *The State Records of North Carolina, 1777–1790*, 16 vols. [numbered consecutively after a preceding series] (Raleigh, N.C.: P. M. Hale, 1886–1907), 15:138; W. H. Browne et al., eds., *Archives of Maryland*, 71 vols. (Baltimore: Maryland Historical Society, 1883–), 45:473; William P. Palmer, ed., *Calendar of Virginia State Papers*, 11 vols. (Richmond, 1875–1893), 1:477–78; and Quarles, *Negro in the American Revolution*, especially pp. 115–32. The effect of internal dissension of slavery has not yet been fully assayed, but Ronald Hoffman, *A Spirit of Dissension: Economics, Politics, and the Revolution in Maryland* (Baltimore: Johns Hopkins University Press, 1973), pp. 147–48, 152–53, 184–88, is suggestive. Gerald W. Mullin, *Flight and Rebellion: Slave Resistance in Eighteenth-Century Virginia* (New York: Oxford University Press, 1972) documents the relationship between acculturation and patterns of resistance in the most important Upper South colony and state.

8. An understanding of the relationship between the American Revolution and the ideological opposition to slavery must begin with Jordan, *White Over Black*, pp. 269–475, and Davis, *The Problem of Slavery in the Age of Revolution*. Davis is especially insightful on the ambiguities and limitation of antislavery thought. Robert McColley, *Slavery and Jeffersonian Virginia* (Urbana, Ill.: University of Illinois Press, 1964), rightly emphasizes the expansion of slavery during the postrevolutionary period, although he ignores the larger pattern of events which threw slavery on the defensive. The long-range implications of these events on slavery are explored by William W. Freehling, "The Founding Fathers and Slavery," *American Historical Review* 77 (1972): 81–93.

9. Arthur Zilversmit, *The First Emancipation: The Abolition of Slavery in the North* (Chicago: University of Chicago Press, 1967); Jordan, *White Over Black*, pp. 315–74; Gary B. Nash, "Slaves and Slaveowners in Colonial Philadelphia," *William and Mary Quarterly*, 3d ser. 30 (1973): 231–32, 236–56, especially 254, 256; Robert William Fogel and Stanley L. Engerman, "Philanthropy at Bargain Prices: Notes on the Economics of Gradual Emancipation," *Journal of Legal Studies* 3 (1974): 377–82, 385–93. Again, Davis's comparative perspective on emancipation in nonplantation societies is instructive. *The Problem of Slavery in the Age of Revolution*, pp. 86–92.

10. Jacob P. Dunn, Jr., *Indiana: A Redemption from Slavery* (Boston: Houghton Mifflin and Co., 1888); Theodore C. Pease, *The Story of Illinois* (Chicago: University of Chicago Press, 1949), pp. 72–78.

11. Wesley M. Gewehr., *The Great Awakening in Virginia, 1740–1790* (Durham, N.C.: Duke University Press, 1930); John B. Boles, *The Great Revival, 1787–1805: The Origins of the Southern Evangelical Mind* (Lexington, Ky.: University of Kentucky Press, 1972); McColley, *Slavery and Jeffersonian Virginia*, pp. 148–62; Donald G. Mathews, *Slavery and Methodism: A Chapter in American Morality, 1780–1845* (Princeton, N.J.: Princeton University Press, 1965), pp. 3–29; Davis, *The Problem of Slavery in the Age of Revolution*, pp. 203–10; Garnett Ryland, *The Baptists of Virginia, 1699–1926* (Richmond, Va.: Baptist

Board of Missions and Education, 1955), pp. 150–55; W. Harrison Daniel, "Virginia Baptists and the Negro in the Early Republic," *Virginia Magazine of History and Biography* 80 (1972): 65–68.

12. Carville Earle and Ronald Hoffman, "The Urban South: The First Two Centuries," *Perspectives in American History,* forthcoming, is the best discussion of economic and demographic changes in the region. Also Lewis C. Gray, *History of Agriculture in the Southern United States to 1860,* 2 vols. (Washington, D.C.: Carnegie Institution, 1933), 2:602–17; Mullin, *Flight and Rebellion,* pp. 124–27; John R. Alden, *The First South* (Baton Rouge, La.: Louisiana State University Press, 1961), pp. 9–10. Although they fail to make regional distinctions, Robert William Fogel and Stanley L. Engerman offer the most accurate information on slave prices during the period. *Time on the Cross: The Economics of American Negro Slavery* (Boston: Little, Brown and Co., 1975), pp. 86–89.

13. Ira Berlin, *Slaves Without Masters: The Free Negro in the Antebellum South* (New York: Pantheon Books, 1974), pp. 29–35.

14. Mullin, *Flight and Rebellion,* pp. 87–88, 117, 156–57; Samuel S. Bradford, "The Negro Iron Workers in Ante Bellum Virginia," *Journal of Southern History* 25 (1959): 195; but see also Charles B. Dew, "David Ross and the Oxford Iron Works: A Study of Industrial Slavery in the Early Nineteenth-Century South," *William and Mary Quarterly,* 3d ser. 31 (1974): 200 n.36.

15. George Drinker to Joseph Bringhurst, 10 December 1804, Pennsylvania Society for Promoting the Abolition of Slavery Papers, Historical Society of Pennsylvania, Philadelphia; Mullin, *Flight and Rebellion,* pp. 83–139 and passim; Berlin, *Slaves Without Masters,* pp. 36–45.

16. The United States census did not distinguish between blacks and mulattoes—meaning, presumably, anyone of mixed African ancestry—until 1850, and at that time about a third of Upper South free Negroes and 22 percent of Maryland's free Negroes were of mixed racial origins. This contrasts sharply with the racial composition of the colonial free Negro population as suggested by the Maryland census of 1755. An enumeration of Negro freemen in the District of Columbia in 1807, soon after it was carved out of Maryland and Virginia, indicates that the shift in the character of the free Negro population from brown to black (although, compared to slaves, still disproportionately brown) took place in the years following the Revolution. *Negro Population of the United States, 1790–1915* (Washington, D.C.: U. S. Department of Commerce, 1918), pp. 109, 221; U.S. Commissioner of Education, *Special Report . . . on the Condition and Improvement of Public Education in the District of Columbia* (Washington, D.C.: Government Printing Office, 1871), p. 195.

17. Unless otherwise noted, the following statistics are computed from *Population of the United States in 1860* (Washington, D.C.: Government Printing Office, 1864), p. 195.

18. St. George Tucker, *A Dissertation on Slavery* (Philadelphia: M. Carey, 1796), p. 72.

19. *Columbian Museum & Savannah Advertiser,* 11 March 1796; W. E. B. DuBois, *The Suppression of the African Slave-Trade to the United States of America, 1638–1870* (Cambridge: Harvard University Press, 1896), pp. 86–87; Patrick S. Brady, "The Slave Trade and Sectionalism in South Carolina," *Journal of Southern History* 38 (1972): 601–20.

20. C. L. R. James, *The Black Jacobins: Toussaint L'Ouverture and the San Domingo Rebellion,* 2d rev. ed. (New York: Vintage Books, 1963); Thomas O. Ott, *The Haitian Revolution, 1789–1804* (Knoxville, Tenn.: University of Tennessee Press, 1973); James G. Leyburn, *The Haitian People* (New Haven, Conn.: Yale University Press, 1941), chap. 1; Berlin, *Slaves Without Masters,* pp. 35–36.

21. Two original works of scholarship have recently reopened the question of acculturation: Mullin, *Flight and Rebellion,* and Peter H. Wood, *Black Majority: Negroes in Colonial South Carolina from 1670 through the Stono Rebellion* (New York: Alfred A. Knopf, 1974). An older, but still insightful formulation of the question is Melville J. Herskovits, "The Negro in the New World: The Statement of a Problem," *American Anthropologists* 32 (1930): 145–55, and *The Myth of the Negro Past* (New York: Harper and Brothers, 1941). Also valuable are Norman E. Whitten, Jr., and John F. Szwed, eds., *Afro-American Anthropology: Contemporary Perspectives* (New York: Free Press, 1970); Roger Bastide, *African Civilisations in the New World* (New York: Harper & Row, 1972); John W. Blassingame,

The Slave Community: Plantation Life in the Ante-Bellum South (New York: Oxford University Press, 1972), pp. 1–40.

22. Jordan, *White Over Black*, pp. 269–582; Berlin, *Slaves Without Masters*, pp. 21–35, 79–107.

23. For Tom Toogood, *Annapolis Maryland Gazette*, 18 June 1795; for Carter, ibid., 3 July 1794; for Mason, Petition from Henrico County, 22 December 1847, Virginia Legislative Papers, Virginia State Library, Richmond; for Green, *Virginia Gazette*, 15 July 1795; for Bishop, *Minutes of the Portsmouth Baptist Association*, 1794, p. 6; for Cook, *Baltimore Federal Gazette*, 14 March 1806; for Wheeler, Anne Arundel County Manumissions, Lib. no. 1, A, p. 289, Maryland Hall of Records, Annapolis. Other names are taken from a survey of Free Negro Registers at the Maryland Hall of Records, Annapolis, Virginia State Library, Richmond, South Caroliniana Library, University of South Carolina, Columbia, South Carolina Archives, Columbia, Georgia Historical Society, Savannah, and the Georgia Department of Archives and History, Atlanta. For a fuller discussion of naming patterns in the postrevolutionary years, see Berlin, *Slaves Without Masters*, pp. 51–53.

24. Robert Carter to Spenser Ball, 23 April 1796, Carter Letterbooks, Library of Congress; A[nn] Ridgely to Henry M. and George C. Ridgely, 17 November 1796, Ridgely Family Papers, DelHR; Johann D. Schoepf, *Travels in the Confederation*, 2 vols. (Philadelphia: W. J. Campbell, 1911), 2:150.

25. Petition from Sussex County, 1786, Misc. Slavery Collection, Historical Society of Delaware, Wilmington; South Carolina House Journal, 1788, pp. 266–67; Charleston Grand Jury Presentment, November 1792, South Carolina Archives, Columbia.

26. Petition from Petersburg, 11 December 1805, Virginia Legislative Papers, Virginia State Library, Richmond; Charleston Grand Jury Presentment, September 1798, South Carolina Archives, Columbia; *Returns of the Whole Number of Persons Within the. . . United States* (Philadelphia: Childs and Swaine, 1791); *Aggregate Amount of Persons Within the United States in the Year 1810* (Washington, D.C.: U.S. Department of State, 1811).

27. Even during this period, however, black unity was far from perfect. Berlin, *Slaves Without Masters*, pp. 56–58.

28. Russell R. Menard, "The Maryland Slave Population, 1658 to 1730: A Demographic Profile of Blacks in Four Counties," *William and Mary Quarterly*, 3d ser. 32 (1975):31–53. For the development of the slave family in eighteenth-century South Carolina, see the C. C. Pinckney [1789–1865] Plantation Book, 1812–1861, Pinckney Family Papers, Library of Congress.

29. Luther P. Jackson, "Manumission in Certain Virginia Cities," *Journal of Negro History* 15 (1930): 285–86; John Hope Franklin, *The Free Negro in North Carolina, 1790–1860* (Chapel Hill, N.C.: University of North Carolina Press, 1943), pp. 31–32; Constance McLaughlin Green, *The Secret City: A History of Race Relations in the Nation's Capital* (Princeton, N.J.: Princeton University Press, 1967), p. 16.

30. *Richmond Virginia Gazette*, 11 December 1793; *Baltimore Maryland Journal*, 25 June 1793; *Annapolis Maryland Gazette*, 6 May 1790; Petition from Accomac County, 3 January 1783, Virginia Legislative Papers, Virginia State Library, Richmond.

31. *Annapolis Maryland Gazette*, 3 April 1783.

32. John C. Fitzpatrick, ed., *The Writings of George Washington*, 39 vols. (Washington, D.C.: Government Printing Office, 1931–1944), 37:267–77; Eugene Prussing, *The Estate of George Washington, Deceased* (Boston: Little, Brown & Co., 1927), pp. 154–60; Benjamin Dawson to Robert Carter, 7 September 1793, Robert Carter Papers, Virginia Historical Society, Richmond; Robert Carter to Benjamin Dawson, 22 July 1794, Robert Carter Letterbooks, Library of Congress, Washington, D.C.; Proposal to Prince and others, 13 February 1793, Robert Carter Papers, Virginia Historical Society, Richmond; Louis Morton, *Robert Carter of Nomini Hall* (Williamsburg: Colonial Williamsburg, 1941), pp. 251–69.

33. McManus, *Black Bondage in the North*, pp. 184–85; Leon F. Litwack, *North of Slavery: The Negro in the Free States, 1790–1860* (Chicago: University of Chicago Press, 1961), pp. 5–6, 101–3, 153–86; Theodore Hershberg, "Free Blacks in Antebellum

Philadelphia: A Study of Ex-Slaves, Freeborn, and Socio-economic Decline," *Journal of Social History* 5 (1972): 186, 198–99; Berlin, *Slaves Without Masters*, pp. 60–62, 96–97, 217–49.

34. Silvio A. Bedini, *The Life of Benjamin Banneker* (New York: Charles Scribner's Sons, 1971); Phillis Wheatley, *Poems on Various Subjects, Religious and Moral* (Philadelphia: Joseph James, 1787); Phillis Wheatley, *Memoirs and Poems of Phillis Wheatley, a Native African and a Slave* (Boston: C.W. Light, 1834); J. Hall Pleasants, "Joshua Johnston, The First American Negro Portrait Painter," *Maryland Historical Magazine* 37 (1942): 120–49.

35. Jackson, "Virginia Negro Soldiers and Seamen," pp. 269, 272, 283; Talbot County, Md., Manumission, 1787, Pennsylvania Society for the Abolition of Slavery Papers, Historical Society of Pennsylvania, Philadelphia, Petition from Charles City County, 21 December 1815, from Petersburg, 9 December 1805, Virginia Legislative Papers, Virginia State Library, Richmond; Peter Williams, *A Discourse, Delivered on the Death of Capt. Paul Cuffe* (New York: B. Young and Co., 1817); George A. Salvador, *Paul Cuffee, the Black Yankee, 1759–1817* (New Bedford, Mass.: Reynolds-DeWalt Printing, 1969); *New York Colored American*, 4 August 1838; there is no adequate study of James Forten.

36. Petition from Norfolk, 7 December 1809, Virginia Legislative Papers, Virginia State Library, Richmond; Petition from John and William Morriss, [1783], South Carolina Legislative Papers, South Carolina Archives, Columbia; Petition from William Nodding, 31 August 1803, from Casper Lott, 4 August 1803, Tennessee Legislative Papers, Tennessee State Library, Nashville; *Annals of Congress*, 4th Cong., 2d sess., pp. 2104–2204; ibid., 6th Cong., 2d sess. 229–45; ibid., 8th Cong., 2d. sess., p. 790; Lorenzo J. Greene, "Prince Hall: Massachusetts Leader in Crisis," *Freedomways* 1 (1961): 244–54; Robert C. Twombly, "Black Resistance to Slavery in Massachusetts," in William L. O'Neill, ed., *Insight and Parallels: Problems and Issues of American Social History* (Minneapolis: Burgess Publishing Co., 1973), pp. 41–53; Dorothy Porter, ed., *Early Negro Writing, 1760–1837* (Boston: Beacon Press, 1971), pp. 13–27, 313–401; Daniel Coker, *A Dialogue Between a Virginian and an African Minister* (Baltimore: Benjamin Edes, 1810).

37. Petition from Thomas Cole, Mathew Webb, P. B. Mathews, and other free Negroes, 1 January 1791, South Carolina Legislative Papers, South Carolina Archives, Columbia; *Charleston City Gazette*, 7 September 1793.

38. WPA, Brown Fellowship Society Papers, South Carolina Historical Society, Charleston; E. Horace Fitchett, "The Traditions of the Free Negro in Charleston, South Carolina," *Journal of Negro History* 25 (1940): 144–45; Kenneth and Anna M. Roberts, eds. and trans., *Moreau de St. Méry's American Journey (1793–1798)* (New York: Doubleday & Co., 1947), p. 48; John Lambert, *Travels Through Lower Canada and the United States of North America*, 3 vols. (London: Richard Phillips, 1810), 1:414, 416.

39. Elmer E. Clark et al., eds., *The Journal and Letters of Francis Asbury*, 3 vols. (London and Nashville, Tenn.: Abingdon Press, 1958), 1:403; Ryland, *Baptists of Virginia*, p. 155; *Minutes of the Portsmouth Baptist Association*, 1794, p. 6., 1798, p. 3; William Wightman, *Life of William Capers. . . Including an Autobiography* (Nashville, Tenn.: Southern Methodist Publishing House, 1858), pp. 124–29; Margaret B. DesChamps, "John Chavis as a Preacher to Whites," *North Carolina Historical Review* 32 (1955): 165–72; Walter H. Brooks, "The Priority of the Sliver Bluff Church and Its Promoters," *Journal of Negro History* 7 (1922), 172–96; Richard Allen and Jupiter Gipson to Ezekiel Cooper, 22 February 1798, Ezekiel Cooper Papers, Garrett Theological Seminary, Evanston, Ill. The pioneering and still invaluable work on the Negro Church is Carter G. Woodson, *The History of the Negro Church* (Washington, D.C.: Associated Publishers, 1921).

40. Roberts and Roberts, eds. and trans., *St. Méry's Journal*, p. 64.

41. See, for example, Lemuel Burkitt and Jesse Read, *A Concise History of the Kehekee Baptist Association from Its Rise Down to 1803* (Halifax, N.C.: A. Hodge, 1803), pp. 258–59.

42. Rush quoted in Jordan, *White Over Black*, p. 424.

43. Robert Semple, *A History of the Rise and Progress of the Baptists in Virginia* (Richmond, Va.: John O'Lynch, 1810), pp. 97, 114–15; *Minutes of the Dover Baptist Association*, typescript, 1793, Virginia Baptist Historical Society, Richmond; Thad W. Tate, Jr., *The Negro in Eighteenth-Century Williamsburg* (Charlottesville, Va.: Colonial Williamsburg,

1965), pp. 158–63. Pamphlet served as a delegate until 1807; *Minutes of the Dover Baptist Association*, 1807.

44. Clark et al., eds., *Journal and Letters of Francis Asbury*, 2:65.

45. Richard Allen, *Life, Experience, and Gospel Labors* (Philadelphia: Lee and Yeocum, 1888), pp. 14–15; William Douglass, *Annals of the First African Church in the USA now styled the African Episcopal Church of St. Thomas, Philadelphia* (Philadelphia: King & Baird, 1862), pp. 10–11; Charles H. Wesley, *Richard Allen: Apostle of Freedom* (Washington, D.C.: Associated Publishers, 1935), pp. 52–53.

46. See, for example, the establishment of the Baltimore African Methodist Church. James A. Handy, *Scraps of African Methodist Episcopal History* (Philadelphia: A. M. E. Book Concern, n.d.), pp. 13–16, 22–24; Daniel A. Payne, *A History of the African Methodist Episcopal Church* (Nashville, Tenn.: A. M. E. Sunday School Union, 1891), pp. 5–8; James H. Wright, *The Free Negro in Maryland, 1634–1860* (New York: Columbia University Press, 1921), pp. 212–13.

47. Woodson, *History of the Negro Church*, pp. 71–99.

48. I hope to address the question of cultural exchanges during the revolutionary era in a separate essay in the near future.

49. Wesley, *Richard Allen*, pp. 124–88.

50. Alexander McCaine to Ezekiel Cooper, 30 September 1802, Ezekiel Cooper Papers, Garrett Theological Seminary, Evanston, Ill.; Mood, *Methodism in Charleston*, p. 64. Many black ministers were forced out of the South. Burkitt and Read, *Kuhekee Baptist Association*, pp. 258–59; Coker, *Dialogue Between a Virginian and An African Minister*, p. 40; David Benedict, *A General History of the Baptist Denomination in America and Other Parts of the World*, 2 vols. (Boston: Lincoln & Edmonds, 1813), 2:509; John W. Davis, "George Liele and Andrew Bryan, Pioneer Negro Preachers," *Journal of Negro History* 3 (1918): 120–21.

51. Berlin, *Slaves Without Masters*, pp. 291–96.

52. Carter G. Woodson, *The Education of the Negro Prior to 1861* (New York: G. P. Putnam's Sons, 1915); William C. Dunlap, *Quaker Education in Baltimore and Virginia Yearly Meetings with an Account of Certain Meetings of Delaware and Eastern Shore Affiliated With Philadelphia* (Philadelphia, 1936), pp. 173ff; *Special Report of the Commissioner of Education*, passim; "Constitution of the African School Society," in the Minutes of the African School Society, Wilmington, 1809–1835, Historical Society of Delaware, Wilmington; *Raleigh Register*, 25 August 1808; *Baltimore American*, 6 June 1805; *Richmond Virginia Argus*, 12 March 1811; Charles C. Andrews, *The History of the New-York African Free-Schools* (New York, 1830), passim.

53. Christopher McPherson, *A Short History of the Life of Christopher McPherson, alias Pherson, Son of Christ, King of Kings and Lord of Lords* . . . 1st ed., ca. 1811 (Lynchburg, Va.: Christopher McPherson Smith, 1855); Edmund Berkeley, Jr., "Prophet Without Honor: Christopher McPherson, Free Person of Color," *Virginia Magazine of History and Biography* 77 (1969): 180–89; quote in *Richmond Virginia Argus*, 12 March 1811.

54. Ibid., 14 March 1811, 16 March 1811.

55. McPherson, *Short History of McPherson*, pp. 6–11, 24.

56. For example, see George Lewis, *Impressions of America and the American Churches* (Edinburg: W. P. Kennedy, 1845), pp. 167–70. Frederick von Raumer, *America and the American People* (New York: J. & H. G. Langley, 1846), pp. 434–35; Frederick Bremer, *The Homes of the New World*, 2 vols. (New York: Harper and Brothers, 1853), 2:234–38; *Charleston Patriot*, 19 September 1835; *Savannah News* quoted in *Louisville Daily Courier*, 6 March 1855; Lillian Foster, *Way-Side Glimpses, North and South* (New York: Rudd & Carleton, 1860), p. 109.

The Illusion of Change:
Women and the American Revolution

Joan Hoff Wilson

Seemingly a symbol of female patriotism, this engraving of a woman with a musket appeared on a broadside, "A New Touch of the Times," issued in 1777 by "A Daughter of Liberty." She lamented the effects of the war on women in the seaport towns and actually ended with a prayer, "Then gracious GOD, now cause to cease/ This bloody war and give us peace!" The picture was used on other broadsides years before the war. New York Historical Society.

As a graduate student at the University of California, Berkeley, in the mid-1960s, I decided not to specialize in the field of Jacksonian Democracy because it would involve too much research in economics and interest group influence on politics, and because of the difficulty of determining the difference between ideology and behavior. As an indirect result of the free speech and antiwar movements on the campus, I have ended up spending most of my time since then in the field of economic foreign policy, dealing, ironically, with the influence (or lack thereof) of business interest groups on twentieth-century American diplomacy, and determining whether or not business ideology is always consistent with business activity.

When I first began to teach women's studies classes in 1970, I did not intend to apply any of the organizational theories or the economic research techniques that I had developed as a historian of foreign policy to the field of women's history. But I have been doing just that. My research in women's history has led me into a variety of projects, such as writing several scripts for *Women and the Law,* a series of video tapes for a nationally distributed law school course; compiling West Coast material for the *Women's History Sources Survey Project;* and integrating women's and ethnic history into secondary school curricula for the State of California Youth Authority.

As a direct result of working on this essay, I have begun a major new project on the impact of the American Revolution on the legal status of women, funded by a grant from the National Endowment for the Humanities. At this writing, I am completing a biography of Anne Henrietta Martin (1875–1951), a leading western suffragist, author, and social critic from Nevada. Clearly I have fallen into a pattern of writing about two seemingly very different aspects of American history —foreign policy and women—both of which may benefit from analysis along structural-functional, interdisciplinary lines.

Joan Hoff Wilson (Ph.D., University of California, Berkeley, 1966), teaches at California State University, Sacramento. She is the author of three books on twentieth century American politics, economics, and foreign policy, the most recent of which is *Herbert Hoover: Forgotten Progressive* (Little, Brown, 1975). The National Endowment for the Humanities awarded her a Younger Humanist Fellowship in 1973–1974, and a research fellowship for 1975–76.

I

To discuss individual women and the American Revolution is to talk about unrequited patriotism. To discuss individual women in relation to any specific historical event like a revolution, a depression, or any other major development in foreign and domestic policy is equally gratuitous. By themselves women seldom fit into the power and prestige categories that characterize standard textbook accounts of this nation's development.[1] Their contributions to history and the important societal conditions affecting them and other subordinate, powerless groups in American history are largely evolutionary in nature. Consequently, they do not dovetail with such common periodizations as the Revolution, the Jacksonian period, Reconstruction, or the Progressive Era.

Therefore, no attempt simply to document the specific individual or group actions of American women between 1763 and 1783 will contribute significantly to assessing their historical importance. One must begin to hypothesize about their collective stage of socioeconomic development *before, during,* and *after* the events leading up to and immediately following the War for Independence. Hence, the time period under discussion will generally be the last half of the eighteenth century and first decade of the nineteenth century, with particular attention given to the years from the end of the French and Indian War in 1763 to 1800. It was a period of war, socioeconomic change, and political upheaval.

This essay may raise more questions than it answers, for I am going to suggest, on the basis of my reading of the secondary scholarship in the field and a foray into a variety of primary sources, several untested conceptual ways of viewing groups of American women who coincidentally were members of the revolutionary generation in eighteenth-century America.[2] To begin to place into perspective the many roles assumed by women in the male-dominated societal processes, structural-functional, interdisciplinary and comparative methodologies, as defined by Robert F. Berkhofer and others, is essential.[3] Whenever possible, the actual status of groups of women should be described *from their point of view* and then compared with the status *usually assigned* to them as isolated objects judged exclusively by male standards. Once these female perceptions are uncovered, we can then assess whether or not they are feminist, depending upon the degree to which women in any time period internalize the values of the man-made world in which they find themselves.

I realize that no single conceptual framework or methodology is completely satisfactory to unravel the complexities of women's history. The application of a functional, comparative analysis will allow historians to more easily question the validity of behavior prescribed for women on the basis of standard patriarchal and often sexist value judgments about their contributions to history. By keeping in mind the differences among various classes and races of women, as well as individual differences among women, we may also move away from traditional generalizations about women as a whole.

Although the societal values assigned to functions performed by individuals or groups vary according to the prevailing norms of their time, women are usually found in low status roles characterized by involutary or forced duties. However necessary these activities are to the development of a country's socioeconomic institutions, in performing such tasks as household work, women seldom determine the parameters of their actions or the monetary value attached to them.[4] Consequently, I will argue that certain types of female functions, leading either to the well-known exploitation of working women or to the ornamental middle-class housewife of the nineteenth century, were abetted by the American Revolution, although not caused by it.

This occurred because the functional opportunities open to women between 1700 and 1800 were too limited to allow them to make the transition in attitudes necessary to insure high status performance in the newly emerging nation. In other words, before 1776 women did not participate enough in conflicts over land, religion, taxes, local politics, or commercial transactions. They simply had not come into contact with enough worldly diversity to be prepared for a changing, pluralistic, modern society. Women of the postrevolutionary generation had little choice but to fill those low status functions prescribed by the small minority of American males who *were* prepared for modernization by enough diverse activities and experiences.[5]

As a result, the American Revolution produced no significant benefits for American women. This same generalization can be made for other powerless groups in the colonies—native Americans, blacks, probably most propertyless white males, and indentured servants. Although these people together with women made up the vast majority of colonial population, they could not take advantage of the overthrow of British rule to better their own positions, as did the white, propertied males who controlled economics, politics, and culture. By no means did all members of these subordinate groups support the patriot cause, and those who did, even among whites, were not automatically accorded personal liberation when national liberation was won. This is a common phenomenon of revolution within subcultures which, because of sex, race, or other forms of discrimination or deprivation of the members, are not far enough along in the process toward modernization to express their dissatisfaction or frustration through effectively organized action.[6]

Given the political and socioeconomic limitations of the American Revolution, this lack of positive societal change in the lives of women and other deprived colonials is to be expected. It is also not surprising that until recently most historians of the period have been content to concentrate their research efforts on the increased benefits of Lockean liberalism that accrued to a relatively small percent of all Americans and to ignore the increased sexism and racism exhibited by this privileged group both during and after the Revolution. They have also tended to ignore the various ways in which the experience of the Revolution either hastened or retarded certain long-term eighteenth-century trends already affecting women.

What has been called in England and Europe "the transformation of the female in bourgeois culture" also took place in America between 1700 and 1800. This process would have occurred with or without a declaration of independence from England. It produced a class of American bourgeoises who clearly resembled the group of middle-class women evident in England a century earlier.[7] However, the changing societal conditions leading up to this transformation in American women were much more complex than they had been for seventeenth-century British women because of the unique roles, that is, functions, that colonial women had originally played in the settlement and development of the New World. The American Revolution was simply one event among many in this century-long process of change. It was a process that ultimately produced two distinct classes of women in the United States—those who worked to varying degrees exclusively in their homes and those who worked both inside and outside of their homes.

To understand this uniquely American process it is necessary to examine five major societal factors defining the status and function of American women throughout the eighteenth century. They were economic, demographic, religious, educational, and legal-political changes that the colonies were experiencing on the road to modernity. This entire process involved the gradual maturation of preindustrial capitalism,[8] and initially it appeared that both men and women were subjected to the same set of transitional economic forces, sociopsychological pressures, and material improvements. Or at least this is the well-preserved illusion of most scholarship on the subject. Instead, it would seem that the first leg of this journey of women into the modern world contained some distinctly different experiences and fewer direct liberalizing benefits and high status functions than it did for men.

Moreover, these five societal conditions had an unequal impact on various classes and groups of colonial women. Their effect was experienced in different degrees, ranging from the middle and upper strata of free white society down to the free and unfree at the bottom of that society: indentured servants and domestics. Black female slaves, native American women, vagabonds, and free, white females living in the most isolated frontier areas sometimes constitute exceptions to the generalizations to be discussed about the changing status and function of eighteenth-century women. Only one aspect of colonial life remained the same for all women. This was the legacy of the "ideology of subordination" inherited from patriarchial Judaic-Christian, western European traditions that produced cultural and economic discrimination against women at all levels of society. At best this ideology was skewed or modified temporarily to meet the immediate needs of colonization, but it was never seriously challenged before 1776 except by isolated seventeenth-century religious radicals like the Puritan Anne Hutchinson or the Quaker Mary Dyer.[9]

After examining these five long-range trends I will turn to the experiences influencing the political consciousness of women during the Revolution and finally to the limitations of the ideology of the most articulate advocates of women's rights—both of which further explain the failure of the Revolution to bring about significant change for women.

II

Before embarking on this lengthy exploration, there is a need to come to grips with two problems that plague almost all students of women's history, whatever the place and period, and especially those who deal with women in a time of revolution: first, the problem of interpreting the semantics of the era, and, second, the problem of defining feminism.

The American Revolution poses special problems of rhetoric which scholars of "ideology" have only recently been giving attention to. The English language was in a process of historical change in the colonies; moreover, individual political words and slogans came to mean different things to women, who were barred from most avenues of public life, than to men, who were not. Consequently we find that a patina of platitudes overlays almost all descriptions of the contributions of "female Patriots," especially during the war. They are described as "patriotic mothers [who] nursed the infancy of freedom," or as forces "for pure living and general righteousness" and as "conservator[s] of moral power." Such statements not only distort but also serve to obliterate the significant historical legacy of this generation of women. As a result, the collective contributions, particularly of lower-class women, to the war effort have been ignored because, like Margaret ("Dirty Kate") Corbin, they cannot be described as having preserved their "virtue and chastity. . .unblemished." In the case of Deborah Sampson Gannett and the legendary "Molly Pitcher," these poor, rugged women have been formed into feminine, genteel nineteenth-century "ladies."[10]

During the 1780s and 1790s there was an increase in similarly flowery rhetoric to describe the importance of "the patriotic Females who their Country saved," of women "instructing their sons in the principles of liberty and government," who had the "reformation of the world" in their power, and the responsibility for keeping the nation independent through their virtuous conduct.[11] It is not unusual for revolutionary generations to be overly concerned with moral standards and to view women as the natural repository of virtue. This had been a common assumption of western culture for many centuries—one that was simply reinforced by revolutionary conditions.

Yet historians of the period have traditionally ignored any system-

atic semantic analysis of this positive rhetoric, as well as the pervasive
negative symbolic portrayal of England by the patriots as the personifi-
cation of an evil, vindictive mother.[12] Obviously these are contrasting
elements in the rhetoric of the revolution. The degree to which one
or the other prevailed in affecting the actual, as opposed to the idealized, status of women or the family during and after the war has yet
to be investigated.

Even in the absence of adequate semantic analysis of the effect of
rhetoric on behavior and values, I see little point in contemporary
historians' continuing to infer, as did most male and female writers of
the late eighteenth century, that through their function as educators
within the home, "traditional womanly virtues were endowed with
political purpose."[13] Indeed, a careful reading of some of the most
articulate women indicates that they were already dimly aware of the
discrepancy between their actual function in society and the exaggerated rhetorical roles assigned to them.

Abigail Adams, for example, grasped the limitations of the educational function of virtuous, upper-class women and of the inadequacy
of their education. Writing in the summer of 1782 to both her husband
and her cousin John Thaxter, she first pointed out that "patriotism in
the female Sex is the most disinterested of all virtues" because women
had no political rights. Hence their patriotism consisted of the un-
heralded act of surviving the loss in battle of "those whom we Love
most." Then she most astutely noted that given the increase in political
corruption and private vice during the war, she did not see how women
could effectively transfer their private virtues to the public realm. How
could they possibly control the virtue of society, as Rousseau had
recommended, when their distinctly inferior female education and
socialization had instilled in them ideas of morality which males did
not necessarily share? Indeed, what means did they have at their dis-
posal for such an enormously pretentious task? It was obvious, at least
to Abigail Adams, that education conducted in the home was not the
way to preserve uncorrupted republicanism. Her friend Mercy Otis
Warren elaborated on some of these thoughts in 1800 when she said
that education was as unnecessary for a woman as virtue was for a
gentleman. In 1805, in her three-volume *History of the Rise, Progress and
Termination of the American Revolution,* she commented negatively on the
decline in virtue of the "children of Columbia," nowhere indicating
that women could stem this counterrevolutionary tide.[14]

The women of the revolution, when not described collectively in platitudinous phrases as paragons of virtue and patriotism, which they supposedly transmitted through their household roles as educators, were usually damned with faint praise, even by those among them who were in a position to know better. Thus, Mercy Warren in her history, as in her earlier patriotic plays and poetry, ignored entirely the significant contributions of women to the Revolution—an indication of the limitations of her "feminism." Instead, her most direct comment on the subject came during the war when she wrote: "Be it known unto Britain even American daughters are politicians and patriots, and will aid the good work with their feeble efforts."[15]

Worse still, perhaps, has been the opposite practice among historians to single out a few identifiable women for acts of military heroism when there is the distinct possibility that numerous camp followers were regularly involved in at least artillery combat. Thus most works on women in the Revolution contain the same descriptions of a handful of women who are assumed to be the only ones to fight or to act as spies and couriers during the war—"Molly Pitcher," Margaret Sybil Ludington, Mary Ludwig Hays McCauly, Nancy Morgan Hart, Lydia Barrington Darragh, Margaret Corbin, Sally St. Clair, and Deborah Gannett Sampson[16] or those who represented extreme examples of personal courage, self-sacrifice, or symbolic action. One of the most celebrated, commonly cited examples of the latter is the story of Betsy Ross and the first flag, which turns out to be apocryphal.[17]

The second major problem in writing about women of this or any other period—defining feminism—may be put this way: Is feminism a historically restricted term, or is its definition necessarily timeless? Can a single unifying feminist factor be found among eighteenth-century women, regardless of class, that falls within the boundaries of such a definition? How broadly can feminist political activity be defined in an age when women had no formal political rights? For purposes of this essay I will begin with Gerda Lerner's general definition of feminism. Lerner has said it "embraces all aspects of the emancipation of American women." Feminism incorporates, therefore, "any struggle to elevate [women's] status, socially, politically, economically, *and in respect to their self concepts,*" whereas the term women's rights movement refers more narrowly to obtaining legal and political rights.[18]

Even this definition, however, does not answer the crucial question of whether or not women who define themselves and their struggle for emancipation exclusively in terms of male rights and standards are indeed feminists. In other words, all feminists support women's rights movements, but not all members of women's rights movements are feminists unless they consciously perceive of themselves as agents for societal change in other than patriarchal terms. In fact, however, most female activists have adhered traditionally to a very narrow definition of equality at best—one, I suggest, that is not feminist unless it encompasses attacks on such traditional patriarchal bailiwicks as the sanctity of motherhood, the family, the institution of marriage, or the prevailing male-dominated economic and political systems. Moreover, they are seldom concerned with preserving or creating a female culture or consciousness separate from one that simply internalizes male standards.

In *Woman as Force in History*, Mary Beard argued logically, if ineffectually, against this limited type of equality and consciousness based on "man the measure of excellence." In taking this position in 1946, she criticized past and present women reformers whom she correctly described as having simplistically portrayed women over the ages as in a state of total subjection. Then she noted that they contradicted themselves by citing examples of exceptional historical women figures when they demanded immediate legal equality, that is, male status as the means for achieving emancipation. Beard also rejected their argument because she did not personally believe that complete equality between men and women would ever be legislated, and because she associated the position with communist and socialist theories of equality.[19]

While I do not agree with all of Beard's reasons for opposing female demands for legal equality, I believe that she not only raised the essential question about their effectiveness, but she also pointed out the basic contradiction in the reasoning that led to them and which continues to exist in most historical studies of women. In fact, neither the total subjection theory nor the exceptional woman extolled for her male qualities provides adequate analytical models for research in the field of women's history or for defining what constitutes feminist activity. The former is obviously contradicted by the existence of the exceptions; the latter continues to make the standards for determining what is important about women in American history the same as those for men. To avoid both the confusion and the contradiction arising from these traditional analytical models, I have already suggested a functional, comparative analysis of women's collective roles in society. I have now offered a definition of feminism based on a conscious, antipatriarchal concept of female behavior and culture that I hope will reduce its indiscriminate application to all types of independent, outspoken women, regardless of the cause or issue they champion.

This definition will make clear why I will argue later that, unlike the English radical theorist Mary Wollstonecraft, the most articulate of late eighteenth-century American women cannot be considered feminists.

III

Since the 1920s an increasing number of historians have argued that during the colonial period women enjoyed a less sex-stereotyped existence than at any time until recently, despite the absence of any significant number of organized or individual feminists. This argument is largely an exaggeration based on inadequate samplings of the small group of women who worked outside the home, or the few who actually appeared in probate records, paid taxes, wrote wills, or asserted their legal and political rights through petitions and occasional voting.

It is true, however, for most of the period up to 1750 that conditions *out of necessity* increased the functional independence and importance of all women. By this I mean that much of the alleged freedom from sexism of colonial women was due to their initial numerical scarcity and the critical labor shortage in the New World throughout the seventeenth and eighteenth centuries. Such increased reproductive roles (economic as well as biological) reflected the logic of necessity and *not any fundamental change* in the sexist, patriarchal attitudes that had been transplanted from Europe. Based on two types of scarcity (sex and labor), which were not to last, these enhanced functions of colonial women diminished as the commercial and agricultural economy became more specialized and the population grew.

A gradual "embourgeoisement" of colonial culture accompanied this preindustrial trend toward modern capitalism. It limited the number of high status roles for eighteenth-century American women just as it had for seventeenth-century English and European women. Alice Clark, Margaret George, Natalie Zemon Davis, and Jane Abray have all argued convincingly that as socioeconomic capitalist organization takes place, it closes many opportunities normally open to women both inside and outside of the family unit in precapitalist times. The decline in the status of women that accompanied the appearance of bourgeois modernity in England, according to Margaret George, "was not merely a relative decline. Precapitalist woman was not simply relatively eclipsed by the great leap forward of the male achiever; she suffered rather, an absolute setback."[20]

In the New World this process took longer but was no less debilitating. Before 1800 it was both complicated and hindered by the existence of a severe labor shortage and religious as well as secular exhortations against the sins of idleness and vanity. Thus, colonial conditions demanded that all able-bodied men, women, and children work, and so the ornamental, middle-class woman existed more in theory than in practice.

The labor shortage that plagued colonial America placed a premium on women's work inside and outside the home, particularly during the war-related periods of economic dislocation between 1750 and 1815. And there is no doubt that home industry was basic to American development both before and after 1776. It is also true that there was no sharp delineation between the economic needs of the community and the work carried on within the preindustrial family until after the middle of the eighteenth century. Woman's role as a household manager was a basic and integral part of the early political economy of the colonies. Hence she occupied a position of unprecedented importance and equality within the socioeconomic unit of the family.[21]

As important as this function of women in the home was, from earliest colonial times, it nonetheless represented a division of labor based on sex-role stereotyping carried over from England. Men normally engaged in agricultural production; women engaged in domestic gardening and home manufacturing—only slave women worked in the fields. Even in those areas of Massachusetts and Pennsylvania that originally granted females allotments of land, the vestiges of this practice soon disappeared, and subsequent public divisions "simply denied the independent economic existence of women." While equality never extended outside the home in the colonial era, there was little likelihood that women felt useless or alienated because of the importance and demanding nature of their domestic responsibilities.[22]

In the seventeenth and eighteenth centuries spinning and weaving were the primary types of home production for women and children (of both sexes). This economic function was considered so important that legal and moral sanctions were developed to insure it. For example, labor laws were passed, compulsory spinning schools were established "for the education of children of the poor," and women were told that their virtue could be measured in yards of yarn.[23] So from the beginning there was a sex, and to a lesser degree a class and educational, bias built into colonial production of cloth, since no formal apprenticeship was required for learning the trade of spinning and weaving.

It has also been recognized that prerevolutionary boycotts of English goods after 1763 and later during the war increased the importance of female production of textiles both in the home and in the early piecework factory system. By mid-1776 in Philadelphia, for example, 4,000 women and children reportedly were spinning under the "putting out system" for local textile plants.[24]

The importance of those few women who fulfilled other economic roles *in addition to* their household activities is not so readily demonstrable. The documentation about bonafide female entrepreneurs remains highly fragmentary and difficult, if not impossible, to analyze with statistical accuracy.[25] Many, if not most, appear to be the widows of "men who had been less affluent." If we take Philadelphia as representative of greater urban specialization and utilization of female workers due to the shortage of labor,[26] we find a significant number of women in only three entrepreneurial occupations up to 1776: shopkeeping, innkeeping, and crafts-making. The first two were obviously sex-role based in that most of the early retail stores and taverns were located in private homes and simply represented an extension of normal household duties. Although craftswomen also often sold their products directly from their individual dwellings, their work was not always related to traditional domestic tasks. Thus, Philadelphia women engaged in roughly thirty different trades ranging from essential to luxury services. They included female silversmiths, tinworkers, barbers, bakers, fish picklers, brewers, tanners, ropemakers, lumberjacks, gunsmiths, butchers, milliners, harnessmakers, potash manufacturers, upholsterers, printers, morticians, chandlers, coachmakers, embroiderers, dry cleaners and dyers, woodworkers, staymakers, tailors, flour processors, seamstresses, netmakers, braziers, and founders.[27]

It is this impressive array of female artisans in Philadelphia and other colonial towns that has led to the conclusion that work for women was much less sex-stereotyped in the seventeenth and eighteenth centuries than it was to become in the nineteenth. The validity of this claim has yet to be documented by a comparative analysis of female artisans in different areas. On the one hand, women found themselves in these essential and nonfamilial roles because they were substituting for dead or absent husbands; on the other hand, it was not considered "inappropriate" according to prevailing socioeconomic norms for women to engage in this wide variety of occupations, carry on the family business if widowed, or become a skilled artisan while still married. Single and married women operating their own shops and taverns were an even more common fact of colonial life.[28]

From tavern licenses issued in Philadelphia, for example, it is clear that between 1762 and 1776 no less than 17 percent, and even as much as 22 percent, of all tavern operators were women,[29] and these figures do not include those women who may have been operating illegally without licenses.[30] Such fragmentary evidence shows there were at least ninety-four female shopkeepers operating in Philadelphia between 1720 and 1776, and that in 1717 nine out of twenty-eight, or 32 percent, of all shopkeepers taking out "freedoms" were women. None of these businesswomen seem to have been given any special attention or consideration—not even the six who signed the nonimportation agreement of 25 October 1765. At the moment there is no way of knowing how representative these figures on innkeepers or "she-merchants" are for other colonial towns on the eve of the American Revolution.[31]

The increasing commerical and agricultural specialization prior to 1776,[32] affected all Americans, but particularly women, whether they were the vast rural majority who engaged in home production or the few who became entrepreneurs in the cities and towns. Probably the most significant changes were an erratic rise in the standard of living and a substantial increase in the number of landless proletarians in the major urban areas. There is now evidence that the uneven and unequal distribution of wealth as shown for Boston existed as well in Philadelphia, Newport, and New York City. Any amount of economic inequality was particularly devastating for widows, who often had dependents to support. The economic plight of the increasingly large number of widows also led to an expansion of their legal rights before 1776, so that they could convert real property into capital for personal support or investment purposes.[33]

American living standards fluctuated with the unequal prosperity that was especially related to wars. Those engaging in craft production and commerce were particularly hard hit after 1750, first by the deflation and depression following the French and Indian War (1754–1763), and then by the War for Independence. In fact, not only were the decades immediately preceding and following the American Revolution ones of economic dislocation, but the entire period between 1775 and 1815 has been characterized as one of "arrested social and economic development." These trends, combined with increased specialization, particularly with the appearance of a nascent factory system, "initiated a decline in the economic and social position of many sections of the artisan class." Thus with the exception of the innkeeping and tavern business, all of the other primary economic occupations of city women were negatively affected by the periodic fluctuations in the commercial economy between 1763 and 1812.[34]

Women artisans and shopkeepers probably suffered most during times of economic crisis because of their greater difficulty in obtaining credit from merchants. Although research into their plight has been neglected, the documents are there—in the records of merchant houses showing women entrepreneurs paying their debts for goods and craft materials by transferring their own records of indebtedness, and in court records showing an increased number of single women, especially widows sued for their debts, or in public records of the increased number of bankrupt women who ended up on poor relief lists or in debtors' prisons or who were forced to become indentured servants or earn an independent living during hard times.[35]

It was also a difficult time for household spinners and weavers, about whom a few more facts are known. First, this all-important economic function increasingly reflected class distinctions. In 1763 one British governor estimated that only the poor wore homespun clothes, while more affluent Americans bought English imports. Second, it was primarily poor women of the northern and middle colonies who engaged in spinning and weaving for pay (often in the form of credit rather than cash), while black slave women and white female indentured servants performed the same function in the South. Naturally women in all frontier areas had no recourse but to make their own clothing. Beginning with the first boycotts of British goods in the 1760s, women of all classes were urged to make and wear homespun. Several additional "manufactory houses" were established as early as 1764 in major cities specifically for the employment of poor women. Direct appeals to patriotism and virtue were used very successfully to get wealthier women to engage in arduous home-spinning drives, but probably only for short periods of time.[36]

Thus all classes of women were actively recruited into domestic textile production by male patriots with such pleas as, "In this time of

public distress you have each of you an opportunity not only to help
to sustain your families, but likewise to call your mite into the treasury
of the public good." They were further urged to "cease trifling their
time away [and] prudently employ it in learning the use of the spinning
wheel."[37] Beyond any doubt the most well-known appeal was the
widely reprinted 9 November 1767 statement of advice to the "Daughters of Liberty" which first appeared in the *Massachusetts Gazette*. It read
in part:

> First then throw aside your high top knots of pride
> Wear none but your own country linen.
> Of economy boast. Let your pride be the most
> To show cloaths of your make and spinning.

Peak periods in prerevolutionary spinning and weaving were
reached during every major boycott from 1765 to 1777. But the war
and inflation proved disruptive. For example, we know that the United
Company of Philadelphia for Promoting American Manufactures,
which employed 500 of the City's 4,000 women and children spinning
at home, expired between 1777 and 1787, when it was revived. The
record of similar organizations elsewhere was equally erratic.[38]

It is common for developing countries with a labor shortage to
utilize technological means to meet production demands. After the
war, the new republic proved no exception, as the inefficiency and
insufficiency of household spinners became apparent. Ultimately the
"putting out" system was replaced entirely by the factory that employed the same women and children who had formerly been
household spinners. It took the entire first half of the nineteenth
century before this process was completed, and when it was, it turned
out to be at the expense of the social and economic status of female
workers.[39]

At the beginning of this process, however, the early cotton mills
in the last quarter of the eighteenth century utilized skilled immigrants
of both sexes. In fact, according to one recent study, the years between
1763 and 1812 constituted the "non-verbal period of industrial technology" in American history. During this time English technological
"know-how" was transferred to the United States primarily through
artificers who either owned, could build, or could operate the latest
"labour-saving machines." In July 1788, for example, the Pennsylvania
Society located a woman who owned a twisting mill and immediately

employed her "on the best Terms." How many of these migrating artisans were women is not yet precisely known.[40]

Direct employment in these early cotton textile mills was the final way, therefore, in which changing economic conditions affected women. Such employment did not represent a new economic function for women—it simply shifted their place of work from the home to the factory. Economic nationalists like Secretary of the Treasury Alexander Hamilton recognized the contributions of women in the production of cloth under the traditional "domestic system." At the same time he recommended, in his well-known *Report on Manufactures* of 1791, that women and children be utilized in the factory production of cotton goods. All economic nationalists, both Federlist and Republican, openly recognized that the labor of women and children would have to be exploited if the nation were to industrialize.[41]

The position was reinforced in the 1790s by male moralists who preached that poor women who did not take up factory work would be "doomed to idleness and its inseparable attendants, vice and guilt." Through at least the War of 1812, this unholy alliance temporarily prolonged the pragmatic colonial idea that "woman's place was . . . not in the home, . . . but wherever her 'more important' work was."[42] Now, however, this idea became the basis for making a class distinction between women that had not been possible throughout most of the preindustrial colonial period. In other words, the potential economic contribution of women to the new textile industry contrasted sharply with the propagandistic rhetoric of the 1780s and the 1790s, which portrayed them as preservers of republican virtue, exclusively within the home as patriotic wives and educators.

Each role could be (and was) justified in the name of nationalism. But each projected distinctly different future tasks for women, depending upon their socioeconomic status. One led to the dual capitalist exploitation of women as a reserve supply of cheap labor in industry and the home, without any increase in their economic power or personal status; the other led to a less functional and isolated position of women within the modern, middle-class nuclear family, whose domestic duties and responsibilities gradually declined until they consisted primarily of improving male manners and nurturing children. Both were necessary for rapid industrialization in the nineteenth century.

While the industrialization that the War of 1812 stimulated did more to hasten these class distinctions (as well as the low status and

alienating features of women's work inside and outside of the home)
than did the American Revolution, the latter set the stage for what was
to follow both in the attitudes toward women it fostered and the
requirements it set for economic growth.

IV

Before, during, and after the Revolution, American women were
experiencing important demographic changes that ultimately contributed to their socioeconomic subordination in the modern world.
These demographic factors were of such an evolutionary nature, however, that few seem to have been directly affected by the Revolution
itself, save for the temporary disruption of the nuclearity of family life,
as men left home to participate in political or military activities, and
for the lowering of sexual and moral standards that normally accom-
pany wars.

To date most social demographers have concentrated on the seventeenth and early eighteenth centuries rather than the revolutionary
period. Nonetheless, much can be inferred from recent studies of
family reconstitution about the condition of women on the eve of the
American Revolution. While regional differences remain to be studied,[43]
significant strides have been taken with vital statistics from about a half
dozen small New England communities, which suggest trends for the
colonial household in that area. Since such figures could not be obtained from traditional literary sources, earlier assumptions about
mortality rates, domestic stability, family size, child raising, education,
male-female sex roles, and even remarriage rates are now being questioned.[44]

In general, living conditions in New England (but not in the
South) appear to gave been more stable and healthy, especially in the
seventeenth century, than they were in England and Europe. Thus,
there is evidence of increased longevity for adults, decreased deaths
from childbirth, and lower mortality rates for infants and adolescents.
And contrary to what was commonly thought, the duration of first
marriages was quite high—ranging from between twenty and twenty-
five years in some New England towns—while remarriage of widows
was less likely than once assumed.[45]

Even the much heralded and first significant demographic fact
about colonial women, namely their scarcity, has been cast into a new

light by social demographers. It is true, for example, that men outnumbered women by three to one in the initial immigration to New England, and by six to one in the early Virginia settlements. Nevertheless, this extreme imbalance in the sex ratio soon succumbed to the high fertility level among colonial women and to lower mortality rates in the New England colonies at the beginning of the eighteenth century. In the middle and southern colonies fertility was also high, but so were mortality rates. Consequently, in these areas immigration continued to play an important role not only in maintaining population growth but also in contributing to a sex imbalance. In colonies like Virginia and Maryland, for example, there were still about three men for every two women in 1700. Even though women colonists in the South showed a greater resistance than men to disease during the "seasoning" process, they remained scarce for the next twenty or thirty years. In contrast, by 1700 the larger New England coastal towns and small eastern settlements actually experienced a surplus of unmarried women, which continued to increase and whose significance has yet to be evaluated by historians.[46]

By 1750, at least northern colonial America could no longer be considered a "paradise on earth for women," where every free, white female could marry and where a stable, parental dominated marriage system or family of orientation (birth) prevailed. It was in the throes of a "demographic crisis." Among other things, this meant that the age gap narrowed between men and women at the time of their first marriages, with men generally marrying slightly earlier and women slightly later. In addition to facing the possibility of not being able to marry, or remarry, in the case of widows, by the time of the Revolution women had been gradually adjusting to changing courtship and marriage patterns, loosened sexual mores, smaller family size, and (among the wealthier, better educated) to more permissive theories from foreign authors about child raising, romantic love, and sex-stereotyped definitions of feminity.[47] All of these demographic alterations were part of the process of family modernization—that is, the evolution from the family of orientation to the family of procreation. This transition was most pronounced in the late eighteenth and early nineteenth centuries, and is therefore coincidentally connected but not substantially affected by the Revolution.

It was the changing position of women within this gradually evolving conjugal household and its declining socioeconomic importance in general that posed the most serious demographic problems for the revolutionary generation of women—not the exact size or structure of the family unit, which continued to vary from region to region and within local communities. In other words, except for the actual years in which the war was fought, colonial women found more and more of their traditional familial duties and responsibilities syphoned off as the economy became more commercially specialized and as other social institutions such as schools became more commonplace. Only women living in the most isolated frontier areas escaped this experience of declining importance and function within the family unit, and their position was far from enviable because of the physical and mental harshness of frontier life.[48]

The difficult task of documenting this trend toward modernization of the conjugal household through family reconstitution analysis is far from complete. But we do know, for example, that there was no dramatic shift from the so-called extended family structure to a nuclear one. Through the seventeenth and early eighteenth centuries New World households appear to have been largely nuclear in structure, with women of completed fertility producing an average of seven to eight children. The number of children borne by New England women declined in the last half of the eighteenth century to five or six. Once mortality rates and other factors are considered, however, the average number of free persons in each household varied from a crowded 9.3 in Boston to 6.7 in some of the interior counties of Massachusetts in 1764 to an average of around 5.8 (or 6.1 if slaves are included) per household by 1790. Despite this slight decrease both in the number of children borne and in household size in the course of eighteenth century, average American families were still larger than those in England and Europe. No drastic decline in marital fertility rates and household size occurred in the United States until after 1850.[49]

Nonetheless, even this relatively small decline prior to 1800 is interesting both for what it did and did not represent. First, it should be noted that it occurred in urban and rural areas and among all religious groups (including the Quakers). With few exceptions it is doubtful that this can be considered conscious family limitation, yet for reasons not yet clear American parents were beginning to consider large families a liability after 1760. But they did not generally have the modern, small target families in mind. Second, there is some, albeit far from conclusive, evidence from letters and diaries that fewer children and smaller family units produced more intimate, sentimental, and affectionate relationships. This in turn is said to have contributed to the growth of individualism, modern concepts of self and ego development among children, and romantic love ties between husbands and wives. By and large, however, the more permissive, less authoritarian child-centered family of procreation simply had not evolved by 1776, as some scholars have claimed. While there are isolated private examples of a more sentimental view of children and a tendency to glorify motherhood, neither became an established practice until after 1800 in the United States. The same is true of the concept of romantic love that finally led to marriage as a "free act" of the couple involved rather than a parentally controlled affair.[50]

It appears that most eighteenth-century women, even those who had read Locke and Rousseau, were still primarily occupied with how to conquer the wills of their children rather than with the development of individual independence. If anything, the slightly smaller household usually meant that mothers, often weakened or ill from frequent pregnancies, were placed in greater direct contact with their children, since there were fewer relatives or servants present. This led at least upper-class colonial women (and aristocratic foreigners who visited them) in the last half of the century to complain about the recalcitrance of American children and the personal burden they had become. "You can not conceive how my time is taken up," Ester Edwards Burr, the mother of Aaron Burr, confided to her journal in 1756. "Sometimes I never sit down a whole day unless to vittles." Pamela Sedgwick of Massachussetts confided to a spinster friend that she no sooner would "snatch a moment from a crying infant," than two or three of her other "ungoverned children" would begin to make noise the like of which was "as distracting to the brain as a confused din of arms to a timid soldier." She finally wrote her often-absent husband Theodore Sedgwick, in 1790, that she was "tired of living a widow and being at the same time a nurse." Poorer women had neither the time nor the literacy to record their impressions of child raising, but it is doubtful that they were any less strict or less burdened than their better educated counterparts by the late eighteenth century.[51]

A much better indication of the transitional stage of the American family on the eve of the Revolution can be found in the general decline of parental economic control over the marriages of their children. Once again, this generalization applies more to the wealthier than the poorer segment of colonial society. During the seventeenth and up to the middle of the eighteenth century parental control had been exercised largely through delayed property inheritance or the need to support a widowed mother. Such authority was undermined, however, as the legal rights of widows were gradually expanded to make them less economically dependent on their male children, and as primogeniture became less feasible as a means of controlling the marital pattern of eldest sons—it actually made the younger ones, according to Thomas Jefferson, "independent of, and disobedient to their parents."[52]

In the case of women, the increase in those who remained unmarried or who married out of normal sibling sequence was an early indication of the decline in parental authority, and hence a weakening of the family of orientation. Another indication of the gradual separation of girls from their family of birth can be found in the significant drop in the percentage of mother-daughter name-sharing. Before 1700, in Hingham, Massachusetts, 98.5 percent of all families with three or more daughters named one after the mother. By 1780 this had dropped to 53.2 percent, and the practice was to decrease even more by the end of the nineteenth century, although less rapidly for boys than girls because of the potential inheritance value of having the same name as one's father or other close male relative.[53]

Probably the most important, yet often overlooked, of all the indices of changing family patterns was the unprecedented increase in premarital pregnancies among white Americans in the last half of the eighteenth century. A peak in the number of so-called "short-term" babies conceived before marriage was reached between 1761 and 1800, when 16.7 percent of all first babies were born under six months of marriage, 27.2 percent under eight and one-half months, and 33 percent under nine months. The overall figure of 30 percent for premarital pregnancies just before and after the American Revolution was not approximated again until the 1960s. Both high periods reflect more than a simple breakdown in sexual mores encouraged by such external factors as wars, the religious revivalism of the mid-eighteenth century, or the counterculture of the last decade.[54]

Instead, premarital pregnancies are perhaps the strongest demographic indication we have of the family in a period of transition and hence unable to enforce conventional controls over sexual behavior. They represent "a collision between an unchanging and increasingly antiquated family structure and a pattern of individual behavior which is more a part of the past than a harbinger of the future." In other words, a dramatic rise in premarital relations does not mean that all other traditional patterns of the established family in any given time period are also abruptly changed or abandoned. Indeed, premarital pregnancies were no more condoned in the last half of the eighteenth century than they are today, but in both instances they do symbolize a generational conflict and a revolt of the young that presage changing power relationships within conjugal households, which may or may not be liberalizing.[55]

In the case of this first peak period, the process of family change was not completed until the 1820s and 1830s, with the appearance of the established nuclear family of procreation. This new family pattern was not only characterized by the sentimentalization of children and the glorification of motherhood, but also ideally by more consensus, affection, and contractual relations than had existed in the more authoritarian family of orientation. Nonetheless, it was within this newly established, child-oriented household that the socioeconomic functions of women were severely limited and from which sexual restrictions and inhibitions emanated, culminating finally in the excessive sexual repression of the late nineteenth century.[56]

This is not to say that any class of women of the revolutionary generation understood what was happening to the family in the last half of the eighteenth century. In such periods of transition it is common that discrepancies increase between familial attitudes (thought) and behavior (function). It must be remembered that they were accustomed to relying upon external, primarily religious and economic, controls over sexual behavior. As the authority of all orthodox religion began to break down, premarital relations assumed class and gender overtones that had not previously existed. What has been called "a sexually permissive subculture" thus emerged more quickly among poorer groups as colonial society became more economically stratified. Most important, it was encouraged or at least passed on intergenerationally from lower-class mothers to their daughters largely through the practice of bundling. While women like Abigail Adams and Mercy Warren worried over how best to instill virtue in their offspring, at the other end of the social scale young girls were told that bundling was "no sin nor shame, for we your mothers did the same."[57]

At the same time we find male patriots quickly capitalizing on the popularity of the political analogy that symbolized the colonies as children in revolt against the "monstrous" mother country. Yet is is equally evident that they did not want to contribute any further to the generational conflict already in progress or to the generally ambiguous, if not actually contradictory, state of the family of orientation by 1776.[58] Nonetheless, it is difficult to imagine that such antiparental, antifemale rhetoric did not further undermine the existing precarious position of family life during the revolutionary years. It would not be until the first quarter of the nineteenth century, however, that lower-class premarital practices would merge with upper-class theories on permissive child raising and romantic love and courtship to complete the breakdown of the family of orientation and replace it with the family of procreation. Even the best educated women could not realize that they were demographically on their way toward modernization within the family of procreation that offered them the "cult of true womanhood" in place of collective validation and a sense of individual worth. Nor could they be expected to have anticipated other "double standard" limitations associated with this new family pattern, such as increased vicarious fulfillment through their husbands or male children and the psychic burden of the permissive child-centered household that epitomized individualism and modern ego development—for men.[59] Assuming that the rhetoric of the Revolution and the trauma of war had not temporarily obfuscated their view of the future, it is doubtful if the most perspicacious women of this generation could have discerned the degree to which demography, and not the separation from England, would determine the destiny of their daughters and grandchildren.

V

The basic reorientation of colonial religion also affected the functionalism of eighteenth-century American women. Originally, Puritanism had not only fostered strong patriarchal, authoritarian family structures, but also had provided external means for socioeconomic control over peoples' lives that went far beyond religious parameters. As the Puritan and other established clergy lost power and status during the last half of the seventeenth century, women were often made the scapegoats for their personal and professional frustrations.[60]

Many orthodox clergymen, who found themselves challenged by new sects and increasing material wealth that fostered "worldly pride or covetousness" instead of piety, looked for "shapes of the Devil" in all manner of activity, especially if it involved immoderate European fashions for either sex. But more often than not they found it in the actions and dress of women, since they made up the majority of the congregations. Such women were castigated for the "sin of idleness" and constantly compared to the vain, evil figure of Eve, or actually accused of illegal political, criminal, or heretical activity.[61] Simultaneously the teachings of the beleaguered orthodox sects became more sex-stereotyped in regard to the "proper sphere" for women, as traditional authority and social mores in colonial communities broke down and secular, as well as religious, witch-hunts took place around 1700. This trend was later reinforced by the even more clearly defined separate sphere or orbit assigned to women through theories associated with the Enlightenment.[62]

With the appearance of revivalism in the form of the Great Awakening from the 1740s on, many of the religious tensions that had plagued both Protestant clergymen and their congregations disappeared or were subsumed by conversions based on a personal relationship with God. One of the most important features of the Great Awakening was that it was a youth movement. It liberated especially young, ambitious male converts from the guilt stemming from material acquisitiveness and from rebellion against traditional political and religious authority. It also gave their anger against entrenched elites an outlet. The Great Awakening was not, therefore, a mystical or introspective experience in the New World. Instead, it was subversive.[63]

"The revivalists undermined the social order, the other main source of guilt," as Richard L. Bushman puts it, "not by repudiating law and authority, but by denying them sanctifying power." Personal, individual salvation through God's Grace was the way to escape both the moral and civil restraints that inhibited the pursuit of wealth and contained resentment against accepted law and authority. At least this is supposedly what the Great Awakening meant for various classes of younger, free and unfree, white males. Most important, it reaffirmed their virility and contained strong patriarchal, authoritarian overtones often disguised with democratic rhetoric.[64]

What it did for women, young and old, is not so clear. Unlike the earlier Quaker movement, women participated in America's first revival experience largely as followers, not leaders. And unlike European revivals for the same time period, the New World version attracted more male than female converts in some areas and "did not display the sensitive mentality of a movement based on the female population and on introverted minds in general; it was rather a democratic revolt in the sphere of religion expressing the feelings of rough and often boorish communities."[65]

Yet women of all ages and classes, particularly those who were unmarried, proved susceptible to this "spiritual epidemic,"[66] without apparently obtaining the same psychological, material, or political benefits that accrued to men from it. The lower the class or status the more emotionally excessive was the response and conversion. For example, there were proportionately fewer converts from either sex in Boston, where the educational level was generally higher, than in other towns where uneducated male "exhorters" would "lead Captive silly Women, and then the Men. Such of them as have good Voices do great Execution; they move Hearers, make them cry, faint, swoon, fall into Convulsions."[67]

But what were the significant legacies of the First Great Awakening for women? Simply the personal and temporary catharsis of conversion? Greater rationalizations for the increase in premarital preganancies that accompanied religious enthusiasm and hastened the breakdown of sexual mores already in progress? Perhaps the true importance of the Great Awakening for them was that it marked the first step toward the religious justification of the creation of a class of American bourgeoises through the ultimate "glorification of humanitarianism, of decency and sobriety, and the virtues of family life."[68] Deprived of a truly mystical, evangelical experience or greater political and material independence through revivalism, or later through the teachings of the Enlightenment, all classes of women were gradually being prepared to accept narrower familial roles. This diminished domesticity would ultimately affect their psychic well-being and their economic, legal, and political functions in modern society.[69]

It cannot even be argued that religion generally improved the literacy rate of women in the last half of the eighteenth century. We know that the stricter, orthodox religions, especially New England Puritanism, had required minimum literacy among women in order that they might benefit from reading the Bible and the early law codes. Although Protestantism is generally credited with having thus improved or raised the general literacy level in the New World, it should be noted that women were nonetheless regarded largely "as mere passive receptors of the written Word of God." This "passive association between Protestantism and female literacy" meant that even in early colonial times New England women generally could not write as well as they could read, for writing, particularly in the form of signatures on wills, deeds, and mortgages, was an active, positive skill (and an extremely important legal tool) that was primarily reserved for male members of society. Even if one does not subscribe to the currently popular belief among social scientists that literacy automatically produces a "modern" personality type and evokes new attitudes such as individualism, ego development, optimism, and enterprise, it is still possible to interpret rising functional literacy among colonial men in New England as an indication of a greater sense of personal autonomy and a greater capacity to take "political action to gain their own ends."[70]

No similarly qualified and moderate statement can be made about female literacy rates for the New England area. Instead, except for a city like Boston, they stagnated at around 40 percent during the first half of the eighteenth century, while male literacy jumped dramatically toward universality, that is, over 90 percent. In the case of rural women, the most recent study shows a regression in their literacy level between 1705 and 1762. This is in contrast to rural men, who by the latter date were 80 percent literate. Since these years include the progress of the Great Awakening *and* the Enlightenment in America, it cannot be argued that greater illiteracy for men was an inevitable by-product of the orally oriented, basically anti-intellectual nature of revivalism, even in the poorest rural areas. Likewise, it also cannot be argued that Enlightenment theories on education and religion increased literacy rates for *both* men and women. And only the formal education of men was definitely improved; first with the establishment of "log cabin" academies, and ultimately with denominational colleges such as Princeton, Dartmouth, Brown, and Rutgers.[71]

In other words, both types of prerevolutionary religious changes, which completed the shift from pietism to enlightened moralism, acted as intellectual opiates for colonial women, while they expanded traditional educational horizons for men of all classes. Therefore, at the lowest (the Great Awakening) and highest (the Enlightenment) intellectual levels of change within eighteenth-century American Protestantism, "repression and religion were [as] complementary," for women as they had been in the seventeenth century. With the possible exception of the Quakers and the sects under Ann Lee and Jemima Wilkinson, the conversion from piety to moralism did not change the fact that most religious groups remained the major means of external social control through which girls and women "were taught to sublimate anger or aggression" and discouraged from assuming leadership positions. At least this seems to be the case up to 1800.[72]

Nonetheless, regardless of its exact form, religion provided women of the seventeenth and eighteenth centuries with their greatest social and cultural opportunities, limited as those may appear in retrospect. It wasn't until the Second Great Awakening of the first quarter of the nineteenth century that churches began to provide women with a vehicle not only for expanding their self-perceptions and sense of personal autonomy but also for obtaining greater legal and economic rights through participation in reform movements. Ironically this modernized form of Protestantism also encouraged greater internalization of sexual inhibitions among women than ever before.[73]

The American Revolution was in part responsible for the shift from external to internal social controls because of its emphasis on automony and individual choice for the colonies. In this sense, therefore, the rhetoric of the Revolution introduced men and women to an indirect process of socialization in which individuals rather than institutions became responsible for their moral as well as political behavior. Thus, when early nineteenth-century religion advocated free will it touched a responsive chord in many postrevolutionary Americans. So it was ultimately through increased church participation that women, supposedly on their way to modernization, began to internalize and practice sexual repression to a greater degree than did their colonial ancestors.

VI

The stagnant literacy level for most women of the revolutionary generation, regardless of class, raises the question of the general status of female education in the colonial era. This represents the fourth major societal influence on the lives of women. In general, changes in their education were more directly related to the appearance of the less authoritarian, more permissive, smaller, child-centered family in Europe and the New World than they were to religious trends. Even in New England, where early provision had been made for the establishment of free public schools, education of girls traditionally was conducted almost exclusively in private homes throughout the colonies. Initially taught by their own mothers or in kitchens of other untrained housewives, known as "dame schools," education of most women was given little theoretical or systematic attention, except within the confines of a few upper-class homes. Even these privileged few complained about their inadequate intellectual backgrounds.[74]

The special interest that some wealthy fathers personally took in the education of their girl children has been called "the potency of daughterhood" by the historian Page Smith. This practice was, in my opinion, a direct outgrowth of the modern trend away from the family of orientation to the family of procreation, with its attendant decline in parental authority. Hence it was not as positive in its results or motivation as Smith implies.[75]

It cannot be denied that unsually strong father-daughter relationships produced a handful of exceptional women, from Anne Hutchinson, Anne Bradstreet, and Margaret Brent in the seventeenth century to Jane Colden Farquhar, Eliza Lucas Pinckney, Mercy Otis Warren, Eliza Southgate Bowne, Judith Sargent Murray in the eighteenth century and Theodosia Burr in the early nineteenth century. But even in these cases, and certainly in the more traditional advice that men as "enlightened" as Franklin and Jefferson gave their daughters, there were severe sexist limits placed on what was proper for women to study. The new or revitalized categories of modern science, such as electricity, chemistry, medicine, and higher mathematics (as opposed to bookkeeping), which emerged before the American Revolution, were off-limits for even the well-to-do future "daughters of Columbia," who were still primarily "formed and educated for the world of fashion."[76]

A classic example of this type of young woman was Nancy Shippen, the daughter of a prominent Philadelphia doctor, who "because of her education and upbringing," much of which took place during the war, remained "personally untouched by this background and as remote from the great conflict as if she were living in another planet." The most striking contrast between her education and awareness and that of her younger brother can be seen in some of the letters they exchanged in 1777 when she was fourteen and he was twelve. Hers contain no references whatsoever to the revolt in progress, while even the seal on his letters carried the motto: "America possessed of liberty!"[77]

Also, women, despite the claims of wealthy fathers and husbands that they needed a good education in order to help manage the family business or estate, were increasingly *not named* as executrixes in the wills left by such men, and with few exceptions showed little knowledge of property values by the time of the Revolution.[78] While the legal implications of this will be discussed below, it is enough to note here that "the potency of daughterhood" probably represented an assertion of paternal control over girl children (as, for a variety of reasons, it became more and more difficult to control male offspring) more than it represented any attempt to "emancipate" their daughters from patriarchy. And, if anything, educational reform outside of the family reinforced rather than removed this subtly debilitating characteristic of "the potency of daughterhood."

The first significant improvement in the formal education of women came in the 1750s, not so much through their admission in greater numbers to the elementary public schools, but largely through the appearance of private female seminaries. These became the most common institutions of higher education for women following the Revolution, although their functioning was temporarily disrupted by the war.[79] Female seminaries initially appeared to be a great improvement in the education of women in the same way that coeducational institutions would appear to be an unqualified improvement a century later. We now know that the results were not so positive in either case.

Although new academic subjects were added to the curriculum, these seminaries ended up in the late eighteenth and early nineteenth centuries training women "to follow the way of martyrdom and high purpose." This meant that they encouraged greater separation between men's and women's cultural and economic roles, thus institutionalizing a double standard of sex-stereotyped education for men and women and "making the ideas, pursuits, systems of morality, and even the *meanings given words. . . different.*" Small wonder that one historian has recently referred to the female seminary movement as a "mask of oppression," and has questioned whether any of the proposed educational reforms for women from the 1790s to the Civil War offered any description of a "proper sphere" for women that could be considered even remotely liberating in a feminist sense. Most important, these female seminaries became identified with teaching the virtures of "self-sacrifice, piety and domesticity" rather than strictly academic subjects—at the very time when technical and formal education was supplanting the traditional apprentice method for obtaining a professional knowledge of a craft.[80]

For example, early colonial women had exercised a virtual monopoly over the practice of midwifery and had virtually "unlimited freedom" in offering their services as amateur doctors and healers, especially in the South where typhoid fever and other diseases produced a lower life expectancy than in New England. Because it was thought that they had natural healing powers, they were in essence medical practitioners in an era of all too few trained physicians. This occupational potential for American women in a scientific field disap-

peared rapidly with the increased emphasis on professional training
that excluded women—a trend that began before the war, but was
strongly reinforced in the immediate postwar decades in both medicine and the legal professions for basically sexist reasons.[81]

It should also be noted that the appearance of a somewhat smaller
conjugal household temporarily contributed to a decline in apprenticeship training for *both* boys and girls, as parents became more inclined "to keep their children at home, finding it undesirable to
dispatch them to a neighboring household to learn a trade." For boys,
professional and trade schools soon overcame this deficiency. Children were commonly "bound out" into other households in the early
colonial period for a variety of reasons unrelated to learning a trade.[82]
But this practice also declined in the late eighteenth century as parents
gradually became more sentimental and possessive about their own
children. Given the general inadequacy of formal elementary education, this actually represented a decline in educational opportunities
for all children because education had not yet been monopolized by
any school system.

However, the hope with which a small group of urban middle-class
women (and an even smaller group of their male counterparts) embraced educational reform for girls in the 1790s should not be underestimated. Neither should their enthusiasm be mistaken for actual
achievement. It did not result in any greater equality between the sexes
in education, government, or any other field that such letter writers,
novelists, and essayists as Charles Brockden Brown, Susanna Haswell
Rowson, Eliza Southgate Bowne, Benjamin Rush, and Judith Sargent
Murray advocated. In fact, for every bold statement like, "I expect to
see our young women forming a new era in female history," or for
every stanza such as, "By Man, your tyrant lord, / Females, no more
be aw'd/ Let Freedom's sacred word/ Inspire your heart," there were
strictures from these same authors that too much education would
masculinize women. Even Judith Sargent Murray's idea of the perfect
female was "a sensible and informed woman—companionable and
serious—[possessing] also a facility of temper, and united to a congenial mind—blest with competency—and rearing to maturity a promising family of children."[83]

Assuming that female educational reform had lived up to the
highest expectations of its strongest proponents of the 1790s, it still
would not have provided women with the technical, scientific, or professional training essential for high status occupations (functionalism)

in a developing nation like the United States. At the very most, the educational reforms of the 1790s were designed to perpetuate the existing pool of reasonably intelligent, patriotic wives and mothers for middle-class men and to expand the ranks of low-paid elementary school teachers from the growing pool of unmarried women.

VII

The legal and political status of the women of the revolutionary generation constitutes the last societal factor under consideration. The legal losses that women suffered following the Revolution are more important than the political ones because their legal status was qualitatively greater before 1776 than afterward.

From the beginning of the colonial period English common law was modified to fit New World conditions, especially with respect to the rights of married women and widows. These modifications were most apparent in commercial, urban areas where such women were declared "feme-sole traders"—a title that gave them the right to sue, conduct businesses, be sued, enter into contracts, sell real property, and have the power of attorney in the absence of their husbands. Whether single or married, seventeenth- or eighteenth-century women could not act as attorneys-at-law, but they often were attorneys-in-fact. Nonetheless, no individual married woman (feme couverte) ever obtained equal legal status with the single or widowed woman (feme sole). But prior to 1776 some middle- and upper middle-class married women did take advantage of equity jurisprudence to protect the property and possesions they had brought with them to marriage.[84]

In fact, there is evidence that there had been a gradual but steady merging of the two systems of equity and common law jurisprudence in American legal practice, especially in debt and criminal cases. This trend and the fact that common law remained subsidiary to local customs and the practices of ecclesiastical courts liberalized the legal treatment of women for much of the colonial period, even with respect to divorce, at least in Puritan Massachusetts. Nonetheless, legal penalties remained more severe for black, native American, and white, female indentured servants than for other classes of women. For a time during the extreme inflation of the revolutionary years, there was a lowering of terms of servitude for debt offenders because the rapidly depreciating continental currency made the imposed fines much higher than they had been under normal economic conditions. The same increased leniency can be seen in the greater number of divorces granted Massachusetts women between 1775 and 1786.[85]

None of these more lenient trends prevented a very negative legal development from taking place in the immediate postrevolutionary decades with respect to women, save for indentured servants, whose numbers decreased. It resulted largely from an increasing reliance upon Blackstone's *Commentaries* as a guide both in the training of professional lawyers and in codfying American law. Not only were free, white women more stringently prevented from acting as attorneys-in-fact because of the greater professionalization of law following the Revolution, but the new law codes did not "admit in words some conditons which in the exigencies of previous times had been tactly permitted" women.[86]

This legal loss of power for the vast majority of women who were married or widowed was not entirely precipitated by the Revolution. Some legal losses for both sexes were inevitable given the legal conservatism that prevailed before, during, and after the break with England, especially for women whose enhanced legal status had never been accompanied by adequate political rights. Also, it was necessary for all early colonial women to be as productive (economically and biologically) as possible. Naturally this need decreased as their numbers increased. In addition, the very absence of a professional class of lawyers in seventeenth-century colonial America had permitted a liberalizing and humanizing of New World laws in general and for married women in particular. This had changed by the middle of the eighteenth century, largely as secular law practices came to prevail over theological ones and as increased mercantilism demanded greater stability and hence a closer application of the more conservative aspects of English common law. While bar associations and professional training for lawyers were increasingly evident before the Revolution, even greater legal conservatism prevailed in its wake.[87]

For instance, with the exception of laws pertaining to debtors, there was a substantial increase "in penalties for crimes against property," and in some of the new states like Massachusetts grounds for which absolute divorces could be granted were limited. "Seduced by . . . Blackstone," as Jefferson later concluded, many young postrevolutionary lawyers "began to slide into Toryism." While much has been made of certain legal changes concerning laws of descent and property distribution, which were dictated more by economic necessity than they were by legal liberalism, the fact remains that there was no legal revolution in the newly found United States for men, let alone for women, where there appears to have been actual legal regression not yet adequately documented. In general, the greatest societal setback for women, which was a direct result of the Revolution, came with the codification of the laws of the United States in the 1820s and the 1830s.[88]

Before the Revolution, however, a regressive change in the legal status of women had already occurred and can be traced through wills and probate records. One of the major legal functions that women had performed from the beginning of the colonial period was the writing of wills, or acting as the beneficiaries of wills. Under common law, widows could not be heirs, that is, they could not be accorded the property rights of their deceased husbands as head of the household. But they could be named sole executrixes of their husbands' property and were often accorded dower rights that were "interpreted by the courts in a manner which was in many instances at variance with common law rules."[89] While widows were "considered a community responsibility" and were technically unable to sell any real property that they had not already possessed at the time of marriage, in practice both their proprietary and contractual rights were expanded in the course of the seventeenth and first half of the eighteenth centuries in order to provide them with greater economic independence. The Revolution does not appear to have fostered these legally liberating colonial trends.[90]

In Virginia, for example, throughout the seventeenth century men clearly favored their wives as heirs, and often provided them with more than the law required. Also, because of the initially higher mortality rates, southern wills also included a wider variety of non-kin than can be found in New England. Increasingly, however, in both geographical areas wills were written during the eighteenth century that made widows more likely to have to share part of a house with the surviving son who had received the bulk of the inheritance. This trend developed even though there is some indication that widows would have preferred (as today) to live with their daughters and sons-in-law. It may have reflected a distinct, yet tacit, disagreement over lineal descent between husbands and wives within the slightly smaller conjugal family. If so, it was a basic disagreement over power (in terms of property inheritance) that women lost in the course of the eighteenth century. This loss became most noticeable statistically in the decades immediately preceding and following the American Revolution, according to a recent study of Hingham, Massachusetts. Prior to 1720 no less than 27 percent of colonial wives with adult sons were named sole executrixes of their husbands' property. This figure dropped to 6 percent between 1761 and 1800, with 85 percent of the male wills naming sons as executors.[91] If these percentages turn out to be representative, they would indicate a significant loss in the legal and economic status of middle- and upper-class women, who had more commonly exercised such responsibility and power in the seventeenth century.

Finally, the differences between female and male colonial wills indicated not only lower levels of literacy among women, as already noted, but also, and most importantly, because they had so little that they could legally leave, the wills of married women (as opposed to those of widows) were of necessity "expressive" or "affective," rather than "instrumental" or of any great material importance. In addition, what they did leave was more often to their daughters or other female relatives (even though they could only do this through their sons-in-law or other male members of the family) rather than to their sons. Naturally part of this female intergenerational transmission along other than direct male blood lines was dictated by the nature of the willed items themselves and the individual woman's knowledge and/or actual control over her possessions. But it should also be noted that widows of property also tended *not* to make their sons their heirs to the degree that men of property did—another indication that women did not endorse the smaller nuclear family model of kinship or lineage, that is, of male children-as-heirs, to the degree that their husbands did.[92] Once again it was a losing battle, especially after the Revolution.

What limited political rights women had possessed before 1776 were also specifically denied them or implicitly discouraged under the new state constitutions. Throughout the colonial period, even though unmarried women with enough property technically could qualify to vote on local issues, few exercised this right except for a handful of strongly independent Dutch, English, or Quaker women in Massachusetts, New York, New Jersey, Rhode Island, and Pennsylvania. Without formal political rights colonial women were obviously quite limited in exercising political influence and fulfilled any civic aspirations vicariously through their husbands or other male members of their families. As usual, it is possible to point out several exceptions, almost all in the seventeenth century, like Lady Deborah Dunch Moody, who established a town in Long Island in 1646, Margaretta Van Schlectenhorst, a widow who supported the cause of the Albany rebel leader Jacob Leisler, and widows like Margaret Sheppard and Mary Loker, who voted in small towns in Massachusetts. Women also figured prominently in Bacon's Rebellion, and at least one, Sarah Drummond, later petitioned the English government for redress against the action taken against her rebel husband. And of course there was the celebrated case of the futile attempt of Margaret Brent, executrix for Governor Leonard Calvert, to vote in the Maryland Assembly in 1647.[93]

As to other forms of political action, there appears to have been a greater tendency for southern, rather than northern women, to present petitions to officials. Julia Cherry Spruill has noted that the petitions drafted by southern women in the seventeenth century disclosed "no doubts regarding their ability to understand and explain the political issues of the time or their right to interpose in matters of public concern." But after the American Revolution the "vigor and self-reliance of women in wealthier families" declined, and there was a "lessening of their influence in public matters." These postrevolutionary women, according to Spruill, "appear[ed] disinclined to admit any interest in public policy and anxious lest their private requests be mistaken for an unwomanly meddling in politics." She concludes that they were "somewhat effeminate and timid" in contrast to their colonial ancestors.[94] Her thought is suggestive and begs for a comparative analysis.

In any event, none of the new state constitutions granted women the right to vote with the exception of New Jersey. In that state, unmarried women worth fifty pounds could and did vote until that right was rescinded in 1807 as the result of an amendment introduced, interestingly enough, by a *liberal* Republican member of the state legislature. New York was the first state in 1777 to disfranchise women voters by inserting the word *male* into its constitution, and the other original eleven states soon followed suit by specifically forbidding women or actively discouraging them from voting.[95]

Even with these conscious acts of disfranchisement, it cannot be said that the political status or power of women deteriorated drastically as a direct result of the Revolution, because it must be remembered that few had voted or stood for office in the colonial period or even requested such political rights. The important qualitative decline in the political position of women came a few decades later when the franchise was extended to virtually every white male regardless of property holdings. The precedents set in the new revolutionary constitutions only prepared the way for the Jacksonian era, which "witnessed the completion of the retrograde and anti-democratic tendency that had commenced a half century earlier," as far as female suffrage was concerned. This period ended with what Harriet Martineau described as the "political nonexistence of women."[96]

VIII

Why didn't the experiences of the Revolution result in changing the political consciousness of women? Part of the answer lies in the socialized attitudes among female members of the revolutionary generation that set them apart from their male contemporaries. Their attitudes had been molded by the modernization trends encountered by most women in the course of the eighteenth century. Out of the necessity wrought by the struggle with England, women performed certain tasks that appeared revolutionary in nature, just as they had performed nonfamilial tasks out of necessity throughout the colonial period. But this seemingly revolutionary behavior is not necessarily proof of the acceptance of abstract revolutionary principles.

Despite their participation in greater economic specialization, despite their experiences with a slightly smaller conjugal household where power relations were changing, despite a limited expansion of the legal rights and somewhat improved educational opportunities for free, white women, the revolutionary generation of females were less prepared than most men for the modern implications of independence. Their distinctly different experiential level, combined with the intellectually and psychologically limiting impact of the Great Awakening and the Enlightenment on women, literally made it impossible for even the best educated females to understand the political intent or principles behind the inflated rhetoric of the revolutionary era. Words like virtue, veracity, morality, tyranny, and corruption were ultimately given public political meanings by male revolutionary leaders that were incomprehensible or, more likely, misunderstood by most women.

As the rhetoric of the revolution began to assume dynamic, emotional proportions, its obsession with "virtue" versus "corruption" struck a particularly responsive chord among literate women, as evidenced for example, in their patriotic statements as individuals and in groups when supporting the boycott of English goods between 1765 and 1774. While these statements are impressive both in number and intensity of feeling, it can be questioned whether the idea of taking "their country back on the path of virtue" and away from "the oppression of corrupt outside forces" was understood in the same way by female and male patriots, when even men of varying Whig persuasions could not agree on them. Virtue and morality for the vast majority of Americans, but particularly women, do not appear to have had the modernizing implications of pluralistic individualism, that is, of the "acceptance of diversity, the commitment to individual action in pursuit of individual goals, the conception of politics as an arena where these goals contest and the awareness of a national government which is at once the course of political power and the framework for an orderly clash of interest." These are characteristics of "modern man."[97]

How does one prove such a generalization about attitudes behind the behavior of women during the Revolution? Few poor white or black women left records revealing how they felt about the war. Such women, whether Loyalists or patriots, conveyed their sentiments silently with their physical labor. Among the more articulate and educated women there is written testimony to at least an initial sense of pride and importance involved in their participation in the war effort. Thus a young Connecticut woman named Abigail Foote wrote in her diary in 1775 that carding two pounds of whole wool had made her feel "Nationly," while others recorded their contributions in similarly patriotic terms.[98]

But the question remains: did their supportive actions prepare them to accept a vision of society anywhere near the version ultimately conveyed by James Madison's Federalist Number Ten in the fight over the Constitution of 1787? To date there is little evidence that this type of sophisticated political thought was present, either in the writings of women about the Revolution and its results or in the appeals made to them during or immediately following the war. From the popular 1767 statement of advice to the Daughters of Liberty to the 1787 one urging women to use "their influence over their husbands, brothers and sons to draw them from those dreams of liberty under a simple democratical form of government, which are so unfriendly to...order and decency," it is difficult to conclude that women were being prepared to understand the political ramifications of the Revolution.[99]

The same lack of political astuteness appears to underlie even the least traditional and most overtly political activities of women, such as the fifty-one who signed the anti-tea declaration in Edenton, North

Carolina, on 25 October 1774 (later immortalized in a London cartoon). The same could be said of the more than 500 Boston women who agreed on 31 January 1770 to support the radical male boycott of tea; of the Daughters of Liberty in general; and of the 1,600 Philadelphia women who raised 7,500 dollars in gold for the Continental Army. Even Mercy Otis Warren never perceived the modern political system that evolved from the Revolution. Instead she viewed the war and its aftermath as the "instrument of Providence that sparked a world movement, changing thought and habit of men to complete the divine plan for human happiness" largely through the practice of virtue.[100]

Perhaps the most important aspect of the supportive activities among women for the patriot cause was the increase in class and social distinctions they symbolized. For example, it appears unlikely that poor white or black women joined Daughters of Liberty groups, actively boycotted English goods, or participated in any significant numbers in those associations of "Ladies of the highest rank and influence," who raised money and supplies for the Continental Army. On the contrary, it may well have been primarily "young female spinsters" from prominent families and well-to-do widows and wives who could afford the time or the luxury of such highly publicized activities. The vast majority, however, of middle-class female patriots (and, for that matter, Loyalists), whether single or married, performed such necessary volunteer roles as seamstresses, nurses, hostesses, and sometime spies, whenever the fighting shifted to their locales, without any undue fanfare or praise.[101]

The same is true of poorer women, with one important difference: they had no choice. They had all they could do to survive, and although this did lead a few of them to become military heroines, they could not afford the luxury of either "disinterested patriotism" or the detached self-interest and indulgences that some of the richer women exhibited. The very poorest, particularly those in urban areas, had no resources to fall back on when confronted with the personal or economic traumas caused by the War for Independence. As noted above, this was especially evident in the case of women wage earners who, regardless of race or class, had apparently always received lower pay than free men or hired-out male slaves, and who had suffered severely from runaway inflation during the war. Women's services were more likely to be paid for in Continental currency than with specie. Fees for male "doctors," for example, according to one Maryland family account book, were made in specie payment after the middle of 1780, while midwives had to accept the depreciated Continental currency for a longer period of time.[102] Thus, the American Revolution hastened the appearance of greater class-based activities among "daughters of the new republic," with poor women undertaking the least desirable tasks and suffering most from the inflationary spiral that plagued the whole country.[103] It is easy to imagine the impact that inflation had on the rural and urban poor, but it even affected those middle- and upper middle-class women who were left at home to manage businesses, estates, plantations, or farms. Their activities often meant the difference between bankruptcy and solvency for male revolutionary leaders.

Probably the classic example of housewifely efficiency and economic shrewdness is found in Abigail's management of the Adams's family and farm during John's long absences. But in this respect Abigail Adams stands in direct contrast to the women in the lives of other leading revolutionaries like Jefferson, Madison, and Monroe—all of whom were bankrupt by public service in part because their wives were not as capable at land management as she was. This even proved true of the most outspoken of all revolutionary wives, Mercy Otis Warren. Numerous lesser well-known women, however, proved equal to the increased domestic responsibilities placed upon them.[104] Only the utterly impoverished could not resort to the traditional colonial task of household manager.

As the months of fighting lengthened into years, more and more poverty-stricken women left home to join their husbands, lovers, fathers, or other male relatives in the army encampments. Once there, distinctions between traditional male and female roles broke down. While a certain number of free white and black slave women were needed to mend, wash, and cook for officers and care for the sick and wounded, most enlisted men and their women took care of themselves and fought beside each other on many occasions. Moreover, unlike the English, German, and French commanders, American military leaders were often morally offended or embarrassed by the presence of these unfortunate and destitute women, "their hair flying, their brows beady with the heat, their belongings slung over one sholder [sic], chattering and yelling in sluttish shrills as they went and spitting in the gutters."[105]

This puritanical, hostile attitude on the part of patriot army officers toward such a common military phenomenon insured that camp followers of the American forces were less systematically provided for than those of foreign troops. Aside from its class overtones (after all

Martha Washington, Catherine Greene, and Lucy Knox were accepted as respectable camp followers), it is difficult to explain this American attitude, except that in the prevailing righteous rhetoric of the Revolution and of later historians these women were misrepresented as little better than prostitutes. In reality they were the inarticulate, invisible poor whose story remains to be told from existing pension records based on oral testimony. At any rate there is pathos and irony in the well-preserved image of Martha Washington, who visited her husband at Valley Forge during the disastrous winter of 1777–1778, copying routine military communiques and presiding over a sewing circle of other officers' wives, while the scores of combat-hardened women, who died along with their enlisted men, have been conveniently forgotten.[106]

These camp followers, as well as the women who stayed at home, complained about their plight privately and publicly, and on occasion they rioted and looted for foodstuffs. Women rioting for bread or other staples never became a significant or even a particularly common revolutionary act in the New World as it did in Europe, largely because of the absence of any long-term, abject poverty on the part of even the poorest colonials. The most likely exception to this generalization came during the extreme inflation that accompanied the war. Then there is indeed some evidence of what can be called popular price control activity by groups of women who had a definite sense of what were fair or legitimate marketing practices. At the moment we have concrete evidence of only a half-dozen seemingly spontaneous instances of "a corps of female infantry" attacking merchants. Other examples will probably be discovered as more serious research into the "moral economy of the crowd" is undertaken by American historians.[107]

What is interesting about the few known cases is that the women involved in some of them did not simply appear to be destitute camp followers passing through towns stripping the dead and looting at random for food. A few at least were women "with Silk gownes on," who were offering to buy sugar, salt, flour, or coffee for a reasonable price with Continental currency. When a certain merchant insisted on payment with specie or with an unreasonable amount of paper money, the women then, and only then, insisted on "taking" his goods at their price. These appear, therefore, to be isolated examples of collective behavior by women where there was, at the least, a very strongly held cultural notion of a moral economy.[108]

Nevertheless, there is still no clear indication of an appreciable change in the political consciousness of such women. Perhaps it was because even the poorest who took part in popular price control actions primarily did so, like the Citoyennes Républicaines Révolutionnaires during the French Revolution, out of an immediate concern for feeding themselves and their children and not for feminist reasons growing out of their age-old economic plight as women in a patriarchal society.[109] In addition, except for camp followers and female vagabonds, the principal concern of most members of this generation of primarily rural women remained the home and their functions there. During the home-spinning drives and during the war when their men were away, their domestic and agricultural duties became all the more demanding, but not consciousness-raising.

They were after all a generation for whom war had become commonplace. Many, like Abigail Adams, had been born around the time of King George's War; married during or shortly after the French and Indian War; and raised their first children during the prerevolutionary activities of the 1760s and early 1770s. Perhaps they were more inured to war than any previous generation of colonists, particularly those who had actually encountered Indian fighting in the frontier areas, and therefore more self-possessed, more enduring. And endure they did, performing all the traditional behind-the-scenes duties expected of women during wartime.[110]

Once independence was won, however, these same women, particularly those forced to become camp followers, naturally welcomed the chance to withdraw to what had been their more normal prewar private lives within the physical and psychic safety of their homes. Collective validation and vicarious fulfillment through their families, rather than individual assertion, continued to satisfy most of them. In fact, their desire to end the increased familial hardships and dislocation created by the Revolution is clearly indicated in the one common characteristic all women exhibited regardless of class: an affective response not only to the Revolution specifically, but also to all legal-political matters in general—and most important, to one another.

For example, there were similar personal complaints about the war from patriot and Loyalist women alike. It is even conceivable that their expressed fears about anti-British (or anti-American) activity and their pleas to their men to stay at home or to become less involved produced many so-called reluctant revolutionaries and many of the more neutral and "disaffected" leaders on both sides. We know from Washington's complaints to his officers that such statements as, "I am without bread, & cannot get any, the Committee will not supply me, my Children will Starve... *Pray Come Home,* "ultimately contributed to many desertions among the rank and file of soldiers.[111]

One of the most interesting types of complaints came from Loyalist women and reflects in reverse what Abigail Adams meant about patriotism being a "most disinterested" virtue among her sex. In spite of their husbands' political opposition to the war and the threat to their own physical well-being, a number of female Loyalists were apparently opposed to leaving the country because of personal relationships. While the vast majority of American women refugees followed or preceded their male relatives into exile, the most recent study of 468 women who later petitioned for compensation and pensions indicates their overwhelming concern with family and friends rather than politics.[112]

This affective response of Loyalist and patriot women should not be exaggerated, but it was very much a normal part of their often passionate, yet ambivalent or disinterested, allegiance. Even Abigail finally asked John Adams in March 1782 to return home from his thankless ambassadorial duties abroad: "...let me intreat you to withdraw. Let me beg of you to resign; your Health suffers; my Health suffers from a dejection of Spirits which I cannot overcome...." If women were consistently loyal it was within what has been called their "homosocial networks" of "shared experiences and mutual affection," as their private letters and diaries clearly indicate.[113] This consistent existence of female love and friendship even in time of war is often obscured or denied in traditional accounts of leading male Loyalists and patriots because it was best expressed and acted out by women (and other powerless groups) who had little to gain in a personal, political, or material sense from victory or defeat.[114]

To the degree that they succeeded in maintaining some consistency between their emotional, physical, and intellectual commitment to one side or another, this paricular generation of late eighteenth-century women suffered most from unrequited loyalty when it became apparent that neither side had a monopoly on virtue or righteousness. Like the rank and file of American men they were psychologically unprepared to accept the many compromises that public life forced upon male revolutionary leaders. In addition, their individual self-perceptions, and economic, legal, and political notions were so under-developed, that these American women who experienced the war never attempted, as French women did later, to organize on their own behalf when their specific needs and mild material requests were not satisfied.

Their familial duties, particularly seemingly incessant child-bearing, were still so demanding and obviously important that they were, in other words, nowhere near what Chalmers Johnson has referred to as the conscious condition of "multiple dysfunctionalism," or what Anthony F. C. Wallace has described as that condition of "panic stricken anxiety, shame, guilt, depression, or apathy" so characteristic of those "culturally disillusioned" people, who are the catalysts of revolutionary change. Indeed, it has taken most of the twentieth century for even American middle-class women to recognize the decline in their functional status, to obtain the necessary prerequisites for their own emancipation, and to begin to envision a society based on other than patriarchal lines.[115] As a result, with the exception of the few military heroines who received pensions from the United States government, none of the supportive actions of these women were rewarded. Nor was there any organized feminist demand that they should be.

IX

Lastly, in explaining the failure of the equalitarian ideals of the Revolution to bear even limited fruit for women, one must analyze the narrow ideological parameters of even those few who advocated women's rights, persons such as Abigail Adams, Judith Sargent Murray, Elizabeth Southgate Bowne, Elizabeth Drinker, and Mercy Otis Warren.

These women, as I have already suggested, were not feminists. Like most of the better organized, but no less unsuccessful Républicaines of France, they seldom, if ever, aspired to complete equality with men except in terms of education. Moreover, none challenged the institution of marriage or defined themselves "as other than mothers and potential mothers." They simply could not conceive of a society whose standards were not set by male, patriarchal institutions, nor should they be expected to have done so. Instead of demanding equal rights, the most articulate and politically conscious American women of this generation asked at most for privileges and at least for favors —not for an absolute expansion of their legal or political functions, which they considered beyond their proper womanly sphere.[116] Man was indeed the measure of equality to these women, and given their societal conditioning, such status was beyond their conception of themselves as individuals.

Ironically it is this same sense of their "proper sphere" that explains why the most educated female patriots did not feel obliged to organize to demand more from the Founding Fathers. It is usually overlooked that in the famous letter of 31 March 1776 where Abigail asks John Adams to "Remember the Ladies," she justified this mild request for "more generous and favourable" treatment on the grounds that married women were then subjected to the "unlimited power" of their husbands. She was not asking him for the right to vote, only for some legal protection of wives from abuses under common law practices. "Regard us then," she pleaded with her husband, "as Beings placed by providence under your protection and in imitation of the Supreme Being make use of that power only for our happiness." Despite an earlier statement in this letter about the "Ladies" being "determined to foment a Rebellion" and refusing to be "bound by any Laws in which we have no voice, or Representation," Abigail Adams was not in any sense demanding legal, let alone political or individual, equality with men at the beginning of the American Revolution.[117] If anything, her concept of the separateness of the two different spheres in which men and women operated was accentuated by the war and the subsequent trials of the new republic between 1776 and 1800.

This idea that men and women existed in two separate spheres or orbits was commonly accepted in the last half of the eighteenth century as one of the natural laws of the universe. While European Enlightenment theories adhered strictly to the inferiority of the natural sphere that women occupied, in colonial America they were tacitly challenged and modified by experience—as were so many other aspects of natural law doctrines.[118] On the other hand, the degree to which educated, upper-class women in particular thought that their sphere of activity was in fact equal, and the degree to which it actually was accorded such status by the male-dominated culture, is all important. Historians have tended to place greater emphasis on the former rather than the latter, with misleading results about the importance of the roles played by both colonial and revolutionary women.

It is true that Abigail Adams was an extremely independent-minded person who firmly criticized books by foreign authors who subordinated the female sphere to that of the male. Writing to her sister Elizabeth Shaw Peabody in 1799, she said that "I will never consent to have our sex considered in an inferior point of light. Let

each planet shine in their own orbit, God and nature designed it so—
if man is Lord, woman is *Lordess*—that is what I contend for." Thus,
when her husband was away she deemed it was within her proper
sphere to act as head of the household on all matters, including the
decision to have her children innoculated against smallpox without his
permission. At the same time, however, she always deferred to his
ambitions and his inherent superiority, because the equality of their
two separate orbits did not make them equal as individuals. In general
Abigail Adams and other women of her class accepted the notion that
while they were mentally equal to men their sphere of activity was
entirely private in nature, except on those occasions when they substituted for their absent husbands. "Government of States and Kingdoms, tho' God knows badly enough managed," she asserted in 1796,
"I am willing should be solely administered by the lords of creation.
I should contend for Domestic Government, and think that best administered by the female."[119] Such a strong belief in equal, but separate, spheres is indeed admirable for the times, but it should not be
confused with feminism.

Nor should it be interpreted to mean that educated women were
obliged to remain ignorant of politics.

> "Never were [there] greater politicans than the several knots of
> ladies, who met together," wrote a wealthy young widow from
> South Carolina 1779. "All trifling discourse of fashions . . . was
> thrown by, and we commenced perfect statesmen. Indeed, I don't
> know but if we had taken a little pains, we should have been
> qualified for prime ministers, so well could we discuss several
> important matters in hand. . . . I won't have it thought, that be-
> cause we are the weaker sex as to *bodily* strength, my dear, we are
> capable of nothing more than minding the dairy, visiting the
> poultry-house, and all such domestic concerns; our thoughts can
> soar aloft, we . . . have as just a sense of honor, glory, and great
> actions, as the 'Lords of the Creation.' . . . They won't even allow
> us the liberty of thought, and that is all I want. I would not wish
> that we should meddle in what is unbecoming female delicacy,
> but sure we may have sense enough to give our opinions . . .
> without being reminded of our spinning and household affairs as
> the only matters we are capable of thinking or speaking of with
> justness or propriety. I won't allow it, positively won't."

Eliza Wilkinson concluded in this portion of her letter, only to
ruefully reflect a few pages later: "What will the men say if they should
see this? I am really out of *my sphere* now, and must fly to Homer for

direction and instruction on household matters."[120]

To have asked for individual or political equality with men would not only have violated their belief in two separate, but equal, spheres of duty, but it also would have automatically meant asking for a role in the public realm that was literally considered a physical impossibility by most eighteenth-century women. Their dawn-to-dusk domestic duties as household managers, and their health problems from frequent childbirth and inadequate diets relegated all classes of colonial women to lives of domesticity in the broadest sense of that term. This was philosophically reinforced by the political theories and physical laws of the universe associated with the Enlightenment that deemed it "natural" for public affairs to be conducted exclusively by men.[121]

Only unusual male feminists like Thomas Paine asked that women be accorded "the sweets of public esteem" and "an equal right to praise." It was Paine—not the female patriots—who also took advantage of American revolutionary conditions to attack the institution of marriage. Later, in the 1790s, only a few isolated women in the United States supported Mary Wollstonecraft's demand for the right to public as well as private fulfillment on the grounds that "private duties are never properly fulfilled unless the understanding enlarges the heart and that public virtue is only an aggregate of private...." Her criticisms of marital bondage were never seriously considered by American women in this postrevolutionary decade.[122]

The reasons for this unresponsiveness to the feminism of both Paine and Wollstonecraft are complex, for it was not only opposed by the sexist Founding Fathers, but by most women. Again we must ask —why?

The physical and mental hardships that most women had endured during the war continued to varying degrees in the economic dislocation that followed in its wake. Sheer personal survival, not rising social or material expectations, dominated the thinking and activities of lower and even some middle- and upper-class women. Probably more important, the few well-educated American women, fortunate to have the leisure to reflect, clearly realized the discrepancy that had occurred between the theory and practice of virtue in the course of the war and its aftermath. While it was discouraging for them to view the corruption of morals of the society at large and particularly among men in public life, they could take some satisfaction in the greater consistency between the theory and practice of virtue in their own private lives. Such postrevolutionary women found their familial duties and homosocial relationships untainted by the corruption of public life. They considered themselves most fortunate and they *were,* compared to their nineteenth-century descendants, who had to pay a much higher price for similar virtuous consistency and spiritual purity.[123]

It was natural, therefore, for the educated among this generation to express disillusionment with politics, as they saw republican principles corrupted or distorted, and then to enter a stage of relative quiescence that marked the beginning of the transitional period between their war-related activities and a later generation of female reformers who emerged in the 1830s. They cannot be held responsible for not realizing the full extent of the potentially debilitating features of their withdrawal to the safety of modern domesticity—where virtue becomes its own punishment instead of reward.

A final factor that helps to explain the absence of feminism in the behavior of women during the Revolution and in their attitudes afterward is related to the demographic changes that were taking place within the family unit between 1760 and 1800. Middle- and upper-class women were increasingly subjected to foreign and domestic literature stressing standards of feminity that had not inhibited the conduct of their colonial ancestors. While the rhetoric of this new literature was that of the Enlightenment, its message was that of romantic love, glamorized dependence, idealized motherhood, and sentimentalized children within the ever-narrowing realm of family life. At poorer levels of society a new family pattern was emerging as parental control broke down, and ultimately these two trends would merge, leaving all women in lower status domestic roles than they had once occupied.[124]

In general it appears that the American Revolution retarded those societal conditions that had given colonial women their unique function and status in society, while it promoted those that were leading toward the gradual "embourgeoisement" of late eighteenth-century women. By 1800 their economic and legal privileges were curtailed; their recent revolutionary activity minimized or simply ignored; their future interest in politics discouraged; and their domestic roles extolled, but increasingly limited.

Moreover, at the highest *and* lowest levels of society this revolutionary generation of women was left with misleading assumptions: certain educated women believing strongly in the hope that immediate improvement for themselves and their children would come with educational reform, and some lower-class women believing that improvement would come through work in the "manufactories." Both admitted, according to Mercy Otis Warren, that their "appointed sub-ordination" to men was natural, if for no other reason than "for the sake of Order in Families."[125] Neither could be expected to anticipate that this notion would limit their participation in, and understanding of, an emerging modern nation because the actual (as opposed to idealized) value accorded their postrevolutionary activities was not yet apparent.

A few, like Priscilla Mason, the valedictorian of the 1793 graduat-ing class of the Young Ladies' Academy of Philadelphia, might demand an equal education with men and exhort women to break out of their traditional sphere, but most ended up agreeing with Eliza Southgate Bowne when she concluded her defense of education for women by saying: "I believe I must give up all pretension to *profundity,* for I am much more at home in my female character." And the dominate male leadership of the 1790s could not have agreed more.[126]

For women, the American Revolution was over before it ever began. Their "disinterested" patriotism (or disloyalty, as the case may be) was accorded identical treatment by male revolutionaries following the war: conscious neglect of female rights combined with subtle edu-cational and economic exploitation. The end result was increased loss of function and authentic status for all women whether they were on or under the proverbial pedestal.

I am especially indebted to Alfred F. Young for his advice and patient editing throughout the many months that we worked together on this essay. Margaret George, Daniel Scott Smith, and Anne H. Sherrill also offered valuable comments and sugges-tions when I began revising the first draft, but none of them should be held responsible for the essay's flaws or conclusions.

1. Since 1922, when Arthur M. Schlesinger, Sr., first noted the absence of women in American textbooks, the situation has only improved in the last few years. One recent study of twenty-seven college-level textbooks disclosed that material on women ranged from a low of .05 percent to a high of 2 percent, with the latter percentage occurring in Charles and Mary Beard's *Basic History of the United States* (New York: New Home Library, 1944), a book now out of print. See Arthur M. Schlesinger, Sr., *New Viewpoints in American History* (New York: Macmillan Co., 1922), p. 126, and Earl R. and Delores Barracano Schmidt, "The Invisible Women: The Historian as Professional Magician; An Analysis, Quantitative and Qualitative, of 27 Textbooks Designed for College Survey Courses in American History," dittoed, 1971.

2. For confirmation of the need to develop new conceptual frameworks in the field of women's history, see Gerda Lerner, "New Approaches to the Study of Women in American History," *Journal of Social History* 3 (Fall 1969): 53–62; idem, "On the Teaching and Organization of Feminist Studies," *Female Studies* 5 (Pittsburgh: Know, Inc., 1973); Patricia Branca and Peter N. Stearns, "On the History of Modern Women," *AHA Newslet-ter* 12 (September 1974): 6; Berenice A. Carroll, "Mary Beard's *Woman as Force in History:*

A Critique," in *Woman: An Issue,* eds. Lee R. Edwards, Mary Heath, and Lisa Baskin (Boston: Little, Brown and Co., 1972), pp. 125–43; Linda Gordon et al., "Historical Phallicies: Sexism in American Historical Writing," dittoed and expanded version of a paper delivered at the December 1970, American Historical Association; Ann D. Gordon et al., *Women in American Society: An Historical Contribution* (Cambridge, Mass.: Radical America, 1971), pp. 3–18; Lois W. Banner, "On Writing Women's History," *Journal of Interdisciplinary History* 11 (Fall 1971): 345–58; Ruth A. Hepburn, "Too Little Ado: A Review of the Literature on America's First Feminist Movement," dittoed Santa Barbara, Calif., 1973; Ruth Rosen, "Sexism in History or Writing Women's History is Tricky Business," *Journal of Marriage and Family* 33 (August 1971): 541–55.

3. Robert F. Berkhofer, Jr., *A Behavioral Approach to Historical Analysis* (New York: Free Press, 1969), pp. 169–210, 243–70; Richard P. McCormick, "The Comparative Method: Its Application to American History," *Mid-America* 56 (October 1974): 231–47; Annette K. Baster, "Women's Studies and American Studies: The Uses of the Interdisciplinary," *American Quarterly* 26 (October 1974): 433–39. An invaluable set of papers on "Conceptual Frameworks for Studying Women's History" was delivered at the Sarah Lawrence College Women's Studies Symposium, 15 March 1975, by Gerda Lerner (Sarah Lawrence College), Joan Kelly-Gadol (The City College of New York), Marylin B. Arthur (Brooklyn College), and Renate Bridenthal (Brooklyn College). They are scheduled for publication in future issues of *Feminist Studies.*

4. Margaret Benston, "The Political Economy of Women's Liberation," *Monthly Review* 21 (September 1969): 13–27.

5. Obviously I have taken liberty here with Kenneth A. Lockridge's theories about modernization to suggest that women lagged far behind men in this process. See Lockridge, "Social Change and the Meaning of the American Revolution," *Journal of Social History* 6 (Summer 1973): 404, 427.

6. Linda Grant De Pauw, "Land of the Unfree: Legal Limitations on Liberty in Pre-Revolutionary America," *Maryland Historical Magazine* 68 (Winter 1973): 355–57; Edwin G. Burrows and Michael Wallace, "The American Revolution: The Ideology and Psychology of National Liberation," *Perspectives in American History* 7 (1972): 305–6; James A. Henretta, *The Evolution of American Society, 1700–1815: An Interdisciplinary Analysis* (Lexington, Mass.: D. C. Heath and Co., 1973), pp. 169–71.

7. Margaret George, "From 'Goodwife' to 'Mistress': The Transformation of the Female in Bourgeois Culture," *Science and Society* 37 (Summer 1973): 152–77.

8. Henretta, *Evolution of American Society,* pp. 41–81; Thomas C. Cochran, *Business in American Life: A History* (New York: McGraw-Hill, 1972), pp. 9–27; William Appleman Williams, "The Age of Mercantilism: An Interpretation of the American Political Economy, 1763 to 1828," *William and Mary Quarterly* 15 (October 1958): 419–37.

9. Douglas Jones (Brandeis University), "Female Vagabonds in Massachusetts," paper delivered at 1975 Conference on Women in the Era of American Revolution; Carol Ruth Berkin, "Within the Conjurer's Circle: Women in Colonial America," University Programs Modular Studies (Morristown, N.J.: General Learning Press, 1974), pp. 2–3; Mary Sumner Benson, *Women in Eighteenth-Century America: A Study of Opinion and Social Usage* (New York: Columbia University Press, 1935), pp. 11–78; Kai Erikson, *Wayward Puritans: A School in the Sociology of Deviance* (New York: John Wiley & Sons, 1966), pp. 77–83, 85–91, 120–23.

10. Mrs. J. L. McArthur, "Women of the Revolution," *Proceedings of the New York State Historical Association* (New York: Kraus Reprint Corporation, 1968; a reprint of the original 1905 edition), pp. 155–56; Julia Ward Stickley, "The Truth about Deborah Sampson Gannett," J. Todd White, "The Truth about Molly Pitcher," both papers delivered at the 1975 conference on Women in the Era of the American Revolution. Numerous similar statements can be found in Elizabeth F. Ellet, *The Women of the American Revolution,* 3 vols. (New York: Charles Scribner, 1853–1854). Based largely on oral, genteel sources for over 170 women, this work has been a standard, albeit misleading, reference for historians.

11. Alexander Garden, *Anecdotes of the American Revolution* (Charleston, S.C.: A. E. Miller, 1828), p. 59; Linda K. Kerber, "Daughters of Columbia: Educating Women for the Republic, 1787–1805," in *The Hofstadter Aegis: A Memorial, 1916–1970,* eds. Stanley Elkins and Eric McKitrick (New York: Alfred A. Knopf, 1974), pp. 56–57.

12. Burrows and Wallace, "American Revolution," pp. 167–306. The psychological and political impact of the familial analogy used by the patriots to describe their struggle with England is analyzed in detail in this essay, but the authors make no attempt to determine what, if any, antifemale bias was encouraged by the more numerous references to England as an old woman rather than a man, often as a diseased prostitute, and by references to the "child colony" as a young, strong male. It seems to me that the excessive use of this negative mother-male child image could only have contributed to increased sexism in the postrevolutionary decades.

13. Kerber, "Daughters of Columbia," p. 58, passim; Benson, *Women in Eighteenth Century America*, p. 248; Frederick Rudolph, ed., *Essays on Education in the Early Republic* (Cambridge: Harvard University Press, 1965), pp. 27–28, 36–37. Benjamin Rush went so far as to say that if women were "educated properly,...they will not only *make and administer its laws,* but form its manner and character" (emphasis added).

14. L. H. Butterfield and Marc Friedlaender, eds., *Adams Family Correspondence,* 4 vols. (Cambridge: Harvard University Press, Belknap Press, 1963, 1973), vol. 1, *December 1761–May 1776,* pp. 85–87; vol. 2, *June 1776–March 1778,* pp. 93–94, 391–92; vol. 3, *April 1778–September 1780,* pp. 52–55; vol. 4, *October 1780–September 1782,* pp. 75, 184, 328–31, 344 [hereafter referred to as *AFC,* vol.: page]; Anne H. Sherrill (Mills College), "Abigail Adams and the American Enlightenment," paper delivered at University of San Francisco Symposium, August 1974, p. 23; Mercy Otis Warren, *History of the Rise, Progress and Termination of the American Revolution: Interspersed with Biographical, Political and Moral Observations,* 3 vols. (Boston: Manning and Loring, 1805), 3:413–36; Thomas Woody, *A History of Women's Education in the United States* (New York: Science Press, 1929), 1:135; Benson, *Women in Eighteenth-Century America,* p. 263.

15. Amelia Day Campbell, "Women of New York State in the Revolution," *The Quarterly Journal of the New York State Historical Association* 3 (July 1922): 155.

16. White, "Truth About Molly Pitcher," pp. 12–14; Linda Grant De Pauw, *Four Traditions: Women of New York During the American Revolution* (Albany: New York State American Revolution Bicentennial Commission, 1974), pp. 19–33; Samuel Stelle Smith, *A Molly Pitcher Chronology* (Monmouth Beach, N.J., 1972); Mollie Somerville, *Women and the American Revolution* (n.p., Judd & Detweiler, 1974), pp. 6–17, 24–35, 42–45, 56–62; John Adams Vinton, ed., *Life of Deborah Sampson: The Female Soldier in the War of the Revolution* (New York: William Abbat, 1916 for no. 47 of *The Magazine of History with Notes and Queries;* reprint of the original 1866 Wiggin and Lunt edition); Elizabeth Cometti, "Women in the American Revolution," *The New England Quarterly* 20 (September 1947): 344–45; E. Merton Coulter, "Nancy Hart, Georgia Heroine of the Revolution: The Story of the Growth of a Tradition," *Georgia Historical Quarterly* 39 (June 1955): 118–151; Campbell, "Women of New York in the Revolution," pp. 155–68; David J. Harkness, *Southern Heroines of the American Revolution,* University of Tennessee Continuing Education Series, vol. 49, no. 2 (June 1973); Ellet, *Women of the Revolution,* 3 vols., passim; Mary Ormsbee Whitton, *These were the Women, U.S.A.: 1776–1860* (New York: Hastings House, 1954), pp. 1–29; Henry Addington Bayley Bruce, *Women in the Making of America* (Boston: Little, Brown and Co., 1912), pp. 81–114; Eugenie Andruss Leonard, *The Dear-Bought Heritage* (Philadelphia: University of Pennsylvania Press, 1965), pp. 537–65; Mary S. Logan, *The Part Taken by Women in American History* (New York: Arno Press, 1972; reprint of original 1912 Perry-Nalle Publishing Co. edition), pp. 105–204; Phoebe A. C. Hanaford, *Daughters of America* (Boston: B. B. Russell, 1883), pp. 37–64; Mary Beard, ed., *America Through Women's Eyes* (New York: Macmillan Co., 1934), pp. 54–87; Sally Smith Booth, *The Women of '76* (New York: Hastings House, 1973), pp. 238–70, passim.

17. In addition to works cited in n.16, see Warren, *History of American Revolution,* 2:202–5; Cometti, "Women in Revolution," pp. 329–43; James Austin Holden, "Influence of Death of Jane McCrea on the Burgoyne Campaign," *Proceedings of the New York State Historical Association* 12 (1913): 249–310; Alice Morse Earle, *Colonial Dames and Good Wives* (New York: Frederick Ungar Publishing Co., 1962; reprint of original 1895 edition, n.p.), pp. 240–75; Sommerville, *Women and Revolution,* pp. 52–54; Rev. Roderick Terry, "Experiences of a Minister's Wife in the American Revolution," *The Connecticut Magazine* 2 (Winter 1907): 523–32; Mrs. Donald McLean, "The Baroness de Riedesel," *Proceedings of the New York State Historical Association* 3 (1903): 39–44; Walter Hart Blumenthal, *Women Camp Followers of the American Revolution* (Philadelphia: George St. McManus

Co., 1952), pp. 57–90; Wallace Brown, *The Good Americans: The Loyalists in the American Revolution* (New York: William Morrow & Co., 1969); Theodore D. Gottlieb, *The Origin and Evolution of the Betsy Ross Flag: Legend or Tradition* (Newark, N.J.: n.p., 1938).

18. Gerda Lerner, "Women's Rights and American Feminism," *American Scholar* 40 (Spring 1971): 236 (emphasis added). William O'Neill's definition, the exact reverse of Lerner's, can be found in "Feminism as a Radical Ideology," in *Dissent: Explorations in the History of American Radicalism*, ed. Alfred F. Young (DeKalb: Northern Illinois University Press, 1968), p. 276. For further elaboration on the use of the term in the United States, see Alice S. Rossi, ed., *The Feminist Papers: From Adams to de Beauvoir* (New York: Bantam Books, 1974), pp. xii–xiii.

19. Mary R. Beard, *Woman as Force in History: A Study in Traditions in Realities* (New York: Macmillan Co., Collier Books, 1962; reprint of original 1946 Macmillan edition), pp. 157–80; Carroll, "Mary Beard," pp. 127–42.

20. Margaret George, *One Woman's "Situation": A Study of Mary Wollstonecraft* (Urbana: University of Illinois Press, 1970), p. 16; idem, "From 'Goodwife' and 'Mistress'," pp. 155–56; Natalie Zemon Davis, "Women on Top: Sexual Inversion and Political Disorder in Early Modern Europe," in *Society and Culture in Early Modern France: Eight Essays* (Stanford, Calif.: Stanford University Press, 1975), p. 126; Jane Abray, "Feminism and the French Revolution," *AHR* 80 (February 1975): 44; Alice Clark, *Working Life of Women in the Seventeenth Century* (New York: Augustus M. Kelley, 1968; reprint of the original 1919 Cass edition), pp. 9–13, 93–149.

21. Edith Abbott, *Women in Industry: A Study in American Economic History* (New York: Source Book Press, 1970; reprint of original 1910 Appleton edition), pp. viii, 11–12; Meta Stern Lilienthal, *From Fireside to Factory* (New York: Rand School of Social Science, 1916), pp. 7–15; Mary P. Ryan, *Womanhood in America: From Colonial Times to the Present* (New York: New Viewpoints, 1975), pp. 21–22, 26, 32, 64.

22. Herbert B. Adams, "Allotments of Land in Salem to Men, Women and Maids," *Essex Institute Historical Collections* 19 (1882): 167–75; Ryan, *Womanhood in America*, p. 35; Edmund S. Morgan, *American Slavery—American Freedom: The Ordeal of Colonial Virginia* (New York: W. W. Norton, 1975), pp. 235, 310.

23. Miriam Schnier, "Women in the Revolutionary Economy," paper delivered April 1975, Organization of American Historians Convention, pp. 2–3; Cotton Mather, *Ornaments for the Daughters of Zion, or the Character and Happiness of a Virtuous Woman* (London: Thomas Parkhurst, 1694), pp. 6–7; Abbott, *Women in Industry*, pp. 20–34; Marcus Wilson Jernegan, *Laboring and Dependent Classes in Colonial America, 1607–1783* (New York: Frederick Ungar Publishing Co., 1931) pp. 84–128; Leonard, *Dear-Bought Heritage*, pp. 156–87; Morgan, *American Slavery—American Freedom*, pp. 321–24. The primary purpose of compulsory education in the colonies was to teach a trade to prevent pauperism and only secondarily to educate for literacy.

24. Frances May Manges, "Women Shopkeepers, Tavernkeepers and Artisans in Colonial Philadelphia" (Ph.D. diss., University of Pennsylvania, 1958), p. 35; Henretta, *Evolution of American Society*, p. 194.

25. Mary Beth Norton, "Eighteenth-Century American Women: The Loyalists as a Test Case," paper delivered at Second Berkshire Conference on the History of Women, 27 October 1974, p. 10. This study of a cross section of female Loyalists indicates only 9.2 percent worked outside the home. Whether these figures are representative of most late eighteenth-century women remains to be documented.

26. For examples of the expansion of female services and functions in port towns, ranging from paid domestic servants, wet nurses, and prostitutes to that of a small group of wealthy women consumers, see Ryan, *Womanhood in America*, pp. 73, 86–87, 91–99; Virginia Bever Platt (Bowling Green State University), "The Working Women of Newport Rhode Island," paper delivered at 1975 Conference on Women in the Era of the American Revolution. According to Platt's figures, female laborers in Newport (whether free, indentured, or hired-out as slaves, and regardless of race) were paid approximately 30 percent less than the lowest paid unskilled, free, white male workers and 20 percent less than hired-out male slaves.

27. Abbott, *Women in Industry*, pp. 13–20, 149–56; Manges, "Women Shopkeepers, Tavernkeepers and Artisans," pp. xxxi–xxxii, 40–41, 44(n. 101), 69–117(n. 290); Carl Bridenbaugh, *The Colonial Craftsman* (Chicago: University of Chicago Press, Phoenix

Books, 1961; reprint of original 1950 New York University Press edition), pp. 105–8; Earle, *Colonial Dames and Good Wives*, pp. 45–87; Carl Holliday, *Women's Life in Colonial Days* (New York: Frederick Ungar Publishing Co., 1922), pp. 291–312; Elisabeth Anthony Dexter, *Colonial Women of Affairs: Women in Business and the Professions in America before 1776*, 2d ed., rev. (Boston: Houghton Mifflin Co., 1931), passim; Ryan, *Womanhood in America*, pp. 34, 92–94.

28. Daniel Scott Smith, "Family Limitation, Sexual Control and Domestic Feminism in Victorian America," *Feminist Studies* 1 (Winter-Spring 1973): 46; Manges, "Women Shopkeepers, Tavernkeepers and Artisans," pp. xii–xxiii, 40–115, 118–119; Page Smith, *Daughters of the Promised Land* (Boston: Little, Brown and Co., 1970), p. 54; Carl N. Degler, *Out of Our Past: Forces that Shaped Modern America* (New York: Harper and Brothers, 1959), pp. 59–60; Mary R. Beard, *Women as Force in History*, pp. 78–80, 106–21. For more details about the socioeconomic activities of colonial women, see Julia Cherry Spruill, *Women's Life and Work in the Southern Colonies* (New York: W. W. Norton & Co., 1972; reprint of original 1938 University of North Carolina Press edition), pp. 255–313, 340–66; Earle, *Colonial Dames and Good Wives*, pp. 45–87; Holliday, *Woman's Life in Colonial Days*, pp. 291–312; Elisabeth Anthony Dexter, *Career Women of America, 1776–1840* (Clifton, N.J.: Augustus M. Kelley Publishers, 1972; reprint of original 1950 Houghton Mifflin edition), passim; Leonard, *Dear-Bought Heritage*, pp. 118–236; Abbott, *Women in Industry*, pp. 10–47; Helen Campbell, *Women Wage Earners: Their Past, Their Present, and Their Future* (New York: Arno Press, 1972; reprint of original 1893 Roberts Brothers edition), pp. 57–76; Annie Nathan Meyer, *Woman's Work in America* (New York: Henry Holt and Co., 1891), passim; Benson, *Women in Eighteenth-Century America*, pp. 34–78, 100–35.

29. Manges, "Women Shopkeepers, Tavernkeepers and Artisans," p. xxiii. Manges's figures indicate that the low of 17 percent was recorded from July 1763 to July 1764 when 52 women were granted licenses out of a total of 308. The high of 22 percent was recorded from July 1770 to July 1771 when 60 women were granted licenses out of a total of 284. Between 1762 and 1776 the average number of years that each woman held a tavern license was 3.8, according to my analysis of her figures. For Boston taverns, see Carl Bridenbaugh, *Cities in Wilderness: The First Century of Urban Life in America, 1624–1742* (New York: Alfred A. Knopf, 1955) p. 72; idem, *Colonial Craftsmen*, pp. 121–22.

30. Manges, "Women Shopkeepers, Tavernkeepers and Artisans," pp. xxiii, 71, 75, 76, 78–81(n. 205), 96, 116, 118.

31. Elisabeth Anthony Dexter's widely quoted statement that approximately 10 percent of all colonial shop managers or "she-merchants" in Boston were women is obviously based on an inadequate sampling of newspaper advertisements. On the other hand she provides evidence for the relative decline in women shopkeepers in the postrevolutionary period and their almost exclusive relegation to the sale of dry goods and clothes for their own sex. See Dexter, *Colonial Women of Affairs*, pp. 34–35, 37–38, 162–65; idem, *Career Women of America*, p. 139.

32. See Bernard Bailyn, *The New England Merchants in the Seventeenth Century* (New York: Harper & Row, Harper Torchbook, 1964; reprint of original 1955 Harvard University Press edition), passim; Richard B. Morris, *Government and Labor in Early America* (New York: Columbia University Press, 1946), pp. 1–54; Thomas C. Cochran, *Business in American Life*, pp. 28–57; idem, "The Business Revolution," *The American Historical Review* 79 (December 1974): 1449–66; Samuel Rezneck, "The Rise and Early Development of Industrial Consciousness in the United States, 1760–1830," *Journal of Economic and Business History* 4 (August 1932): 784–86; David J. Jeremy, "British Textile Technology Transmission to the United States: The Philadelphia Region Experience, 1770–1820," *Business History Review* 47 (Spring 1973): 24–29; Henretta, *Evolution of American Society*, pp. 95–112, 174–200; Manges, "Women Shopkeepers, Tavernkeepers and Artisans," pp. 8, 14–15, 17, 20, 25, 33, 37, 38, 42, 118.

33. James Henretta, "Economic Development and Social Structure in Colonial Boston," *William and Mary Quarterly* 22 (January 1965): 80–83, 85; Philip J. Greven, Jr., *Four Generations: Population, Land, and Family in Colonial Andover, Massachusetts* (Ithaca: Cornell University Press, 1970), pp. 281–82; Richard L. Bushman, *From Puritan to Yankee: Character and the Social Order in Connecticut, 1690–1765* (Cambridge: Harvard University Press, 1967), pp. 267–88; Burrows and Wallace, "American Revolution," pp. 255–67;

Jacob M. Price, "Economic Function and the Growth of American Port Towns in the Eighteenth Century," *Perspectives in American History* 8 (1974): 130–37; Allan Kulikoff, "The Progress of Inequality in Revolutionary Boston," *William and Mary Quarterly* 28 (July 1971): 376, 378, 380, 383–84, 388–89, 406–9; James T. Lemon and Gary B. Nash, "The Distribution of Wealth in Eighteenth Century America: A Century of Changes in Chester County, Pennsylvania, 1693–1802," *Journal of Social History* 2 (1968–1969): 9–12; Kenneth Lockridge, "Land, Population and the Evolution of New England Society, 1630–1790," *Past and Present*, no. 39 (April 1968), pp. 62–80; Alexander Keyssar, "Widowhood in Eighteenth-Century Massachusetts: A Problem in the History of the Family," *Perspectives in American History* 8 (1974): 100–101, 114–15, 117–18; Platt, "Working Women of Newport," pp. 8, 11.

34. Henretta, *Evolution of American Society*, pp. 42, 72, 159, 188–89; idem, "Economic Development and Social Structure in Colonial Boston," pp. 72–92.

35. Henretta, *Evolution of American Society*, p. 196; Morris, *Government and Labor*, pp. 188–207, 354–63; *AFC*, 4:258; Manges, "Women Shopkeepers, Tavernkeepers and Artisans," pp. 34–35, 69; F. T. Carlton, "Abolition of Imprisonment for Debt in the United States," *Yale Review* 17 (1908): 339–44; Spruill, *Women's Life and Work*, pp. 338–39; Keyssar, "Widowhood in Eighteenth-Century Massachusetts," pp. 112–13; Kulikoff, "The Progress of Inequality in Revolutionary Boston," pp. 383–84, 408–9.

36. Platt, "Working Women of Newport," pp. 9–10; William R. Bagnall, *The Textile Industries of the United States* (New York: Augustus M. Kelley, 1971; reprint of the original 1893 Riverside Press edition), pp. 28–88; Rolla M. Tryon, *Household Manufactures in the U.S., 1640–1860* (Chicago: University of Chicago Press, 1917), pp. 58–59, 100–107, 112–15; Victor S. Clark, *History of Manufactures in the United States*, vol. 1, *1607–1860* (New York: Peter Smith, 1949; reprint of the original 1929 Carnegie Institution edition), pp. 116, 117, 188–91; Jernegan, *Laboring and Dependent Classes*, p. 18; Caroline Gilman, ed., *Letters of Eliza Wilkinson* (New York: Arno Press, 1969; reprint of original 1839 Samuel Colman edition), p. 105; Schneir, "Women in the Revolutionary Economy," p. 8, passim; Leonard, *Dear-Bought Heritage*, pp. 188–99.

37. Quoted from the *Pennsylvania Packet*, 7 August 1775 and 19 December 1774.

38. Jeremy, "British Textile Technology Transmission," pp. 28–29; Abbott, *Women in Industry*, pp. 36–37; Herbert Heaton, "The Industrial Immigrant in the United States, 1783–1812," *Proceedings of the American Philosophical Society* 95 (1951): 522–23; Rezneck, "Industrial Consciousness," pp. 786–90, 795–96; Cometti, "Women in American Revolution," pp. 332–33; Bagnall, *Textile Industries*, pp. 79–88; Leonard, *Dear-Bought Heritage*, pp. 199–203.

39. Cochran, "Business Revolution," pp. 1455, 1465; Abbott, *Women in Industry*, pp. 37–47; Jeremy, "British Textile Technology Transmission," pp. 31, 47; Manges, "Women Shopkeepers, Tavernkeepers and Artisans," pp. 27, 35, 37, 44–70, 119–20; Gerda Lerner, "The Lady and the Mill Girl: Changes in the Status of Women in the Age of Jackson," in *Our American Sisters*, eds. Jean E. Friedman and William G. Shade (Boston: Allyn and Bacon, 1973), pp. 89–90; Leonard, *Dear-Bought Heritage*, pp. 203–7; Elizabeth Faulkner Baker, *Technology and Women's Work* (New York: Columbia University Press, 1964), pp. 12–13; Abbott, *Women in Industry*, pp. 95–97, 109–47.

40. Jeremy, "British Textile Technology Transmission," pp. 24–52, 53–56 (quotations from pp. 29–30); Heaton, "Industrial Immigrant," p. 519; Mildred Campbell, "English Emigration on the Eve of the American Revolution," *The American Historical Review* 61 (October 1955): 4, 6–7. Campbell's study showed that out of 6,000 emigrants to the New World from December 1773 to April 1776, 12 percent or 720 of these were adult females, of whom 23 percent or 165 "were working women with some skill or occupation" outside of that of housewife. Hopefully, the study in progress by David J. Jeremy will reveal a clearer picture of their contribution to the transmission of textile skills and technology between Britain and America.

41. Abbott, *Women in Industry*, pp. 46, 47, 88; Jeremy, "British Textile Technology Transmission," p. 36; Jacob E. Cooke, ed., *The Reports of Alexander Hamilton* (New York: Harper and Row, 1964), pp. 130–31. For the ways in which economic nationalists rationalized the exploitation of female labor, see Rezneck, "Industrial Consciousness," pp. 790–99.

42. Cochran, "Business Revolution," p. 1465; Baker, *Technology and Women's Work*,

pp. 6–7. For earlier Puritan references to the "sin of idleness," see n. 61 below.

43. For demographic studies of the southern colonies see Lorena S. Walsh and Russell R. Menard, "Death in the Chesapeake: Two Life Tables for Men in Early Colonial Maryland," *Maryland Historical Magazine* 69 (Summer 1974): 211–27; Wesley Frank Craven, *White, Red, and Black: The Seventeenth-Century Virginian* (Charlottesville, Va.: University of Virginia Press, 1971); Russell R. Menard, "Immigration to the Chesapeake Colonies in the Seventeenth Century: A Review Essay," *Maryland Historical Magazine* 68 (1973): 323–29; Irene W. D. Hecht, "The Virginia Muster of 1624/5 as a Source for Demographic History," *William and Mary Quarterly* 30 (1973): 65–92.

44. I am referring here to recent works on demography and social structure by John Demos, Philip J. Greven, James Henretta, Kenneth A. Lockridge, Robert V. Wells, Daniel Scott Smith, Darrett Rutman, Alexander Keyssar, and Richard Alterman that question some of the earlier prescriptive conclusions reached by Bernard Bailyn, Edmund Morgan, Oscar Handlin, Arthur W. Calhoun, Perry Miller, and Thomas Johnson based on research into literary sources.

45. Henretta, *Evolution of American Society,* pp. 12–13; Greven, *Four Generations,* pp. 21–40, 29, 110–11, 192–94; David E. Stannard, "Death and the Puritan Child," *American Quarterly* 26 (December 1974): 463–66; Keyssar, "Widowhood in Eighteenth-Century Massachusetts," pp. 88–94, 108–9; Walsh and Menard, "Death in the Chesapeake," pp. 222–27; Maris A. Vinovskis, "Mortality Rates and Trends in Massachusetts Before 1860," *Journal of Economic History* 32 (March 1972): 184–89, 190–91, 194–203, 212–13; John Demos, "Notes on Life in Plymouth Colony," *William and Mary Quarterly* 22 (1965): 271–72.

46. Daniel Scott Smith, "The Demographic History of Colonial New England," *Journal of Economic History* 32 (March 1972): 170–73; Herbert Moller, "Sex Composition and Correlated Culture Patterns of Colonial America," *William and Mary Quarterly* 2 (April 1945): 118, 124–25; Henretta, *Evolution of American Society,* p. 172; Greven, *Four Generations,* pp. 121–22; John Demos, "Families in Colonial Bristol, Rhode Island: An Exercise in Historical Demography," in *Quantitative History,* eds. D. K. Rowney and J. Q. Graham, Jr. (Homewood, Ill: Dorsey Press, 1969), pp. 301, 305; Keyssar, "Widowhood in Eighteenth-Century Massachusetts," pp. 95–97. Between 1721 and 1760 as many as 15 percent of all adult women remained unmarried at least until the age of 45 in certain towns in Massachusetts and Rhode Island.

47. Moller, "Sex Composition," p. 140; Demos, "Life in Plymouth," pp. 272–73, 275–76; Henretta, *Evolution of American Society,* p. 132; Bruce E. Steiner, "Demographic Studies," *New England Quarterly* 43 (September 1970): 482–89; Daniel Scott Smith, "Parental Power and Marriage Patterns: An Analysis of Historical Trends in Hingham, Massachusetts," *Journal of Marriage and the Family* 35 (August 1973): 419–28; Ryan, *Womanhood in America,* pp. 106–111; Greven, *Four Generations,* pp. 272–75; Smith and Hindus, "Premarital Pregnancy," pp. 561–64.

48. Smith, "Parental Power and Marriage Patterns," p. 427; Keyssar, "Widowhood in Eighteenth-Century Massachusetts," pp. 117–18; Ryan, *Womanhood in America,* pp. 86–91. Since none of the new demographic studies have dealt with actual frontier conditions I see no reason to deny the validity of the axiom that "the frontier was great for men and dogs, but hell for horses and women." There is a tendency among some historians who have recently rediscovered the functional importance of women within the seventeenth century colonial household to confuse conditions in newly settled coastal areas with those of frontier America, which continued well into the nineteenth century. The former were generally organized efforts characterized by the immediate establishment of stable family life and kinship networks, while the latter were often isolated and unplanned or poorly planned ventures into the wilderness where male dominance reigned supreme and where isolated women, whether they were there as status symbols, slaves, civilizers, or prostitutes, had no institutionalized protection (such as the proximity of their families of orientation) from the physical hardships imposed both by the environment and the men. It appears that this dominance diminished to some degree as the first elements of law and order were introduced and small communities with more balanced sex ratios developed—only to return when these settlements became fully "civilized" and well within the cultural and economic standards set by the older coastal towns. By saying this, I do not want to diminish the socioeconomic impor-

tance of the western frontier woman; but at the same time I do not want to romanticize it.

49. Smith, "Parental Power and Marriage Patterns," pp. 421, 427; idem, "Demographic History of Colonial New England," pp. 165 (n. 2), 170–73; Greven, *Four Generations*, 14–16, 30, 111–13, 118–23, 261–68; Wilson H. Grabill, Clyde V. Kiser, and Pascal K. Whelpton, "A Long View," in *The American Family in Social-Historical Perspective,* ed. Michael Gordon (New York: St. Martin's Press, 1973), pp. 375, 379; idem, eds. *The Fertility of American Women* (New York: John Wiley and Sons, 1958), pp. 9–10; Philip J. Greven, Jr., "The Average Size of Families and Households in the Province of Massachusetts in 1764 and in the United States in 1790: An Overview," in *Household and Family in Past Time,* ed. Peter Laslett (London: Cambridge University Press, 1972), pp. 551, 556, 557–58, 559; Demos, "Families in Colonial Bristol," pp. 297, 299, 305.

50. J. William Frost, *The Quaker Family in Colonial America* (New York: St. Martin's Press, 1973), pp. 70, 86–88; Robert V. Wells, "Family Size and Fertility Control in Eighteenth-Century America: A Study of Quaker History," *Population Studies* 25 (1971): 73–82: idem, "Demographic Change and the Life Cycle of American Families," *Journal of Interdisciplinary History* 2 (Spring 1975): 743–49; Smith, "Parental Power and Marriage Patterns," pp. 421, 426; idem, "Demographic History of Colonial New England," pp. 166, 178, 179(n. 17), 180(n. 19), 182–83; Grabill, Kiser, and Whelpton, "A Long View," pp. 383–84; Ryan, *Womanhood in America,* pp. 48, 62, 121, 124–35; Lawrence Stone, "The Massacre of the Innocents," *New York Review of Books,* 14 November 1974, p. 31; Greven, *Four Generations,* pp. 279–84; Bushman, *Puritan to Yankee,* pp. 183–95, 235–66; Burrows and Wallace, "American Revolution," pp. 255–67, 283–89; Gordon S. Wood, "Rhetoric and Reality in the American Revolution," *William and Mary Quarterly* 23 (1966): 25–31; John J. Waters, Jr., *The Otis Family in Provincial and Revolutionary Massachusetts* (Chapel Hill: University of North Carolina Press, 1968), pp. 128–34; David J. Rothman, "A Note on the Study of the Colonial Family," in *Education in American History,* ed. Michael B. Katz (New York: Praeger Publishers, 1973), pp. 22–28; Steiner, "Demographic Studies," pp. 482–89. All statements, even those as qualified as Greven's (p. 282), about the transition taking place in the family unit being complete in 1776, must be viewed with caution especially when Burrows and Wallace suggest (p. 283), "families provide the political system with the personality type it requires."

51. John F. Walzer, "Eighteenth-Century American Childhood," in *The History of Childhood,* ed. Lloyd deMause (New York: The Psychohistory Press, 1974), pp. 352–53, 358, 360–75, 378 (n. 50); Ann Hulton, *Letters of a Loyalist Lady* (Cambridge: Harvard University Press, 1927), pp. ix, 37, 49–50, 63; Spruill, *Women's Life and Work,* pp. 55–63; Stewart Mitchell, ed., *New Letters of Abigail Adams, 1788–1801* (Boston: Houghton Mifflin Co., 1947), pp. xxviii–xxix, 35–36, 109, 129, 130–31, 174; Philip J. Greven, Jr., ed., *Child-Rearing Concepts, 1628–1861* (Ithaca, Ill.: F. E. Peacock Publishers, 1973), pp. 1–6, 46–51, passim. Also see n. 14 for the child-rearing views of Abigail Adams and Mercy Warren.

52. Keyssar, "Widowhood in Eighteenth-Century Massachusetts," pp. 87–91, 100–101, 114, 117, 118; Smith, "Parental Power and Marriage Patterns," pp. 420–24; Greven, *Four Generations,* pp. 72–99, 280–86; Demos, "Notes on Life in Plymouth Colony," pp. 273–75; idem, *Little Commonwealth,* pp. 149–70; (on pages 169–70 Demos appears to contradict some of his own evidence and Greven's by denying "that parents deployed their ownership of property so as to maintain effective control over their grown children" in the seventeenth century); Paul Leicester Ford, ed., *The Works of Thomas Jefferson* (New York: G. P. Putnam's Sons, 1904), 2:269.

53. Joseph E. Illick, "Child-Rearing in Seventeenth-Century England and America," in *History of Childhood,* pp. 324–25; Smith, "Parental Power and Marriage Patterns," pp. 425–26 (n. 9).

54. Smith and Hindus, "Premarital Pregnancy," pp. 537, 561, passim; Daniel Scott Smith, "The Dating of the American Sexual Revolution: Evidence and Interpretation," in *American Family in Social-Historical Perspective,* p. 323; Moller, "Sex Composition," pp. 142–45; Arthur W. Calhoun, *A Social History of the American Family* (New York: Barnes and Noble, 1917), vol. 1: *Colonial Period,* pp. 51–64; Greven, *Four Generations,* pp. 113–16; Demos, "Families in Colonial Bristol, R. I.," p. 306; Henretta, *Evolution of American Society,* pp. 132–33.

55. Smith and Hindus, "Premarital Pregnancy," pp. 537–41, 549, 553 (quotation), 555–60.

56. Ibid.; Greven, *Child-Rearing Concepts*, pp. 4–5. See also nn. 48 and 50 above.

57. Smith and Hindus, "Premarital Pregnancy," pp. 547–51. Bundling has been described by these two authors as "an eighteenth century compromise between persistent parental control and pressures of the young to subvert traditional familial authority" (p. 556). See n. 14 for views of Adams and Warren on virtue.

58. Ibid., p. 557; Michael Paul Rogin, *Fathers and Children* (New York: Alfred A. Knopf, 1975), pp. 30, 34. See n. 50 above and section on education for confirmation of conservative views about the family held by the Founding Fathers.

59. Rogin, *Fathers and Children*, pp. 63–64, 70–71. For representative examples of the general submissiveness and the vicarious aspects of the lives of the middle- and upper-class women in the late eighteenth century which ultimately led to a culmination of the double standard in the cult of idleness and "true womanhood," see Linda Grant De Pauw, "The American Revolution and the Rights of Women: The Feminist Theory of Abigail Adams," paper delivered at the 1975 meeting of the Organization of American Historians; Hulton, *Letters of a Loyalist Lady*, p. 6; Woody, *History of Women's Education*, 1:133–34; Alice Morse Earle, ed., *Diary of Anna Green Winslow: A Boston School Girl of 1771* (Detroit: Singing Tree Press, 1970; reprint of the original 1894 Houghton Mifflin edition), passim; Eliza Southgate Bowne, *A Girl's Life Eighty Years Ago* (New York: Charles Scribner's Sons, 1887), pp. 15–19, 50–51; Ethel Armes, ed., *Nancy Shippen: Her Journal Book: The International Romance of a Young Lady of Fashion of Colonial Philadelphia with Letters to Her and About Her* (Philadelphia: J. B. Lippincott, 1935), pp. 41–42; passim; AFC, 2:407; 3:xxxiii; 4:210, 221, 258; Keith Thomas, "The Double Standard," *Journal of the History of Ideas* 20 (April 1959): 195–216; E. Willett Cunington, *Feminine Attitudes in the Nineteenth Century* (New York: MacMillan and Co., 1936), pp. 201–35; Barbara Welter, "The Cult of True Womanhood: 1820–1860," *American Quarterly* 18 (Summer 1966): 151–74; Ryan, *Womanhood in America*, pp. 137–91.

60. Calhoun, *American Family*, 1:83–103; Greven, *Four Generations*, pp. 72–99; Stone, "Massacre of Innocents," p. 30; Bushman, *From Puritan to Yankee*, pp. 3–38, 147–82; Erikson, *Wayward Puritans*, pp. 54–64; Thomas Jefferson Wertenbaker, *The Puritan Oligarchy: The Founding of American Civilization* (New York: Charles Scribner's Sons, 1947), pp. 183–251; Gaustad, *Great Awakening*, pp. 1–15; Thomas Szasz, *Ceremonial Chemistry* (Garden City, N.Y.: Doubleday & Co., Anchor Books, 1974), pp. 65–66; idem, *The Manufacture of Madness* (New York: Harper and Row, 1970), pp. 99–100; Spruill, *Women's Life and Work*, pp. 326–30.

61. Moller, "Sex Composition," pp. 151–52; Bushman, *From Puritan to Yankee*, pp. 188, 196–98; Erikson, *Wayward Puritans*, pp. 64–136, 163–81; Smith, *Daughters of the Promised Land*, pp. 47–50; Mather, *Ornaments for the Daughters of Zion*, pp. 98, 119–27, passim; Jernegan, *Laboring and Dependent Classes*, pp. 87–88; Abbott, *Women in Industry*, p. 34; Edmund S. Morgan, *The Puritan Family* (Boston: Trustees of the Public Library, 1944), pp. 65, 66–67, 74, 147; Morris, *Government and Labor*, pp. 4–5.

62. Robert Middlekauff, *The Mathers: Three Generations of Puritan Intellectuals, 1596–1792* (New York: Oxford University Press, 1971), pp. 148–61, 340; Ryan, *Womanhood in America*, pp. 76–81; Smith, *Daughters of the Promised Land*, pp. 54–58; Erikson, *Wayward Puritans*, pp. 137–59; Howard W. Haggard, *Devils, Drugs and Doctors* (New York: Harper and Brothers, 1939), p. 69; George L. Kittredge, *Witchcraft in Old and New England* (New York: Russell, 1956), pp. 329–73, 579–98; Benson, *Women in Eighteenth-Century America*, pp. 104–8; Marlow, "Ideology of Woman's Movement," pp. 100–123; Keith E. Melder, "The Beginnings of the Women's Rights Movement in the United States, 1800–1940" (Ph.D. diss., Yale University, 1964), pp. 1–51; Woody, *History of Women's Education*, 1:92–96, 160, 162, 166, 175–76, 184, 186, 239–68; Paul Boyer and Stephen Nissenbaum, *Salem Possessed: The Social Origins of Witchcraft* (Cambridge: Harvard University Press, 1974), pp. 22–36, 179–216 (n. 59); Ryan, *Womanhood in America*, pp. 74–81.

63. Cedric B. Cowing, "Sex and Preaching in the Great Awakening," *American Quarterly* 20 (Fall 1968): 628–29, 635; Lockridge, "Social Change and the Meaning of the American Revolution," pp. 412, 416–17; Gaustad, *Great Awakening*, p. 18; Lawrence A. Cremin, *American Education: The Colonial Experience, 1607–1783* (New York: Harper and Row, 1970), p. 319; William Howland Kenney, III, "George Whitefield and Colonial

Revivalism: The Social Sources of Charismatic Authority, 1737–1770" (Ph.D. diss., University of Pennsylvania, 1966), pp. 149–53; Moller, "Sex Composition," pp. 126, 152–53.

64. Bushman, *From Puritan to Yankee,* pp. 187–95, 235–66 (quotation from p. 193); Burrows and Wallace, "American Revolution," p. 288; Cowing, "Sex and Preaching," pp. 629–38, 644.

65. Moller, "Sex Composition," pp. 146–47, 152–53 (quotation from p. 152); Benson, *Women in Eighteenth-Century America,* pp. 263–73; Cowing, "Sex and Preaching," pp. 629–35.

66. Herbert L. Osgood, *The American Colonies in the Eighteenth Century,* 4 vols. (New York: Columbia University Press, 1924), 3:417–18; Charles Francis Adams, "Some Phases of Sexual Morality and Church Discipline in New England," *Massachusetts Historical Society Proceedings* 6 (1891): 501; Cederick B. Cowing, "Sex and Preaching in the Great Awakening," *American Quarterly* 20 (1968): 624–44; Benson, *Women in Eighteenth-Century America,* pp. 259–61; Melder, "Beginnings of the Women's Rights Movement," pp. 69–70.

67. Gaustad, *Great Awakening,* p. 72; Cowing, "Sex and Preaching," pp. 632–33.

68. Moller, "Sex Composition," p. 153; Cowing, "Sex and Preaching," pp. 624–25; Ryan, *Womanhood in America,* p. 50. The small prayer circles formed by young women were few, unstable, and very likely conservative. See Benson, *Women in Eighteenth-Century America,* pp. 259–62. Smith and Hindus, "Premarital Pregnancy," pp. 537, 541, 549, 553.

69. Smith and Hindus, "Premarital Pregnancy," pp. 549–58; Cowing, "Sex and Preaching," passim; Melder, "Beginnings of the Women's Rights Movement," pp. 69–94; Whitney R. Cross, *The Burned-Over District: The Social and Intellectual History of Enthusiastic Religion in Western New York, 1800–1850* (New York: Harper and Row, Harper Torchbook, 1965; reprint of original 1950 Cornell University Press edition), pp. 3–13, passim.

70. Kenneth A. Lockridge, *Literacy in Colonial New England: An Inquiry into the Social Contest of Literacy in the Early Modern West* (New York: W. W. Norton, 1974), pp. 7, 26–31, 126–28 (quotations from pp. 31 and 127–28).

71. Lockridge, *Literacy in Colonial New England,* pp. 13–27, 38–42, 45, 127–28, 140; Cremin, *American Education,* pp. 320–32, 494–96, 517–43.

72. Woody, *Women's Education,* 1: 245–46; Benson, *Women in Eighteenth-Century America,* p. 145; Smith and Hindus, "Premarital Pregnancy," pp. 549–51; Illick, "Child-Rearing in Seventeenth Century," pp. 315, 342–43 (n. 79); Flexnor, *Century of Struggle,* p. 343. See also n. 69.

73. Smith and Hindus, "Premarital Pregnancy," pp. 550–51.

74. Mary F. Eastman, "The Education of Women in the Eastern States," May Wright Sewall, "The Education of Women in the Western States," and Cristine Ladd Franklin, "The Education of Women in the Southern States," all in *Woman's Work in America,* ed. Annie Nathan Meyer (New York: Henry Holt and Co., 1891), pp. 3–19, 54–57, 89–91; Spruill, *Women's Life and Work,* pp. 185–207; Clifton Johnson, *Old-Time Schools and School-Books* (New York: Macmillan Co., 1925), pp. 24–68; Cremin, *American Education,* p. 123–37; Armes, *Nancy Shippen,* pp. 36–37; Jean Fritz, *Cast for a Revolution: Some American Friends and Enemies, 1728–1814* (Boston: Houghton Mifflin Co., 1972), pp. 8–10; Edgar W. Knight, ed., *A Documentary History of Education in the South before 1860* (Chapel Hill: University of North Carolina Press), p. 326; Woody, *History of Women's Education,* 1:92, 106–8, 124–300, 305; Leonard, *Dear-Bought Heritage,* pp. 237–97; Geraldine Brooks, *Dames and Daughters of the Young Republic* (New York: Thomas Y. Crowell and Co., 1901), pp. pp. 96–98; Holliday, *Women's Life in Colonial Days,* 70–94; Benson, *Women in Eighteenth-Century America,* pp. 108–9, 116–19. For complaints from women about their inadequate educations, see *AFC,* 1:36; 2:93–94, 391–93; 3:52–53; 4:74–75, 94; Bowne, *A Girl's Life,* pp. 55–56, 58–63; Armes, *Nancy Shippen,* pp. 19, 21–22; Woody, *History of Women's Education,* 1:93, 129–37, Katherine Anthony, *First Lady of the Revolution: The Life of Mercy Otis Warren* (Port Washington, N.Y.: Kennikat Press, 1972; reprint of original 1958 edition), p. 188.

75. Smith, *Daughters of the Promised Land,* pp. 39–40, 46–47; Daniel Scott Smith, "Parental Power and Marriage Patterns: An Analysis of Historical Trends in Hingham, Massachusetts," *Journal of Marriage and the Family* 35 (August 1973): 423, 426–27. For

a criticism of Page Smith's book, especially his attitude toward women and his theory of the "potency of daughterhood" (which is based on only six documented examples and neglects all those women who apparently resisted their fathers' attempts to "emancipate" them), see Banner, "On Writing Women's History," pp. 356–57 and Linda Gordon et al., "Historical Phallicies," pp. 21–25.

76. Elizabeth Wade White, "The Tenth Muse—A Tercentenary Appraisal of Anne Bradstreet," *William and Mary Quarterly* 8 (July 1951): 355; Holliday, *Woman's Life in Colonial Days*, pp. 86–94; Earle, *Diary of Anna Green Winslow*, pp. iii–vi, passim; Benson, *Women in Eighteenth-Century America*, pp. 100–135; Holliday, *Woman's Life in Colonial Days*, p. 86; Julian P. Boyd, ed., *The Papers of Thomas Jefferson* (Princeton: Princeton University Press, 1952), 6:359–60; Eliza Southgate Bowne, *A Girl's Life Eighty Years Ago* (New York: Charles Scribner's Sons, 1887), pp. iv, 4–18, 30–31; Vena Bernadette Field, "Constantia: A Study of the Life and Works of Judith Sargent Murray, 1751–1820," *Maine Bulletin* 33 (February 1931): 15–16; Joan Hoff Wilson, "Dancing Dogs of the Colonial Period: Women Scientists," *Early American Literature* 7 (Winter 1973): 225–35; idem, "What Does a Woman Want?: Toward a Theory of Feminist Humanism," dittoed, Sacramento, Calif., 1971, pp. 1–6; idem, "Woman as a Declining Force in American History," in *Image, Myth and Beyond: American Women and American Studies*, vol. 2, ed. Betty E. Chmaj (Pittsburgh: Know, Inc., 1974), pp. 224–38; Straub, "Benjamin Rush's Views on Women's Education," p. 153; Wilson Smith, ed., *Theories of Education in Early America, 1655–1819* (Indianapolis and New York: Bobbs-Merrill Co., 1973), pp. 252–53; J. D. Bernal, *Science in History*, vol. 2: *The Scientific and Industrial Revolutions* (Cambridge: M.I.T. Press paperback, 1971; reprint of original 1954 C. A. Watts edition), pp. 516, 599–617, 636–38, 653–59.

77. Armes, *Nancy Shippen*, pp. 19, 21, 43.

78. Daniel Scott Smith, "Inheritance and the Position and Orientation of Colonial Women," paper delivered at the Second Berkshire Conference on the History of Women, 27 October 1974, pp. 12–13.

79. *AFC*, 4:344; Woody, *Women's Education*, 1:329–41; Cremin, *American Education*, pp. 564–70; Melder, "Beginning of the Women's Rights Movement," pp. 94–100.

80. Woody, *History of Women's Education*, 1:563–65; Melder, "Mask of Oppression," pp. 1–3, 6, 16–17; idem, "Beginnings of the Women's Rights Movement," pp. 100–124; Gerda Lerner, "Women's Rights and American Feminism," pp. 238–39; idem, "The Lady and the Mill Girl," pp. 85–87; Benson, *Women in Eighteenth-Century America*, pp. 157–61, 173; Eleanor Flexnor, *Century of Struggle* (New York: Atheneum, 1970; reprint of original 1959 Belknap edition), pp. 23–24.

81. Wilson, "Dancing Dogs: Women Scientists," pp. 225, 230; Morgan, *American Slavery—American Freedom*, pp. 158–64. Manges, "Women Shopkeepers, Tavernkeepers and Artisans," pp. xxxii–xxxiii; Lerner, "Lady and Mill Girl," pp. 85–88; Spruill, *Women's Life and Work*, pp. 267–76; Barbara Ehrenreich and Deirdre English, *Witches, Midwives and Nurses—A History of Women Healers* (Glass Mountain Pamphlets, 1972), pp. 18–32; Abbott, *Women in Industry*, pp. 266–67 (n. 4).

82. David J. Rothman, "A Note on the Study of the Colonial Family," in *Education in American History: Readings on the Social Issues*, ed. Michael B. Katz (New York: Praeger Publishers, 1973), p. 25; John Demos, "Notes on Life in Plymouth Colony," *William and Mary Quarterly* 22 (1965): 283–86.

83. Kerber, "Daughters of Columbia," pp. 36, 48–57; Benson, *Women in Eighteenth-Century America*, pp. 172–87; Bertha Monica Stearns, "Early Philadelphia Magazines for Ladies," *Pennsylvania Magazine of History and Biography* 64 (October): 483; Straub, "Benjamin Rush's Views on Women's Education," pp. 147–57; Rudolph, *Essays on Education*, pp. 26–40; Clara M. and Rudolf Kirk, eds., *Charlotte Temple: A Tale of Truth* (New York: Twayne Publishers, 1964), pp. 11–24, passim; William S. Kable, ed., *Three Early American Novels* (Columbus, Ohio: Charles E. Merrill Publishing Co., 1970), pp. 4–14, passim; Bowne, *A Girl's Life*, pp. 54–62; Field, *Constantia*, pp. 65–68, passim.

84. Richard B. Morris, *Studies in the History of American Law: With Special Reference to the Seventeenth and Eighteenth Centuries* (New York: Octagon Books, 1963; reprint of original 1959 John M. Mitchell edition), pp. 128–35, 175–200; Sophie H. Drinker, "Women Attorneys of Colonial Times," *Maryland Historical Magazine* 56 (December 1961): 335, 338, 341, 342, 347; Eleanor M. Boatwright, "The Political and Civil Status of Women

in Georgia, 1783–1860," *The Georgia Historical Quarterly* 25 (December 1941): 301–3; Beard, *Woman as Force in History,* pp. 117–18; Susie M. Ames, "Law-in-Action: The Court Records of Virginia's Eastern Shore," *William and Mary Quarterly* 4 (April 1947): 184–86; Spruill, *Women's Life and Work,* pp. 340–66; George Lee Haskins, *Law and Authority in Early Massachusetts: A Study in Tradition and Design* (New York: Macmillan Publishing Co., 1960) pp. 116, 180–81, 182, 214–15, 280; Paul Samuel Reinsch, "English Common Law in the Early American Colonies," *Bulletin of the University of Wisconsin,* no. 31 (October 1899), pp. 19, 25, 53–59, passim; George Athan Billias, ed., *Selected Essays: Law and Authority in Colonial America* (Barre, Mass.: 1965), pp. 1–31, 74–135; David H. Flaherty, ed., *Essays in the History of Early American Law* (Chapel Hill: University of North Carolina Press, 1969), pp. 3–280.

85. Billias, *Law and Authority in Colonial America,* p. 26; Haskins, *Law and Authority,* pp. 165, 167, 183, 265; Flaherty, *Essays in Early American Law,* pp. 281–391, 433–50; Beard, *Woman as Force in History,* pp. 134–44; Richard B. Morris, *Government and Labor in Early America* (New York: Columbia University Press, 1946), pp. 347–48, 363; D. Kelly Weisberg, " 'Under Greet Temptations Heer': Women and Divorce in Puritan Massachusetts," *Feminist Studies* 2, nos. 2/3 (1975): 183–93; Nancy F. Cott, "Adultery, Divorce, and the Status of Women," forthcoming in *William and Mary Quarterly*; Kathryn Turner Preyer, "Joseph Story, the Supreme Court and the Question of a Federal Common Law Jurisdiction over Crimes," paper, Organization of the American Historians, 1970.

86. Flaherty, *Essays in Early American Law,* pp. 24–25, 74, 452–57; Beard, *Woman as Force in History,* pp. 144–55; Drinker, "Women Attorneys," p. 351; Dexter, *Colonial Women of Affairs,* pp. 190–93.

87. Richard B. Morris, "Legalism versus Revolutionary Doctrine in New England," *New England Quarterly* 4 (April 1931): 195–215; Flaherty, *Essays in Early American Law,* pp. 392–417; Weisberg, "Women and Divorce," pp. 185–90.

88. F. T. Carlton, "Abolition of Imprisonment for Debt in the United States," *Yale Law Review* 17 (1908): 339–44; Morris, *Government and Labor,* p. 363; idem, "Legalism versus Revolutionary Doctrine," pp. 203–4; Boatwright, "Political and Civil Status of Women," pp. 318–19; Flaherty, *Essays in Early American Law,* pp. 204, 240–41, 341, 458–71; Gordon S. Wood, "Rhetoric and Reality in the American Revolution," *William and Mary Quarterly* 23 (January 1966): 29–30; Maxwell Bloomfield, "William Sampson and the Codifiers: The Roots of American Legal Reform, 1820–1830," *American Journal of Legal History* 11 (1967): 234–52.

89. Keyssar, "Widowhood in Eighteenth-Century Massachusetts," pp. 101, 118; Haskins, *Law and Authority,* pp. 180–82; Billias, *Law and Authority in Colonial America,* pp. 23–26.

90. Kulikoff, "Progress of Inequality in Revolutionary Boston," p. 388; Keyssar, "Widowhood in Eighteenth-Century Massachusetts," p. 118; Morris, *History of American Law,* pp. 128–30.

91. Morgan, *American Slavery—American Freedom,* pp. 164–68, 304; Smith, "Inheritance and the Position and Orientation of Colonial Women," pp. 6, 10, 11, 13.

92. Ibid., pp. 8–10; Norton, "Eighteenth-Century American Women," pp. 10–12; Lockridge, *Literacy in Colonial New England,* p. 12.

93. Sophie H. Drinker, "Votes for Women in 18th-Century New Jersey," *Proceedings of the New Jersey Historical Society* 80 (January 1962): 34–42; Boatwright, "The Political and Civil Status of Women in Georgia, 1783–1860," pp. 301–3; Albert Edward McKinley, *The Suffrage Franchise in the Thirteen English Colonies in America* (New York: Burt Franklin, 1905), pp. 473–74; Mrs. Henry W. Edwards, "Lady Deborah Moody," *Essex Institute Historical Collections* 31 (1894): 96–102; De Pauw, *Four Traditions,* pp. 12–13; Spruill, *Women's Life and Work,* pp. 232–45; "Virginia in 1677: The Case of Sarah, Widow of William Drummond," *Virginia Magazine of History and Biography* 22 (July 1914): 234–43.

94. Spruill, *Women's Life and Work,* pp. 241–45.

95. Mary Philbrook, "Women's Suffrage in New Jersey," *Proceedings of the New Jersey Historical Society* 57 (1939): 87–98; Drinker, "Votes for Women in New Jersey," pp. 31–45; Edward Raymond Turner, "Women's Suffrage in New Jersey, 1790–1807," *Smith College Studies in History* 1 (July 1916): 165–87; McKinley, *Suffrage Franchise,* passim; Marchette Chute, *The First Liberty: A History of the Right to Vote in America, 1619–1850* (New York: E. P. Dutton, 1969), pp. 17 n., 119, 289–90, 314–16; Chilton Williamson, *American*

Suffrage From Property to Democracy (Princeton: Princeton University Press, 1960), pp. 92–116; Kirk H. Porter, *A History of Suffrage in the United States* (New York: Greenwood Press, 1969; reprint of 1918 University of Chicago Press edition), pp. 7–14.

96. Lerner, "Lady and Mill Girl," pp. 90–91; Edward Pessen, *Jacksonian America* (Homewood, Ill.: Dorsey Press, 1969), pp. 86–87.

97. Gordon S. Wood, "Rhetoric and Reality in the American Revolution," *William and Mary Quarterly* 23 (January 1966): 31, passim; Lockridge, "Social Change and the Meaning of the American Revolution," pp. 424, 426–27, 433; Bernard Bailyn, *The Ideological Origins of the American Revolution* (Cambridge: Harvard University Press, Belknap Press, 1967), pp. viii–ix, 160–229; Burrows and Wallace, "The American Revolution," pp. 268–94.

98. Alice Morse Earle, *Home Life in Colonial Days* (New York: Macmillan, 1898), p. 253; Schneir, "Women in the Revolutionary Economy," pp. 15–17.

99. *Pennsylvania Gazette*, 6 June 1787; Lockridge, "Social Change and Meaning of the Revolution," p. 425. See also n. 37 above.

100. *AFC*, 3:380; William Raymond Smith, *History as Argument* (The Hague: Mouton & Co., 1966), pp. 117 (quotation), passim; Somerville, *Women and the American Revolution*, pp. 18–22; Earle, *Colonial Dames and Good Wives*, pp. 251–53; Leonard, *Dear-Bought Heritage*, pp. 548–59, 555–59.

101. *AFC*, 3:378, 380; Leonard, *Dear-Bought Heritage*, p. 548–49; Ellet, *Women of the Revolution*, passim; Earle, *Colonial Dames and Good Wives*, pp. 247–49; Gilman, *Letters of Eliza Wilkinson*, pp. 23, 27, 58, 60, 64, 78–79, 86–87; Armes, *Nancy Shippen*, pp. 21, 22, 41, 43, 44, 58, 62; Earle, *Diary of Anna Green Winslow*, passim.

102. Platt, "Working Women of Newport," pp. 8, 11, 13; Cometti, "Inflation in Maryland," pp. 228–33, 234.

103. *AFC*, 2:212; 4:7, 296; Handlin, "Revolutionary Economic Policy in Massachusetts," pp. 2–26; "Extracts from the Journal of Mrs. Henry [Elizabeth] Drinker, of Philadelphia, from September 25, 1777, to July 4, 1778" *Pennsylvania Magazine* 13 (1889): 300, 301.

104. *AFC*, 1:117, 119, 218, 232, 329, 359, 375, 380, 398–99, 407–8, 416; *AFC*, 2:212, 238–39; *AFC*, 3:xxxi, 61–62, 65–66, 95–96; *AFC*, 4:7, 255–59, 258, 327, 345–46; Booth, *Women of '76*, p. 11; Sherrill, "Abigail Adams," pp. 28–29; Ellet, *Women of the Revolution*, passim; Earle, *Colonial Dames and Good Wives*, pp. 258–75.

105. Blumenthal, *Women Camp Followers*, pp. 58–66, 72–79; Booth, *Women of '76*, pp. 181–88 (quotation from page 183); White, "Truth About Molly Pitcher," pp. 5–6, 10–14.

106. Cometti, "Women in the Revolution," p. 344; Blumenthal, *Women Camp Followers*, pp. 58, 79–82, 85; White, "Truth About Molly Pitcher," pp. 3–5, 10 (n. 63), 12–14.

107. Booth, *Women of '76*, p. 182; Leonard, *Dear-Bought Heritage*, pp. 554–55; Handlin, "Revolutionary Economic Policy in Massachusetts," p. 21; Cometti, "Women in the Revolution," pp. 330–31, 336; E. P. Thompson, "The Moral Economy of the English Crowd in the Eighteenth Century," *Past and Present*, no. 50 (February 1971), pp. 76–136; *AFC*, 2:295–96.

108. White, "Truth About Molly Pitcher," p. 11; *AFC*, 2:196; Thompson, "Moral Economy of the English Crowd," pp. 76–79; Jesse Lemisch, "Bailyn Besieged in his Bunker," critique delivered at the April 1975 OAH meeting, pp. 10–13; Pauline Maier, "Popular Uprisings and Civil Authority in Eighteenth-Century America," *William and Mary Quarterly* 27 (1970): 3–35; Kulikoff, "Progress of Inequality in Revolutionary Boston," pp. 410–11.

109. Abray, "Feminism in the French Revolution," pp. 52, 62.

110. Sherrill, "Abigail Adams," p. 8; McArthur, "Women of the Revolution," pp. 156–57, 159–60; Campbell, "Women of New York in the Revolution," pp. 155–68; Cometti, "Women in the Revolution," pp. 332–35, 340–41, 344–46; Somerville, *Women and the American Revolution*, pp. 40–41, 46–51; Blumenthal, *Women Camp Followers*, pp. 57–58; Wheeler, *Life and Writings of Paine*, pp. 192–93; Mary A. Livermore, "Women in the State," in *Woman's Work in America*, ed. Meyer, pp. 255–59; Terry, "Experiences of a Minister's Wife in the American Revolution," pp. 523–32; Earle, *Colonial Dames and Good Wives*, pp. 240–57; Cometti, "Women in the Revolution," pp. 336–39, 342–44;

Garden, *Anecdotes of the Revolution*, pp. 11, 44–45, 48, 52–59; McArthur, "Women of the Revolution," p. 156; *AFC*, 1:391, 406; Booth, *Women of '76*, pp. 25–82. See also nn. 16, 17, and 101 above.

111. *AFC*, 1:276; 2:301, 407; 4:255–57, 294; Smith, *John Adams*, 1:205; Ann Hulton, *Letters of a Loyalist Lady*, pp. 22–27, 28–30, 58–59, 70–72, 81–83, 85–86, 87–88, 91–92; Marvin L. Brown, Jr., trans. and ed., *Baroness von Riedesel and the American Revolution: Journal and Correspondence of a Tour of Duty, 1776–1783* (Chapel Hill: University of North Carolina Press, 1965), passim; Blumenthal, *Women Camp Followers*, pp. 66–67, 75–81; Garden, *Anecdotes of the Revolution*, pp. 28–41; Cometti, "Women in the Revolution," p. 330; Ellet, *Women of the American Revolution*, 3:200–204; Gilman, *Letters of Eliza Wilkinson*, passim.

112. Norton, "Eighteenth Century American Women," pp. 16–18 (n. 26).

113. *AFC*, 4:294; Carroll Smith-Rosenberg, "The Female World of Love and Ritual: Relations between Women in Nineteenth-Century America," *Signs: Journal of Women in Culture and Society* 1 (Autumn 1975): 9–10.

114. The exceptions to this generalization, of course, were those Loyalists who were native Americans, i.e. "Indians" (many of whom were influenced by Molly [Mary] Brant, the Mohawk widow of Sir William Johnson), and particularly those blacks who fought for the British in return for the promise of freedom. See De Pauw, *Four Traditions*, pp. 17–18; Mary Beth Norton, "The Fate of Some Black Loyalists of the American Revolution," *The Journal of Negro History* 58 (October 1973): 402–26; H. Pearson Gundy, "Molly Brant, Loyalist," *Ontario History* (Summer 1953).

115. Chalmers Johnson, *Revolutionary Change* (Boston: Little, Brown, 1966), pp. 44–45, 80–81, 106–7; Anthony F. C. Wallace, *Culture and Personality* (New York: Random House, 1961), pp. 143–44. For discussion of the preconditions necessary for feminist emancipation, see Lerner, "Women's Rights and American Feminism," p. 237, and Joan Hoff Wilson, "What Does a Woman Want?: Toward a Theory of Feminist Humanism," pp. 1–6; idem, "Woman as a Declining Force in American History," pp. 224–38.

116. Bowne, *A Girl's Life*, pp. 60–61; Berkin, "Conjurer's Circle," p. 17; Kerber, "Daughters of Columbia," pp. 49–50. For descriptions of woman's "proper sphere" according to theories of the Enlightenment based on natural law, see Holt Carleton Marlow, "The Ideology of the Woman's Movement, 1750–1860" (Ph.D. diss., University of Oklahoma, 1966), pp. 7–15, 100–123; Benson, *Women in Eighteenth-Century America*, pp. 11–33, 100–103; Abray, "Feminism in the French Revolution," p. 52; Gilman, *Letters of Eliza Wilkinson*, p. 61. For women's fears about exceeding their "proper spheres," see *AFC*, 2:109–10; Ellett, *Women of the American Revolution*, 1:84–85; Kerber, "Daughters of Columbia," pp. 53–55; Anthony, *First Lady of the Revolution*, pp. 32–33, 188; Adams, *Correspondence between Adams and Warren*, p. 485; Gilman, *Letters of Eliza Wilkinson*, p. 66.

117. *AFC*, 1:370; Benson, *Women in Eighteenth-Century America*, p. 247.

118. Adrienne Koch, ed., *The American Enlightenment: The Shaping of the American Experiment in a Free Society* (New York: George Braziller, 1965), pp. 19–45; idem, *Power, Morals, and the Founding Fathers: Essays in the Interpretation of the American Enlightenment* (Ithaca, N.Y.: Cornell University Press, Great Seal Books, 1961), pp. 3–5; Melder, "Beginnings of the Women's Rights Movement," pp. 7–13.

119. Other independent and influential positions taken by Abigail Adams include her private opposition to the institution of slavery, her indirect responsibility for the fact that John Adams's first draft of a constitution for the new state of Massachusetts did not specify "male" for citizen, and her decisive role in his negotiation of a new loan with the Dutch in 1799. See *AFC*, 1:162, 332, 369, 380, 400; 2:15, 24, 37, 45–48, 50; 3:226–28; Page Smith, *John Adams* (Garden City, N.Y.: Doubleday & Co., 1962), vol. 2, *1784–1826*, pp. 727–30, 1006 (quotation); Anthony, *First Lady of the Revolution*, pp. 186–89; Janet Whitney, *Abigail Adams* (Boston: Little, Brown, 1974), pp. 155, 290.

120. Gilman, *Letters of Eliza Wilkinson*, pp. 17, 61, 66.

121. Spruill, *Women's Life and Work*, pp. 51–53, 232–54; Benson, *Women in Eighteenth-Century America*, pp. 223–73.

122. See in particular "An Occasional Letter on the Female Sex," and "Reflections on Unhappy Marriages," in Daniel Edwin Wheeler, ed., *Life and Writings of Thomas Paine*, 10 vols. (New York: V. Parke, 1908), vol. 5. Both appeared originally in the *Pennsylvania Magazine* for August 1775. Mary Wollstonecraft, *A Vindication of the Rights of Woman With*

Strictures on Political and Moral Subjects, ed. Charles W. Hagelman, Jr. (New York: W. W. Norton & Co., 1967), passim; Melder, "Beginnings of Women's Rights Movement," p. 127.

123. Sherrill, "Abigail Adams," pp. 3, 5–7; Rogin, *Fathers and Children,* p. 71. See also n. 14.

124. Smith, "Parental Power and Marriage Patterns," pp. 425–27; Ryan, *Womanhood in America,* pp. 106–7, 123–26, 134–35.

125. Anthony, *First Lady of the Revolution,* p. 188.

126. Kerber, "Daughters of Columbia," pp. 47–53, 55–56; Bowne, *Girl's Life,* p. 62; Benson, *Women in Eighteenth-Century America,* pp. 136–70; Ryan, *Womanhood in America,* pp. 126–27.

Afterword

Alfred F. Young

The devil inspiring British ministers to do their evil deeds, a frequent theme of patriot cartoons, especially in Boston. This engraving is from the *Boston Gazette*, 24 February 1766, after the Stamp Act demonstrations, when Bostonians hung British officials in effigy on the town gallows. Lord Bute, to the left, is depicted in Scottish kilts, a symbol linking him to the despised Stuart monarchs.

Alfred F. Young, editor of this volume, also edited *Dissent: Explorations in the History of American Radicalism* (Northern Illinois University Press, 1968) which the Press now looks on as the first in a series that will continue to explore major themes in the history of American radicalism. He is also co-general editor, with Leonard W. Levy, of the *American Heritage Series* (Indianapolis: Bobbs Merrill Co.) comprising some 45 volumes of original source materials.

He is the author of *The Democratic Republicans of New York: The Origins, 1763–1797* (University of North Carolina Press, 1967), winner of the Institute of Early American History Award. His book, *The Crowd and the Coming of the Revolution: From Ritual to Rebellion in Boston,* will soon be published. It will be followed by an interpretive study of the role of artisans and laborers in the shaping of the nation, 1760–1820. His recent research has been supported by a Guggenheim Foundation fellowship and grants from Northern Illinois University.

What directions do these essays point to in our overall understanding of the American Revolution?

In taking off my cap as editor and putting on my cap as fellow historian of the Revolution, I will confine myself to commenting on what I find challenging in these essays and worthy of further inquiry. I hope to avoid the danger I warned about in the Foreword of synthesizing what it is too early to synthesize.

For me, the essays are exciting as demonstrations of what further research may uncover about the Revolution as to (1) the importance of class, (2) the allegiances of those at the bottom of society and on the outside, (3) the active role played by common people in shaping events, (4) the kind of ideas we may expect to find at the bottom, and (5) the impact of radicalism, both in its achievements and in its failures.

If my comments stimulate readers to different reactions, that is all to the good. The purpose of this volume is to open discussion, not foreclose it, or perhaps to reopen discussion on some themes of the Revolution that somehow endure through all the shifting currents of scholarship.

The essays point first of all to the continued value of analyzing the colonial and revolutionary eras in terms of class. They give convincing evidence of societies in which class differences, class consciousness, and class antagonisms were important. Gary Nash, in showing a history of growing class antagonisms in the cities prior to the onset of the conflict with Britain, makes even more credible the rudimentary class feeling Dirk Hoerder finds in Boston from 1765 to 1775, and that which Eric Foner encounters in more sophisticated political forms in Philadelphia from 1775 through the war. The Regulator movement that dominated the backcountry of North Carolina is clearly better understood in Marvin L. Michael Kay's terms as a movement of poor and middling western farmers directed against the upper classes in their midst than as a sectional conflict of the frontier against eastern aristocracy. And Foner is able to unlock some of the mysteries surrounding Paine's radicalism by relating him to a context of class differences in Philadelphia. The "disaffection" that Ronald Hoffman shows to be so widespread in the wartime South takes on meaning in the context of class antagonisms intensified by wartime demands of the elite on the poor.

All of this is not to claim that the Revolution was a lower-class revolution—far from it—or that the struggle over "who shall rule at home" was as important as the conflict for home rule against Britain —although for some people it clearly was just that. Of necessity, the essays leave open the larger question of how much class conflict. Revolutionary America was a big and varied place, and the volume cannot cover all the ground. But to me, the essays offer evidence enough that class conflict was neither scanty, sporadic, nor muted by the war, as some scholars have claimed. We should continue to be alert to its importance, giving much more attention to defining class and measuring various types of consciousness of class.

Second, the essays suggest a great deal about the allegiances of the common people in the Revolution, about what side they chose— or did not choose—in the conflict of patriot against Britain. To me, they suggest a number of seemingly contradictory trends: how important certain segments of the lower and middling classes were to the patriot side; how much of a stereotype it is to regard the common people as uniformly patriot; and how limited the categories are by which historians have sorted out allegiances of those down below: "patriot," "loyalist," "neutral."

One's class, one's group identity, one's degree of deprivation and subordination, whether one was a slave or a woman, obviously had something to do with how one reacted, or failed to react, to the patriot cause. Indeed, we have to consider far more seriously the possibility that a kind of inverted class feeling may have led many of the poor and middling sort, as well as many blacks, to loyalism or "disaffection."

For the cities alone, our essays leave us with the distinct impression that the artisan and laboring classes—the mechanics—were by and large patriot and that their internal radicalism merged with the external radicalism towards Britain. This trend, which Hoerder finds in Boston and Foner in Philadelphia, others have also found in the seaboard cities in variant forms; and Jesse Lemisch has found it in a major occupational group, the merchant seamen.[1] The hypothesis is reinforced by Nash's findings of the process of politicization underway in the cities long before 1765.

For the countryside, our essays do most to dispel the notion that among the classes at the bottom of white society common people equals patriot. (Had they concentrated on the yeomanry of New England, the story would doubtless be different.) Hoffman's vivid portrayal of the "disaffected" among the rural poor in Maryland—those who refused to be mobilized by either side and whose motto he feels is summed up by the slogan "Don't Tread on Me"—can be extended, his evidence suggests, to the Delaware–Maryland–Virginia peninsula and parts of the Lower South. The fact that Kay is uncertain about the allegiances of the Regulators of 1766–1771 suggests that this same class distrust of the gentry of both sides was true of backcountry North Carolina. And the southern pattern is similar to the one Staughton Lynd found earlier for the tenants of the Hudson Valley[2], and which Edward Countryman verifies and finds elsewhere in the North. It may be that such a response occurred in the countryside wherever there was a prior history of intense class antagonisms and where patriot leaders were from the elite.

Such a hypothesis has implications for the study of lower-class loyalism. In recent years scholars have taken great pains to stress that all Loyalists were not rich men and that loyalism could be found through the social spectrum. But in establishing that there were Loyalists in all classes, they have muddied the class character of the various types of loyalism. And in focusing on the Loyalists who left the country and filed reparations claims in Britain, they have not done justice to the mass of Loyalists and neutralists who stayed behind.

Loyalist or neutralist may not even be the right terms for large numbers of these people; Hoffman's term "disaffected" may apply to them, too. Perhaps we should broaden the analysis of all such lower-class groups and see to what extent they fit the concept Eric Hobsbawm has developed so effectively to describe somewhat similar "pre-political people" in other premodern societies: "primitive rebels."[3] The patriotic stereotype is perhaps easiest to pierce in confronting the way blacks responded to the Revolution. We know that there were as many as five hundred thousand slaves in the colonies, (perhaps as much as one-fifth of the total population), that they were in the North and the South, and that there was a very small population of free blacks. Of all these blacks, a very small minority took up arms for, or aided, the patriot cause; a much larger group, it seems, aided the British, and the largest number of all voted with their feet against either side, that is, they fled to freedom under whatever circumstances they could. Jefferson's estimate that Virginia alone lost thirty thousand slaves in one year, 1778, covers many times the number of blacks who took up arms for the patriots and British combined. Ira Berlin, in identifying the emergence of a free black community as the most important development in black history for the period, in effect confirms how relatively little the political conflict aroused the mass of blacks.

We continue to hear so much about black patriots because blacks are required to prove that "we too contributed to America" in order to compensate for the history that, as Bill Cosby put it some years ago, was "lost, strayed, or stolen." This is certainly understandable. But must ethnic groups accept the dominant patriotic criterion of what is a "contribution" so as to gain the respect they deserve? The most recent scholar to examine the black Loyalists concludes "that they were less pro-British than they were pro-black."[4] Black Loyalists, black neutralists, or blacks who simply ran away were concerned for their personal freedom, no less than black patriots. Amazingly, scholars are only beginning to write the history of slavery in the eighteenth century. Until we know much more about the forces shaping black culture—the African heritage and evangelical religion—and the forms resistance to slavery took, we will not be able to set the black response to the American Revolution in perspective.

The traditional patriotic stereotypes about women in the Revolution are challenged in a variety of ways by Joan Hoff Wilson's essay. Molly Pitcher, Deborah Sampson, Abigail Adams, and Mercy Warren "were there," and male historians have generally left them out or used them as tokens. The question, however, is whether we should permit their images alone to dominate our vision of woman in the revolutionary era, any more than we should permit Crispus Attucks and the blacks who fought at Bunker Hill and crossed the Delaware with Washington to dominate our vision of blacks in the Revolution. Perhaps women's history can leap over the phase of proving that "we too were there," adopting the norms of male society. Women very likely divided, to the extent that they were political, in the same proportion that the male population did. We really don't know. More important, Joan Hoff Wilson suggests that if women showed any distinctive consciousness during the war it was an "affective" concern for family and loved ones, which transcended allegiance to a political cause.

Given the inequalities of colonial society (which were very much worsened during the war), given the predemocratic character of the political scene and the premodern character of life for much of the country, it should not surprise us that many ordinary Americans had higher priorities than freedom from Britain. Blacks wanted their personal freedom; landless farmers wanted land; and women wanted the traditional concern of their "sphere," the maintenance of hearth and home. Perhaps the wonder is that so many other Americans of humble circumstance saw their own aspirations bound up with independence. Historians still have to put the proportions in focus.

Third, in demonstrating class conflict and diversity of allegiances, the essays offer evidence for what E. P. Thompson calls the "agency" of working people, "the degree to which they contributed by conscious efforts to the making of history."[5] The essays show people creating movements, participating in crowd actions, organizing committees, making individual acts of defiance. In other words, they show people in motion, on their own, acting in their own self-interest.

It is necessary to dwell on this theme, because our understanding of the role of common people in the Revolution has long been blocked by two stereotypes, both of which, it is reassuring to learn from George Rudé, are also to be found among Englishmen and Frenchmen when they look at their revolutionary pasts. One is the stereotype of the common people as a mob manipulated by outside propagandists and agitators. The other is that of the "glorious people" who rise up as one in unison with their leaders. Both concepts had their origin in the limited vision or political purposes of eighteenth-century contemporaries.[6]

The belief that all crowds were manipulated mobs had its origin in contemporary elite circles. In England there were indeed, as Rudé has made clear, crowds led by "mob captains" whose strings were pulled by men "behind the curtain"—all contemporary phrases. This, in fact, was the only way in which elites could comprehend action by masses of people presumed to be ignorant and mindless. There were also such crowds in America, in particular in the first wave of resistance to Britain, the Stamp Act crisis of 1765. Where historians have gone astray is in failing to recognize that even these crowds were far more complex and in projecting an unchanging single "model" of the 1765 crowd onto all the crowd actions of the decade that followed.

The second stereotype had its origin in America among those patriot leaders who tried to lead crowds and who were at great pains to claim credit for orderly respectable events (such as the Tea Party), while disassociating themselves from "mere mobs"—those they could not control and whose radicalism was a source of embarrassment. Recently, scholars bent on correcting the first stereotype have run the risk of fortifying the second. They have taken another crowd that Rudé found common in the eighteenth century—the lower middle-class crowd, or crowd of mixed class composition, with fixed and limited targets, who were the victims of violence, rather than its practitioners —and projected this as typical of all American crowds. In Bernard Bailyn's judgment, this type of crowd "shared actively the attitudes and fears of the Revolutionary movement."[7] Thus, in place of the mindless crowd, we have been given a crowd with the mind of the patriot leaders. This second version, albeit far less pernicious, still does not allow for the agency of ordinary people in shaping crowd actions.

The importance of Dirk Hoerder's scholarship is to suggest something of this range of crowd actions: that there were self-led crowds as well as outside-led crowds; that there were crowds which shared the goals and methods of the Sons of Liberty leaders and others which did not. From Pauline Maier's scholarship we have convincing evidence that the Sons of Liberty leaders were engaged in a decade-long struggle to control or contain the crowd. What she has perceived through the eyes of the leaders, Hoerder has tried to get at from the vantage point of the people in the crowd.[8] It is difficult to do.

What is equally extraordinary is the long and varied line of self-organized rural "rioters" that our essays parade before us: New Jersey land rioters, New York tenants, Vermont land claimants, North Carolina Regulators, and the disaffected in the wartime South.

Our essays also show that the agency of ordinary people extended beyond crowd activity. Foner, in synthesizing the research of other scholars, is able to show us how, in Philadelphia, by 1775–1776 the lower and middling classes had created a world of committees, especially among militia, who formed the urban political base of the radical democrats who wrote the Pennsylvania constitution. The Philadelphia scene has overtones of the famous army debates of the English Revolution of the 1640s; one wonders whether it is duplicated elsewhere.

Fortunately, the study of this aspect of popular participation in the Revolution is growing, and it may soon be possible to differentiate types and levels of popular movements with greater precision.

Fourth, the essays are exciting as to the kind of ideas we are likely to encounter if we were to launch a full-scale search for the ideology of the Revolution from the bottom up. In place of the "mindless mob" or the mob of one mind with their leaders, we may say (at the least) that we have evidence of ordinary people (in mobs and out) with minds of their own, or perhaps better put, of many minds. The ideas our essays cast up are in several realms: political economy, evangelical religion, and democratic thought.

The value of Joseph Ernst's research is that he brings us back to the question of the economic origins of the Revolution (long exiled by most historians), but focuses on the plane of ideas—political economy —in the context of long-range changes in the Anglo-American economy. Hopefully, this will lift the debate above the arid and worn out discussion of the advantages and disadvantages of mercantilism and get us to the economic assumptions underlying the debate over political and constitutional issues. If this line of inquiry is pursued beyond elite circles, it may be possible to construct not only a political economy of the merchant and planter classes but a related political economy of farmers and artisans.

Edward Countryman's synthesis of northern rural rioters reminds us, with particular force, how central land was to farmers who were landless or whose title to land was uncertain. American rural riots were land riots, not, as in England, bread riots. At the same time, there are tantalizing glimpses in our essays that there may have been among Americans something akin to what E. P. Thompson has identified in England as the "moral economy of the poor,"—that is, "a consistent traditional view of social norms and obligations, of the proper economic functions of several parties within the community." Nash and Hoerder offer hints of this; so does Joan Hoff Wilson in the occasional food riots women engaged in during the war. But, most strikingly, Foner describes how, in Philadelphia, radicals divided over the issue of popular price control, which came to a head during the war in the armed clash at James Wilson's house. These are outcroppings; the evidence we have of food riots much earlier in the colonial period and much later in the nineteenth century suggest that these ideas of a "moral economy" either were of very long duration or possibly were renewed by successive waves of immigrants.[9]

The evangelical realm of popular ideology is also a motif in several essays. Rhys Isaac's depiction of a democratic culture of "vital religion" among the common folk of Virginia, distinct from the aristocratic life-style of the gentry, is so graphic as to prompt us to ask at once where else the Great Awakening left two such divergent cultures in its wake. Berlin shows the impact of the same religion in the churches shaped by free blacks, syncretized with an African heritage (epitomized, for example, by the name African Methodist Episcopal Church). Joan Hoff Wilson finds the evangelical effect on women's consciousness not at all liberating. But what are we to say of the man in the Philadelphia Stamp Act crowd who calls out, "No King but King Jesus," save that we must know much more about the effects on ordinary people of the waves of evangelical religion that swept the colonies in the decades before the Revolution, and of the many ways in which as Alan Heimert put it "dissenter animosity was translated into social terms."[10] Historians have recently rediscovered the millenial streak in the American Revolution. Is it possible we might also discover American versions of the kind of millenialists and radical sectarians Christopher Hill has portrayed for the English Revolution of the 1640s, men with visions of "a world turned upside down"?[11] Hermon Husband, proscribed North Carolina Regulator and sometime Quaker, fled to western Pennsylvania, where he preached a vision of a New Jerusalem of the west made up of yeoman farmers and ended up, in the 1790s, as a radical leader of the Whiskey Rebellion. Clearly, we will not know unless we look.[12]

Eric Foner's essay on Paine brings us to the third and best known realm of popular ideology: the democratic. In Foner's version of Paine we see a political ideology knit together with a political economy and located, as it has not been done before, in a particular social context and placed in continuity with an English democratic tradition we had all but forgotten. This illuminates Paine, in my opinion, in a way we have not understood him before. How widespread was his constellation of ideas? We cannot say at this point, but it is interesting to see in this volume a variant in the person of Dr. Thomas Young, whom we encounter in no less than three essays: as a foe of landlords and land speculators, in Countryman's story of rural rebellion in New York and Vermont; as one of Samuel Adams's more radical co-workers, in Hoerder's Boston; and as coauthor of Pennsylvania's radical constitution, in Foner's Philadelphia, who also tried to induce his Vermont friends to emulate Pennsylvania. Here is a native American Thomas Paine, rooted in struggles over land, in struggles with conservative merchants over tactics towards Britain, and, like Paine, in the deist conflict with orthodoxy.[13] How many more were there like him? And what ideas and cultural values are we likely to discover when we attempt to reconstruct the careers of people, a cut below Paine and Young, who left us diaries, memoirs, and autobiographies by the score?[14]

Political economy (perhaps a "moral economy"), evangelical religion, democratic thought—these I would say are strands of a popular ideology. Doubtless there are others. They do not permit us to claim a distinct ideology among those below; but neither should they permit scholars to continue on the bland assumption of a consensus behind a single patriot ideology descended from a single English tradition.

Finally, what do the essays point to about the impact of common people and of radical movements on the Revolution and of the Revolution on them?

Here we must keep in mind the distinctions between the two kinds of radicalism, external and internal, and deal separately with those at the bottom of white society and those on the outside: blacks, Indians, and women.

We have already touched on the effect of the movements from below on the larger movement for independence from Britain. These effects are fairly well known to historians. In 1776, the people clearly were ahead of their leaders, and Thomas Paine's pamphlet *Common Sense,* which both articulated and crystallized sentiment for independence and democratic political aspirations, was of major importance in converting a movement for resistance into a revolution. In this process the artisans and laboring population of the cities and the yeomanry of the New England towns—a group neglected in these pages—played a major role. How much the rural radicalism of the other sort—tenant protest, smoldering Regulator discontent, the fear of conscription—held back the movement for independence is more difficult to measure. The move to declare independence and establish a new government was designed in part to curb such dangerous tendencies, including "domestic insurrection," a phrase in the Declaration of Independence. How much lower-class disaffection affected the war itself is also difficult to measure.

But what of the effects of the radical movements that sought internal change? Were they not all short lived, sporadic, and confined to a particular geographic area? Were they not failures, and of minimum impact in shaping policy?

My first temptation is to draw upon Richard Cobb's response to the same question when it is asked about the same thing in the French Revolution. The "question commonly asked: 'Why did the popular

movement fail in the course of the French Revolution?' " he writes is
"largely irrelevant since the movement never had any chance at all of
success, at least under its own momentum and without outside help.
It should be replaced by the question, 'How did a popular movement
in its own right ever emerge at all?' for this is perhaps the most
astonishing fact about the history of the French Revolution."[15]

Perhaps this should be our attitude, too, towards the American
radicals that appear in these pages. How astonishing in the first place
that several thousand badly outnumbered Regulators fought at the
Battle of the Alamance, that New York's tenants rose in rebellion not
once but many times, that the Green Mountain boys were so obdurate
in the pursuit of their claims, that Maryland farmers were so vulgarly
undeferential in defying conscription, that apprentices and artisans in
the lower trades in Philadelphia formed a Committee of Privates, that
there were so many crowds in Boston which Samuel Adams and his
friends had nothing to do with—and the list could go on.

But Cobb's insight, however tantalizing, should not be the stopping place in our thinking. The essays suggest to me that more can be
claimed for the popular movements of the American Revolution discussed in this volume, and still more if we examined a good many
others.

How does one measure the success of popular movements? If, for
example, we measure them by their capacity to endure, were the movements depicted here ephemeral? Free blacks, as outcasts of white
society, demonstrated an extraordinary capacity to build institutions.
The same is true of master artisans who, after the war, built self-
interest organizations and engaged in sustained political activity, and
of the men and women who built the evangelical churches. But even
where there was not continuity of organization, there was a capacity to
sustain protest. The reappearance of tenant dissidence in the Hudson
Valley is a good example: a rebellion suppressed in 1766; another
suppressed in 1777; protest in the 1790s, partly legal, partly extralegal,
and, finally, a successful movement of mass proportions against land-
lordism in the nineteenth century—the "down rent wars."[16] To understand such protest, we need to pay much more attention to the way
tradition was transmitted orally from one generation to another. Rituals of protest in the Revolution, which had their origin in England—
effigy burning, liberty poles, tar and feathering—in turn became the
forms of protest for later generations.[17] We understand such "primitive rebels" poorly.

If we measure the success of radical movements by their capacity to influence those in power, an even more compelling case can be made. We have an intriguing set of images in our essays: the Continental Congress and the British sending emissaries to the old Regulators beseeching their support; the younger Charles Carroll of Maryland arguing with his reactionary father of the need to accommodate and not supress disaffection; a Virginian on the hustings desperately trying to reach his farmer audience in the language of classical oratory alien to them, in contrast to Patrick Henry, the new patriot leader whose political strength rested on a style of oratory, and indeed a life-style, that reached both commoner and gentry.

These scenes suggest to me a process by which the pressures of the internal radicalism forced the creation not only of a new style but of a sophisticated kind of American conservatism. The rulers had to learn "the propriety of Swimming with a Stream which it is impossible to stem"; they had to "yield to the torrent if they hoped to direct its course," as one of them put it.[18] One way of measuring more exactly the effects of the popular movements would be to focus on the wing of the ruling elite that mastered this tactic. We need a fuller picture of the radicalism of the 1780s—of Shaysism, and not only Daniel Shays's rebellion in Massachusetts. When we have it, it may be that we will see that this process was brought to a climax when the Founding Fathers—the men who shaped the federal Constitution in 1787—created a government which attempted to take into account "the people out of doors" and adjusted to the "temper" or the "genius" of the American people—these being the phrases they used.

The same process of accommodation did not work for the outsiders, the Indians, blacks, and women. They had relatively little impact on the Revolution, although the Revolution had a major and largely negative impact on them.

Indians were always outsiders in a physical sense—tribal societies on the frontier. They were in the way, and the colonists wanted to push them back. Francis Jennings makes a good case to give more weight to the Quebec Act—which made it more difficult for speculators and settlers to get at Indian lands—as a cause of the Revolution. The Indians—or most of them—fought on the wrong side, and the American victory, opening the gates to further expansion, was for them a disaster, only postponed by their continued military resistance.

Blacks, in a way, became outsiders even more in the wake of the Revolution. The northern states eliminated slavery by 1800; Southern slaveholders certainly did not fight the Revolution to do away with slavery. And the creation of the first large population of free blacks was due primarily to the efforts of blacks rather than the benevolence of white masters. The fact that blacks created their own separate institutions so soon is evidence that most whites—even those who disliked slavery—wanted a racially segregated society in which blacks would remain outsiders.

As to women, neither the collective activities nor individual acts they undertook—the mass spinning bees or boycotts before the war, or the home front efforts during the war—lifted them out of what was commonly regarded as the "women's sphere." Nothing like a women's rights movement emerged; Abigail Adams and Mercy Warren seem exceptional, even among middle-class women, and their pleas were based on assumptions that accepted more or less the same limited role for women. In measuring results, John Adams's put-down of Abigail is more significant than her eloquent plea to "remember the ladies." No spark of liberty leaped from the battle cries against Britain to inspire males to take up the cause of women.

From the perspectives of these groups, in the eyes of our essayists, the Revolution indeed looks different. For the Indians, it was one more in a series of calamities; for blacks, it was a fortuitous event; for women, it was largely irrelevant. There was a "revolution" in the life of each of these groups, but our essayists locate it elsewhere than in the American Revolution per se. From the Indian perspective, as Jennings so aptly puts it, the American Revolution was a "baron's revolt" against the Crown, but their revolution was a "series of peasant wars" against the barons. For blacks, the "revolution in black life" lay in the creation of a free black community. For the American woman, it lay in her transformation into a bourgeois woman, a process that had begun several centuries before and would leave her worse off when it was completed in the nineteenth century than before.

Moreover, for none of these groups was the Revolution a case of "ideals betrayed" or "ideals unfulfilled." For none of them did the revolutionary generation, including most of those we have identified as internal radicals, even make promises.

Is the judgment of our scholars too harsh? Perhaps. It may simply be the result of recognizing that the history of the groups outside the dominant culture runs on different tracks and with different timetables. There is no reason to start with the assumption that the American Revolution should have been an event of transforming importance in their history. We will do better if we attempt to set the American Revolution within the larger and longer frame of reference of the history of Indians, blacks, and women, rather than force their history into the framework of American political history and its periodization. And perhaps we can start to think of other lower-class groups who have their own culture in the same way.

Striking a balance between the failures and achievements of the Revolution may be the most difficult task of all. It is not at all certain as to where the scholarship in this volume is leading as to the meaning of the Revolution. The task is not one for historians alone. Perhaps it is time for everyone, celebrant and dissenter, to go back to the Revolution with some of the qualities our scholars bring to it: a sense of humility before a many-sided event not easily reduced to a simple formula; an understanding that there is not one tradition, but that there are many traditions that come out of the Revolution; and an awareness that insofar as ordinary people are concerned, the history of the American Revolution, as the history of the United States, is yet to be written.

1. Charles S. Olton, *Artisans for Independence: Philadelphia Mechanics and the American Revolution* (Syracuse, N.Y.: Syracuse University Press, 1975); Staughton Lynd, *Class Conflict, Slavery and the United States Constitution: Ten Essays* (Indianapolis: Bobbs-Merrill Co., 1967), chap. 4; Richard Walsh, *Charleston's Son of Liberty: A Study of the Artisans, 1763–1789* (Columbia: University of South Carolina Press, 1959); Jesse Lemisch, "The Radicalism of the Inarticulate Merchant Seamen in the Politics of Revolutionary America," in *Dissent: Explorations in the History of American Radicalism,* ed. Alfred F. Young (DeKalb: Northern Illinois University Press, 1968); and "Listening to the 'Inarticulate': William Widger's Dream and the Loyalties of American Revolutionary Seamen in British Prisons," *Journal of Social History* 3 (Fall 1969): 1–29.

2. Lynd, *Class Conflict,* chaps. 2, 3.

3. Eric Hobsbawm, *Primitive Rebels: Studies in Archaic Forms of Social Movement in the 19th and 20th Centuries* (New York: W. W. Norton & Co., 1965), p. 2.

4. James W. St. G. Walker, "Blacks as American Loyalists: The Slaves' War for Independence," *Historical Reflections* (Department of History, University of Waterloo, Canada) 2, no. 1 (Summer 1975): 53. Professor Walker kindly allowed me to read his essay in MS.

5. E. P. Thompson, *The Making of the English Working Class* (New York: Pantheon Books, 1963), p. 12.

6. George Rudé, *The Crowd in History, 1730–1848* (New York: John Wiley & Sons, 1964), introduction.

7. Bernard Bailyn, ed., *Pamphlets of the American Revolution 1750–1776* (Cambridge: Harvard University Press, 1965), p. 583.

8. Pauline Maier, *From Resistance to Revolution: Colonial Radicals and the Development of American Opposition to Britain, 1765–1776* (New York: Alfred A. Knopf, 1972). For another recent effort to probe the "lower-class crowd," see Steven J. Rosswurm, " 'That They Were Grown Unruly': The Crowd and Lower Classes in Philadelphia, 1765–1780," (Master's thesis, Northern Illinois University, 1974).

9. Herbert G. Gutman, "Work, Culture, and Society in Industrializing America, 1815–1919," *American Historical Review* 78, no. 3 (June 1973): 574–75; Michael Smuksta, "Food Riots in America, 1710–1865," (Masters' thesis, Northern Illinois University, 1974).

10. Alan Heimert, *Religion and the American Mind from the Great Awakening to the Revolution* (Cambridge: Harvard University Press, 1966), p. 381.

11. Christopher Hill, *The World Turned Upside Down: Radical Ideas During the English Revolution* (New York: Viking Press, 1972).

12. Mark Jones, "Hermon Husband: Millenarian, Carolina Regulator and Whiskey Rebel" (Ph.D. diss. in progress, Northern Illinois University).

13. For a somewhat different interpretation, which she has kindly allowed me to see in MS, see Pauline Maier, "Reason and Revolution: The Radicalism of Dr. Thomas Young," to be published in *American Quarterly*.

14. For what can be done with such material, see Jesse Lemisch, "The American Revolution and the American Dream: A Life of Andrew Sherburne, a Pensioner of the Navy of the Revolution," (unpublished paper presented to the Columbia University Seminar in Early American History and Culture, October 1975); and Walter Wallace, " 'Oh Liberty! Oh Virtue! Oh My Country!' An Exploration of the Minds of New England Soldiers During the American Revolution" (Master's thesis, Northern Illinois University, 1974), based on an examination of 168 New England soldiers' diaries and journals.

15. R. C. Cobb, *The Police and the People: French Popular Protest, 1789–1820* (London and New York: Oxford University Press, 1970), p. xiv.

16. Alfred F. Young, *The Democratic Republicans of New York: The Origins, 1763–1797* (Chapel Hill: University of North Carolina Press, 1967), pp. 13, 26, 60–61, 203–7, 533–35.

17. I will develop this theme in "The Crowd and the Coming of the Revolution: From Ritual to Rebellion in Boston ," (to be published).

18. Robert R. Livingston to William Duer, 12 June 1777, R.R.Livingston Papers, New York Historical Society, cited in Young, *Democratic Republicans*, p. 15.

Index

A Note on the Text

This book was designed by Peter Coveney. The text is set in ten-point Baskerville with two points leading; the display type is Caslon Antique.

The keyboarding was done at Northern Illinois University Press via the University's 367-70 IBM computer and using WYLBUR, an interactive text-editing system developed at the Stanford University Computation Center and at the Computer Center, Division of Computer Research and Technology, National Institutes of Health, Bethesda, Maryland, as adapted for use at Northern Illinois University. A fully coded, 9-track, 1600 bpi magnetic tape was sent to the compositor, Datagraphics Press, Inc., Phoenix, Arizona. The tape was processed on an RCA Videocomp unit. The book was printed and bound by R. R. Donnelley & Sons Company, Chicago, Illinois.

The Index was prepared by Laura English using WYLBUR and an IBM Key Word Out of Context (KWOC) program.